Number 4.

Three sequels now to the original *Big Book of Logos*.

Logo designers all over the world know the importance of keeping "in the loop," of having a source that shows the fresh new designs that are being produced by outstanding creative people.

The Big Book of Logos series IS that source.

The Big Book of Logos 4 is packed full of new designs that will inspire you, challenge you, and serve as a creative springboard.

For all those who create logos, this book will be your constant source for "solitary brainstorming."

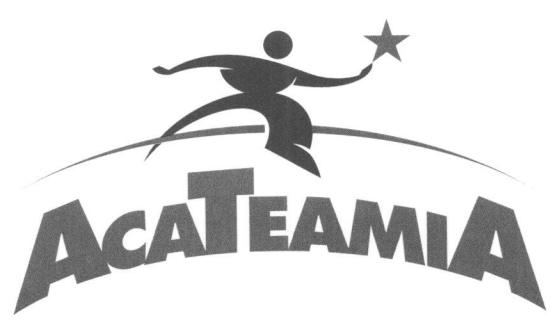

1.

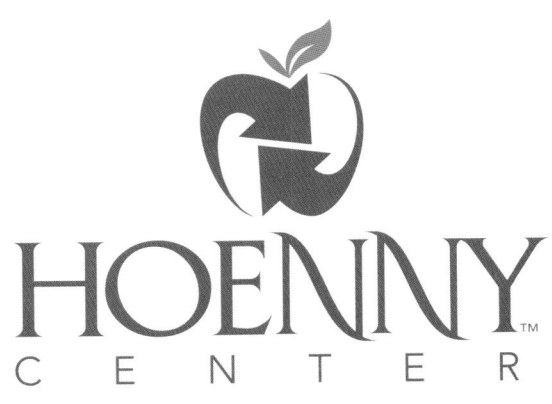

2.

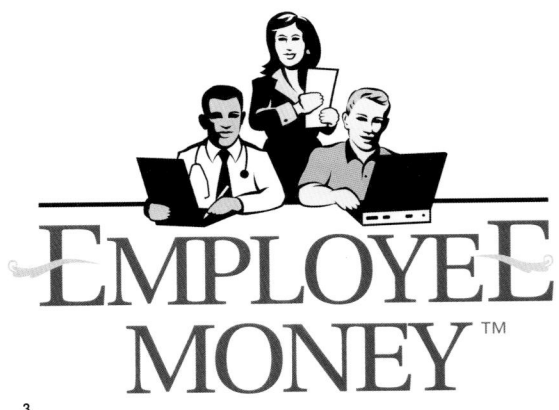

3.

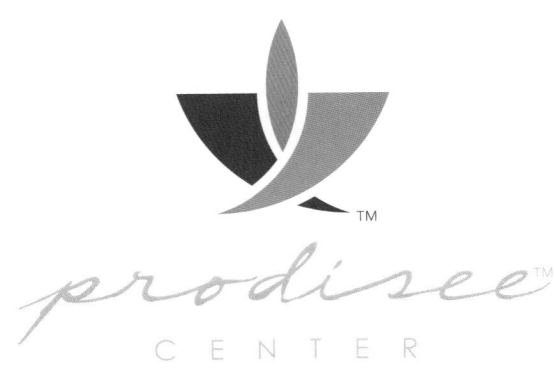

4.

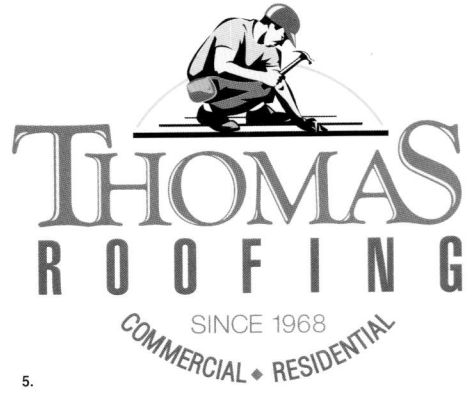

5.

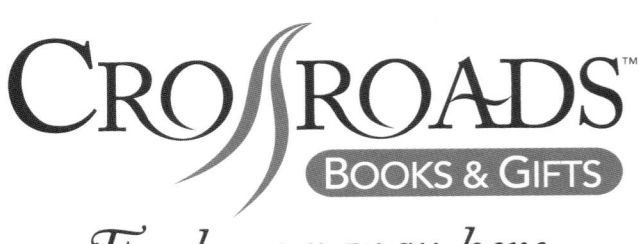

6.

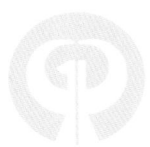

7.

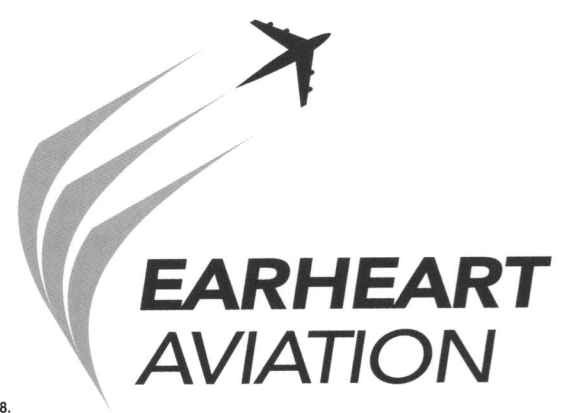

8.

The BIG BOOK of LOGOS 4

David E. Carter

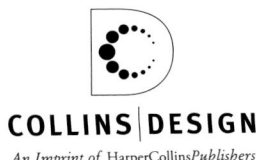

COLLINS DESIGN

An Imprint of HarperCollinsPublishers

THE BIG BOOK OF LOGOS 4
Copyright © 2006 by COLLINS DESIGN

HarperCollins books may be purchased for educational, business, or sales promotional use.
For information, please write: Special Markets Department, HarperCollins Publishers Inc.,
10 East 53rd Street, New York, NY 10022

First Paperback Edition

First published in hardcover in 2004 by:
Collins Design
An Imprint of HarperCollins*Publishers*
10 East 53rd Street
New York, NY 10022
Tel: (212) 207-7000
Fax: (212) 207-7654
collinsdesign@harpercollins.com
www.harpercollins.com

Distributed throughout the world by:
HarperCollins*Publishers*
10 East 53rd Street
New York, NY 10022
Fax: (212) 207-7654

Book Design by **Designs by You!**
Suzanna and Anthony Stephens

Library of Congress Control Number: 2004110152

ISBN-10: 0-06-089194-7
ISBN-13: 978-0-06-089194-7

Printed in China
First Paperback Printing, 2006

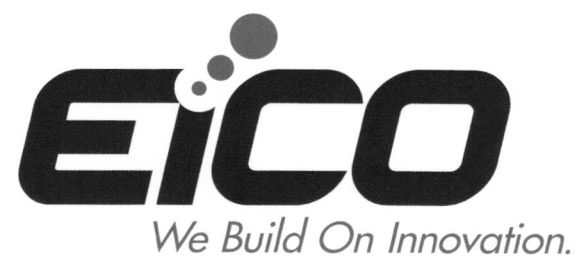

9.

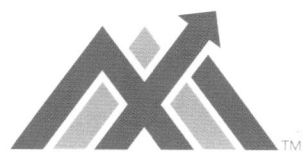

The MAXAlliance™

Trans *Action*™

10.

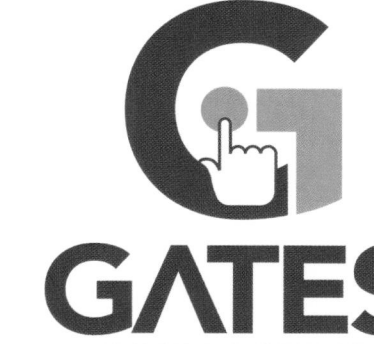

11.

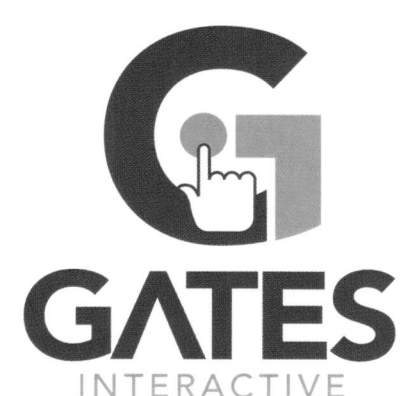

12.

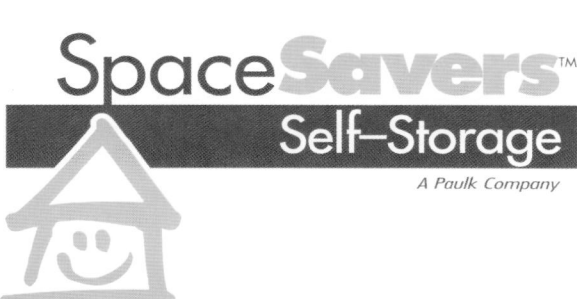

13.

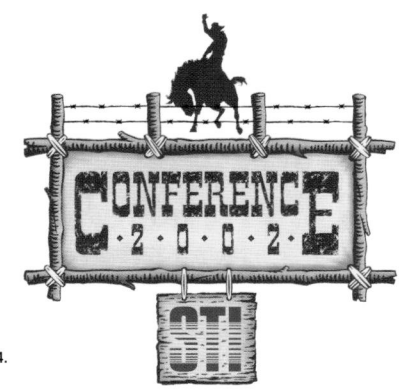

14.

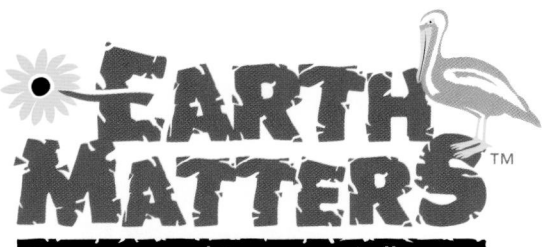

15.

1 - 15
Design Firm **Pixallure Design**
1.
  Client   *Acateamia*
  Designer Steven Lutz
2.
  Client   *Hoenny Center*
  Designers Steven Lutz, Terry Edeker
3.
  Client   *Employee Money*
  Designers Steven Lutz, Billie Green,
            Terry Edeker
4.
  Client   *Prodisee Center*
  Designers Joel Lamascus, Terry Edeker
5.
  Client   *Thomas Roofing*
  Designers Steven Lutz, Terry Edeker
6.
  Client   *Crossroads Books & Gifts*
  Designers Steven Lutz, Terry Edeker
7.
  Client   *Greene & Phillips*
  Designer Joel Lamascus

8.
  Client   *Earheart Aviation*
  Designer Steven Lutz
9.
  Client   *EICO*
  Designer Steven Lutz
10.
  Client   *Max Alliance*
  Designer Terry Edeker
11.
  Client   *InsTrust Insurance Group*
  Designer Steven Lutz
12.
  Client   *Gates Interactive*
  Designer Terry Edeker
13.
  Client   *Space Savers*
  Designer Terry Edeker
14.
  Client   *Software Technology Inc.*
  Designers Steven Lutz, Terry Edeker
15.
  Client   *Daphne Public Library*
  Designers Steven Lutz, Terry Edeker

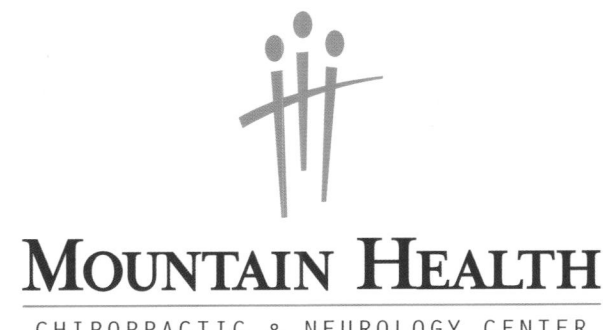

1.

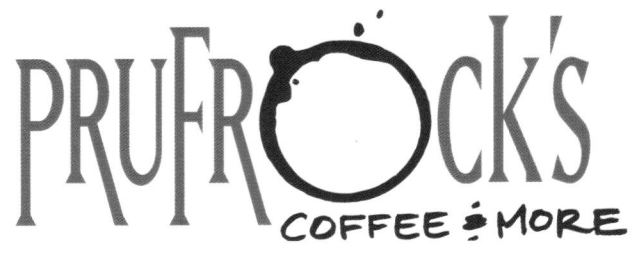

2.

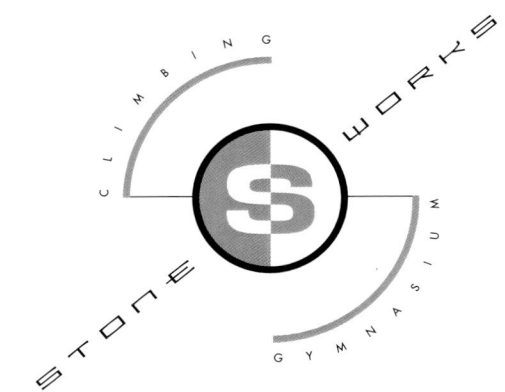

3.

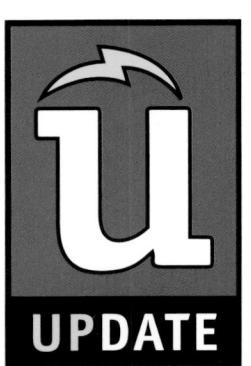

4.

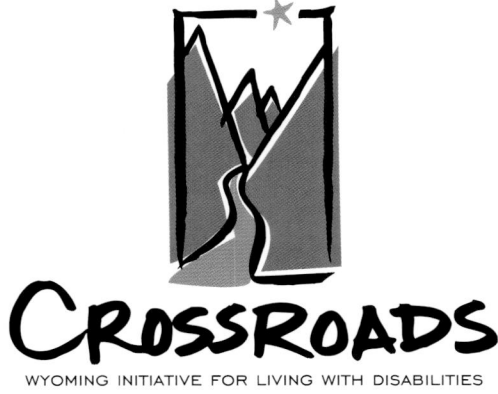

5.

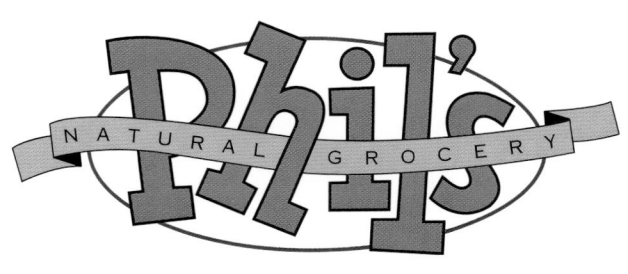

6.

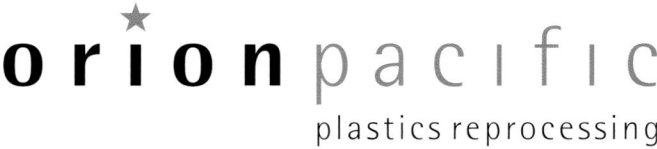

7.

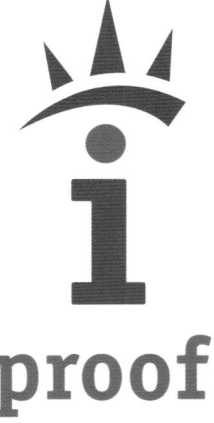

8.

FIRST AMERICAN FUNDS™

9.

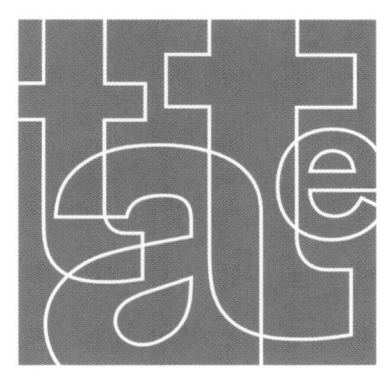 ARCOLA MILLS

10.

LΛNDMARK
C E N T E R

11.

tate

12.

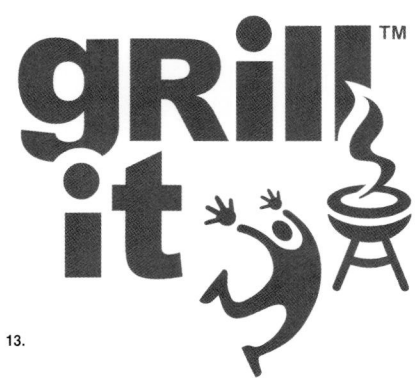 gRill it™

13.

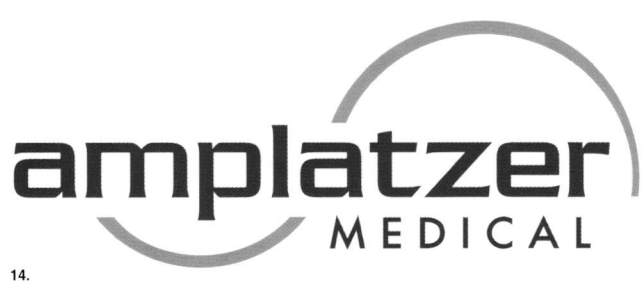 amplatzer MEDICAL

14.

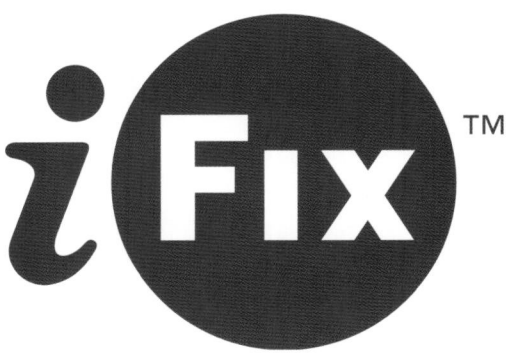 iFix™

15.

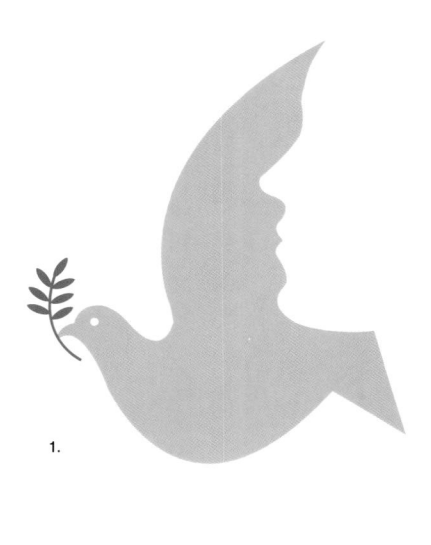

1.

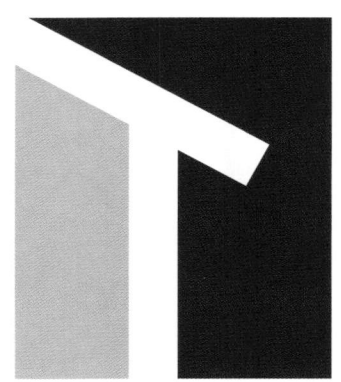

2.

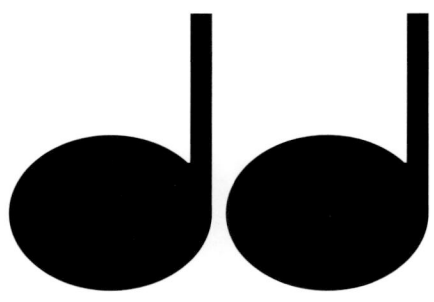

3.

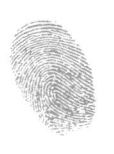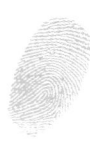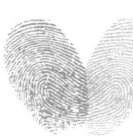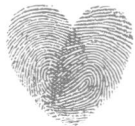

4.

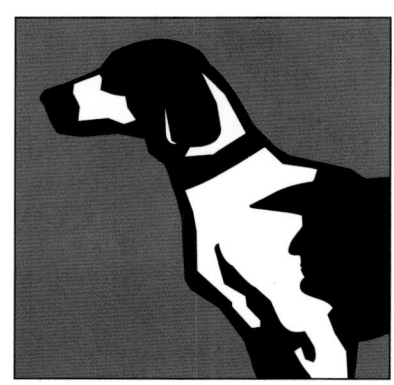

5.

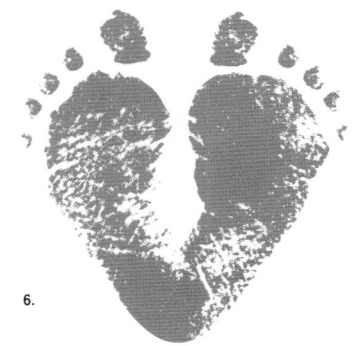

6.

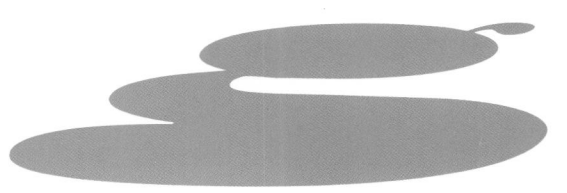

7.

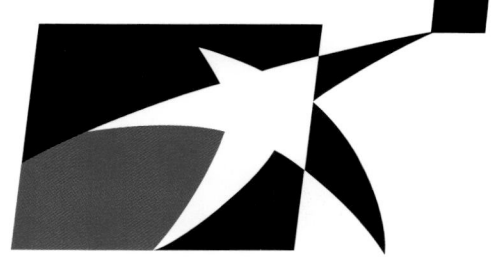

8.

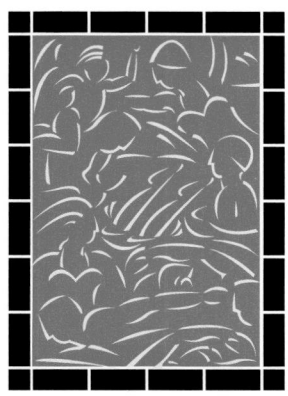

9.

10.

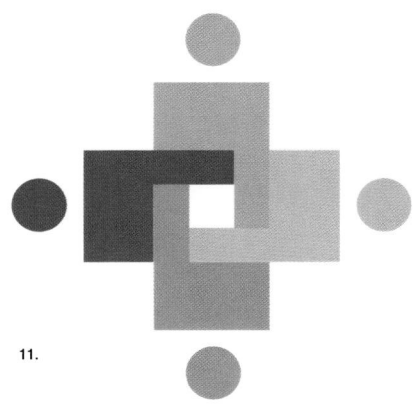

11.

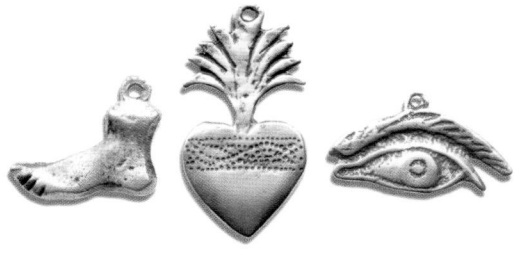

12.

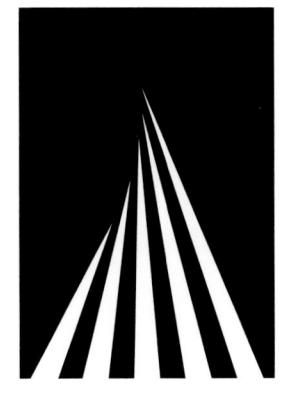

13.

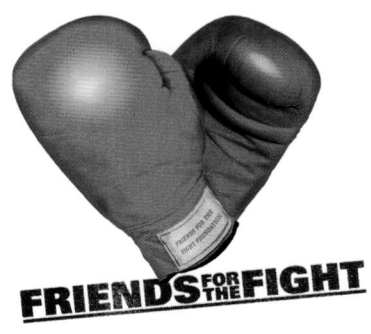

14.

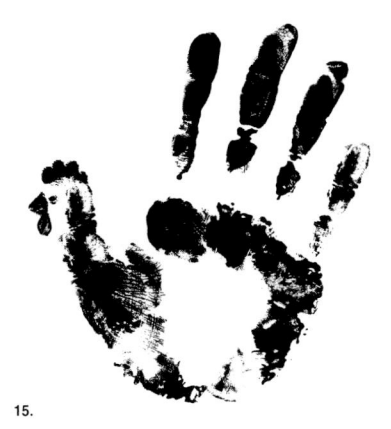

15.

1 - 15
Design Firm **Bradford Lawton Design Group**

1.
| Client | New Heights Methodist Church |
| Designer | Jody Laney |

2.
| Client | True Slate |
| Designers | Bradford Lawton, Jody Laney |

3.
| Client | KPAC Texas Public Radio |
| Designers | Jody Laney, Bradford Lawton |

4.
| Client | Marriage and Family Counseling |
| Designer | Bradford Lawton |

5.
| Client | Rick Smith Dog Training |
| Designer | Jody Laney |

6.
| Client | Sav-A-Baby |
| Designers | Becky Haas, Bradford Lawton |

7.
| Client | Gary Pools |
| Designers | Becky Haas, Bradford Lawton |

8.
| Client | Lone Star Overnight |
| Designer | Bradford Lawton |

9.
| Client | Alamo Heights Pool |
| Designers | Jody Laney, Bradford Lawton |

10.
| Client | Family Violence Prevention Service |
| Designer | Jody Laney |

11.
| Client | University Physicians Group |
| Designers | Bradford Lawton, Jody Laney |

12.
| Client | Texas Diabetes Institute |
| Designer | Bradford Lawton |

13.
| Client | Air Force Federal Credit Union |
| Designer | Jennifer Zinsmeyer Murillo |

14.
| Client | Friends for the Fight |
| Designer | Leslie Magee |

15.
| Client | Wing Basket |
| Designer | Jennifer Zinsmeyer Murillo |

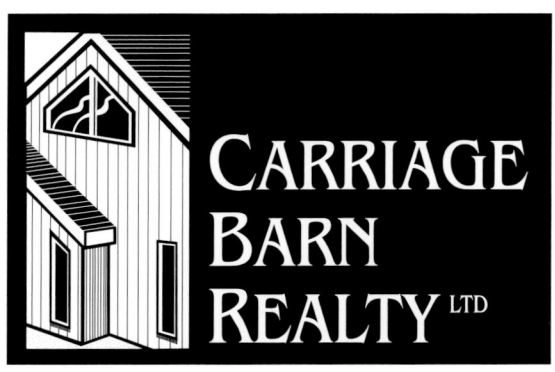

1.

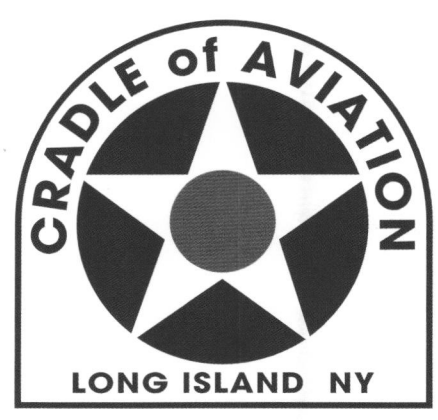

2.

DCI

DESIGN COMMUNICATIONS INC

3.

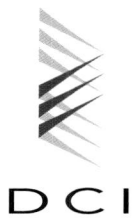

kasl

company llc

4.

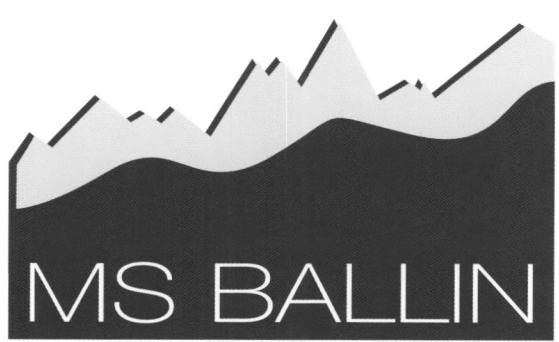

MS BALLIN

5.

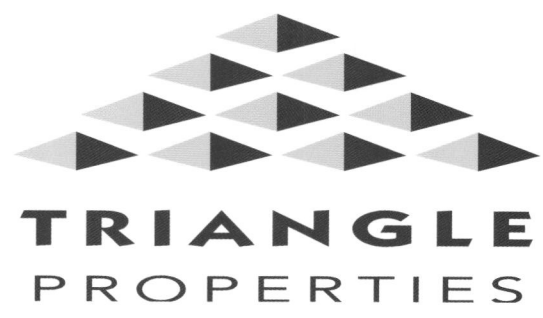

TRIANGLE
PROPERTIES

6.

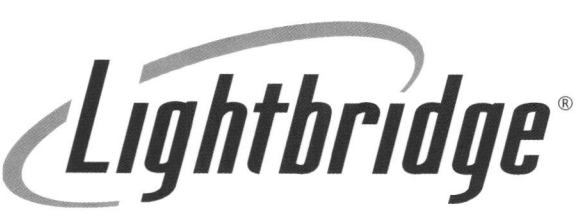

Lightbridge®

7.

1 - 6
Design Firm **Guarino Graphics & Design Studio**

7
Design Firm **Monderer Design**

1.
Client   *Carriage Barn Realty*
Designer   Jan Guarino

2.
Client   *Cradle of Aviation*
Designer   Jan Guarino

3.
Client   *DCI Communications*
Designer   Jan Guarino

4.
Client   *KASL Company LLC*
Designer   Jan Guarino

5.
Client   *MS Ballin*
Designer   Jan Guarino

6.
Client   *Triangle Properties*
Designer   Jan Guarino

7.
Client   *Lightbridge*
Designers   Jason CK Miller,
            Stewart Monderer

(opposite)
Client   *Flying Star Cafe*
Design Firm **Vaughn Wedeen Creative**
Designer   Pamela Chang

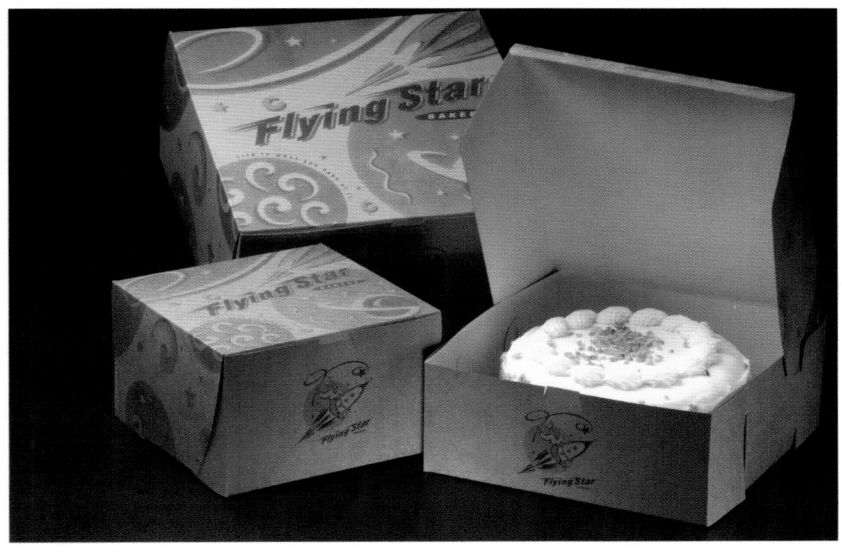

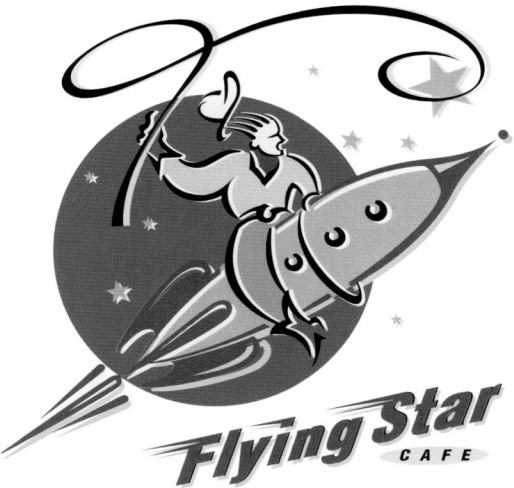

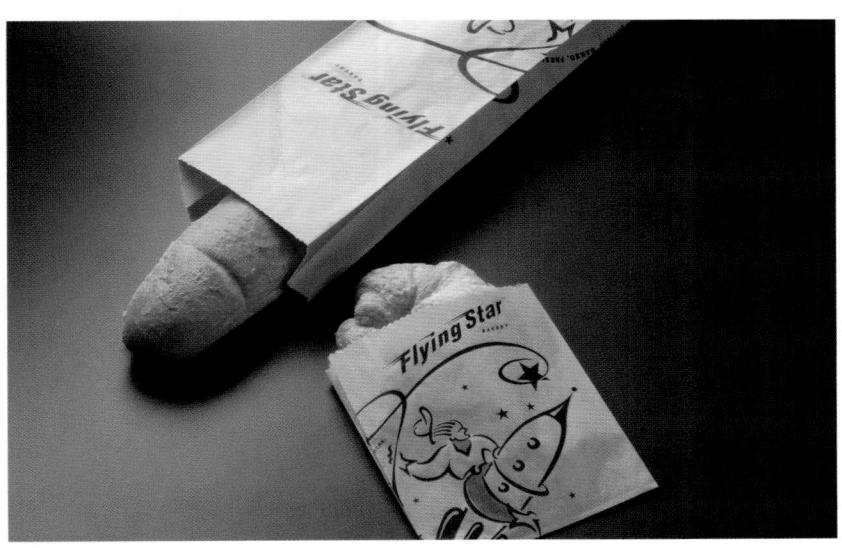

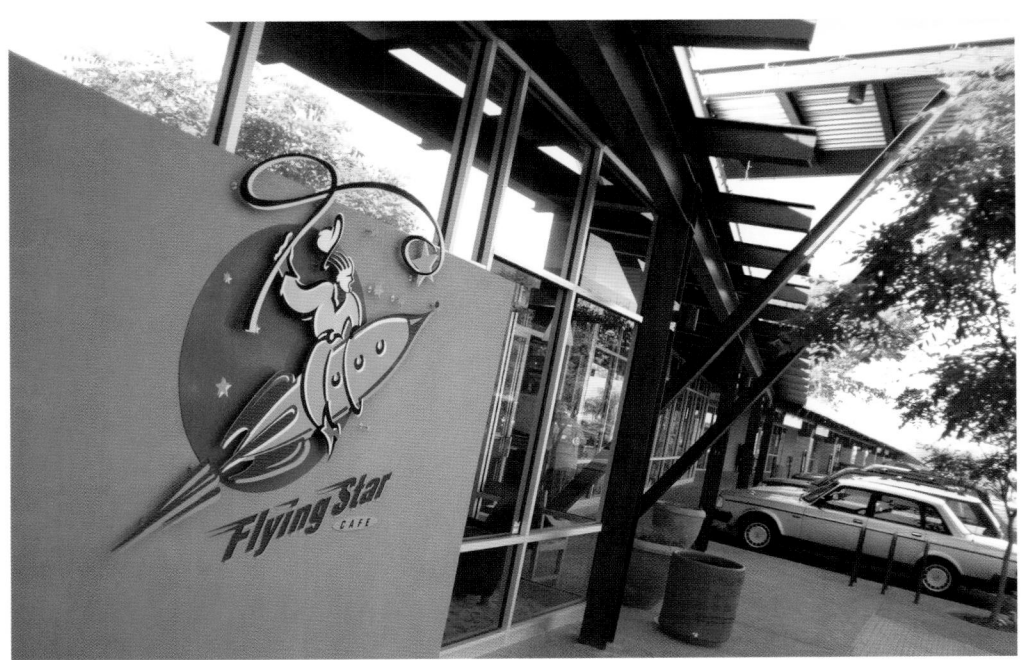

SPACE

1.

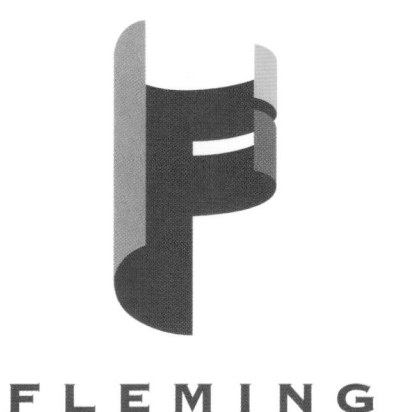

FLEMING

2.

3.

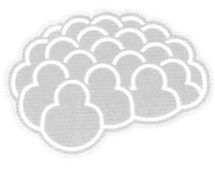

CREATIVE CLUB *of* SAN ANTONIO

4.

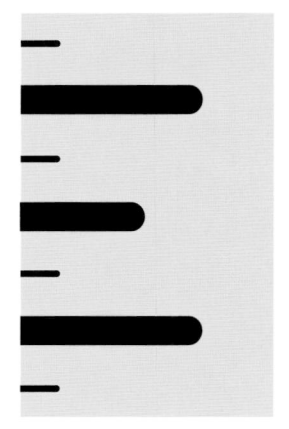

WINGS & CO.

5.

SAN ANTONIO RIVER FOUNDATION

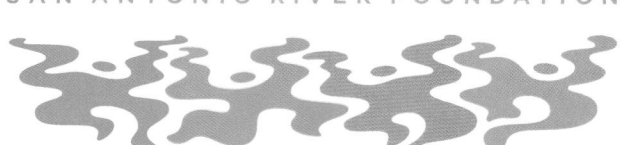

6.

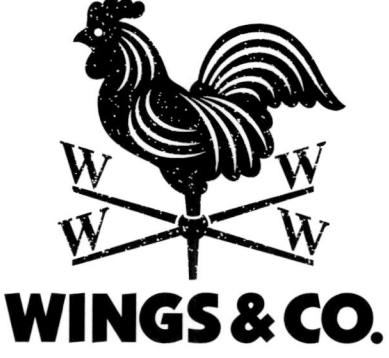

7.

The Birth Place
AT SOUTHWEST GENERAL HOSPITAL

8.

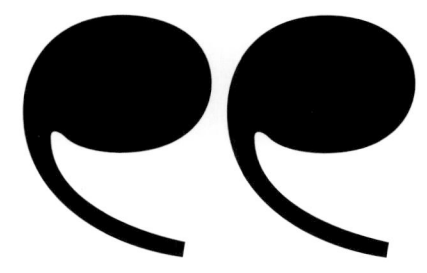

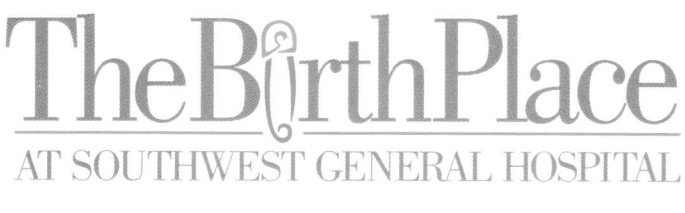

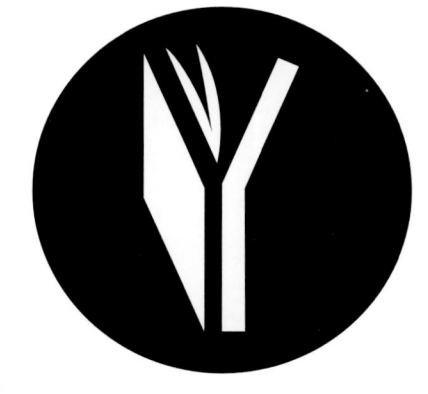

9.

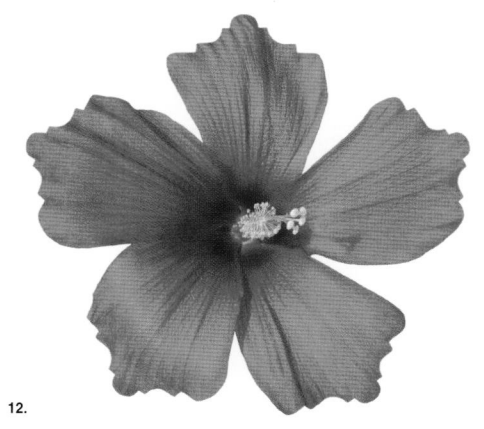

10.

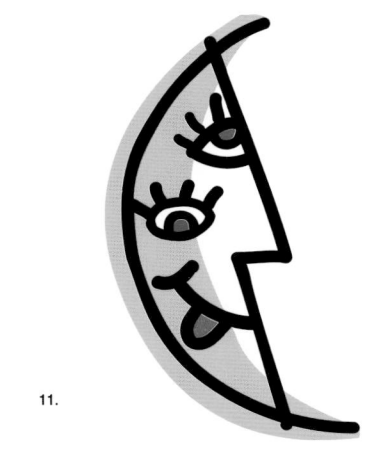

11.

13.

cielos

14.

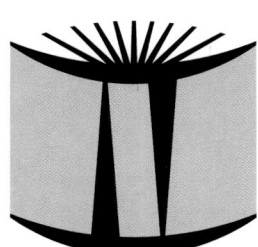

15.

1 - 15
Design Firm **Bradford Lawton Design Group**

1.
Client   *BBtt*
Designer   Bradford Lawton

2.
Client   *Fleming*
Designer   Bradford Lawton

3.
Client   *Easy Inch Loss Program*
Designer   Leslie Magee

4.
Client   *Creative Club of San Antonio*
Designer   Rolando M. Murillo

5.
Client   *Wings Basket*
Designer   Rolando M. Murillo

6.
Client   *San Antonio River Foundation*
Designers   Rolando M. Murillo, Bradford Lawton

7.
Client   *KSTX Texas Public Radio*

8.
Client   *Southwest General Hospital*
Designers   Bradford Lawton, Jody Laney

9.
Client   *San Antonio Youth Literacy*
Designer   Jennifer Zinsmeyer Murillo

10.
Client   *Williams Landscaping*
Designer   Bradford Lawton

11.
Client   *Luna C Restaurant*
Designers   Bradford Lawton, Jody Laney

12.
Client   *San Antonio Botanical Society*
Designer   Bradford Lawton

13.
Client   *Creative Surgeons*
Designers   Bradford Lawton, Jody Laney

14.
Client   *Frontier Ent.*
Designers   Rolando Murillo, Bradford Lawton

15.
Client   *Gemini Ink*
Designers   Leslie Magee

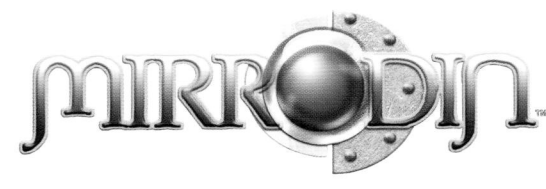

1.

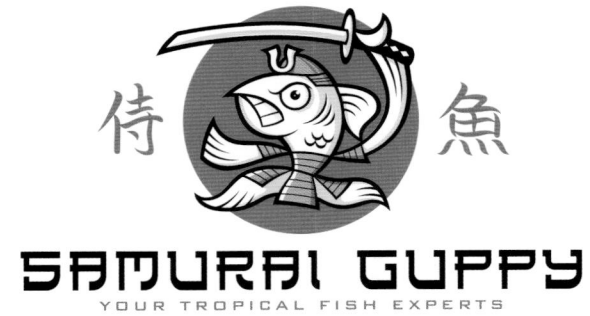

2.

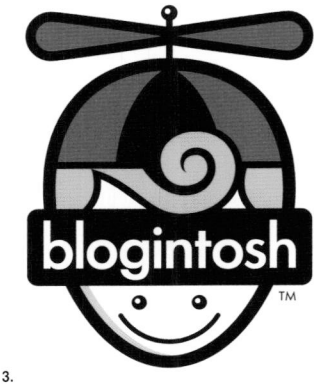

3.

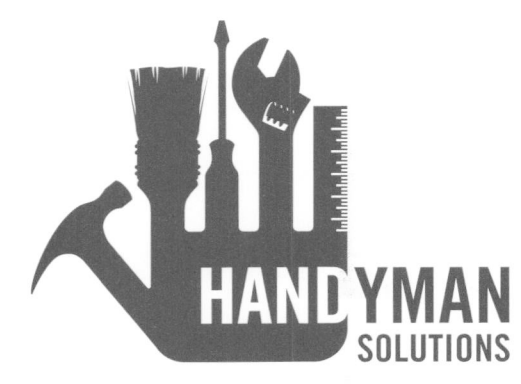

4.

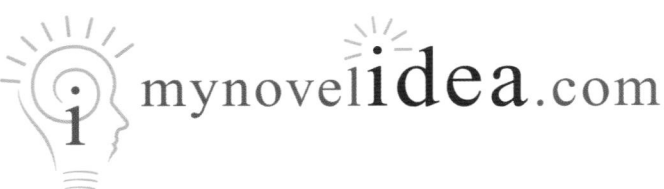

5.

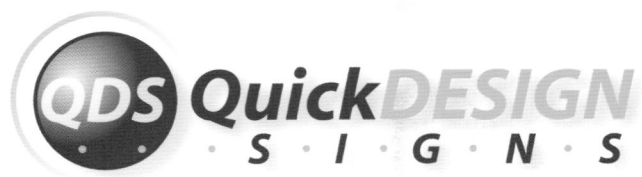

6.

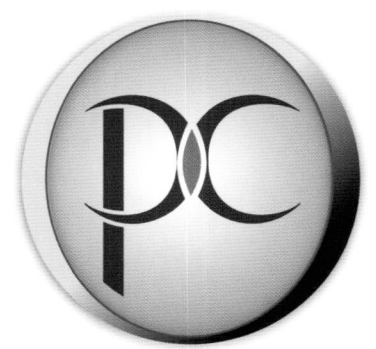

7.

1
Design Firm **Wizards of the Coast**
2 - 4
Design Firm **Glitschka Studios**
5 - 7
Design Firm **End2End Integration, LLC**
1.
Designers Jeremy Cranford,
Yasuyo Dunnett
2.
Client *Samurai Guppy*
Designer Von R. Glitschka
3.
Client *www.blogintosh.com*
Designer Von R. Glitschka
4.
Client *Handyman Solutions*
Designer Von R. Glitschka

5.
Client *My Novel Idea*
Designer Scott Wyss
6.
Client *Quick Design Signs*
Designer Scott Wyss
7.
Client *Party Campus*
Designer Scott Wyss
(opposite)
Client *Satellite Coffee*
Design Firm **Vaughn Wedeen Creative**
Designer Pamela Chang

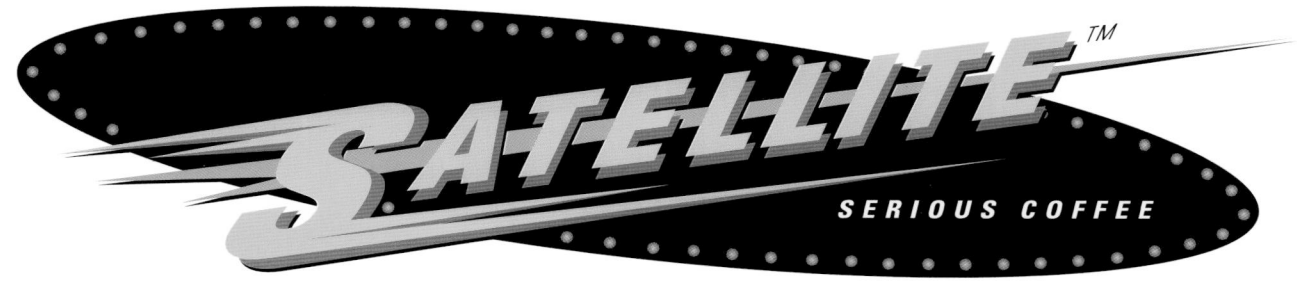

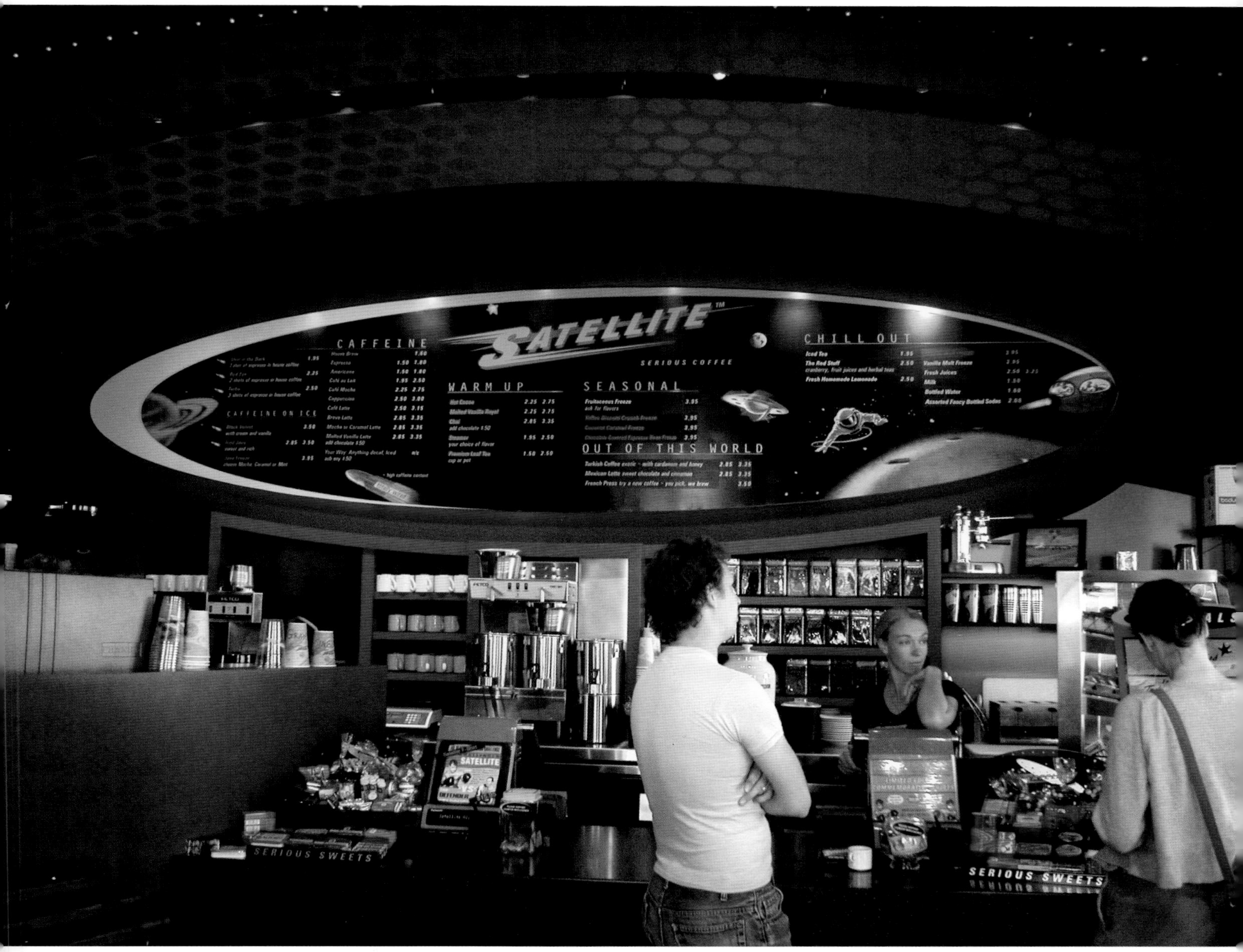

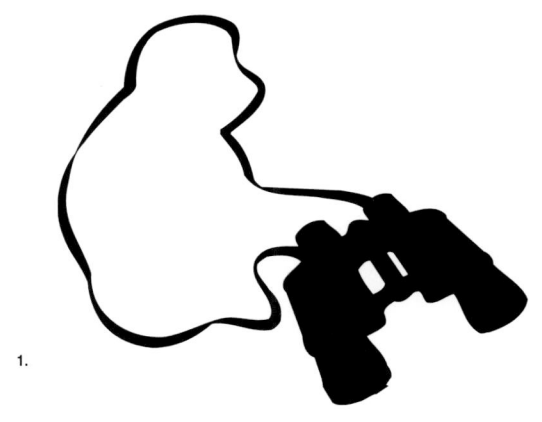

1.

2.

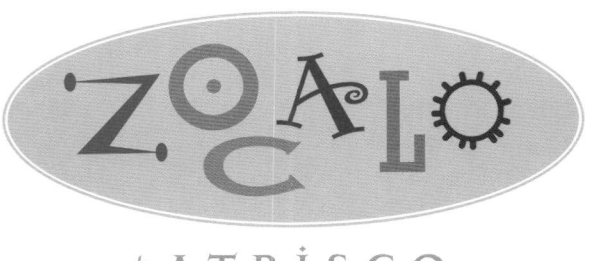

3.

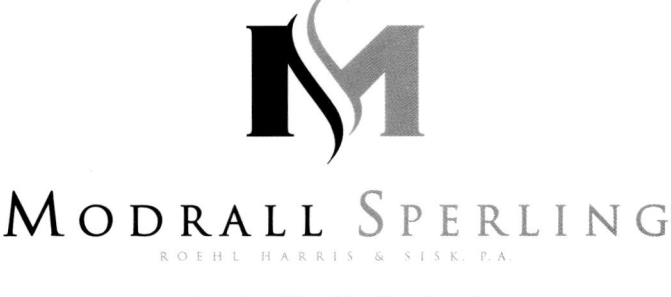

4.

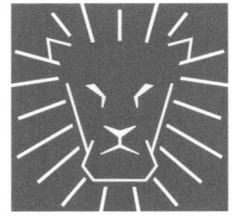

Amy Biehl

High School

5.

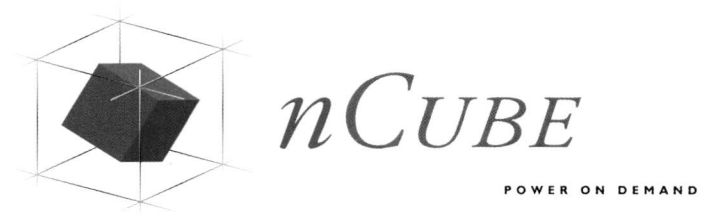

6.

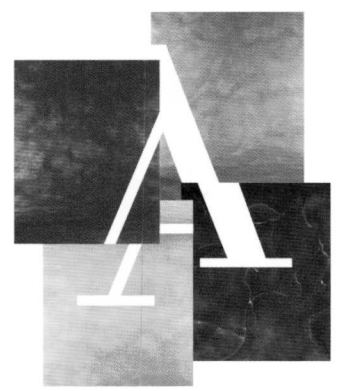

7.

8.

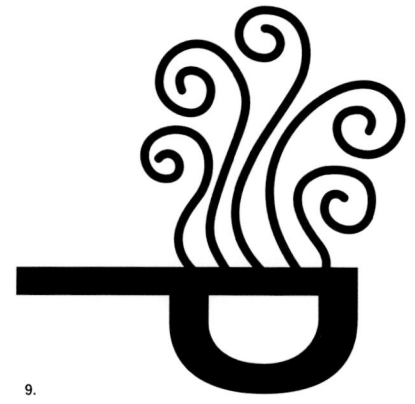

9.

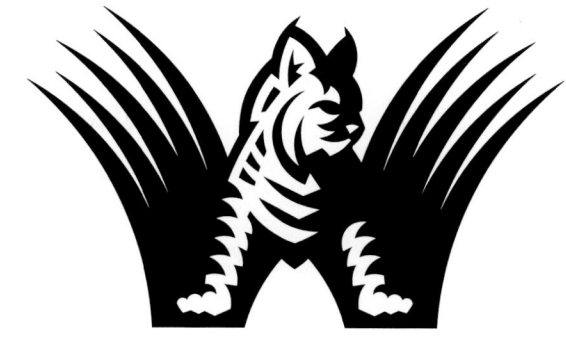

10.

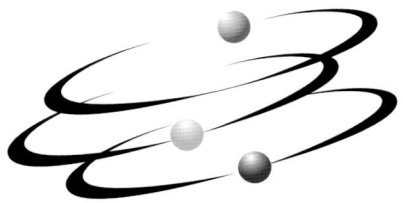

biosgroup

science for business

11.

DK

DENISH + KLINE ASSOCIATES

12.

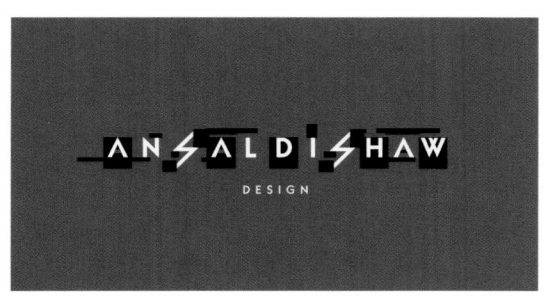

13.

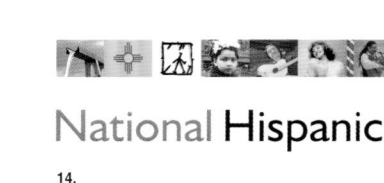

National **Hispanic** Cultural Center

14.

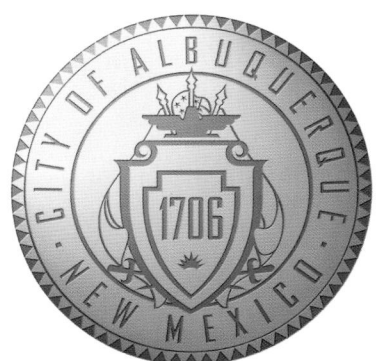

15.

1, 2, 9, 10
Design Firm **Bradford Lawton Design Group**
3 - 8, 11 - 15
Design Firm **Vaughn Wedeen Creative**

1.
Client   *Texas Primate Observatory*
Designer   Bradford Lawton

2.
Client   *Railtex*
Designers   Bradford Lawton, Jody Laney

3.
Client   *Zocalo LLC*
Designer   Rick Vaughn

4.
Client   *Modrall Sperling Lawyers*
Designer   Pamela Chang

5.
Client   *Amy Biehl High School*
Designers   Steve Wedeen, Pamela Chang

6.
Client   *nCube*
Designer   Pamela Chang

7.
Client   *Academy Printers*
Designer   Pamela Chang

8.
Client   *AguaVida*
Designer   Pamela Chang

9.
Client   *Premier Catering*
Designers   Bradford Lawton, Jody Laney

10.
Client   *Wildlife Rescue & Rehabilitation*
Designer   Rolando Murillo

11.
Client   *BiosGroup*
Designer   Pamela Chang

12.
Client   *Denish + Kline Associates*
Designer   Pamela Chang

13.
Client   *Ansaldi Shaw Design/Architecture*
Designer   Steve Wedeen

14.
Client   *National Hispanic Cultural Center*
Designers   Steve Wedeen, Pamela Chang

15.
Client   *City of Albuquerque, New Mexico*
Designer   Rich Vaughn

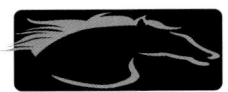

CALIFORNIA HORSE PARK
A STATE OF THE ART EQUINE SHOW FACILITY

1.

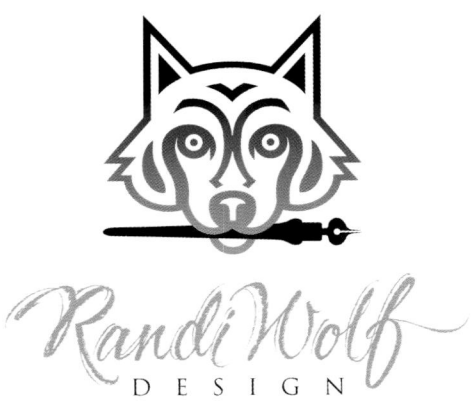

3.

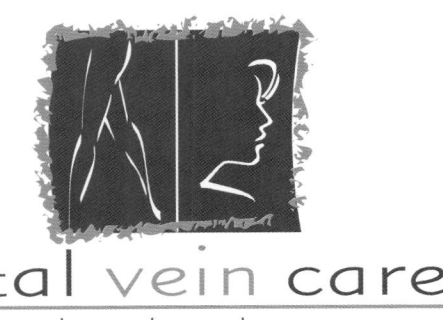

total vein care
vein and aesthetic laser center

2.

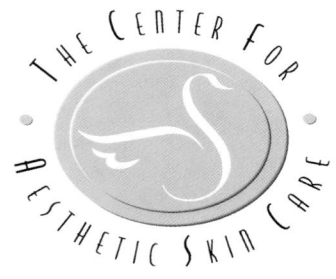

Marc S. Cohen, MD, FACS • Nancy G. Swartz, MS, MD, FACS
Ophthalmic Plastic and Cosmetic Surgeons

4.

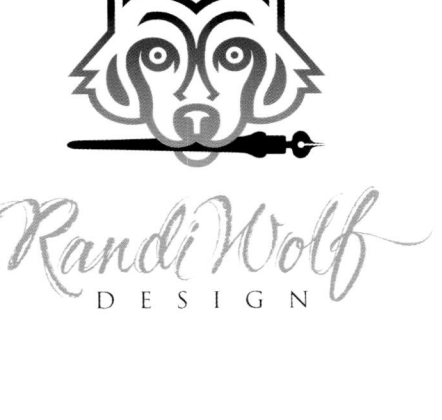

GALEÁNA
WOOD PRODUCTS

5.

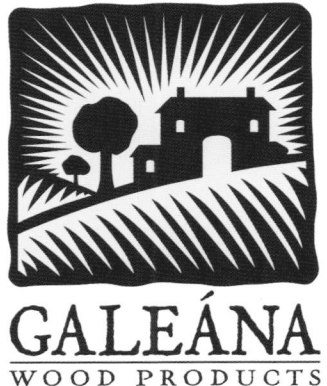

GALEÁNA
WOOD PRODUCTS

6.

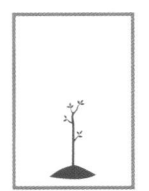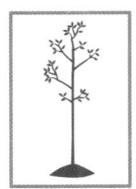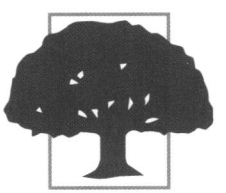

LITTLETON PUBLIC SCHOOLS FOUNDATION
If You Want Oak Trees, You Have To Plant Acorns

7.

1, 2
Design Firm **Market Street Marketing**
3, 4
Design Firm **Randi Wolf Design**
5 - 7
Design Firm **Hat Trick Creative, Inc.**
1.
Client — California Horse Park
Designer — Kathleen Downs
2.
Client — Total Vein Care
Designer — Kathleen Downs
3.
Client — Randi Wolf Design
Designer — Randi Wolf
4.
Client — Dr. Marc Cohen,
Dr. Nancy Swartz
Designer — Randi Wolf

5, 6.
Client — Galeána Wood Products
Designers — Charlie Pate, Lance Brown
7.
Client — Littleton Public Schools
Foundation
Designers — Lance Brown, Charlie Pate
(opposite)
Client — Albuquerque Isotopes
Design Firm **Vaughn Wedeen Creative**
Designer — Pamela Chang

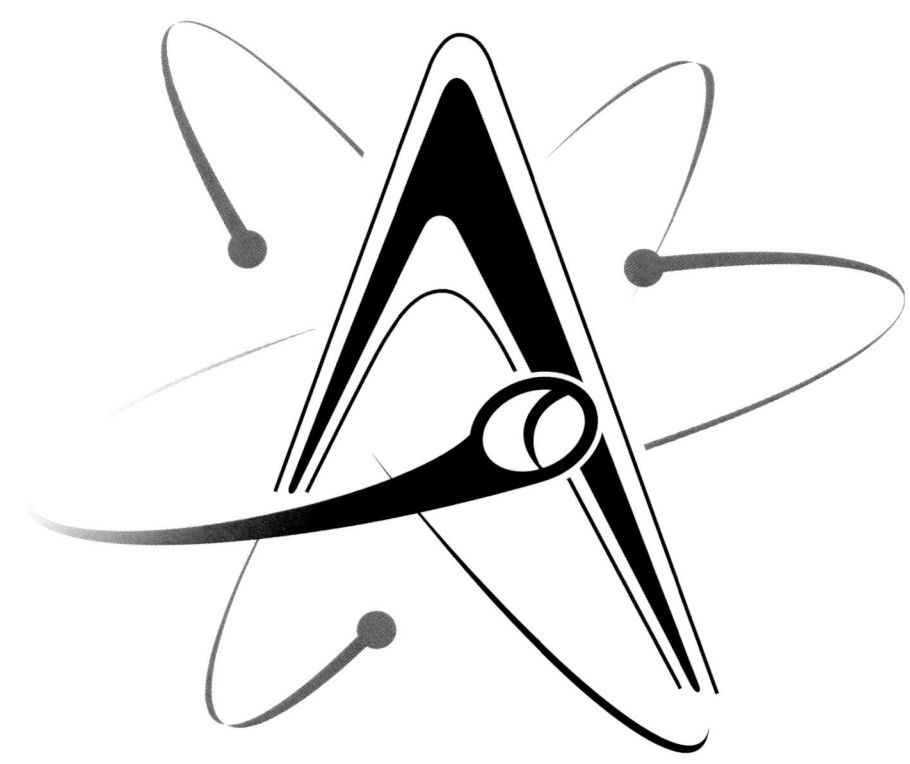

Albuquerque

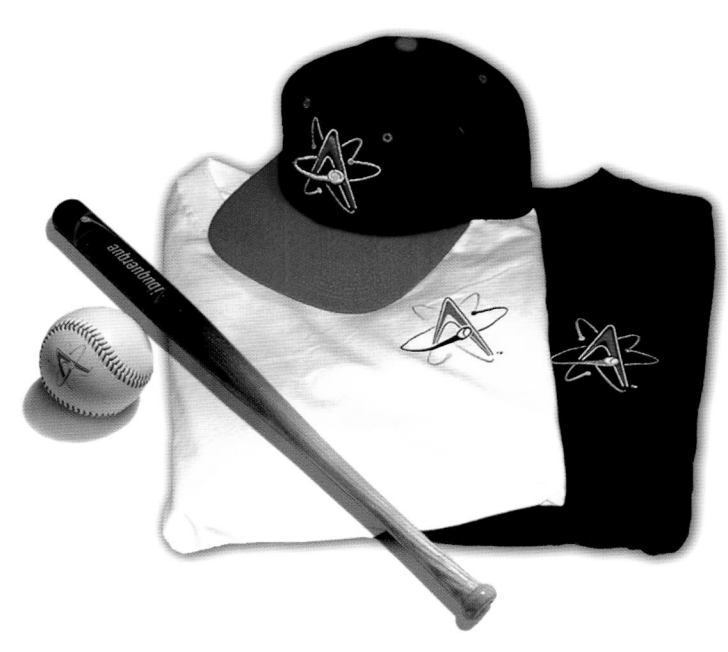

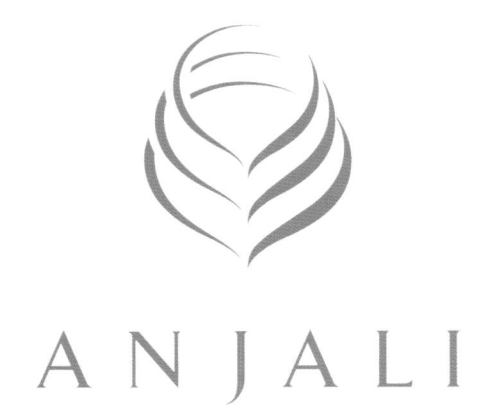

1.

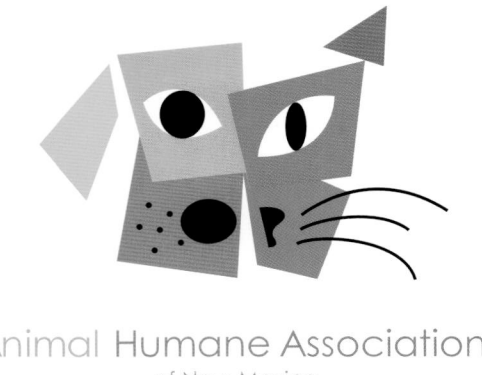

2.

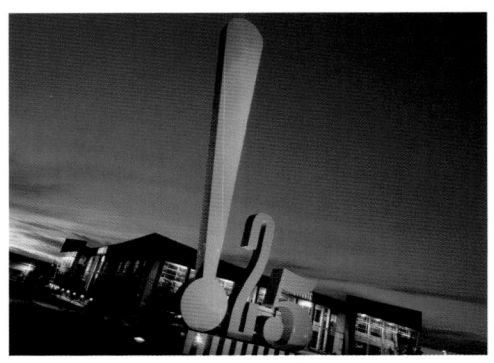

3.

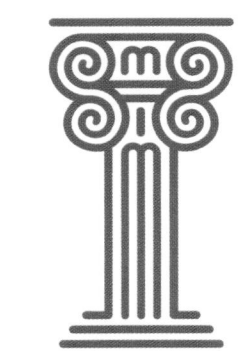

4.

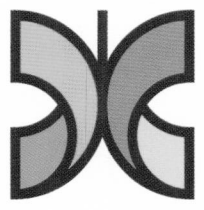

5.

6.

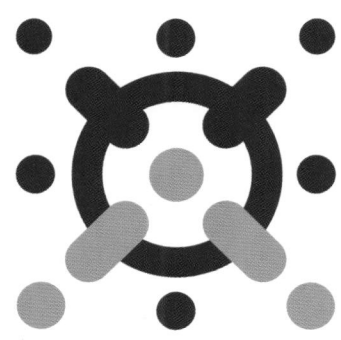

7.

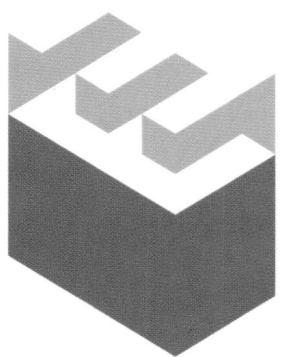

8.

9.

UltraSafe

10.

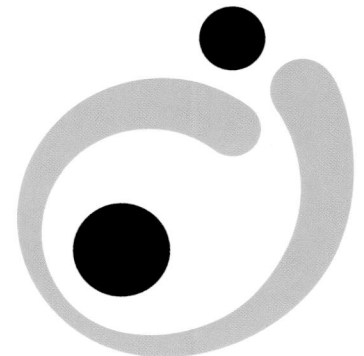

11.

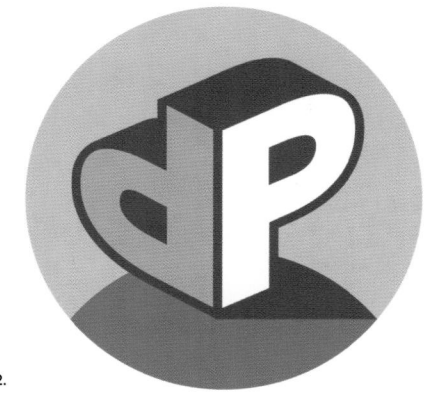

12.

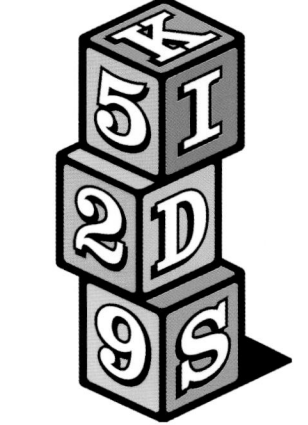

13.

ALTRAMED

14.

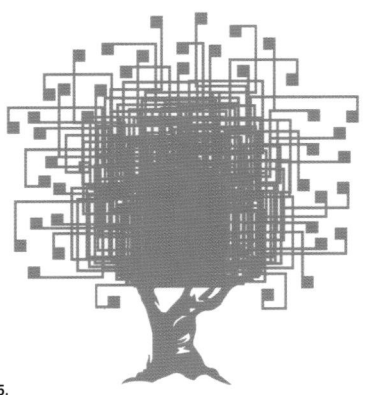

15.

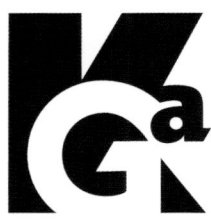

Kensington | GLASS ARTS | Incorporated

1.

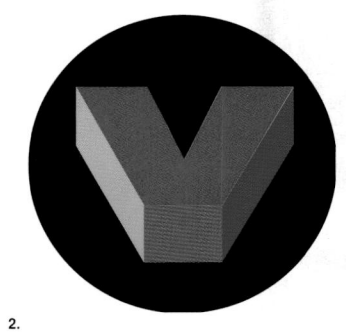

2.

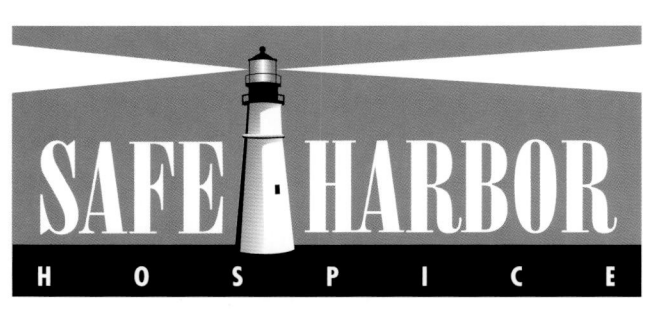

3.

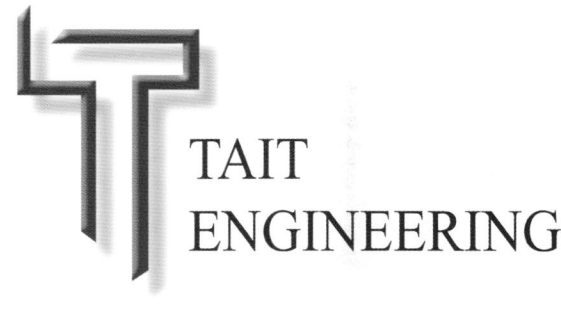

TAIT ENGINEERING

4.

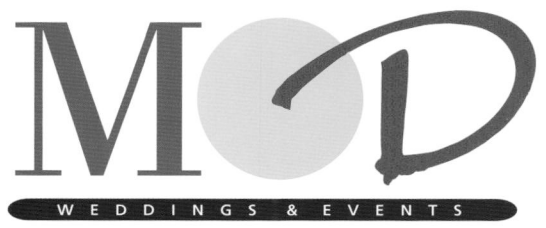

5.

CAIRNS + ASSOCIATES

6.

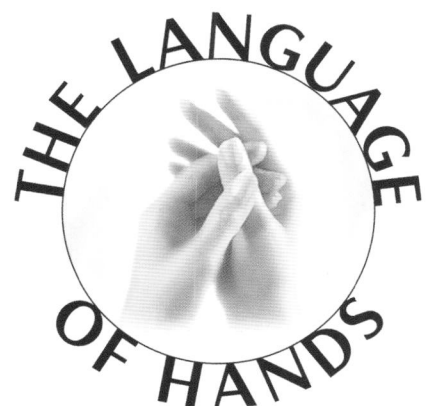

7.

1
Design Firm **Jill Tanenbaum Graphic Design & Advertising**
2, 3
Design Firm **VanPelt Creative**
4
Design Firm **Erisa Creative**
5, 6
Design Firm **Ethan Ries Designs**
7
Design Firm **Cairns + Associates**

1.
Client   *Kensington Glass Arts Incorporated*
Designer   Sue Sprinkle
2.
Client   *VanPelt Creative*
Designer   Chip VanPelt

3.
Client   *Safe Harbor Hospice*
Designer   Chip VanPelt
4.
Client   *Tait Engineering*
Designer   Erin May
5.
Client   *MOD Weddings & Events*
Designer   Ethan Ries
6.
Client   *Cairns + Associates*
Designer   Ethan Ries
7.
Client   *Vaseline Intensive Care Lotion*
Designer   Ethan Ries
(opposite)
Client   *Goldline Controls, Inc.*
Design Firm **DynaPac Design Group**
Designer   Lee A. Aellig

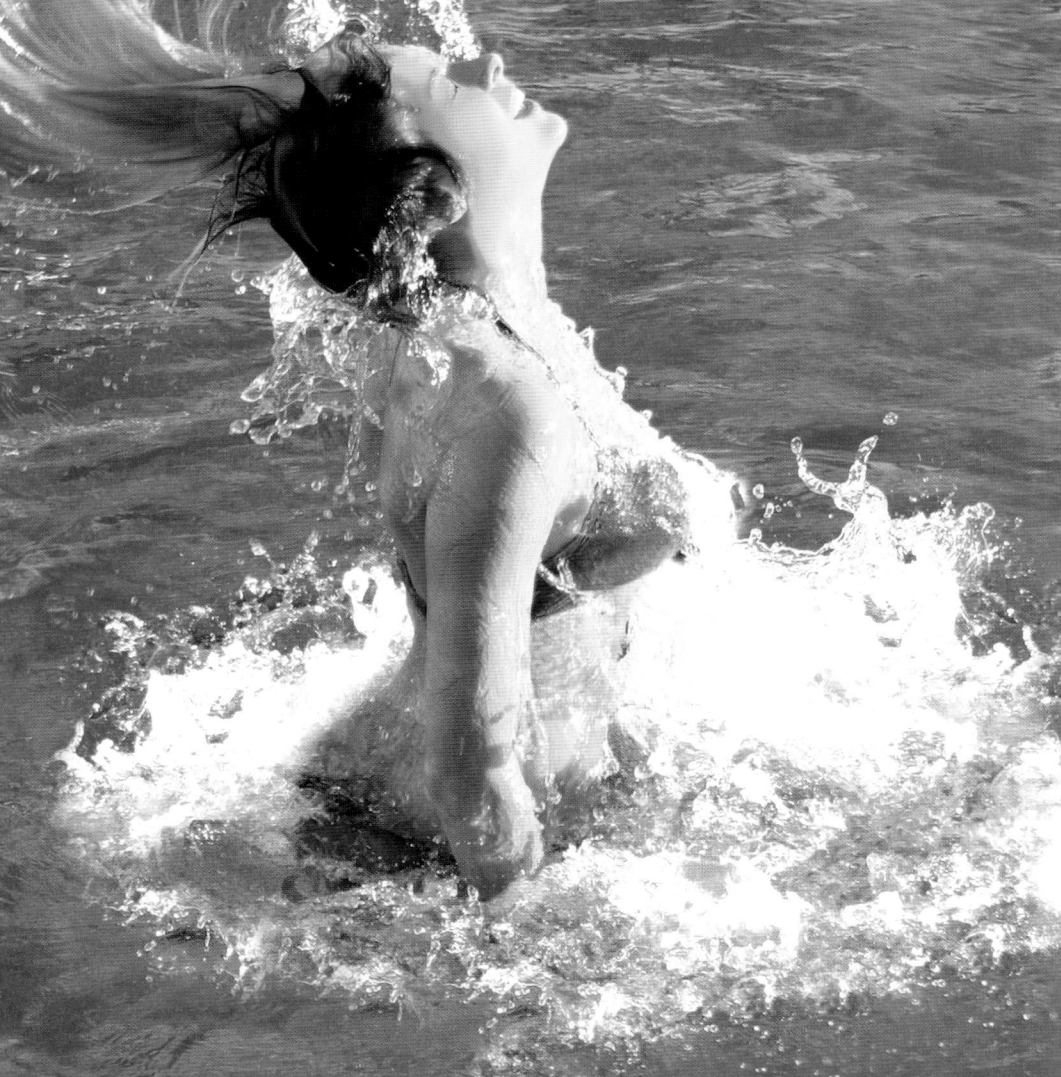

AQUA LOGIC

Automation and Chlorination

THE LOGICAL SOLUTION
FOR PURE SWIMMING PLEASURE

GOLDLINE
CONTROLS INC.

IMAGINE

changing the world

1.

BURNS
AND COMPANY
CONSULTING

2.

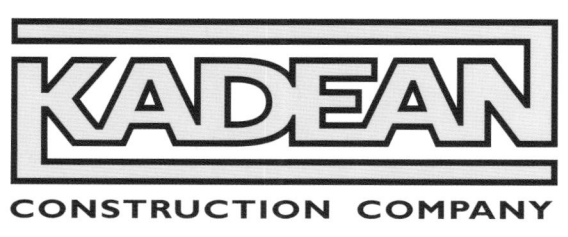

CONSTRUCTION COMPANY

3.

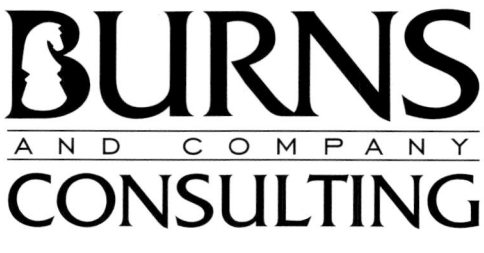

WEINBAUER & ASSOCIATES, INC.
Tax & Financial Services

4.

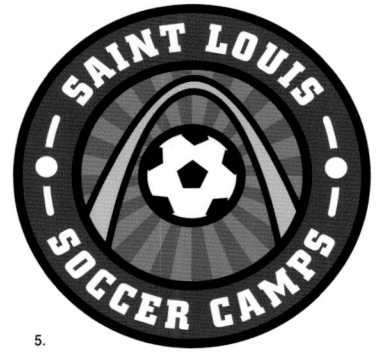

5.

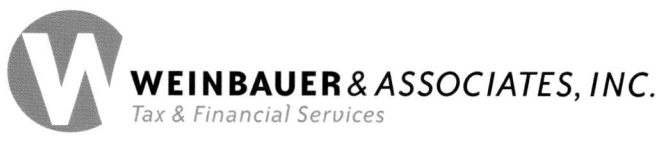

6.

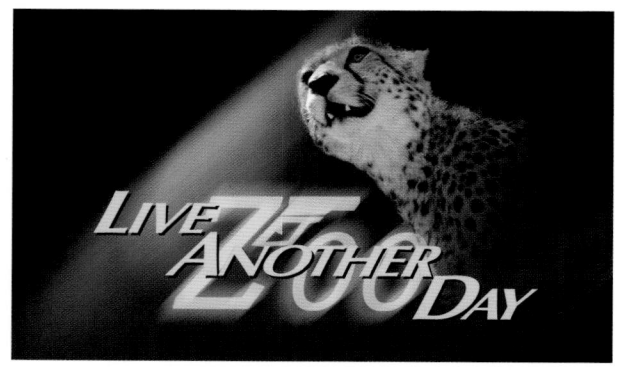

7.

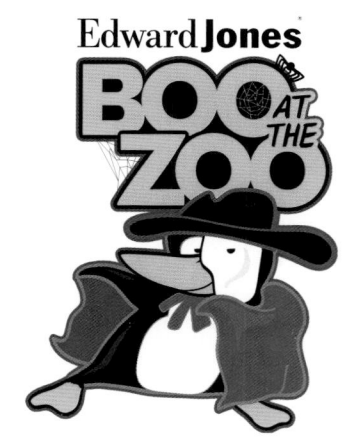

8.

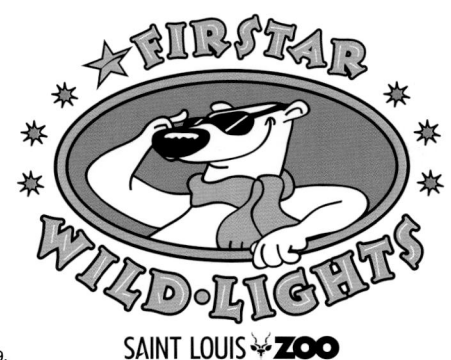

9.

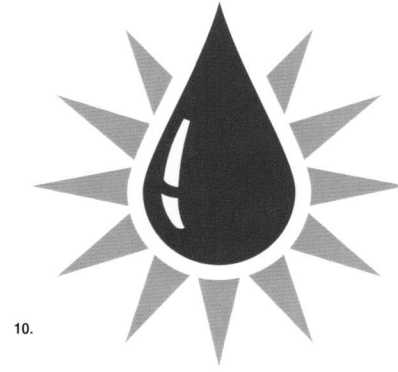

10.

BRIGHT RAIN

C R E A T I V E

11.

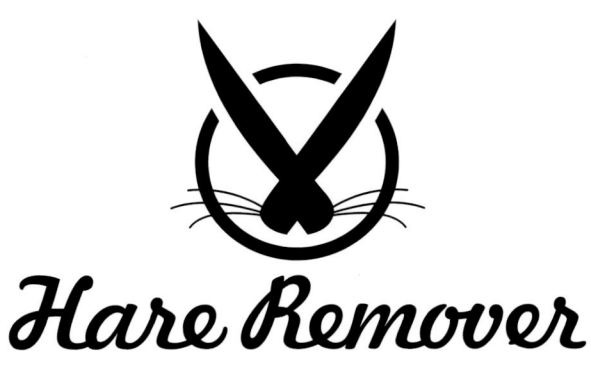

12.

GOLF DAY
2002

13.

Triple 40

14.

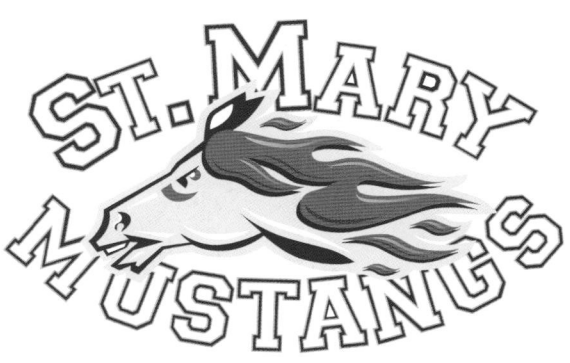

15.

1 - 13
Design Firm **Bright Rain Creative**
14, 15
Design Firm **Pixallure Design**
1.
Client   *St Louis Young Presidents Organization*
Designer   Matt Marino
2.
Client   *Burns and Company Consulting*
Designer   Kevin Hough
3.
Client   *Kadean Construction Company*
Designer   Matt Marino, Bill Rice
4.
Client   *Weinbauer & Associates, Inc.*
Designer   Matt Marino
5, 6.
Client   *St. Louis Soccer Camps*
Designer   Matt Marino
7.
Client   *Saint Louis Zoo*
Designer   Kevin Hough

8, 9.
Client   *Saint Louis Zoo*
Designer   Matt Marino
10, 11.
Client   *Bright Rain Creative*
Designers   Kevin Hough, Matt Marino
12.
Client   *Bob Abrams Idea Company*
Designer   Matt Marino
13.
Client   *Clayco Construction Company*
Designer   Kevin Hough
14.
Client   *Triple 40*
Designer   Steven Lutz`
15.
Client   *St. Mary Catholic School*
Designer   Terry Edeker

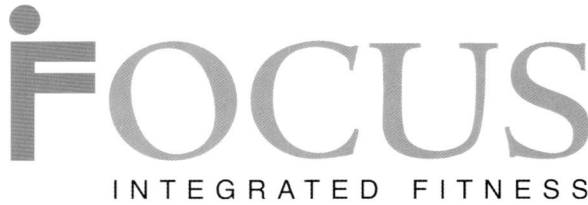

1.

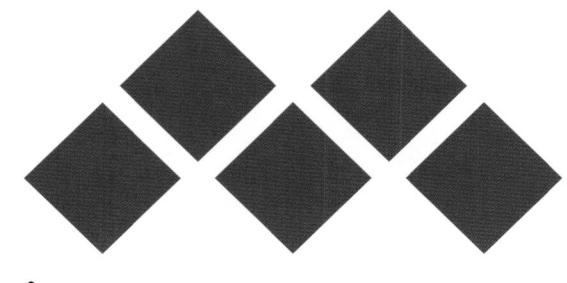

2.

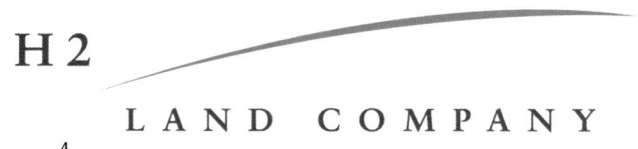

3.

H 2

LAND COMPANY

4.

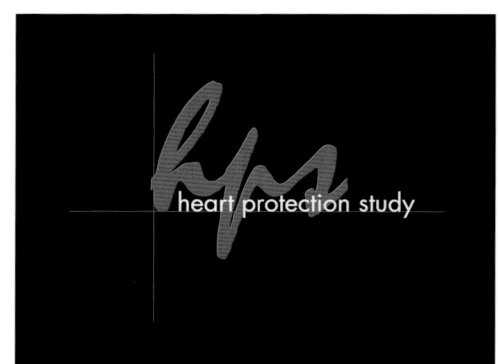

5.

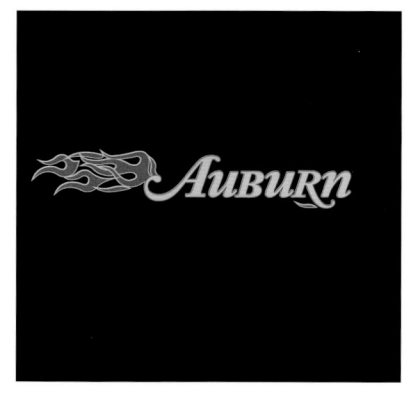

6.

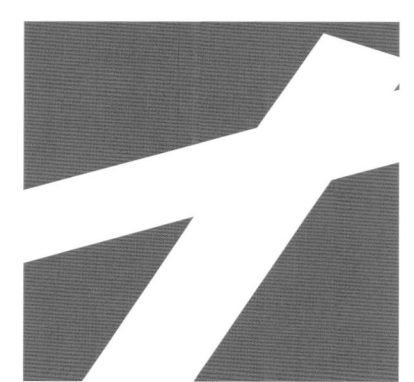

7.

1
Design Firm **inc3**
2
Design Firm **Studio Hill Design**
3, 4
Design Firm **Lomangino Studio Inc.**
5
Design Firm **Merck Worldwide**
6
Design Firm **Atomic Design**
7
Design Firm **Robert Talarczyk Design**

1.
Client   *Focus Integrated Fitness*
Designers Harvey Appelbaum,
John Sexton,
Christopher Nystrom

2.
Client   *Milestone Imports*
Designers Sandy Hill,
Sean Michael Chavez

3.
Client   *Foster/Searing*
Designer Kim Pollock

4.
Client   *H2 Land Company*
Designer Michael Mateos

5.
Client   *Zocor hps*
Designer Robert Talarczyk

6.
Client   *Auburn*
Designer Lewis Glaser

7.
Client   *Robert Talarczyk Design*
Designer *Robert Talarczyk*

(opposite)
Client   *Auto Care Products, Inc.*
Design Firm **DynaPac Design Group**
Designer Lee A. Aellig

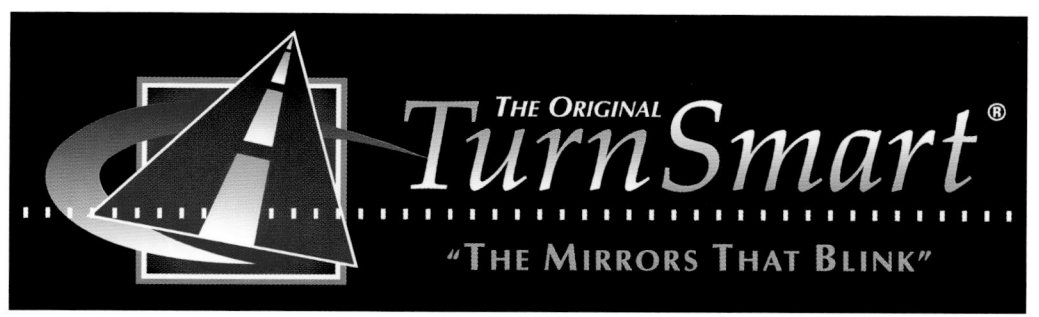

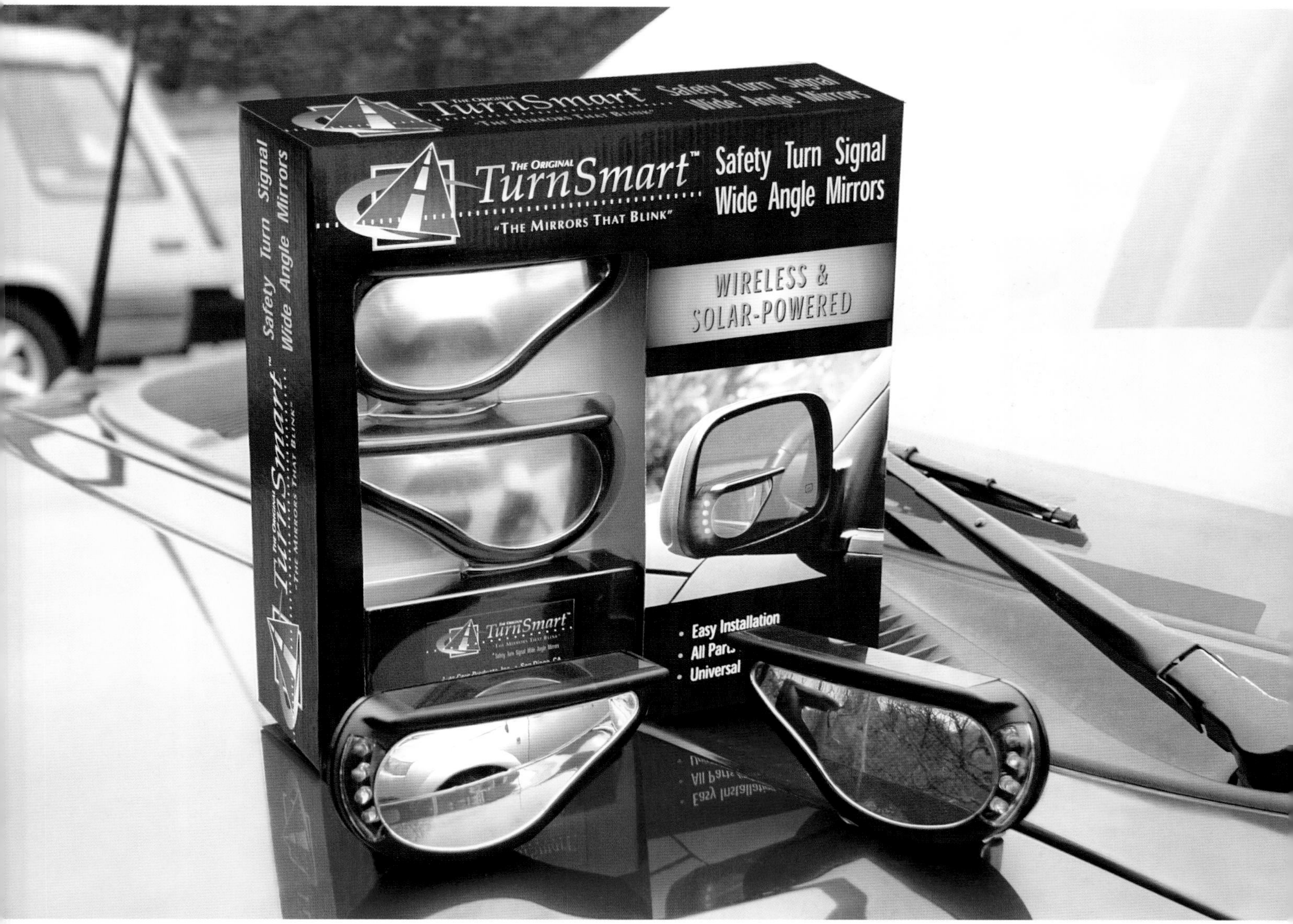

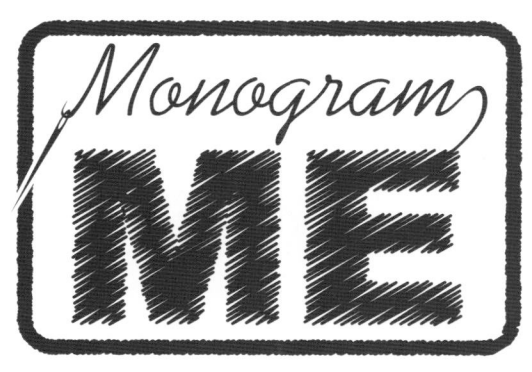

1.

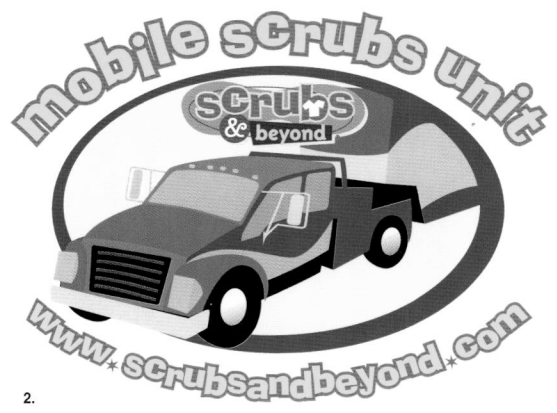

2.

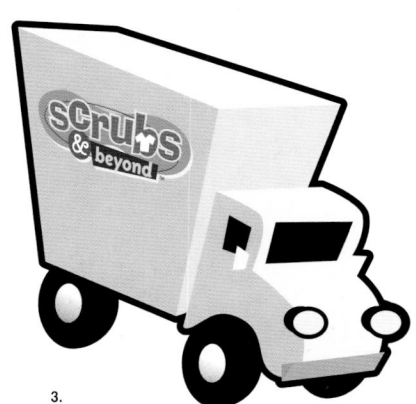

3.

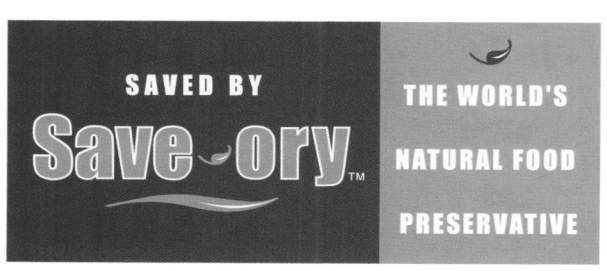

4.

5.

ST. LUKE'S
FAMILY PRACTICE

6.

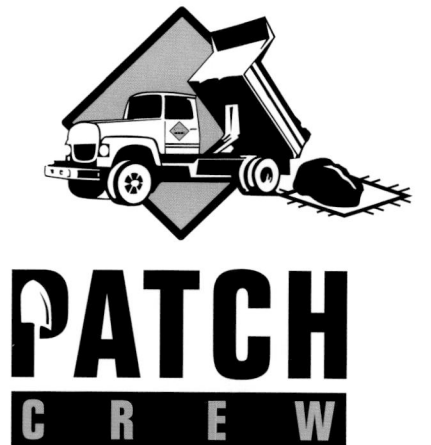

7.

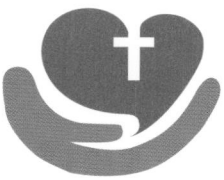

8.

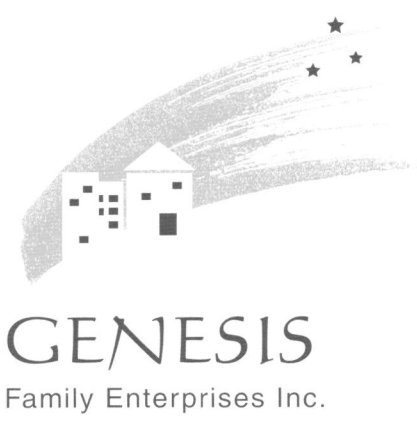

GENESIS
Family Enterprises Inc.

9.

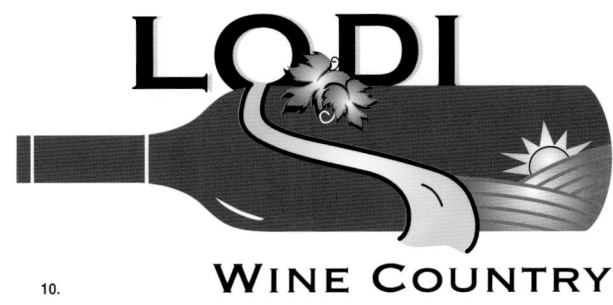

10.

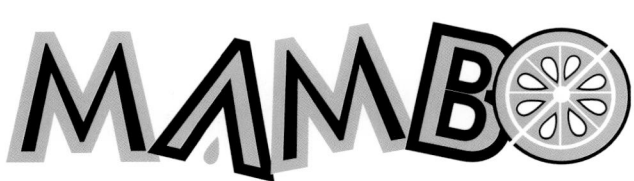

Marketing With A Twist!

11.

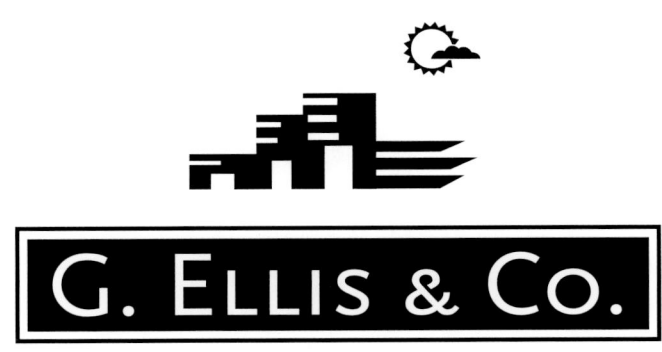

G. ELLIS & CO.

COMMERCIAL REAL ESTATE

12.

NuCal Foods Inc.

Eggs can't get any fresher.

13.

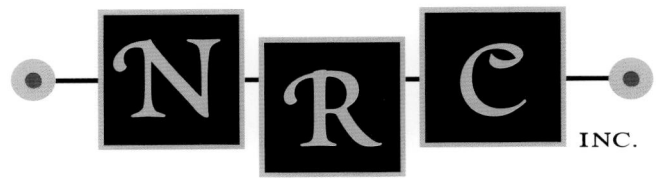

INSURANCE AGENCY

14.

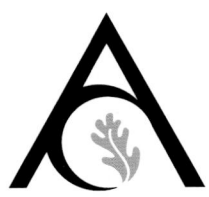

AGILE OAK ORTHOPEDICS

15.

1 - 4
Design Firm **Bright Rain Creative**
5 - 15
Design Firm **Marcia Herrmann Design**

1, 2.
Client   *Scrubs & Beyond*
Designers   Kevin Hough, Matt Marino

3, 4.
Client   *Scrubs & Beyond*
Designer   Matt Marino

5.
Client   *Meitetso Corporation*
Designer   Marcia Herrmann

6.
Client   *St. Lukes Family Practice*
Designer   Marcia Herrmann

7.
Client   *Patch Crew*
Designer   Marcia Herrmann

8.
Client   *Archworks*
Designer   Marcia Herrmann

9.
Client   *Genesis Family Enterprises*
Designer   Marcia Herrmann

10.
Client   *Lodi Wine Country*
Designer   Marcia Herrmann

11.
Client   *Mambo*
Designer   Marcia Herrmann

12.
Client   *G. Ellis & Co.*
Designer   Marcia Herrmann

13.
Client   *NuCal Eggs*
Designer   Marcia Herrmann

14.
Client   *NRC Insurance Agency Inc.*
Designers   Marcia Herrmann,
            Sylvia Magdalena

15.
Client   *Agile Oak Orthopedics*
Designer   Marcia Herrmann

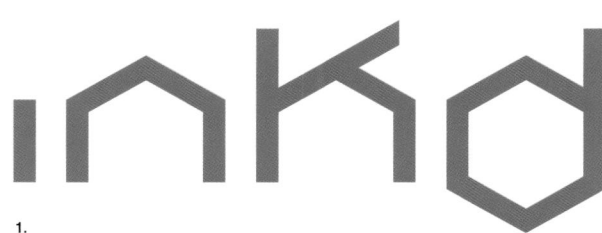

1.

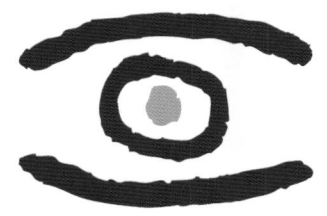

2.

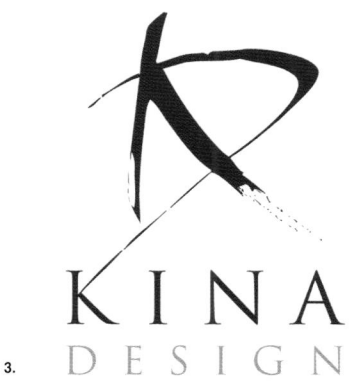

3.

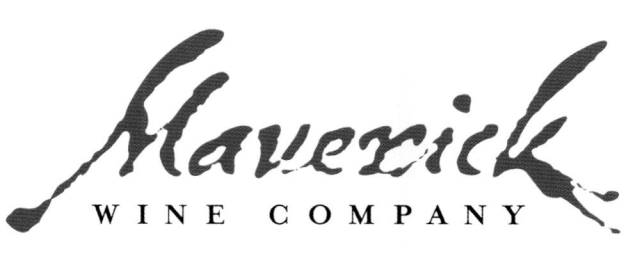

4.

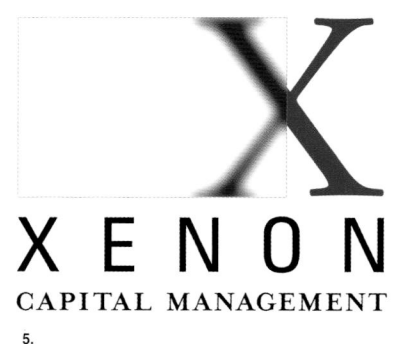

5.

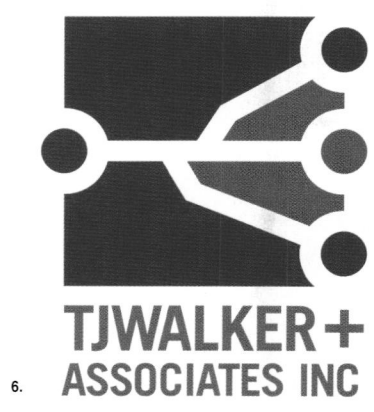

6.

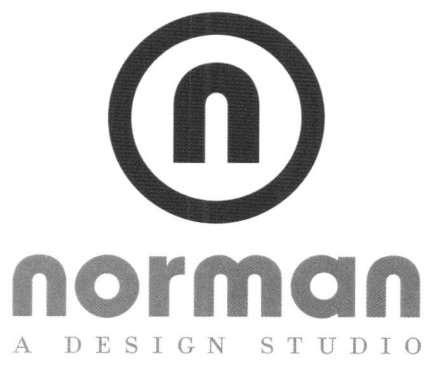

7.

1
Design Firm **Lahn Nguyen**
2 - 7
Design Firm **Norman Design**
1.
Client   *INKD Clothing*
Designer Lahn Nguyen
2.
Client   *The Keen Eye*
Designer Claudia Renzi
3.
Client   *Kina Design*
Designer Armin Vit
4.
Client   *Maverick Wine Company*
Designer Armin Vit
5.
Client   *Xenon Capital Management*
Designer Armin Vit

6.
Client   *TJ Walker & Associates Inc.*
Designer Armin Vit
7.
Client   *Norman Design*
Designer Armin Vit
(opposite)
Client   *Putt Meister, Inc.*
Design Firm **DynaPac Design Group**
Designer Lee A. Aellig

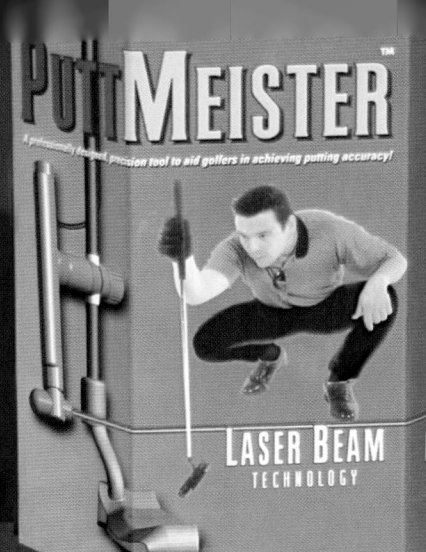

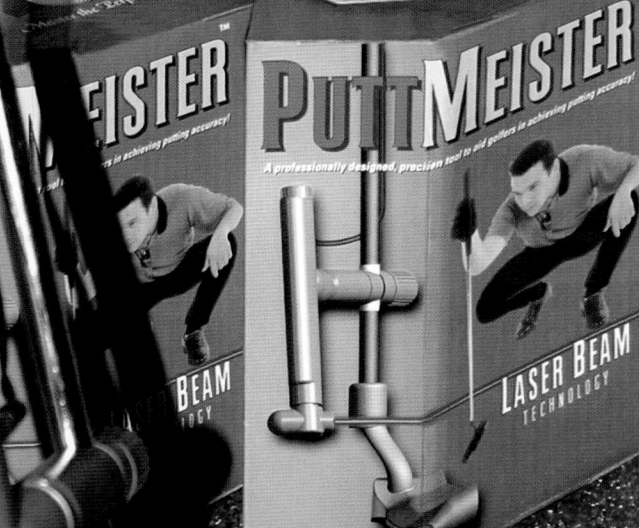

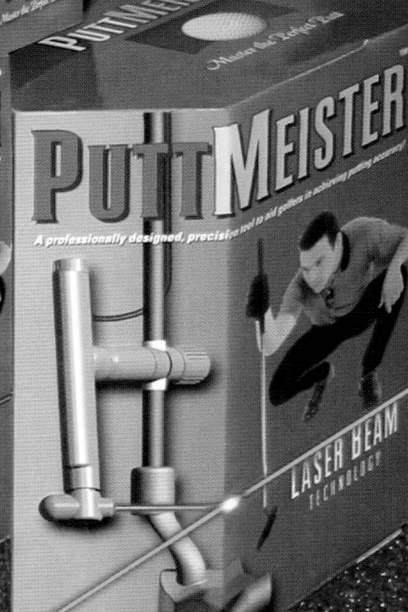

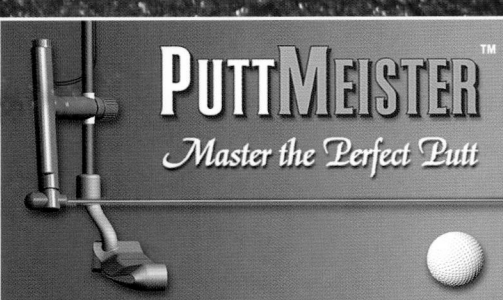

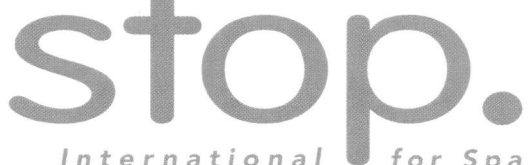

stop.
International for Spa

1.

Swadden Virgin & Young

2.

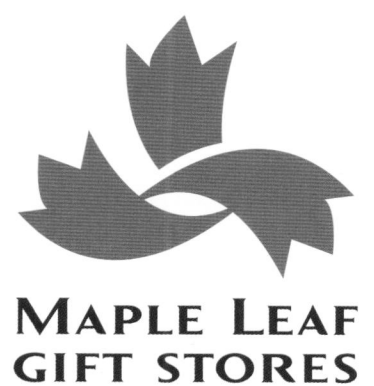

WILDEN LOFTS

3.

HEALTH POINT

The new model of Primary Care

4.

MERCEDES OLIVE

5.

MARIA MANNA 乩 LIFE SPA

6.

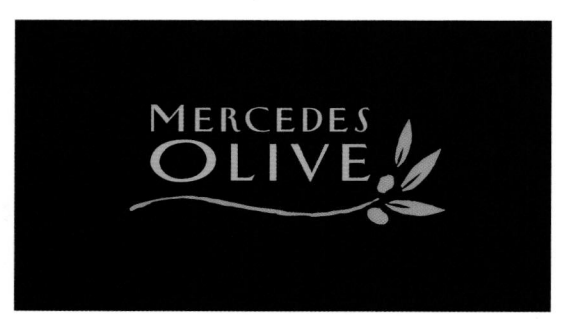

MAPLE LEAF GIFT STORES

7.

2020

DOWNTOWN VICTORIA
2020

8.

ART IN BLOOM

9.

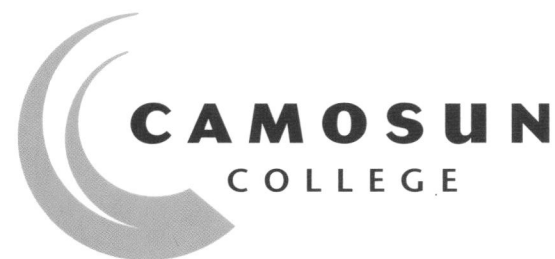

CAMOSUN COLLEGE

10.

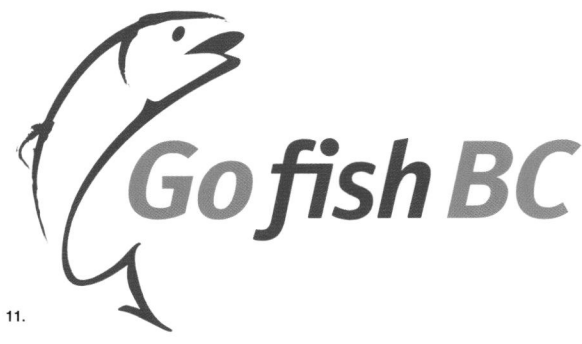

Go fish BC

11.

Glazin Sisco

executive search

12.

together we care

GREATER VICTORIA HOSPITALS FOUNDATION

13.

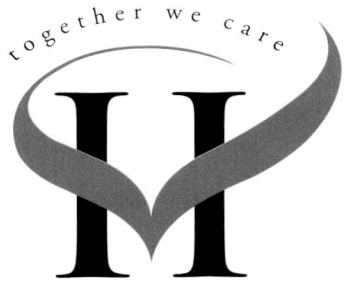

Hard·Hats®
Job training • Job filled • Job done

14.

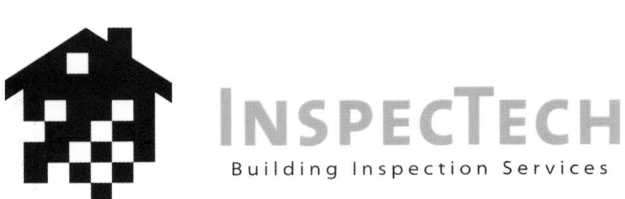

INSPECTECH
Building Inspection Services

15.

1 - 15		
Design Firm	**Trapeze Communications**	
1.		
Client	*Stop. Hand & Foot Spa*	
Designer	Mark Bawden	
2.		
Client	*Swadden, Virgin & Young*	
Designer	Mark Bawden	
3.		
Client	*Wilden Lofts*	
Designer	Mark Bawden	
4.		
Client	*Vancouver Island Health Authority*	
Designer	Mark Bawden	
5.		
Client	*Mercedes Olive*	
Designers	Mark Bawden, Joe Hedges	
6.		
Client	*Maria Manna*	
Designer	Neil Tran	
7.		
Client	*Maple Leaf Gifts*	
Designer	Joe Hedges	

8.	
Client	*Downtown Victoria 2020*
Designer	Marianne Unger
9.	
Client	*Art Gallery of Greater Victoria*
Designers	Mark Bawden, June Paulovich
10.	
Client	*Camosun College*
Designer	Mark Bawden
11.	
Client	*Freshwater Fisheries Society of British Columbia*
Designer	Joe Hedges
12.	
Client	*Glazin Sisco*
Designers	Mark Bawden, Marianne Unger
13.	
Client	*Greater Victoria Hospitals Foundation*
Designers	Mark Bawden, Marianne Unger
14.	
Client	*Grant Thornton*
Designer	Neil Tran
15.	
Client	*Inspectech*
Designers	Mark Bawden, June Paulovich

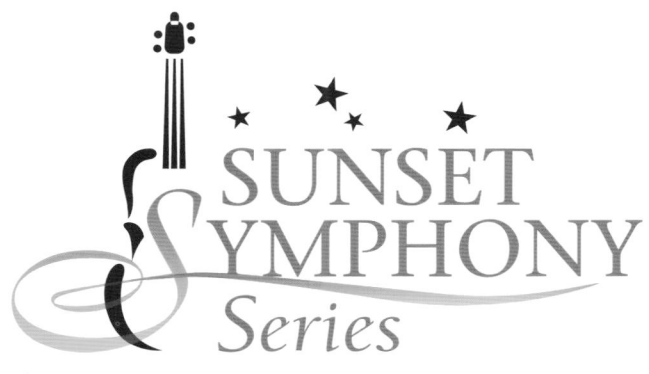

1.

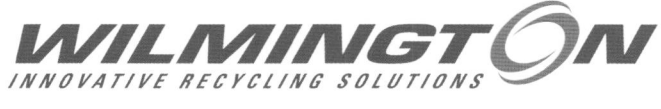

2.

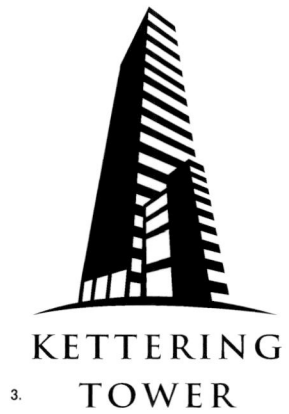

3.

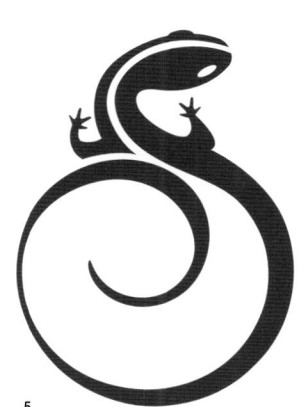

4.

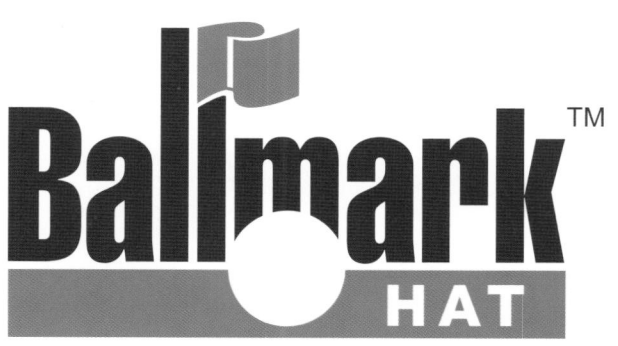

5.

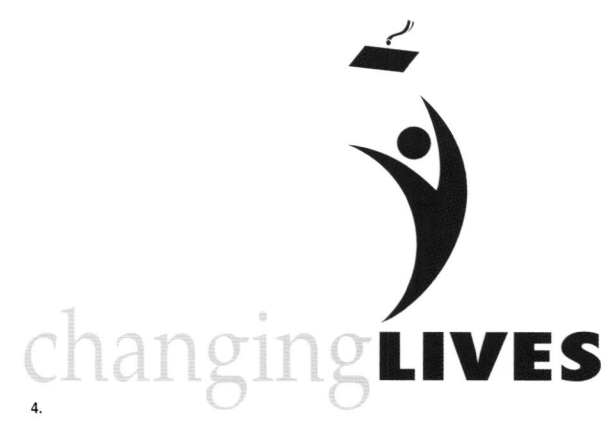

6.

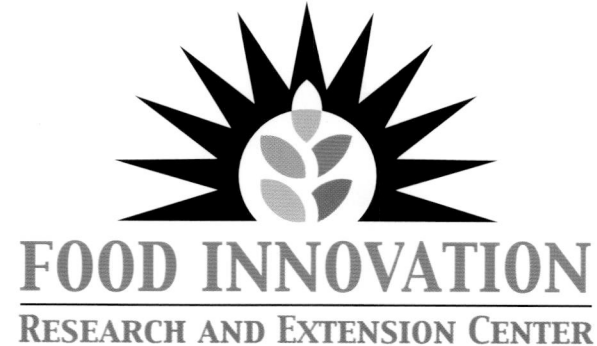

7.

1 - 4
Design Firm **Nova Creative Group**

5
Design Firm **Grafik Marketing Communications**

6
Design Firm **Rutgers University**

7
Design Firm **Fleming & Roskelly, Inc.**

1.
Client   *Dayton Philharmonic Orchestra*
Designer   Dwayne Swormstedt

2.
Client   *Wilmington Iron & Metal*
Designer   Jack Denlinger

3.
Client   *Miller Valentine*
Designer   Jack Denlinger

4.
Client   *Sinclair Community College Foundation*
Designers   Dwayne Swormstedt, Ben Robinson

5.
Client   *Market Salamander*
Designers   Michelle Mar, Judy Kirpich, Heath Dwiggins

6.
Client   *Food Innovation Research and Extension Center*
Designer   John Van Cleaf

7.
Client   *Adams Headwear*
Designers   Tom Roskelly, Deb Moniz
(opposite)
Client   *Mexotic Foods*
Design Firm **DynaPac Design Group**
Designer   Lee A. Aellig

NEW

Includes Gourmet Sauce Tub & Cheese Packet for Added "MEXCITING™" Flavor

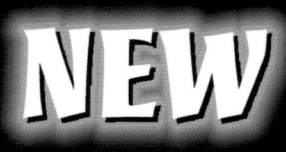

AMERICA'S FINEST

MEXOTIC™

GOURMET CUISINE

PREMIUM FOODS

LOADED with "MEXCEPTIONAL™" QUALITY!

▼

FINEST INGREDIENTS and MASTERFUL TECHNIQUE CREATES SMOOTH, SUPERIOR TASTE!

▼

Previously Handled Frozen For Your Protection, Refreeze Or Keep Refrigerated

All Individually Sealed

FULLY COOKED • JUST HEAT & SERVE • READY IN ④ MINUTES

READY-TO-EAT

BEEF ESPECIAL

2 Premium Beef Wraps
with Gourmet Red Chili Sauce and Cheese

Suggested serving

NET WT. 9.23 OZ. (262g)

U.S. INSPECTED AND PASSED BY DEPARTMENT OF AGRICULTURE EST. 31595

Read Learning Centre

1.

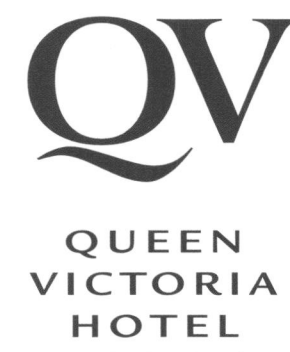

QUEEN VICTORIA HOTEL AND SUITES

2.

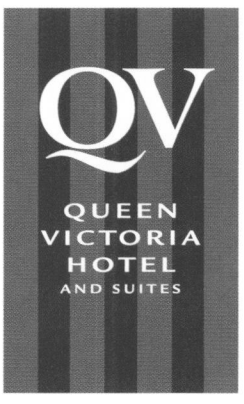

3.

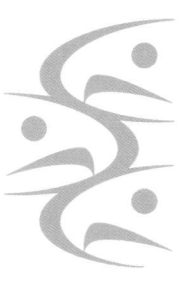

VICTORIA CONFERENCE CENTRE

4.

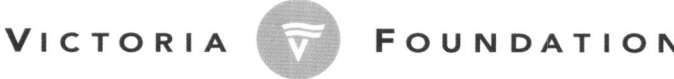

5.

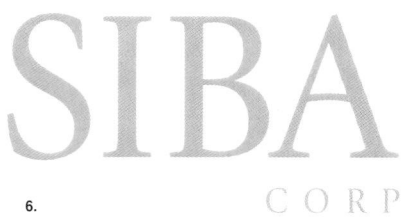

6.

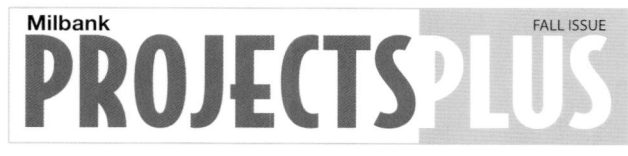

7.

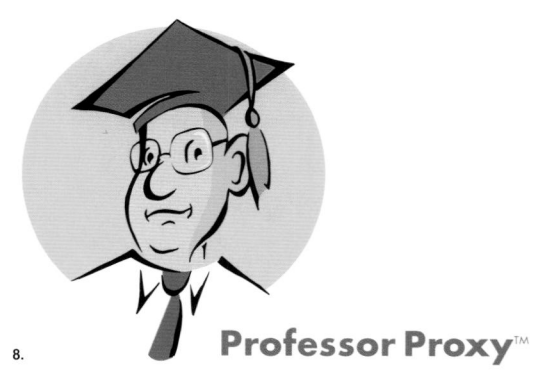

8.

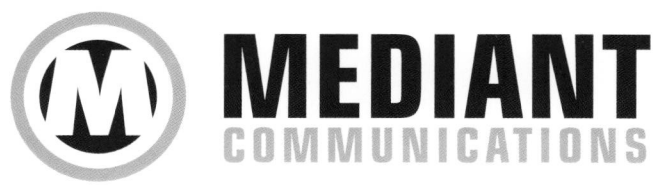

MEDIANT
COMMUNICATIONS

9.

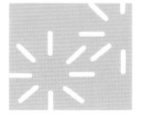

JS Public Relations

10.

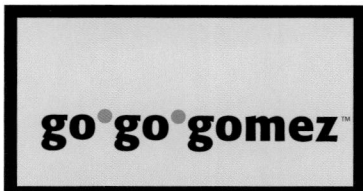

go·go·gomez™

g

11.

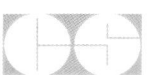

*Cantor***SEINUK**

STRUCTURAL ENGINEERS

12.

CDR
Credit Derivatives Research LLC

13.

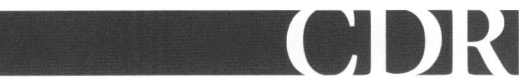

Gimme Credit™

14.

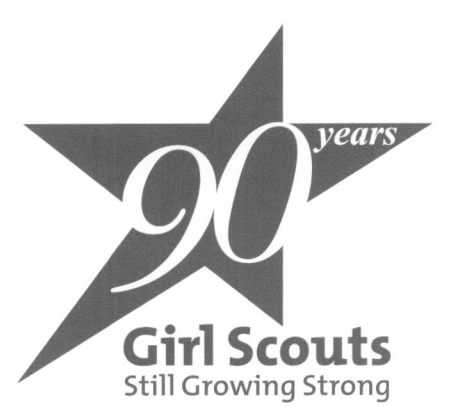

90 years

Girl Scouts
Still Growing Strong

15.

1 - 5
Design Firm **Trapeze Communications**
6 - 15
Design Firm **Rappy & Company**
1.
  Client   *Victoria Read Society*
  Designers   Mark Bawden, Marianne Unger
2 - 3.
  Client   *Queen Victoria Inn*
  Designers   Mark Bawden, Joe Hedges
4.
  Client   *Victoria Conference Centre*
  Designers   Mark Bawden, Chris Paul
5.
  Client   *Victoria Foundation*
  Designers   Joe Hedges, Mark Bawden
6.
  Client   *SIBA Corp.*
  Designers   Floyd Rappy, Nicole Picarillo
7.
  Client   *Milbank*
  Designers   Floyd Rappy, Brian Santiago

8.
  Client   *Mediant Communications*
  Designers   Floyd Rappy, Amanda Skudlarek
9.
  Client   *Mediant Communications*
  Designers   Floyd Rappy, Jamie Flohr
10.
  Client   *JS Public Relations*
  Designer   Floyd Rappy
11.
  Client   *Go Go Gomez*
  Designers   Floyd Rappy, Kristina Schmidt
12.
  Client   *Cantor Seinuk*
  Designers   Floyd Rappy, Mary Smith
13.
  Client   *Credit Derivatives Research LLC*
  Designers   Floyd Rappy, Brian Jones,
              Kristina Schmidt
14.
  Client   *Gimme Credit*
  Designers   Floyd Rappy, Soohyen Park
15.
  Client   *Girl Scouts of the USA*
  Designer   Floyd Rappy

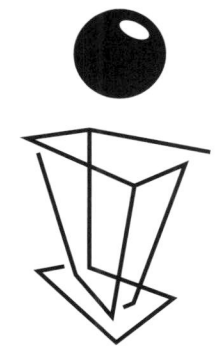

industrial modeling corporation

1.

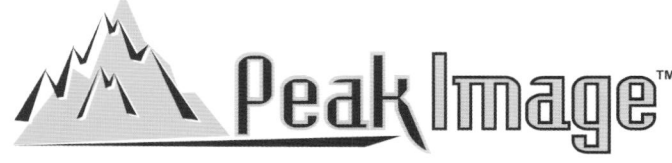

2.

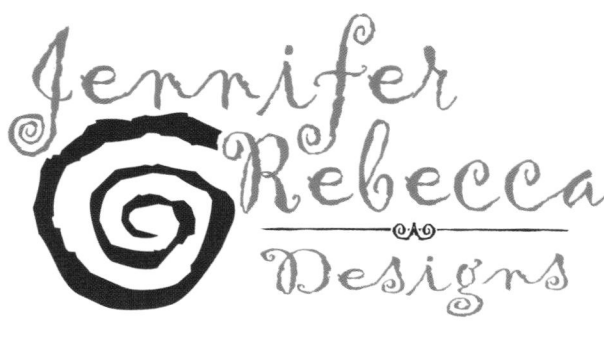

3.

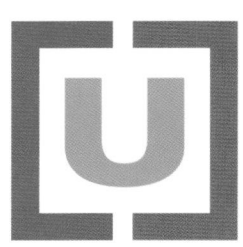

UNIVERSITYSQUARE

4.

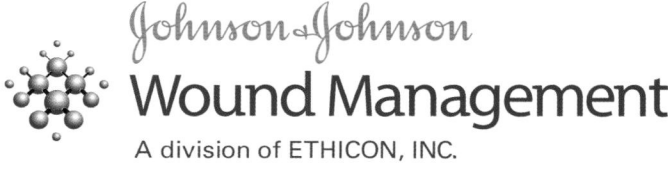

5.

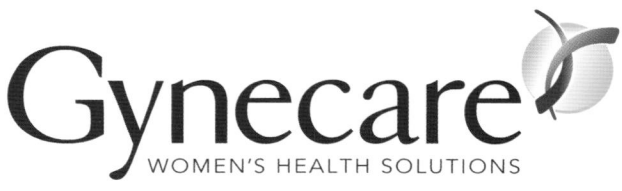

6.

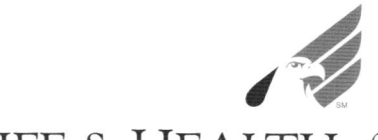

7.

1
Design Firm **DrrtyGrrl Designs**
2, 3
Design Firm **JenGraph**
4 - 7
Design Firm **The Bailey Group**
1.
Client   *Industrial Modeling Corporation*
Designer   Debbi Murray
2.
Client   *Guentherman Consulting, Inc.*
Designer   Jennifer A. Niles
3.
Client   *Jennifer Rebecca Designs*
Designer   Jennifer A. Niles
4.
Client   *University of Pennsylvania*
Designers   Jerry Corcoran, Steve Perry,
             Dave Fiedler

5.
Client   *Ethicon*
Designers   Steve Perry, Wendy Slavish,
             Lizzy Lee
6.
Client   *Ethicon*
Designer   Ann marie Malone
7.
Client   *Life & Health of America*
Designers   Dave Fiedler, Jerry Corcoran
(opposite)
Client   *Nestle Chocolates*
Design Firm **TD2, S.C.**
Designers   Rafael Rodrigo Córdova,
             Rafael Treviño M.

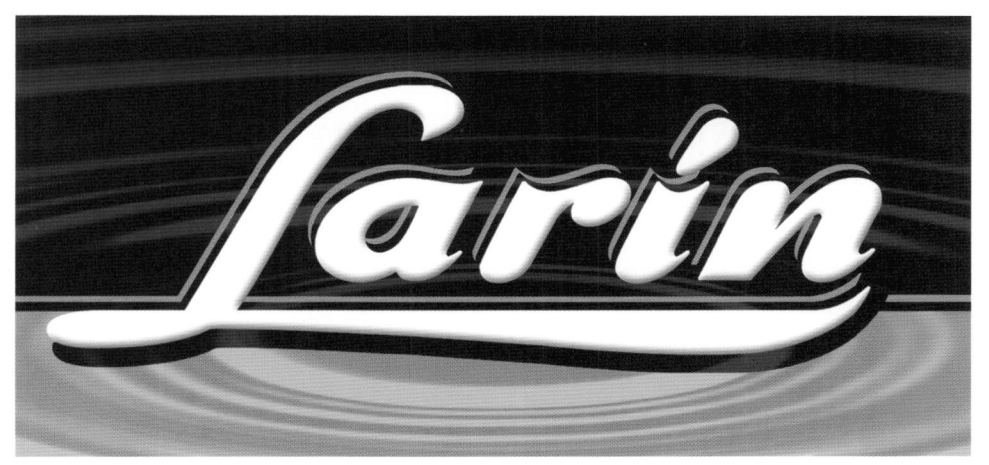

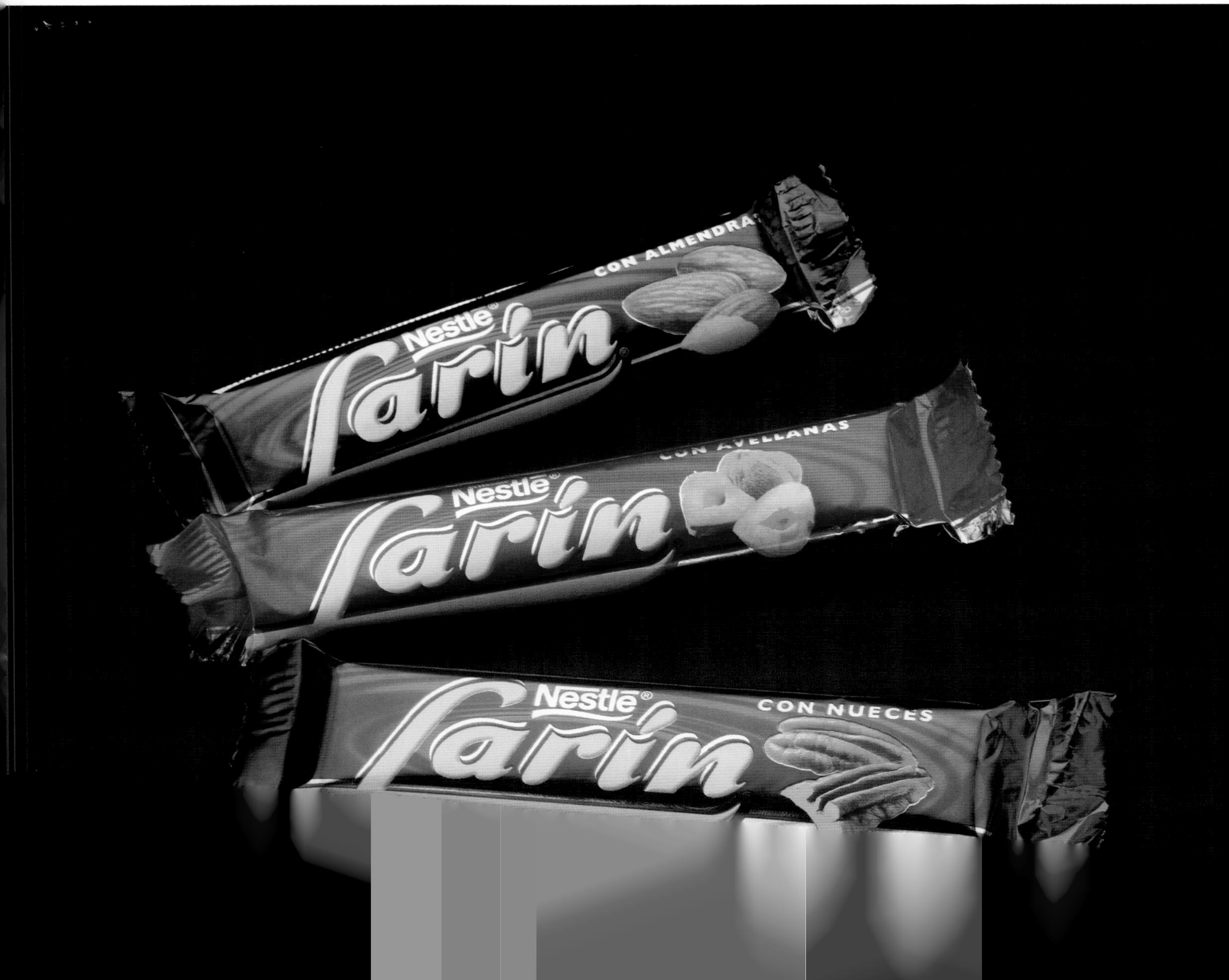

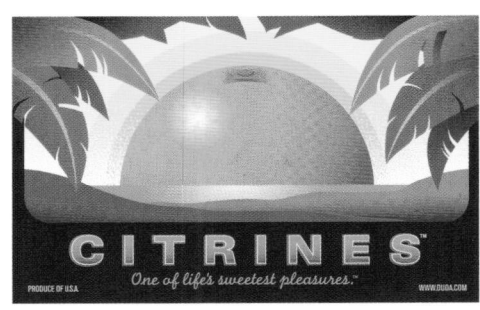

1.

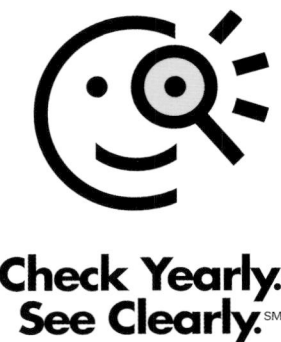

**Check Yearly.
See Clearly.**SM

2.

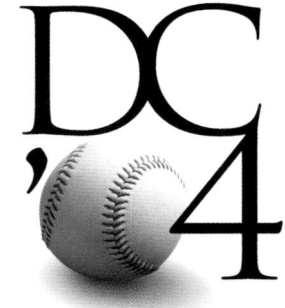

3.

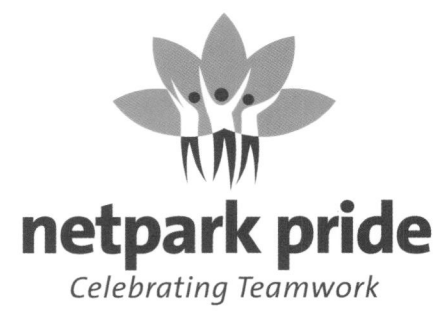

4.

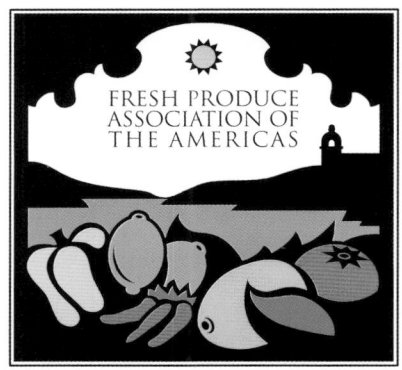

5.

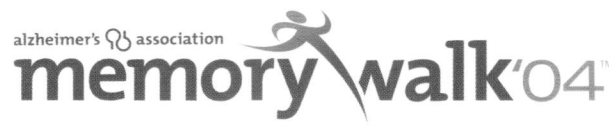

6.

  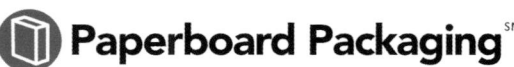

7.

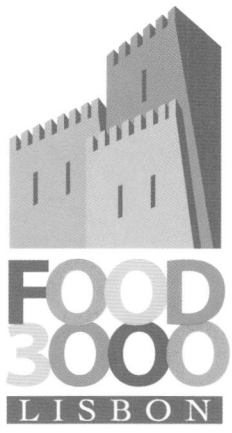

8.

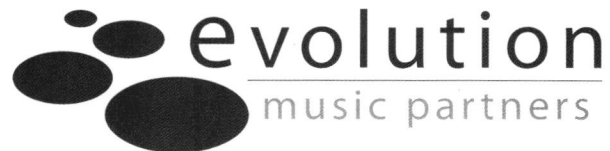

9.

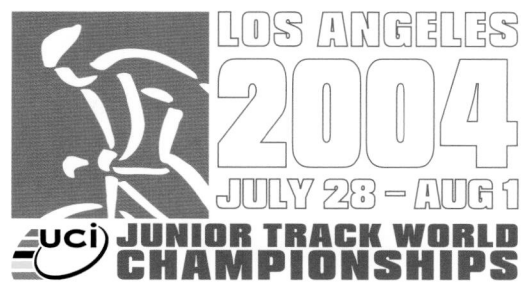

10.

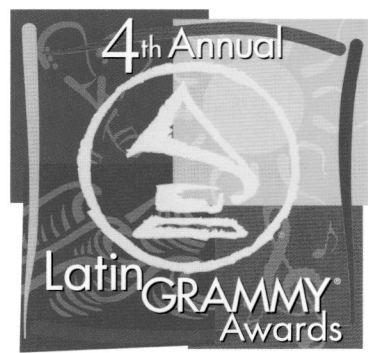

SEPTEMBER 3, 2003 • 9PM ET/PT • CBS

11.

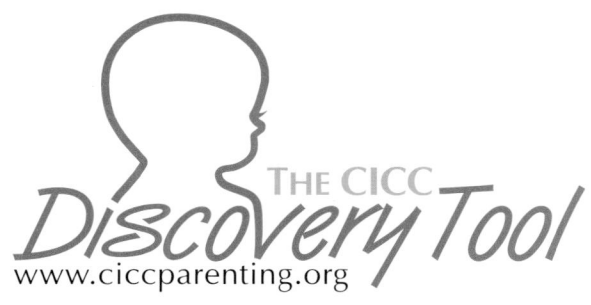

12.

MACKWORKS

FURNISHINGS & DESIGN

13.

BREWER & TOMINAGA

14.

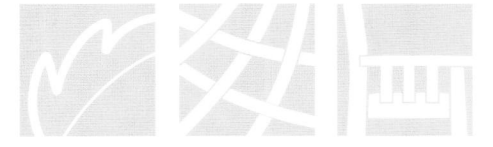

Knowledge @ Technology's Edge

15.

1 - 8
Design Firm **Porter Novelli**
9 - 15
Design Firm **Mark Deitch & Assoc., Inc.**

1.
Client   *DUDA*
Designer   Todd Metrokin

2.
Client   *Vision Council of America*
Designers   Penny Rigler, Peter Buttecali

3.
Client   *Washington DC Baseball*
Designers   Rebecca Mabie, Matt Stevenson

4.
Client   *Medco*
Designers   Todd Metrokin, Penny Rigler

5.
Client   *Fresh Produce Association
of the Americas*
Designer   Todd Metrokin

6.
Client   *Alzheimer's Association*
Designers   Todd Metrokin, Allyson Hummel

7.
Client   *American Forest & Paper
Association*
Designers   Todd Metrokin, Mike Gallagher,
Penny Rigler

8.
Client   *Food Forum 3000*
Designer   Penny Rigler

9.
Client   *Evolution Music Partners*
Designer   Dvorjac Riemersma

10.
Client   *AEG*
Designer   Lisa Clark

11.
Client   *Latin Academy of Recording
Arts & Sciences*
Designer   Lisa Clark

12.
Client   *Center for Improvement of
Child Caring*
Designer   Dvorjac Riemersma

13.
Client   *Mackworks*
Designer   Dvorjac Riemersma

14.
Client   *Brewer & Tominaga*
Designer   Dvorjac Riemersma

15.
Client   *VEDA*
Designer   Dvorjac Riemersma

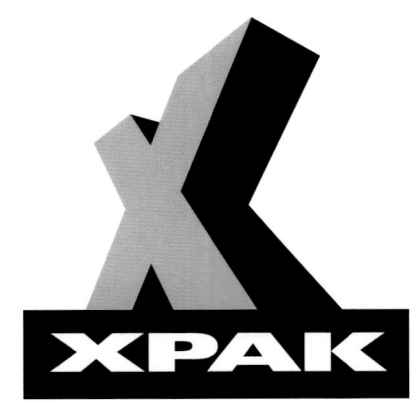

1.

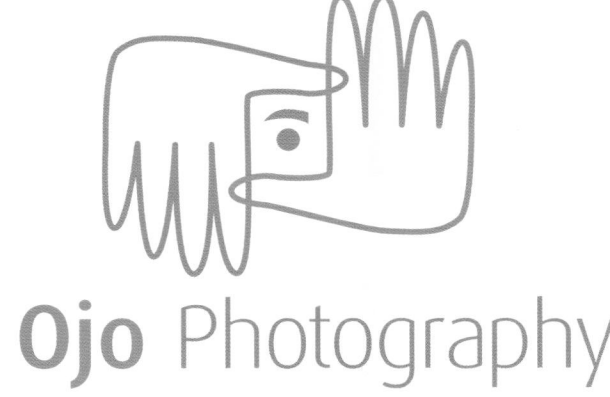

Ojo Photography

2.

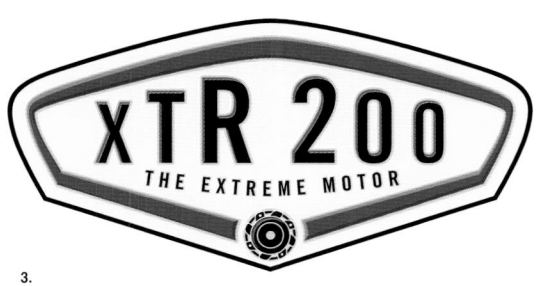

3.

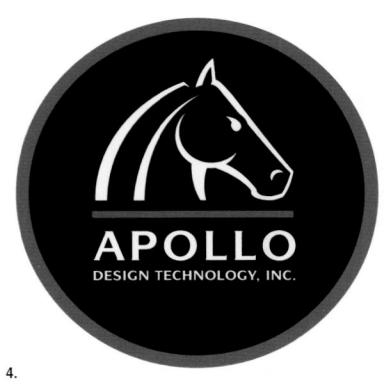

4.

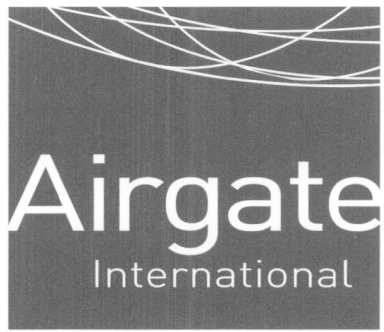

5.

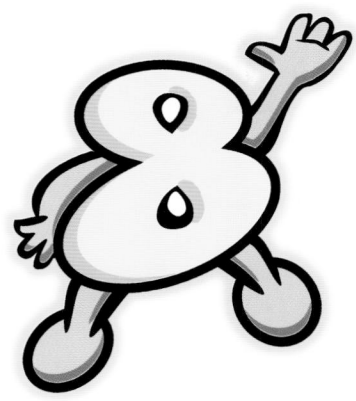

6.

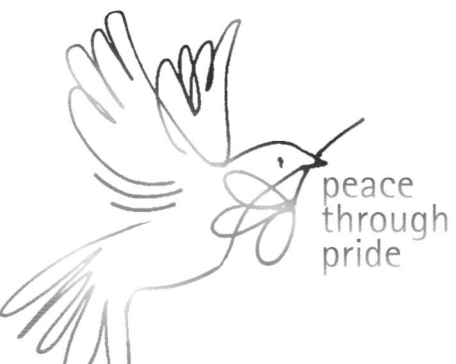

peace
through
pride

7.

1
Design Firm **Proximity Canada**
2
Design Firm **Jenny Kolcun Design**
3
Design Firm **Brad Terres Design**
4
Design Firm **Boyden & Youngblutt**
5
Design Firm **Strategy One, Inc.**
6, 7
Design Firm **Stephen Burdick Design**

1.
Client   *Polyair Envelope Manufacturer*
Designers   Paul Wiersma, Curtis Wolowich

2.
Client   *Ojo Photography*
Designer   Jenny Kolcun

3.
Client   *Casablanca Fan Company*
Designers   Brad Terres, Matt Meehan

4.
Client   *Apollo Design Technology*
Designer   Todd Lemley

5.
Client   *Airgate International*
Designers   Brian Danaher, Jason Thompson

6.
Client   *Technical Assistance Collaborative*
Designer   Stephen Burdick

7.
Client   *Wainwright Bank*
Designer   Stephen Burdick

(opposite)
Client   *Printegra*
Design Firm **TD2, S.C.**
Designer   Rafael Rodrigo Córdova

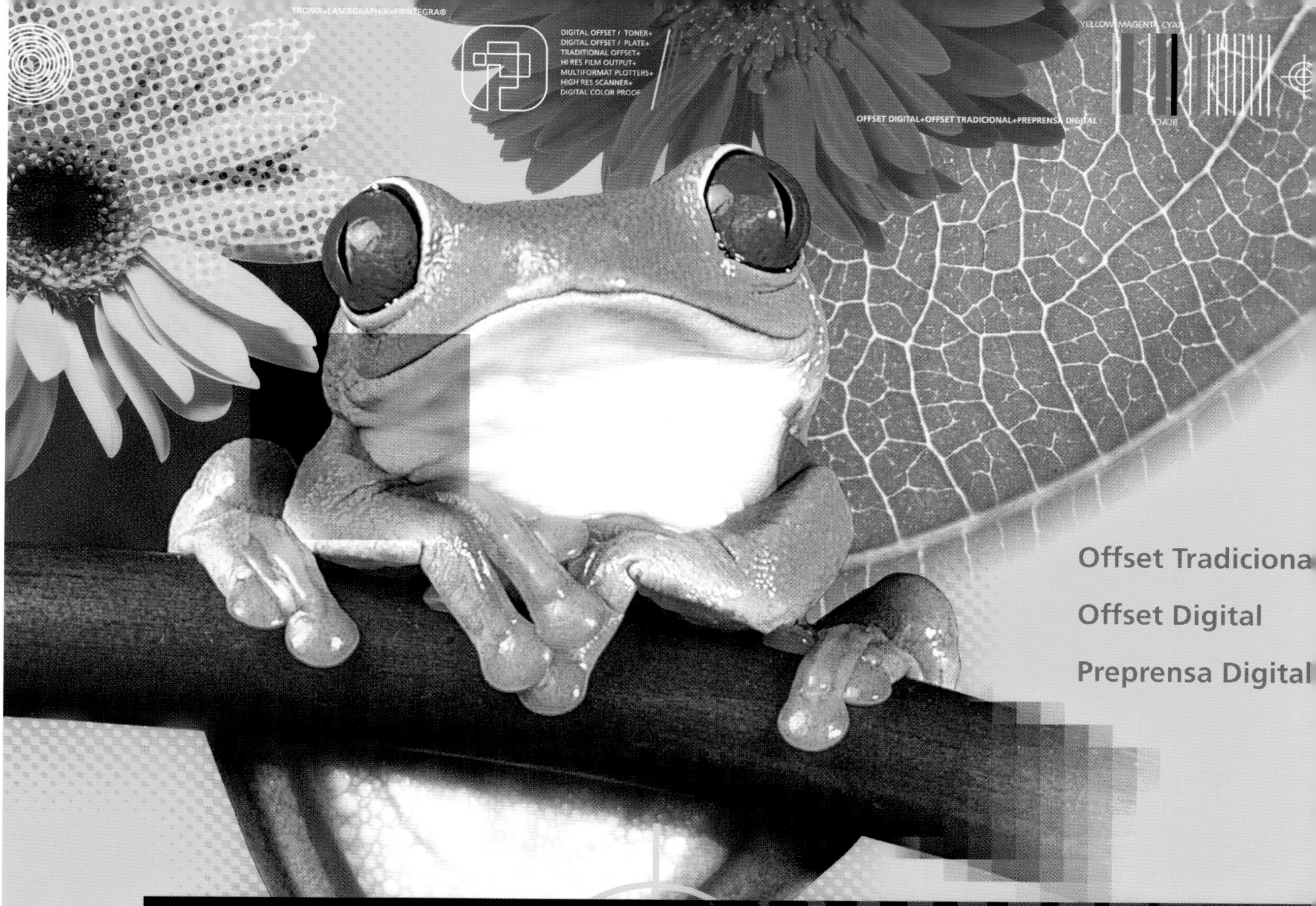

Offset Tradiciona

Offset Digital

Preprensa Digital

Trabajando juntos

Ahora somos **Printegra**®.

Trónix y Lasergraphix nos unimos multiplicando nuestras capacidades.

Nos mantenemos a la vanguardia poniendo en tus manos la tecnología de impresión

más adecuada para cada tipo de proyecto. Ahora no importará el tamaño, el tiraje,

la técnica o el sustrato... En **Printegra**® nuestro trabajo será tu satisfacción.

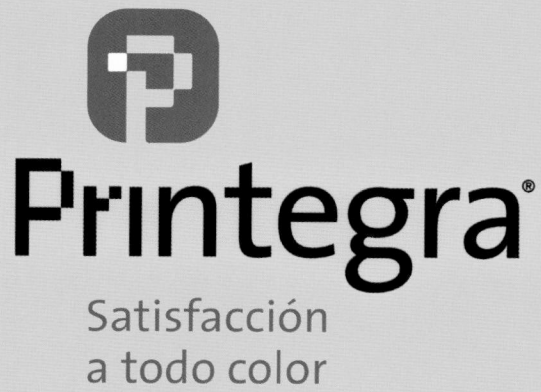

Printegra®

Satisfacción
a todo color

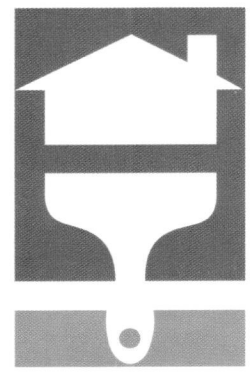

1.

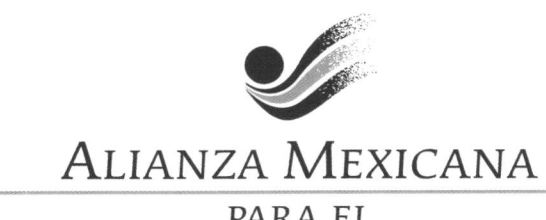

2.

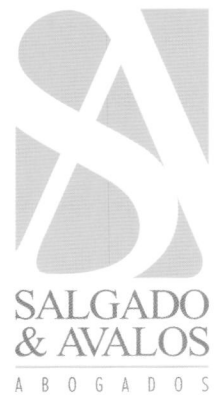

3.

4.

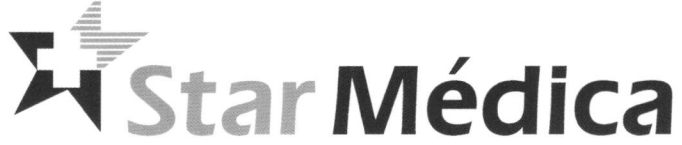

5.

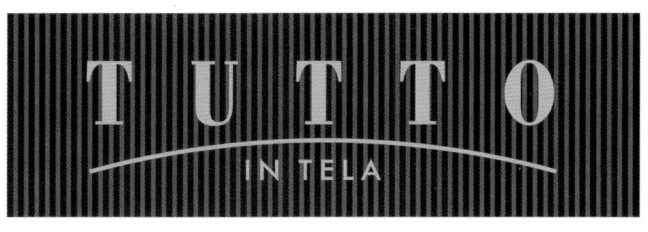

6.

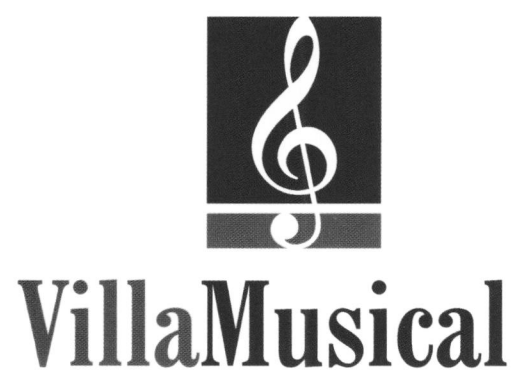

7.

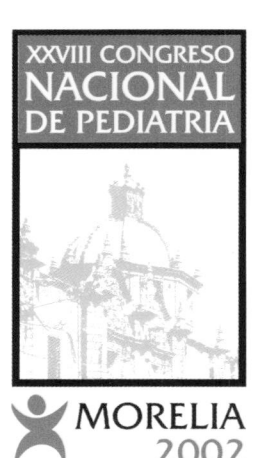

8.

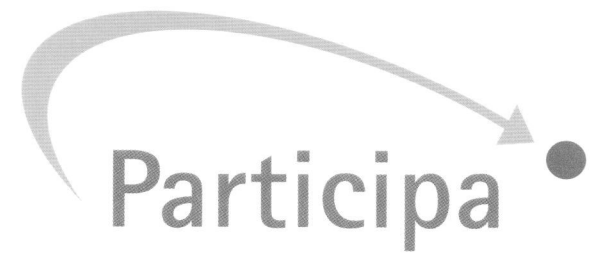

9.

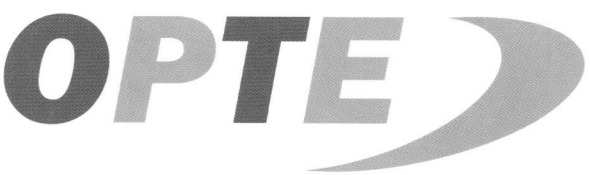

10.

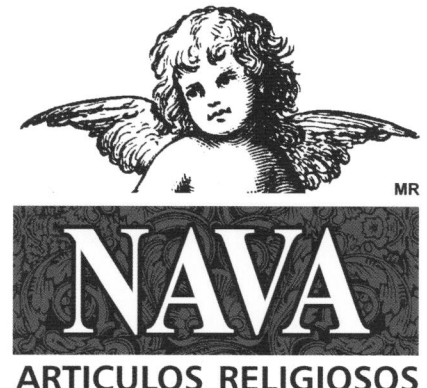

MR

11.

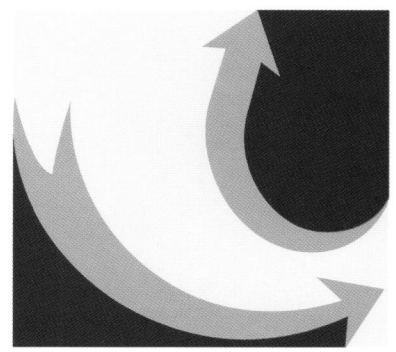

12.

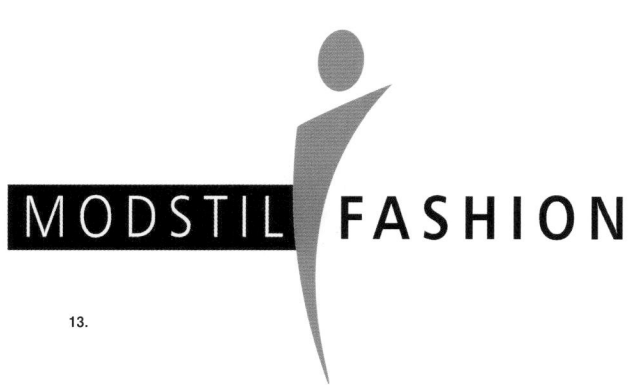

13.

14.

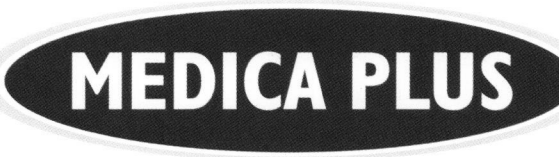

15.

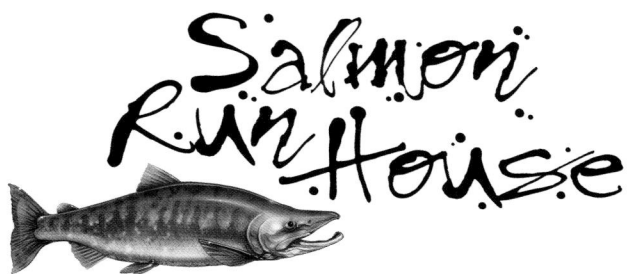

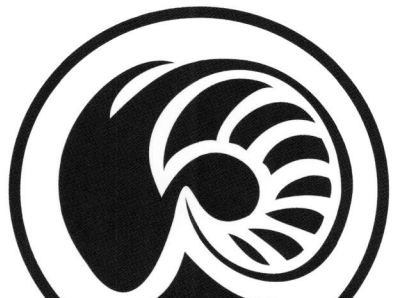

1.

2.

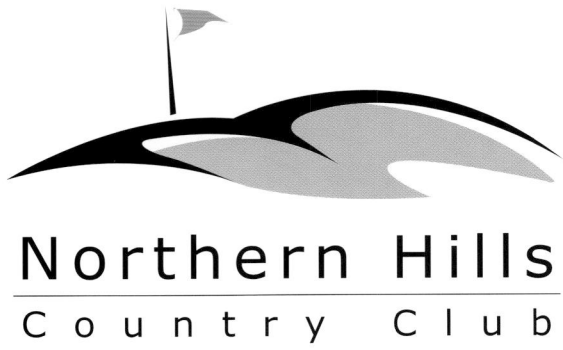

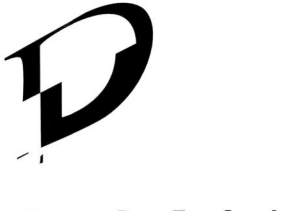

3.

4.

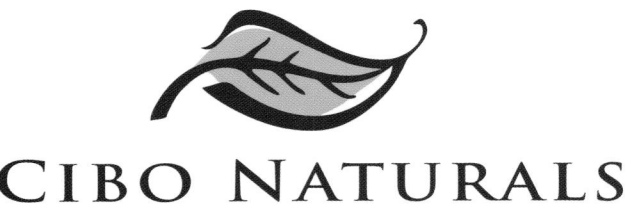

CIBO NATURALS

5.

6.

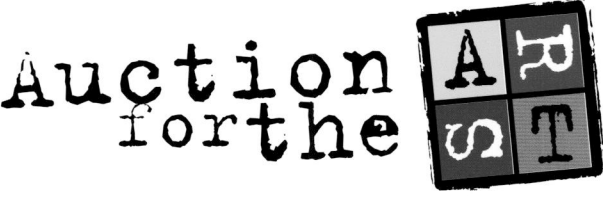

7.

1 - 7
Design Firm **Daigle Design**
1.
Client   *Salmon Run House*
Designers   Candace Daigle, Jessi Carpenter
2.
Client   *Sakai Village*
Designer   Jane Shasky
3.
Client   *Rockford Asset Management*
Designer   Paul Dunning
4.
Client   *Northern Hills Country Club*
Designer   Dan Thompson
5.
Client   *Daigle Design*
Designer   Kim Tebb

6.
Client   *Cibo Naturals*
Designers   Candace Daigle, Jane Shasky,
   Gloria Chen
7.
Client   *Bainbridge Island Performing Arts*
Designers   Candace Daigle, Paul Dunning
(opposite)
Client   *Nestle*
Design Firm **TD2, S.C.**
Designer   Rafael Rodrigo Córdova,
   Liliana Ramírez

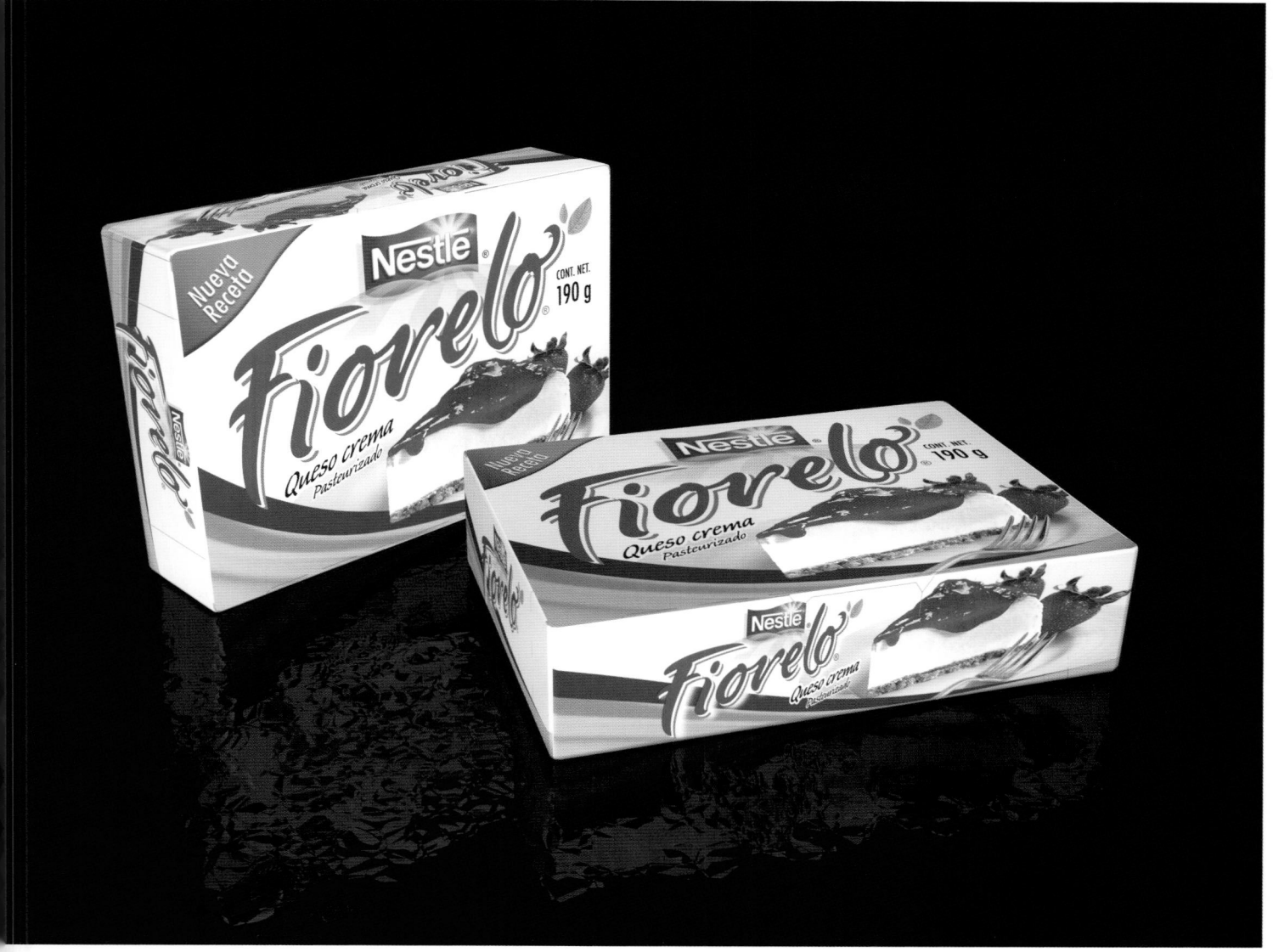

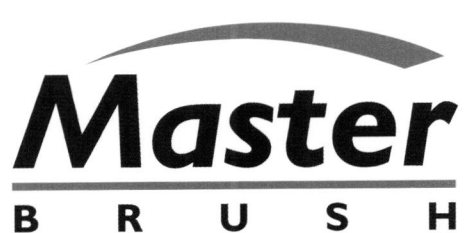

1.

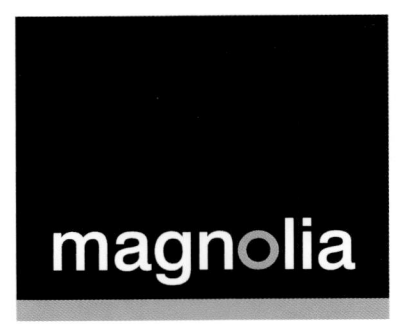

2.

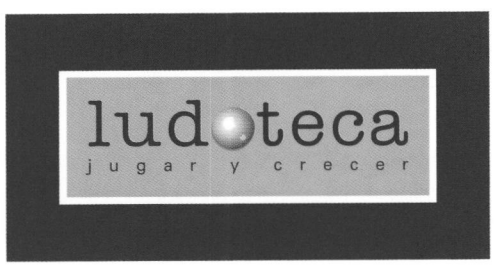

3.

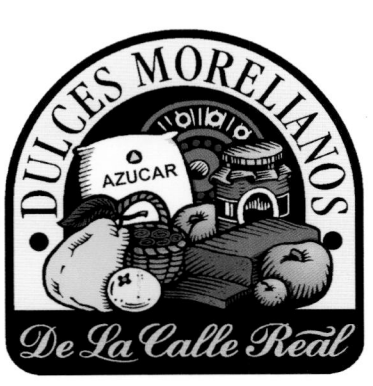

4.

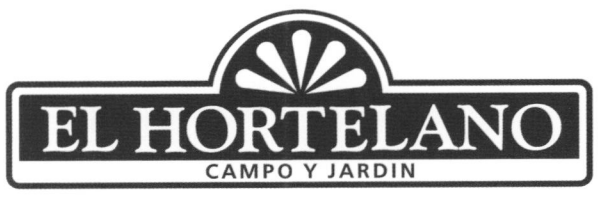

5.

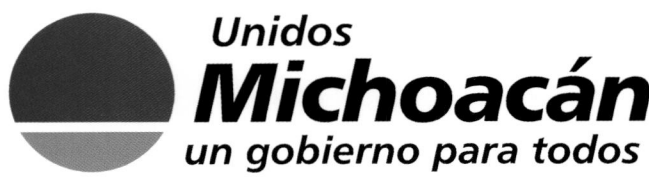

6.

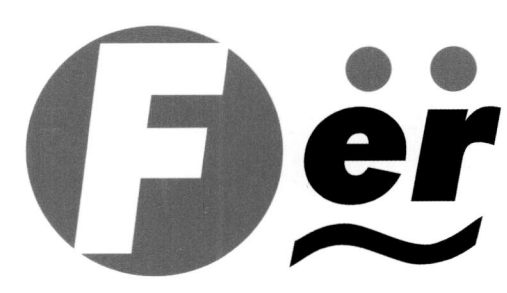

7.

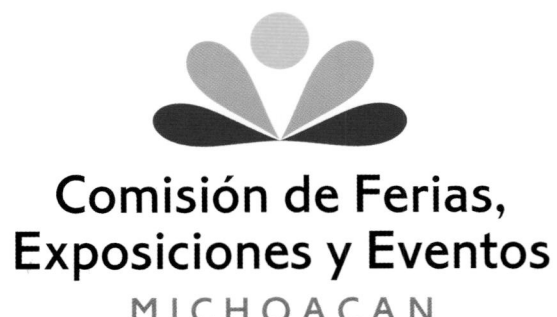

8.

EX IMPORT

9.

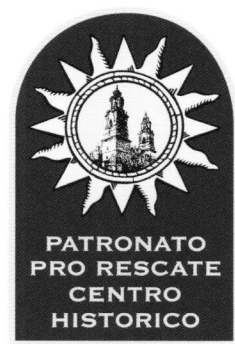

10.

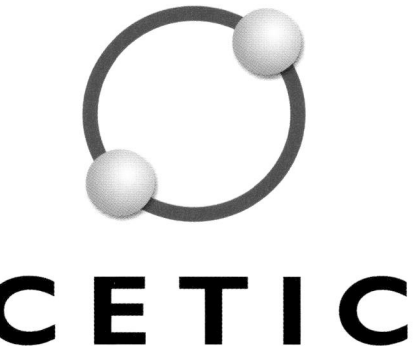

CETIC

11.

PATRONATO
PRO RESCATE
CENTRO
HISTORICO

Morelia

12.

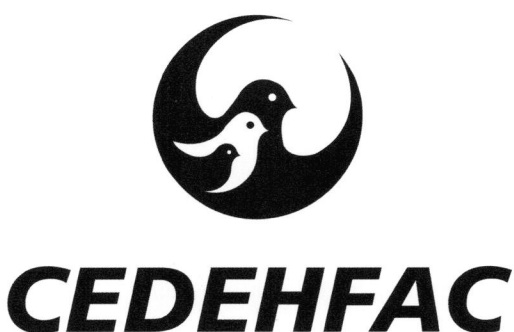

CEDEHFAC

13.

Iberotel

14.

EL
CARACOL
CONSULTORES EN DISEÑO

15.

1 - 15		**8.**	
Design Firm	**Caracol Consultores SC**	Client	*Comisión de Ferias y Exposiciones de Michoacán*
1.		Designer	Luis Jaime Lara
Client	*Master Brush*	**9.**	
Designer	Luis Jaime Lara	Client	*EXIMPORT*
2.		Designer	Luis Jaime Lara
Client	*Magnolia Pisos y Recubrimientos*	**10.**	
Designers	Luis Jaime Lara, Myriam Zavala	Client	*Congreso Nacional de Escuelas particulares*
3.		Designer	Luis Jaime Lara
Client	*Gobierno del Estado de Michoacán (Ludotecas)*	**11.**	
		Client	*Gob. del Estado de Michoacán (Centro de Informática)*
Designers	Myriam Zavala, Luis Jaime Lara	Designers	Luis Jaime Lara, Raúl Elizondo, Carlos Chávez, Victor Rodríguez
4.			
Client	*Dulces Morelianos De La Calle Real*	**12.**	
Designer	Luis Jaime Lara	Client	*Patronato pro—rescate del Centro Histórico*
5.			
Client	*Hortelano Campo y Jardín*	Designers	Luis Jaime Lara, Elizabeth Viveros S.
Designers	Luis Jaime Lara, Georgina Luengas M.	**13.**	
		Client	*Centro de Desarrollo Humano y Familiar*
6.			
Client	*Gobierno del Estado de Michoacán*	Designer	Luis Jaime Lara, Elizabeth Viveros
		14.	
Designer	Luis Jaime Lara	Client	*Ibertol*
7.		Designer	Luis Jaime Lara
Client	*Fer Material Didáctico Infantil*	**15.**	
Designer	Luis Jaime Lara	Client	*Caracol Consultores SC*
		Designers	Luis Jaime Lara, Georgina Luengas

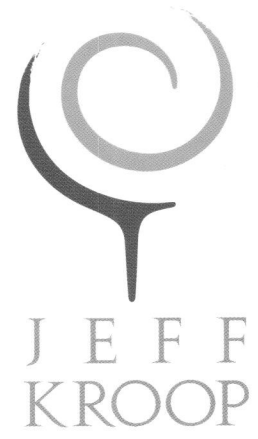

JEFF
KROOP

1.

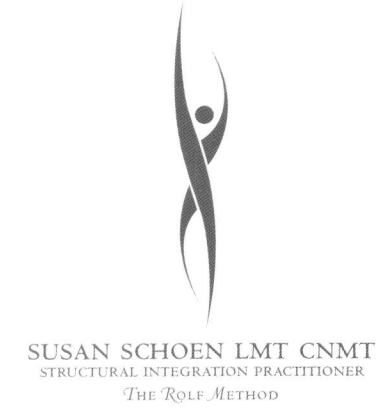

SUSAN SCHOEN LMT CNMT
STRUCTURAL INTEGRATION PRACTITIONER
The Rolf Method

2.

LATIN
access

3.

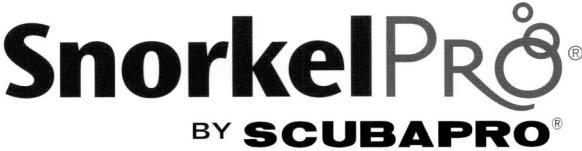

SnorkelPro ®
BY **SCUBAPRO** ®

4.

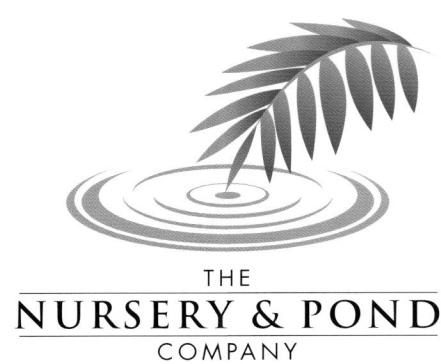

THE
NURSERY & POND
COMPANY

5.

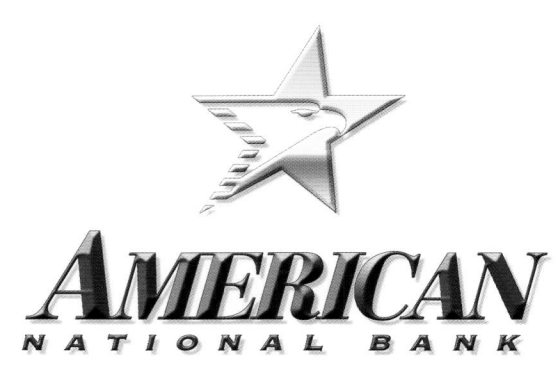

AMERICAN
NATIONAL BANK

6.

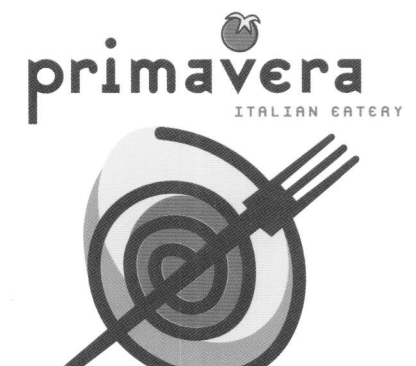

primavera
ITALIAN EATERY

7.

1, 2
Design Firm **Gouthier Design**
3
Design Firm **Smith Design**
4
Design Firm **Laura Coe Design**
5
Design Firm **Rick Cooper, Inc.**
6
Design Firm **Dotzler Creative Arts**
7
Design Firm **Dana Design**
1.
Client   *Jeff Kroop, Inc.*
Designers   Jonathan Gouthier, Mami Awamura
2.
Client   *Susan Schoen LMT, CNMT*
Designers   Jonathan Gouthier, Kiley Del Valle

3.
Client   *Filmation*
Designer   Eileen Berezni
4.
Client   *Scub Pro*
Designers   Tracy castle, Laura Coe Wright
5.
Client   *The Nursery & Pond Company*
Designer   Rick Cooper
6.
Client   *American National Bank*
Designer   Dotzler Creative Arts
7.
Client   *Primavera, Italian Eatery*
Designer   Dana Ezzell Gay
(opposite)
Client   *Patricia Gabriela Peláez*
Design Firm **TD2, S.C.**
Designer   Rafael Rodrigo Córdova

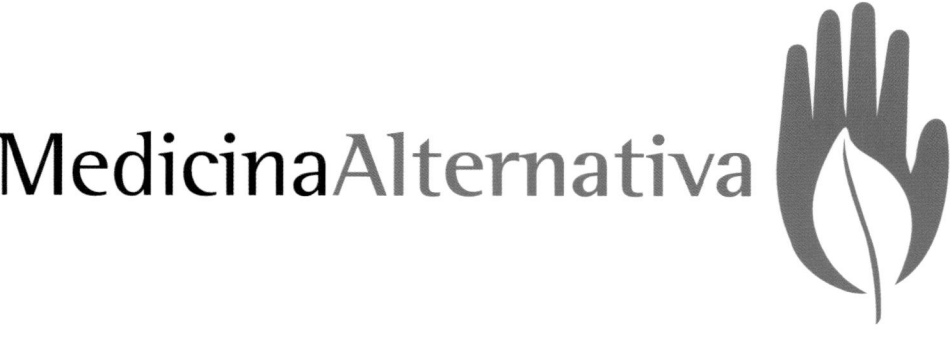

MedicinaAlternativa

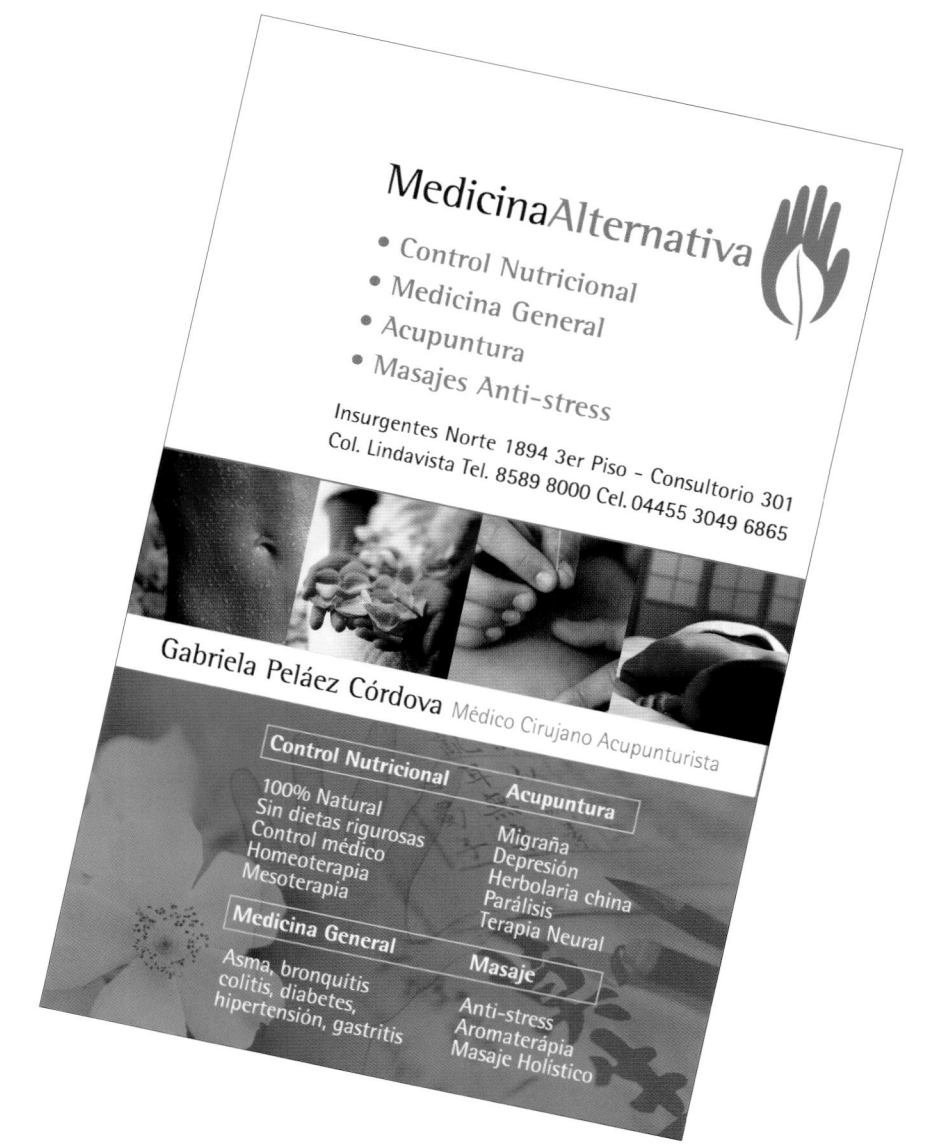

MedicinaAlternativa
- Control Nutricional
- Medicina General
- Acupuntura
- Masajes Anti-stress

Insurgentes Norte 1894 3er Piso - Consultorio 301
Col. Lindavista Tel. 8589 8000 Cel. 04455 3049 6865

Gabriela Peláez Córdova Médico Cirujano Acupunturista

Control Nutricional | **Acupuntura**

100% Natural
Sin dietas rigurosas
Control médico
Homeoterapia
Mesoterapia

Migraña
Depresión
Herbolaria china
Parálisis
Terapia Neural

Medicina General | **Masaje**

Asma, bronquitis
colitis, diabetes,
hipertensión, gastritis

Anti-stress
Aromaterápia
Masaje Holístico

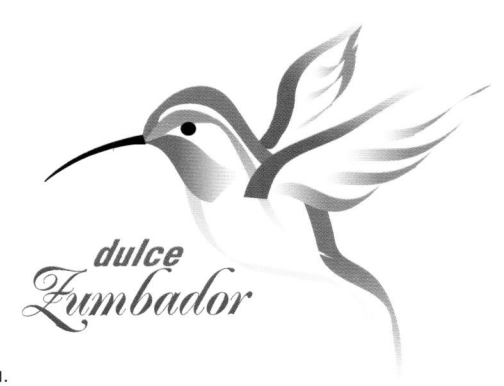

1.

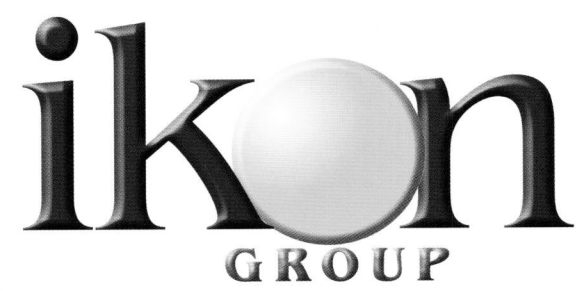

2.

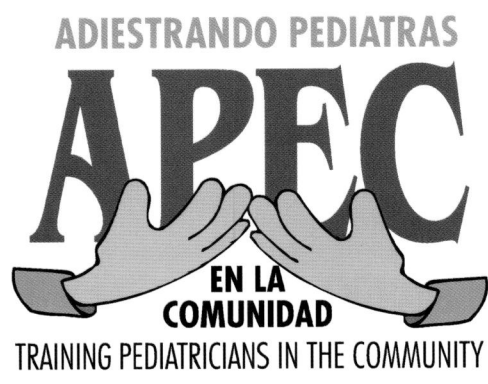

3.

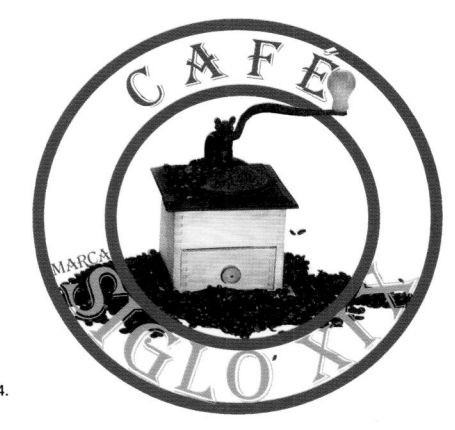

4.

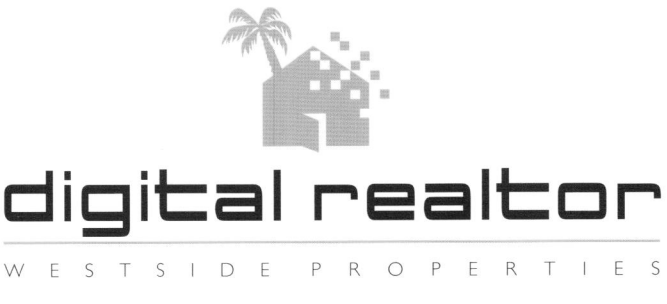

5.

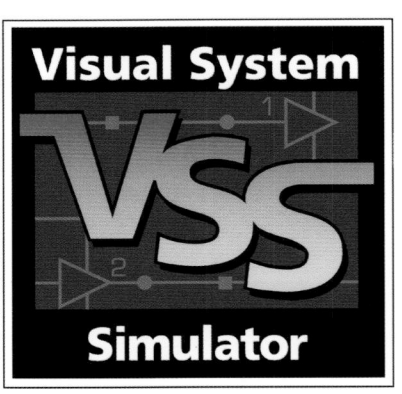

6.

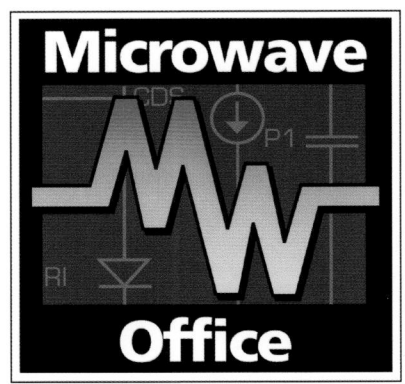

7.

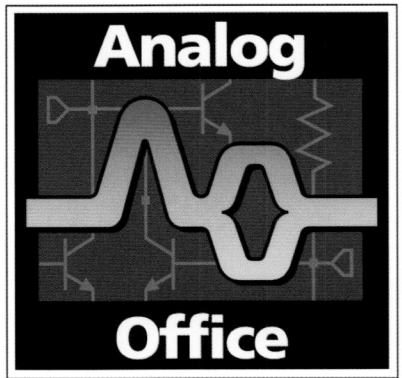

8.

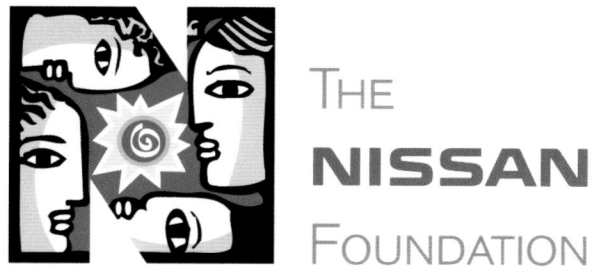

9.

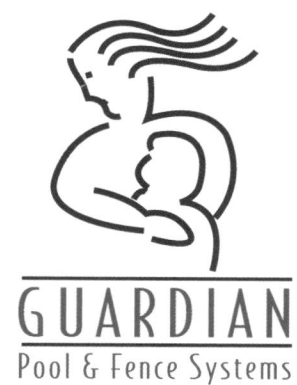

10.

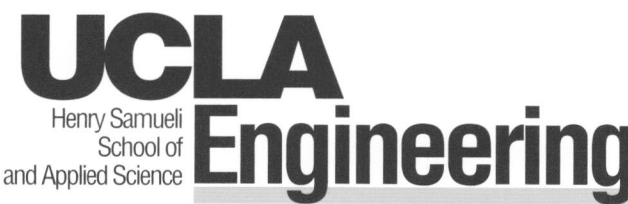

11.

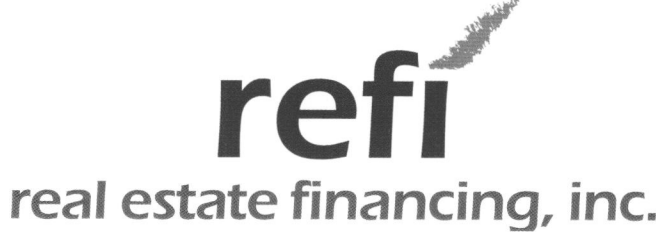

12.

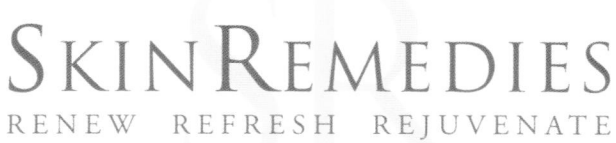

13.

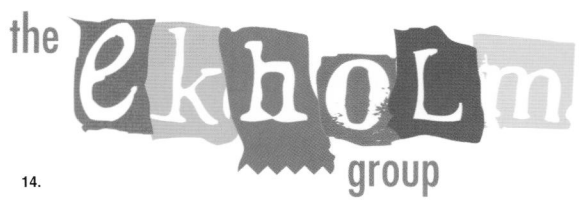

14.

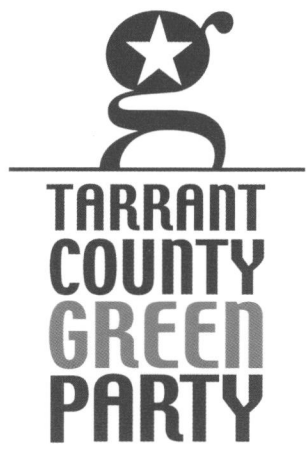

15.

1 - 4			6 - 8.		
Design Firm	**Maremar Graphic Design**		Client	*Applied Wave Research, Inc.*	
5 - 13			Designer	Suleman Poonja	
Design Firm	**Poonja Design, Inc.**		9.		
14,15			Client	*Nissan North America, Inc.*	
Design Firm	**Michael Niblett Design**		Designer	Suleman Poonja	
1.			10.		
Client	*Lilia Molina*		Client	*Guardian Pool and Fence Company*	
Designer	Marina Rivón		Designer	Suleman Poonja	
2.			11.		
Client	*Omar Haedo*		Client	*University of California, Los Angeles*	
Designer	Marina Rivón		Designer	Suleman Poonja	
3.			12.		
Client	*UPR Pediatrics Dept.*		Client	*Real Estate Financing, Inc.*	
Designer	Marina Rivón		Designer	Suleman Poonja	
4.			13.		
Client	*Ivan Irizarry*		Client	*Skin Remedies*	
Designer	Marina Rivón		Designer	Suleman Poonja	
5.			14.		
Client	*Digital Realtor*		Client	*The Eckholm Group*	
Designer	Suleman Poonja		Designer	Michael Niblett	
			15.		
			Client	*Green Party of Tarrant County*	
			Designer	Michael Niblett	

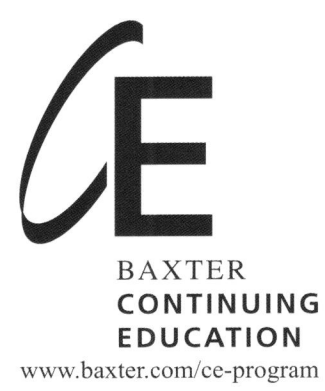

1.

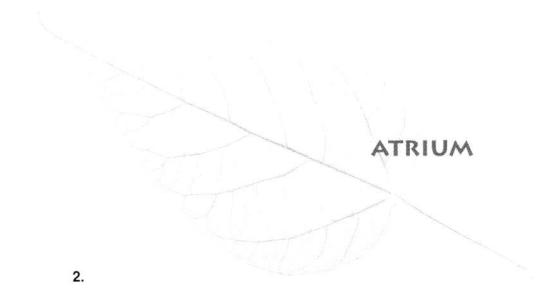

2.

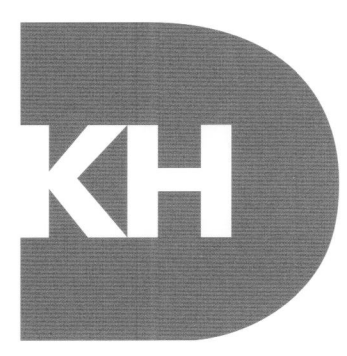

3.

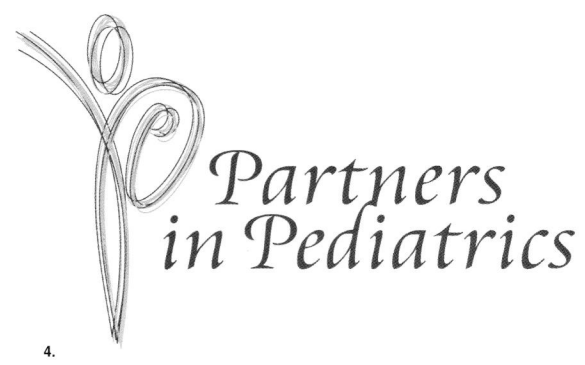

4.

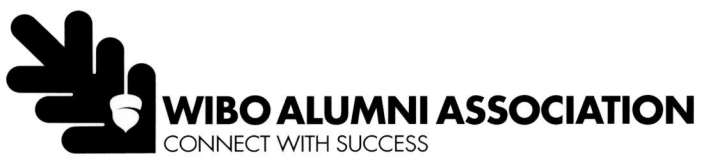

5.

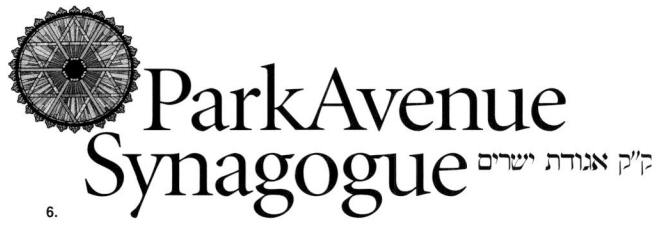

6.

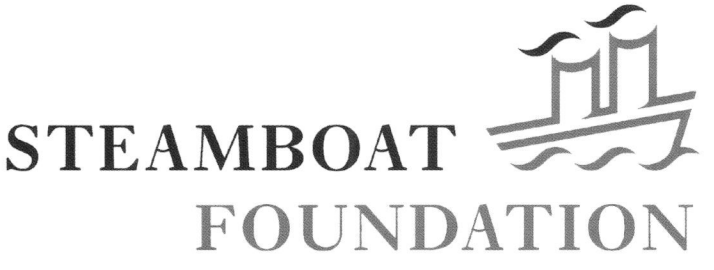

7.

1, 2
Design Firm **Design Moves, Ltd.**
3
Design Firm **Kevin Hall Design**
4
Design Firm **Parsons and Maxson, Inc.**
5 - 7
Design Firm **Namaro Graphic Designs, Inc.**

1.
Client   *Baxter Healthcare*
Designers   Laurie Medeiros Freed,
         April Weaver

2.
Client   *Atrium Landscape Design*
Designers   Laurie Medeiros Freed,
         April Weaver

3.
Client   *Kevin Hall Design*
Designer   Kevin Hall

4.
Client   *Partners In Pediatrics, PC*
Designer   Sean Caldwell

5.
Client   *Workshop in*
         Business Opportunities
Designer   Nadine Robbins

6.
Client   *Park Avenue Synagogue*
Designers   Nadine Robbins, Molly Ahearn

7.
Client   *Steamboat Foundation*
Designers   Nadine Robbins, Molly Ahearn
(opposite)
Client   *Labatt USA*
Design Firm **HMS Design**
Designer   Josh Laird

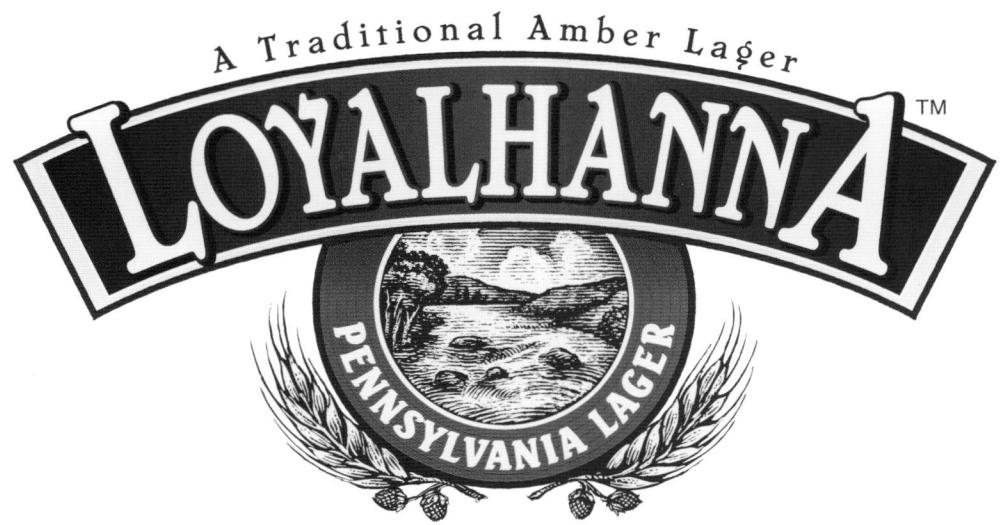

A Traditional Amber Lager

LOYALHANNA™

PENNSYLVANIA LAGER

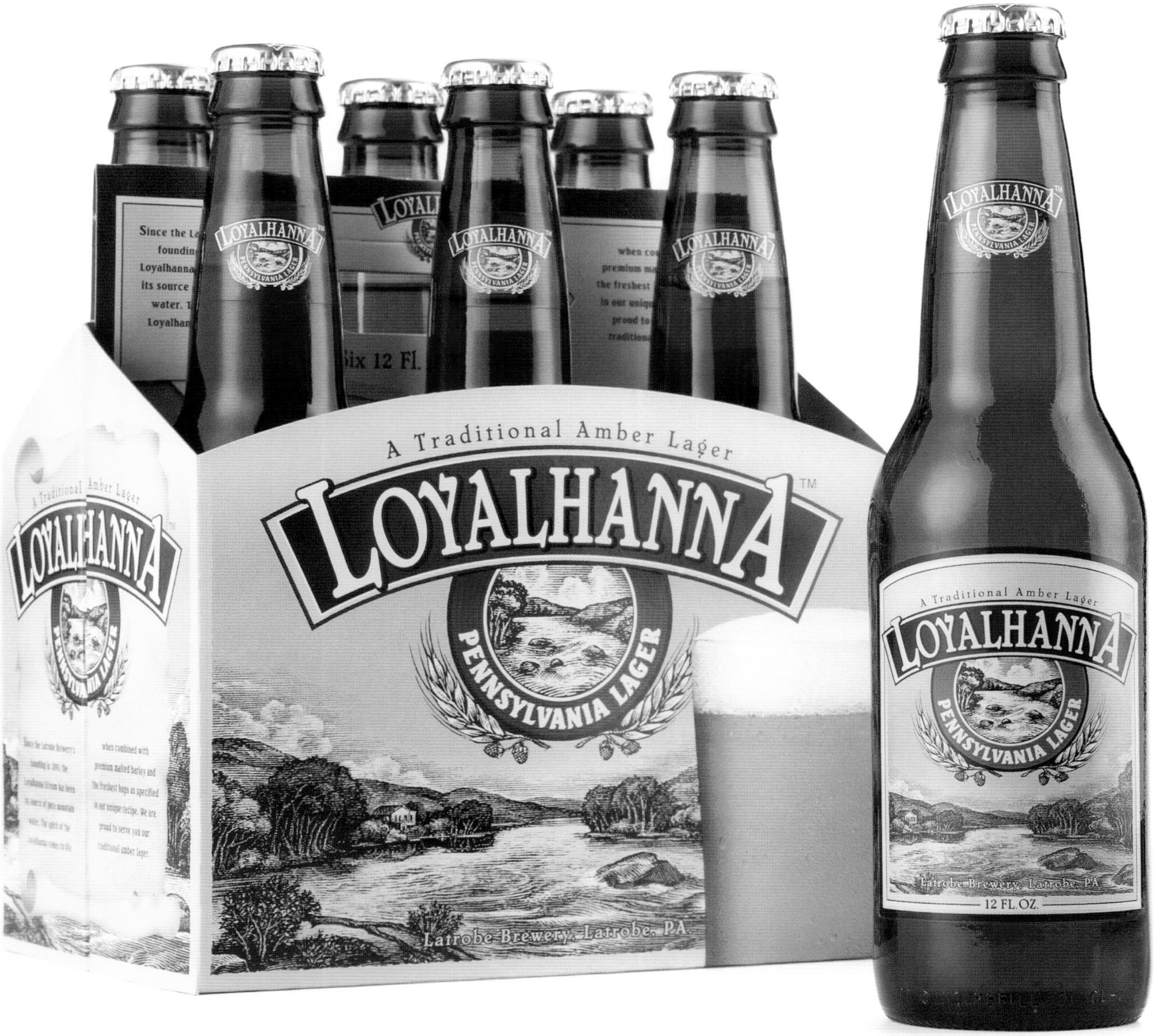

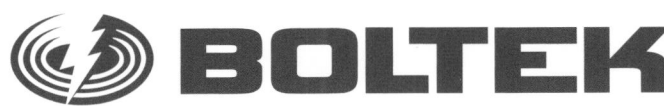

1.

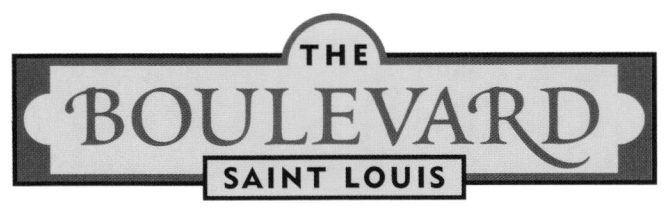

2.

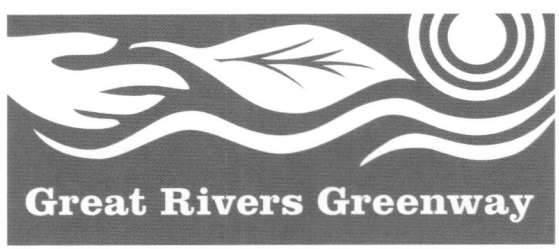

3.

Real kitchen™

4.

St. Louis Mills SM

5.

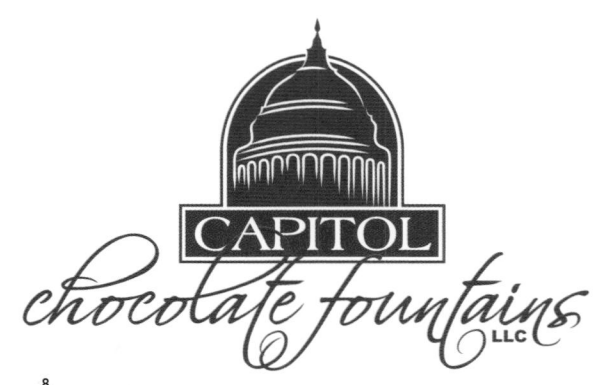

6.

Average Girl
THE MAGAZINE

7.

CAPITOL
chocolate fountains LLC

8.

Insight GENETICS

9.

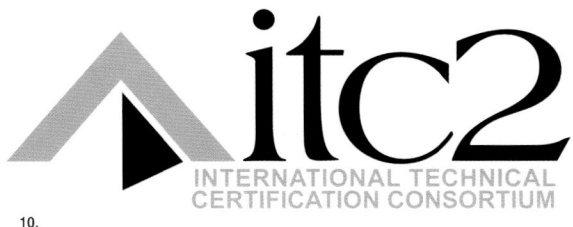

10.

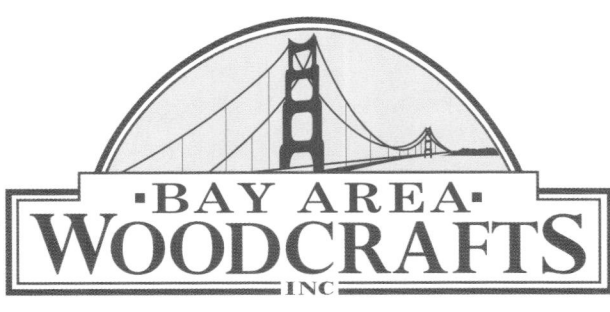

11.

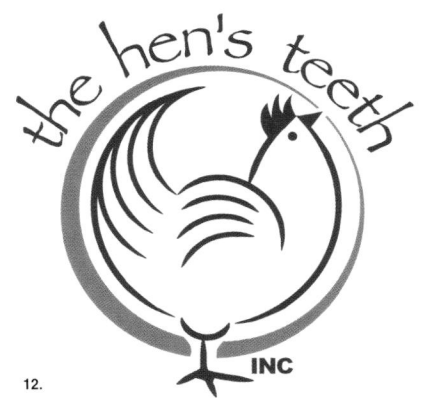

12.

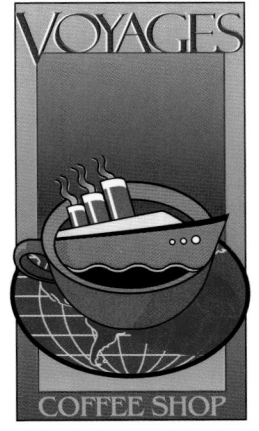

13.

FURMAN KALLIO
INTELLECTUAL PROPERTY & TECHNOLOGY LAW

14.

15.

1, 7 - 14
Design Firm **Nancy Carter Design**
2 - 6, 15
Design Firm **Kiku Obata & Company**
1.
Client   *Boltek*
Designer   Nancy Carter
2.
Client   *Pace Properties*
Designer   Todd Mayberry
3.
Client   *Great Rivers Greenway*
Designers   Teresa Norton-Young,
     Troy Guzman
4.
Client   *Real Kitchen*
Designer   Eleanor Safe
5.
Client   *The Mills Corporation*
Designer   Joe Floresca
6.
Client   *Pin-up Bowl*
Designer   Rich Nelson
7.
Client   *Average Girl, The Magazine*
Designer   Nancy Carter

8.
Client   *Capitol Chocolate Fountains*
Designer   Nancy Carter
9.
Client   *Insight Genetics*
Designer   Nancy Carter
10.
Client   *ITC2*
Designer   Nancy Carter
11.
Client   *Bay Area WoodCrafts*
Designer   Nancy Carter
12.
Client   *The Hen's Teeth*
Designer   Nancy Carter
13.
Client   *Voyages Coffee Shop*
Designer   Nancy Carter
14.
Client   *Furman—Kallio*
Designer   Nancy Carter
15.
Client   *Craft Alliance*
Designer   Amy Knopf

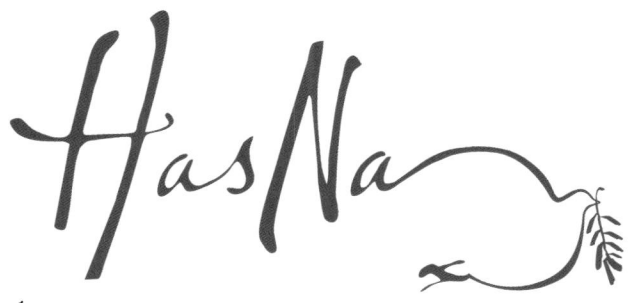

1.

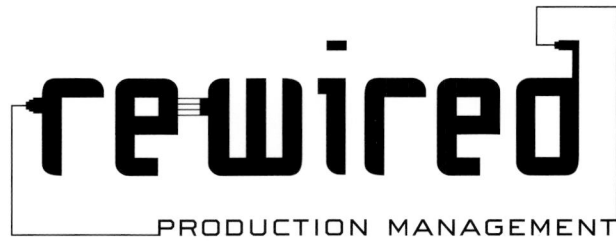

2.

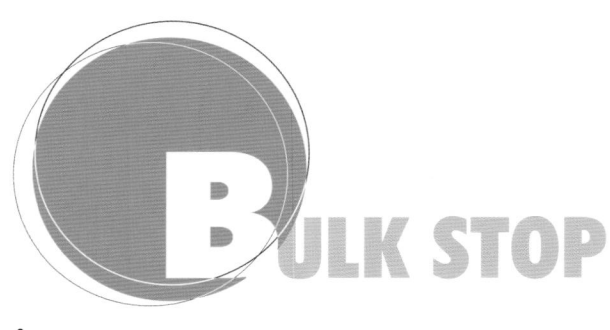

3.

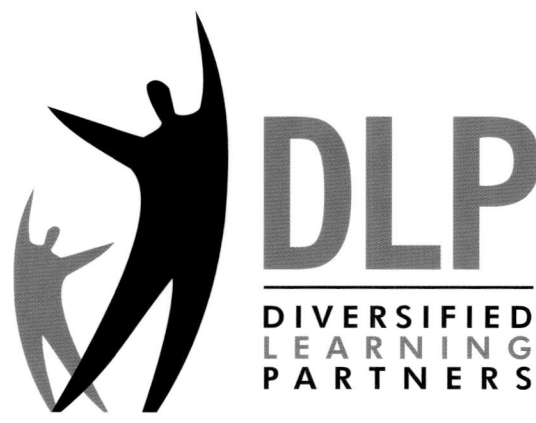

4.

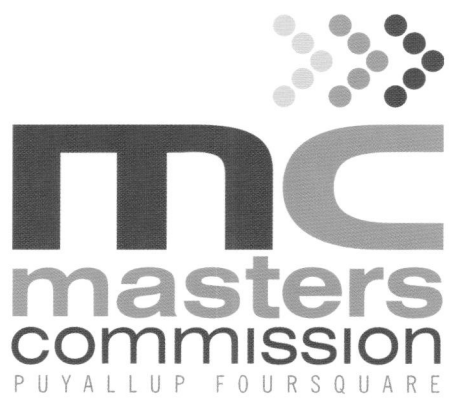

5.

6.

refresh

inspiring results

7.

1, 2
Design Firm **Jill Bredthauer**
3
Design Firm **B² Communications**
4, 5
Design Firm **Drotz Design**
6, 7
Design Firm **Peggy Lauritsen Design Group**
1.
Client   *Hasna Inc.*
Designer Jill Bredthauer
2.
Client   *Rewired Production Management*
Designer Jill Bredthauer
3.
Client   *Bulk Stop*
Designer Brian Berry
4.
Client   *DLP*
Designer Dallas Drotz
5.
Client   *Puyallup Foursquare*
Designer Dallas Drotz

6.
Client   *Direct Source, Inc.*
Designer Michelle Ducayet
7.
Client   *Lawson Software*
Designer John Haines
(opposite)
Client   *Labatt USA*
Design Firm **HMS Design**
Designer Jeff Meyer

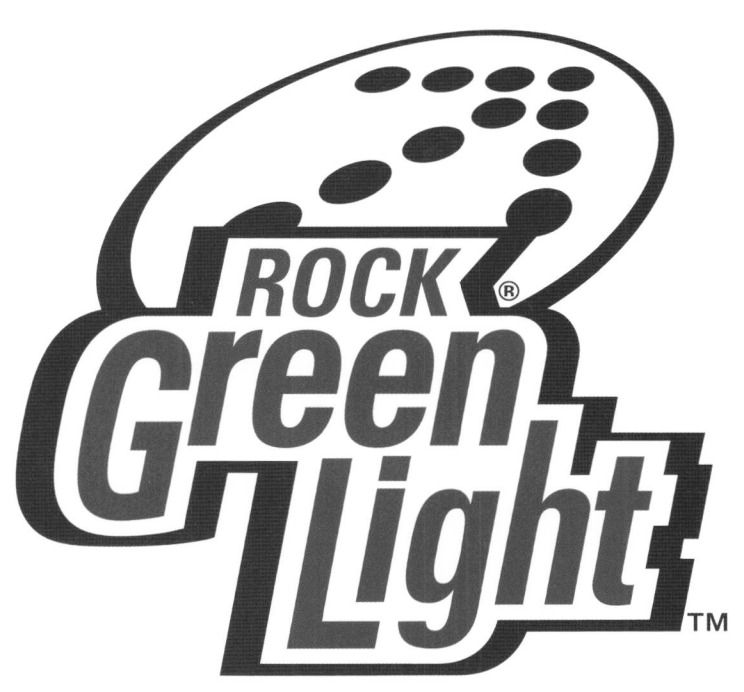

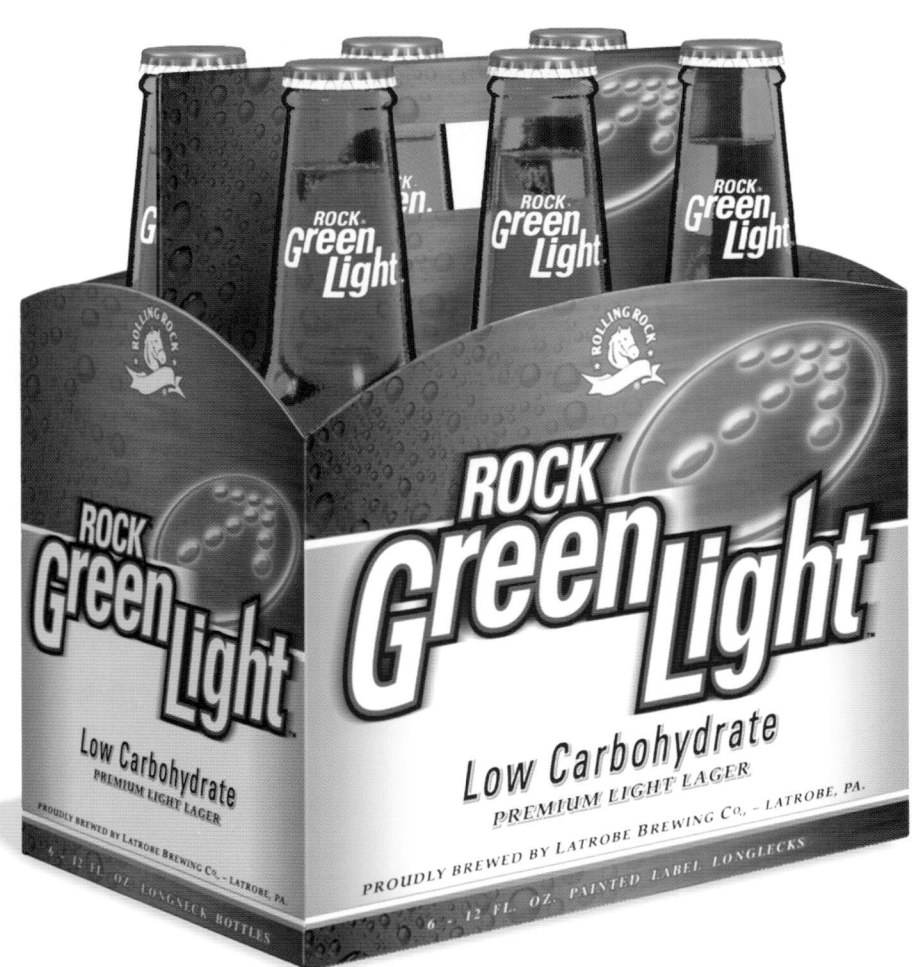

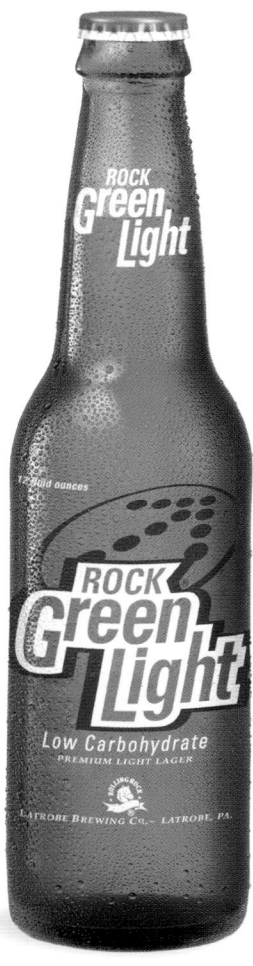

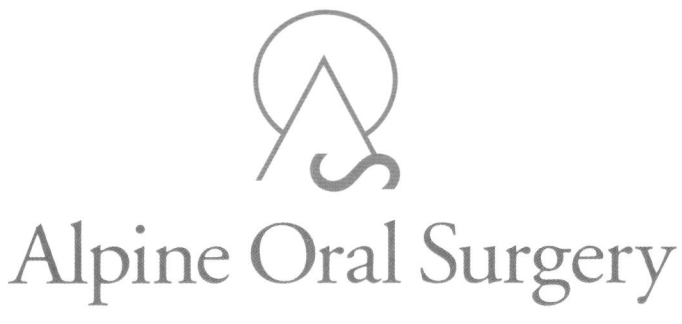

Alpine Oral Surgery

1.

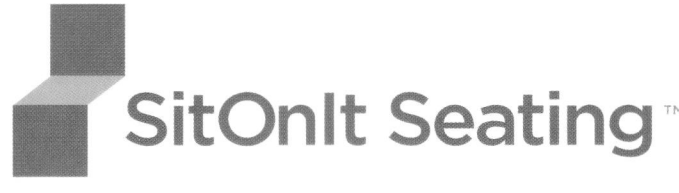

SitOnIt Seating™

2.

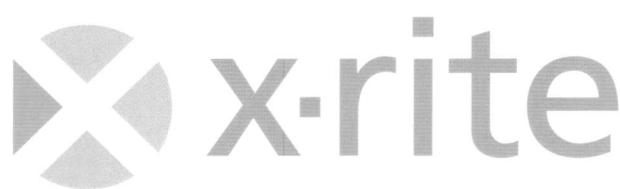

x·rite

3.

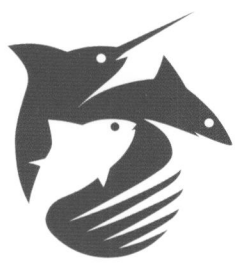

University of Miami
Center for Sustainable Fisheries

4.

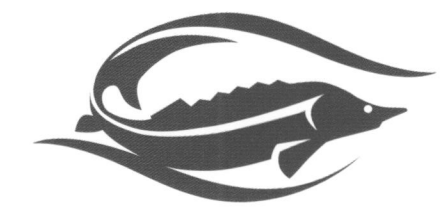

STURGEON
Aqua Farms

5.

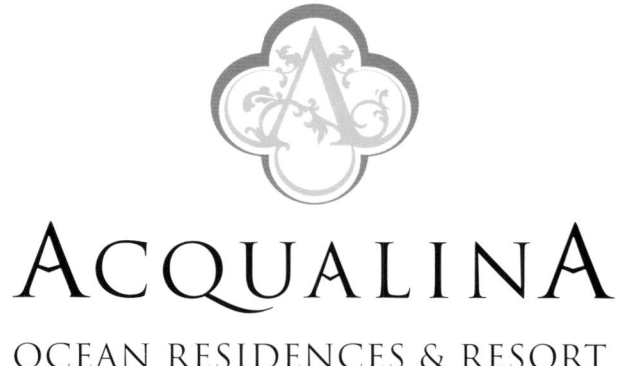

ACQUALINA
OCEAN RESIDENCES & RESORT

6.

ISLAND CITY
T R A D E R S
HOME & GARDEN

7.

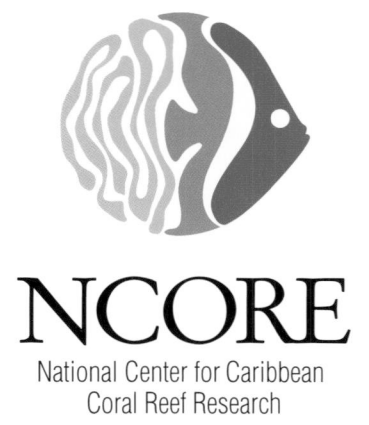

NCORE
National Center for Caribbean
Coral Reef Research

8.

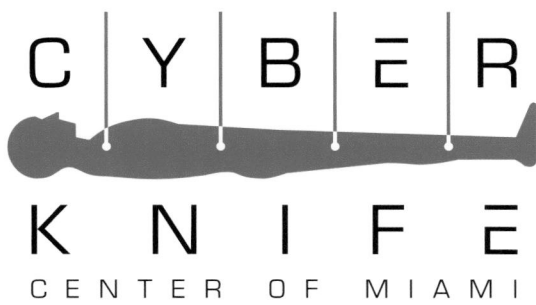

9.

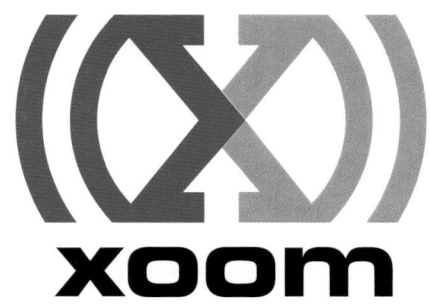

10.

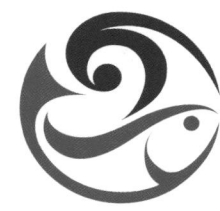

PEW INSTITUTE FOR OCEAN SCIENCE

11.

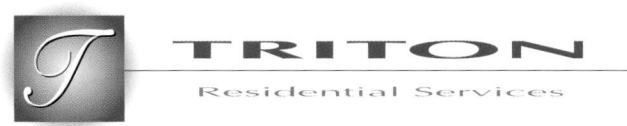

12.

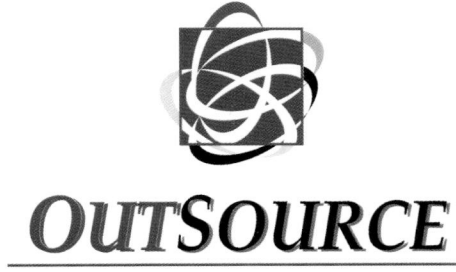

OutSource
Technical Solutions
bringing it all together

13.

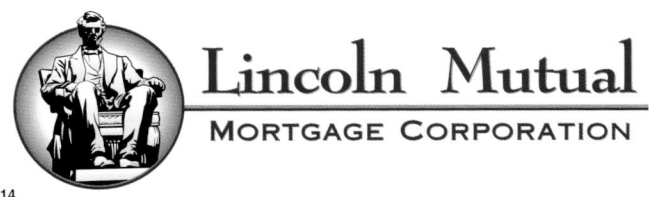

14.

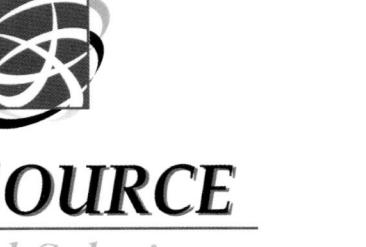

15.

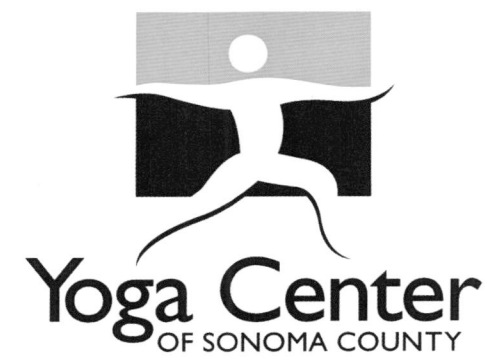

1.

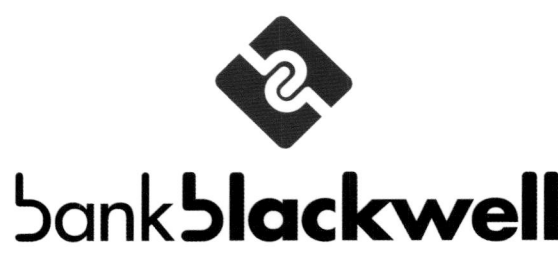

2.

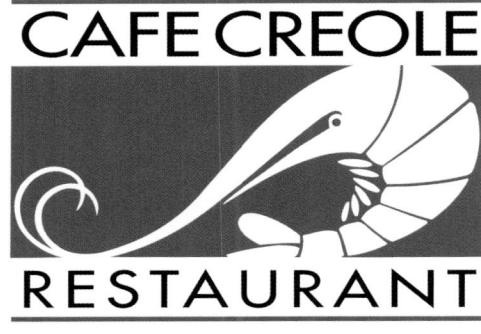

3.

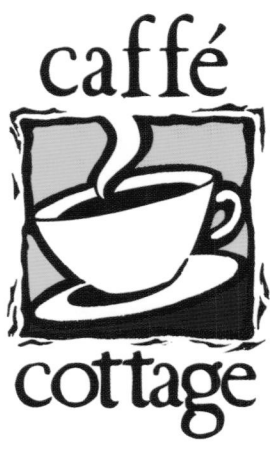

4.

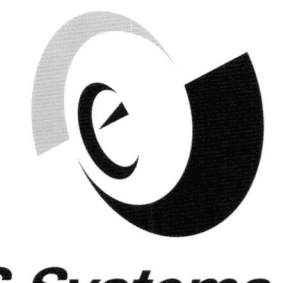

E.S.Systems,Inc.

5.

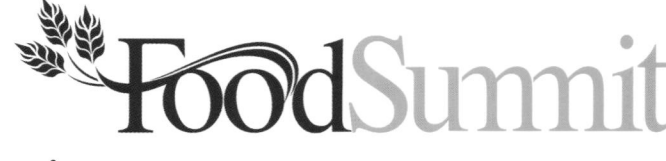

6.

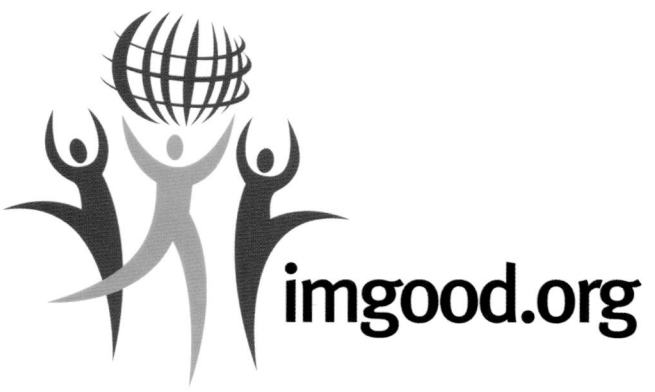

7.

1 - 7
Design Firm **Creative Madhouse**
1.
Client   Yoga Center of Sonoma County
Designer   Madelyn Wattigney
2.
Client   BankBlackwell
Designer   Madelyn Wattigney
3.
Client   Cafe Creole Restaurant
Designer   Madelyn Wattigney
4.
Client   Caffe Cottage
Designer   Madelyn Wattigney
5.
Client   E.S. Systems, Inc.
Designer   Madelyn Wattigney
6.
Client   FoodSummit
Designer   Madelyn Wattigney
7.
Client   ImGood.org
Designer   Madelyn Wattigney

(opposite)
Client   Wm. Bolthouse Farms
Design Firm **HMS Design**
Designer   Josh Laird

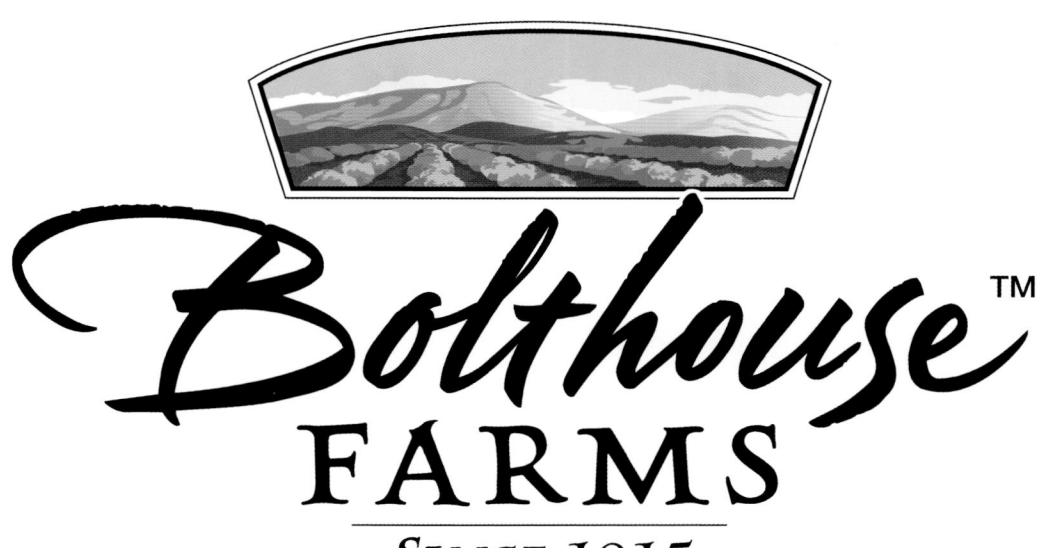

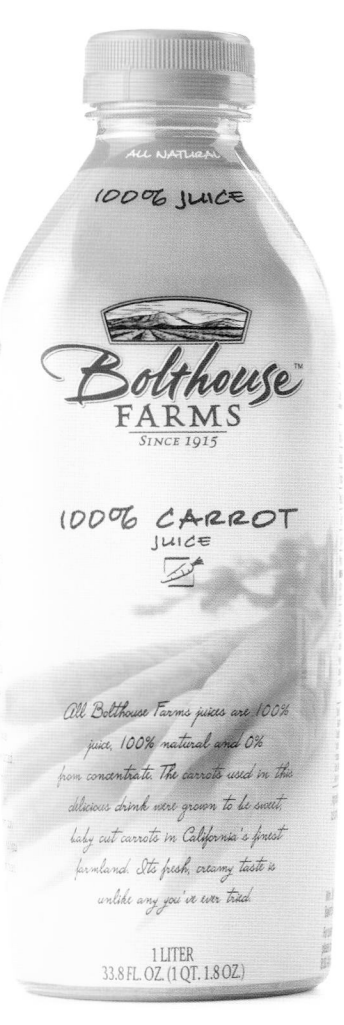

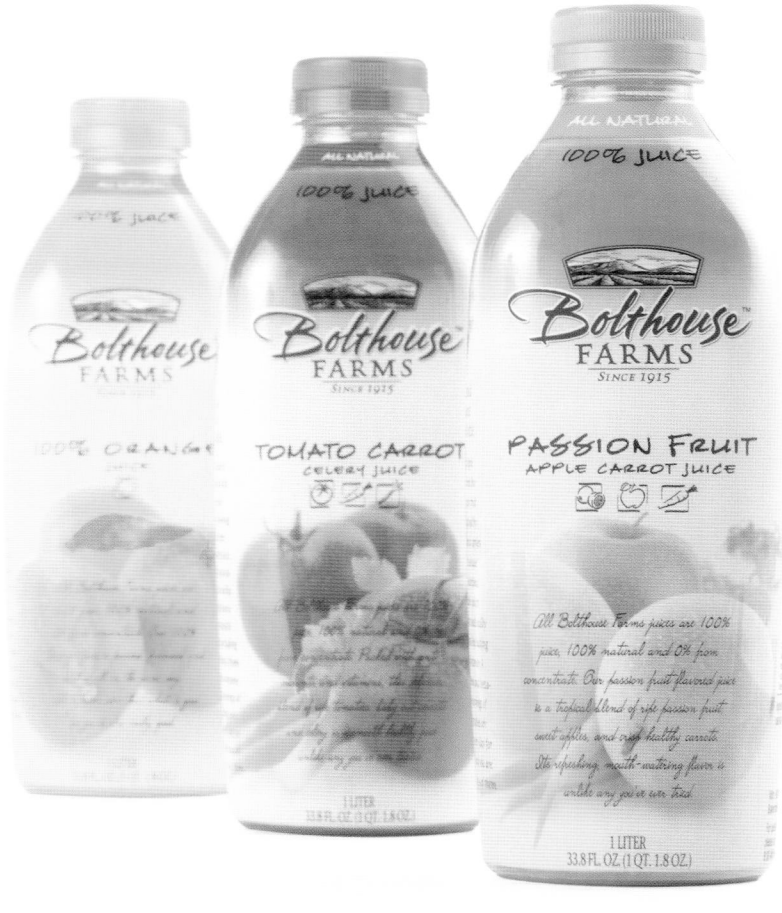

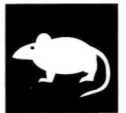 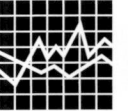 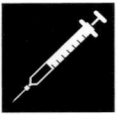 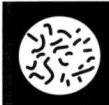 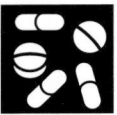 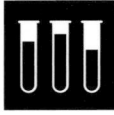 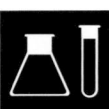

1.

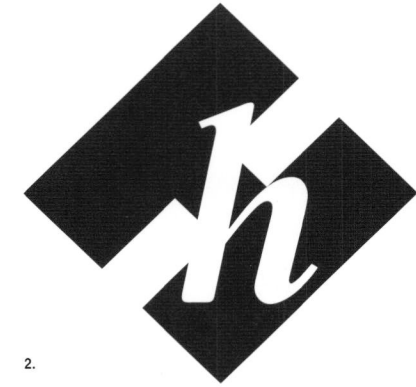

2.

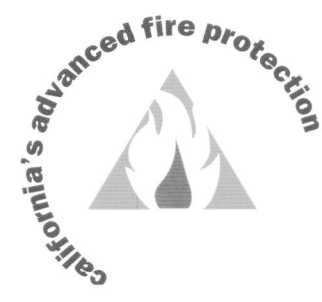 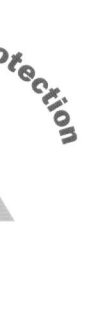

California's advanced fire protection

3.

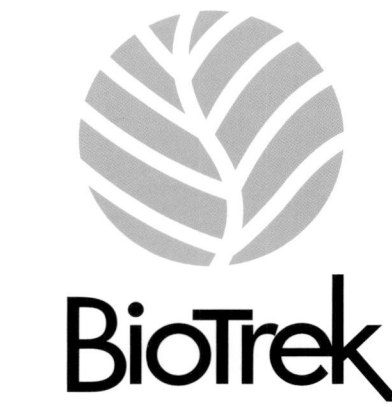

BioTrek

4.

JASNA
Los Angeles 2004

5.

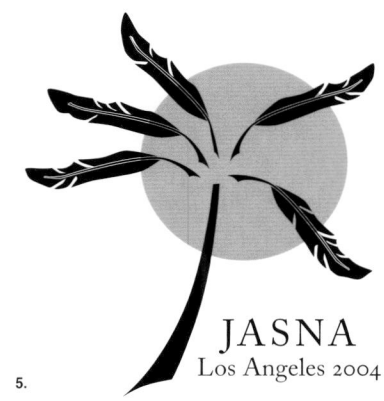

6.

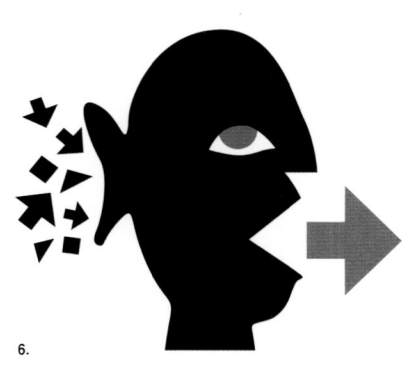

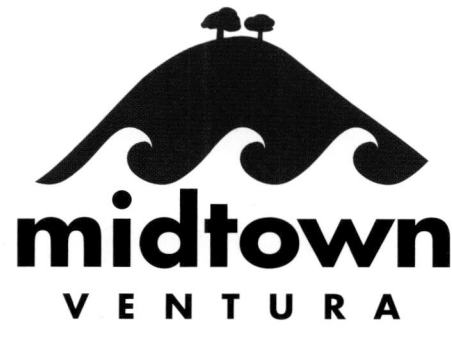

midtown
VENTURA

7.

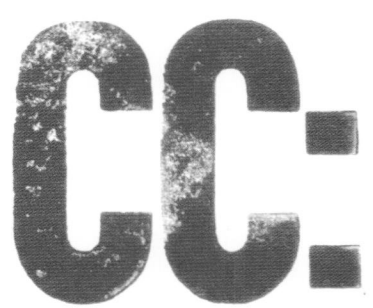

8.

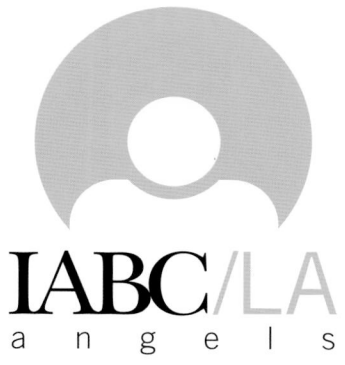

IABC/LA
a n g e l s

9.

Montrachet

PREMIER APARTMENT HOMES

10.

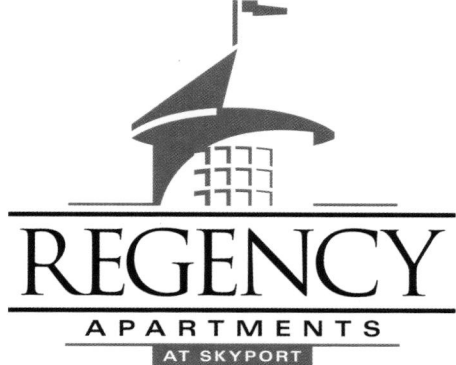

REGENCY
APARTMENTS
AT SKYPORT

11.

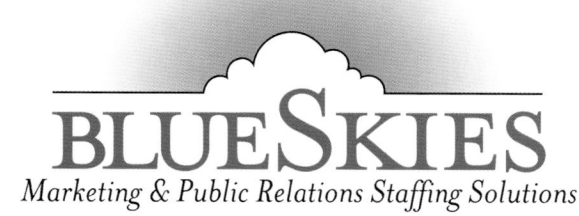

BLUESKIES
Marketing & Public Relations Staffing Solutions

12.

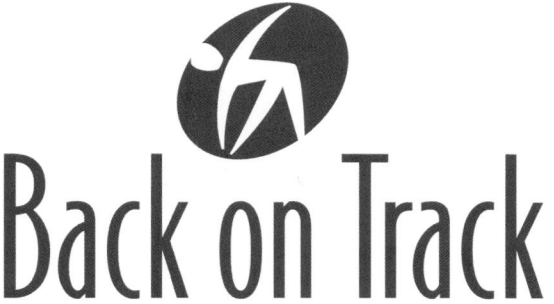

Back on Track

13.

CMC

14.

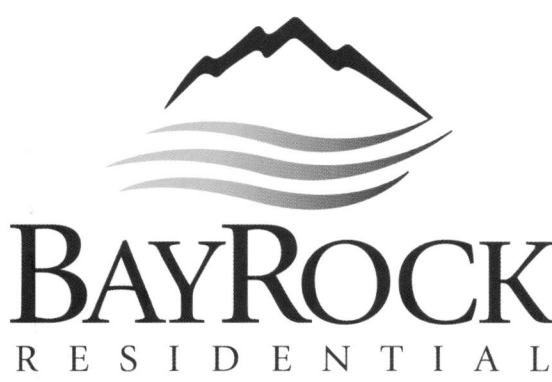

BAYROCK
R E S I D E N T I A L

15.

1 - 9		
Design Firm	**Gunnar Swanson Design Office**	
10 - 15		
Design Firm	**Shawver Associates, Inc.**	
1.		
Client	Hanham Consulting	
Designer	Gunnar Swanson	
2.		
Client	Halstead Communication	
Designer	Gunnar Swanson	
3.		
Client	California's Advanced Fire Protection	
Designer	Gunnar Swanson	
4.		
Client	California State Polytechnic University Pomona	
Designer	Gunnar Swanson	
5.		
Client	Jane Austen Society of North America	
Designer	Gunnar Swanson	
6.		
Client	Gunnar Swanson Design Office	
Designer	Gunnar Swanson	

7.	
Client	Midtown Ventura Community Council
Designer	Gunnar Swanson
8.	
Client	County Communicators
Designer	Gunnar Swanson
9.	
Client	IABC/LA The Los Angeles Chapter of the International Association of Business Communicators
Designer	Gunnar Swanson
10.	
Client	Bay Rock
Designer	Rich Costa
11.	
Client	SSR Realty
Designers	Rich Costa, Kyle Ogden
12.	
Client	Blue Skies
Designer	Amy Krachenfels
13.	
Client	Back on Track
Designer	Amy Krachenfels
14.	
Client	CMC
Designers	Rich Costa
15.	
Client	Bay Rock Residential
Designers	Rich Costa

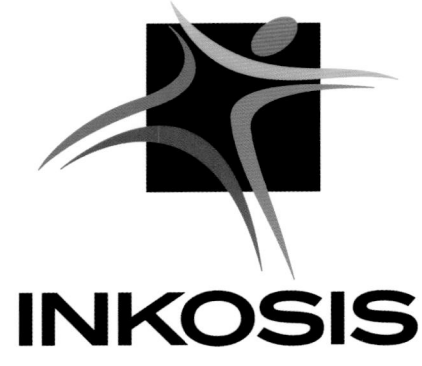

INKOSIS

1.

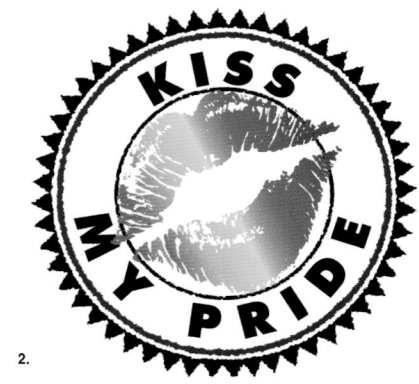

2.

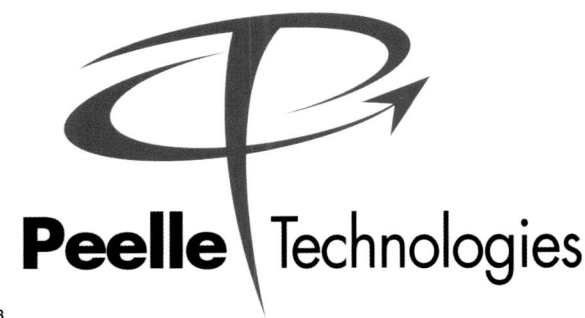

Peelle Technologies

3.

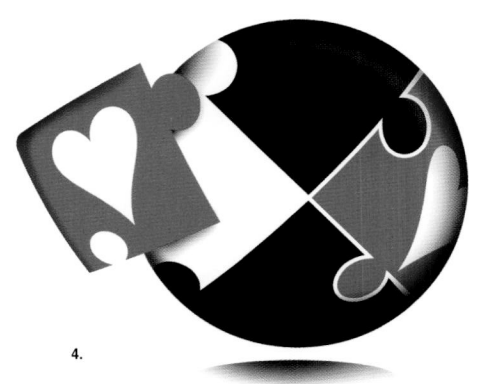

4.

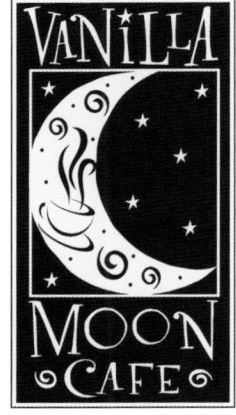

5.

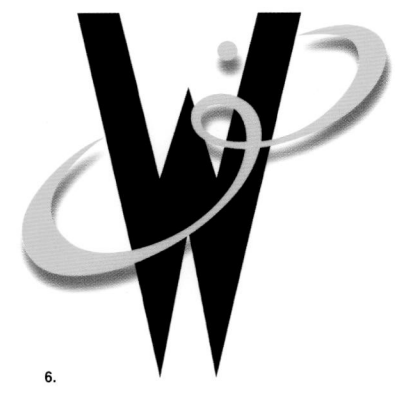

6.

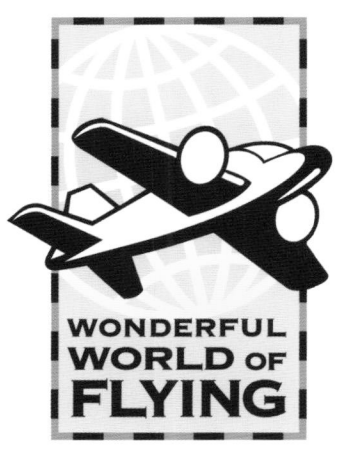

7.

1 - 7
Design Firm **Creative Madhouse**
1.
Client   *Inkosis*
Designer   Madelyn Wattigney
2.
Client   *Kiss My Pride*
Designer   Madelyn Wattigney
3.
Client   *Peelle Technology*
Designer   Madelyn Wattigney
4.
Client   *Two Topia*
Designer   Madelyn Wattigney
5.
Client   *Vanilla Moon Cafe*
Designer   Madelyn Wattigney
6.
Client   *W3 Master*
Designer   Madelyn Wattigney
7.
Client   *Wonderful World of Flying*
Designer   Madelyn Wattigney

(opposite)
Client   *Atlantic Maintenance Corp.*
Design Firm **Fiorentino Associates**
Designer   Andy Eng

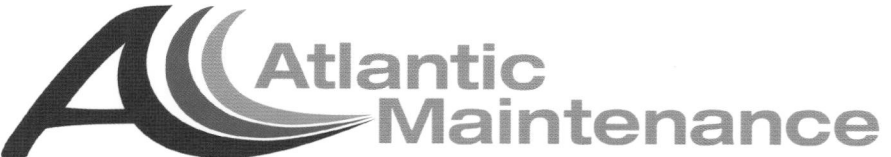

The cleaning and maintenance professionals
that know the outside, inside out.

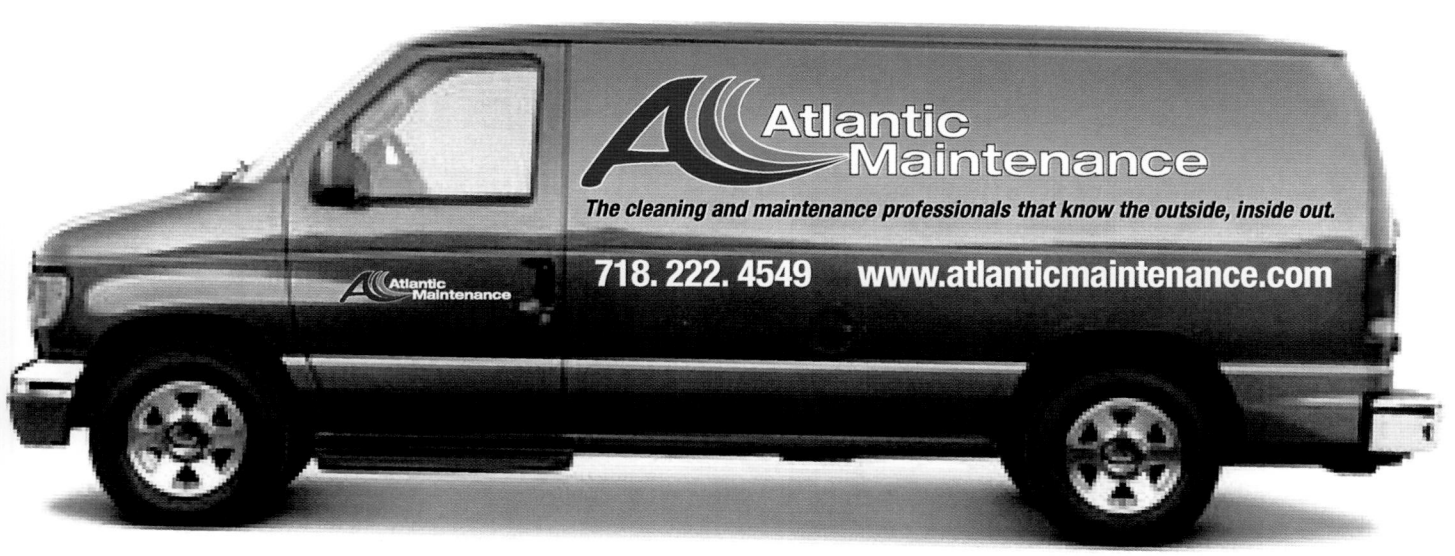

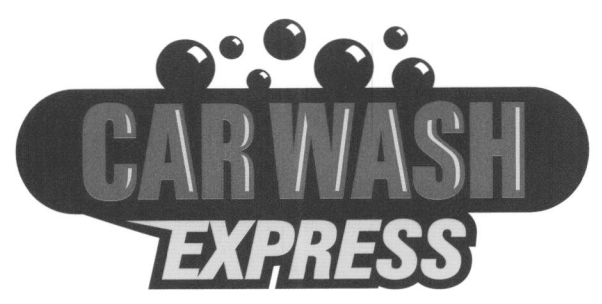

1.

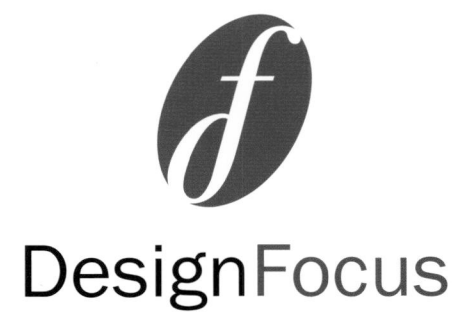

2.

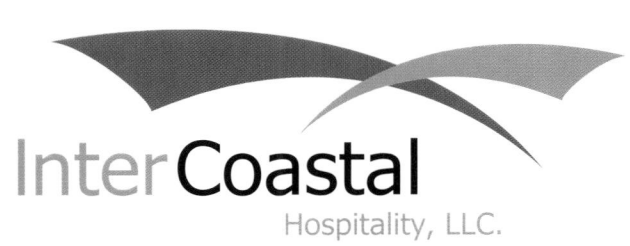

3.

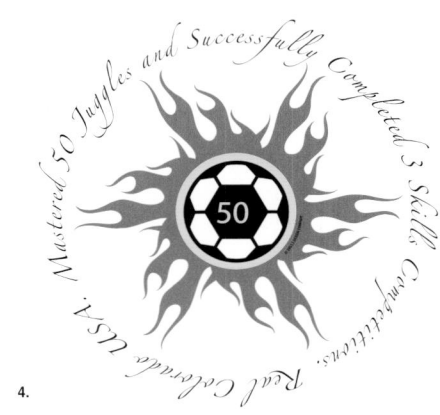

4.

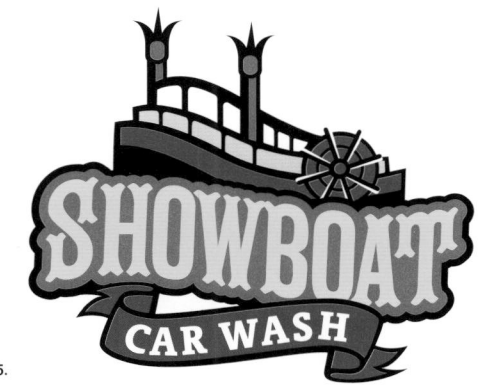

5.

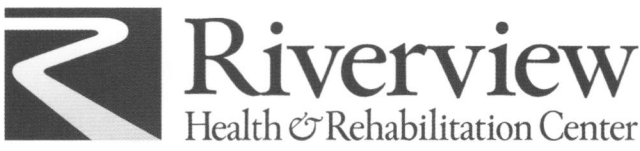

6.

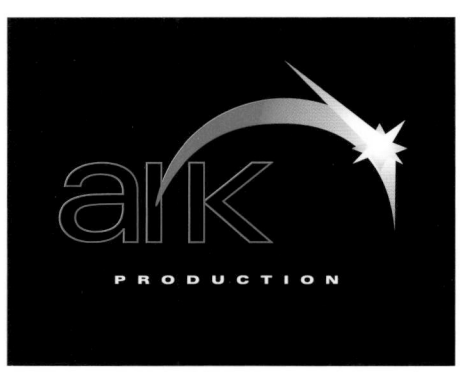

7.

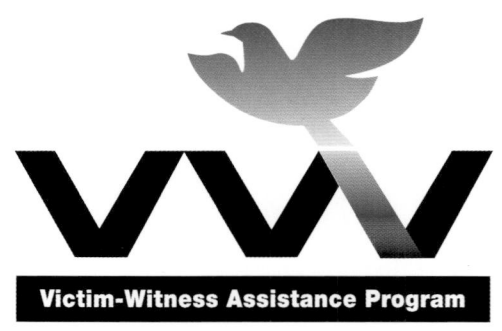

8.

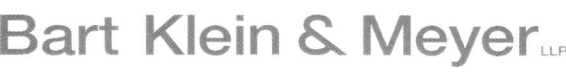

9.

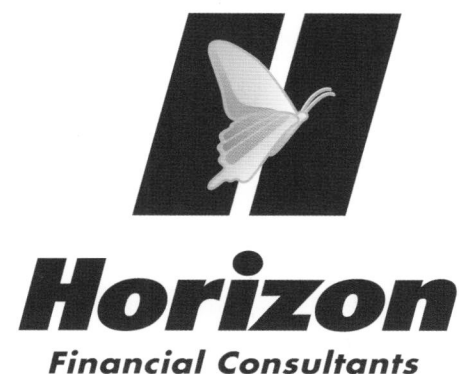

10.

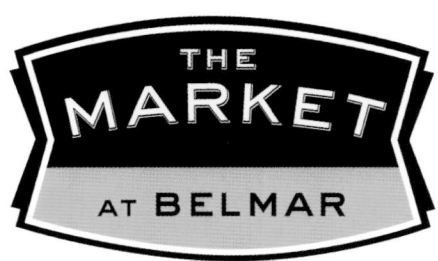

FARMERS, ARTISANS, FRIENDS

EVERY SUNDAY AT BELMAR

11.

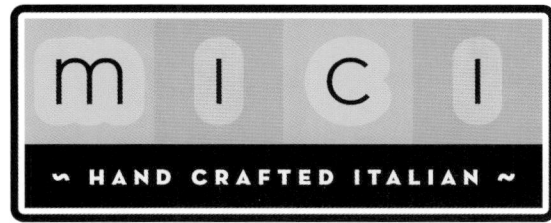

12.

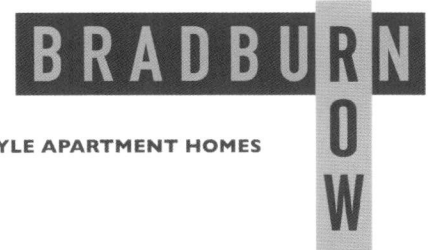

URBAN STYLE APARTMENT HOMES

13.

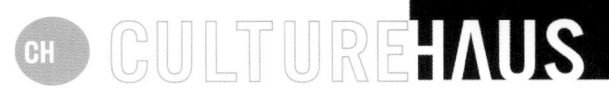

14.

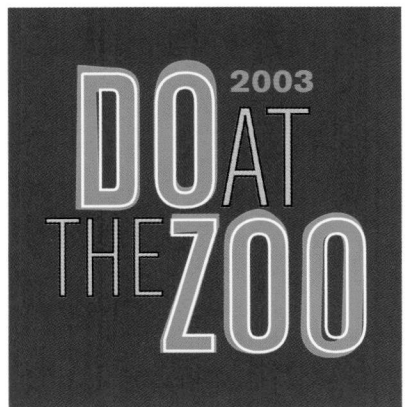

15.

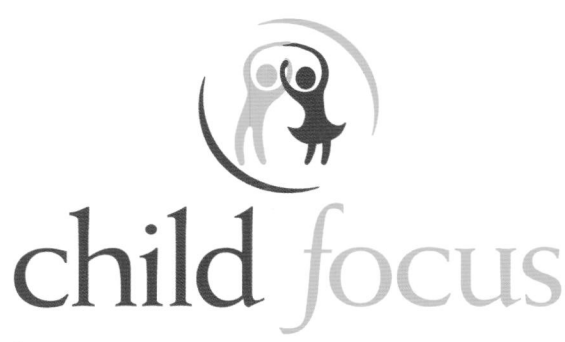

1.

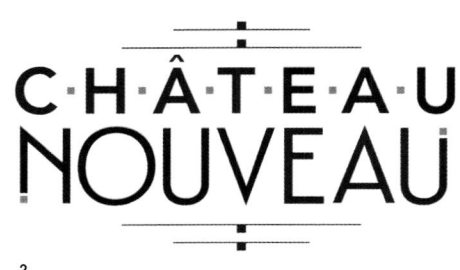

2.

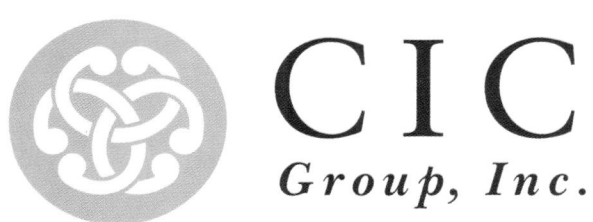

3.

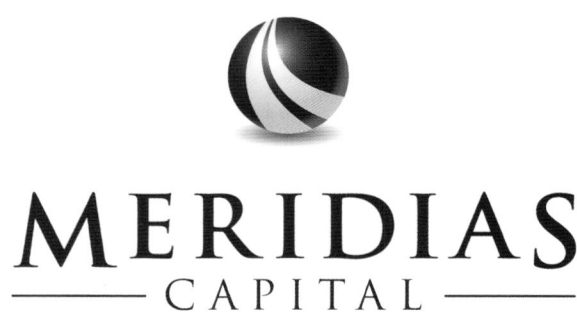

4.

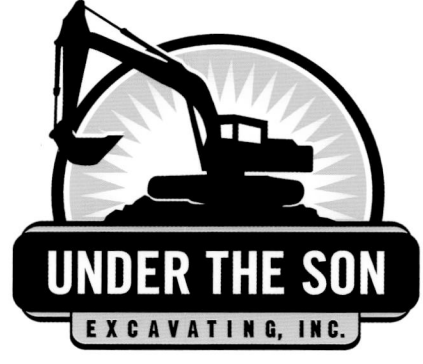

5.

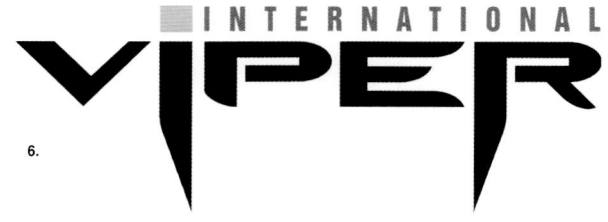

6.

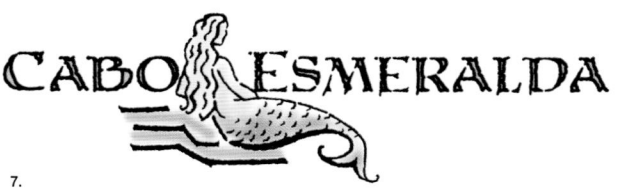

7.

1 - 7
Design Firm **CDI Studios**
1.
Client   *Child Focus of Nevada*
Designer Henry Martinez III
2.
Client   *Pacific Properties*
Designer Mackenzie Walsh
3.
Client   *Capital Investment Company*
Designers Michelle Georgilas,
          Eddie Roberts
4.
Client   *Meridias Capital*
Designers Michelle Georgilas,
          Eddie Roberts
5.
Client   *Under the Son Excavating*
Designers Victoria Hart,
          Mackenzie Walsh

6.
Client   *Viper International*
Designer Casey Corcoran
7.
Client   *Bernard Realty*
Designer Victoria Hart
(opposite)
Client   *Tasty Baking Company*
Design Firm **Munroe Creative Partners**
Designer Mike Cavallaro

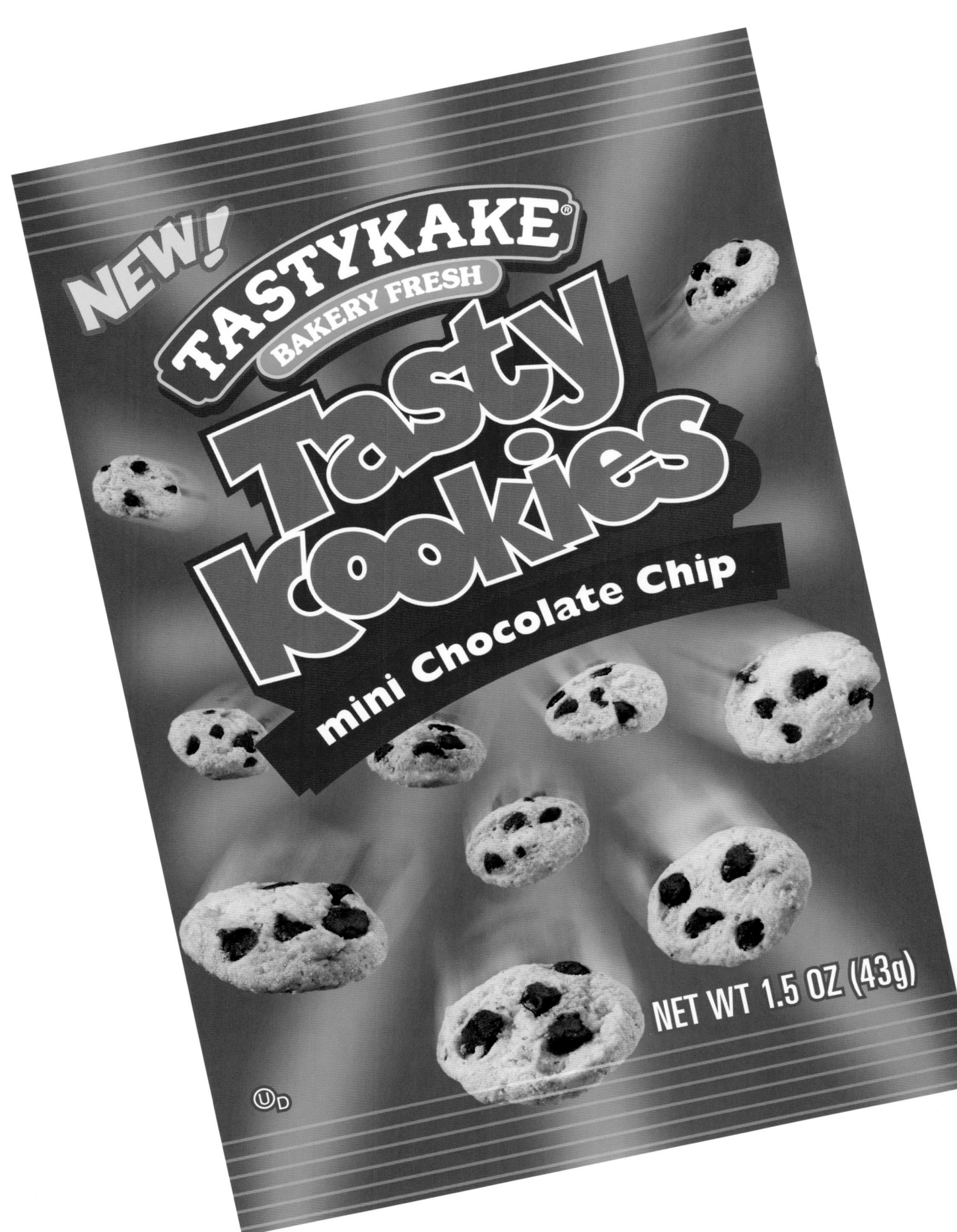

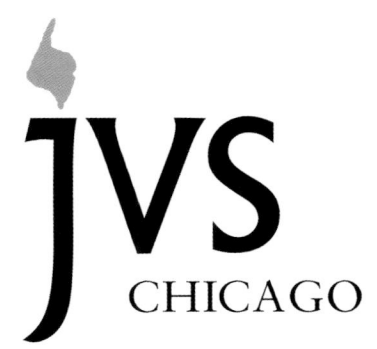

1.

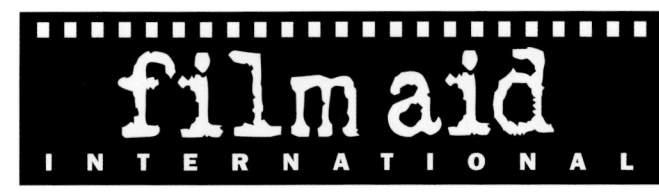

2.

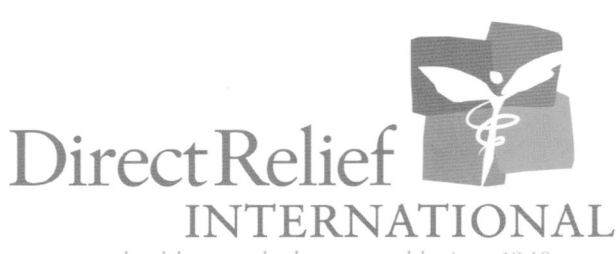

3.

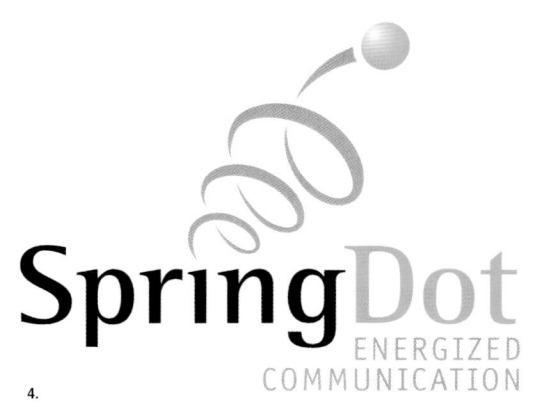

4.

5.

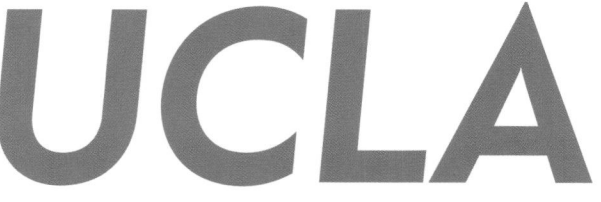

6.

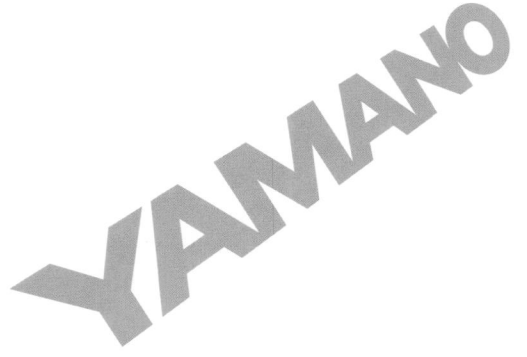

7.

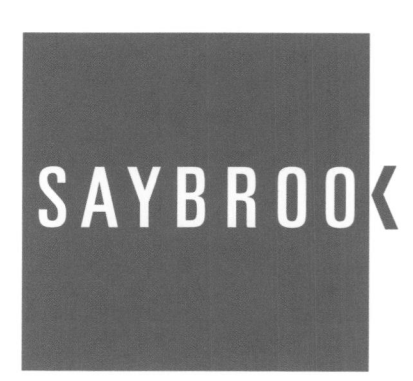

8.

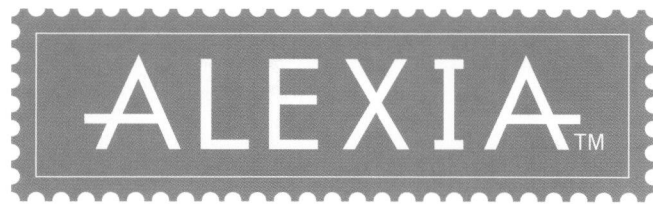

9.

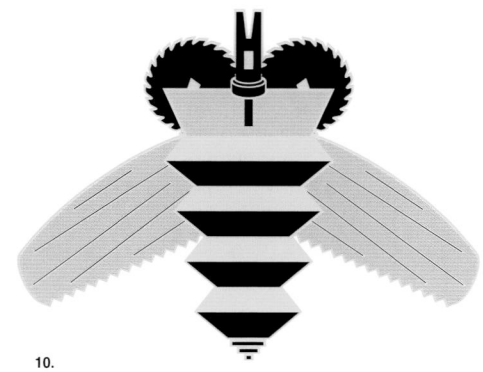

10.

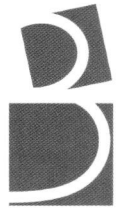

BLOCK CONSULTING

11.

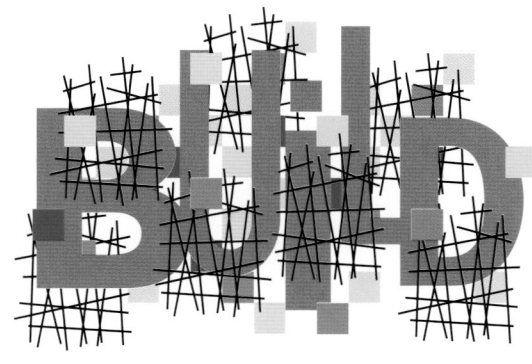

12.

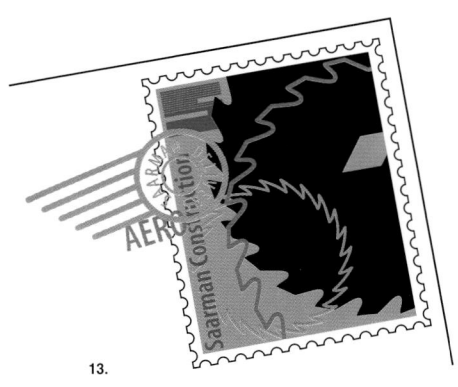

13.

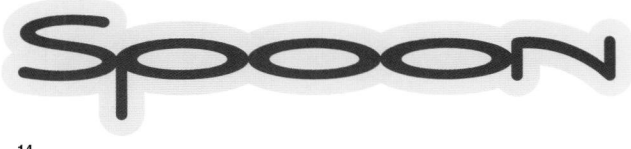

14.

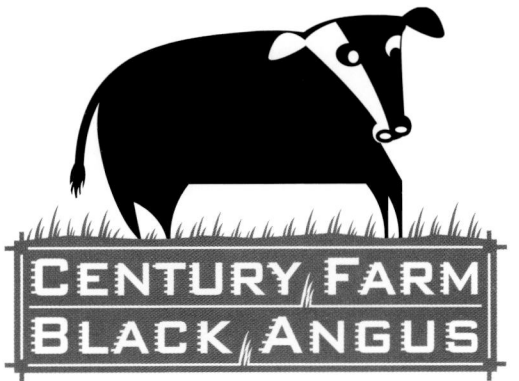

15.

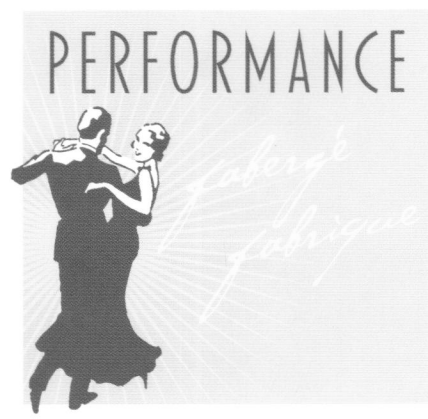

1.

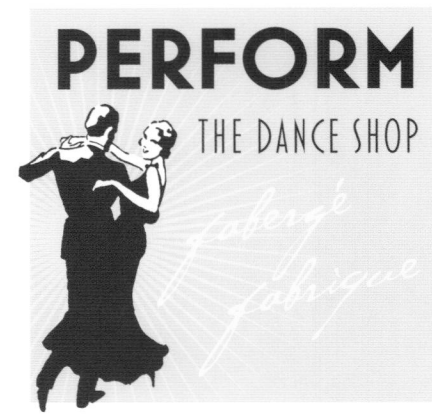

2.

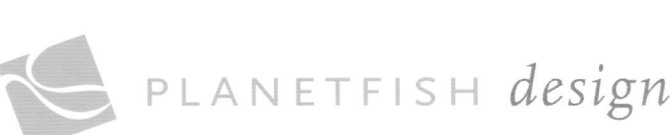

3.

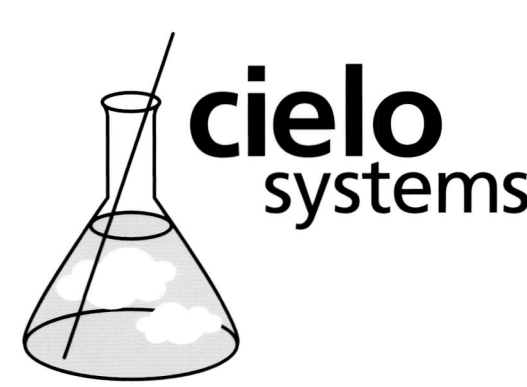

4.

5.

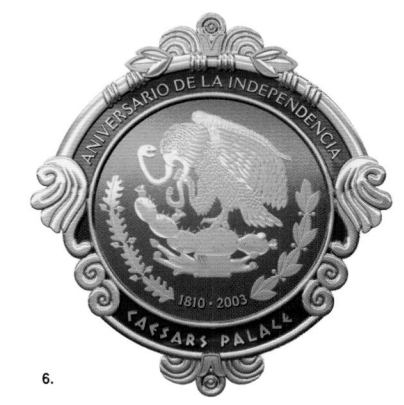

6.

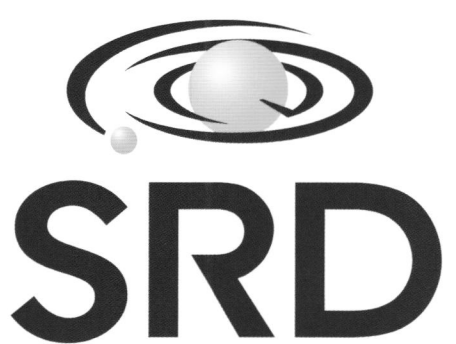

7.

1 - 4
Design Firm **PlanetFish Design**
5 - 7
Design Firm **CDI Studios**

1, 2.
Client   *Fabergé Fabrique*
Designer   Felicia Lo

3.
Client   *PlanetFish Design*
Designer   Felicia Lo

4.
Client   *Cielo Systems*
Designer   Felicia Lo

5.
Client   *Connection Power*
Designers   Eddie Roberts,
Victoria Hart

6.
Client   *Ceasars Palace*
Designers   Victoria Hart,
Henry Marting III,
Eddie Roberts

7.
Client   *Systems Research
Development*
Designers   Eddie Roberts,
Victoria Hart

(opposite)
Client   *Pinnacle Foods*
Design Firm **Zunda Design Group**
Designers   Todd Nickel, Charles Zunda,
Tom James

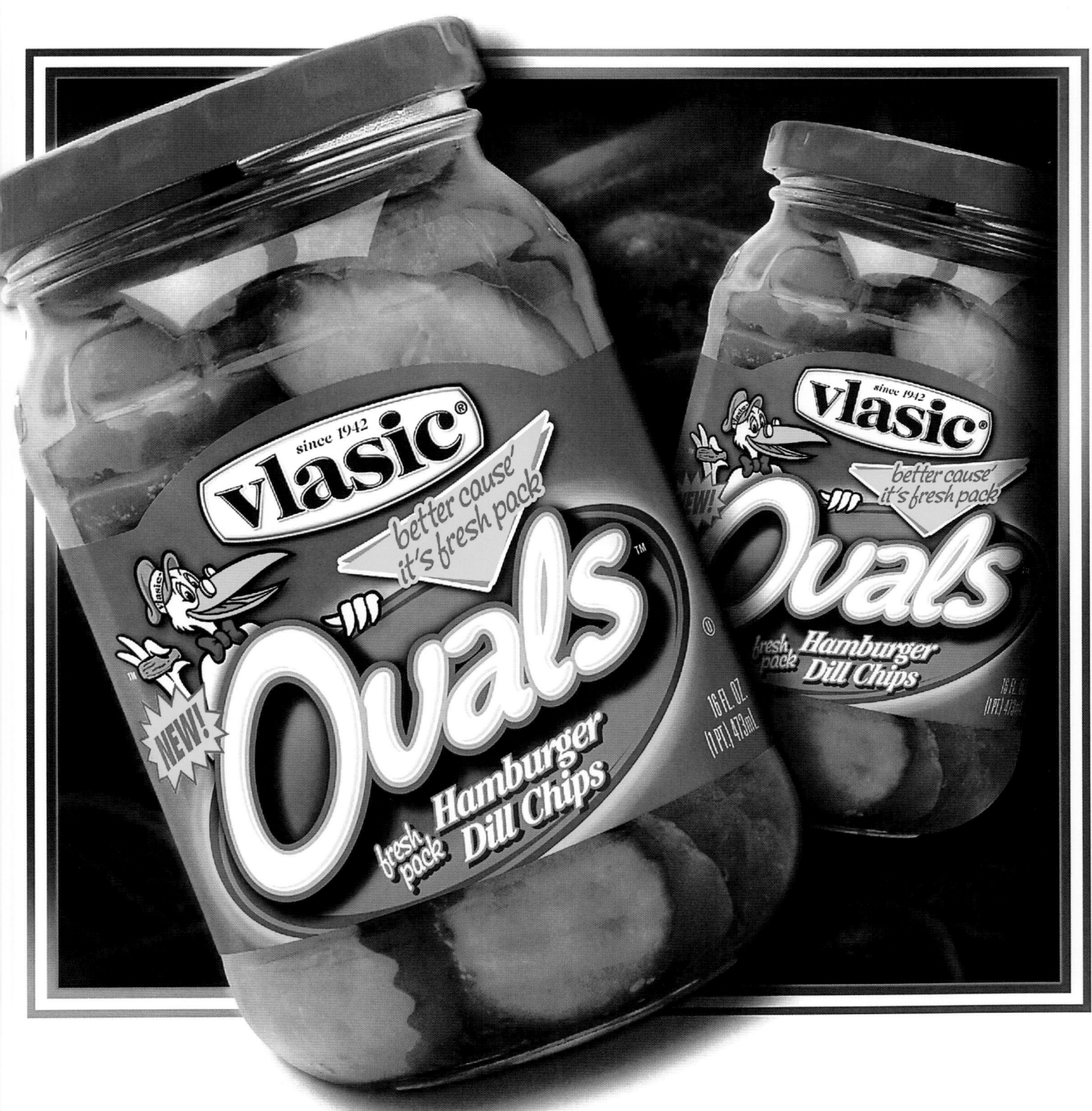

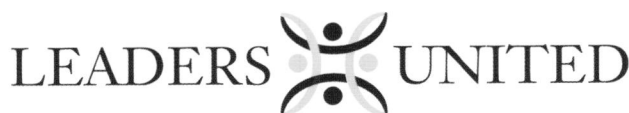

1.

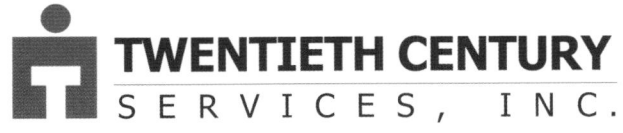

2.

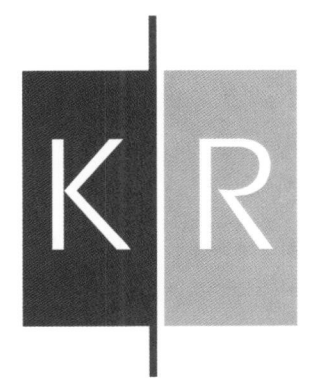

3.

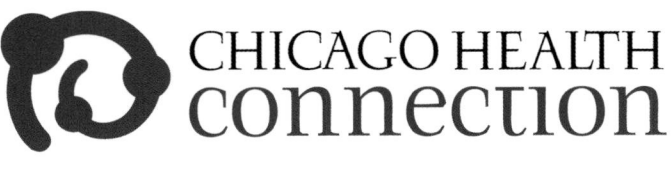

4.

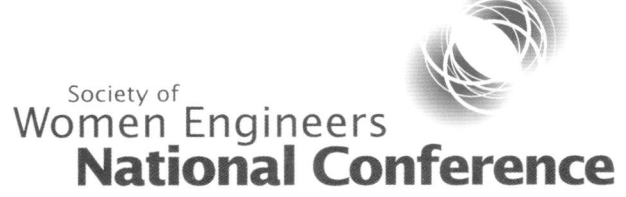

5.

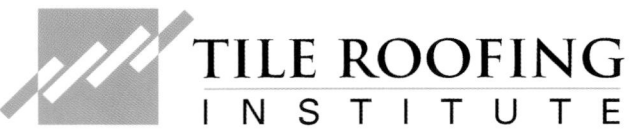

6.

Funk FL Linko

7.

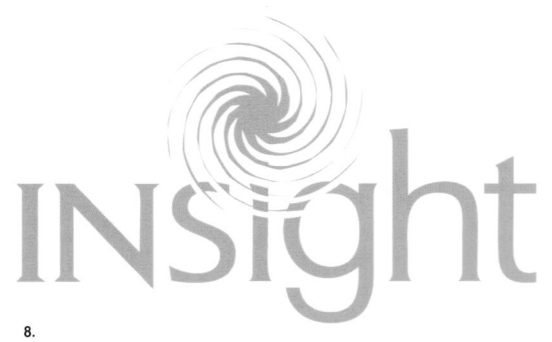

8.

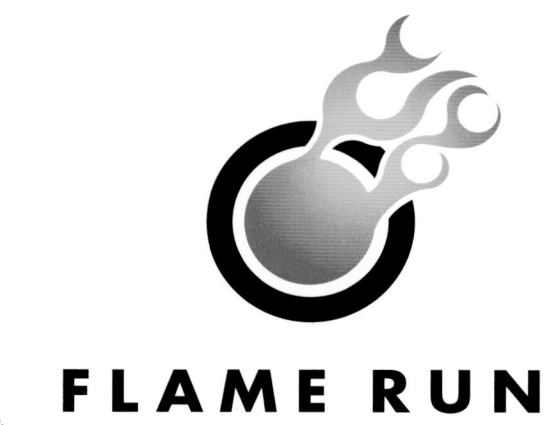

FLAME RUN

9.

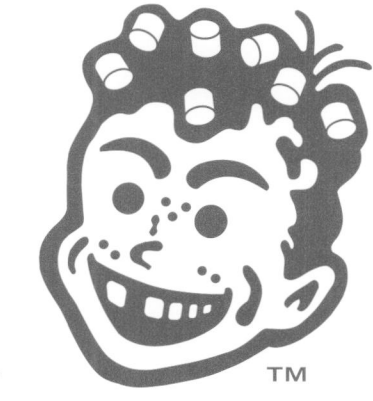

TM

10.

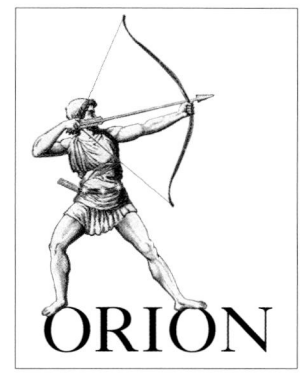

ORION

11.

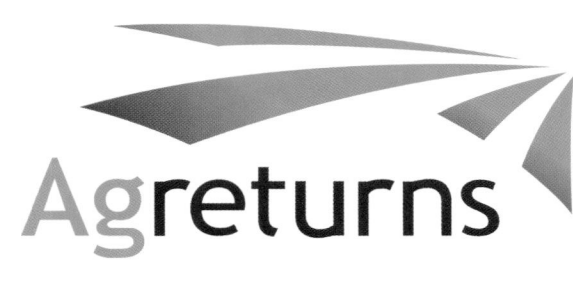

coffeesmiths

12.

Whitlock

TAVERN

13.

Agreturns

14.

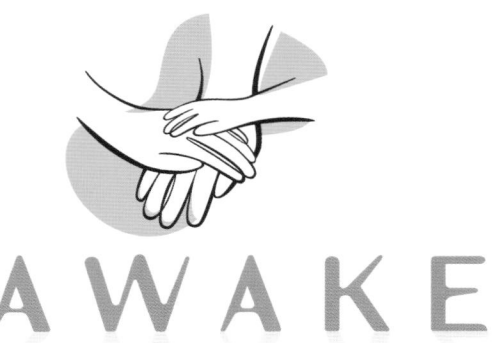

AWAKE

15.

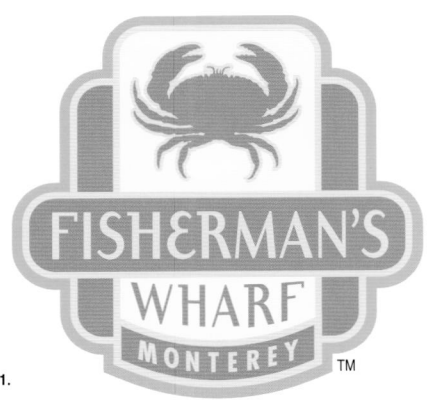

1.

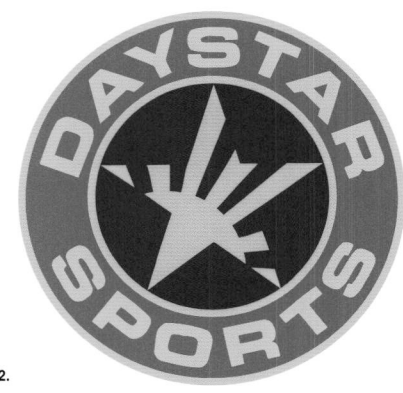

2.

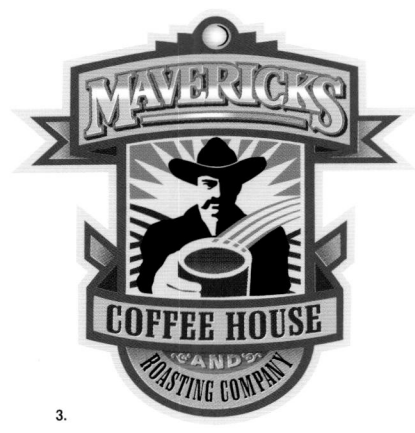

3.

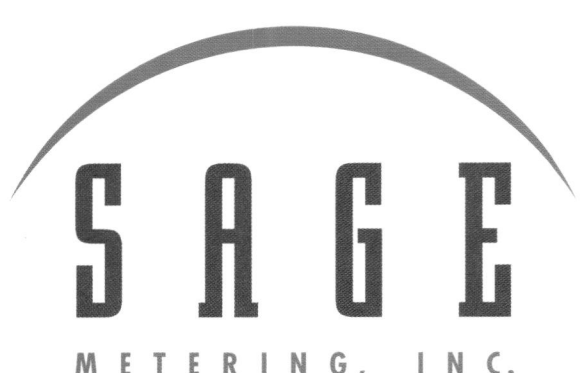

4.

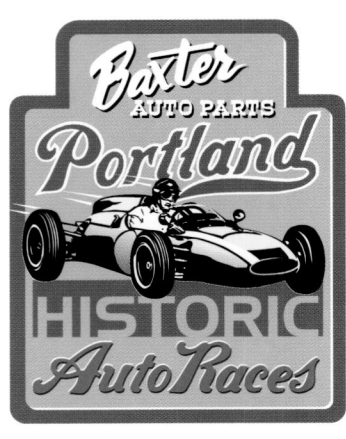

5.

GREENBLOCK

6.

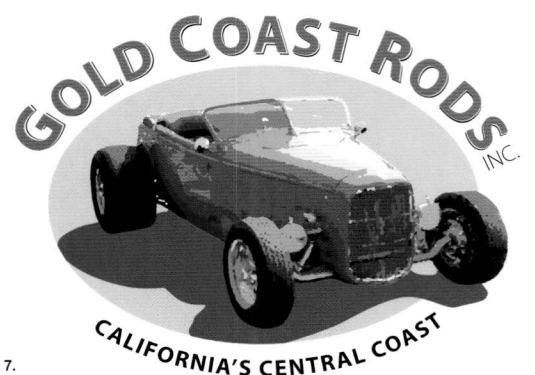

7.

1 - 7
Design Firm **The Wecker Group**
1.
Client *Fisherman's Wharf Monterey*
Designer Robert Wecker
2.
Client *Daystar Sports*
Designer Robert Wecker
3.
Client *Mavericks Coffee House &
Roasting Company*
Designer Robert Wecker
4.
Client *Portland Historic
Automobile Races*
Designer Robert Wecker
5.
Client *Sage Metering*
Designer Robert Wecker
6.
Client *Greenblock*
Designers Robert Wecker,
Matt Gnibus

7.
Client *Gold Coast Rods, Inc.*
Designer Robert Wecker
(opposite)
Client *Drinks Americas, Inc.*
Design Firm **Zunda Design Group**
Designers Pat Sullivan,
Charles Zunda

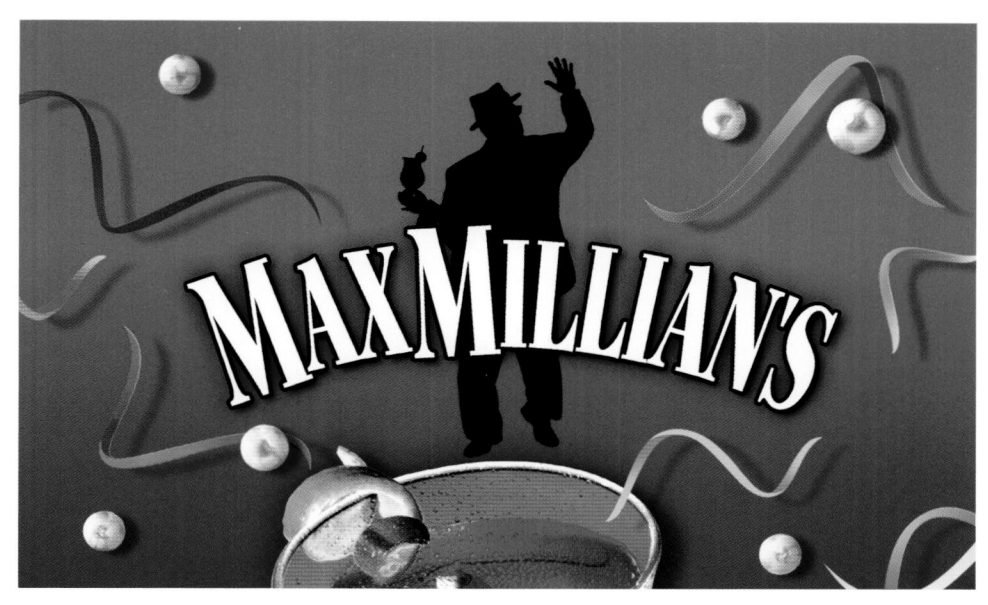

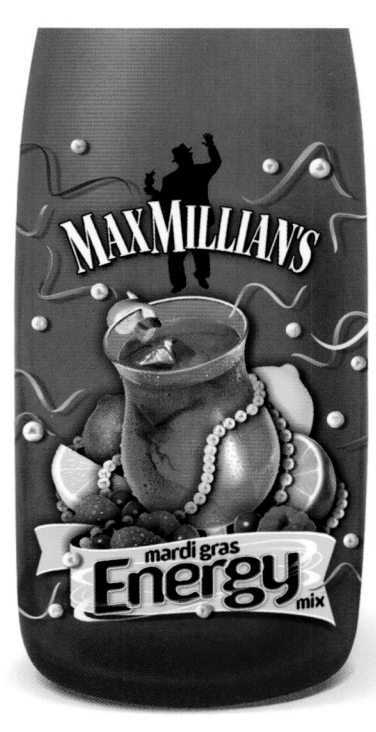

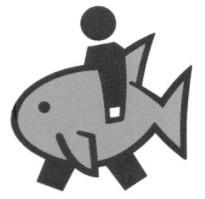

fischers fritzz

1.

Wild World
JAGDCENTER DORSTEN

2.

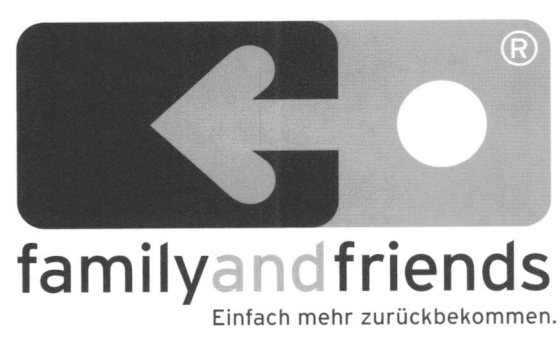

family and friends
Einfach mehr zurückbekommen.

3.

ascos
ruhrgas positioning services

4.

wortundtat

5.

EDDIE'S MILLION DOLLAR COOK-OFF

6.

C A R E
Center for Activity
Research and Education

7.

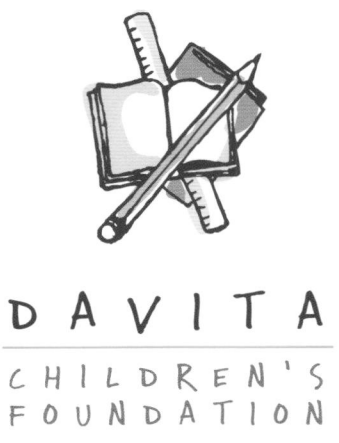

DAVITA
CHILDREN'S FOUNDATION

8.

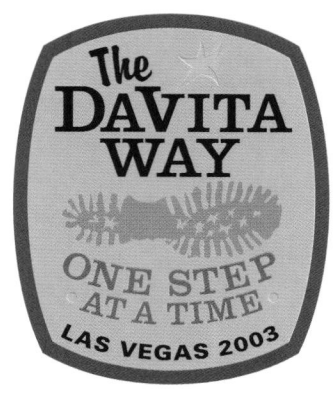

9.

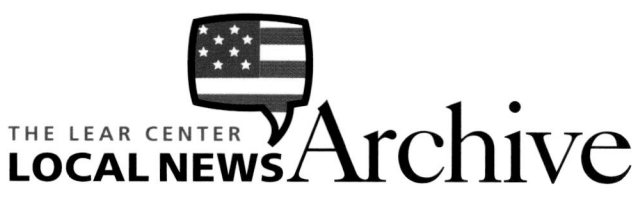

A Project of the USC Annenberg School and the University of Wisconsin

10.

USC CENTER ON
PublicDiplomacy

A Partnership of the USC Annenberg School for Communication and the USC College of Letters, Arts & Sciences' School of International Relations

11.

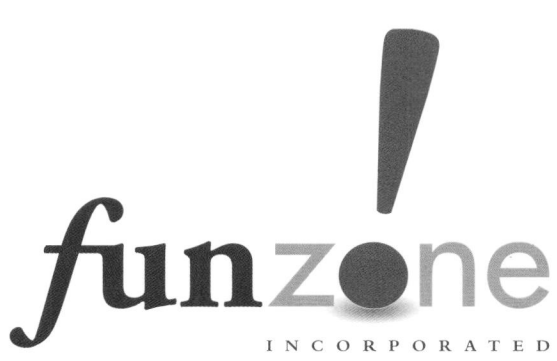

12.

OnSmile.com
the fine art of dentistry

13.

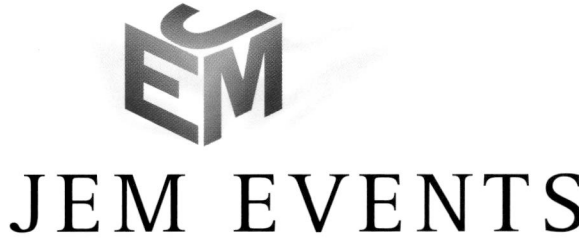

JEM EVENTS

14.

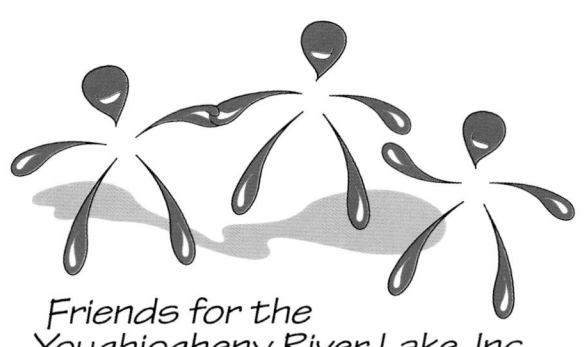

Friends for the Youghiogheny River Lake, Inc.

15.

1 - 5
Design Firm **Buttgereit und Heidenreich**
6 - 14
Design Firm **IE Design + Communications**
15
Design Firm **Freelance Visual Artist**

3.
Client   *family and friends*
Designers   Michael Buttgereit, Wolfram Heidenreich

4.
Client   *Ruhrgas AG, Essen, Germany*
Designer   Michael Buttgereit

5.
Client   *Wort und Tat e.v., Essen, Germany*
Designers   Michael Buttgereit, Wolfram Heidenreich

6.
Client   *Disney*
Designers   Marcie Carson, Cya Nelson

7.
Client   *CARE*
Designers   Marcie Carson, Amy Klass

8.
Client   *Davita Healthcare*
Designers   Marcie Carson, Cya Nelson

9.
Client   *Davita Healthcare*
Designer   Marcie Carson

10 - 11
Client   *University of Southern California*
Designers   Marcie Carson, Cya Nelson

12.
Client   *Fun Zone*
Designer   Marcie Carson

13.
Client   *OnSmile*
Designer   Marcie Carson

14.
Client   *JEM Events*
Designer   Marcie Carson

15.
Client   *Friends for the Youghiogheny River Lake, Inc.*
Designer   Chris M. Brioady

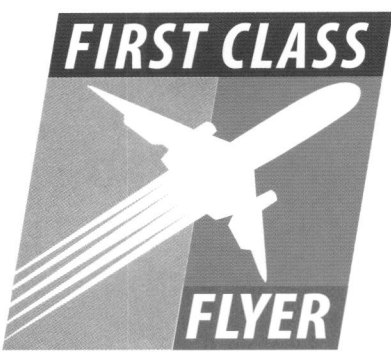

1.

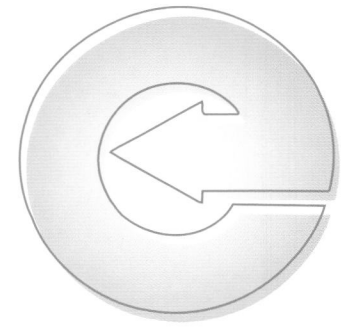

2.

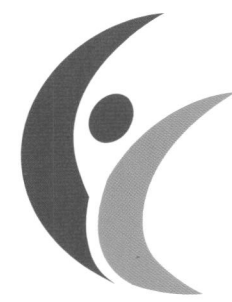

"Here for Good"

Community Foundation for Monterey County

3.

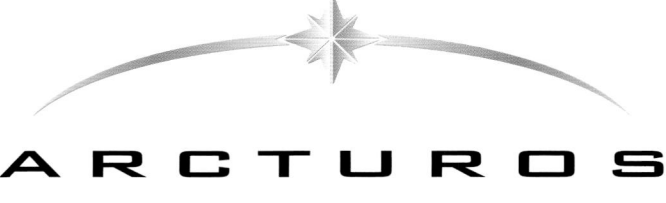

4.

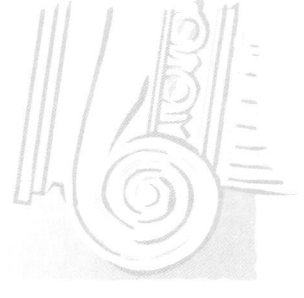

SAMUEL B. BENAVIDES, AIA

5.

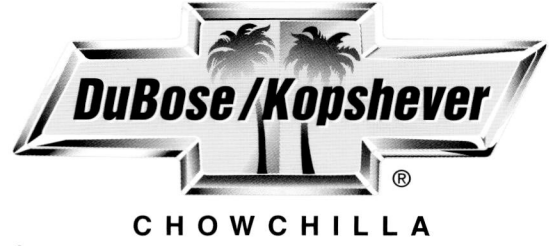

CHOWCHILLA

6.

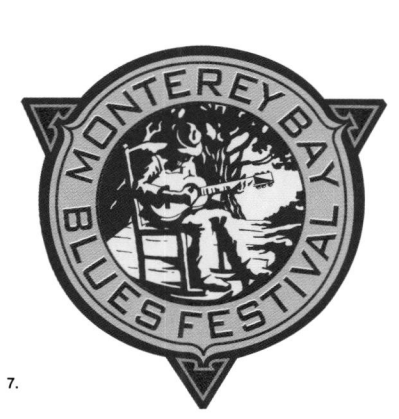

7.

1 - 7
Design Firm **The Wecker Group**

1.
Client — First Class Flyer
Designers — Robert Wecker,
Matt Gnibus

2.
Client — Entersports
Designer — Robert Wecker

3.
Client — Community Foundation for Monterey County
Designer — Robert Wecker

4.
Client — Arcturos Yachts
Designers — Robert Wecker, Matt Gnibus

5.
Client — Benavides Architects
Designer — Robert Wecker

6.
Client — DuBose/Kopshever Chevrolet
Designers — Robert Wecker, Matt Gnibus

7.
Client — Monterey Bay Blues Festival
Designers — Robert Wecker, Harry Briggs

(opposite)
Client — Pinnacle Foods
Design Firm **Zunda Design Group**
Designers — Todd Nickel, Charles Zunda, Tom James

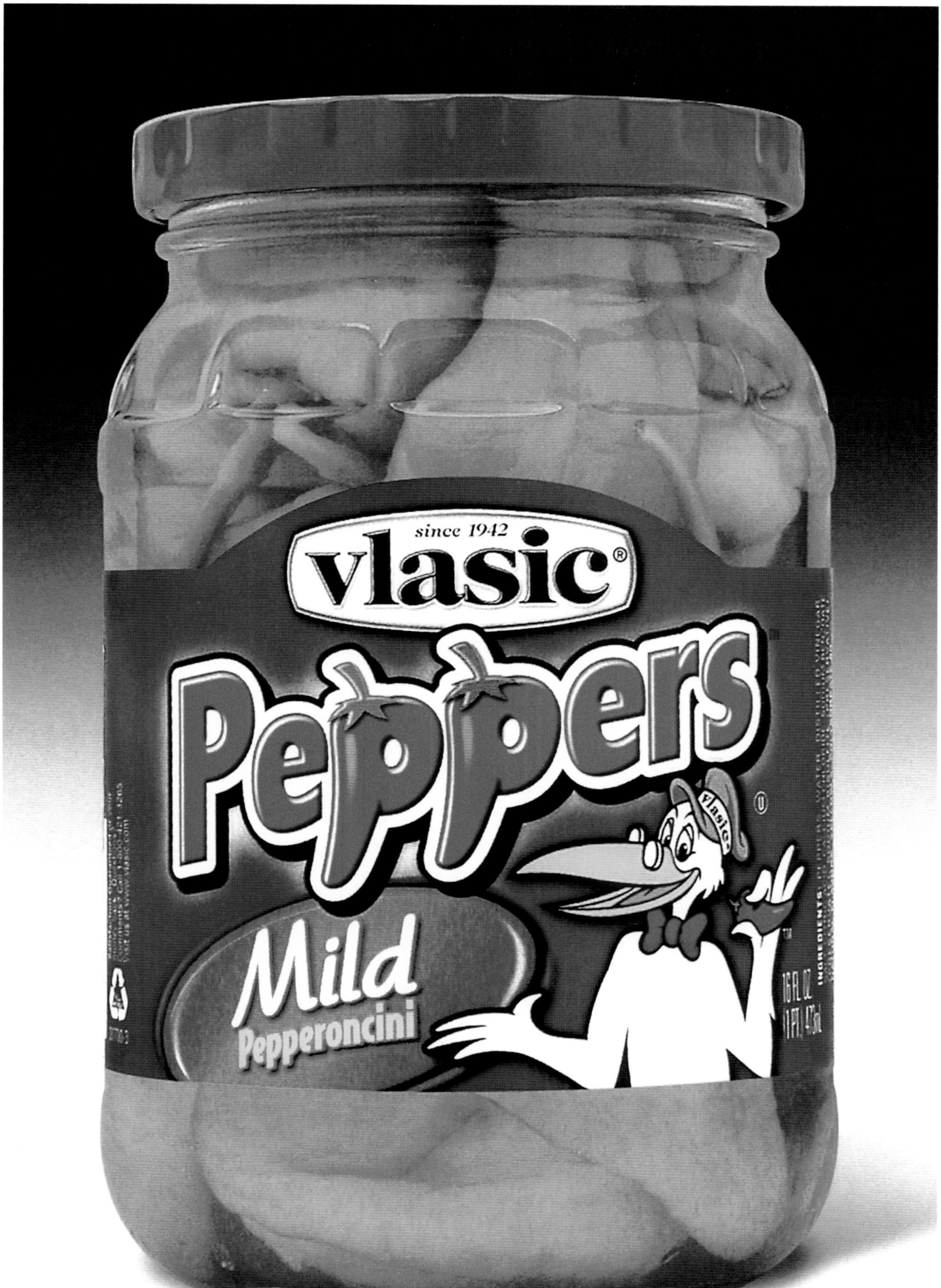
since 1942
vlasic
Peppers
Mild
Pepperoncini

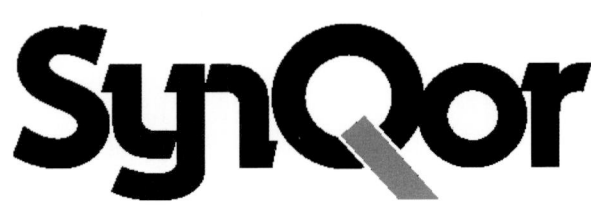

1.

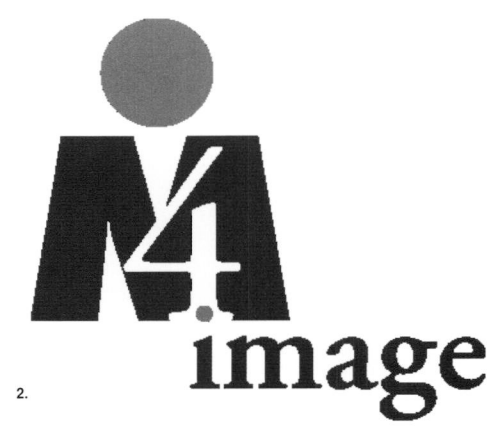

2.

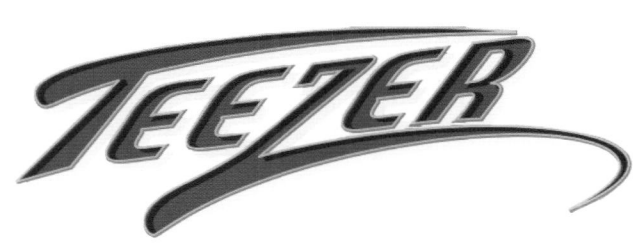

3.

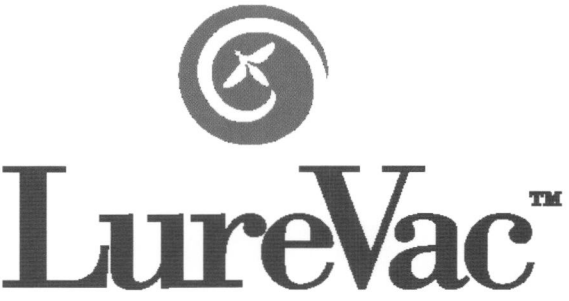

4.

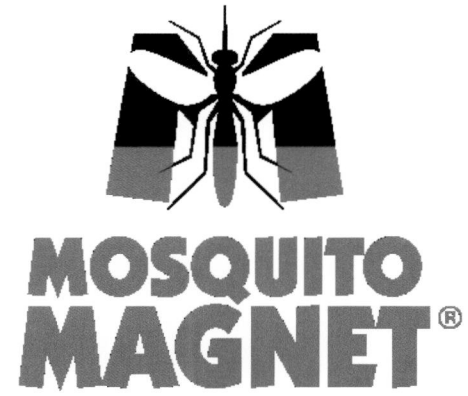

5.

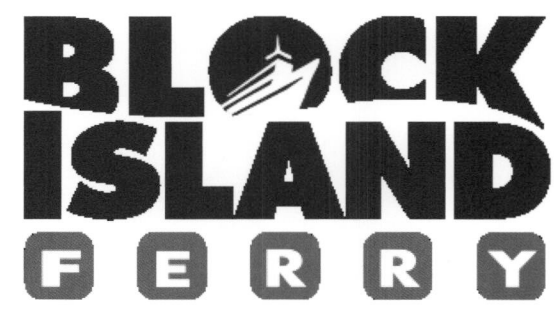

6.

7.

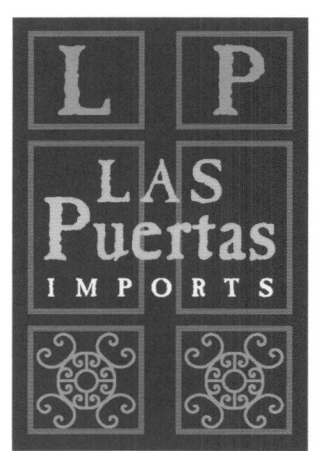

8.

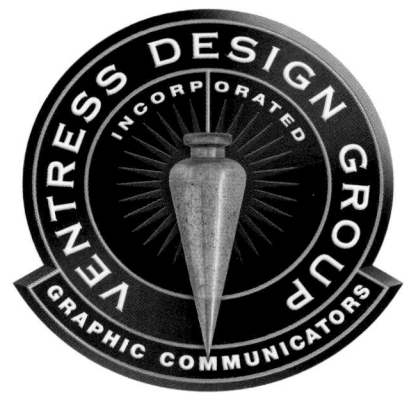

9.

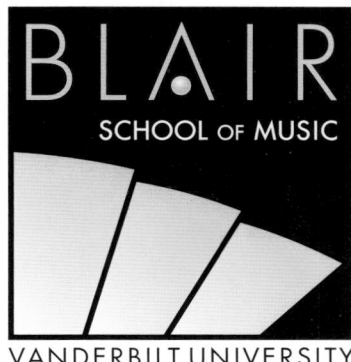

10.

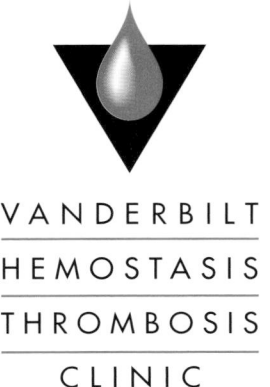

VANDERBILT
HEMOSTASIS
THROMBOSIS
CLINIC

11.

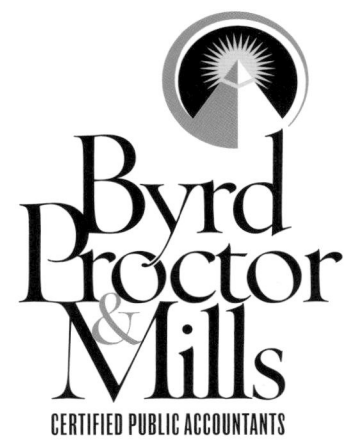

12.

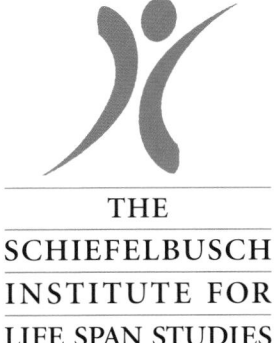

THE
SCHIEFELBUSCH
INSTITUTE FOR
LIFE SPAN STUDIES

13.

14.

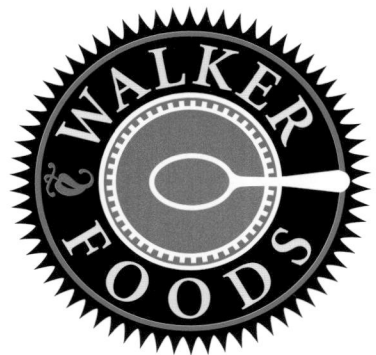

15.

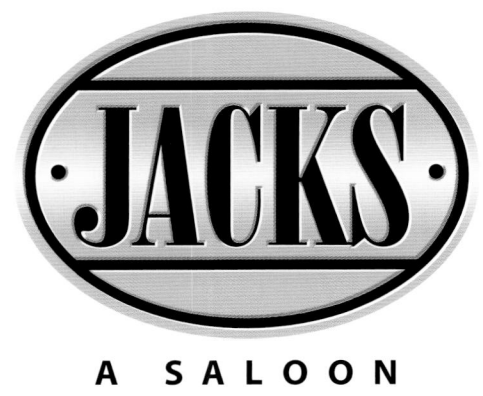

1.

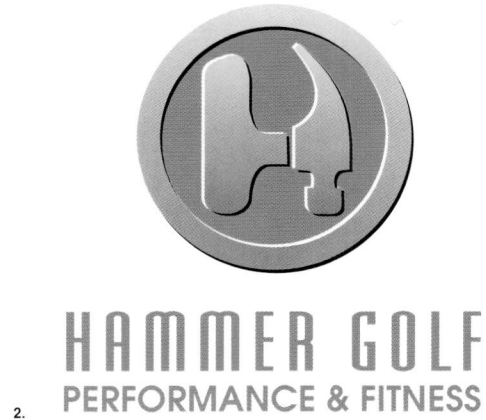

2.

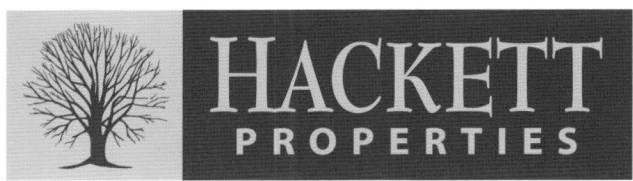

3.

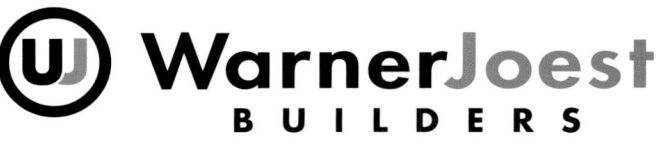

4.

Tools for Decision

™

5.

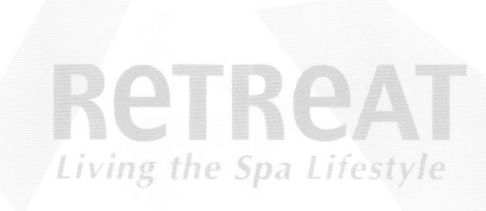

TAYLOR BAY YACHTS, LLC

6.

RetReat
Living the Spa Lifestyle

7.

1 - 7
Design Firm **The Wecker Group**
1.
Client   *Doubletree Hotel/Monterey*
Designer   Robert Wecker
2.
Client   *Hammer Golf Performance*
Designers Robert Wecker,
           Matt Gnibus
3.
Client   *Hackett Properties*
Designer   Robert Wecker
4.
Client   *Warner Joest Builders*
Designers Robert Wecker,
           Tremayne Cryer
5.
Client   *Tools for Decision*
Designers Robert Wecker,
           Matt Gnibus
6.
Client   *Taylor Bay Yachts*
Designers Robert Wecker,
           Matt Gnibus

7.
Client   *Retreat*
Designer   Robert Wecker
(opposite)
Client   *American Heritage Billiards*
Design Firm **Berni Marketing & Design**
Designers Carlos Seminario,
           Stuart Berni

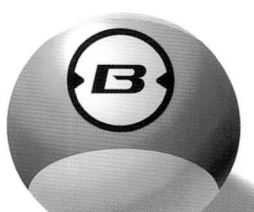

American Heritage

Challenge

To uncover consumer buying habits and reposition the #2 billiards company in the U.S. to stimulate sales growth.

Solution

Repositioned American Heritage through the creation of a new branding strategy and research-based tagline that appeals to consumers looking "For the Finishing Touch" to complete a room's décor. Developed a dynamic corporate identity and website. Designed an innovative kiosk and POP display system that serves as a customizable tool to improve the buying experience.

Result

Right on cue: new positioning and kiosk/sales resonate with target audience yielding exponential sales growth.

Quote

"Our new corporate identity and repositioning have really improved our image. The interactive point of purchase system is a first in the industry and consumers really love it. We look forward to working with Berni for years to come."

Joe Pucci, President

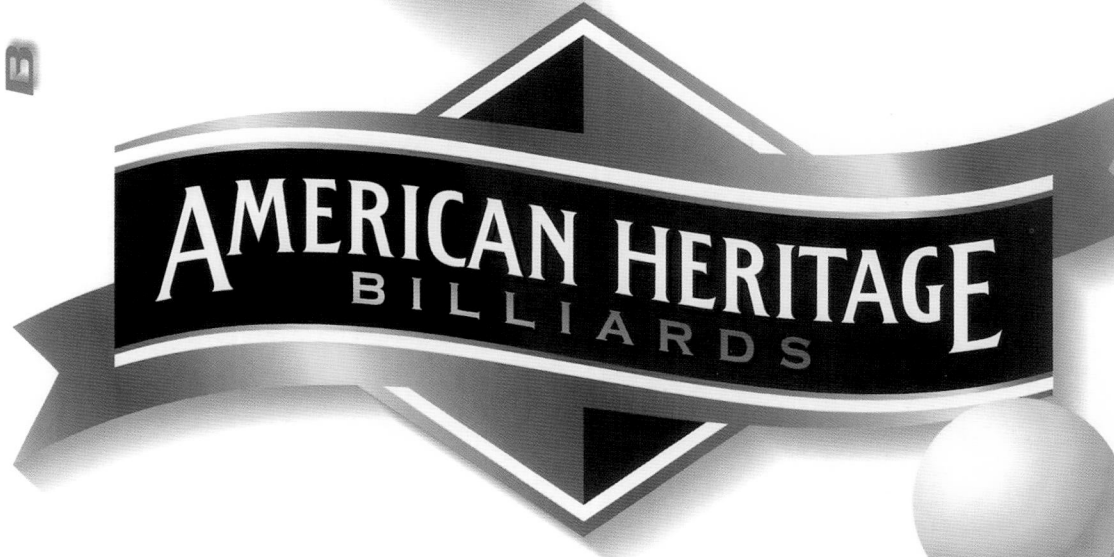

◆ F O R   T H E   F I N I S H I N G   T O U C H ◆

www.bernidesign.com

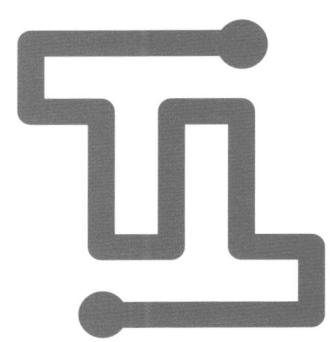

1.

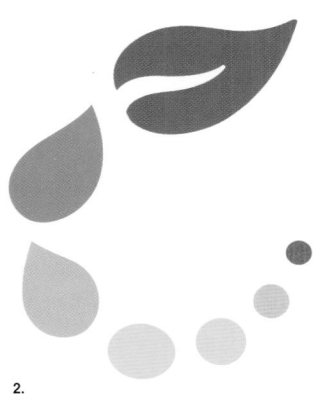

2.

FREE▂MOTION™

3.

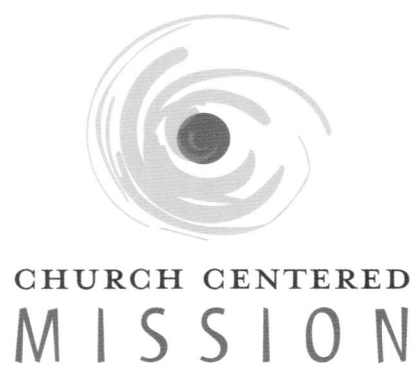

CHURCH CENTERED
MISSION

4.

rai.2028
RESPONSIVE ARTIFICIAL INTELLIGENCE

5.

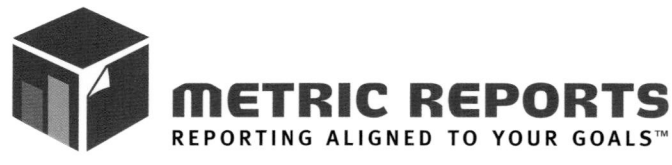

6.

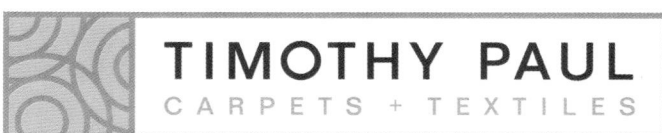

TIMOTHY PAUL
CARPETS + TEXTILES

7.

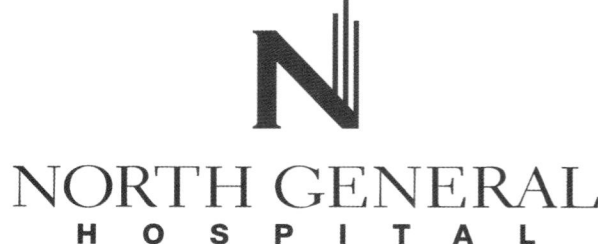

NORTH GENERAL
HOSPITAL

Growing With Our Community, Caring For Your Health

8.

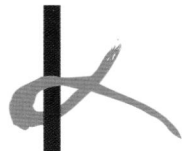

KOOCHES
hand made carpets

9.

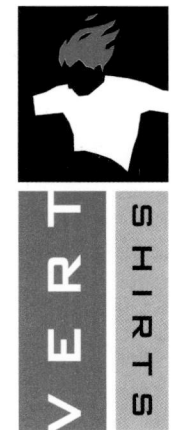

10.

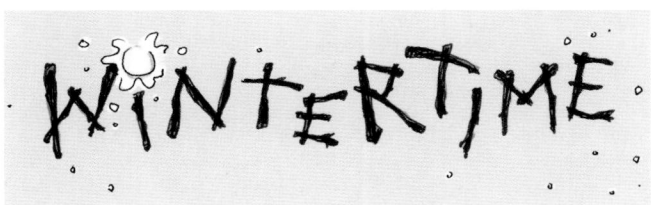

11.

design nut

12.

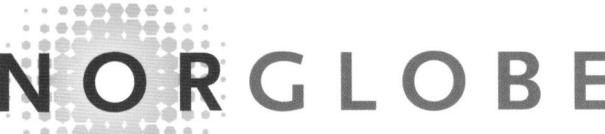

13.

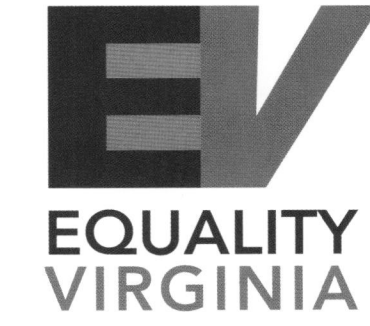

EQUALITY VIRGINIA

14.

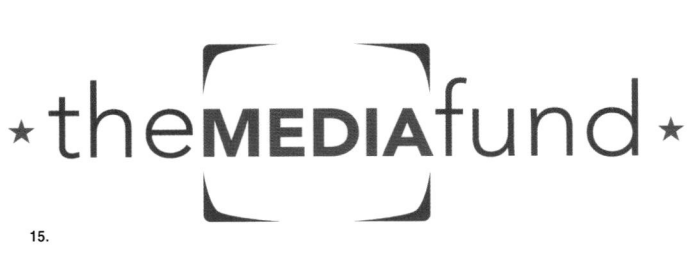

15.

1 - 3
Design Firm **Hornall Anderson Design Works**
4 - 6
Design Firm **StudioNorth**
7 - 15
Design Firm **Design Nut**

1.
Client TruckTrax
Designers Jack Anderson, Gretchen Cook, Kathy Saito

2.
Client Pace International
Designers Jack Anderson, Sonja Max, Andrew Smith, Kathy Saito

3.
Client FreeMotion
Designers Jack Anderson, Kathy Saito, Sonja Max, Henry Yiu, Alan Copeland

4.
Client Joel Holm Ministries
Designers Allison Misevich, Chris Trinco

5.
Client StudioNorth
Designer Mark Schneider

6.
Client Metric Reports
Designer Allison Misevich

7.
Client Timothy Paul Carpets + Textiles
Designer Brent M. Almond

8.
Client North General Hospital/Sutton Group
Designer Brent M. Almond

9.
Client Kooches Hand Made Carpets
Designer Brent M. Almond

10.
Client David Cohen
Designer Brent M. Almond

11.
Client Round House Theatre/Kircher, Inc.
Designer Brent M. Almond

12.
Client Design Nut, LLC
Designer Brent M. Almond

13.
Client NorGlobe, LLC
Designer Brent M. Almond

14.
Client Equality Virginia
Designer Brent M. Almond

15.
Client The Media Fund/Elevation
Designer Brent M. Almond

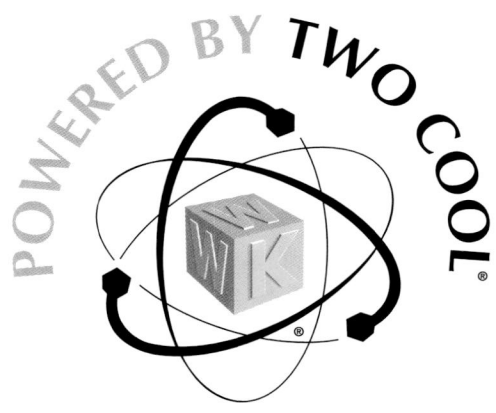

1.

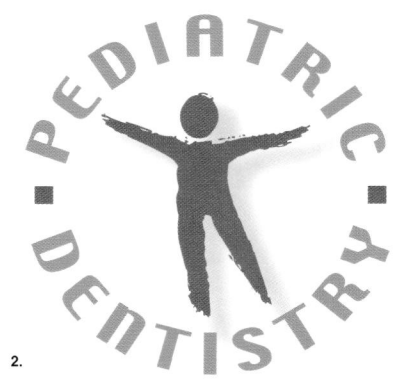

2.

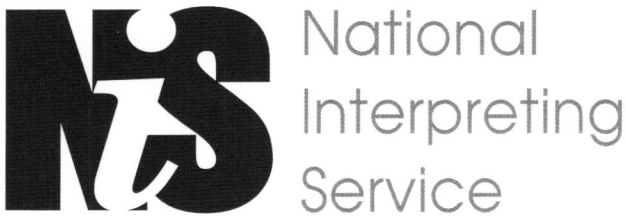

3.

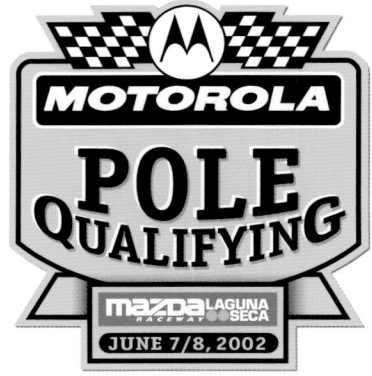

4.

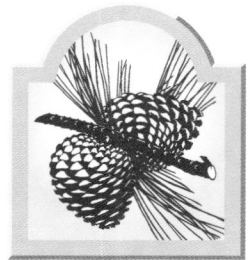

MONTEREY
PENINSULA
COUNTRY CLUB
PEBBLE BEACH, CA

5.

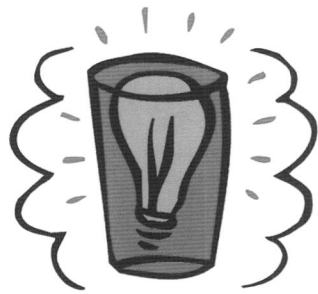

6. **The Drink Tank**

MYTHMAKER
CREATIVE SERVICES

7.

1 - 5
Design Firm **The Wecker Group**
6, 7
Design Firm **Faia Design**
1.
Client   *Wright Williams & Kelly*
Designers   Robert Wecker,
      Matt Gnibus
2.
Client   *Monterey Peninsula*
      Dental Group
Designer   Robert Wecker
3.
Client   *Language & Line Services*
Designer   Robert Wecker
4.
Client   *Mazda Raceway Laguna Seca*
Designer   Robert Wecker
5.
Client   *Monterey Peninsula Country Club*
Designer   Robert Wecker
6.
Client   *Odwalla, Inc.*
Designer   Don Faia

7.
Client   *Mythmaker Creative Services*
Designers   Don Faia,
      Tom Dill
(opposite)
Client   *Owensby Development*
Design Firm **Berni Marketing & Design**
Designers   Carlos Seminario,
      Stuart Berni

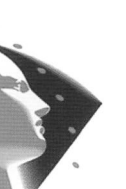

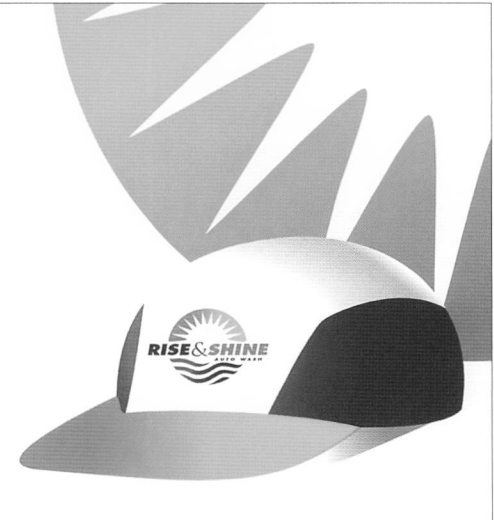

Owensby Development

Challenge

To launch a dynamic
national brand
for a car wash
chain with broad
demographic appeal.

Solution

Creation of shiny, new name and
identity system that is leveraged
into multiple consumer touch-points
to build brand equity.

Result

On time, on target, and on budget.
Positive perception of quality service
achieved with consumers.

Quote

"We needed the look and feel of a national brand
right out of the gate. Berni's expertise and experience
working with startups made all the difference.
We hit the ground running."

Charles Owensby, Principal

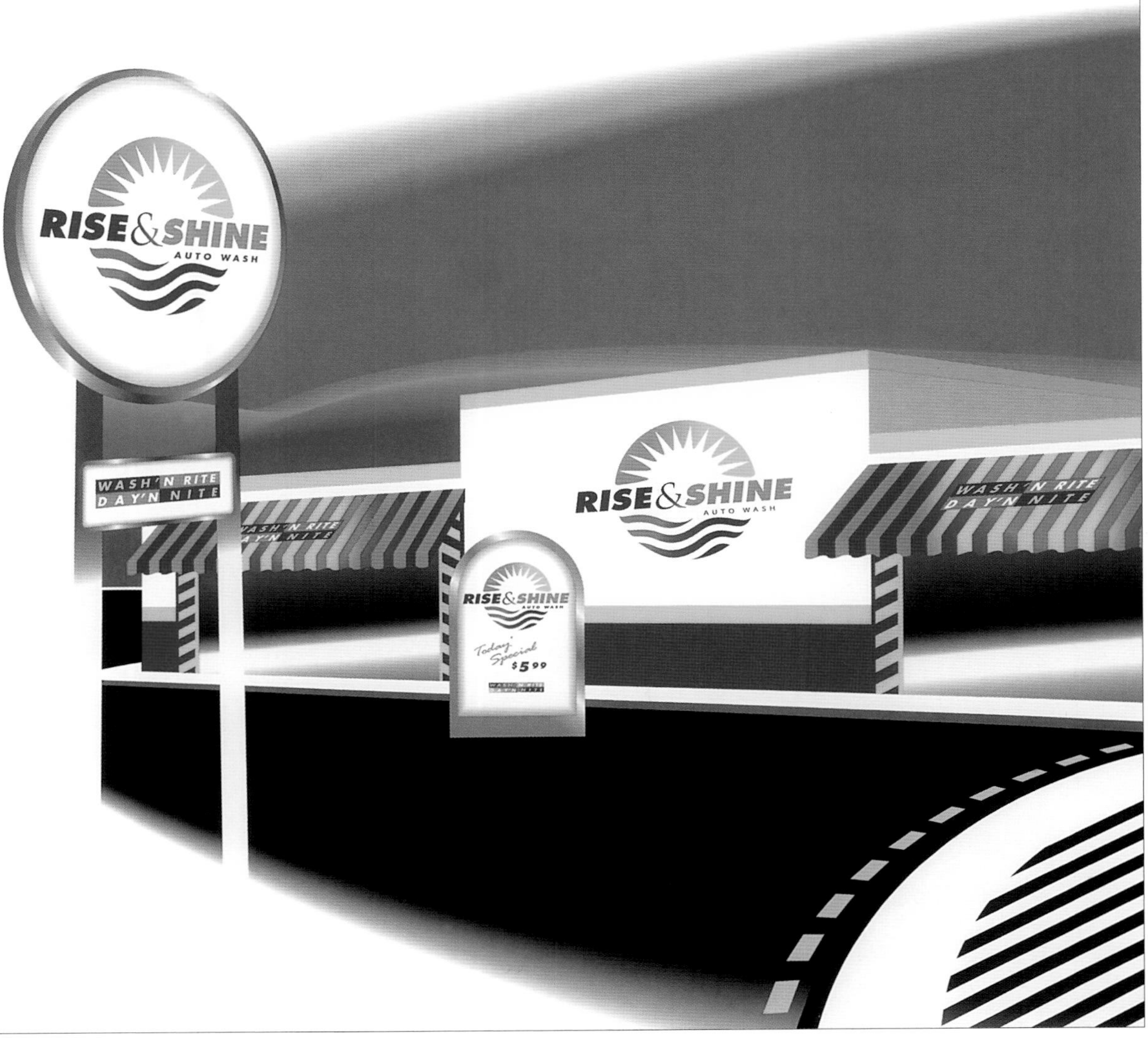

www.bernidesign.com

BERNI

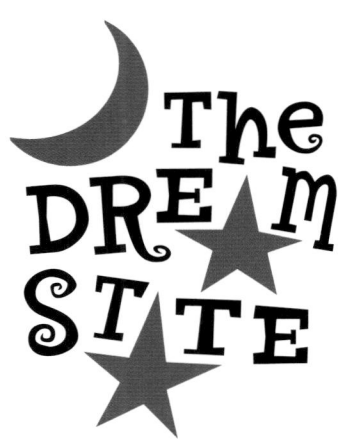

1.

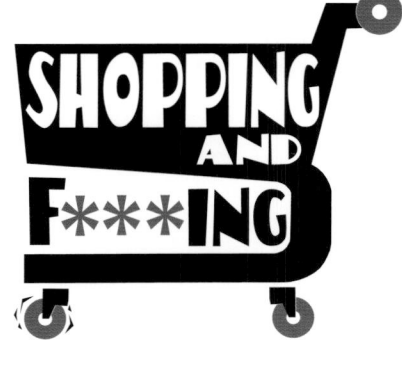

2.

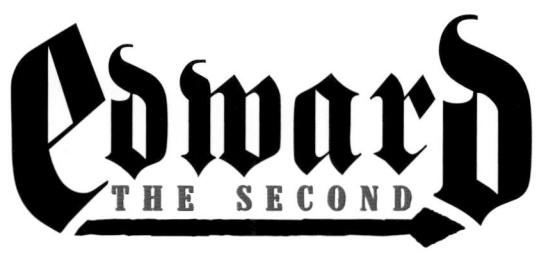

3.

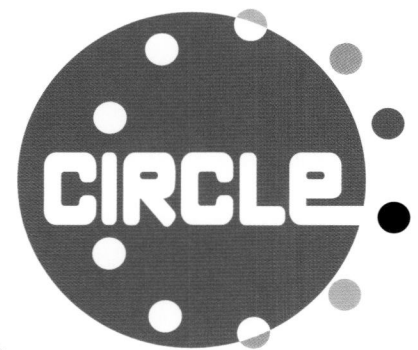

4.

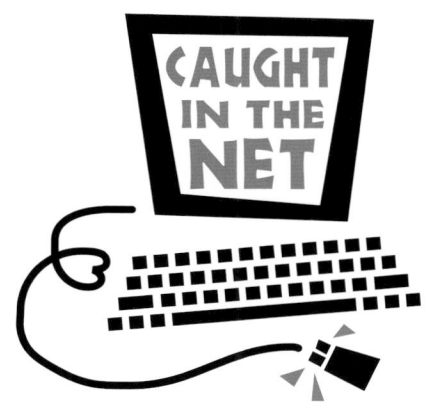

5.

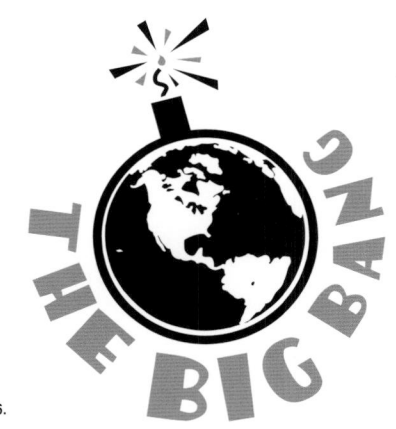

6.

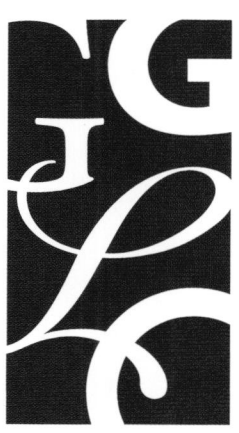

7.

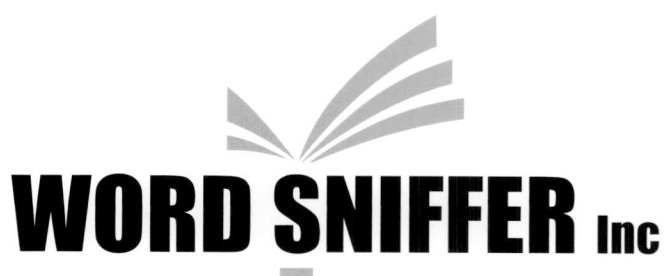

8.

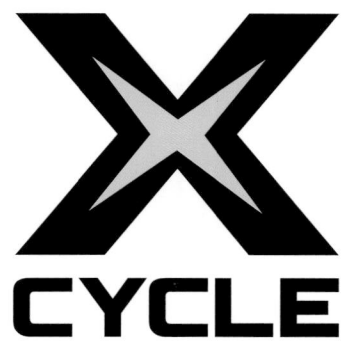

CYCLE

9.

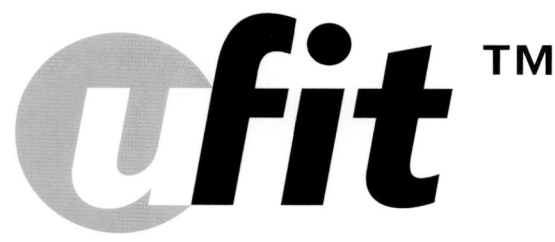

ufit ™

10.

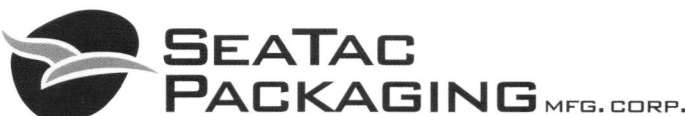

SeaTac
Packaging MFG. CORP.

11.

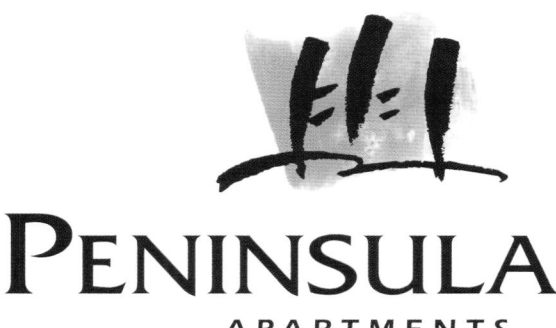

PENINSULA
APARTMENTS

12.

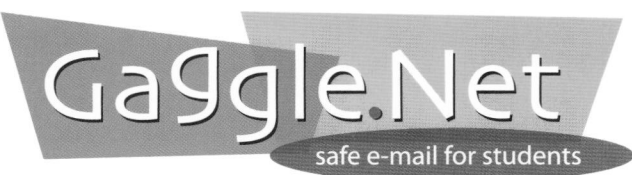

Gaggle.Net
safe e-mail for students

13.

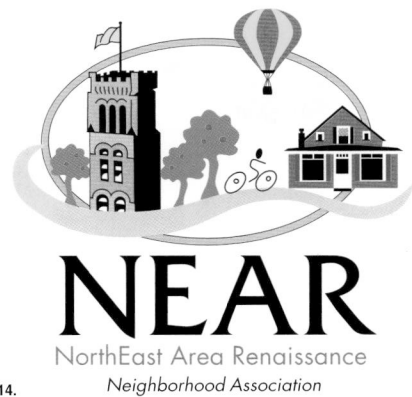

NEAR
NorthEast Area Renaissance
Neighborhood Association

14.

A
AGAPE
CHRISTIAN
C H U R C H

15.

1 - 6
Design Firm **Jeff Fisher LogoMotives**
7
Design Firm **Hornall Anderson Design Works**
8 - 12
Design Firm **Gloria Chen**
13
Design Firm **ZENN Graphic Design**
14
Design Firm **Minx Design**
15
Design Firm **Redpoint Design**
1 - 6.
Client   *triangle productions!*
Designer   Jeff Fisher
7.
Client   *Freerein*
Designers   Jack Anderson, Mark Popich,
            Tobi Brown, John Anicker,
            Bruce Stigler, Steffanie Lorig,
            Ensi Mofasser, Elmer dela Cruz,
            John Anderle, Gretchen Cook

8.
Client   *Word Sniffer, Inc.*
Designer   Gloria Chen
9, 10.
Client   *SportsArt American, Inc.*
Designers   Gloria Chen, David Littrell
11.
Client   *SeaTac Packaging Mfg. Corp.*
Designer   Gloria Chen
12.
Client   *Peninsula Apartments*
Designer   Gloria Chen
13.
Client   *Gaggle.Net*
Designer   Zengo Yoshida
14.
Client   *Northeast Area Renaissance*
Designer   Cecilia Sveda
15.
Client   *Agape Christian Church*
Designer   Clark Most

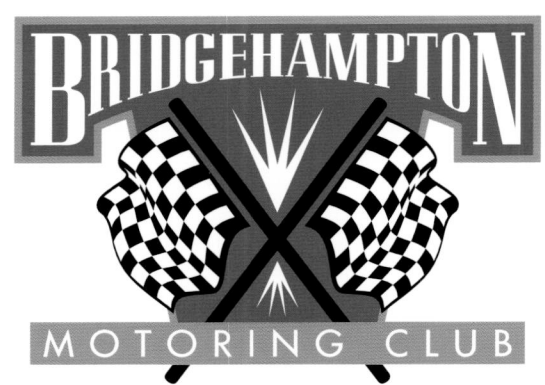

1.

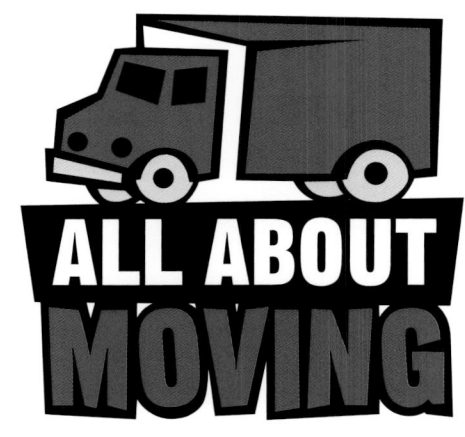

2.

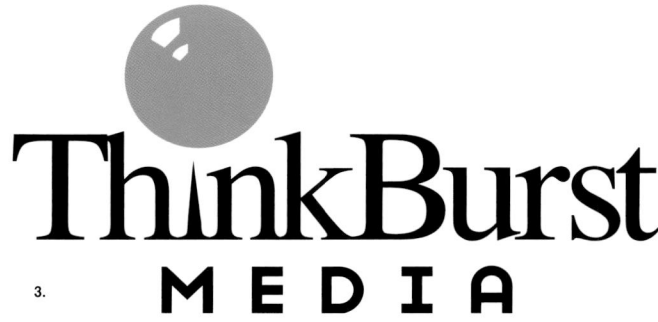

3.

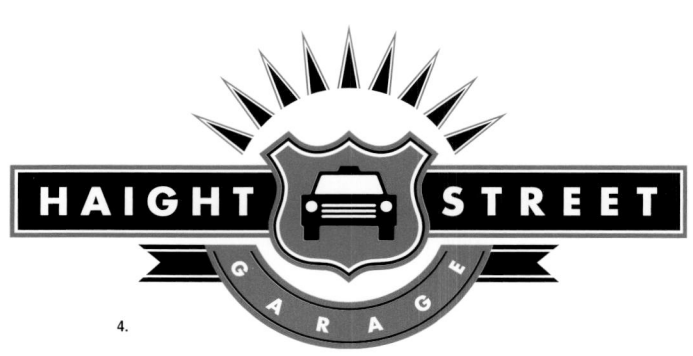

4.

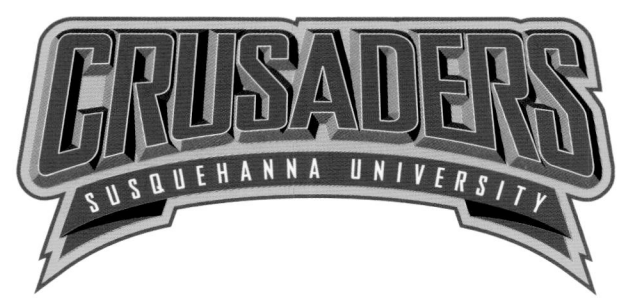

5.

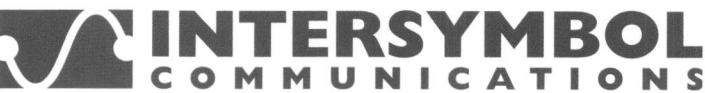

6.

CollegeLabels.com

7.

1 - 7
Design Firm **MFDI**
1.
Client   *Bridgehampton Motoring Club*
Designer   Mark Fertig
2.
Client   *All About Moving*
Designer   Mark Fertig
3.
Client   *Think Burst Media*
Designers   Mark Fertig,
             Kevin Pitts
4.
Client   *Luxor Cab Company*
Designer   Mark Fertig
5.
Client   *Susquehanna University*
Designer   Mark Fertig
6.
Client   *Intersymbol Communications*
Designer   Mark Fertig
7.
Client   *Labels-R-Us*
Designers   Mark Fertig,
             Kevin Pitts

(opposite)
Design Firm **Berni Marketing & Design**
Designers   Carlos Seminario,
             Stuart Berni

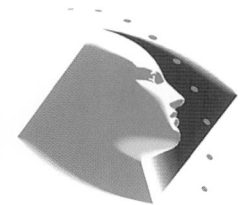

FarmStores Dairy

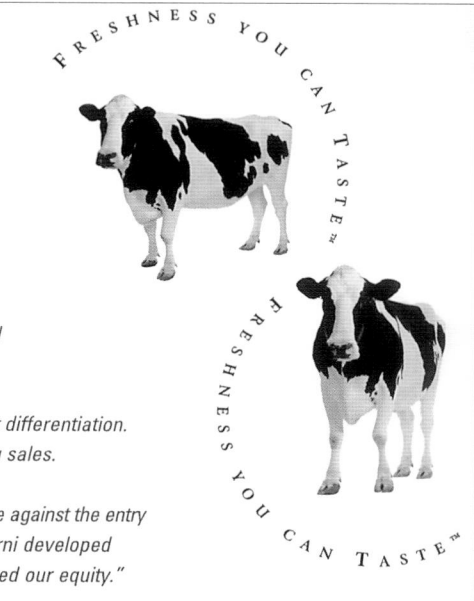

FRESHNESS YOU CAN TASTE™

FRESHNESS YOU CAN TASTE™

Challenge

To update the brand
identity of a dominant
local retailer to
compete against
national brands with
a complete line
of dairy products.

Solution

Refreshed positioning and packaging
graphics to create a memorable brand
that capitalizes on farm-fresh taste.

Result

Greater shelf presence due to product differentiation.
Enhanced customer perception. Rising sales.

Quote

"We needed a fresh new look to compete against the entry
of national brands into our market. Berni developed
a terrific branding system that leveraged our equity."

Manny Portuondo, Owner

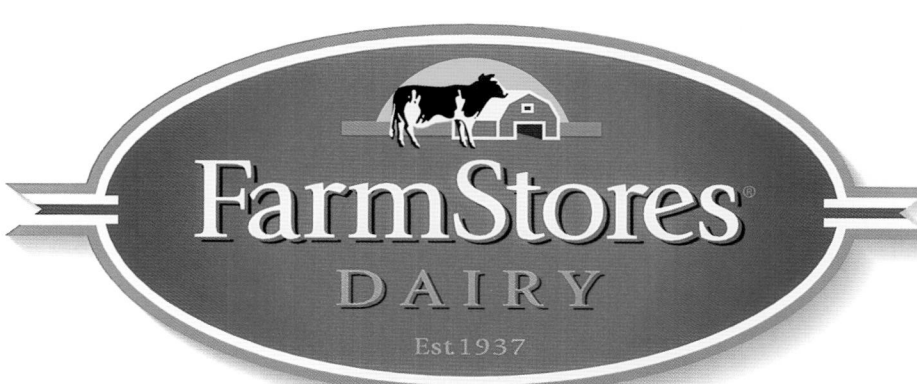

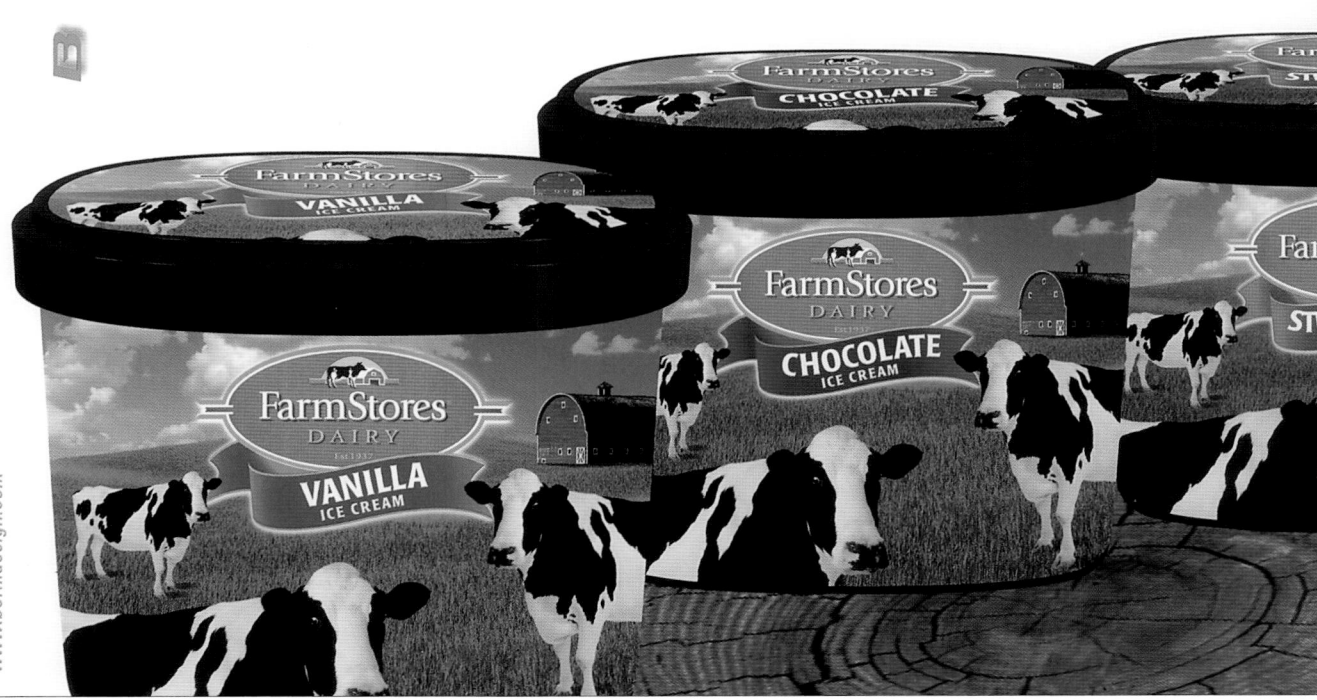

www.bernidesign.com

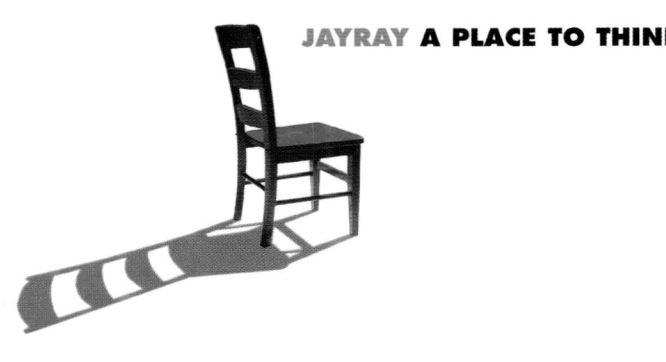

JAYRAY **A PLACE TO THINK**

1.

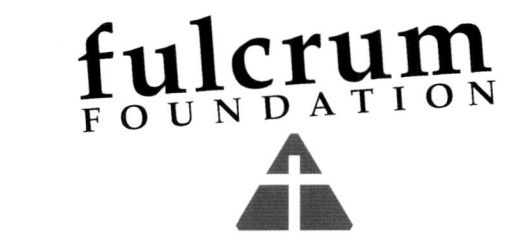

2.

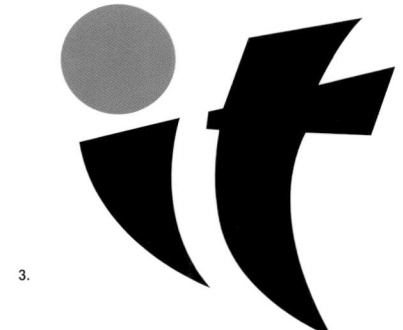

3.

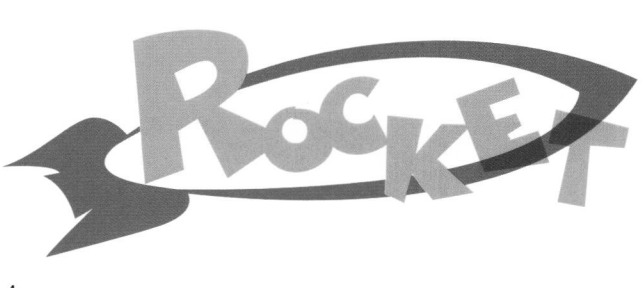

4.

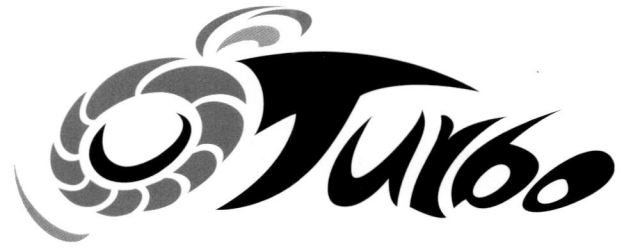

5.

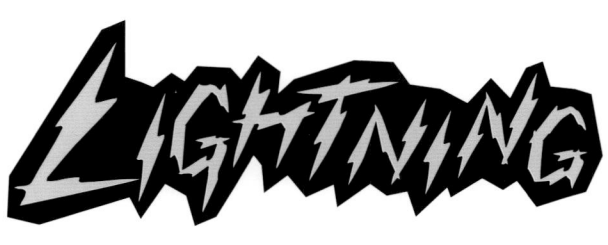

6.

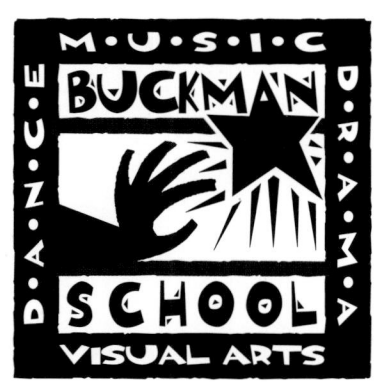

7.

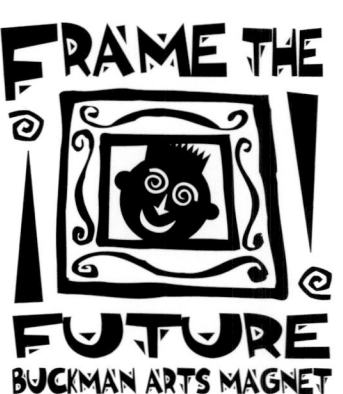

8.

9.

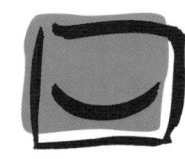

classmates·com®

10.

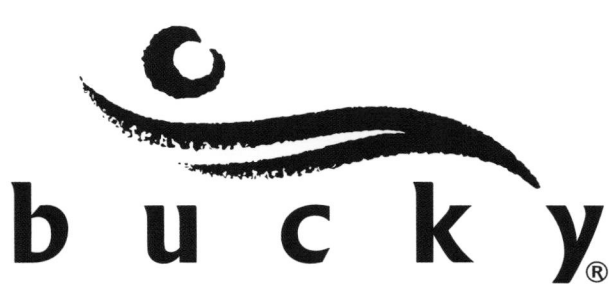

11.

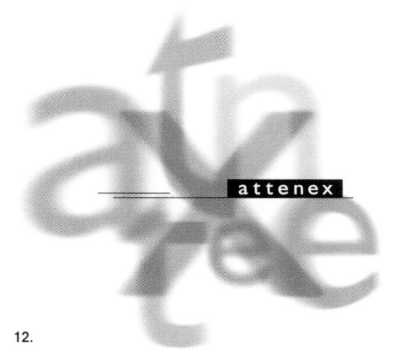

attenex

12.

ORIVO

13.

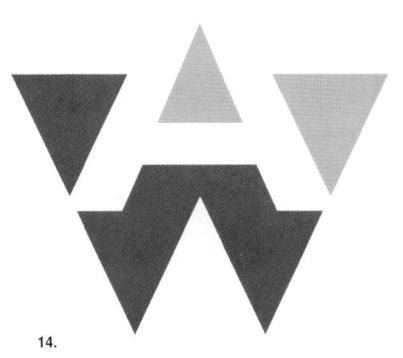

14.

15.

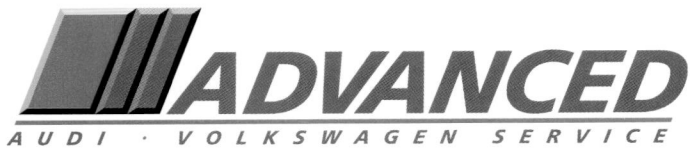

1.

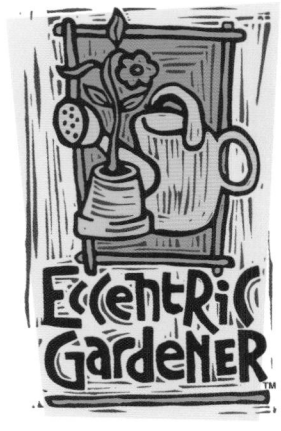

2.

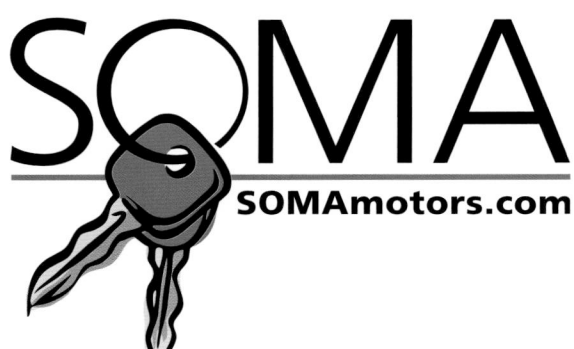

3.

E M B R Y O

4.

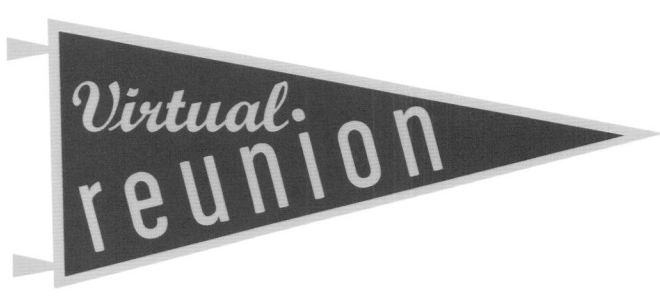

5.

Virtual reunion

6.

SERIOUSLY FUN GAMES

7.

1 - 7
Design Firm **MFDI**
1.
Client   *Advanced Audi Volkswagen*
Designer   Mark Fertig
2.
Client   *The Eccentric Gardener Plant Company*
Designer   Mark Fertig
3.
Client   *True Hire*
Designer   Mark Fertig
4.
Client   *Embryo Media*
Designer   Mark Fertig
5.
Client   *Soma Motors*
Designer   Mark Fertig

6.
Client   *Chat University*
Designers   Mark Fertig, Kevin Pitts
7.
Client   *Seriously Fun Games*
Designer   Mark Fertig
(opposite)
Client   Castleberry Foods
Design Firm **Berni Marketing & Design**
Designers   Carlos Seminario, Stuart Berni

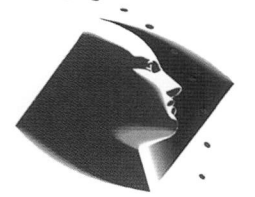

Black Rock Cattle Company

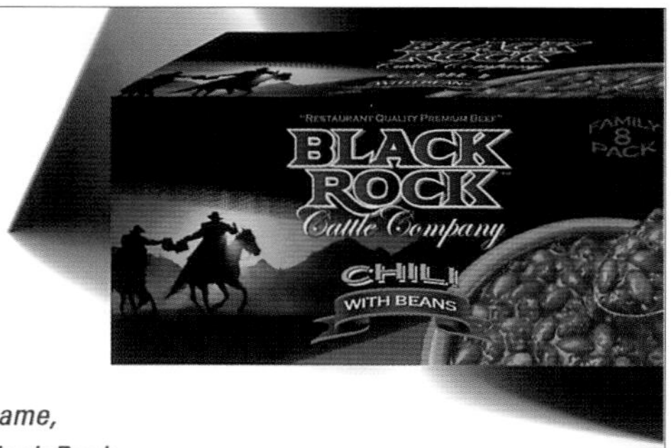

Challenge

To create an entirely new brand that would dominate the premium chili category in today's mass merchandisers.

Solution

Berni develops a compelling new brand name, and then creates the strong and hearty Black Rock brand image which captures the value-conscious consumer looking for a new taste sensation. Results indicated that a western heritage look and feel best supports the overall brand promise.

Result

Right on track: New look, combined with an appetizing multi-pack corralled consumers.

Quote

"The restaurant-quality premium beef Black Rock brand is a gotta have for our stores."

Buyer, Big Box Stores

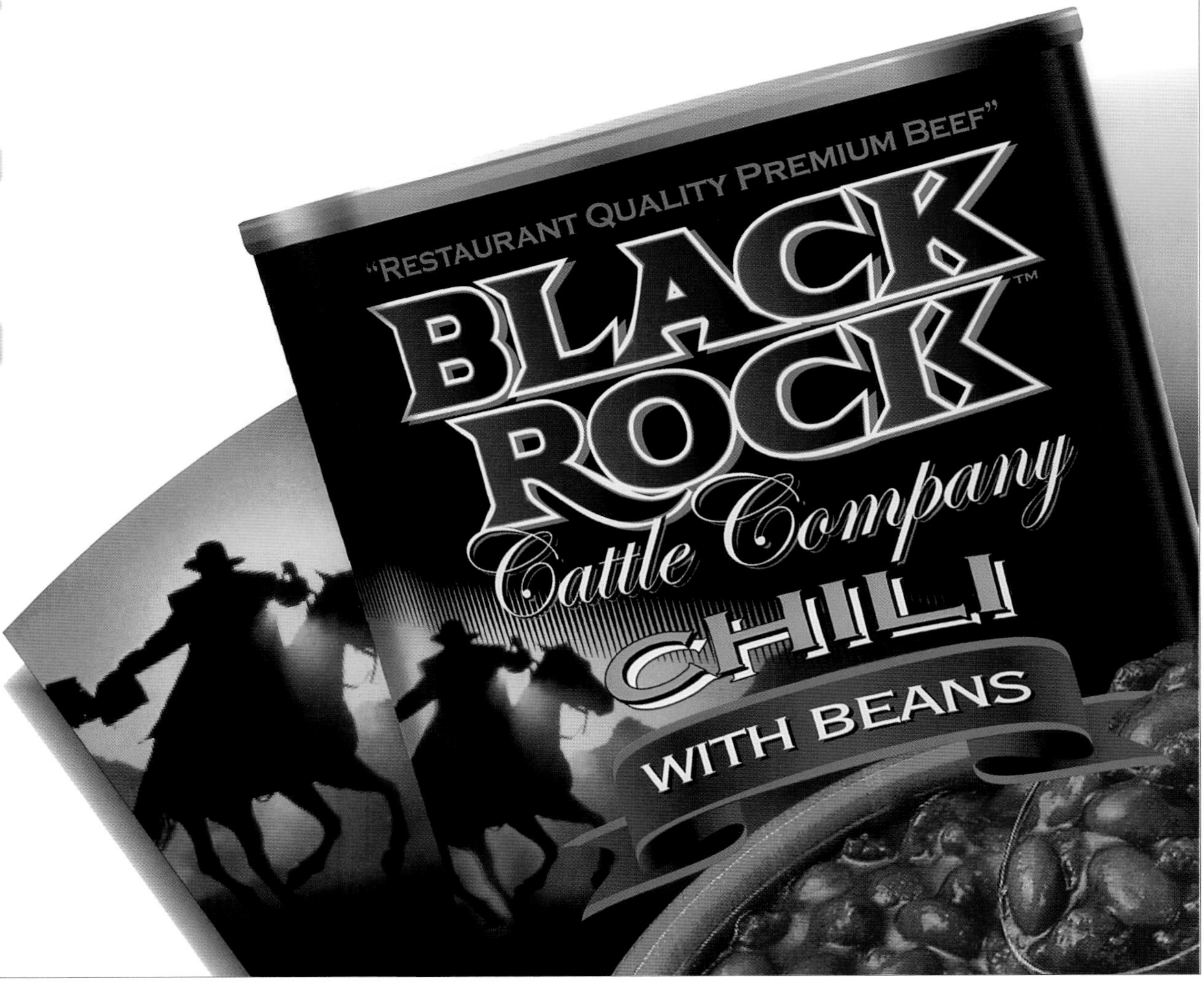

www.bernidesign.com

B E R N I

99

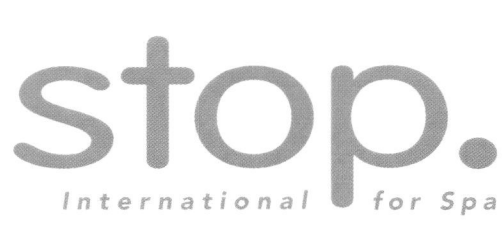

1.

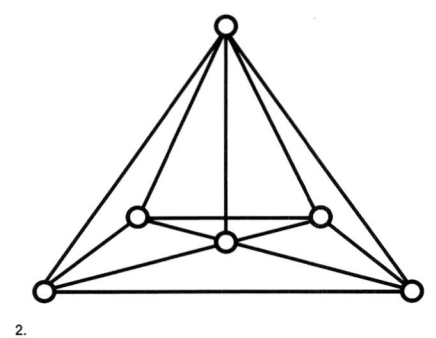

2.

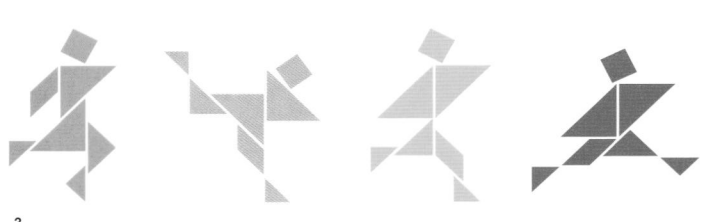

3.

specLo**g**ix

4.

b-hive

5.

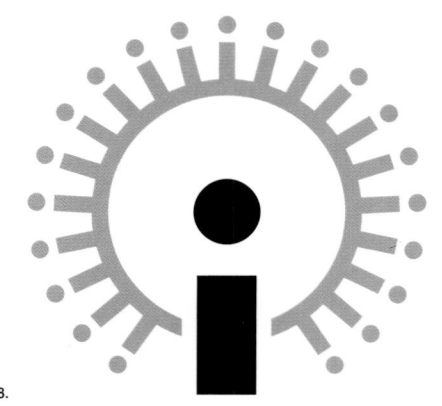

6.

aggregate

7.

8.

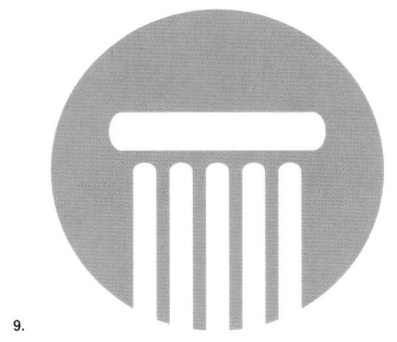

9.

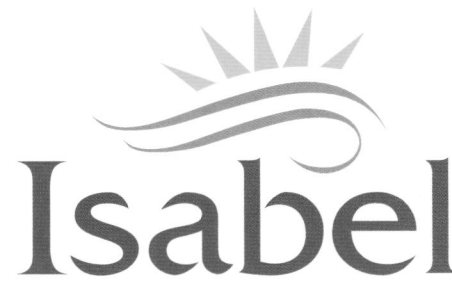

10.

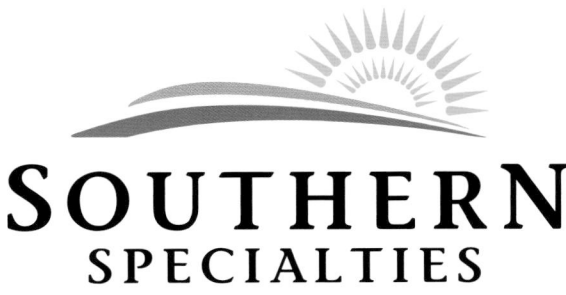

SOUTHERN
SPECIALTIES

11.

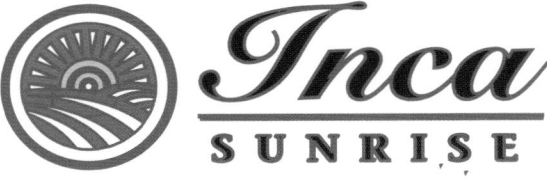

12.

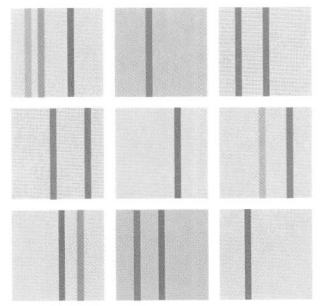

13.

· SEÑOR ROOF ·
TRADITIONAL CRAFTSMANSHIP

14.

15.

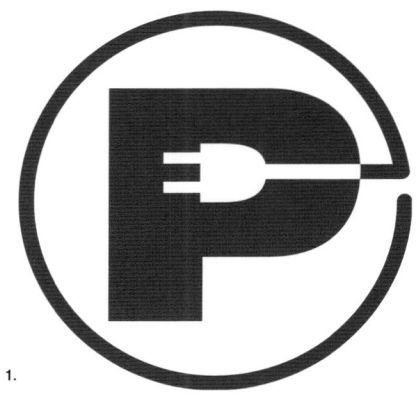

1.

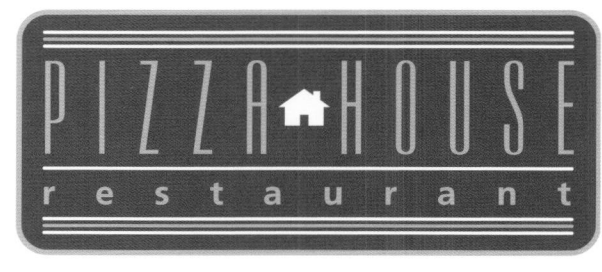

2.

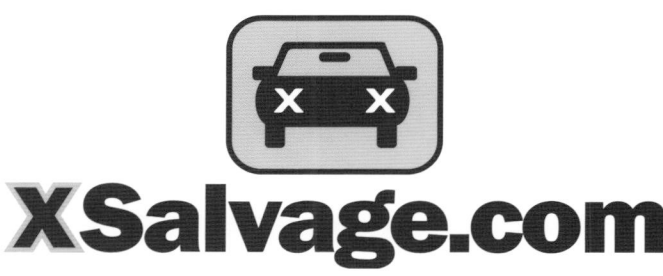

3.

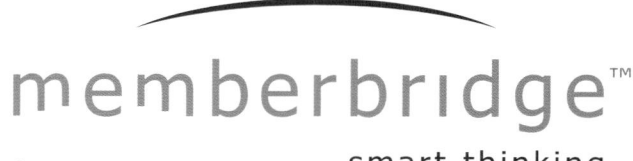

4.

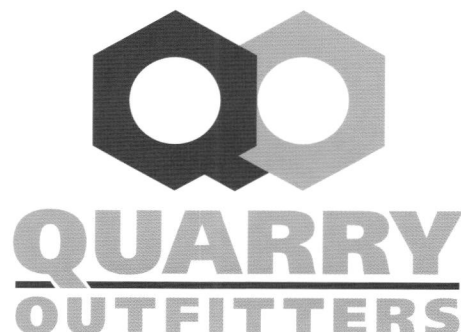

5.

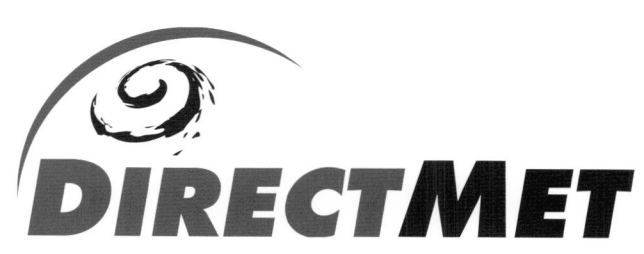

6.

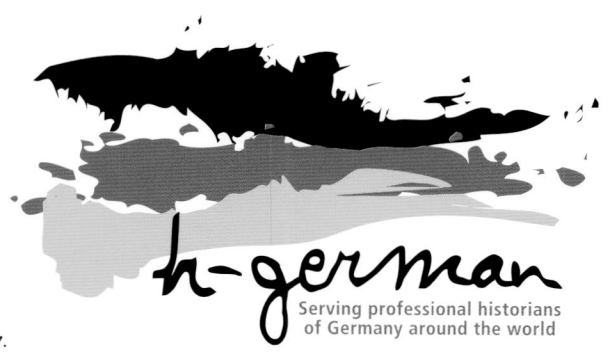

7.

1 - 7
Design Firm **MFDI**

1.
| Client | Computer Environments |
| Designer | Mark Fertig |

2.
| Client | Pizza House Restaurant |
| Designer | Mark Fertig |

3.
| Client | XSalvage.com |
| Designer | Mark Fertig |

4.
| Client | Member Bridge |
| Designer | Mark Fertig |

5.
| Client | Quarry Outfitters |
| Designer | Mark Fertig |

6.
| Client | Direct Met |
| Designer | Mark Fertig |

7.
Client	H-Net.org
Designers	Mark Fertig,
	David Imhoof

(opposite)
Client	SDC Designs
Design Firm	**Berni Marketing & Design**
Designers	Carlos Seminario,
	Stuart Berni

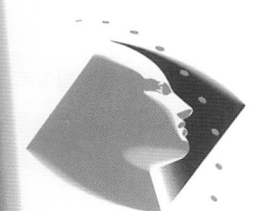

Karishma

B E R N I

Challenge

To launch a new
product line with an
innovative proprietary
brand for a prominent
jewelry wholesaler.

Solution

Romancing both jewelry retailers and consumers
alike, an elegant and captivating brand name and
identity were translated to positioning, POP display,
structural packaging and graphics, and supporting
sales collateral.

Result

Brilliant success. Dazzled retail target market.
Expanded distribution opportunities.

Quote

We needed a partner to launch our first new brand. Berni walked
us through the process and we are delighted with the results.
Sales are up. The Berni team was great to work with."

Abhay Javeri, Principal

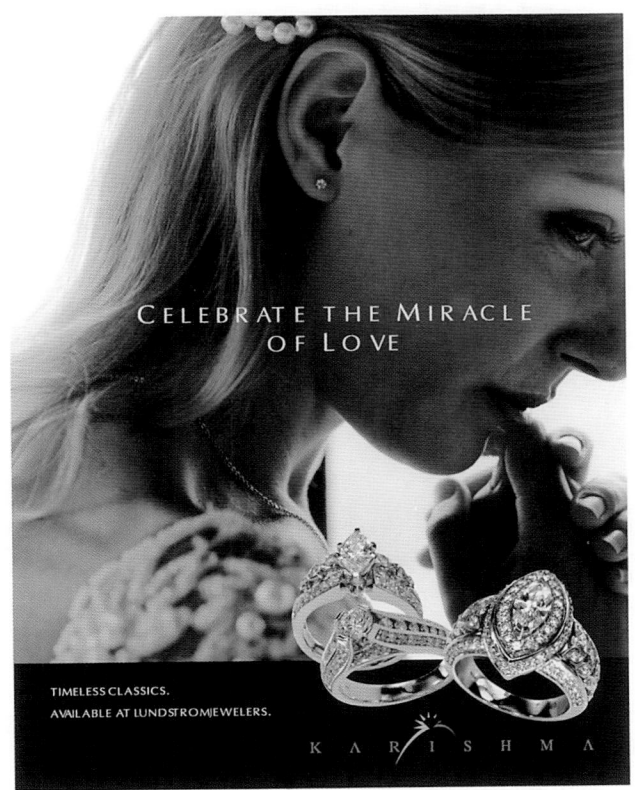

CELEBRATE THE MIRACLE OF LOVE

TIMELESS CLASSICS.
AVAILABLE AT LUNDSTROM JEWELERS.

KARISHMA

www.bernidesign.com

KARISHMA

TIMELESS CLASSICS

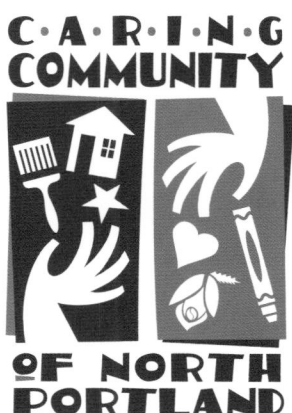

1.

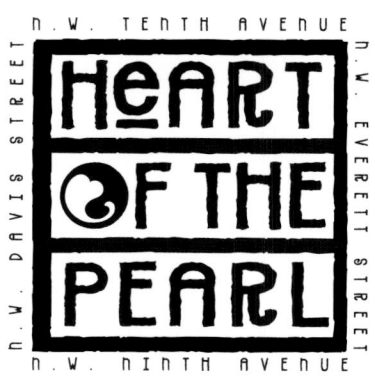

2.

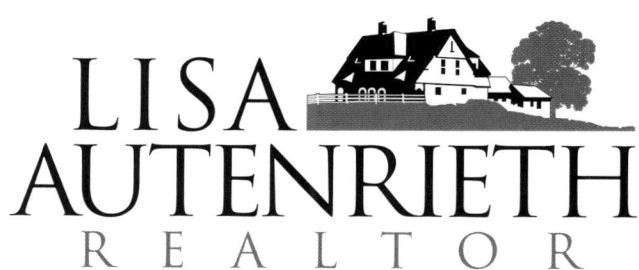

3.

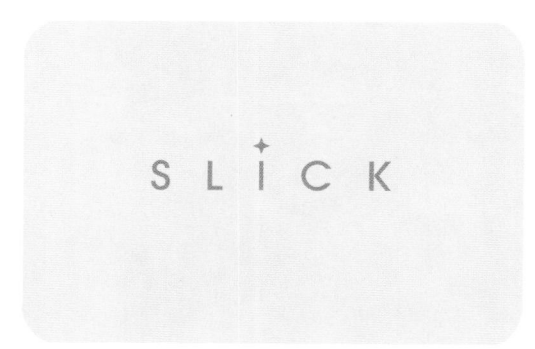

4.

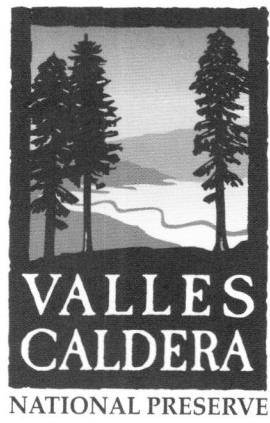

5.

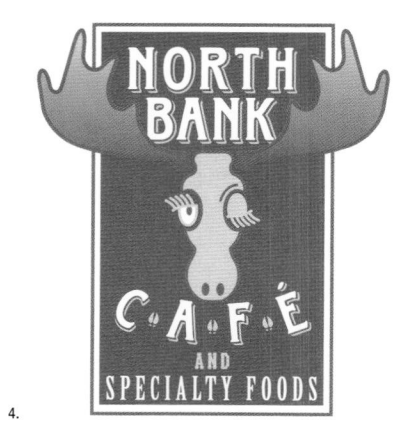

6.

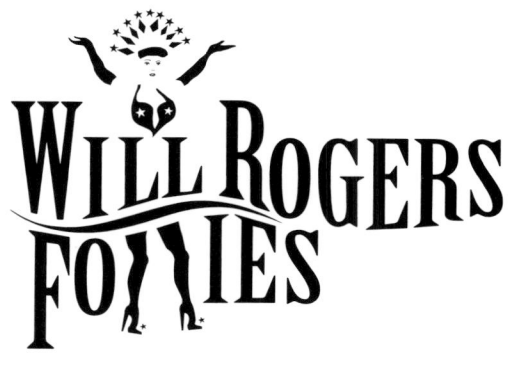

7.

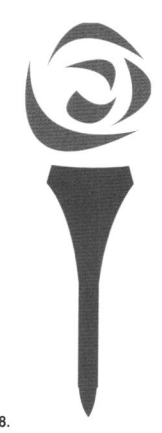

8.

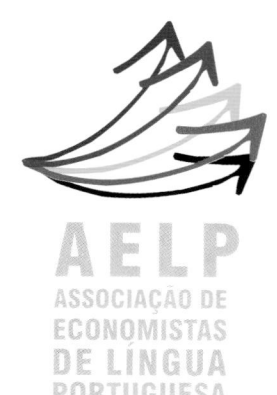

AELP
ASSOCIAÇÃO DE
ECONOMISTAS
DE LÍNGUA
PORTUGUESA

9.

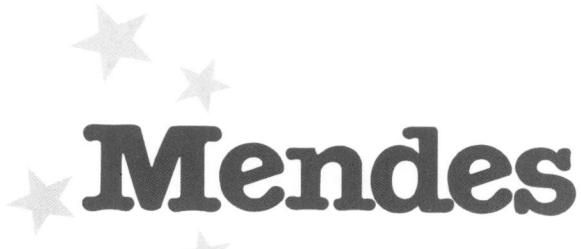

Mendes

10.

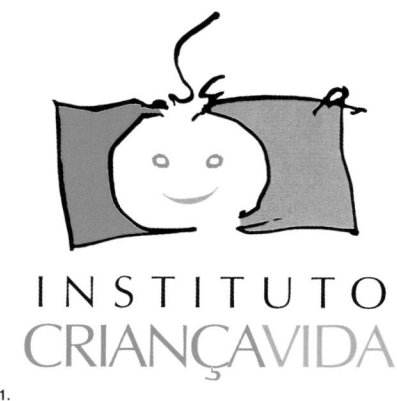

INSTITUTO
CRIANÇAVIDA

11.

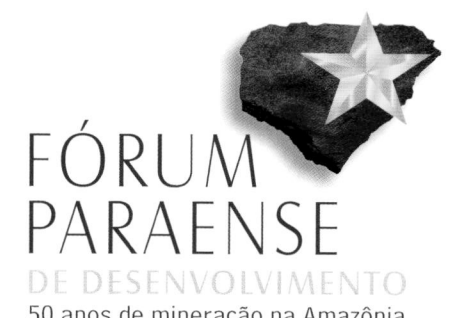

FÓRUM
PARAENSE
DE DESENVOLVIMENTO
50 anos de mineração na Amazônia

12.

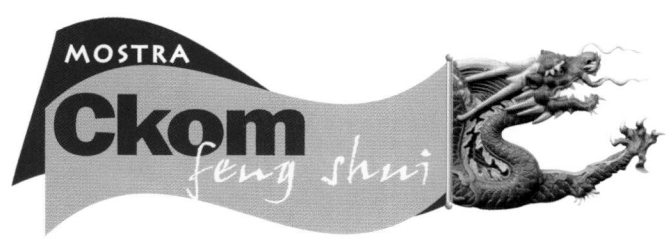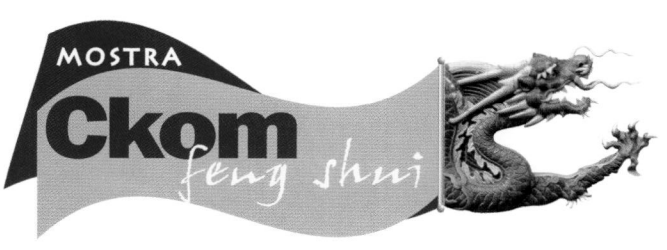

13.

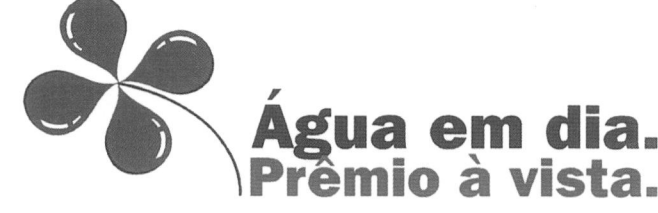

**Água em dia.
Prêmio à vista.**

14.

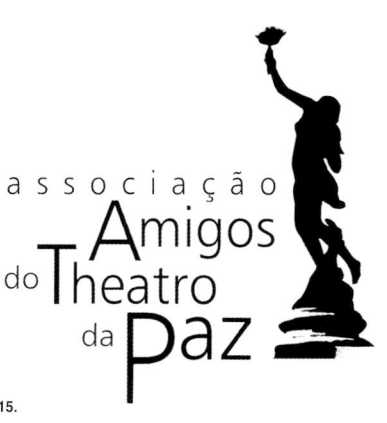

a s s o c i a ç ã o
Amigos
do Theatro
da Paz

15.

1 - 7
Design Firm **Jeff Fisher LogoMotives**
8
Design Firm **Cave**
9 - 15
Design Firm **Mendes Publicidade**

1.
Client *Caring Community of North Portland*
Designer Jeff Fisher
2.
Client *Heart of the Pearl*
Designer Jeff Fisher
3.
Client *Lisa Autenrieth*
Designer Jeff Fisher
4.
Client *North Bank Cafe*
Designer Jeff Fisher
5.
Client *Slick*
Designers Jeff Fisher, Lisa Fritsch
6.
Client *Broadway Rose Theatre Company*
Designer Jeff Fisher

7.
Client *Valles Caldera Trust/*
USDA Forest Service
Designer Jeff Fisher
8.
Client *Adele DeCof Foundation*
Designers David Edmundson, Matt Cave
9.
Client *AELP*
Designer Maria Alice Penna
10.
Client *Mendes Publicidade*
Designers Oswaldo Mendes,
Maria Alice Penna
11.
Client *Instituto Criança Vida*
Designer Maria Alice Penna
12.
Client *Associação Comercial do Pará*
Designer Maria Alice Penna
13.
Client *Ckom Engenharia*
Designer Maria Alice Penna
14.
Client *COSANPA*
Designer Maria Alice Penna
15.
Client *Associação Amigos*
deTheatro da Paz
Designer Maria Alice Penna

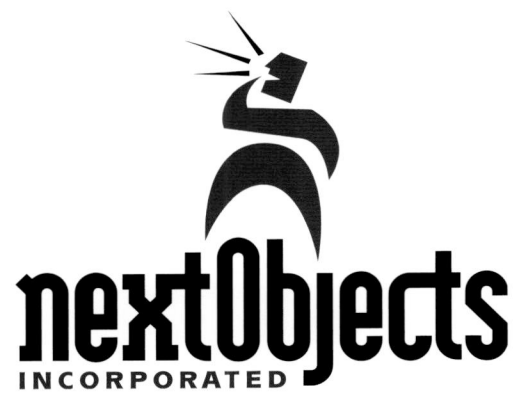

1.

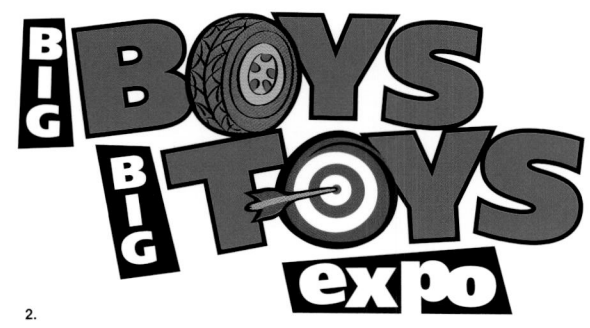

2.

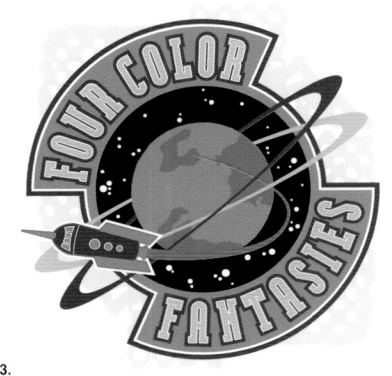

3.

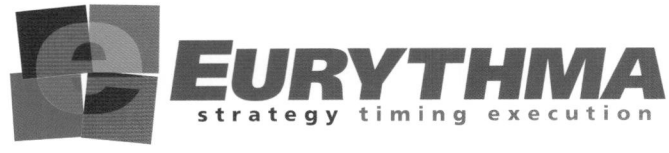

4.

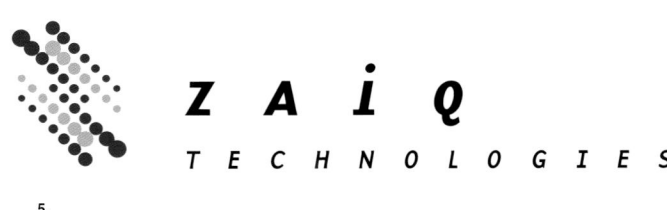

5.

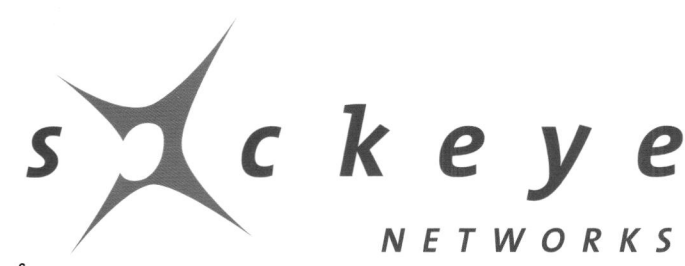

6.

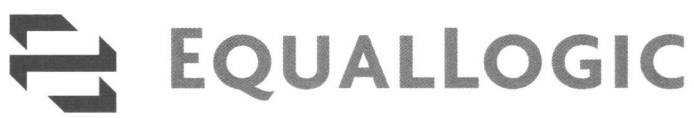

7.

1 - 4
Design Firm **MFDI**
5 - 7
Design Firm **Monderer Design**
1.
   Client   *Next Objects Incorporated*
   Designer Mark Fertig
2.
   Client   *The Daily Item/Sunbury Broadcasting*
   Designers Mark Fertig, Leslie Imhoof, Scott Spector
3.
   Client   *Four Color Fantasies Collectible Comics*
   Designer Mark Fertig

4.
   Client   *Eurythma*
   Designer Mark Fertig
5.
   Client   *Zaiq Technologies*
   Designer Stewart Monderer
6.
   Client   *Sockeye Networks*
   Designes Stewart Monderer, Jeffrey Gobin
7.
   Client   *EqualLogic, Inc.*
   Designer Stewart Monderer
(opposite)
   Client   *Lennar*
   Design Firm **Berni Marketing & Design**
   Designers Carlos Seminario, Stuart Berni

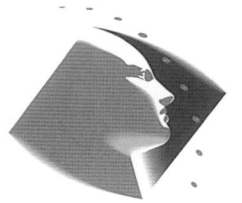

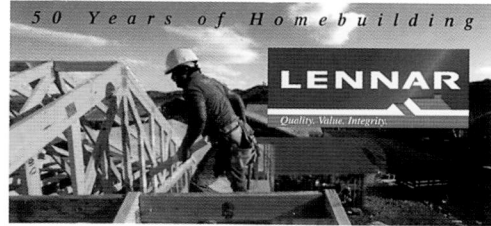

Lennar Corporation

Challenge

How to consolidate over 21 unique brands under one cohesive Brand Architecture System for America's leading home builder.

Solution

Development of a forward looking brand strategy that highlights and promotes Lennar's unique marketing platforms while consolidating twenty-one brands down to two. Update and contemporize corporate identity to build equity with customers and foster teamwork internally.

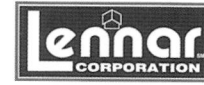

Old brandmark

Result

Launched in their 50th year anniversary, Lennar is now the "darling of Wall Street" with its stock soaring up 60% since initiating the Brand Strategy Program. Its new image and consumer-oriented positioning of "Quality. Value. Integrity." inspires home buyers, Associates and Wall Street simultaneously.

Quote

"Our new identity and slogan more accurately reflect who we are and what we do. The Berni team did a great job with both our brand strategy and execution. Our entire company is excited about our new image."

Kay Howard
Director of Communications

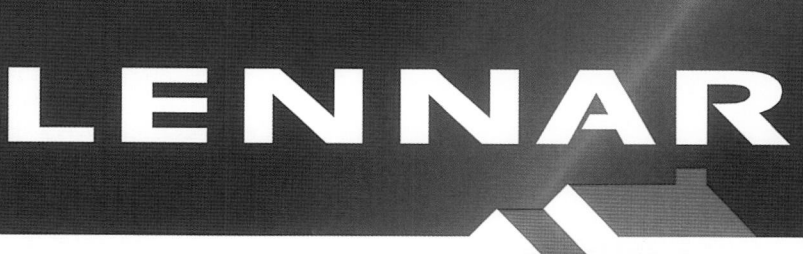

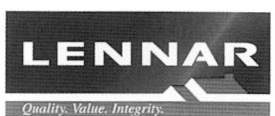

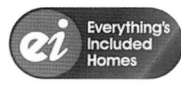

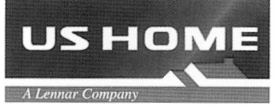

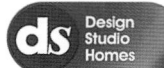

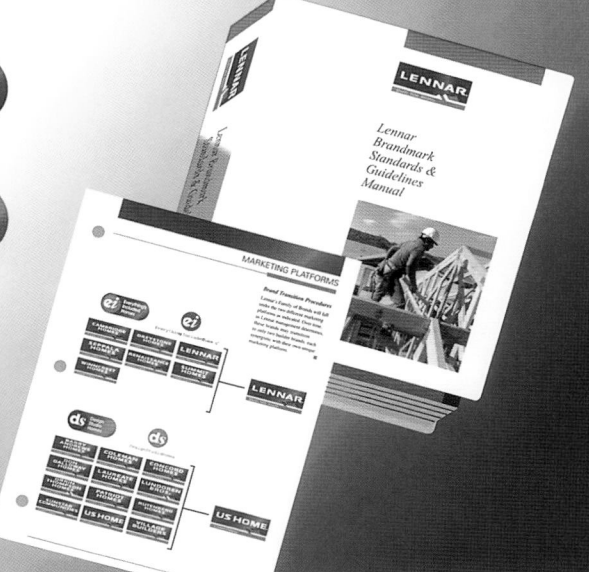

BERNI

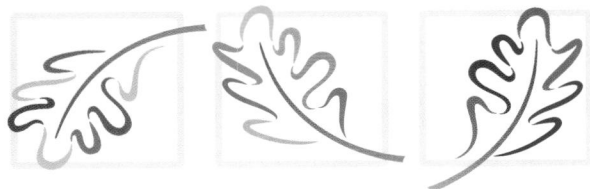

1.

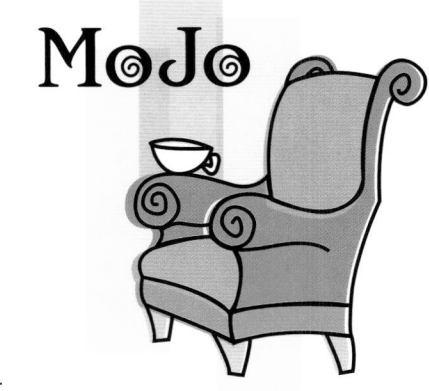

2.

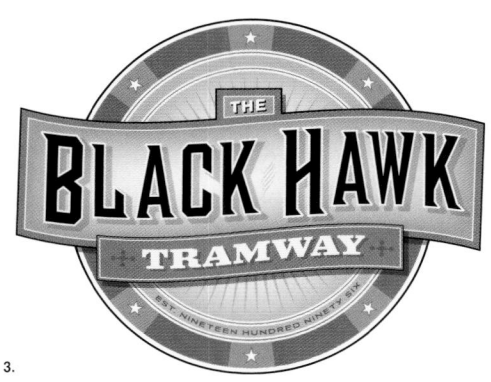

3.

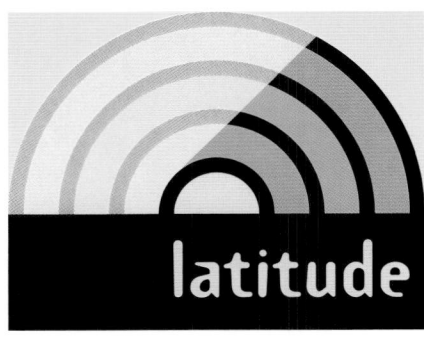

4.

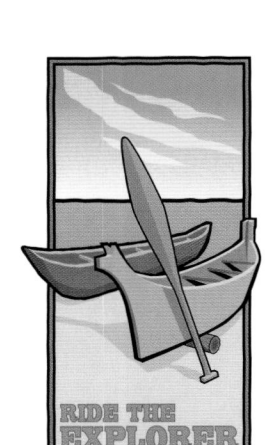

5.

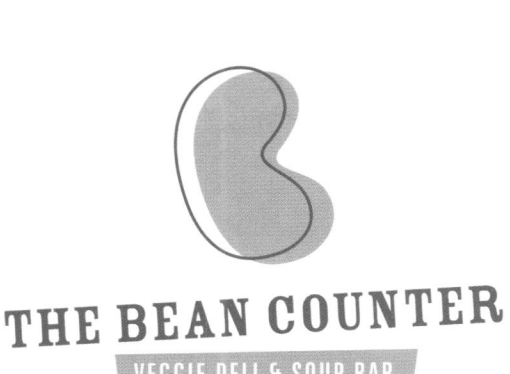

6.

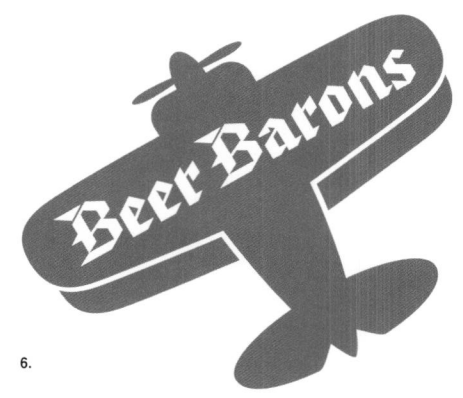

7.

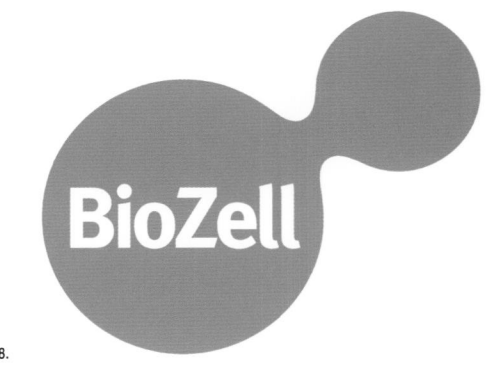

8.

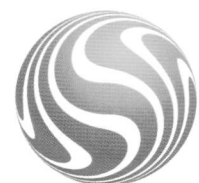

spectrum *media*

9.

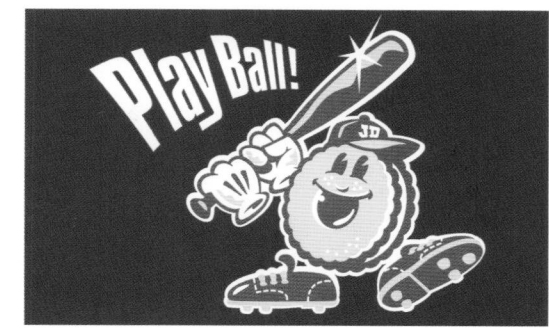

10.

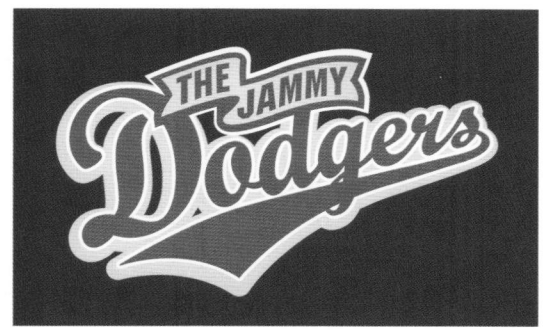

11.

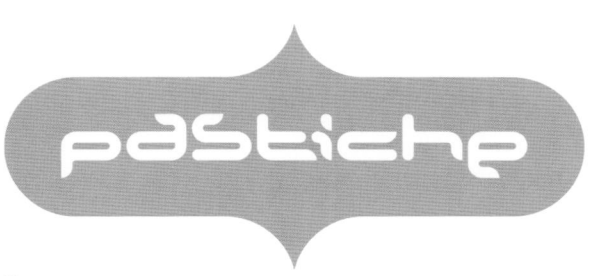

12.

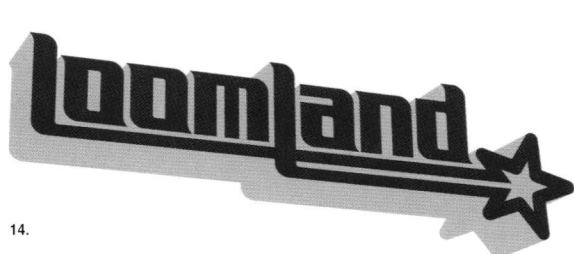

13.

14.

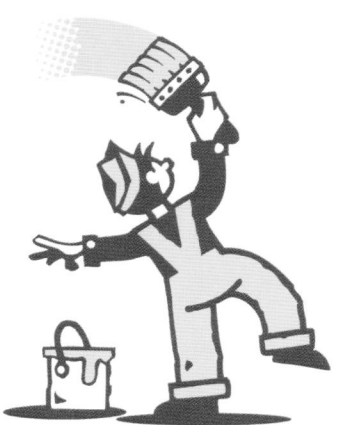

15.

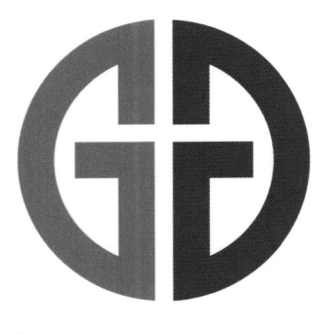

1.

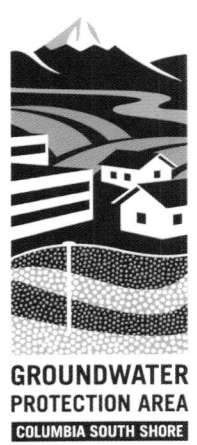

**GROUNDWATER
PROTECTION AREA**
COLUMBIA SOUTH SHORE

2.

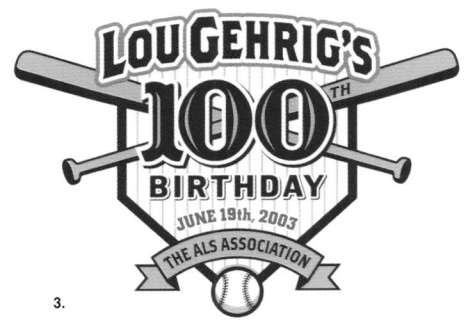

3.

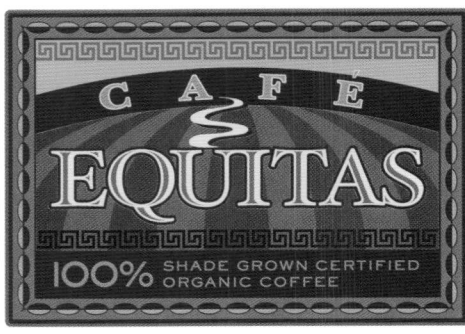

4.

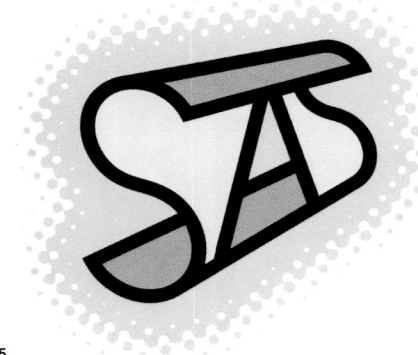

5.

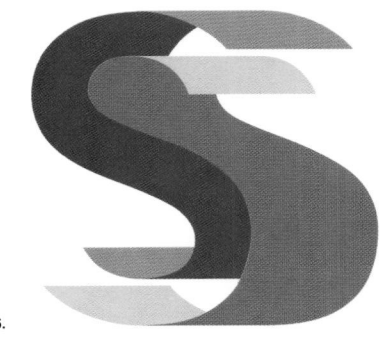

6.

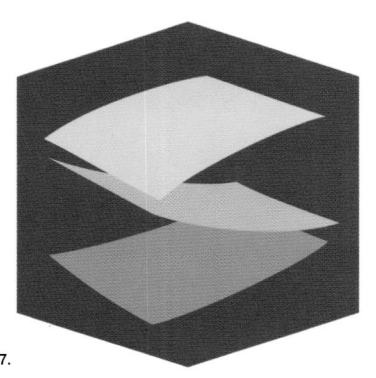

7.

1 - 7
Design Firm **Dotzero Design**
1.
　Client　　Scottsdale Christian Academy
　Designers　Jon Wippich, Karen Wippich
2.
　Client　　Portland Water Bureau
　Designers　Jon Wippich, Karen Wippich
3.
　Client　　ALS Association
　Designers　Jon Wippich, Karen Wippich
4.
　Client　　Davis Agency/Longbottom Coffee
　Designers　Jon Wippich, Karen Wippich
5 - 7.
　Client　　Standard Companies
　Designers　Jon Wippich, Karen Wippich

(opposite)
　Client　　Banco Popular
　　　　　　Dominicano, C. por A.
Design Firm **Muts&Joy&Design**
　Designers　Katherine Hames,
　　　　　　Gisele Sangiovanni,
　　　　　　Tom Delaney

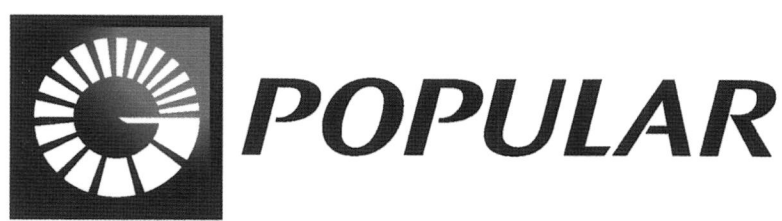

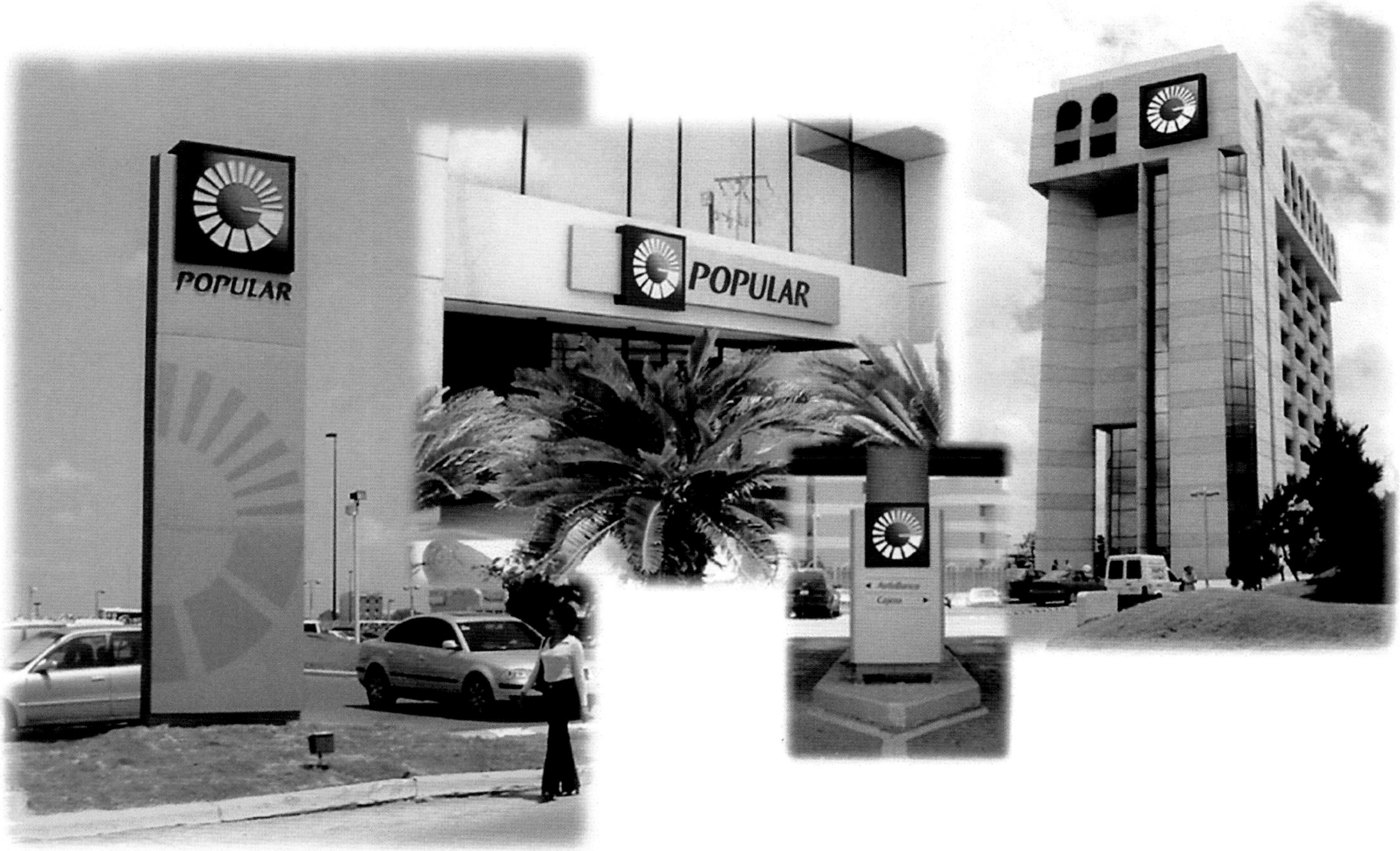

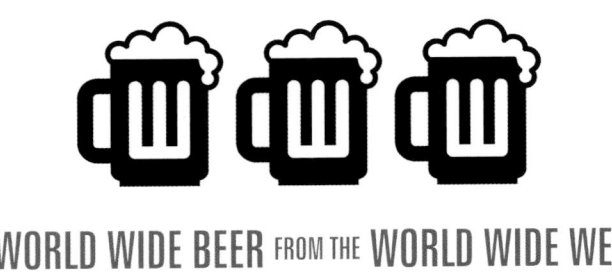

WORLD WIDE BEER FROM THE WORLD WIDE WEB

1.

2.

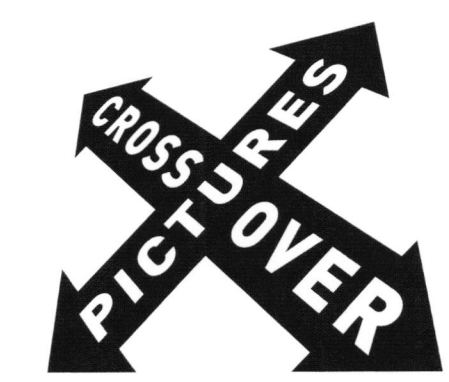

3.

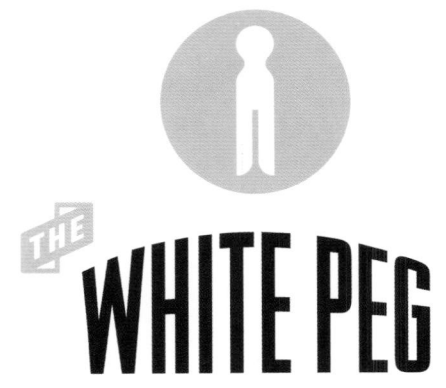

THE WHITE PEG

4.

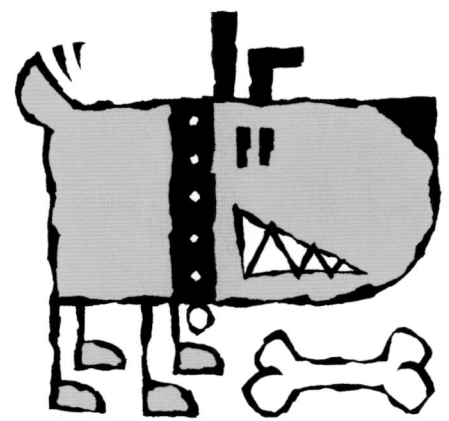

5.

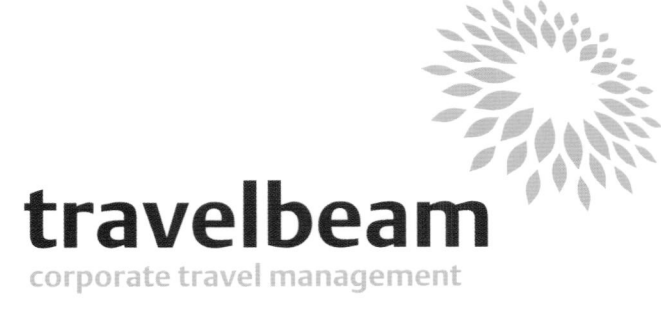

travelbeam
corporate travel management

6.

urban
oasis

7.

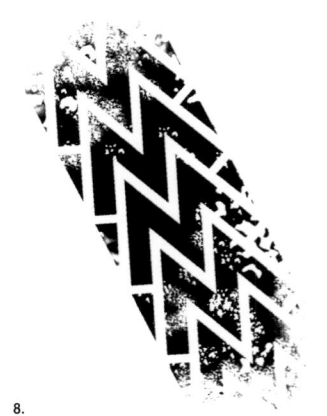

8.

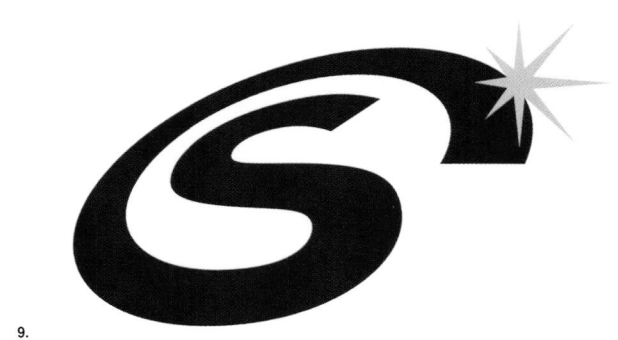

9.

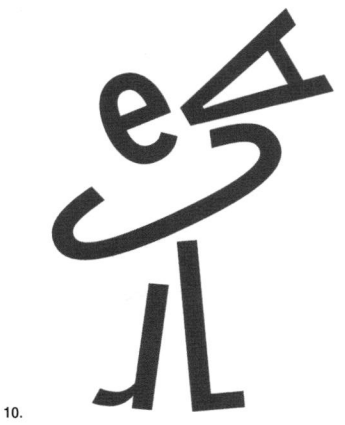

10.

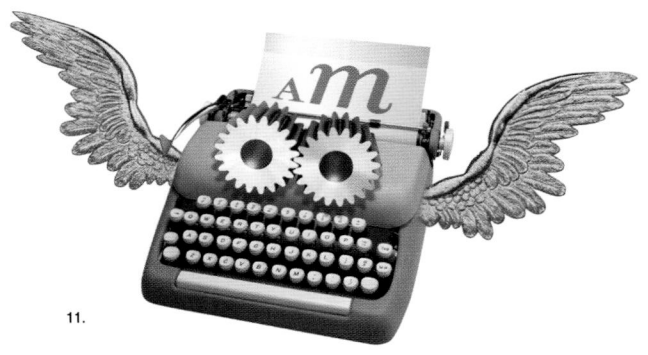

11.

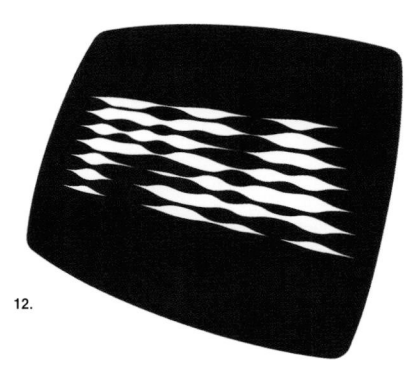

12.

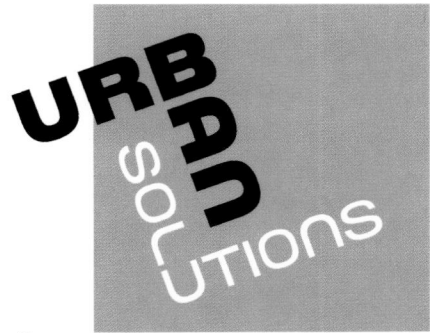

13.

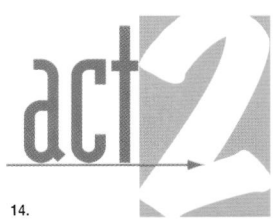

14.

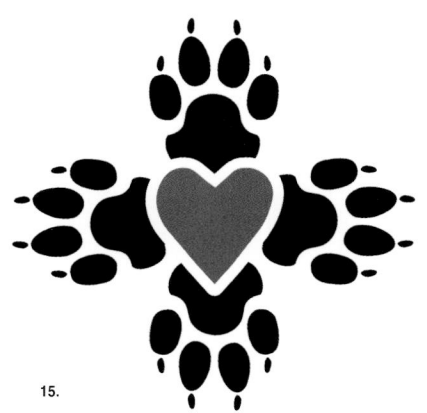

15.

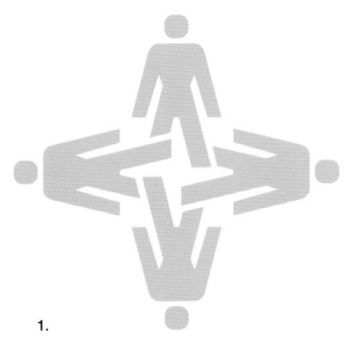

1.

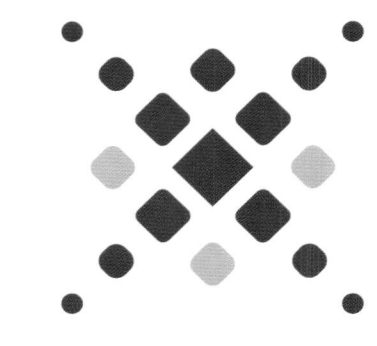

2.

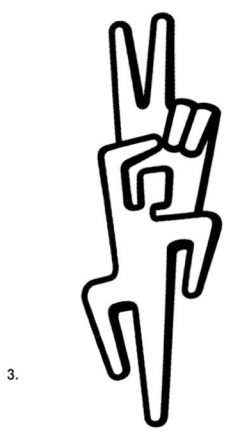

3.

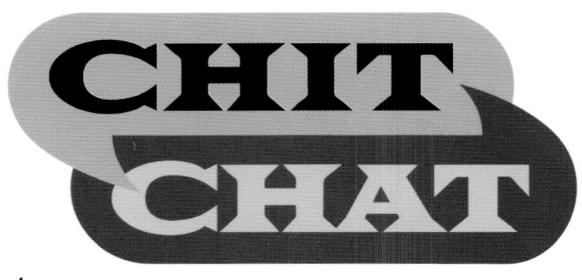

4.

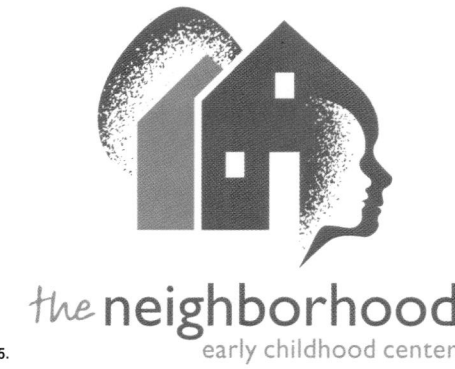

5.

the **neighborhood**
early childhood center

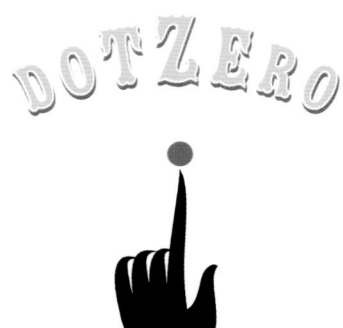

6.

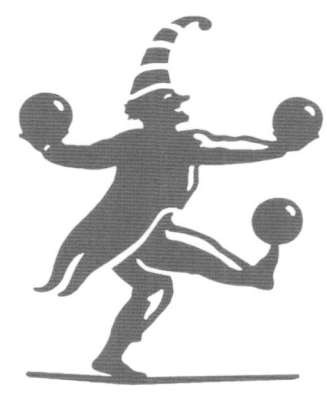

7.

1 - 7
Design Firm **Dotzero Design**
1, 2.
   Client   *Unicru*
   Designers Jon Wippich, Karen Wippich
3.
   Client   *Do It For Peace*
   Designers Jon Wippich, Karen Wippich
4.
   Client   *Chit Chat Coffee Shop*
   Designers Jon Wippich, Karen Wippich
5.
   Client   *The Neighborhood*
   Designers Jon Wippich, Karen Wippich
6.
   Client   *Dotzero*
   Designers Jon Wippich, Karen Wippich

7.
   Client   *CMD/Bridge Port Brewing Co.*
   Designers Jon Wippich, Karen Wippich
(opposite)
   Client   *BancoLeón, S.A.*
   Design Firm **Muts&Joy&Design**
   Designers Muts Yasumura,
               Katherine Hames,
               Gisele Sangiovanni,
               Tom Delaney

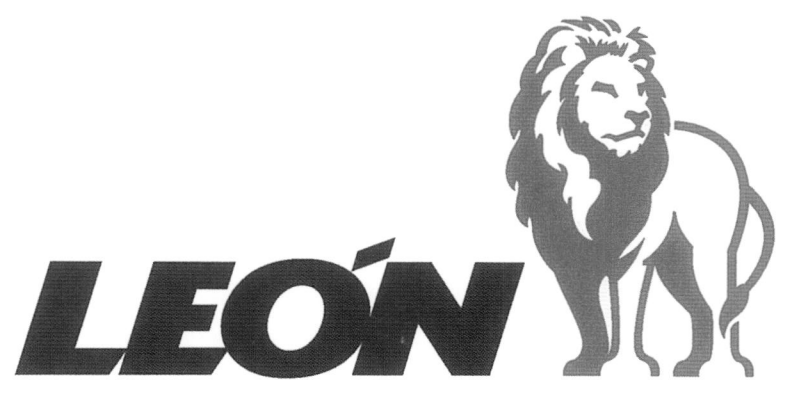

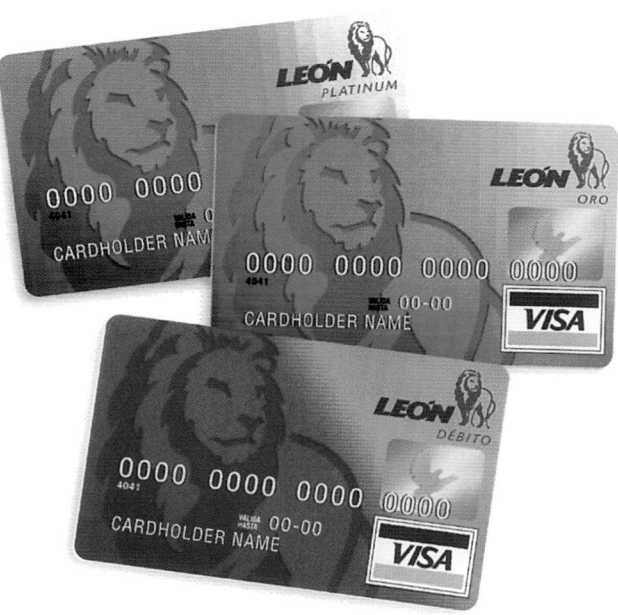

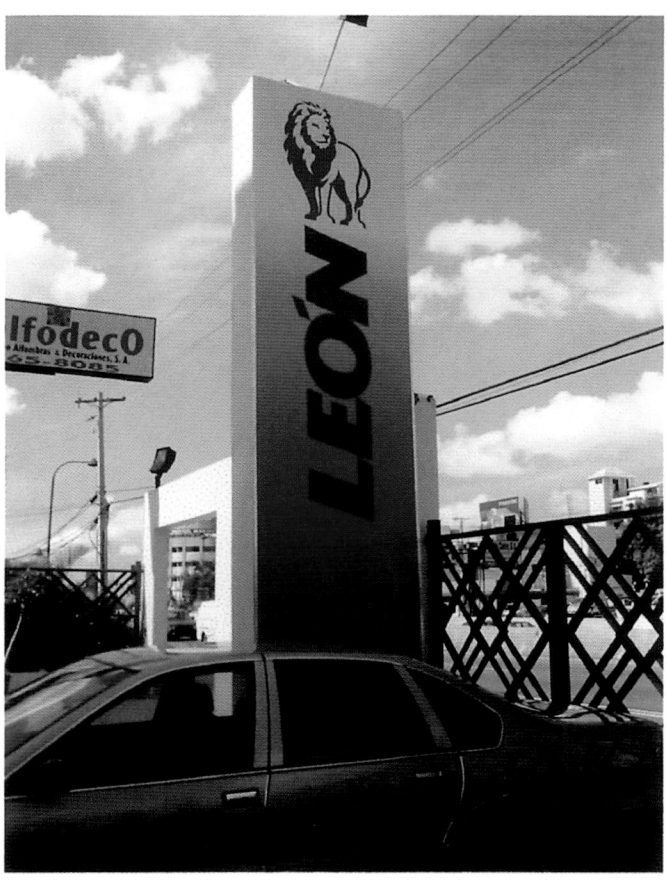

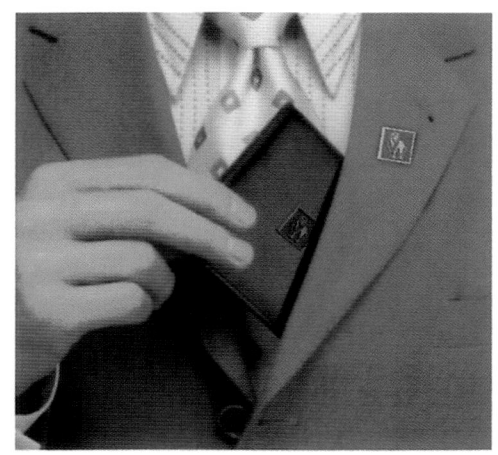

aQuantive

1.

TEAO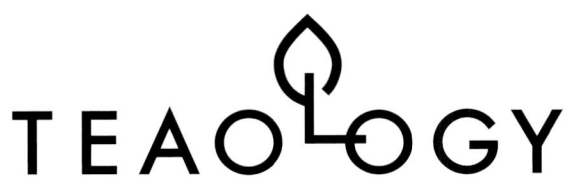GY

2.

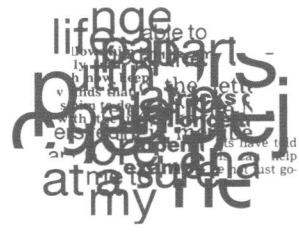

(*poetry center san josé*)

3.

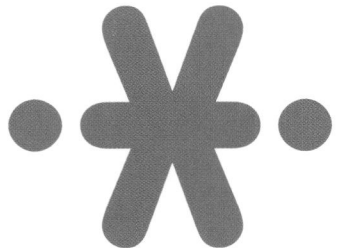

VIAMQ

4.

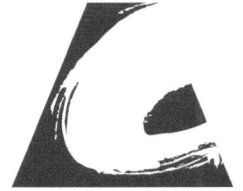

artscouncil
silicon valley

5.

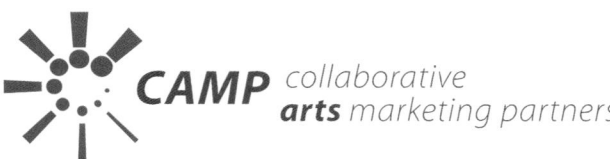

CAMP collaborative
arts marketing partnership

6.

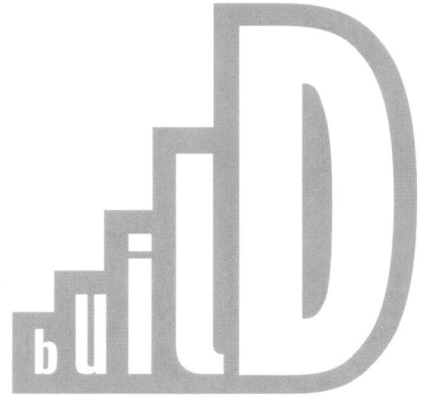

7.

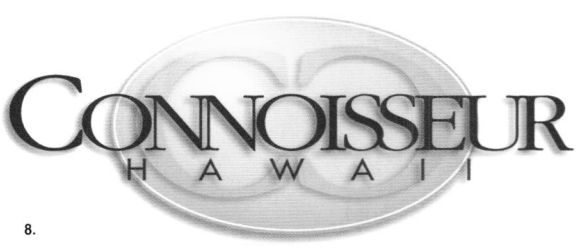

8.

WATERLADIES

9.

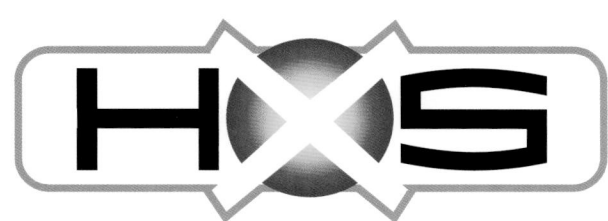

POWER UP Alabama

10.

MAUI BAY

11.

H×S

HAWAIIAN XTREME SPORTS TELEVISION

12.

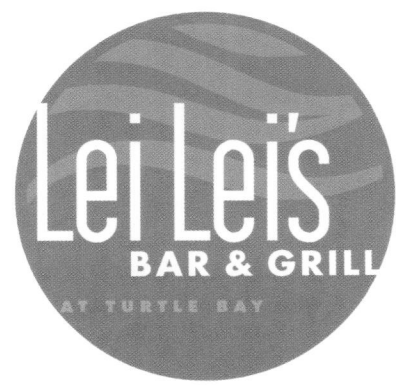

Lei Lei's
BAR & GRILL
AT TURTLE BAY

13.

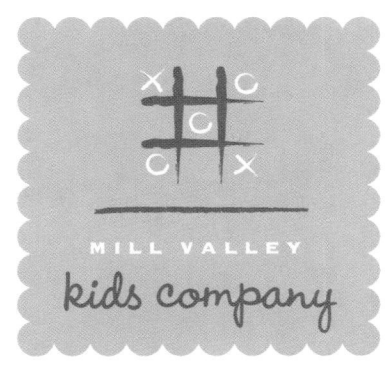

MILL VALLEY
kids company

14.

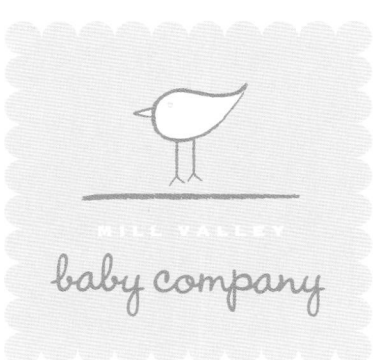

MILL VALLEY
baby company

15.

1, 2.			
Design Firm	**Hornall Anderson Design Works**		
3 - 7			
Design Firm	**Joe Miller's Company**		
8 - 13			
Design Firm	**John Wingard Design**		
14, 15.			
Design Firm	**Studio Moon**		

1.		**7.**	
Client	aQuantive Corporation	Client	Build
Designers	Jack Anderson, Kathy Saito, Henry Yiu, Sonja Max, Gretchen Cook	Designer	Joe Miller
2.		**8.**	
Client	Teaology	Client	Connoisseur Hawaii
Designers	Jana Nishi, Sonja Max, Mary Chin Hutchison	Designer	John Wingard
3.		**9.**	
Client	Poetry Center San Jose	Client	The WaterLadies
Designer	Joe Miller	Designer	John Wingard
4.		**10.**	
Client	Willow Technology	Client	Alabama Rural Electric Association
Designer	Joe Miller	Designer	John Wingard
5, 6.		**11.**	
Client	Arts Council Silicon Valley	Client	Taveuni Development Company
Designer	Joe Miller	Designer	John Wingard
		12.	
		Client	Hawaiian Xtreme Sports Television
		Designer	John Wingard
		13.	
		Client	Lei Lei's Bar & Grill
		Designer	John Wingard
		14.	
		Client	Mill Valley Kids Company
		Designer	Tracy Moon
		15.	
		Client	Mill Valley Baby Company
		Designer	Tracy Moon

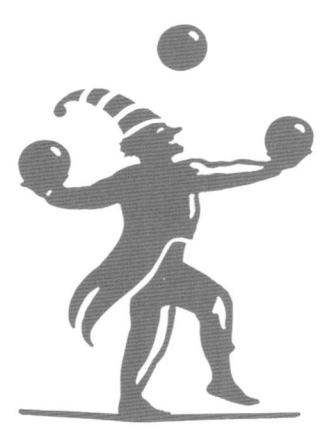

1.

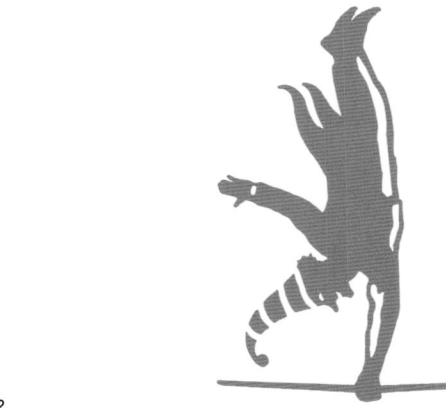

2.

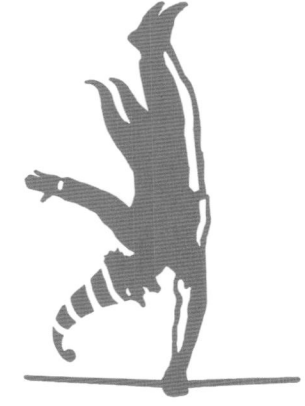

3.

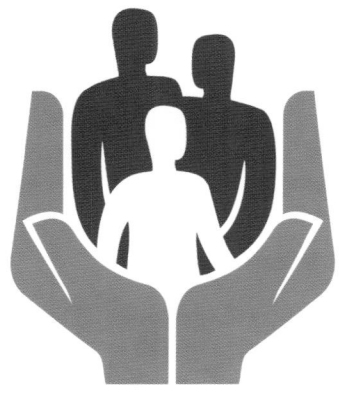

4.

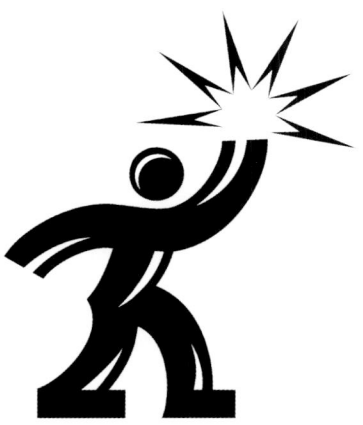

5.

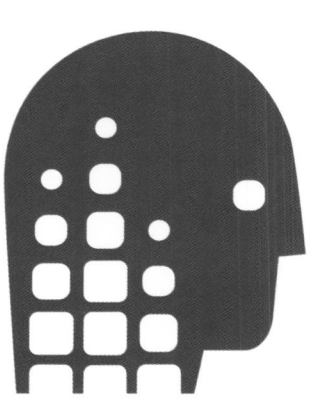

6.

1 - 7
Design Firm **Dotzero Design**
1, 2.
   Client   *CMD/Bridgeport Brewing Co.*
   Designers Jon Wippich, Karen Wippich
3.
   Client   *Scottsdale Christian Academy*
   Designers Jon Wippich, Karen Wippich
4.
   Client   *Kalberer*
   Designers Jon Wippich, Karen Wippich
5.
   Client   *BIA Deaf Translaters*
   Designers Jon Wippich, Karen Wippich
6.
   Client   *Unicru*
   Designers Jon Wippich, Karen Wippich

7.
   Client   *Do It For Peace*
   Designers Jon Wippich, Karen Wippich
(opposite)
   Client   *Varela Hermanos, S.A.*
   Design Firm **Muts&Joy&Design**
   Designers Tom Delaney,
                 Toni Kurrasch

7.

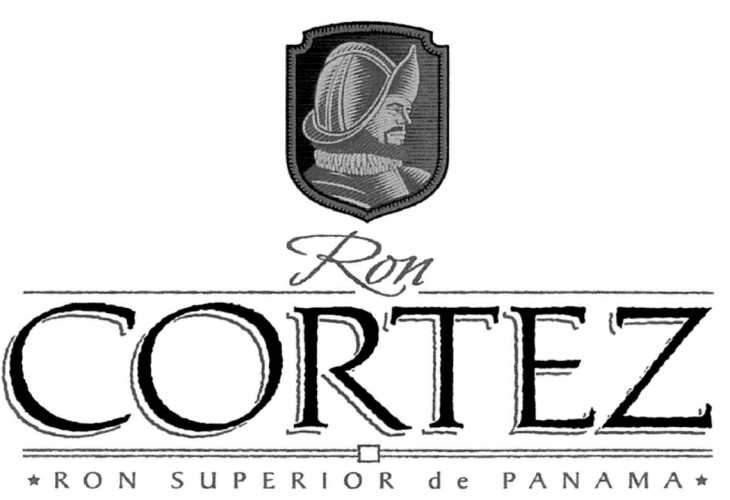

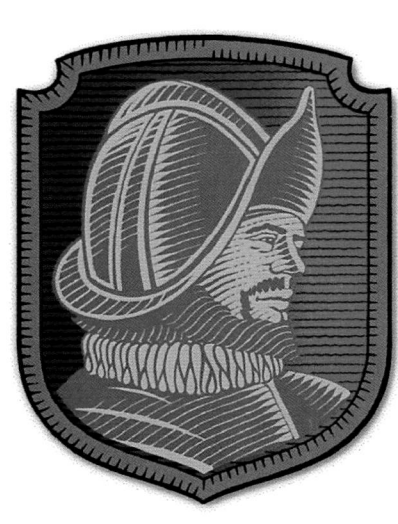
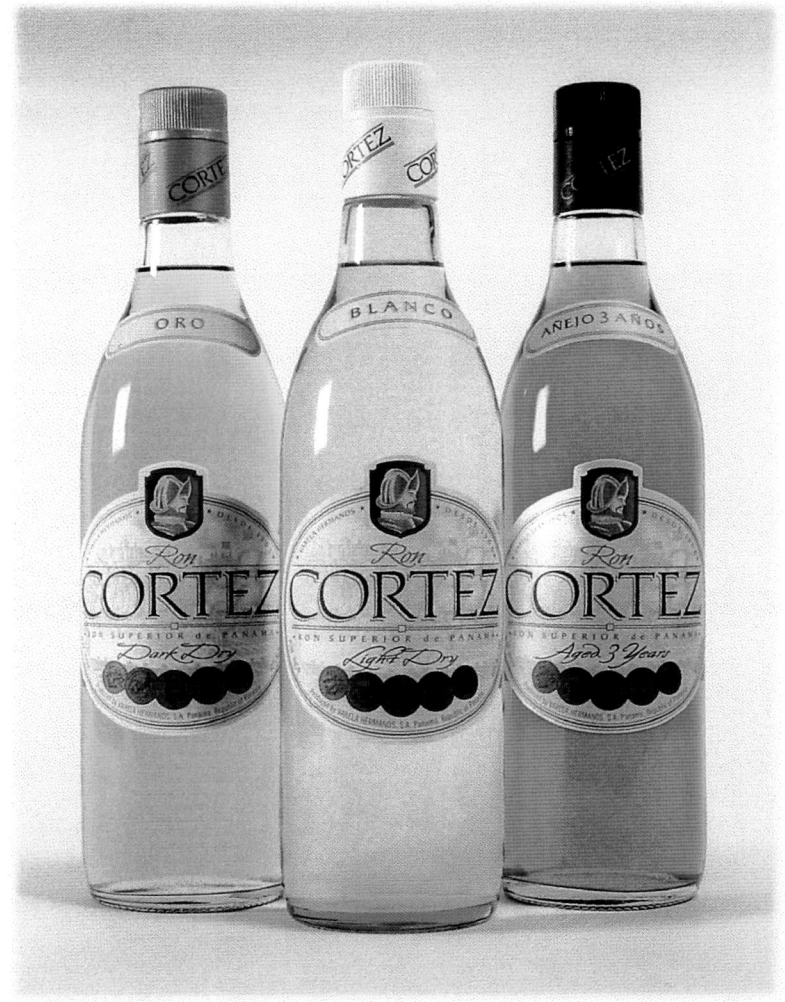

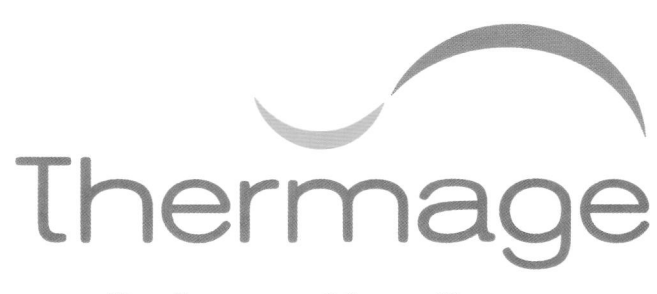

1.

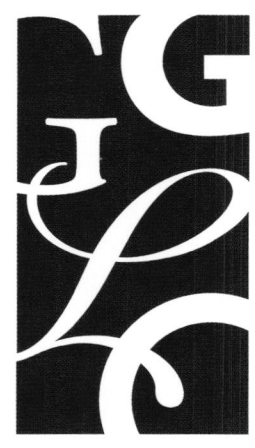

2.

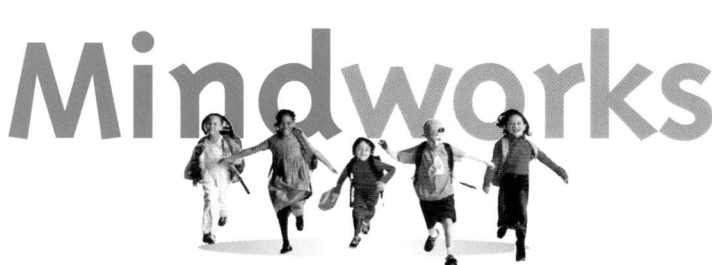

3.

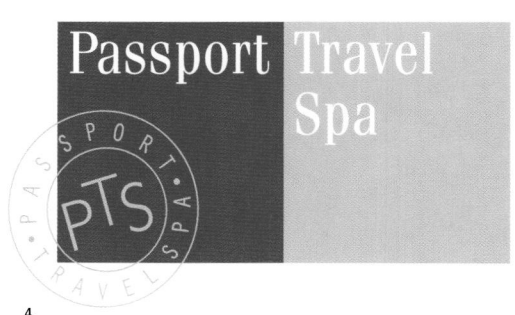

4.

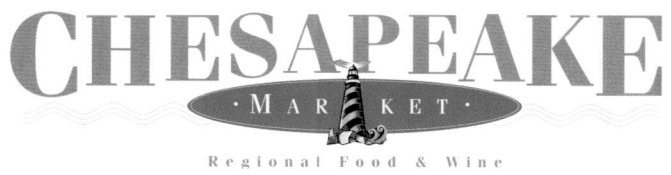

5.

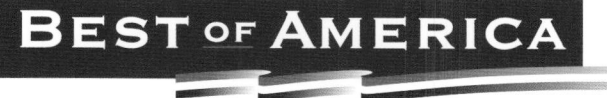

6.

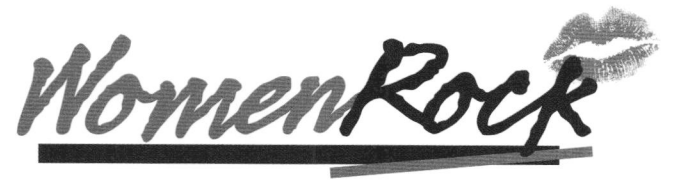

7.

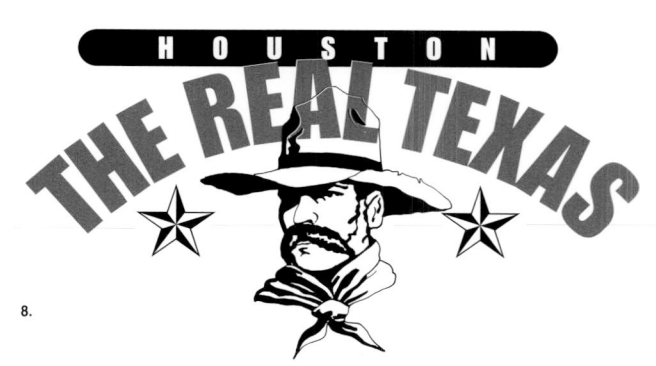

8.

LA COCINA MEXICANA

9.

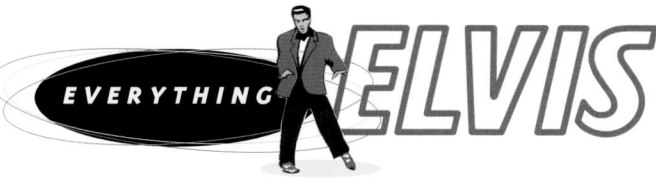

10.

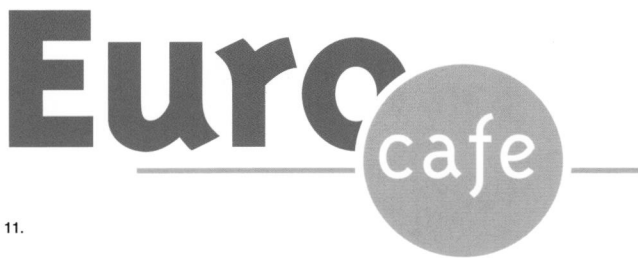

11.

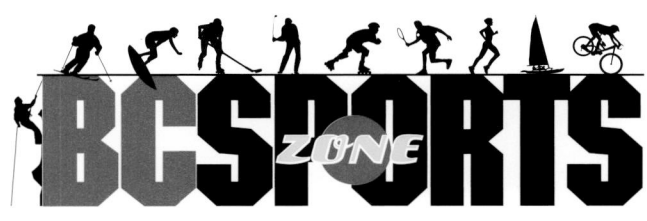

12.

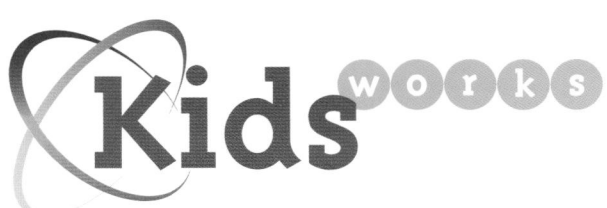

13.

JOURNEY
C H U R C H

14.

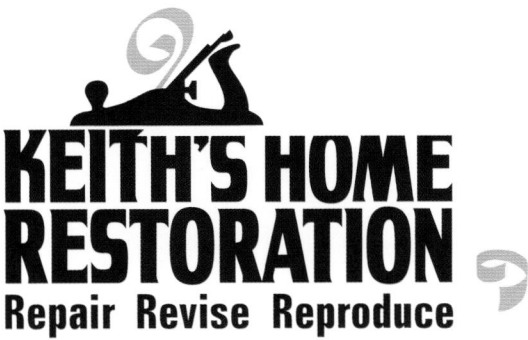

KEITH'S HOME
RESTORATION
Repair Revise Reproduce

15.

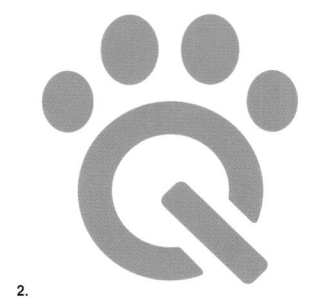

ⓙⓦⓓ john wingard design

1.

publicityconnections

3.

INSight

4.

TravelPORT®
A CENDANT COMPANY

5.

TERRAVIDA COFFEE

6.

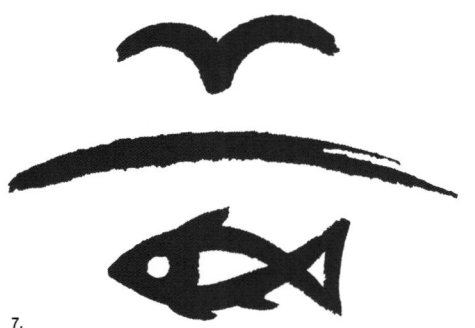

7.

1
Design Firm **John Wingard Design**
2
Design Firm **Cave**
3
Design Firm **Noble Erickson Inc.**
4 - 7
Design Firm **Hornall Anderson Design Works**
1.
Client   *John Wingard Design*
Designer   John Wingard
2.
Client   *Questinghound Technologies*
Designers David Edmundson,
           Matt Cave
3.
Client   *Publicity Connections*
Designer   Jackie Noble
4.
Client   *InSite Works Architects*
Designers John Anicker, Kathy Saito,
           Henry Yiu, Sonja Max

5.
Client   *Travelport*
Designers Lisa Cerveny, Andrew Wicklund,
           Andrew Smith, Jana Nishi,
           Hillary Radbill
6.
Client   *TerraVida Coffee*
Designers Jack Anderson, Sonja Max,
           James Tee, Tiffany Place,
           Elmer dela Cruz, Jana Nishi
7.
Client   *OneWorld Challenge*
Designers Jack Anderson, John Anicker,
           Andrew Smith, Andrew Wicklund,
           Mary Hermes, John Anderle
(opposite)
Client   *Seafarer Baking Co.*
Design Firm **Sabingrafik, Inc.**
Designers Tracy Sabin, Bridget Sabin

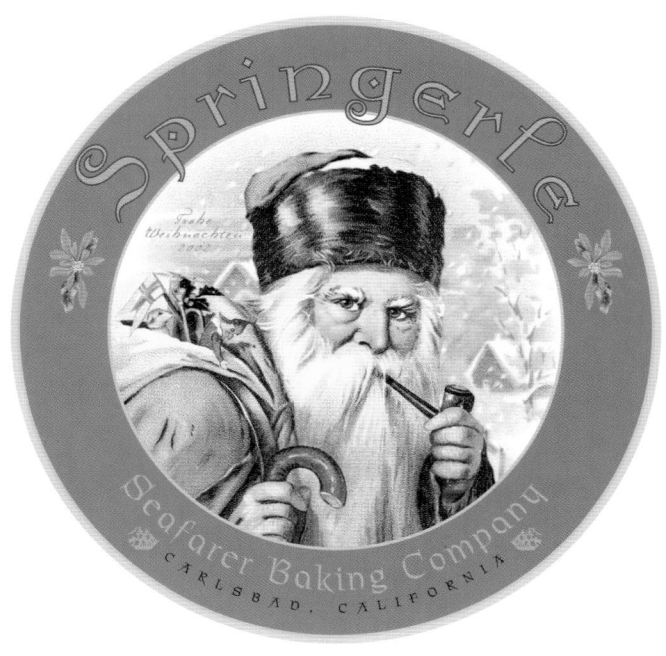

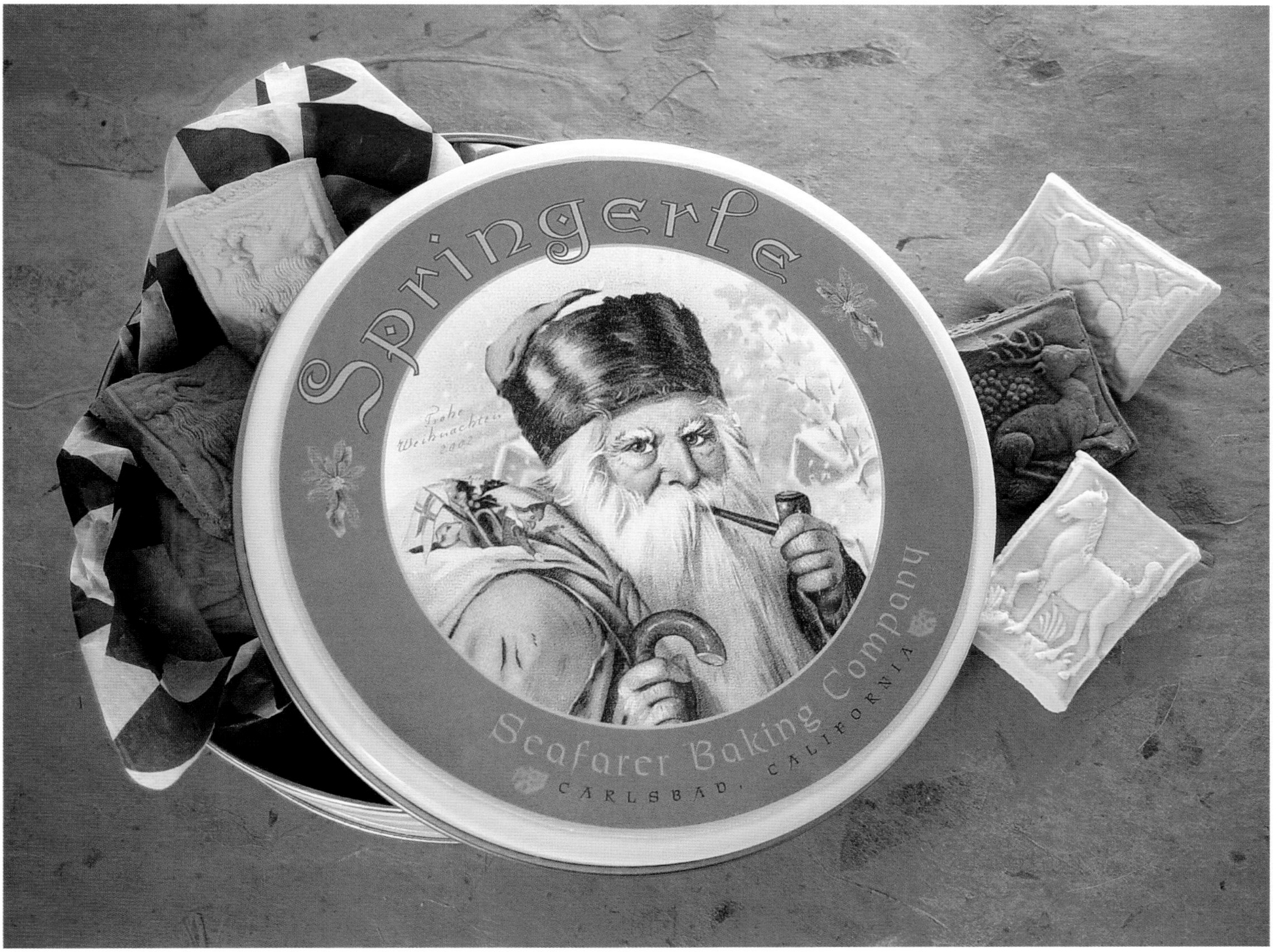

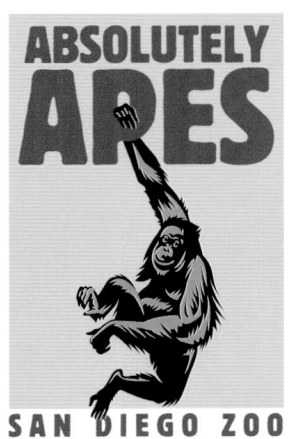

1.

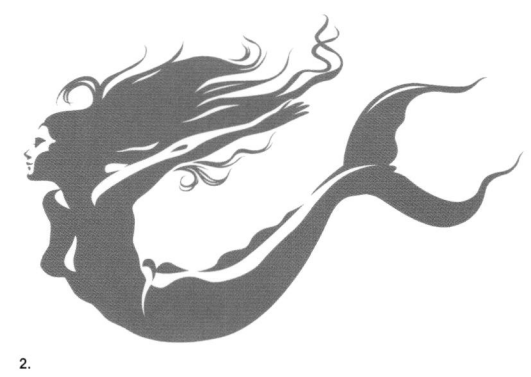

2.

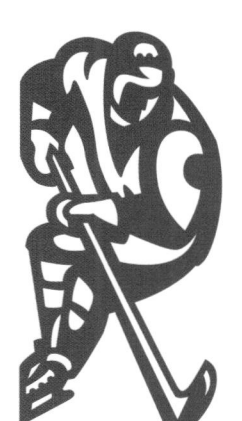

3.

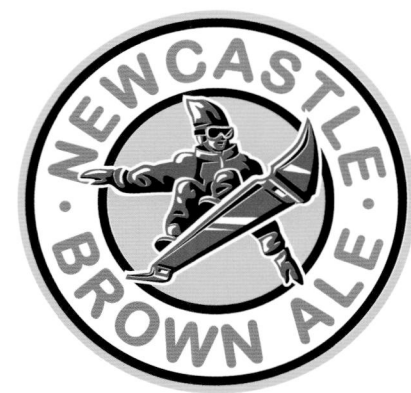

4.

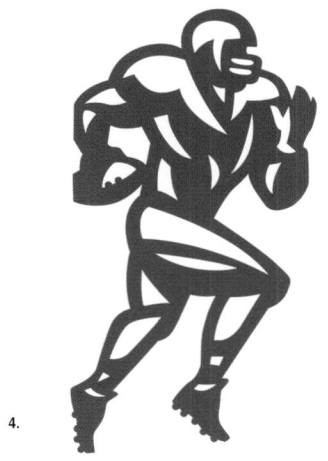

5.

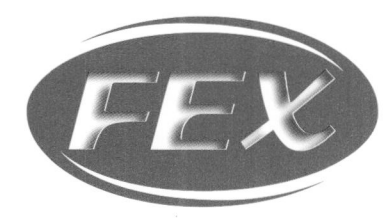

6.

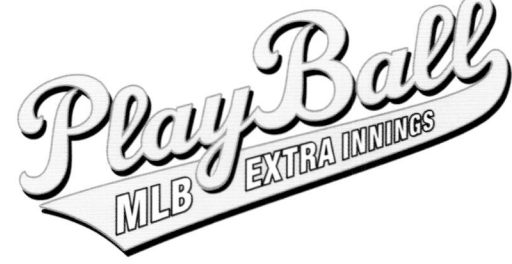

Fitness Equipment Expert

7.

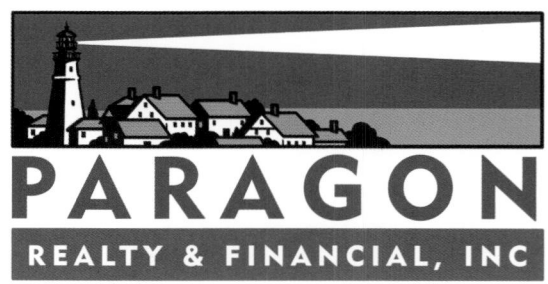

8.

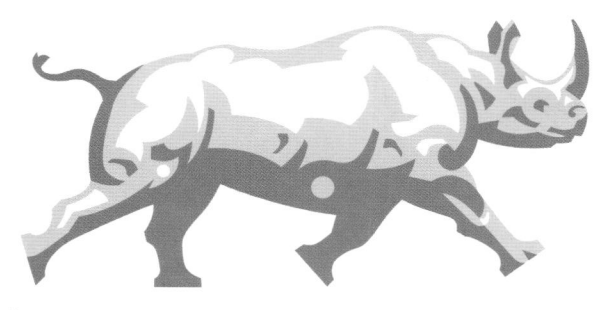

9.

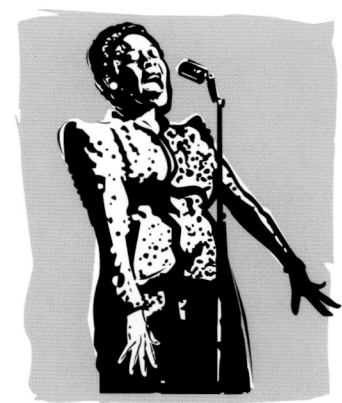

10.

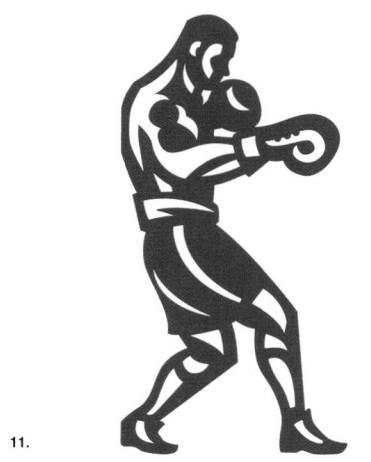

11.

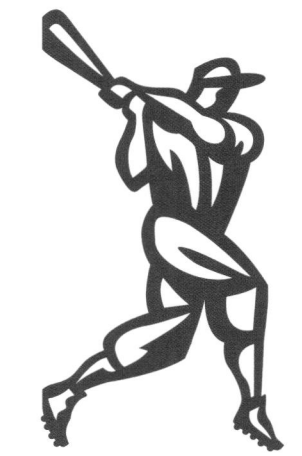

12.

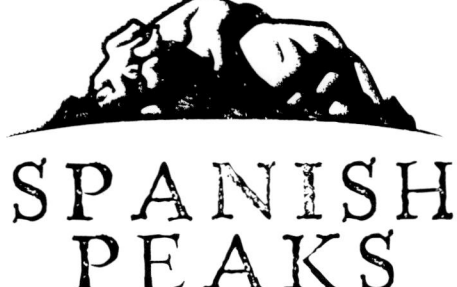

SPANISH PEAKS

BIG SKY MONTANA

13.

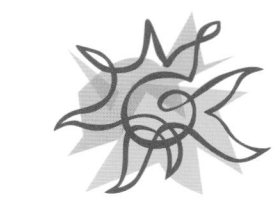

SUNDANCE

14.

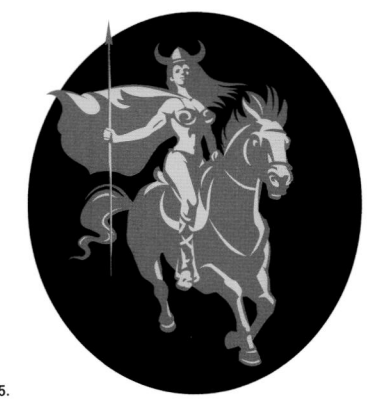

15.

1 - 15
Design Firm **Sabingrafik, Inc.**

1.
Client *San Diego Zoo*
Designers Tracy Sabin, Kevin Stout

2.
Client *Coastal Plastic Surgery*
Designers Tracy Sabin, Cindy White

3, 4.
Client *Amerisports Bar & Grill*
Designers Tracy Sabin, Joel Sotelo

5.
Client *Newcastle Beer*
Designers Tracy Sabin, Mike Brower

6.
Client *MLB Advance Media*
Designers Tracy Sabin, Ian Jensen

7.
Client *Fitness Equipment Expert*
Designers Tracy Sabin, Mary McNulty

8.
Client *Paragon Realty & Financial, Inc.*
Designer Tracy Sabin

9.
Client *Beithan/Hessler*
Designers Tracy Sabin, Peter Oehjne

10.
Client *Bottleneck Blues Bar*
Designers Tracy Sabin, Joel Sotelo

11, 12.
Client *Amerisports Bar & Grill*
Designers Tracy Sabin, Joel Sotelo

13.
Client *Spanish Peaks*
Designers Tracy Sabin, James Wiesinger

14.
Client *Sundance*
Designers Tracy Sabin, Craig Fuller,
Sandra Sharp

15.
Client *TYR Motorsports*
Designers Tracy Sabin, Jim Davis

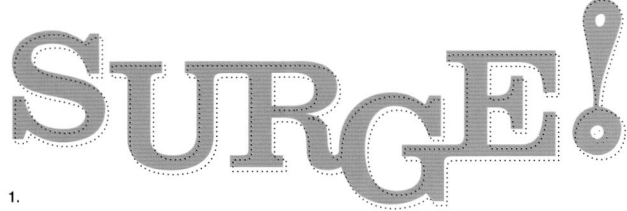

1.

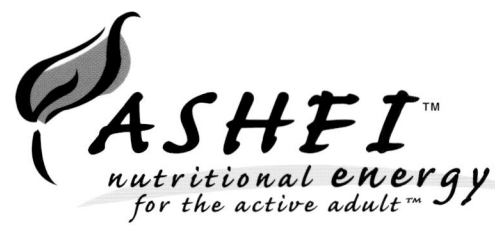

2.

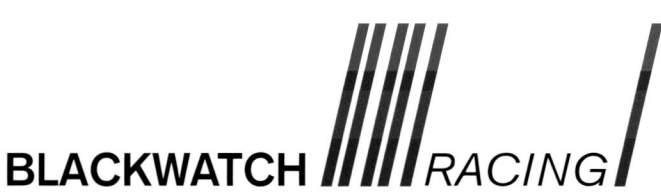

3.

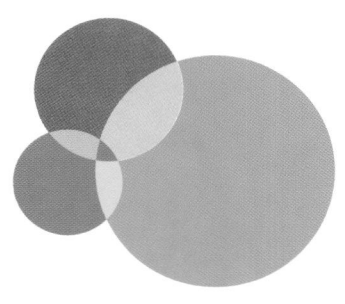

4.

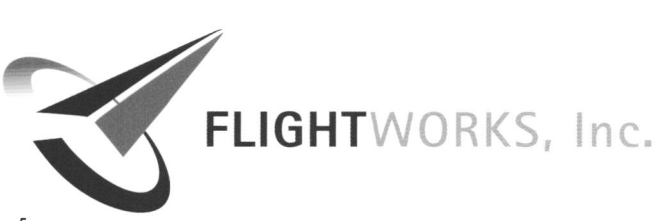

5.

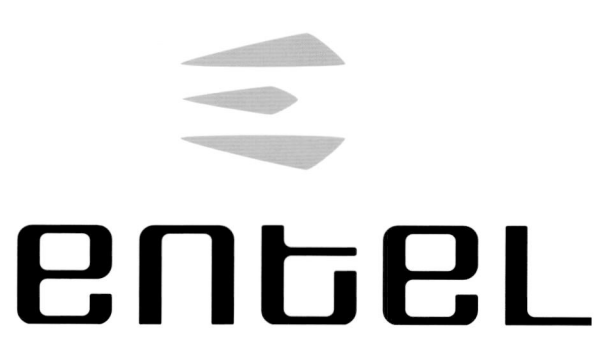

6.

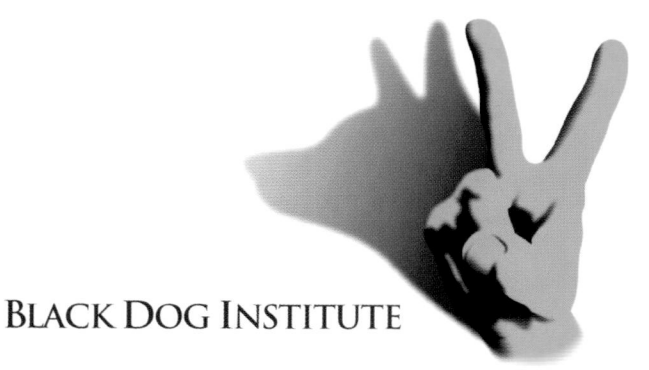

7.

1 - 6
Design Firm **Ciro Design**

7
Design Firm **John Bevins Pty Limited**

1.
Client   *IDSA Western District*
Designer   Katrina Luong

2.
Client   *ASHFI*
Designer   Alisa Schroeder

3.
Client   *Blackwatch Racing*
Designer   Katrina Luong

4.
Client   *Saddleback Packaging*
Designer   Juan Valadez

5.
Client   *Flightworks Inc.*
Designer   Nora Gard

6.
Client   *Entel*
Designer   Jimmy Matsuki

7.
Client   *Black Dog Institute*
Designers John Bevins,
             Cato Purnell Partners

(opposite)
Client   *Adra Soaps*
Design Firm **Sabingrafik, Inc.**
Designer   Tracy Sabin

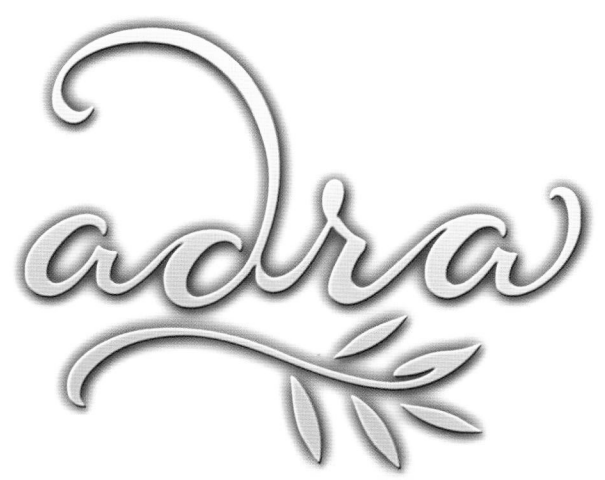

adra

handmade natural soaps

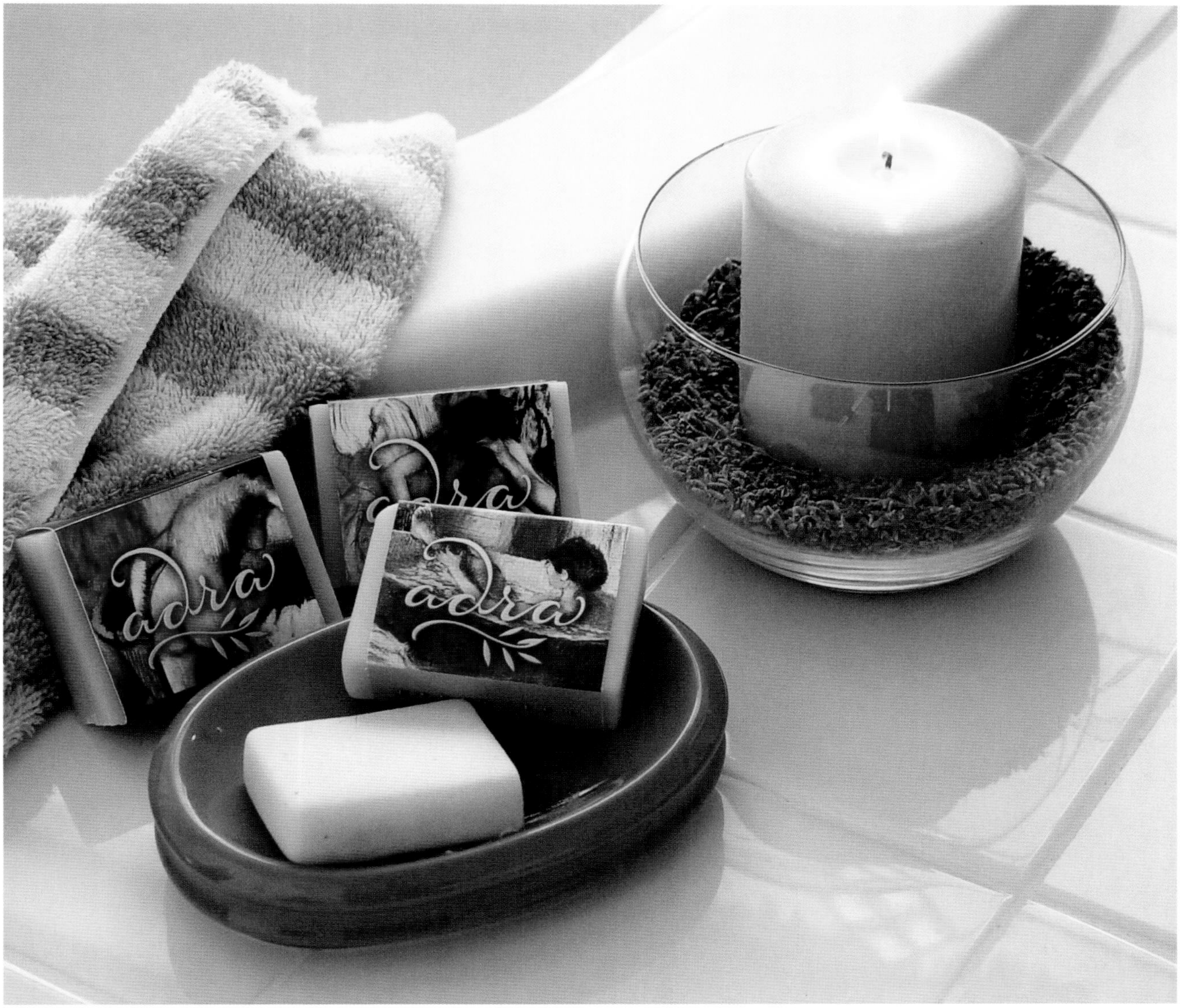

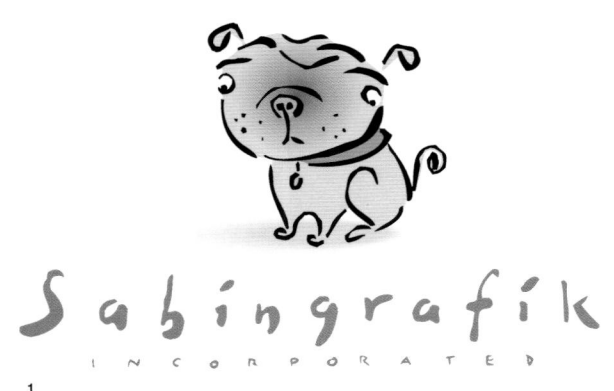

1.

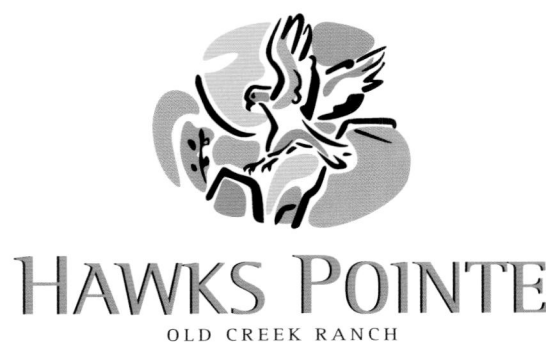

2.

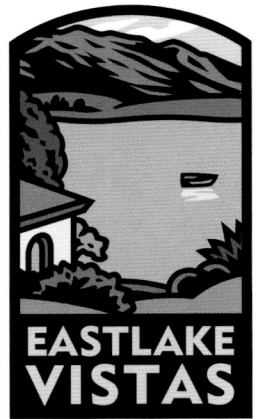

3.

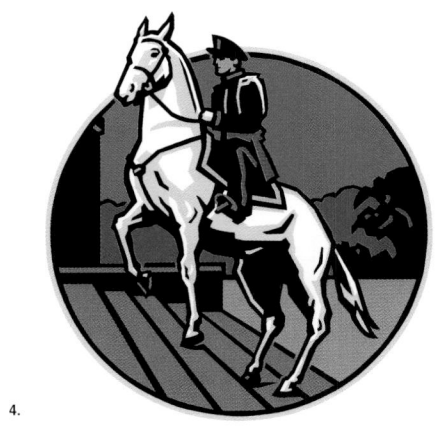

4.

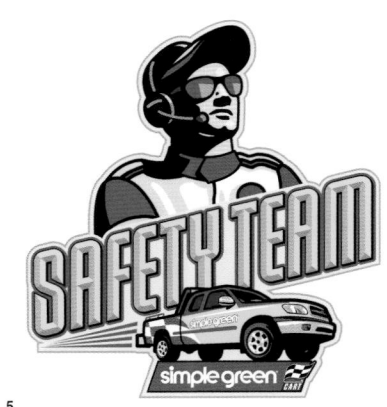

5.

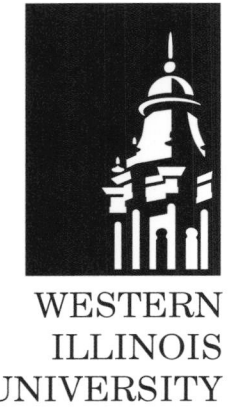

6.

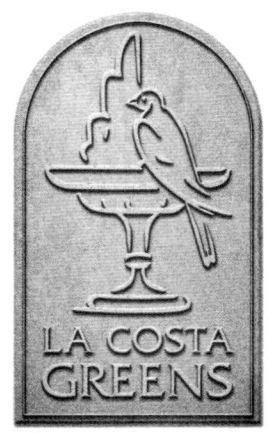

7.

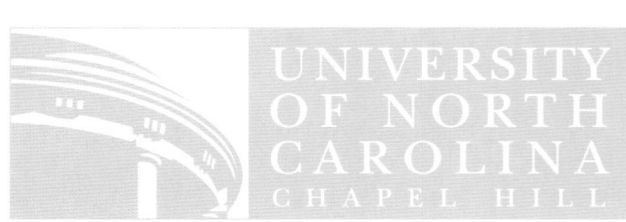

8.

128

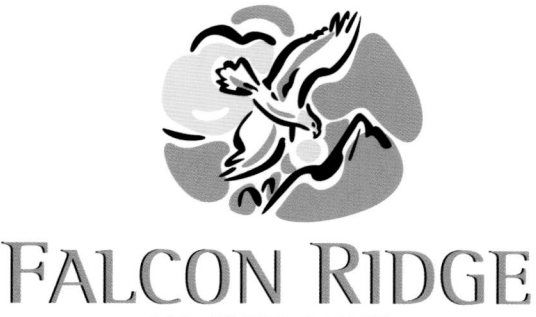

FALCON RIDGE

OLD CREEK RANCH

9.

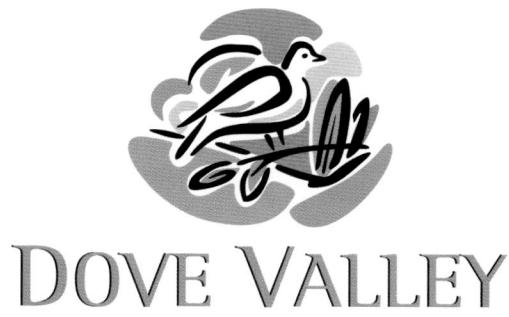

DOVE VALLEY

OLD CREEK RANCH

10.

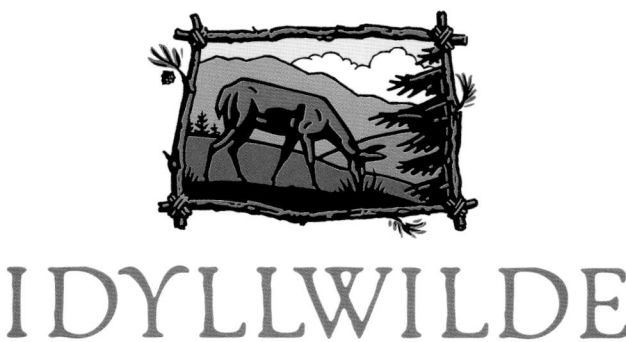

IDYLLWILDE

PARKER COLORADO

11.

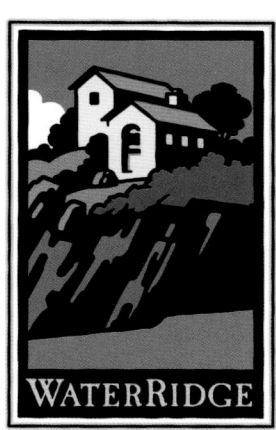

WaterRidge

12.

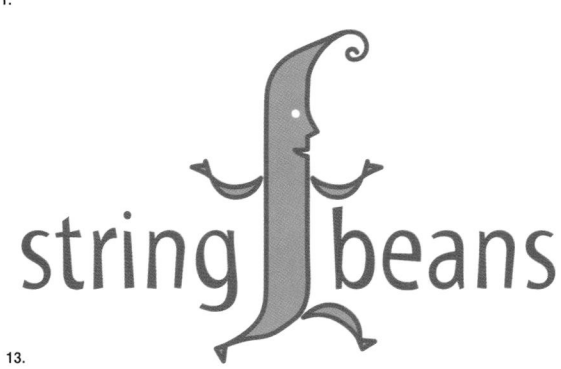

string beans

13.

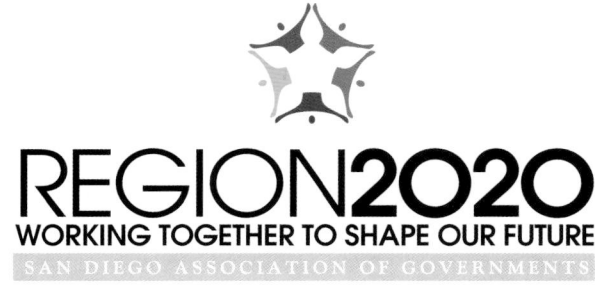

REGION**2020**

WORKING TOGETHER TO SHAPE OUR FUTURE

SAN DIEGO ASSOCIATION OF GOVERNMENTS

14.

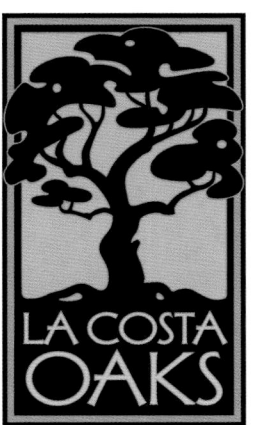

LA COSTA OAKS

15.

1 - 15
Design Firm **Sabingrafik, Inc.**

1.
Client   *Sabingrafik, Inc.*
Designer   Tracy Sabin

2.
Client   *Old Creek Ranch*
Designers   Tracy Sabin, Stephen Sharp

3.
Client   *Eastlake Vistas*
Designers   Tracy Sabin, Dennis Zimmerman

4.
Client   *Sandhurst Foundation*
Designers   Tracy Sabin, James Dewar

5.
Client   *Simple Green*
Designers   Tracy Sabin, Mike Brower

6.
Client   *Western Illinois University*
Designers   Tracy Sabin, Victoria Primicias

7.
Client   *La Costa Greens*
Designers   Tracy Sabin, Stephen Sharp

8.
Client   *University of North Carolina at Chapel Hill*
Designers   Tracy Sabin, Victoria Primicias

9, 10.
Client   *Old Creek Ranch*
Designers   Tracy Sabin, Stephen Sharp

11.
Client   *Idyllwilde*
Designers   Tracy Sabin, Craig Fuller, Sandra Sharp

12.
Client   *WaterRidge*
Designers   Tracy Sabin, Stephen Sharp

13.
Client   *String Beans*
Designers   Tracy Sabin, Mike Nelson

14.
Client   *San Diego Association of Governments*
Designers   Tracy Sabin, Mary McNulty

15.
Client   *La Costa Oaks*
Designers   Tracy Sabin, Stephen Sharp

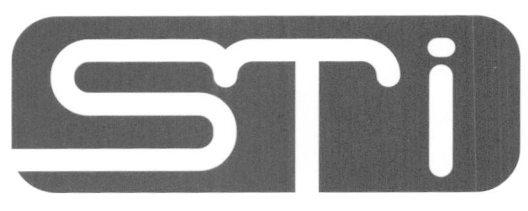

1.

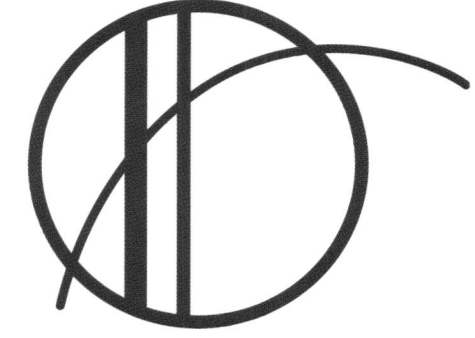

2.

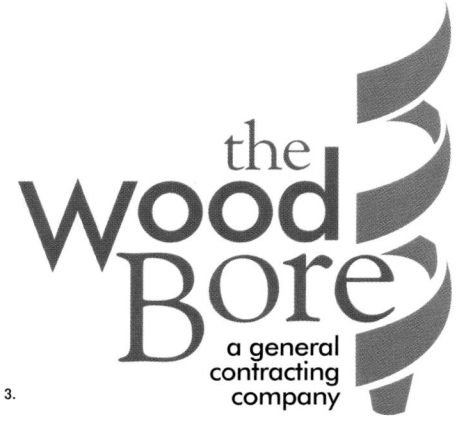

3.

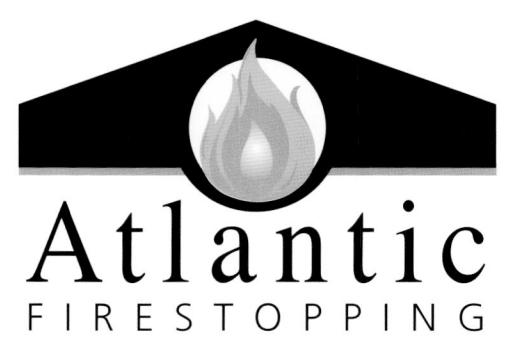

4.

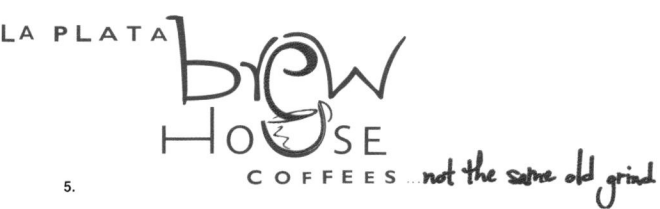

5.

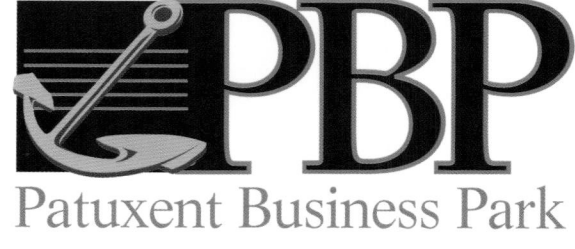

6.

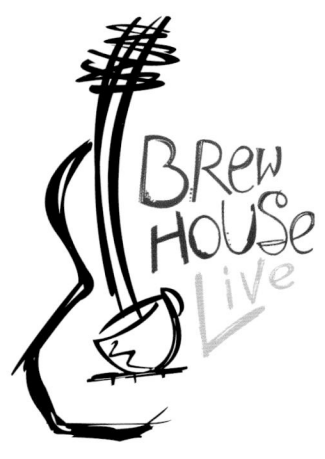

7.

1, 2
Design Firm **The Hayden Group**
3 - 7
Design Firm **Rottman Creative Group**
1.
Client *Sti In-Store Merchandising*
Designer Craig Weber
2.
Client *The Hayden Group*
Designer Ellen Rudy
3.
Client *The Wood Bore Co.*
Designers Gary Rottman,
Jenna Holcombe
4.
Client *Atlantic Firestopping*
Designer Jenna Holcombe

5.
Client *LaPlata BrewHouse Coffee's*
Designer Jenna Holcombe
6.
Client *Calvert County Department of Economical Development*
Designer Gary Rottman
7.
Client *LaPlata BrewHouse Coffee's*
Designer Jenna Holcombe
(opposite)
Client *Caffe Ibis*
Design Firm **One Hundred Church St.**
Designer R.P. Bissland

CAFFE IBIS

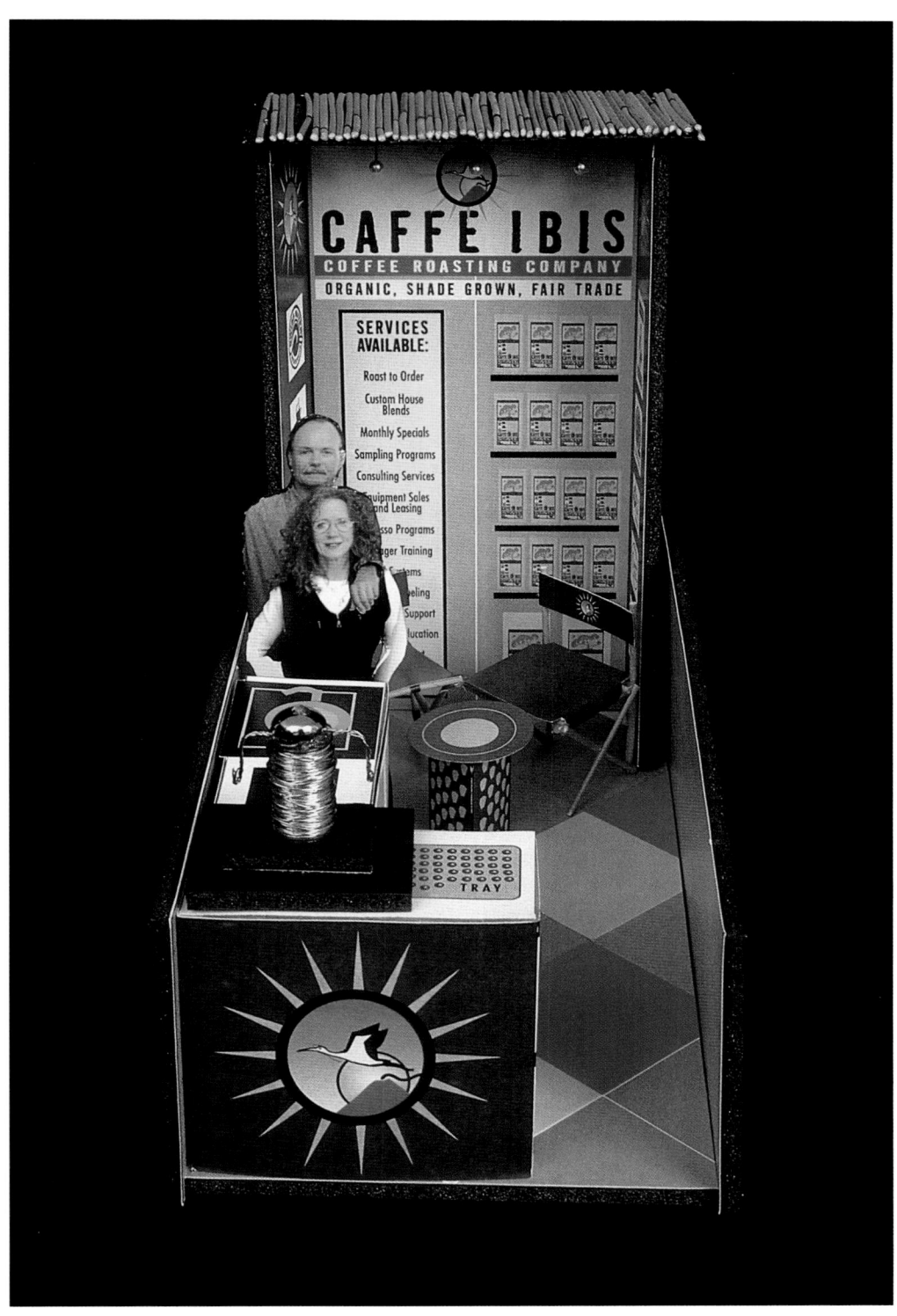

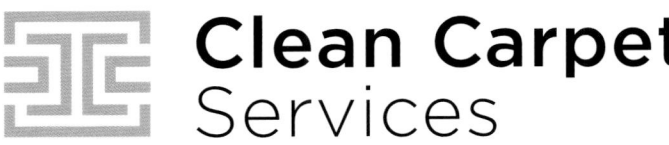

1.

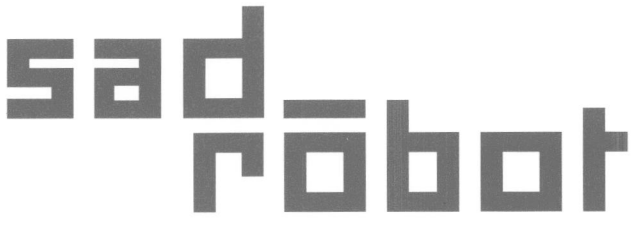

2.

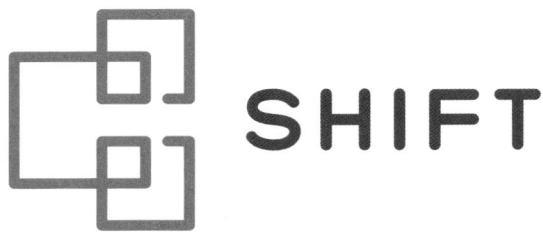

3.

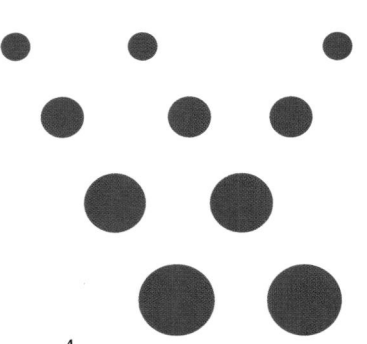

4.

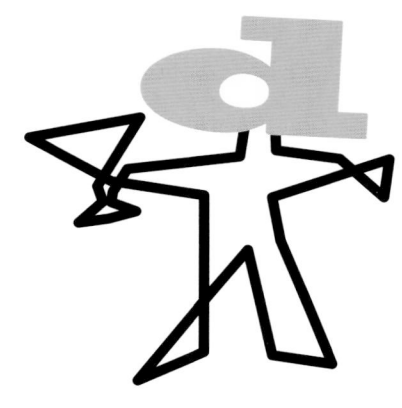

5.

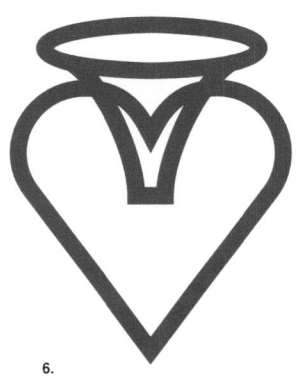

6.

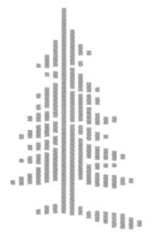

7.

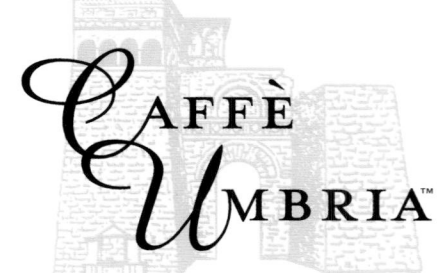

8.

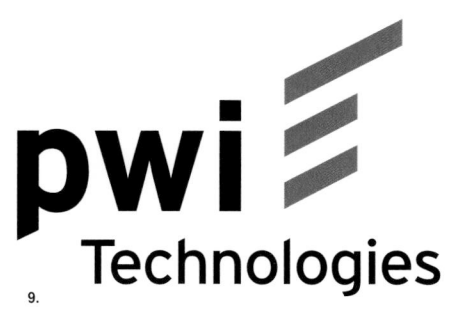

pwi Technologies

9.

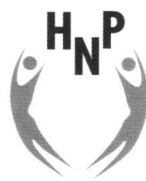

Hemophilia Nurse Partnership

10.

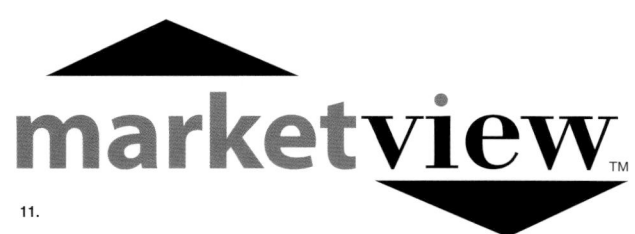

11.

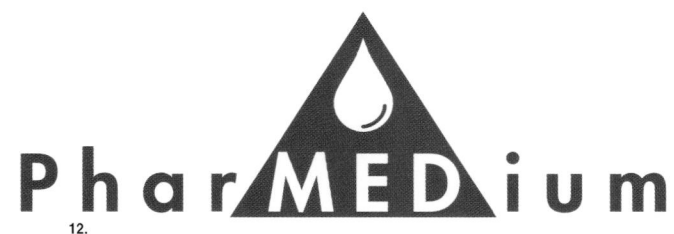

12.

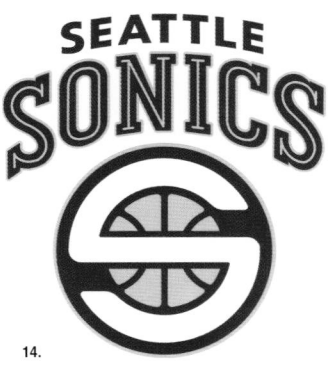

14.

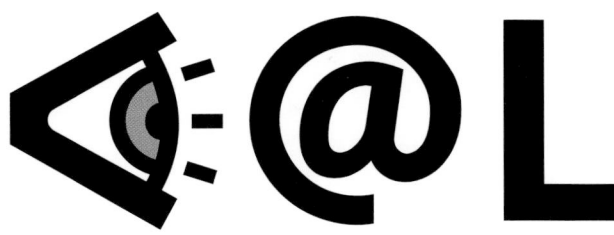

13.

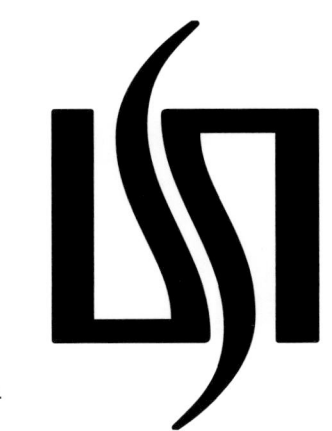

15.

1 - 9
Design Firm **Studio Rayolux**

10 - 12
Design Firm **Design Moves, Ltd.**

13 - 15
Design Firm **Hornall Anderson Design Works**

1.
Client — *Clean Carpet Service*
Designer — Thad Boss

2.
Client — *Sad Robot Records*
Designer — Thad Boss

3, 4.
Client — *Shift*
Designer — Thad Boss

5.
Client — *Drunkinseattle.com*
Designer — Thad Boss

6.
Client — *Vena Cava Records*
Designer — Thad Boss

7.
Client — *Northwest Biotherapeutics*
Designer — Thad Boss

8.
Client — *Caffé Umbria Coffee Roasting Company*
Designer — Thad Boss

9.
Client — *PWI Technologies*
Designer — Thad Boss

10.
Client — *Baxter Healthcare*
Designers — Laurie Medeiros Freed, William R. Sprowl

11.
Client — *GlobalView*
Designers — Laurie Medeiros Freed, William R. Sprowl

12.
Client — *Phar MEDium Healthcare Corporation*
Designers — Laurie Medeiros Freed, William R. Sprowl

13.
Client — *Seattle Convention & Visitors Bureau*
Designers — Lisa Cerveny, Jack Anderson, Bruce Branson-Meyer, Mark Popich

14.
Client — *Seattle Sonics*
Designers — Jack Anderson, Mark Popich, Andrew Wicklund, Elmer dela Cruz

15.
Client — *Lincoln Square*
Designers — Jack Anderson, Katha Dalton, Gretchen Cook, Sonja Max

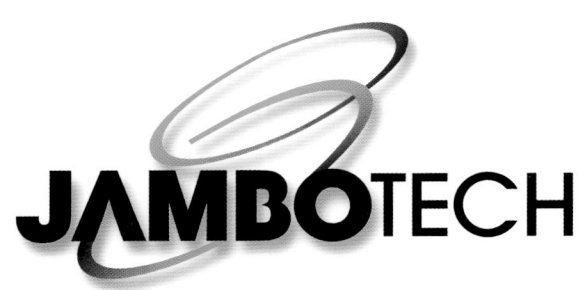

1.

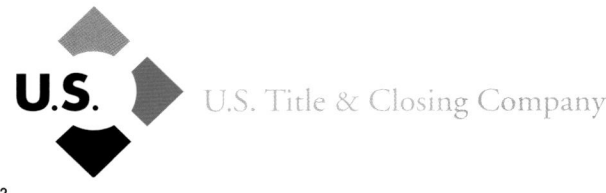

2.

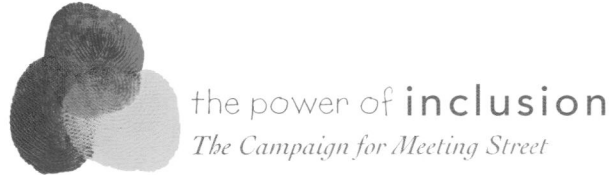

3.

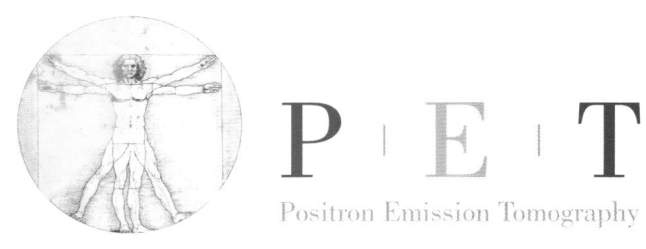

4.

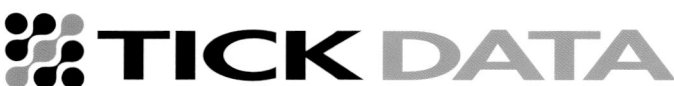

5.

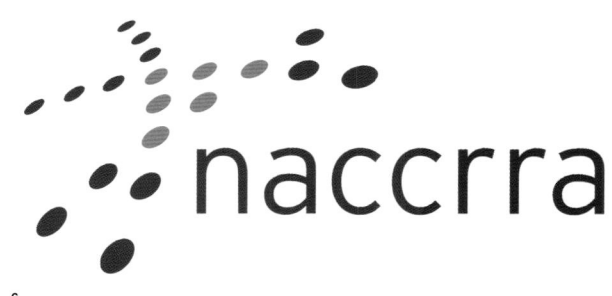

6.

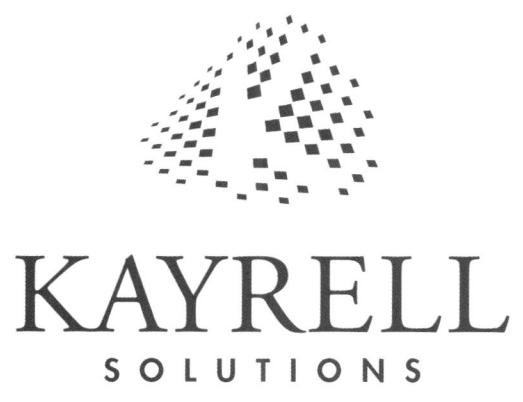

7.

1
Design Firm **Shimokochi—Reeves**
2 - 4
Design Firm **Im-aj Communications & Design, Inc.**
5 - 7
Design Firm **Alliant Studios**

1.
Client — *Jambo Tech*
Designer — Mamoru Shimokochi

2.
Client — *U.S. Title & Closing Company*
Designers — Jami Ouellette, Mark Bevington, Lee Kosa

3.
Client — *Meeting Street*
Designers — Jami Ouellette, Lee Kosa

4.
Client — *Sheilds Health Care*
Designers — Jami Ouellette, Mark Bevington

5.
Client — *Tick Data*
Designers — Mike Domingo, Patrick Dennis

6.
Client — *NACCRRA*
Designer — David McGaw

7.
Client — *Kayrell Solutions*
Designer — Kevin Frank

(opposite)
Client — *Justin Allen Company*
Design Firm **Ciro Design**
Designer — Katrina Luong

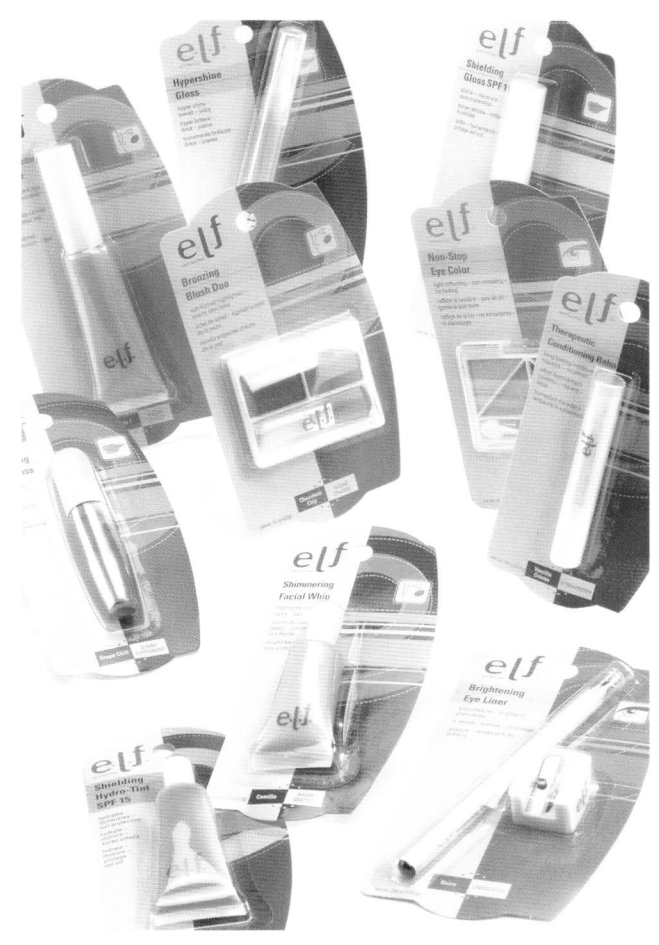

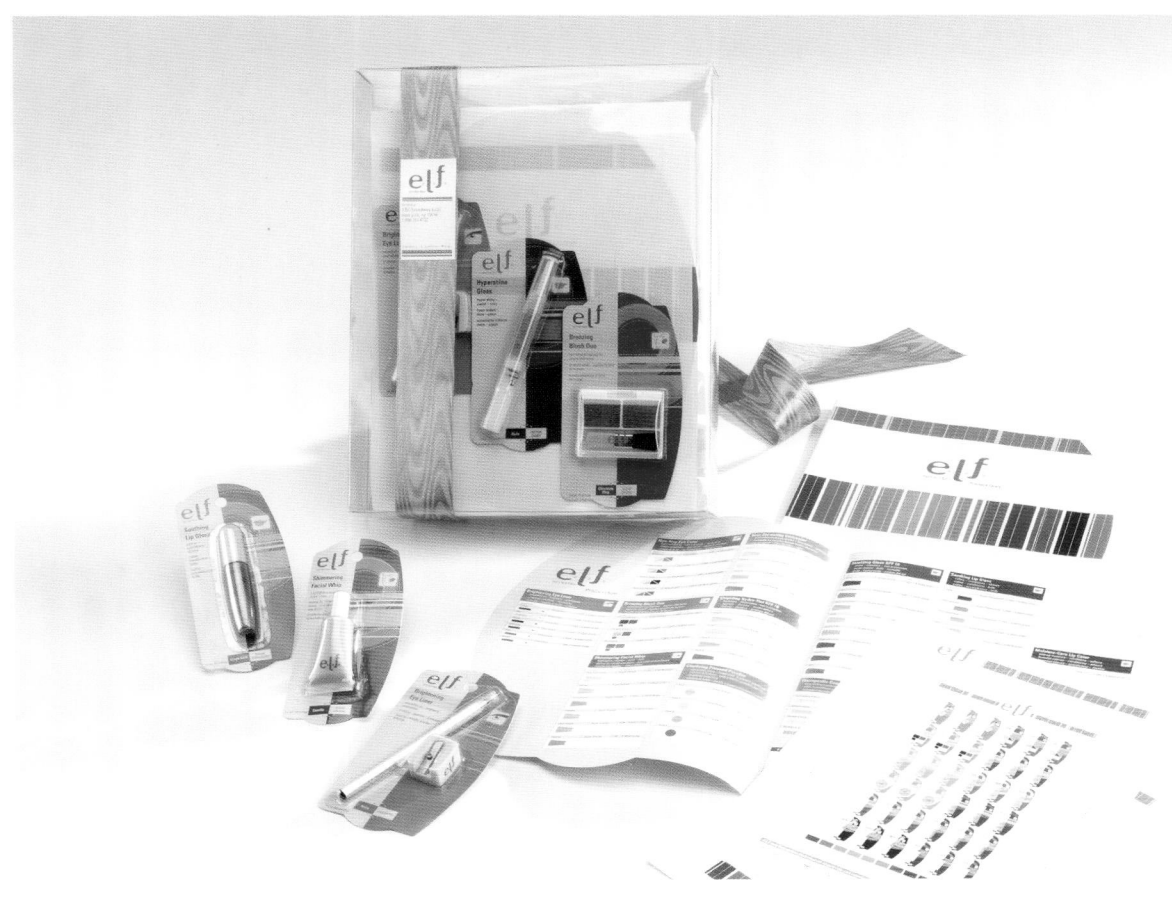

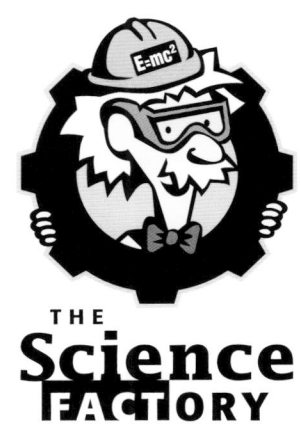

1.

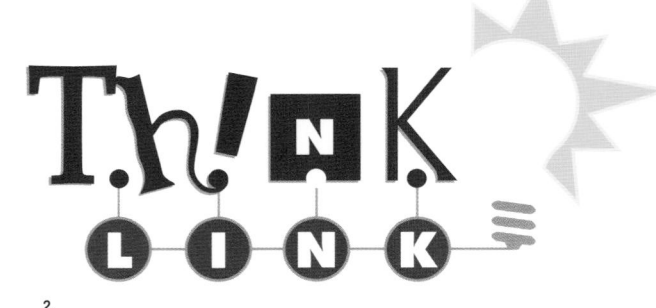

2.

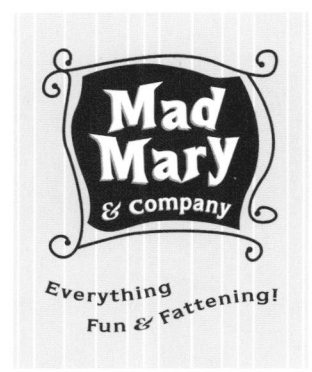

3.

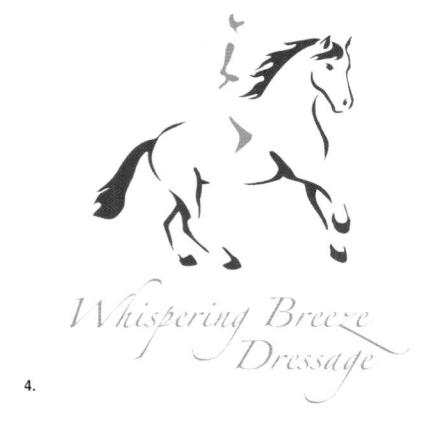

4.

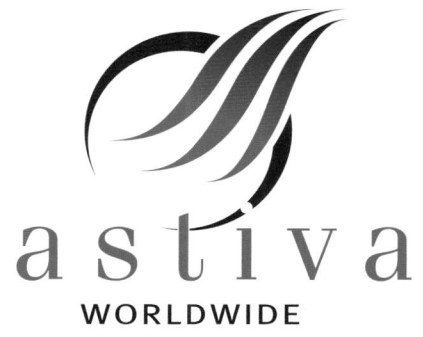

5.

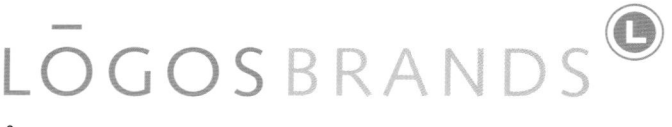

6.

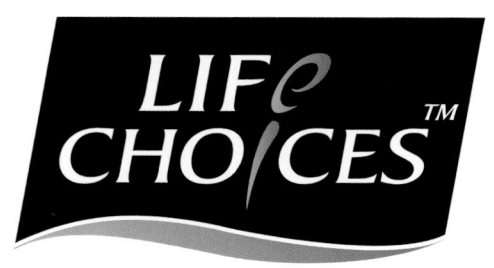

7.

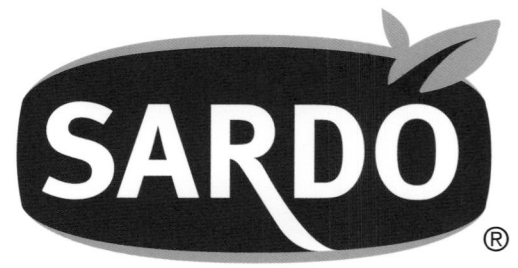

8.

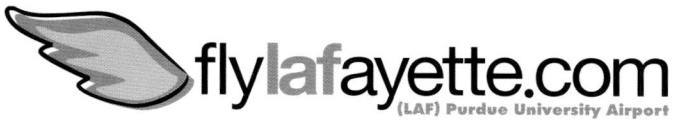

9.

INDESIGN
INDIANA PRODUCT DESIGN EXHIBITION

10.

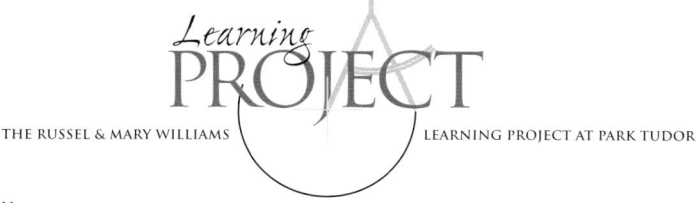

THE RUSSEL & MARY WILLIAMS   LEARNING PROJECT AT PARK TUDOR

11.

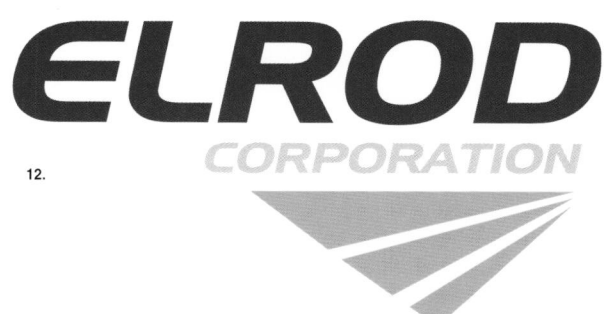

12.

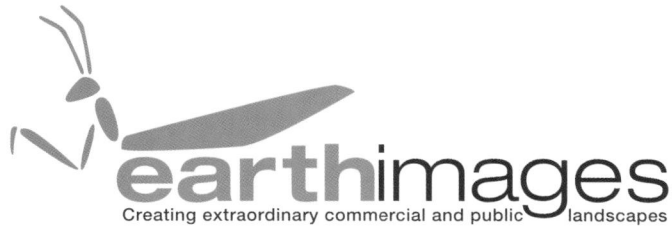

Creating extraordinary commercial and public landscapes

13.

14.

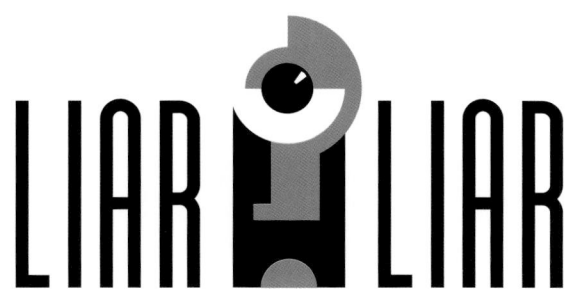

15.

1 - 4
Design Firm **j-creative**
5 - 8
Design Firm **LOGOSBRANDS**
9 - 14
Design Firm **Indiana Design Consortium, Inc.**
15
Design Firm **JFDesign**

1.
Client   The Science Factory
Designer   Joan Gilbert Madsen

2.
Client   Think Link Discovery Museum
           for Children
Designer   Joan Gilbert Madsen

3.
Client   Mad Mary & Company
Designer   Joan Gilbert Madsen

4.
Client   Whispering Breeze Dressage
Designer   Joan Gilbert Madsen

5.
Client   Astiva Worldwide
Designers Gabriella Sousa, Brian Smith

6.
Client   LOGOSBRANDS
Designers Ali Khan, Sunny Chan

7.
Client   LIFE CHOICES Natural Foods
Designers Phil Slous, Franca DiNardo

8.
Client   SARDO Food Importers
Designers Ali Khan, Franca DiNardo

9.
Client   Lafayette Chamber of Commerce
Designer   Andrew R. Schwint

10.
Client   Pro Bono
Designer   Andrew R. Schwint

11.
Client   Park Tudor School
Designer   Kristy Blair

12.
Client   Elrod Corporation
Designers Andrew R. Schwint,
           Debra Pohl Green

13.
Client   Earth Images, Inc.
Designer   Andrew R. Schwint

14.
Client   Bo-Witt Products, Inc.
Designer   Andrew R. Schwint

15.
Client   TDU Toys
Designer   Josie Fertig

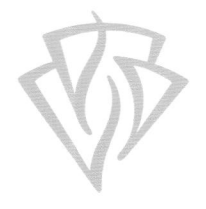

SAN FRANCISCO MARRIOTT

1.

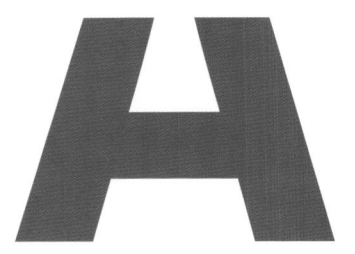

OTOÑO

PLAZA

2.

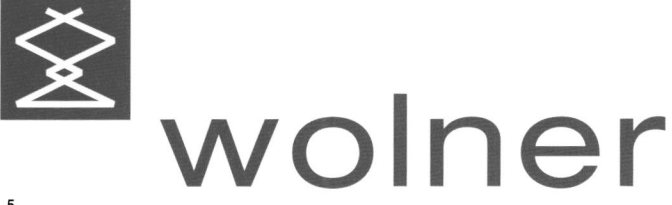

MULVANNY ARCHITECTURE G2

3.

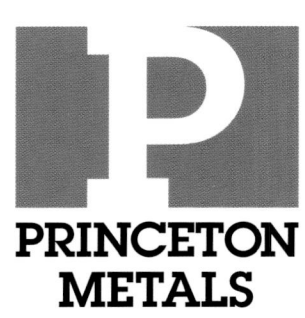

A

4.

wolner

5.

PRINCETON
METALS

6.

Leadership | **Communication**

7.

1 - 4
Design Firm **Hornall Anderson Design Works**
5 - 7
Design Firm **Design Matters, Inc!**

1.
Client   *San Francisco Marriott*
Designers   Jack Anderson, Kathy Saito,
              Sonja Max, Alan Copeland,
              Gretchen Cook

2.
Client   *Otoño Plaza*
Designers   John Anicker, Henry Yiu,
              Kathy Saito, Gretchen Cook,
              Sonja Max

3.
Client   *Mulvanny/G2*
Designers   Jack Anderson, Katha Dalton,
              Jana Nishi, Michael Brugman,
              Hillary Radbill, Henry Yiu, Ed Lee

4.
Client   *Hornall Anderson Design Works*
Designers   Jack Anderson, John Hornall,
              Henry Yiu, Andrew Wicklund,
              Mark Popich

5.
Client   *Stephen Z. Wolner, D.D.S.*
Designers   Stephen M. McAllister,
              Gordon Fraser

6.
Client   *Princeton Metal Company*
Designer   Stephen M. McAllister

7.
Client   *Leadership Communication*
Designers   Stephen M. McAllister,
              Gordon Fraser

(opposite)
Client   *Vegewax Candle Worx*
Design Firm   **LOGOSBRANDS**
Designers   Denise Barac, Franca DiNardo

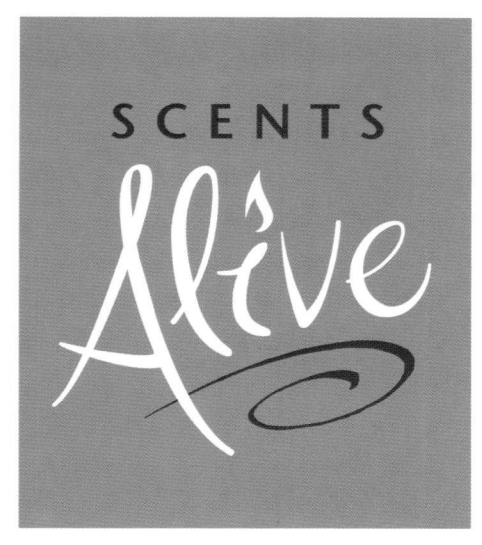

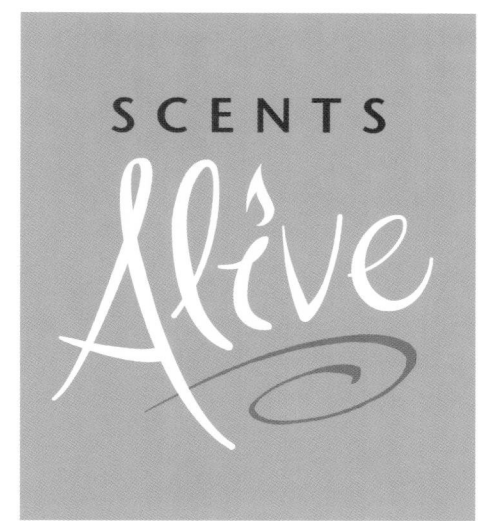

burns
190-210
hours

burns
140-160
hours

Each candle
burns in a
unique
decorative
pattern

SCENTS
Alive

sootfree
burns
longer

soot free
burns
longer

burns
90-110
hours

SCENTS
Alive

Each candle
burns in a
unique
decorative
pattern

4"
PILLAR
CANDLE

6"
PILLAR
CANDLE

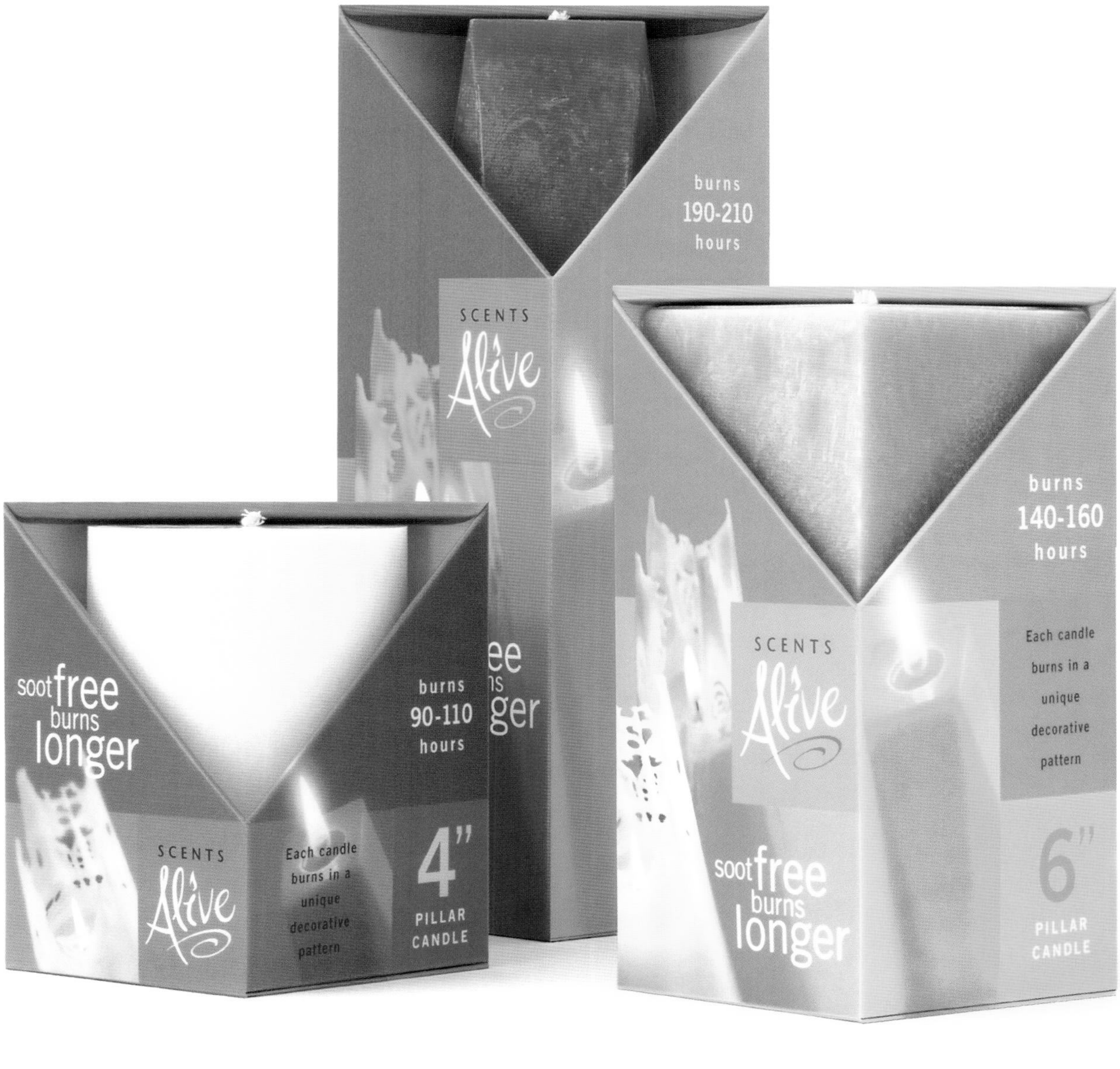

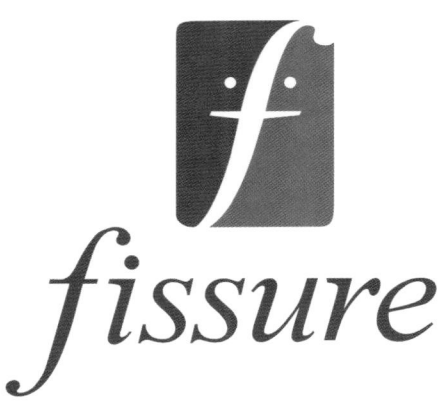

1.

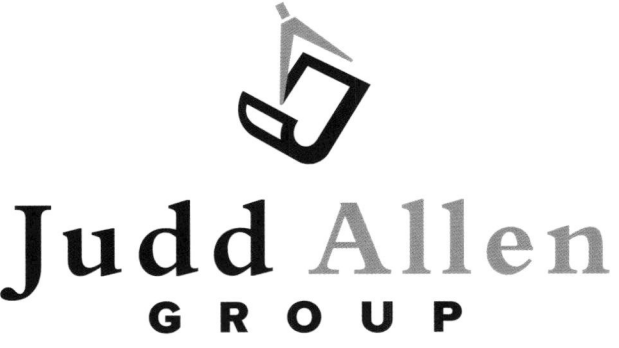

2.

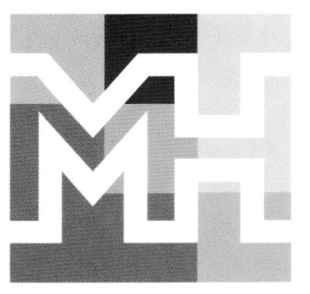

3.

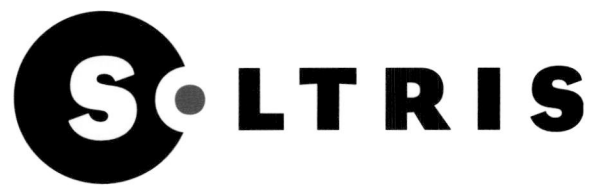

4.

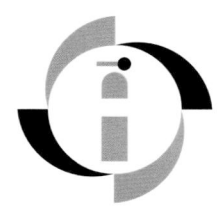

5.

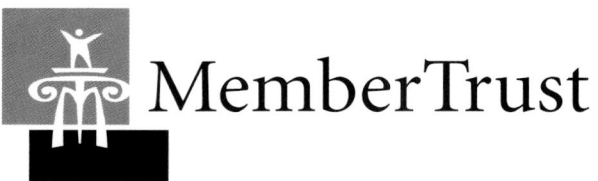

6.

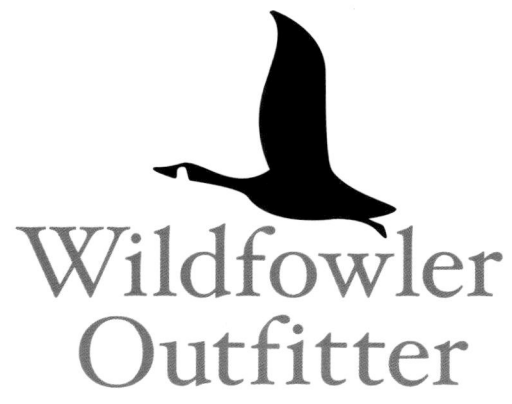

7.

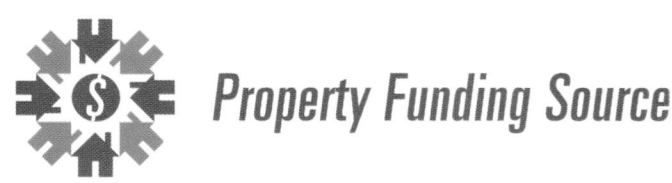

8.

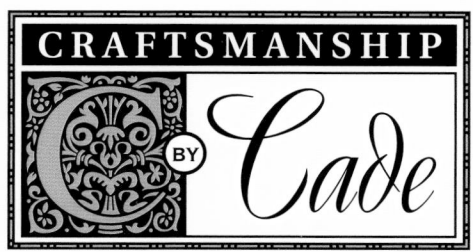

9.

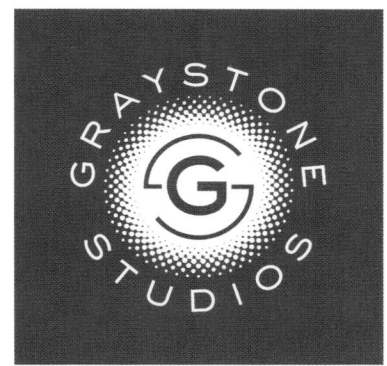

10.

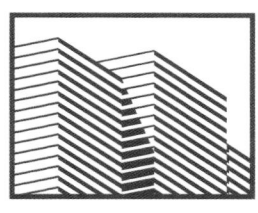

1300

HIGHLAND

CORPORATE DRIVE

11.

12.

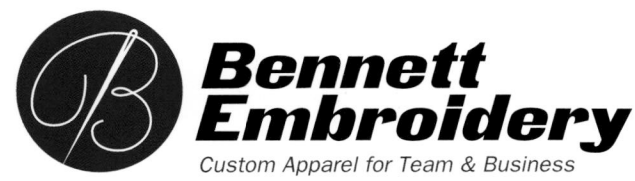

Custom Apparel for Team & Business

13.

14.

FIXEL

DIGITAL COLOR +

IMAGE MANIPULATION

15.

1 - 9
Design Firm **Design Center, Inc.**
10 - 15
Design Firm **Creative Vision Design Co.**

1.
Client — *Fissure*
Designer — Chris Cornejo
2.
Client — *Judd Allen Group*
Designer — Cory Docken
3.
Client — *Mohagen Hansen Architectural Group*
Designers — Sherwin Schwartzrock, Cory Docken
4.
Client — *Soltris*
Designer — Cory Docken
5.
Client — *Integrated Fire Protection*
Designer — Cory Docken
6.
Client — *MemberTrust*
Designer — Sherwin Schwartzrock

7.
Client — *WildFowler Outfitter*
Designer — Chris Cornejo
8.
Client — *Property Funding Source*
Designer — Cory Docken
9.
Client — *Cade Moore Carpentry*
Designer — Sherwin Schwartzrock
10.
Client — *Tracey Gear*
Designer — Greg Gonsalves
11.
Client — *Peregrine Group*
Designer — Greg Gonsalves
12.
Client — *Graystone Studios*
Designer — Greg Gonsalves
13.
Client — *Bennett Embroidery*
Designer — Greg Gonsalves
14.
Client — *S.J. Corio Company*
Designer — Greg Gonsalves
15.
Client — *Fixel*
Designer — Greg Gonsalves

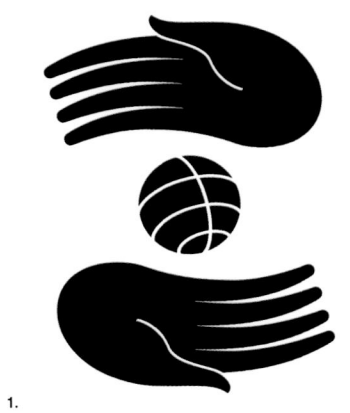

1.

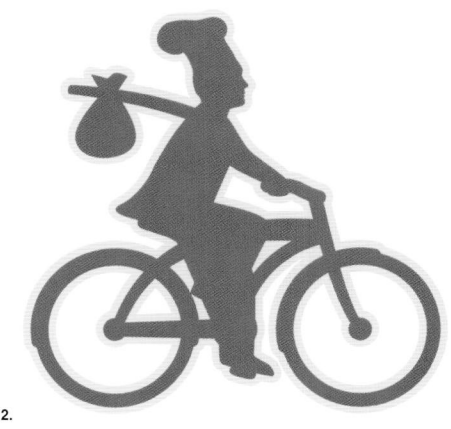

2.

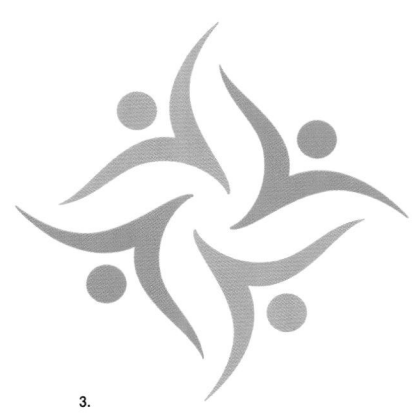

3.

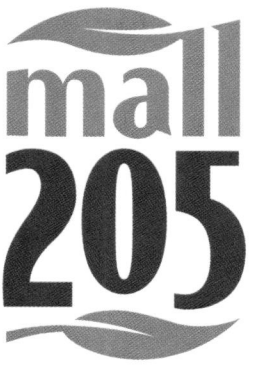

4.

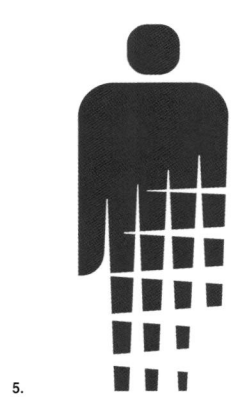

5.

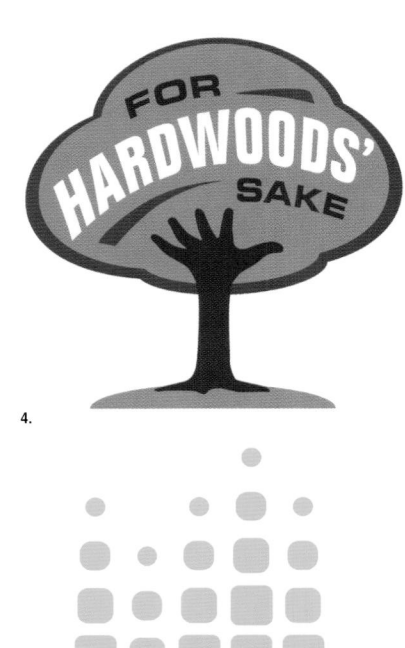

6.

mall 205

7.

1 - 7
Design Firm **Dotzero Design**
1.
   Client   *ALS Association*
   Designers Jon Wippich, Karen Wippich
2.
   Client   *Peddler Bakery*
   Designers Jon Wippich, Karen Wippich
3.
   Client   *National Psoriasis Foundation*
   Designers Jon Wippich, Karen Wippich
4.
   Client   *Healthy Forest*
   Designers Jon Wippich, Karen Wippich
5, 6.
   Client   *Unicru*
   Designers Jon Wippich, Karen Wippich

7.
   Client   *Davis Agency/Mall 205*
   Designers Jon Wippich, Karen Wippich
(opposite)
   Client   Schick Wilkinson Sword
   Design Firm **Muts&Joy&Design**
   Designer   Gisele Sangiovanni

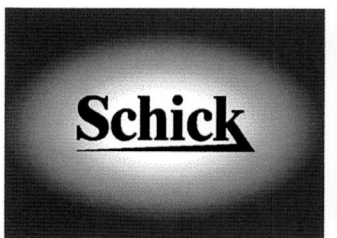
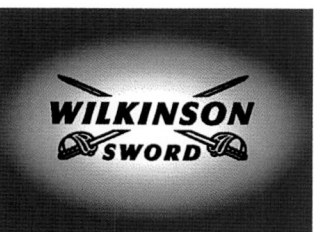

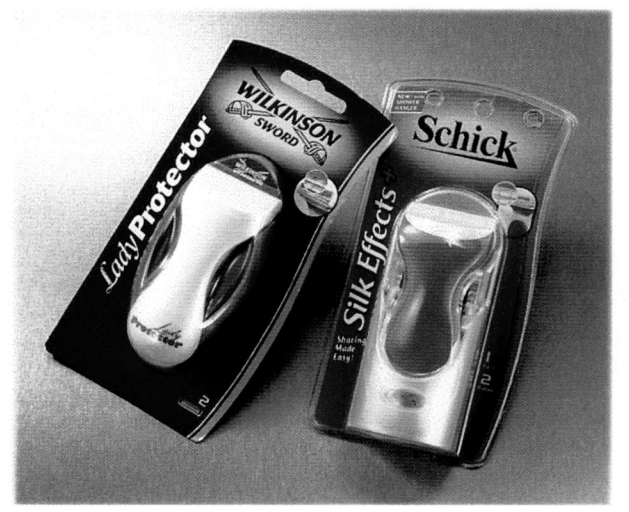

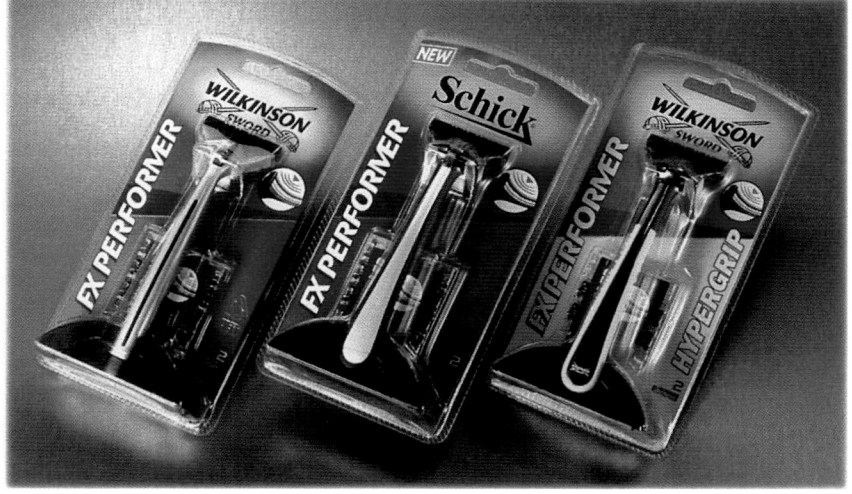

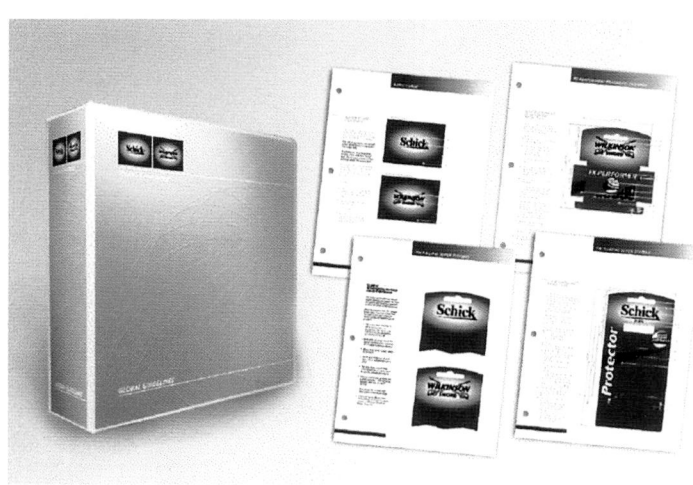

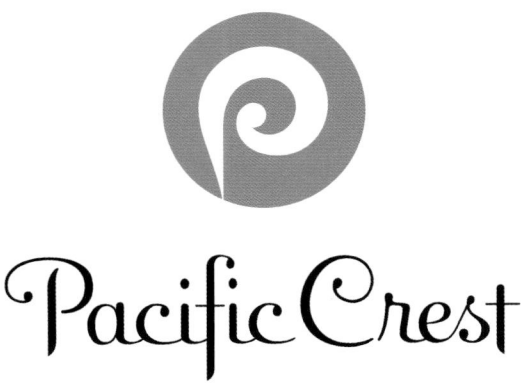

1.

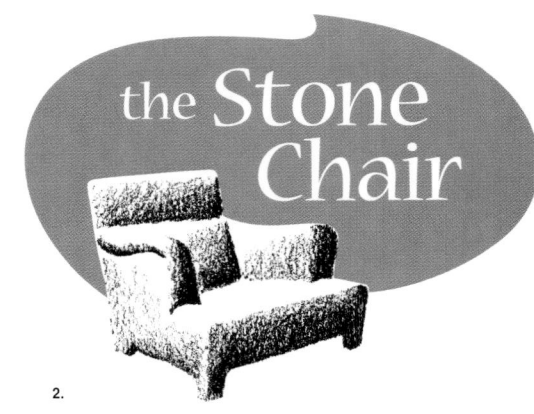

2.

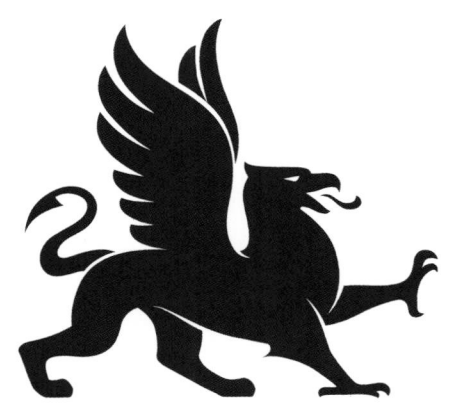

3.

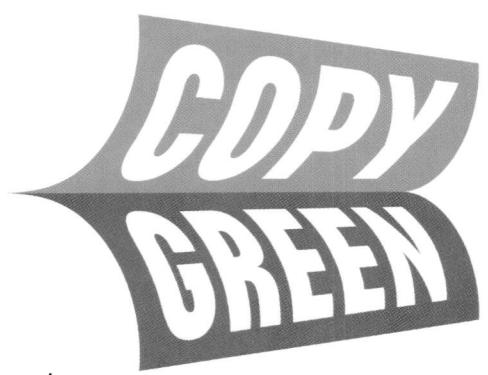

4.

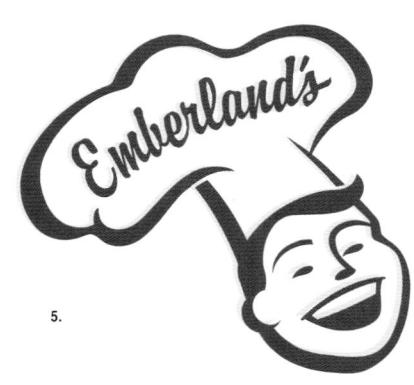

5.

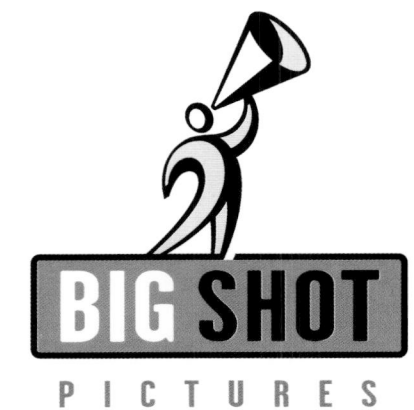

6.

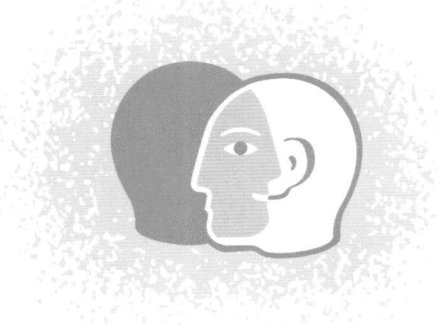

7.

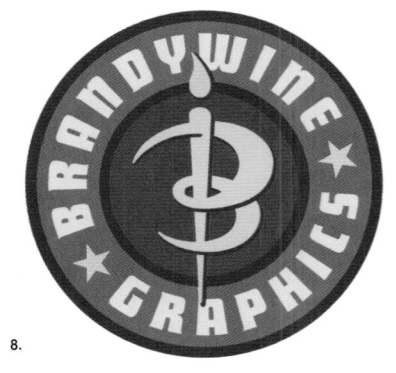

8.

9.

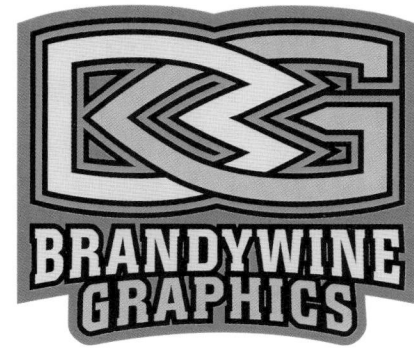

10.

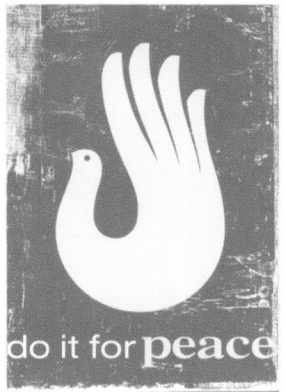

11.

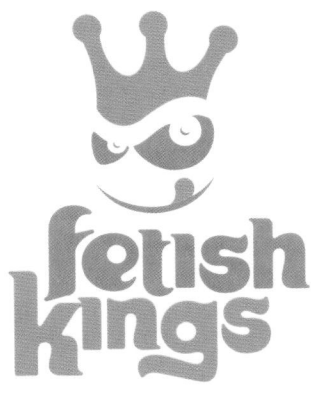

12.

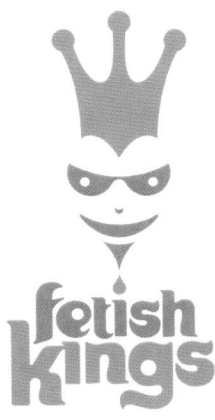

13.

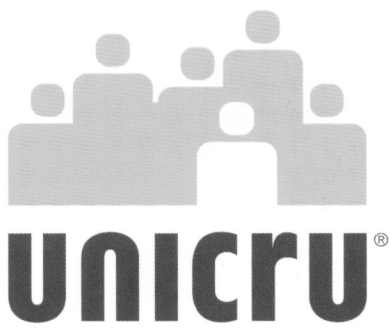

14.

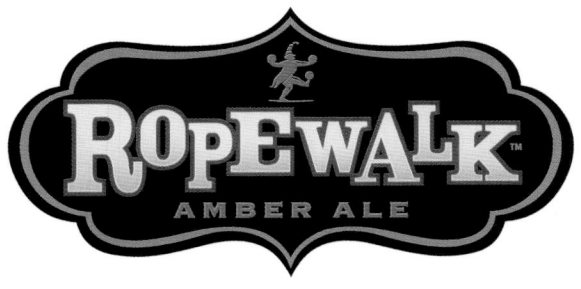

15.

1.

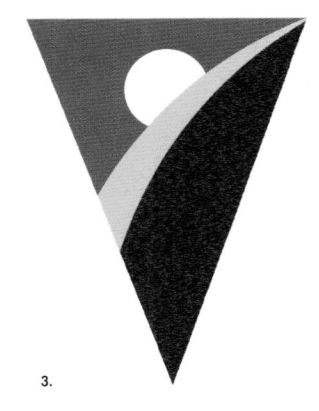

2.

3.

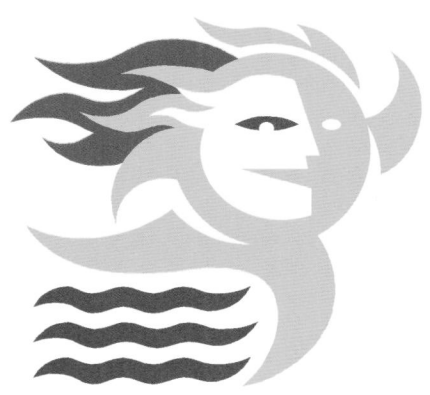

4.

5.

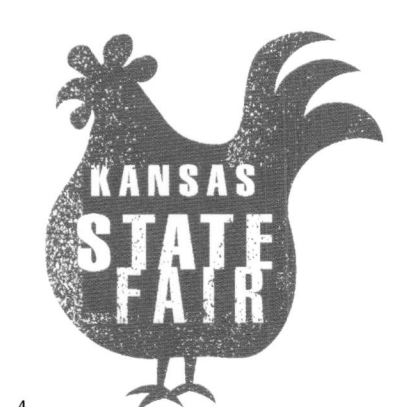

6.

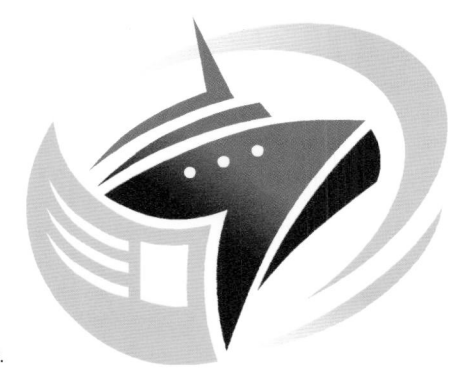

7.

1 - 7
Design Firm **Greteman Group**
1.
Client   *Boise Towne Square*
Designers   Sonia Greteman, James Strange,
              Craig Tomson
2.
Client   *Oak Creek Mall*
Designers   Sonia Greteman, James Strange,
              Craig Tomson
3.
Client   *Verus Bank*
Designers   Sonia Greteman, James Strange
4.
Client   *Kansas State Fair*
Designers   Sonia Greteman, James Strange,
              Craig Tomson
5.
Client   *Butler College*
Designers   Sonia Greteman, James Strange

6.
Client   *Cruise Mailing Services*
Designers   Sonia Greteman, James Strange
7.
Client   *Wichita Festivals*
Designers   James Strange, Sonia Greteman
(opposite)
Client   Banfi Vintners
Design Firm **Muts&Joy&Design**
Designers   Katherine Hames,
              Muts Yasumura

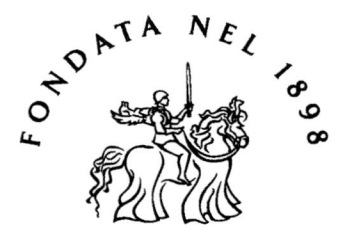

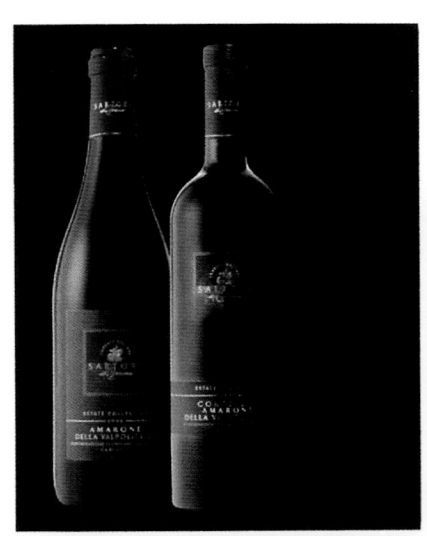

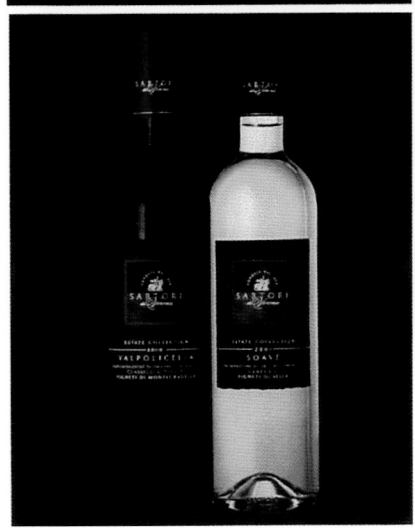

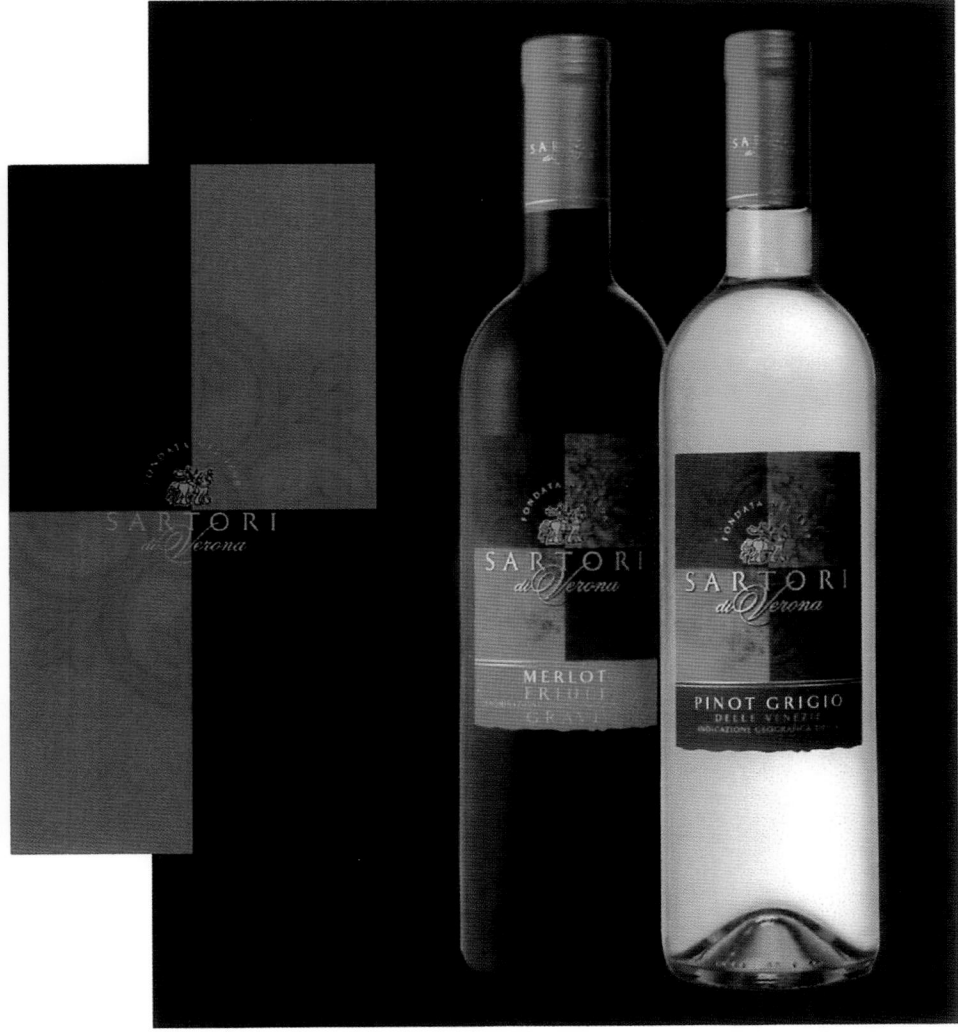

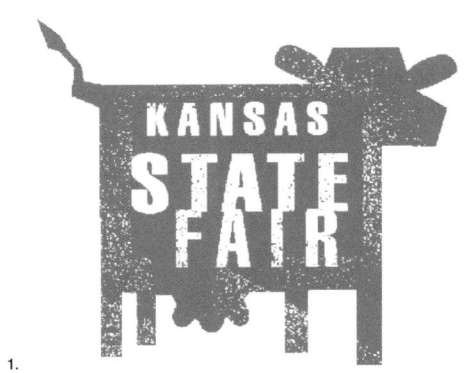

1.

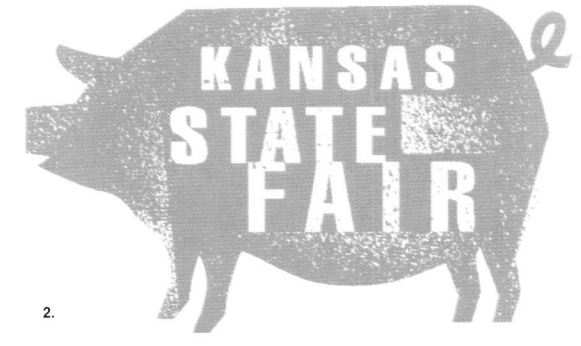

2.

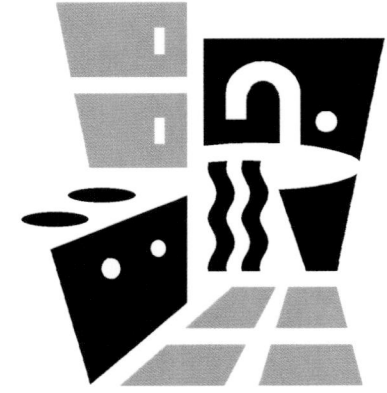

3.

4.

5.

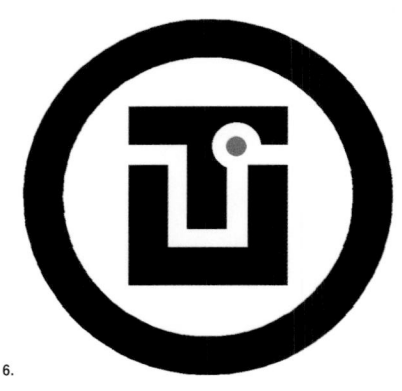

6.

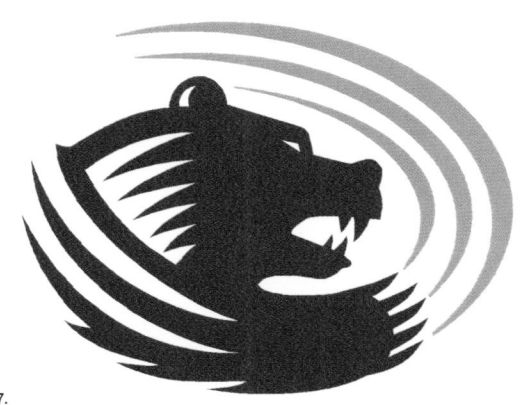

7.

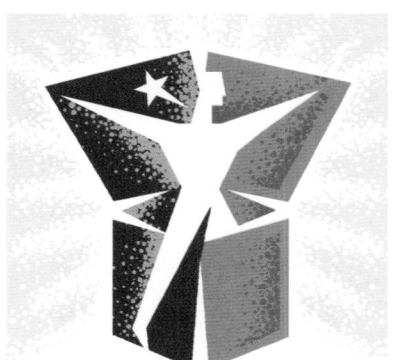

8.

9.

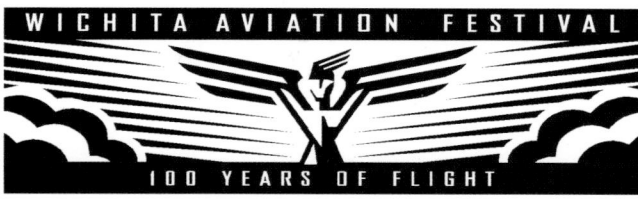

10.

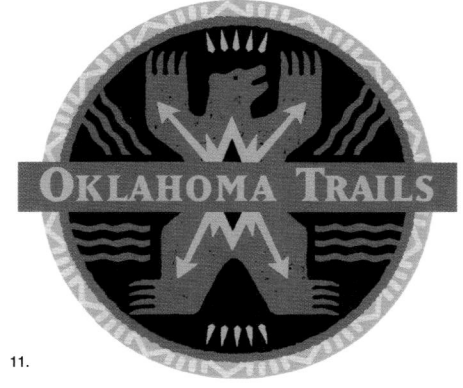

11.

12.

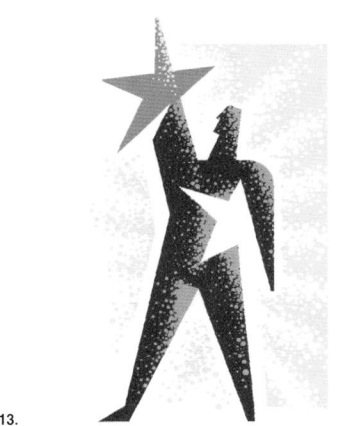

13.

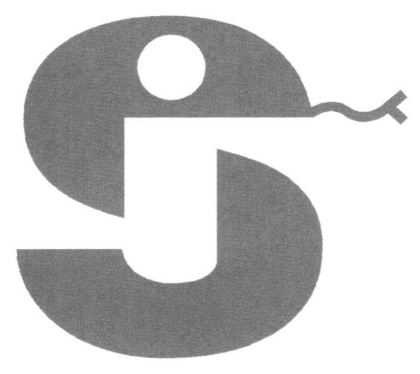

14.

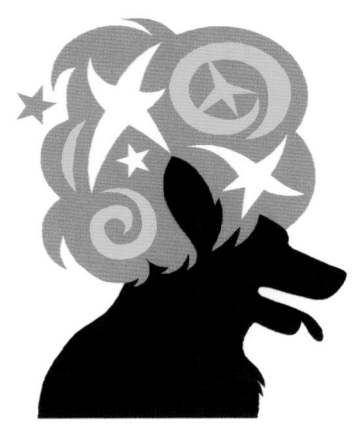

15.

1 - 15
Design Firm **Greteman Group**

1, 2.
Client   *Kansas State Fair*
Designers   Sonia Greteman, James Strange

3.
Client   *Kitchen & Bath Gallery*
Designers   Sonia Greteman, James Strange

4.
Client   *Royal Caribbean Cruises Ltd.*
Designers   Sonia Greteman, James Strange

5.
Client   *Galichia Heart Hospital*
Designers   Sonia Greteman, James Strange

6.
Designers   James Strange

7.
Client   *Butler College Grizzlies*
Designers   Sonia Greteman, James Strange

8.
Client   *Out of the Box*
Designers   Sonia Greteman, James Strange

9.
Client   *Kansas Turnpike Authority*
Designers   Sonia Greteman, James Strange

10.
Client   *Wichita Aviation Festival*
Designers   Sonia Greteman, James Strange

11.
Client   *Oklahoma City Zoo*
Designers   Sonia Greteman, James Strange

12.
Client   *Botanica*
Designers   Sonia Greteman, James Strange

13.
Client   *Above and Beyond*
Designers   Sonia Greteman, James Strange

14.
Client   *Strange Ideas*
Designers   James Strange

15.
Client   *Kansas Humane Society*
Designers   Sonia Greteman, James Strange

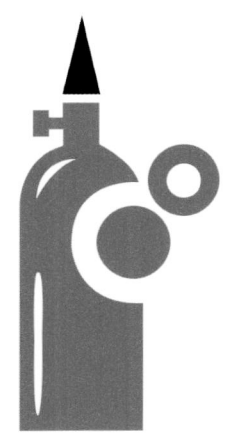

1.

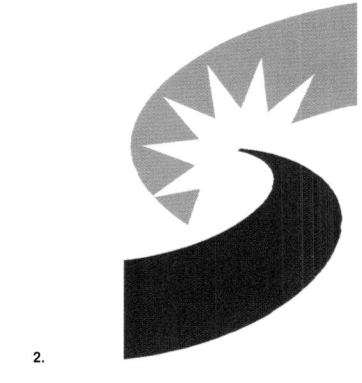

2.

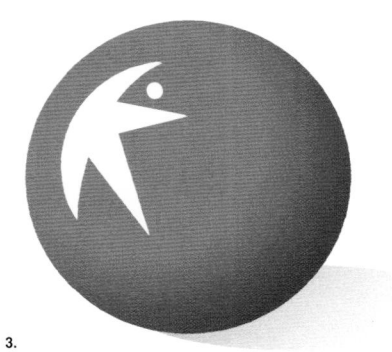

3.

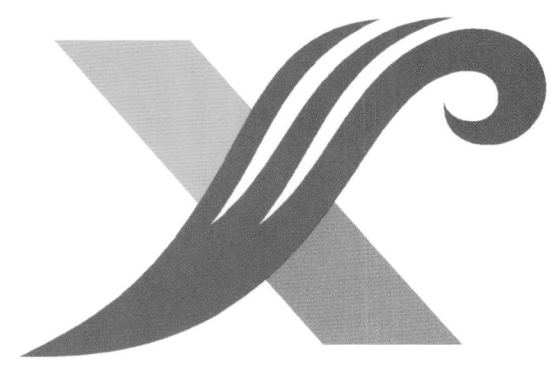

4.

5.

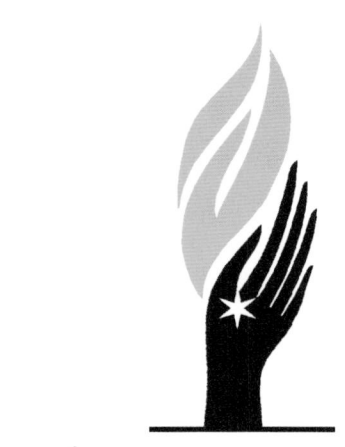

6.

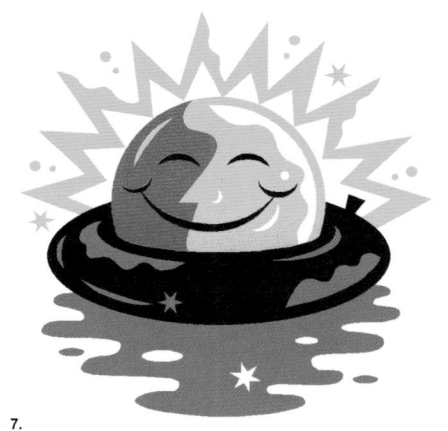

7.

1 - 7
Design Firm **Greteman Group**

1.
Client   *O2 Design*
Designers   Sonia Greteman, James Strange

2.
Client   *Shawnee Mission Hospital*
Designers   Sonia Greteman, James Strange

3.
Client   *Kansas Children's Service League*
Designers   Sonia Greteman, James Strange

4.
Client   *SeaXpress*
Designers   Sonia Greteman, James Strange

5.
Client   *Greteman Group*
Designers   Sonia Greteman, James Strange

6.
Client   *Inspiring Leadership*
Designers   Sonia Greteman, James Strange

7.
Client   *Wichita Festivals*
Designers   Sonia Greteman, James Strange

(opposite)
Client   *Symphony Importers LLC*
Design Firm **Muts&Joy&Design**
Designers   Katherine Hames, Tom Delaney,
              Gisele Sangiovanni

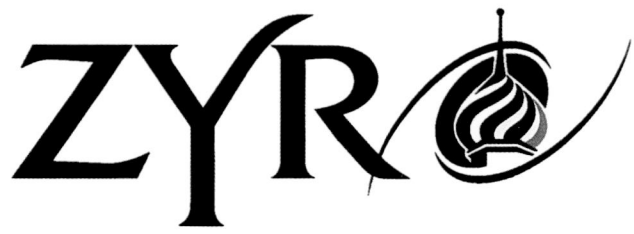

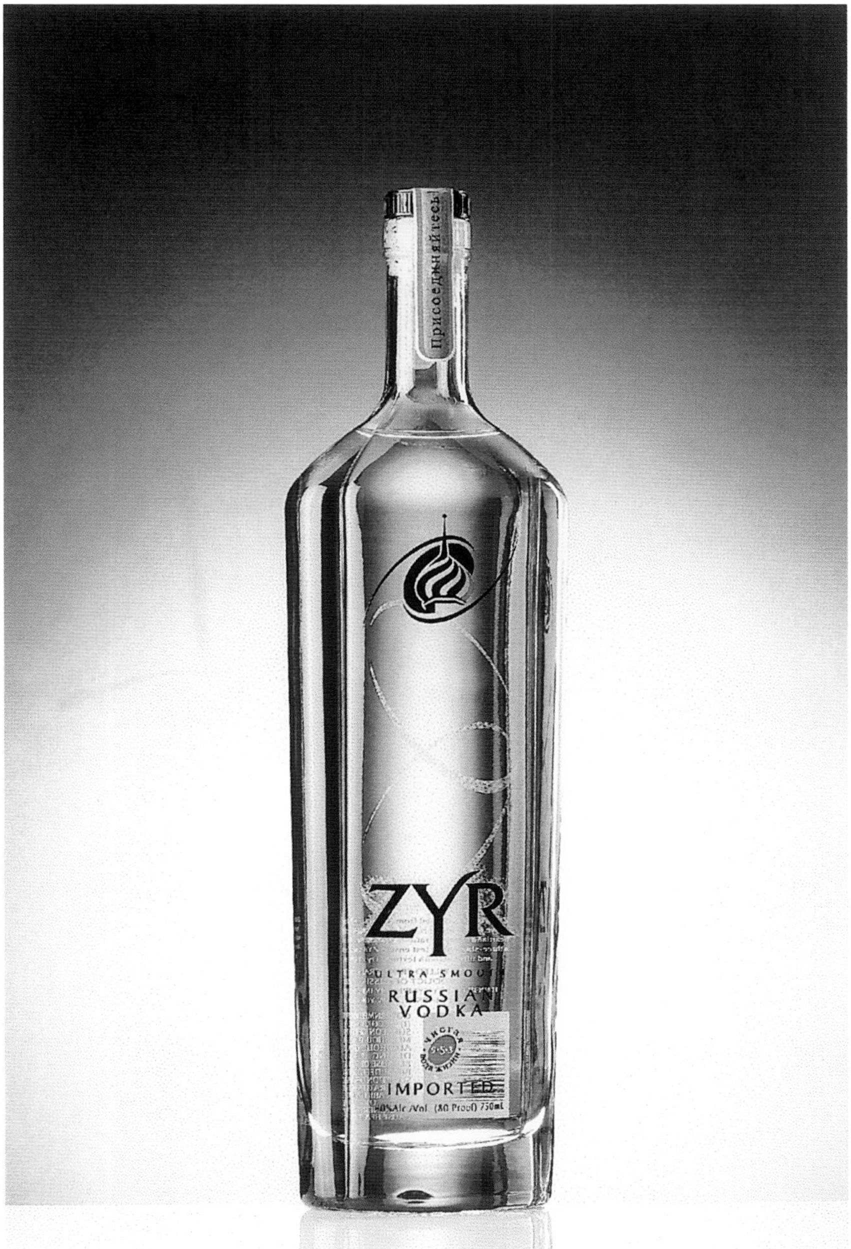

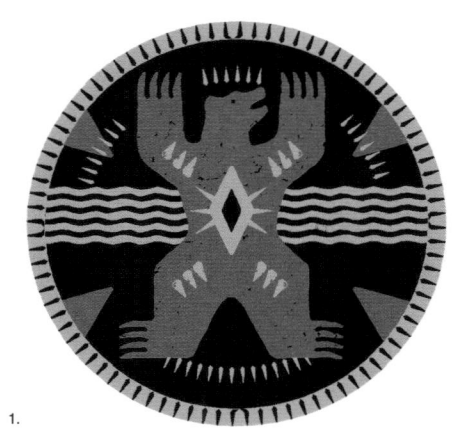

1.

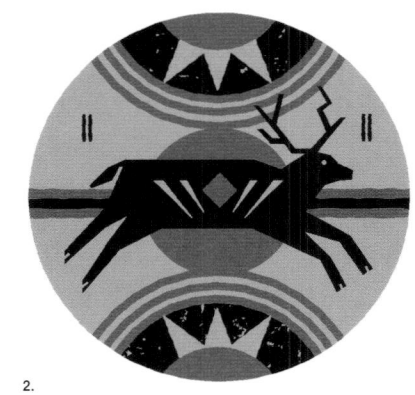

2.

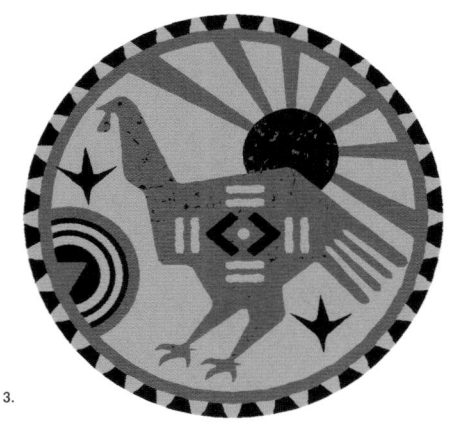

3.

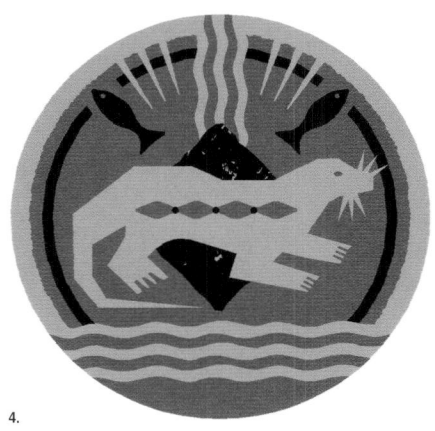

4.

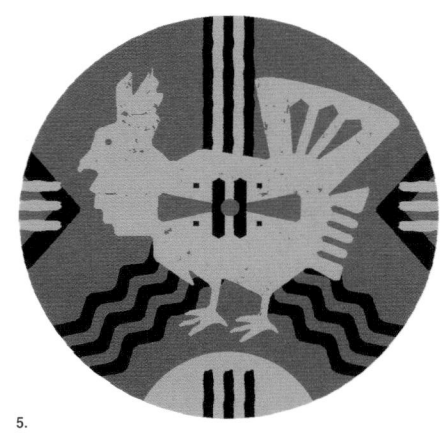

5.

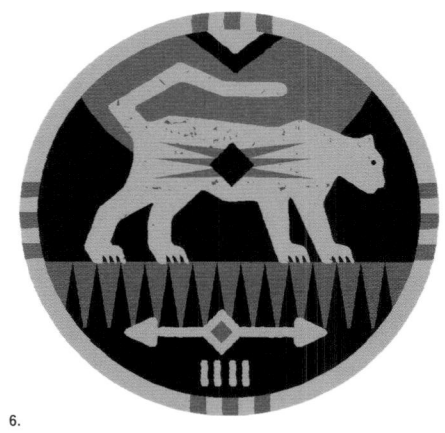

6.

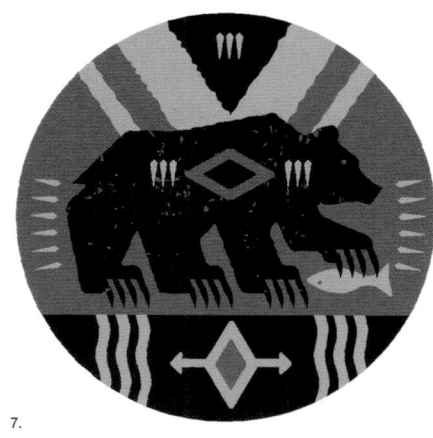

7.

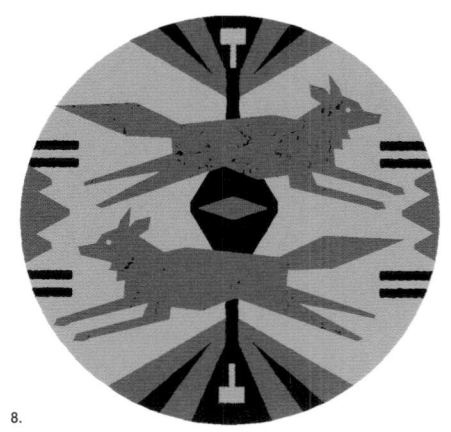

8.

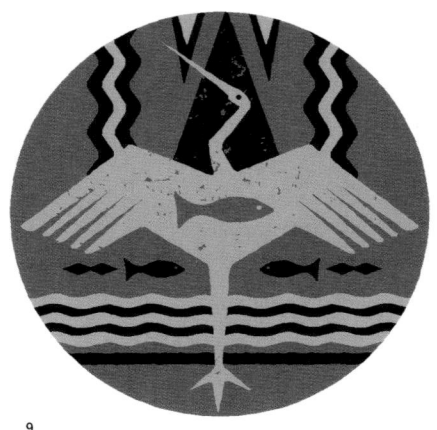

9.

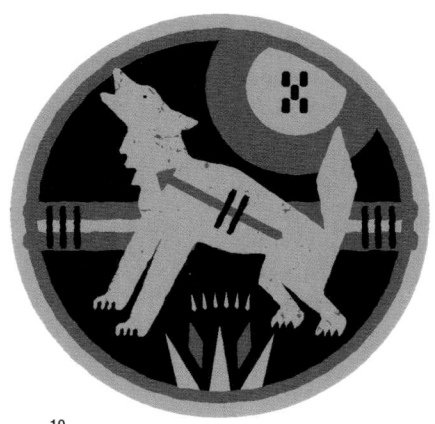

10.

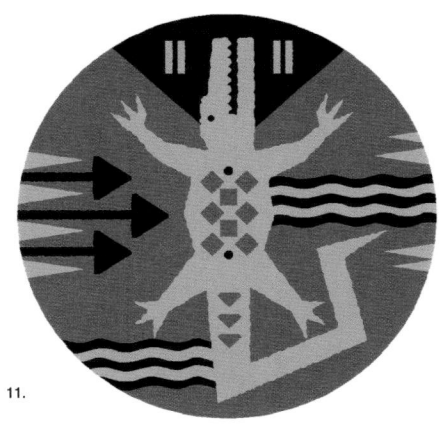

11.

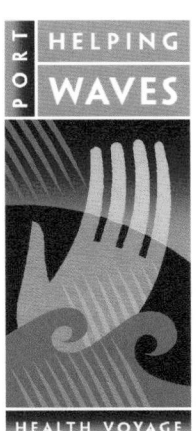

12.

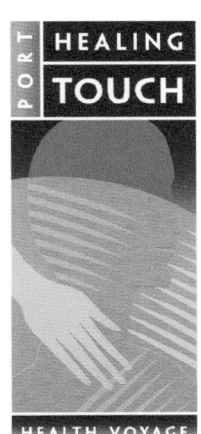

13.

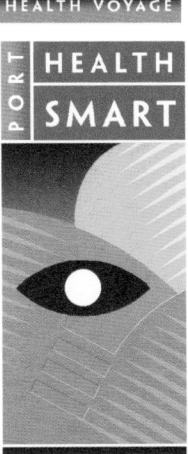

14.

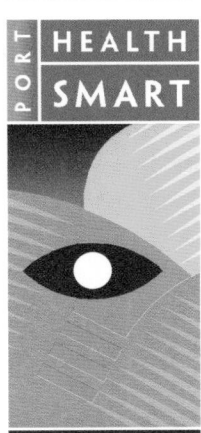

15.

1 - 15
Design Firm **Greteman Group**
1 - 11.
Client   *Oklahoma City Zoo*
Designers Sonia Greteman, James Strange
12 - 15.
Client   *Royal Caribbean Cruises Ltd.*
Designers Sonia Greteman, James Strange

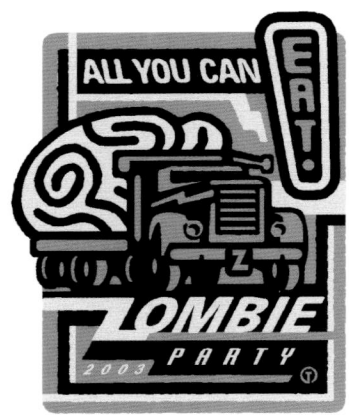

1.

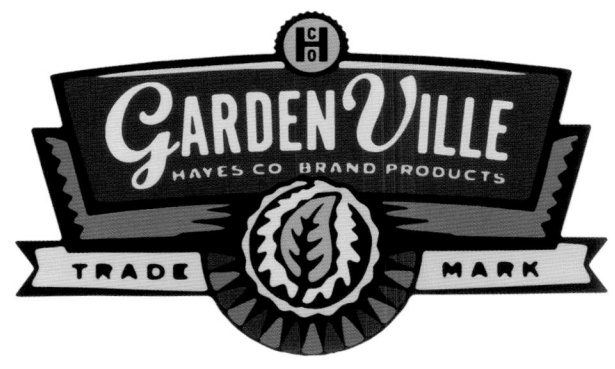

2.

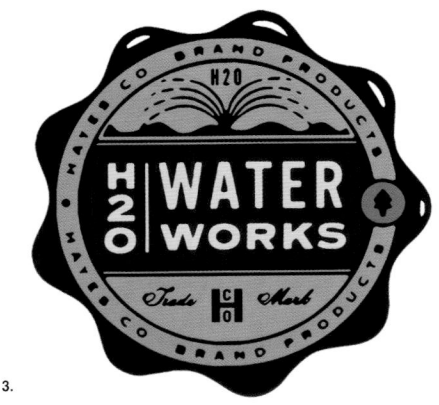

3.

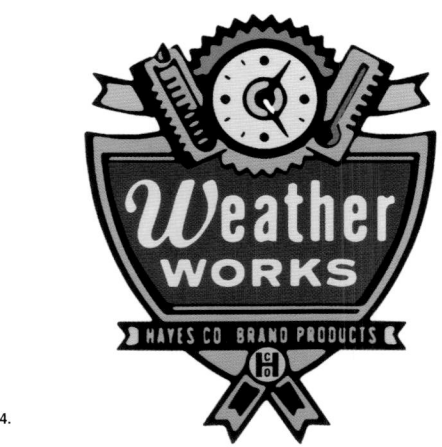

4.

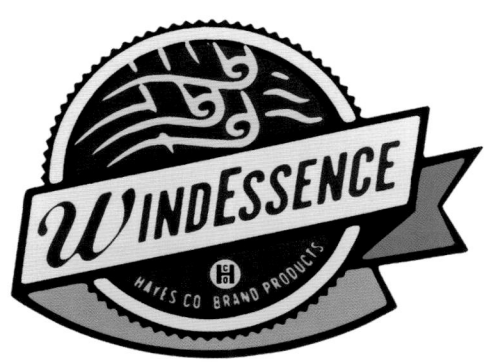

5.

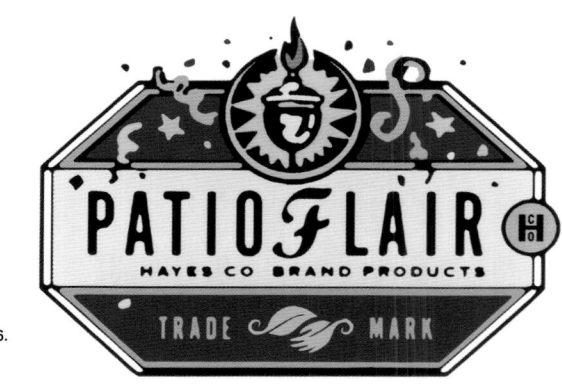

6.

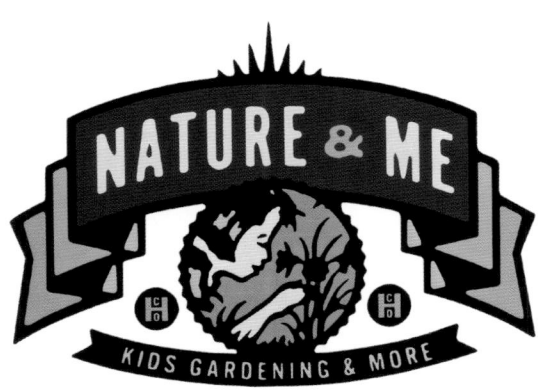

7.

1
  Design Firm **Greteman Group**
2 - 7
  Design Firm **Insight Design Communications**
1.
  Client   *James Strange*
  Designer   James Strange
2 - 7.
  Client   *The Hayes Co., Inc.*
  Designer   Tracy Holdeman

(opposite)
  Client   *Centro Cultural*
              E. León Jimenes
  Design Firm **Muts&Joy&Design**
  Designer   Katherine Hames

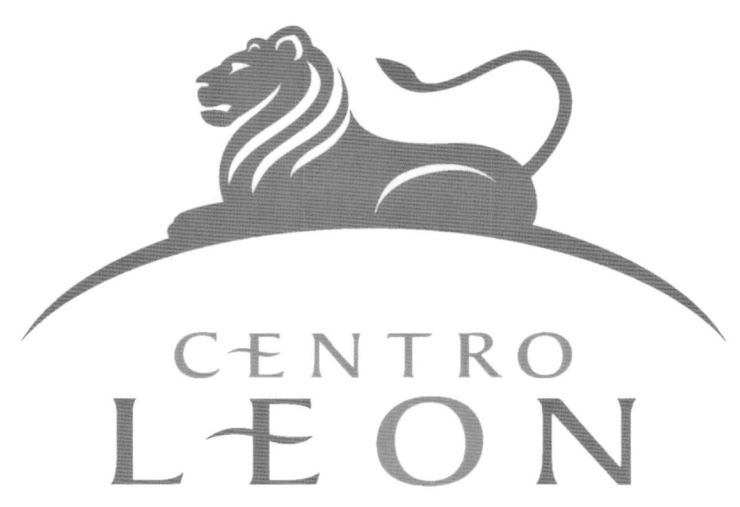

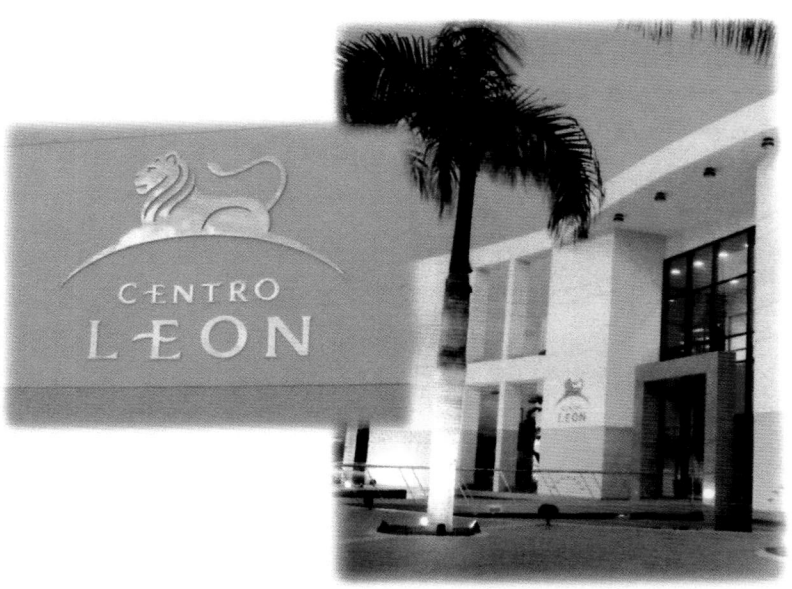

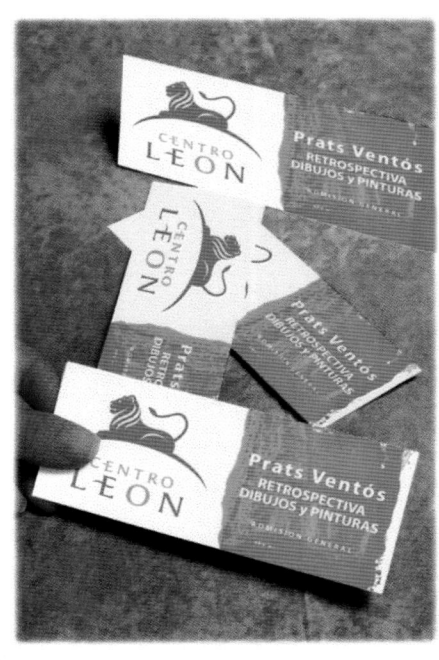

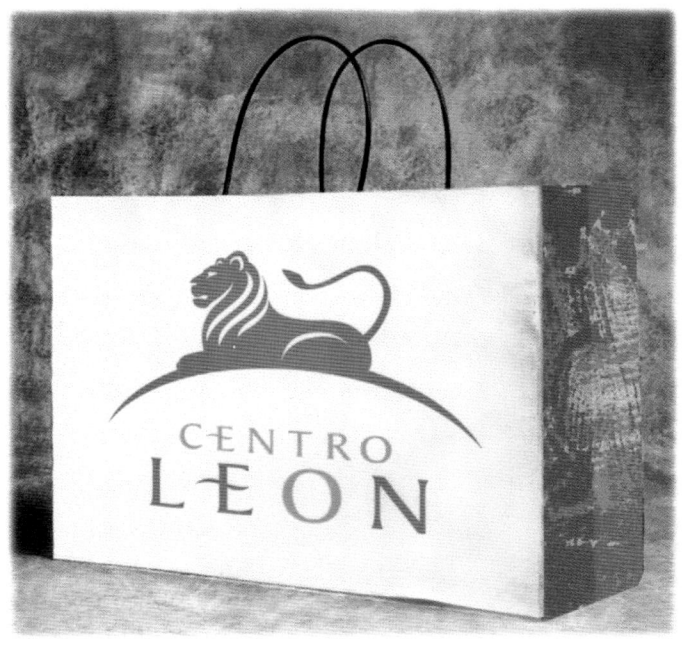

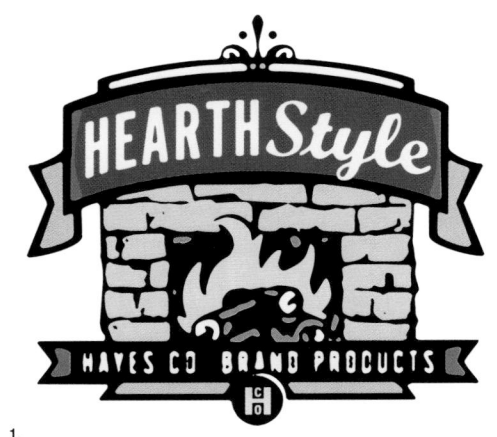

1.

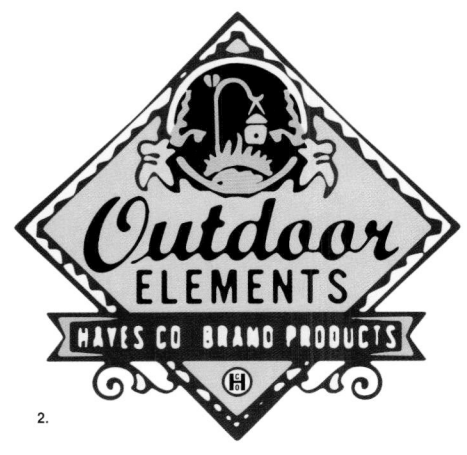

2.

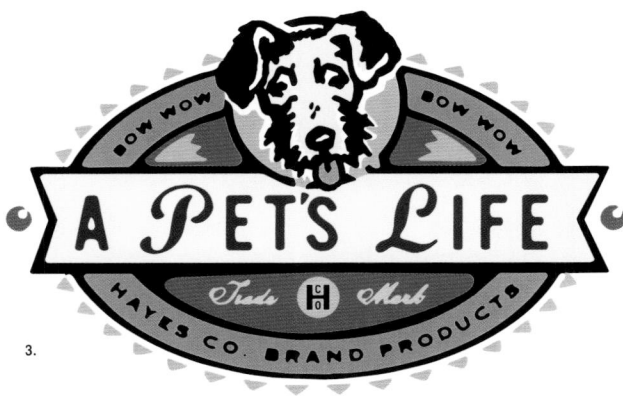

3.

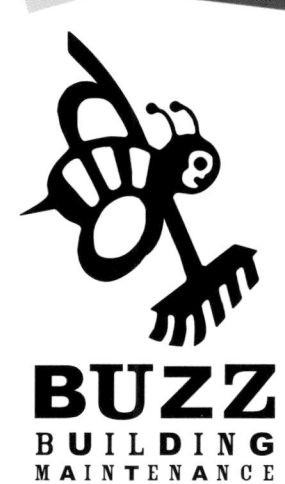

4.

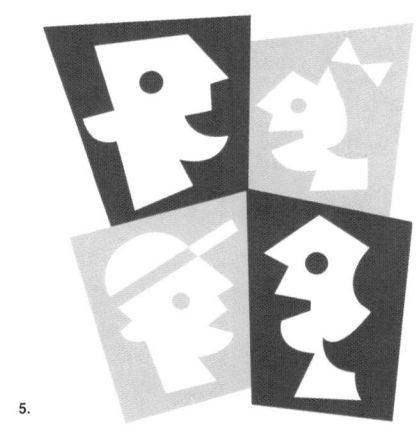

5.

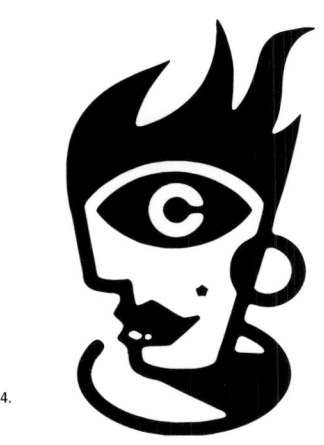

6.

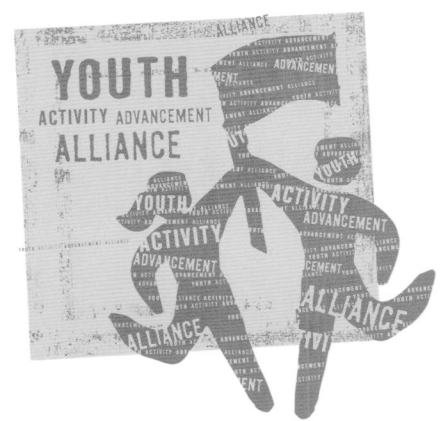

7.

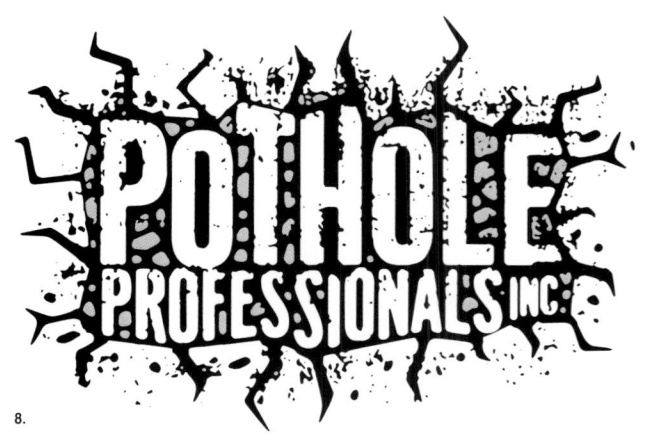

8.

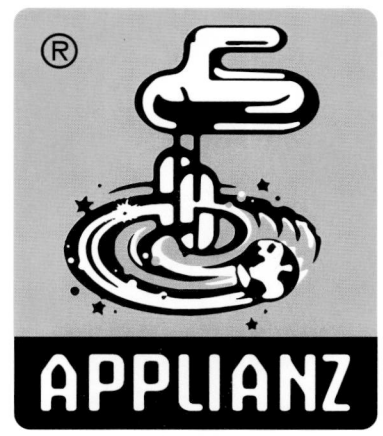

APPLIANZ

9.

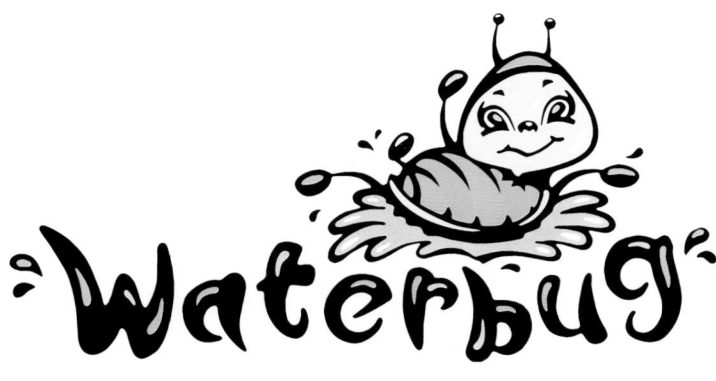

10.

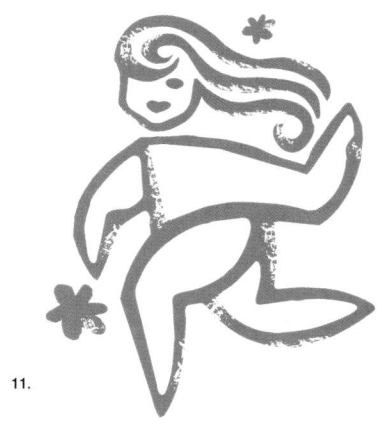

11.

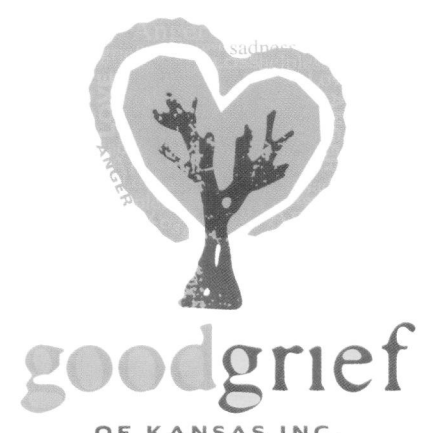

goodgrief
OF KANSAS INC.

12.

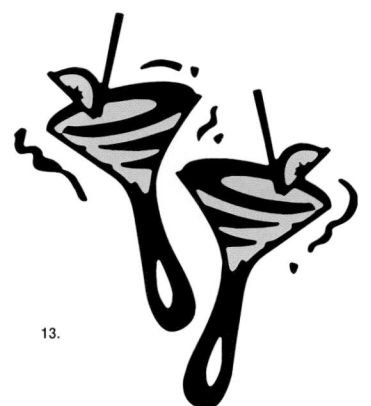

13.

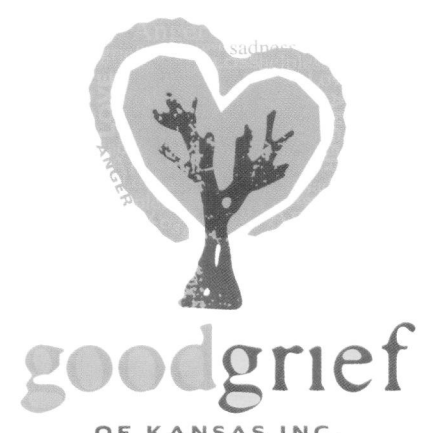

14.

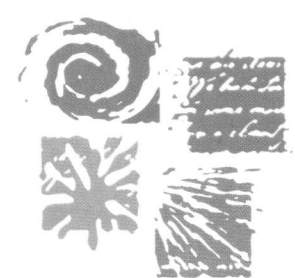

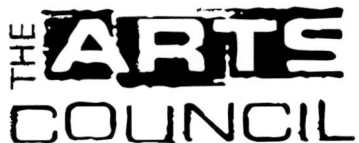

THE **ARTS** COUNCIL

15.

1 - 15		
Design Firm **Insight Design Communications**		
1 - 3.		
Client	*The Hayes Co., Inc.*	
Designer	Tracy Holdeman	
4.		
Client	*Cosmetic Cafe*	
Designer	Tracy Holdeman	
5.		
Client	*Family Matters*	
Designers	Tracy Holdeman,	
	Lea Carmichael	
6.		
Client	*YMCA*	
Designers	Tracy Holdeman,	
	Lea Carmichael	
7.		
Client	*Buzz Building Maintenance*	
Designers	Tracy Holdeman,	
	Lea Carmichael	
8.		
Client	*Pothole Professionals Inc.*	
Designer	Tracy Holdeman	

9.	
Client	*Applianz*
Designer	Tracy Holdeman
10.	
Client	*Floating Swimwear*
Designer	Tracy Holdeman
11.	
Client	*YWCA*
Designers	Tracy Holdeman,
	Lea Carmichael
12.	
Client	*Good Grief*
Designers	Tracy Holdeman,
	Lea Carmichael
13.	
Client	*Carlos O' Kelly's*
Designer	Tracy Holdeman
14.	
Client	*Marketplace Evangelism*
Designer	Tracy Holdeman
15.	
Client	*The Arts Council*
Designer	Tracy Holdeman

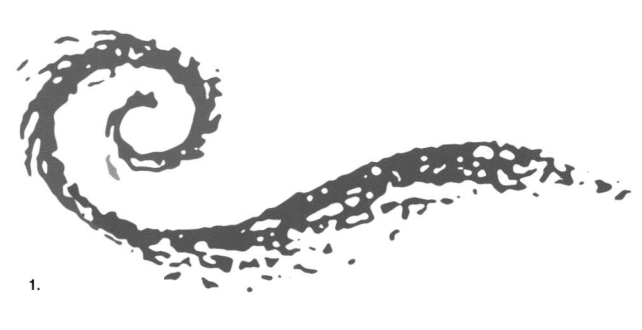

1.

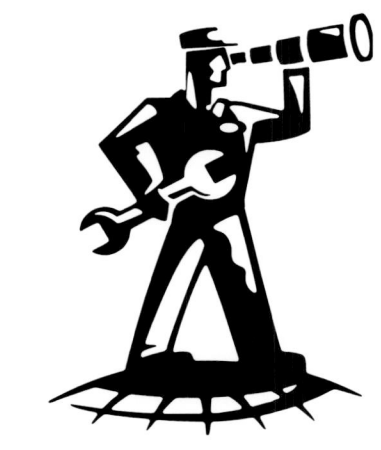

2.

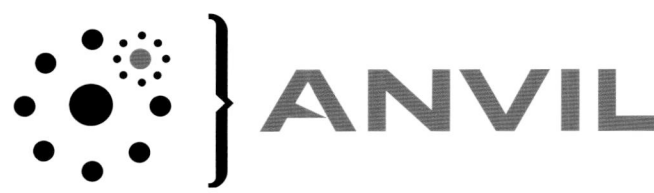

3.

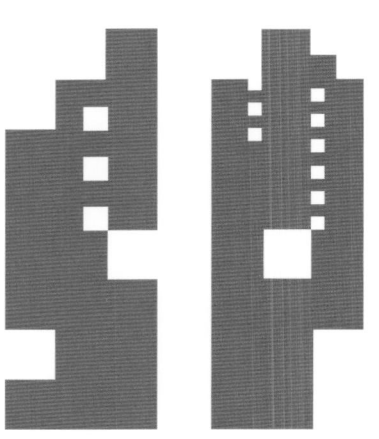

4.

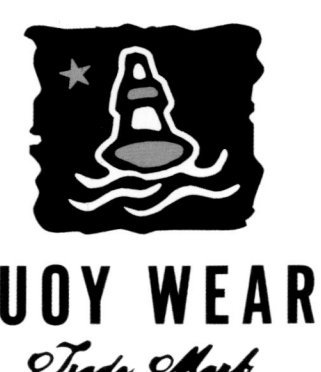

BUOY WEAR

Trade Mark

5.

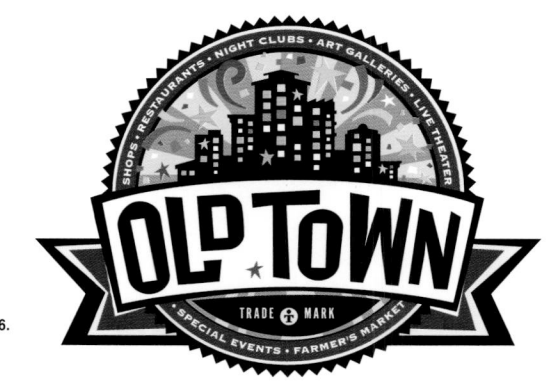

6.

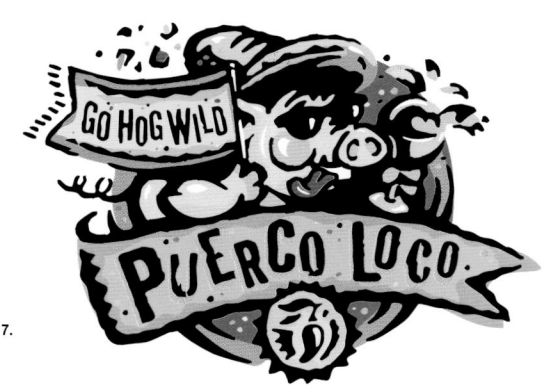

7.

1 - 7
Design Firm **Insight Design Communications**
1.
Client *Floating Swimwear*
Designer Tracy Holdeman
2.
Client *B.G. Automotive Products*
Designer Tracy Holdeman
3.
Client *Anvil Corporation*
Designer Tracy Holdeman
4.
Client *Spangenberg Phillips*
Designer Tracy Holdeman
5.
Client *Floating Swimwear*
Designers Tracy Holdeman, Lea Carmichael
6.
Client *Old Town*
Designer Tracy Holdeman
7.
Client *Carlos O' Kelly's*
Designer Tracy Holdeman

(opposite)
Client *Banco Del Progreso, S.A.*
Design Firm **Muts&Joy&Design**
Designer Gisele Sangiovanni

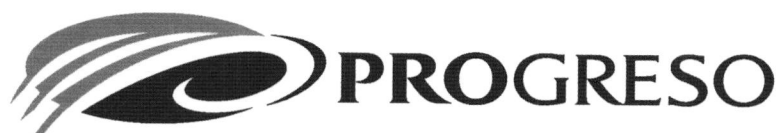

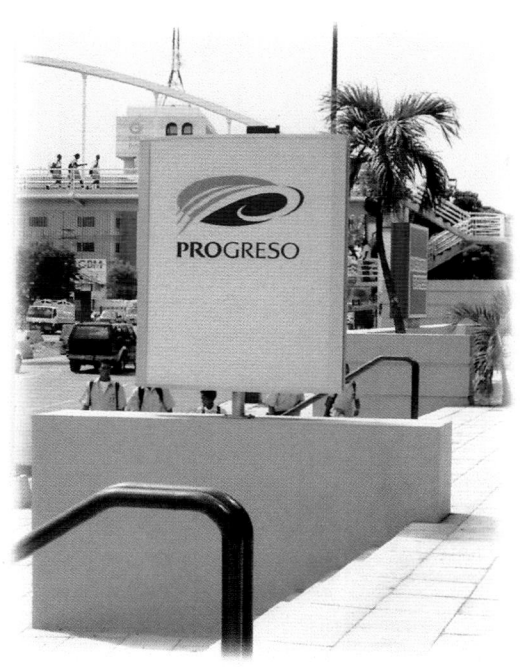

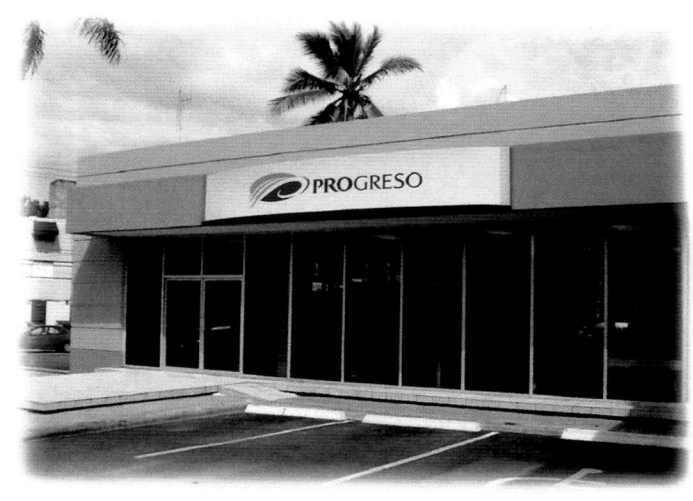

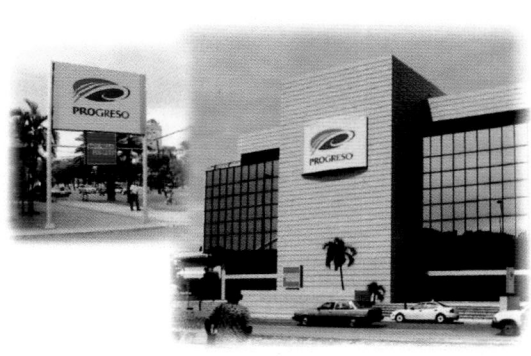

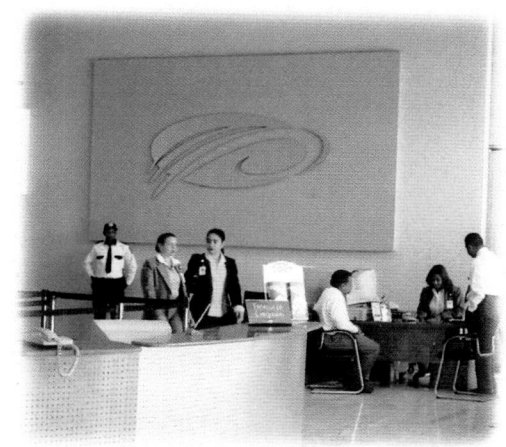

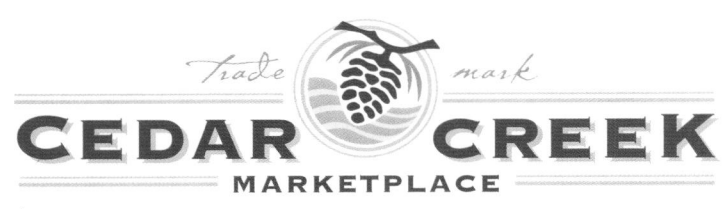

1.

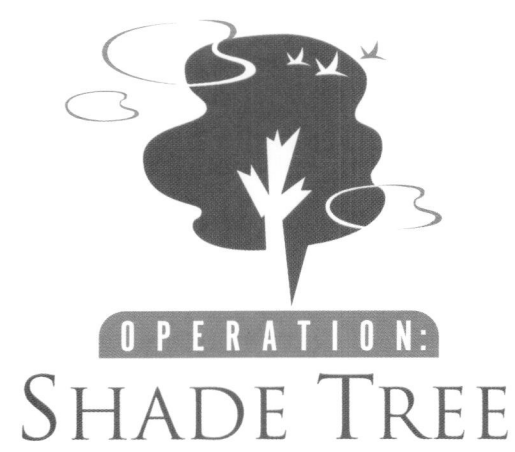

2.

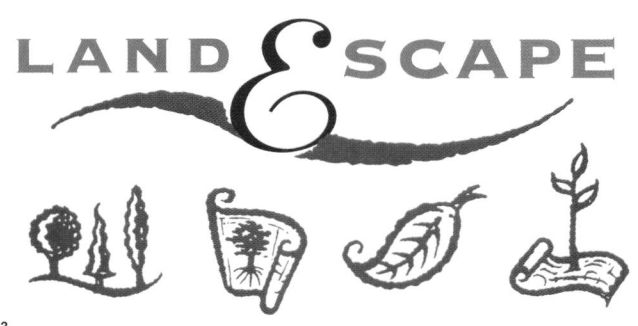

3.

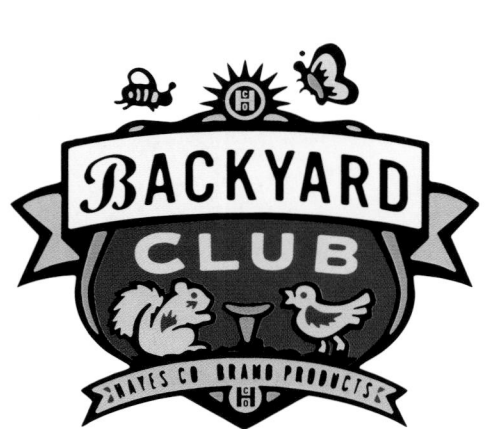

4.

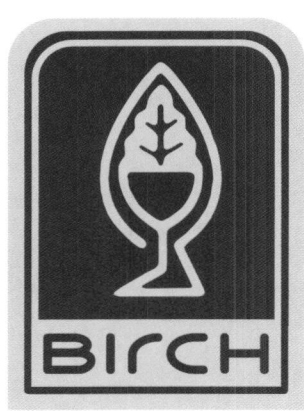

5.

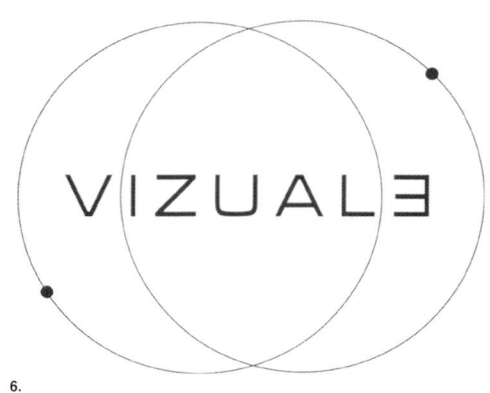

6.

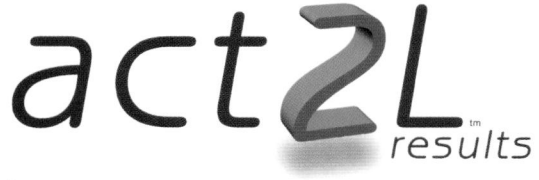

7.

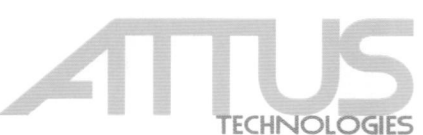

8.

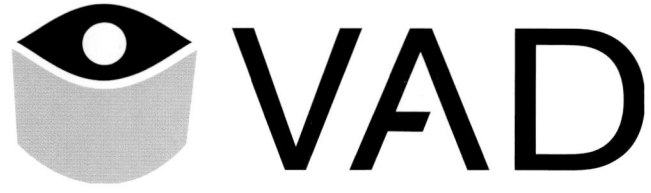

9.

futuretest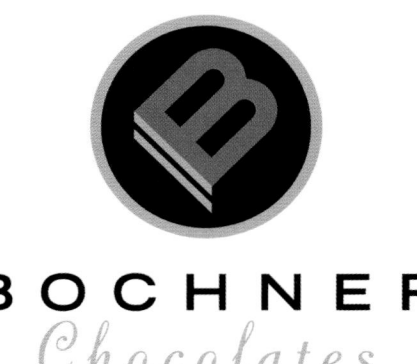

10.

COLLECTIVECAPACITY™

11.

BOCHNER
Chocolates

12.

no boundaries™

13.

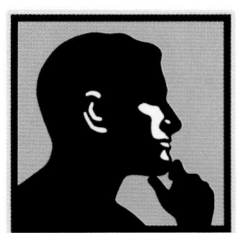

TALASKE
SOUND THINKING™

14.

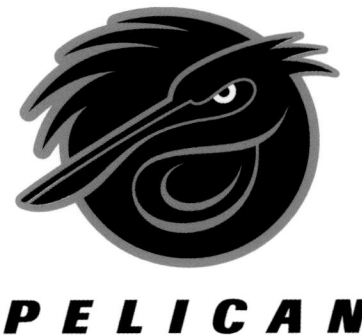

PELICAN

15.

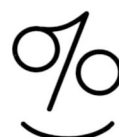

PAUL
WU
+
ASSOCIATES
chartered accountants

604,734,7750

1.

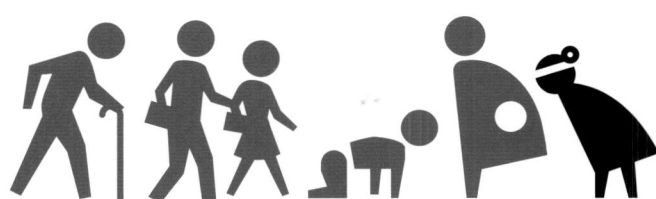

Dr. Winnie Su
FAMILY MEDICINE & OBSTETRICS

2.

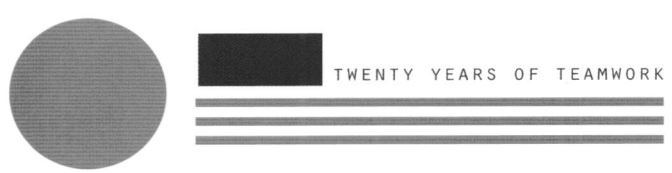

TWENTY YEARS OF TEAMWORK

3.

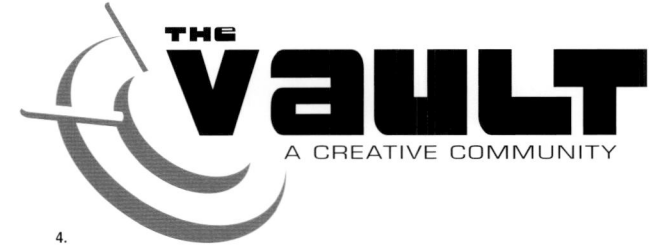

THE VAULT
A CREATIVE COMMUNITY

4.

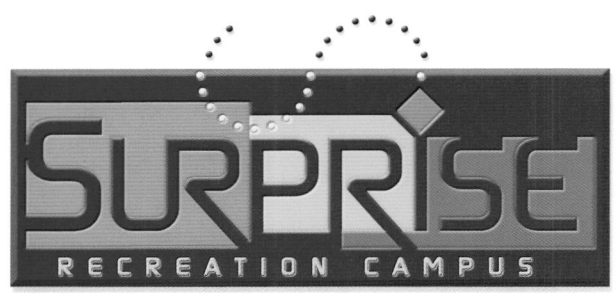

SURPRISE
RECREATION CAMPUS

5.

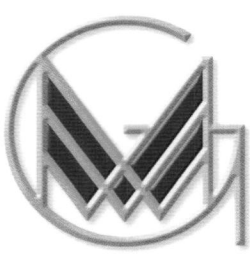

MOMENTUM GROUP

6.

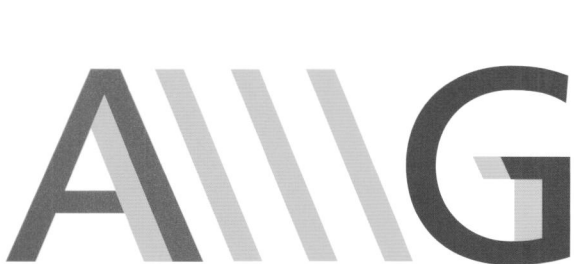

Associated Marketing Group

7.

1, 2
Design Firm **Nancy Wu Design**
3, 4
Design Firm **Iconix, Inc.**
5 - 7
Design Firm **Sullivan Marketing & Communications**
1.
Client   *Paul Wu & Associates Ltd.*
Designer   Nancy Wu
2.
Client   *Dr. Winnie Su, MD*
Designer   Nancy Wu
3.
Client   *GM/Toyota*
Designer   Paul Snyder
4.
Client   *Frenak Photo, Inc.*
Designer   Marina Savic
5.
Client   *City of Surprise AZ*
Designer   Jack Sullivan

6.
Client   *Momentum Group*
Designer   Jack Sullivan
7.
Client   *Associated Marketing Group*
Designer   Jack Sullivan
(opposite)
Client   *Fremont Bank*
Design Firm   **Shawver Associates, Inc.**
Designer   Amy Krachenfels

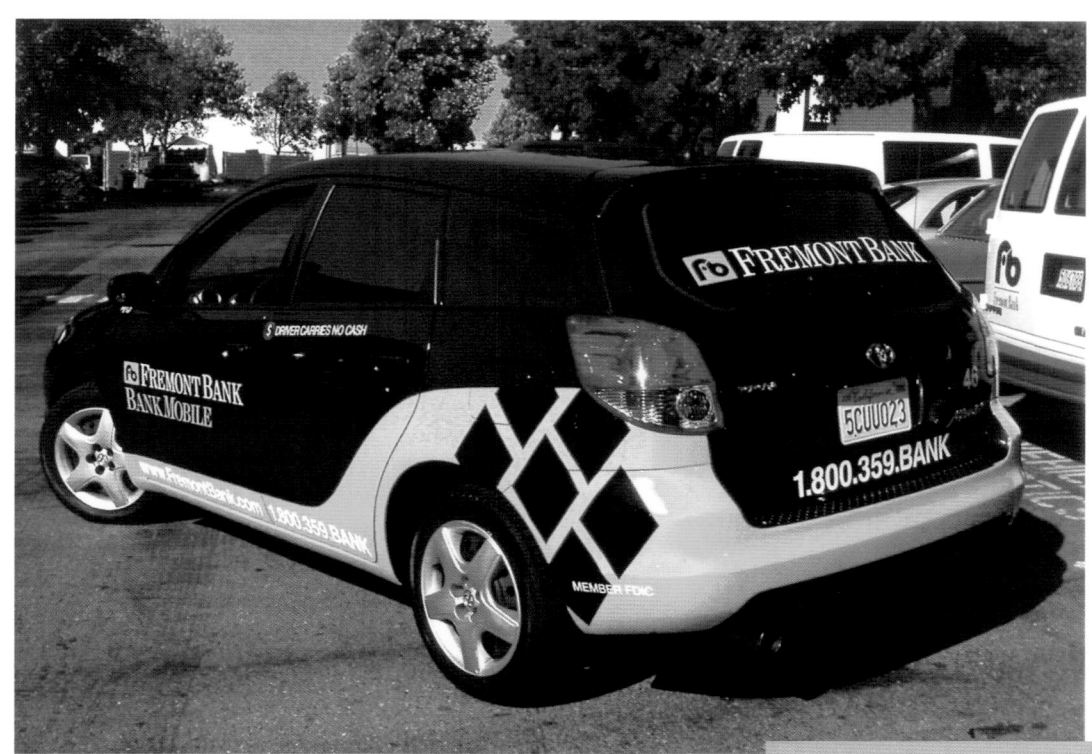

FREMONT BANK

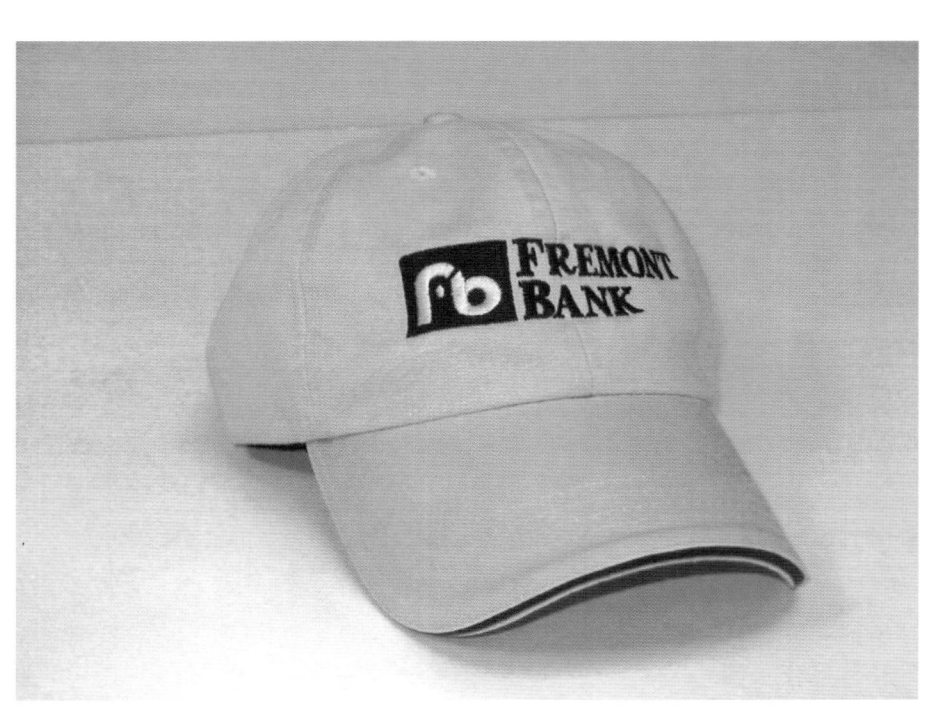

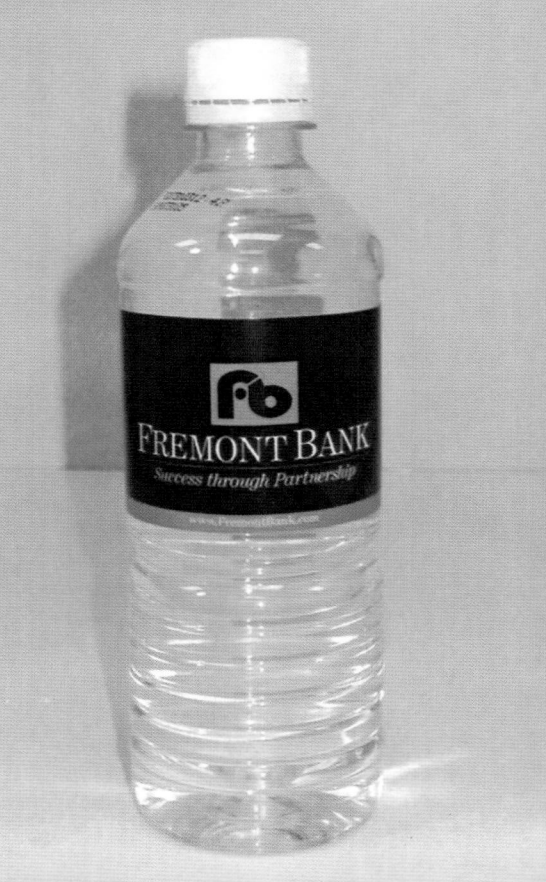

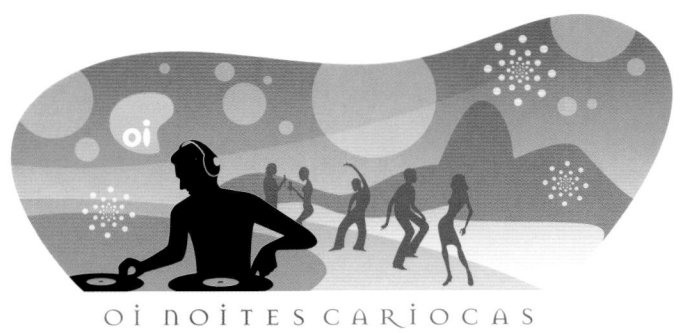

OI NOITES CARIOCAS

1.

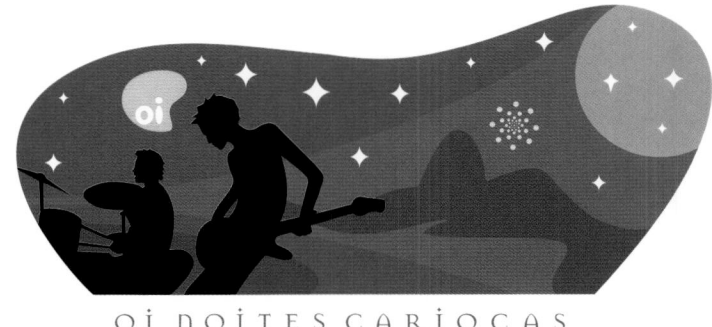

OI NOITES CARIOCAS

2.

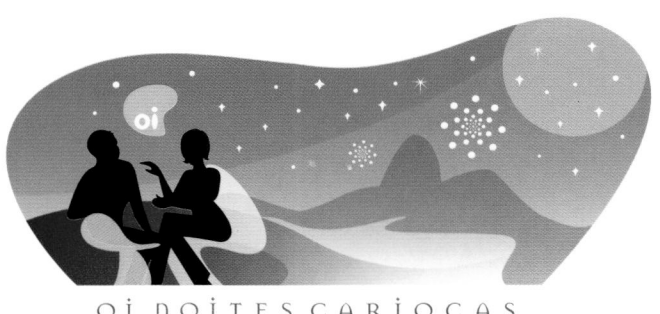

OI NOITES CARIOCAS

3.

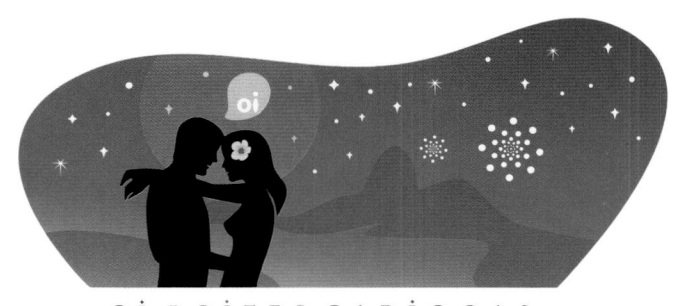

OI NOITES CARIOCAS

4.

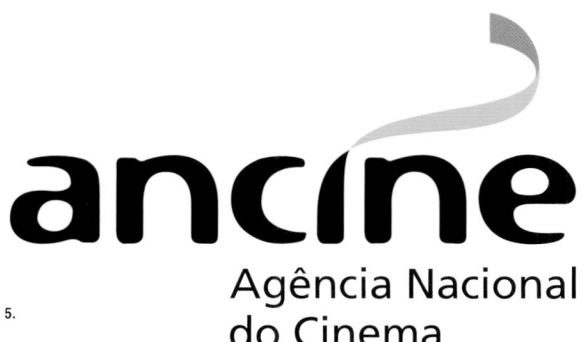

Agência Nacional
do Cinema

5.

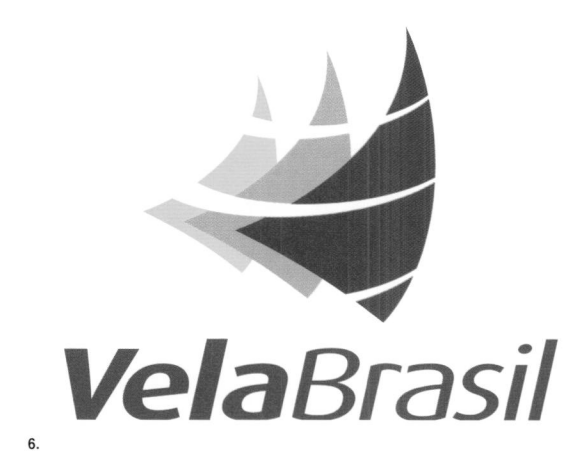

6.

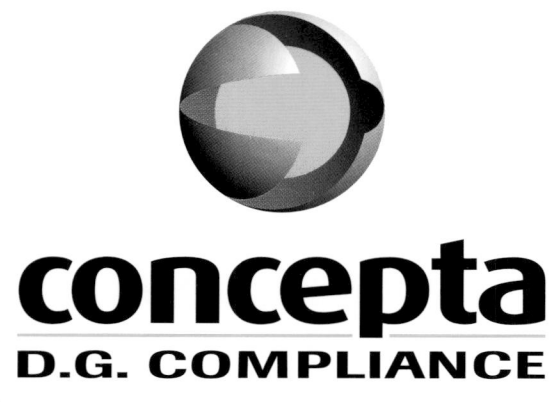

7.

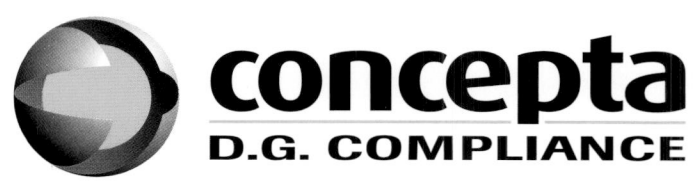

8.

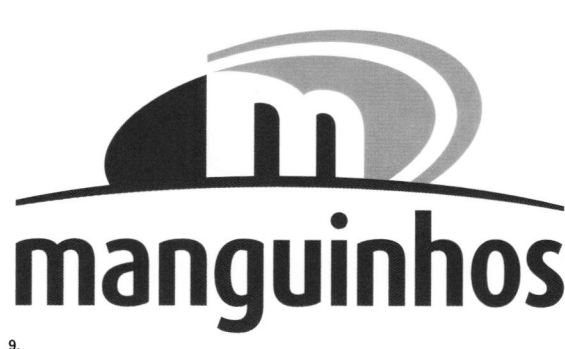

9.

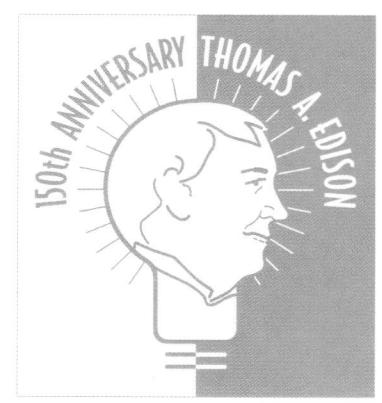

10.

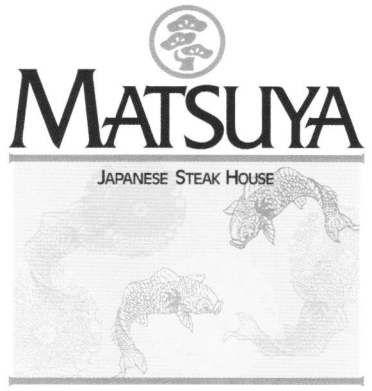

11.

12.

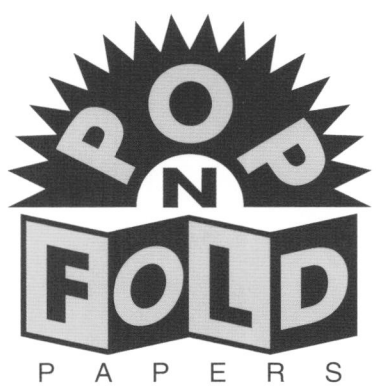

13.

STEPHEN LONGO   DESIGN ASSOCIATES

14.

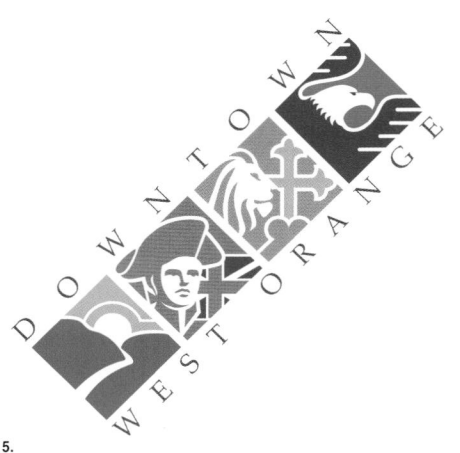

15.

1 - 5		
Design Firm	**Pandora**	
6 - 9		
Design Firm	**Animus Design**	
10 - 15		
Design Firm	**Stephen Longo + Associates**	
1 - 4.		
Client	*Oi Noites Cariocas*	
Designers	Silvia Grossmann,	
	Lauro Machado	
5.		
Client	*Ancine—National Cinema Agency*	
Designer	Silvia Grossmann	
6.		
Client	*Vela Brasil*	
Designers	Marcus Fernandes,	
	Rique Nitzche	
7, 8.		
Client	*Concepta*	
Designers	Marcus Fernandes,	
	Rique Nitzche	
9.		
Client	*Manguinhos*	
Designers	Aldo Moura,	
	Rique Nitzche	

10.		
Client	*U.S. Parks Service*	
Designer	Stephen Longo	
11.		
Client	*Matsuya Restaurant*	
Designer	Stephen Longo	
12.		
Client	*Nabisco*	
Designer	Stephen Longo	
13.		
Client	*Pop N' Fold Papers*	
Designer	Stephen Longo	
14.		
Client	*Stephen Longo*	
	Design Associates	
Designer	Stephen Longo	
15.		
Client	*Township of West Orange*	
Designer	Stephen Longo	

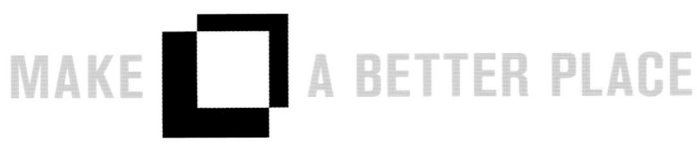

1.

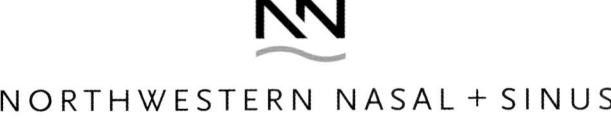

NORTHWESTERN NASAL + SINUS

2.

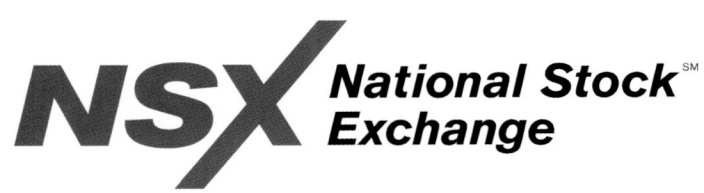

NSX National Stock^{SM} Exchange

3.

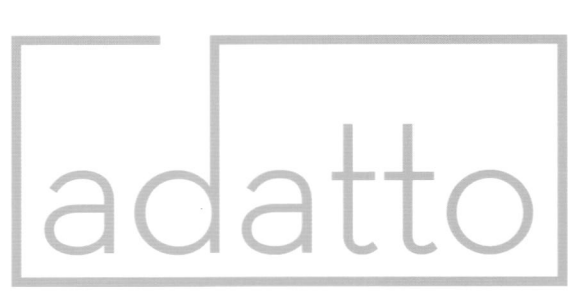

adatto

4.

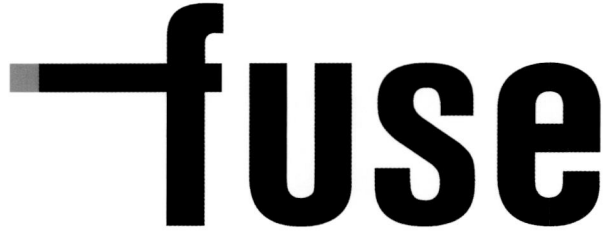

fuse

5.

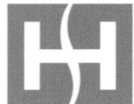 liquidlibrary

6.

HUBBARD
STREET
DANCE
CHICAGO

7.

1 - 7
Design Firm **Liska + Associates, Inc.**
1.
  Client   *Make A Better Place*
  Designer Fernando Munoz
2.
  Client   *Northwestern Nasal + Sinus*
  Designer Hans Krebs
3.
  Client   *National Stock Exchange*
  Designers Liska + Associates Staff
4.
  Client   *Adatto*
  Designer Jonathan Seeds
5.
  Client   *Fuse*
  Designer Brian Graziano

6.
  Client   *liquidlibrary*
  Designers Liska + Associates Staff
7.
  Client   *Hubbard Street Dance Chicago*
  Designer Steve Liska
(opposite)
  Client   St. John's University
  Design Firm **BrandLogic**
  Designers Wynn Medinger,
                 Karen Lukas Hardy

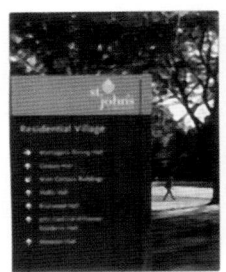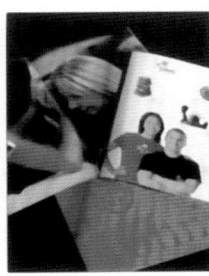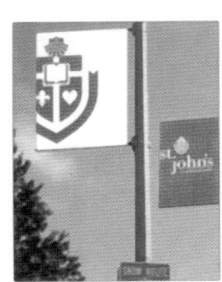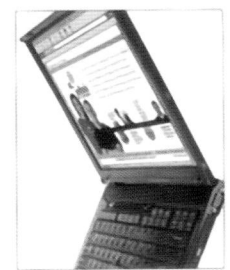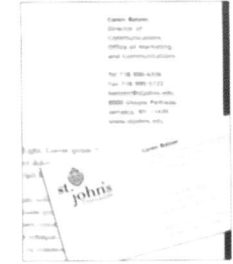

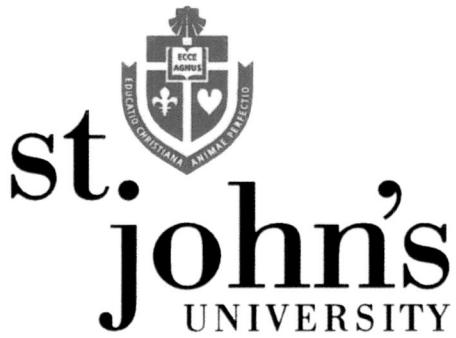

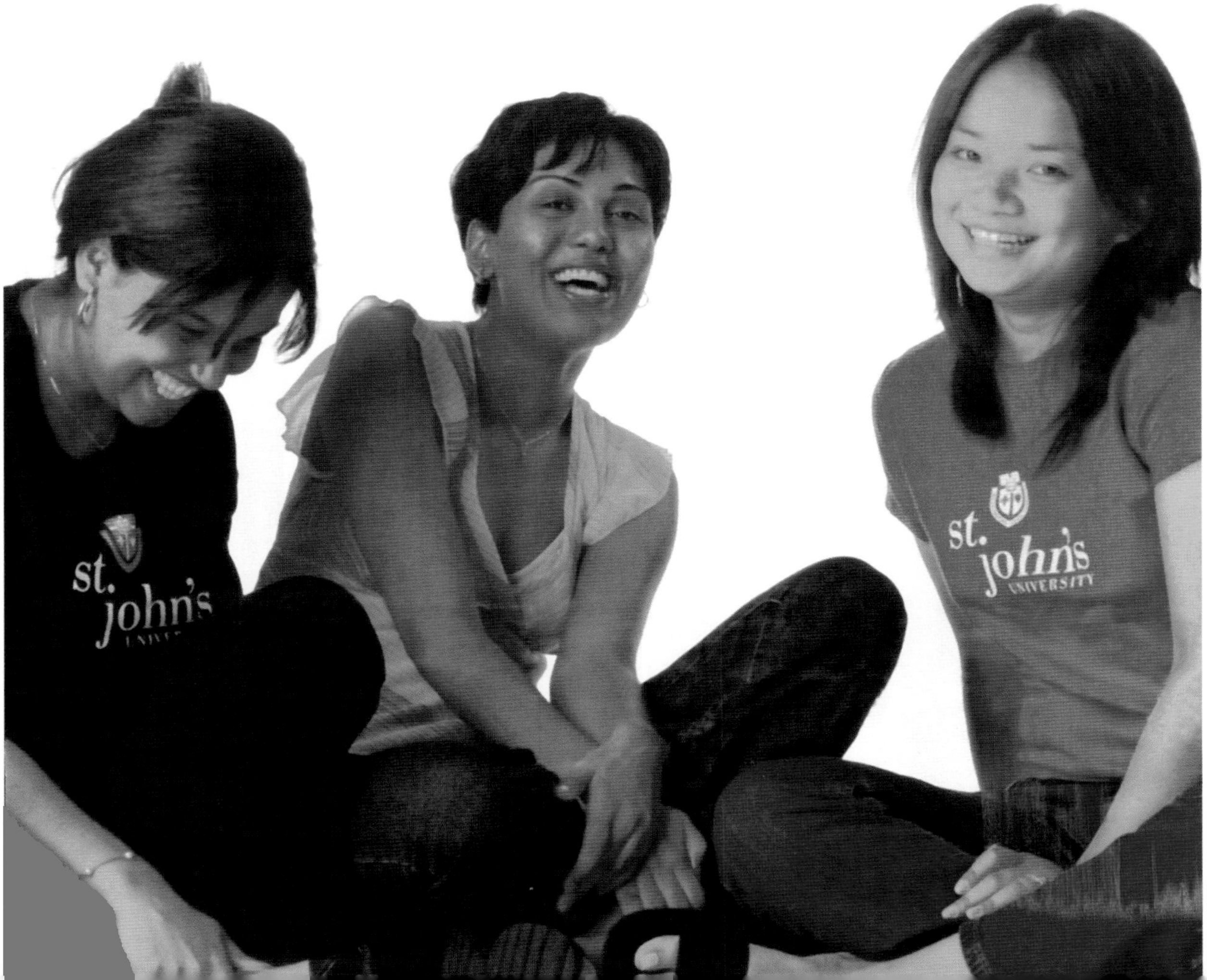

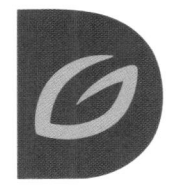

DOUBLEGREEN
LANDSCAPES

1.

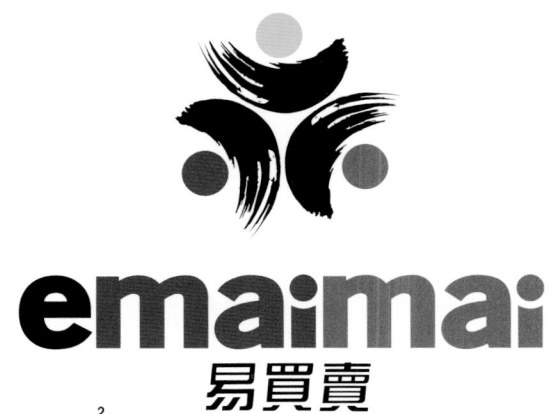

emaimai
易買賣

2.

AVENUE B
Consulting Inc.

3.

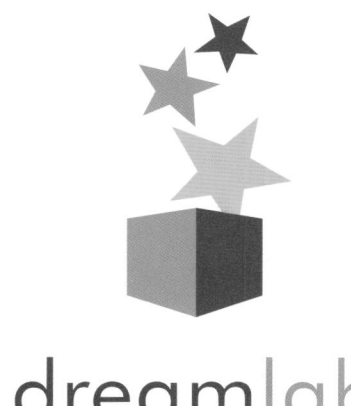

GALLERY C

4.

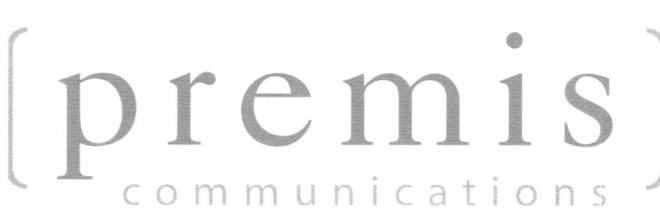

WESTCHESTER

NEIGHBORHOOD
SCHOOL

5.

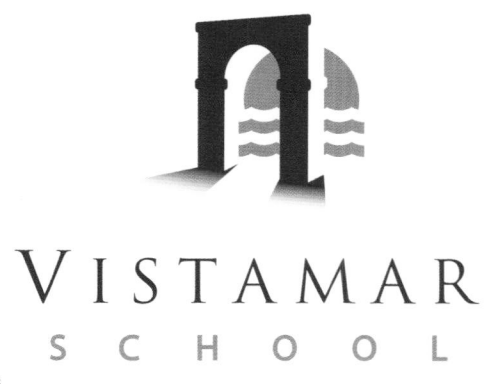

dreamlab

6.

[premis]
communications

7.

VISTAMAR
SCHOOL

8.

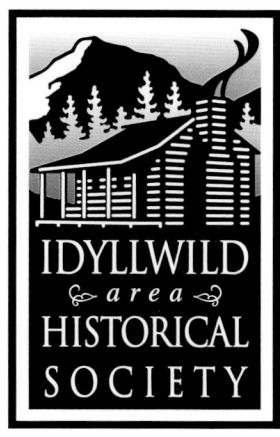

9.

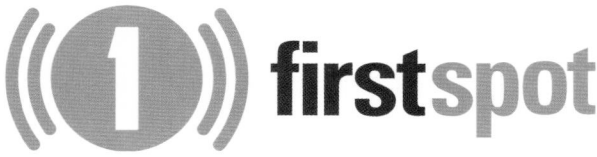

10.

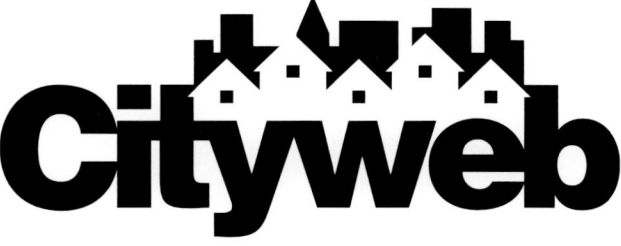

11.

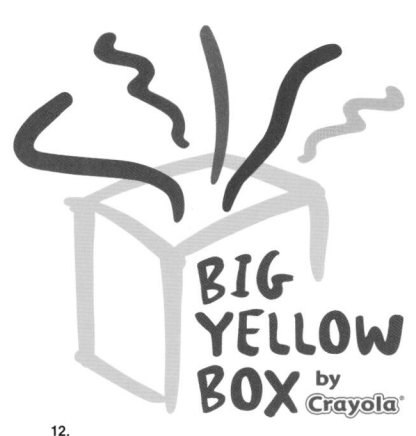

12.

Move Line

13.

LUXI

14.

Jack and Shirley
**Lubeznik
Center
for the Arts**

15.

1 - 13
Design Firm **Evenson Design Group**
14, 15
Design Firm **Liska + Associates, Inc.**

1.
Client   Doublegreen Landscapes
Designer   Judy Lee

2.
Client   Emaimai
Designers   Judy Lee, Mark Sojka

3.
Client   Avenue B Consulting Inc.
Designer   Tricia Rauen

4.
Client   Gallery C
Designer   Mark Sojka

5.
Client   Westchester Neighborhood School
Designers   Ken Loh, Ondine Jarl

6.
Client   Honda
Designers   Mark Sojka, John Han

7.
Client   Premis Communications
Designer   Mark Sojka

8.
Client   Vistamar School
Designer   Mark Sojka

9.
Client   Idyllwild Area Historical Society
Designer   Mark Sojka

10.
Client   FirstSpot
Designer   Kera Scott

11.
Client   Warner Bros. Online
Designer   Mark Sojka

12.
Client   Crayola
Designers   Glen Sokamoto, Kera Scott

13.
Client   Move Line
Designer   Mark Sojka

14.
Client   Luxi
Designer   Jonathan Seeds

15.
Client   Lubeznik Center for the Arts
Designer   Laura Litman

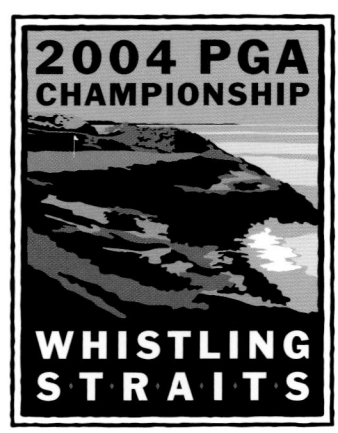

1.

2.

LITERACY
SERVICES

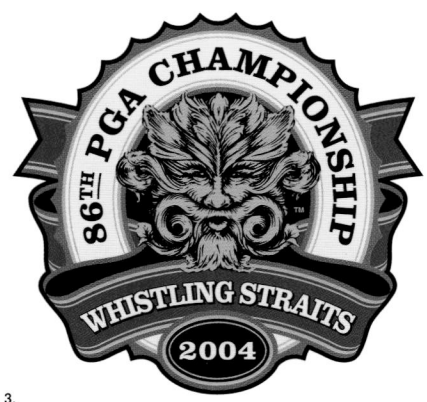

3.

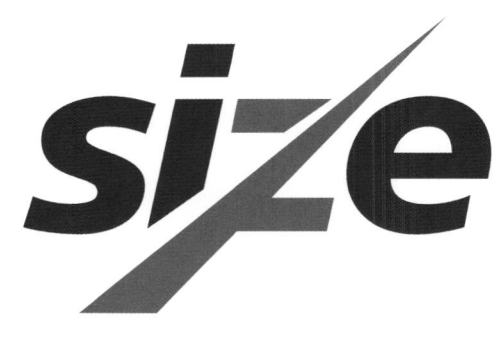

4.

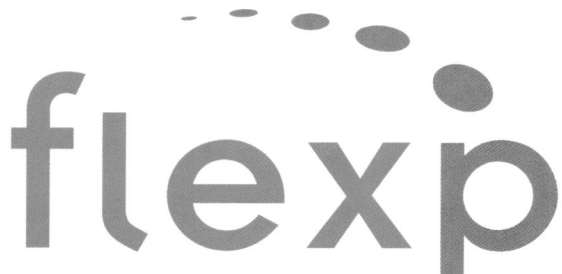

5.

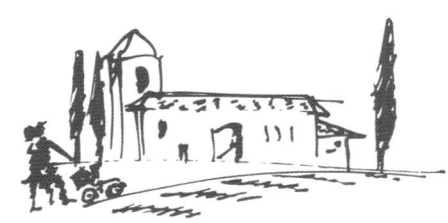

CIAO BAMBINO!

6.

me&b.
MATERNITY

7.

1 - 3
Design Firm **McDill Design Milwaukee**
4 - 6
Design Firm **Look Design**
7
Design Firm **Liska + Associates, Inc.**

1.
Client   *Kohler Company*
Designer Joel Harmeling
2.
Client   *Literacy Services of Wisconsin*
Designer Brad Bedessem
3.
Client   *Kohler Company*
Designer Joel Harmeling
4.
Client   *Size Technologies*
Designers Look Design

5.
Client   *Flex P*
Designers Look Design
6.
Client   *Ciao Bambino!*
Designers Look Design
7.
Client   *me&b Maternity*
Designer Danielle Akstein
(opposite)
Client   Cubby's Coffee House
Design Firm **Evenson Design Group**
Designer John Krause

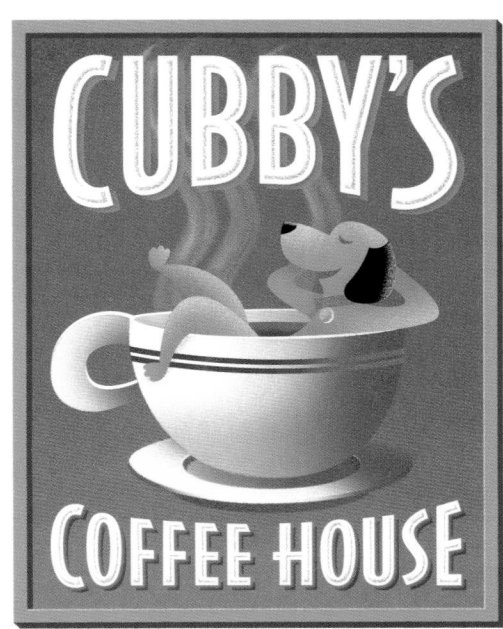

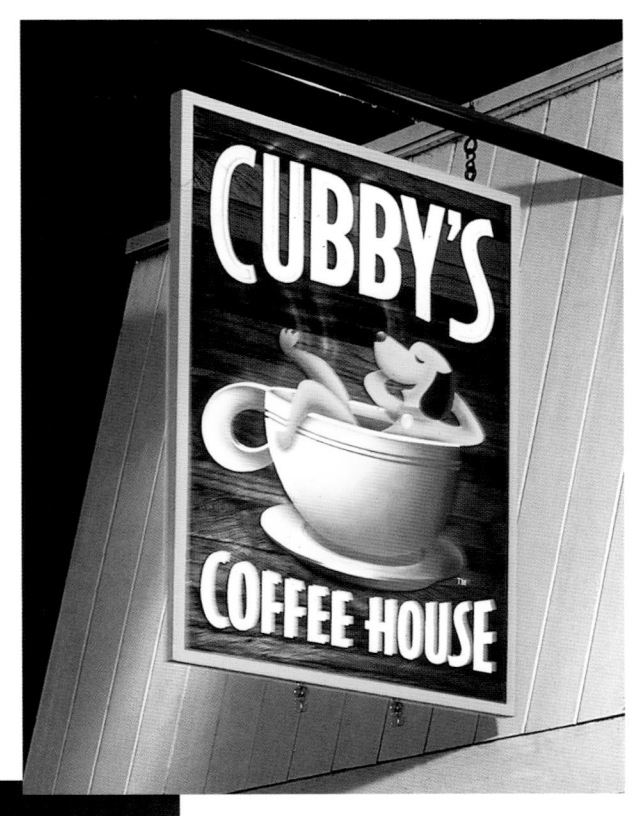

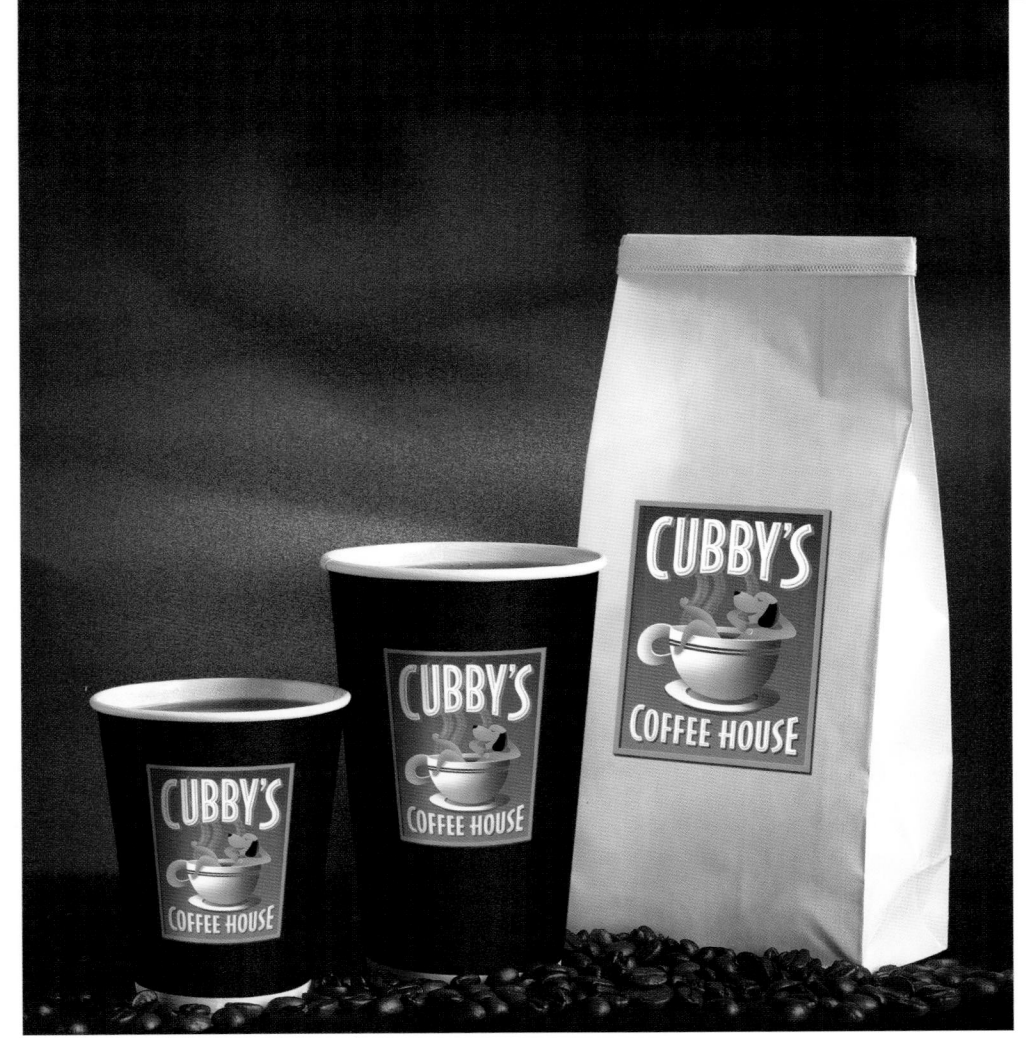

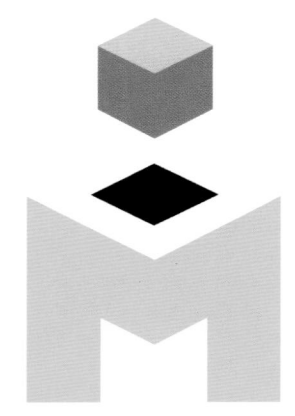

1.

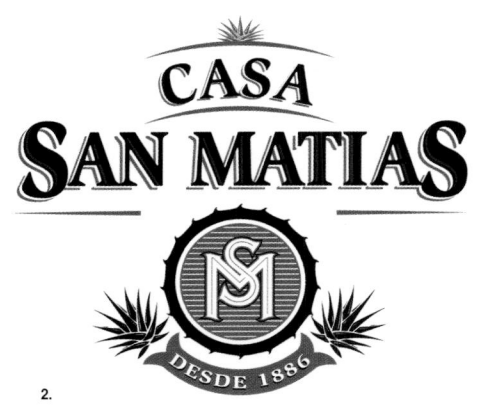

2.

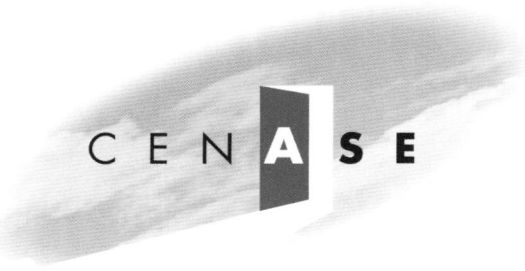

3.

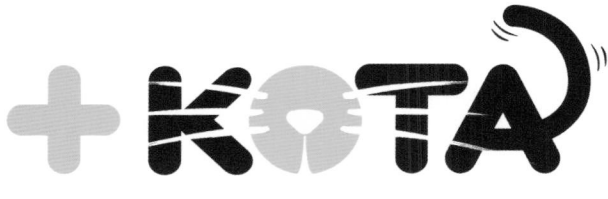

4.

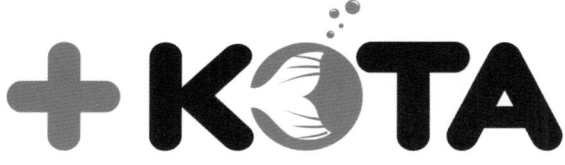

5.

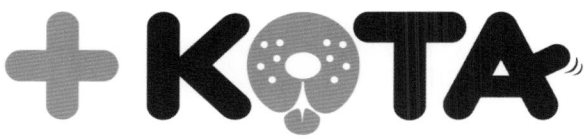

6.

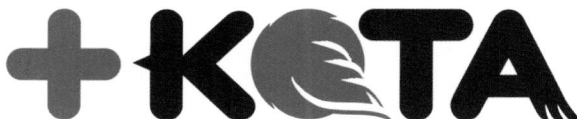

7.

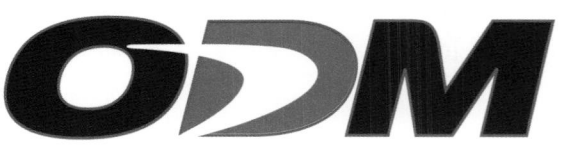

8.

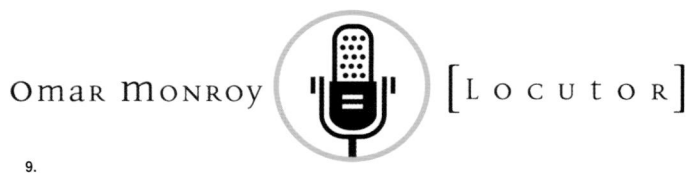

9.

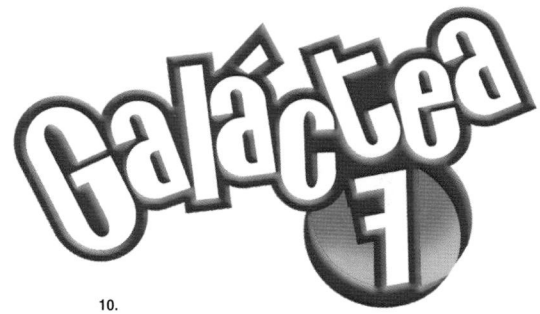

10.

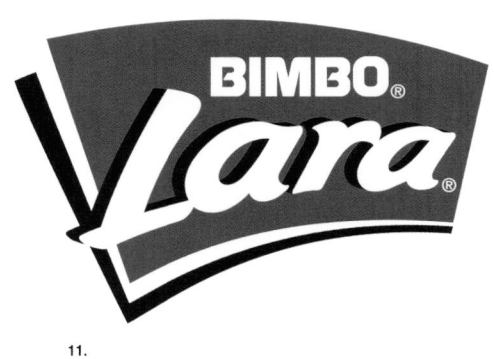

11.

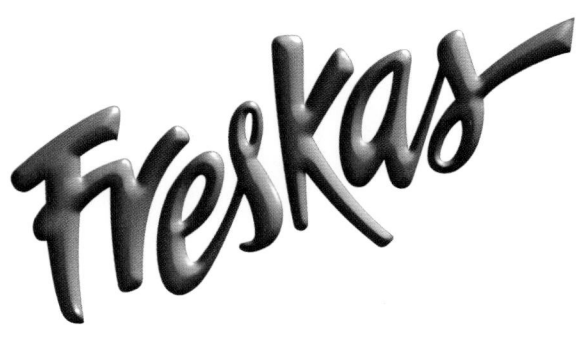

12.

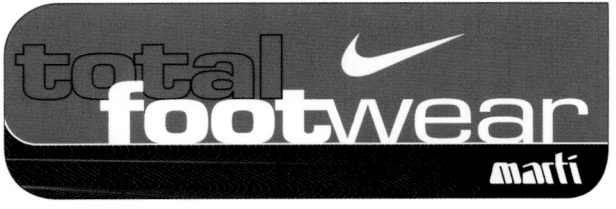

13.

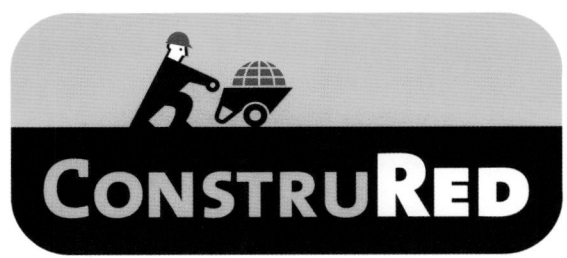

14.

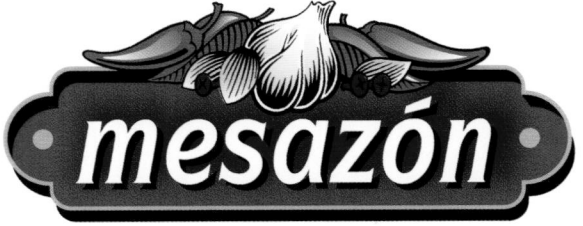

15.

1 - 15
Design Firm **TD2, S.C. Consultores en Identidad**

1.
Client — *A la Medida*
Designers — Jose Luis Patiño, Rafael Treviño M.

2.
Client — *Casa San Matías (Tequila)*
Designers — R. Rodrigo Córdova, Rafael Treviño M., Adalberto Arenas

3.
Client — *CENASA*
Designer — Rafael Treviño M.

4 - 7.
Client — *+KOTA*
Designers — Rafael Treviño, Erika Bravo

8.
Client — *ODM de México*
Designer — Rafael Treviño M

9.
Client — *Omar Monroy*
Designer — Rafael Rodrigo Córdova

10.
Client — *NESTLE Helados*
Designer — Rafael Rodrigo Córdova

11.
Client — *BIMBO*
Designers — Rafael Treviño M., Rafael Rodrigo Córdova

12.
Client — *Nestle Chocolates*
Designer — Rafael Treviño M.

13.
Client — *Nike Mexico*
Designer — Rafael Treviño M.

14.
Client — *Cementos Chihuahua*
Designer — Rafael Treviño

15.
Client — *Mesazón*
Designers — José Luis Patiño, Rafael Treviño M.

1.

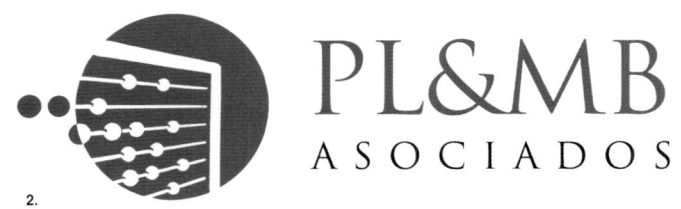

PL&MB
A S O C I A D O S

2.

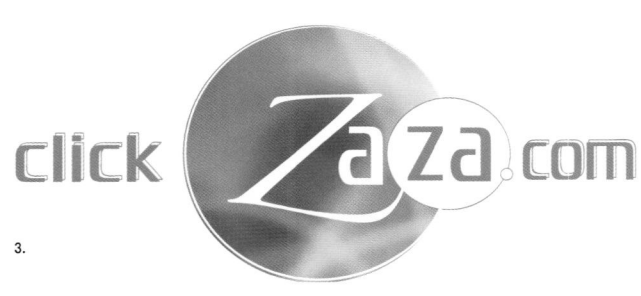

3.

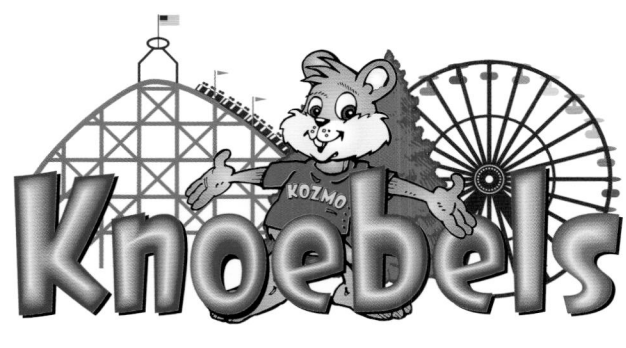

4.

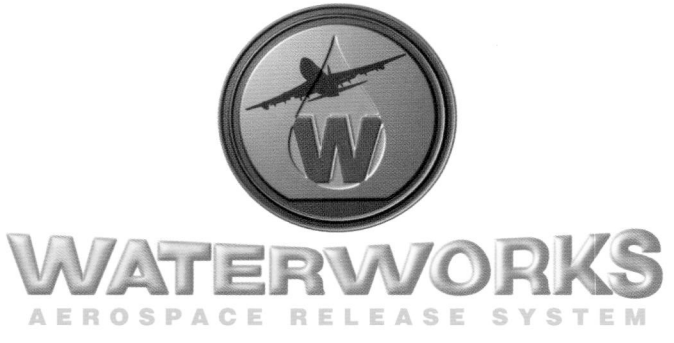

5.

Rentalunits.com

6.

bestlodging.com

VACANCY

7.

1, 2
    Design Firm **TD2, S.C. Consultores en Identidad**
3
    Design Firm **T-1 Productions**
4, 5
    Design Firm **PhaseOne Marketing & Design**
6, 7
    Design Firm **Bondepus Graphic Design**
1.
    Client   *Erika Rodríguez*
    Designers R. Rodrigo Córdova, Miguel Ríos
2.
    Client   *Juana Pérez*
    Designers R. Rodrigo Córdova, Sergio Enriquez
3.
    Client   *Click Zaza*
    Designer Parisa Chum

4.
    Client   *Knoebels Amusement Park*
    Designer Michael Tobin
5.
    Client   *Zyvax, Inc.*
    Designer Matthew Korbar
6.
    Client   *Bestlodging.com*
    Designer Gary Epis, Geordie Lynch
7.
    Client   *Bestlodging.com*
    Designers Gary Epis, Amy Bond
(opposite)
    Client   Boomerang
    Design Firm **Evenson Design Group**
    Designer Mark Sojka

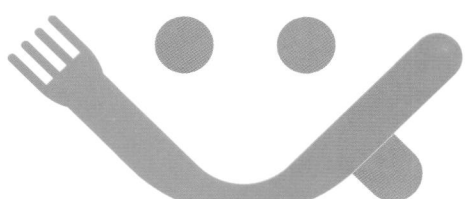

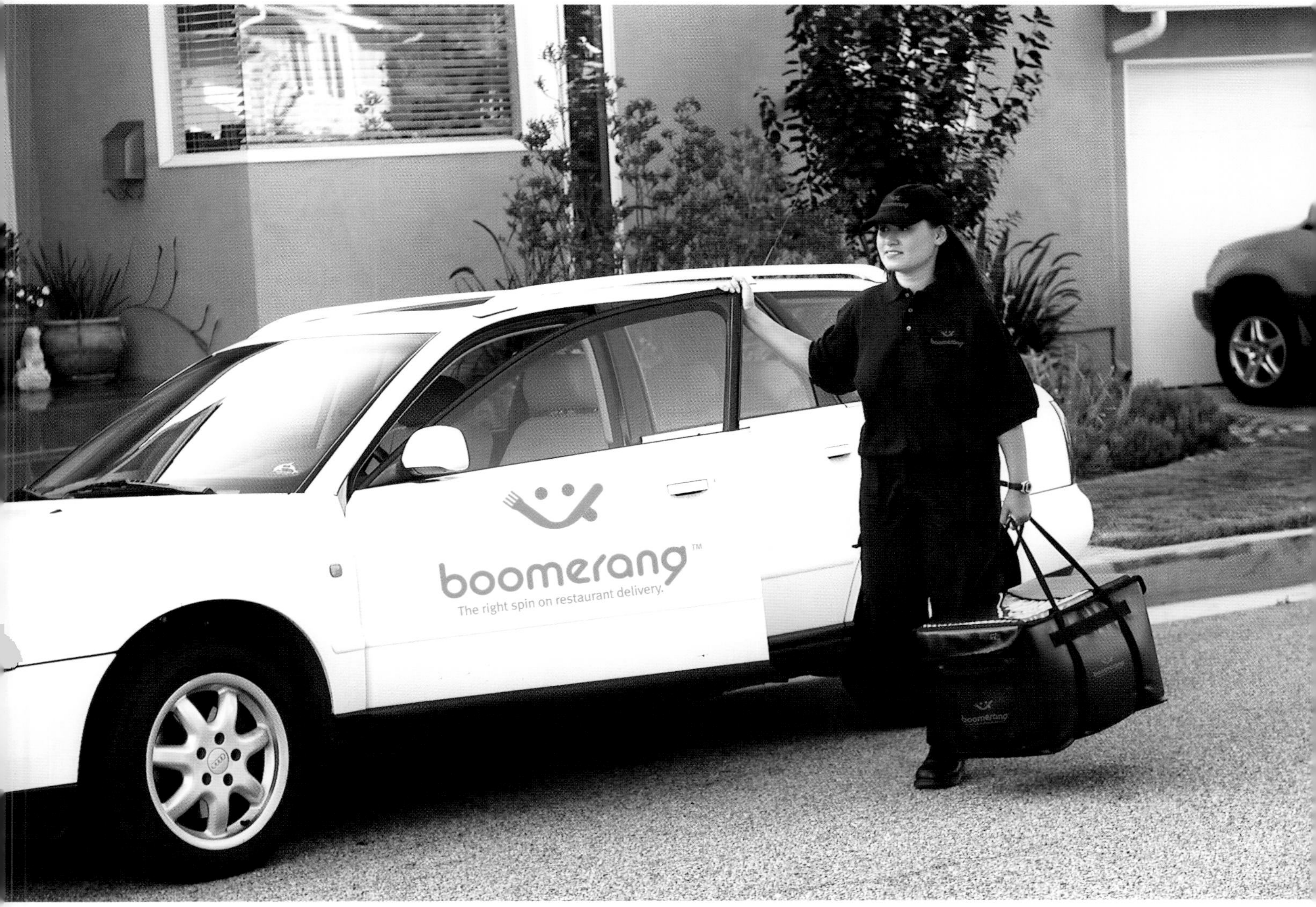

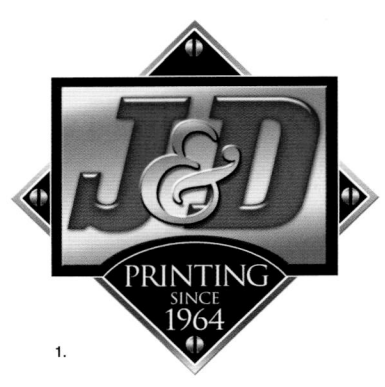

1.

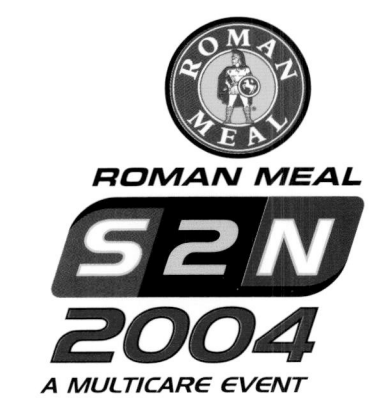

2.

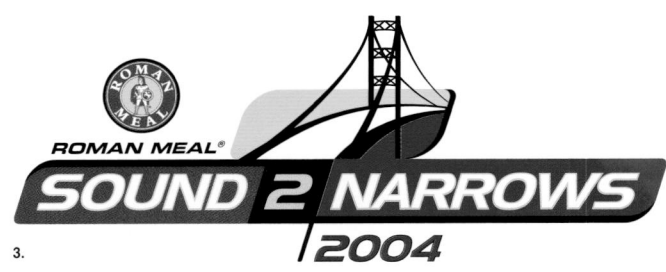

3.

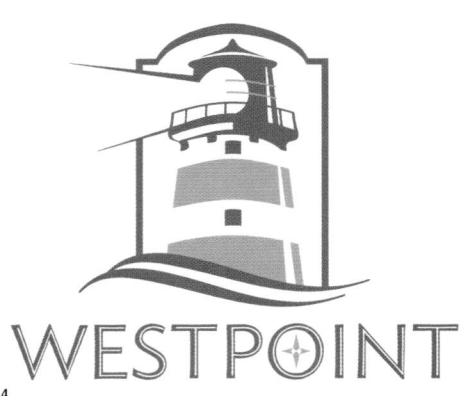

4.

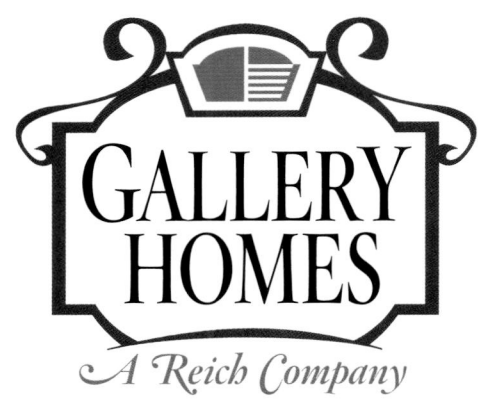

5.

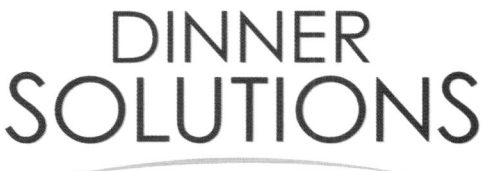

6.

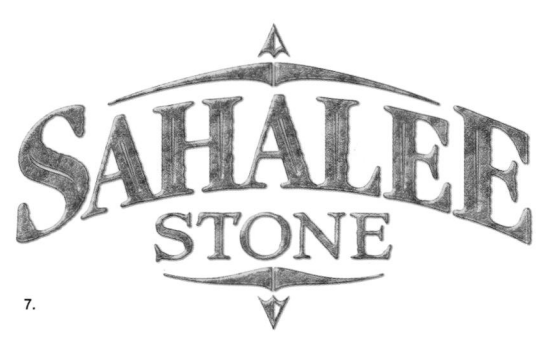

7.

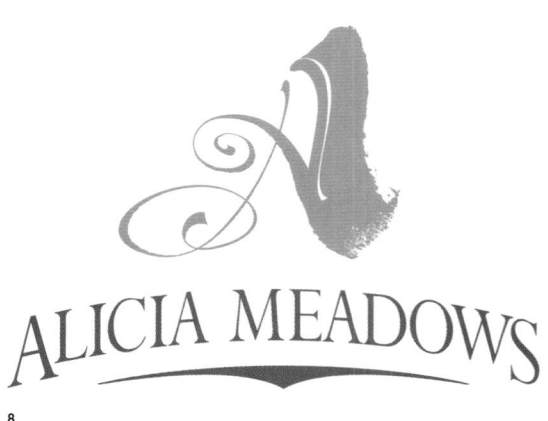

8.

ulmer | berne | llp

ATTORNEYS

9.

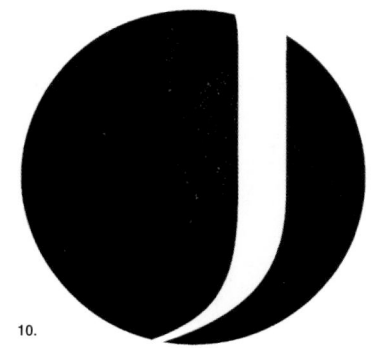

10.

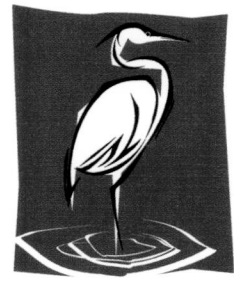

Nature Center
AT SHAKER LAKES

11.

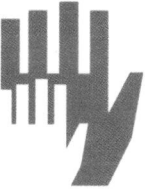

the althans foundation

12.

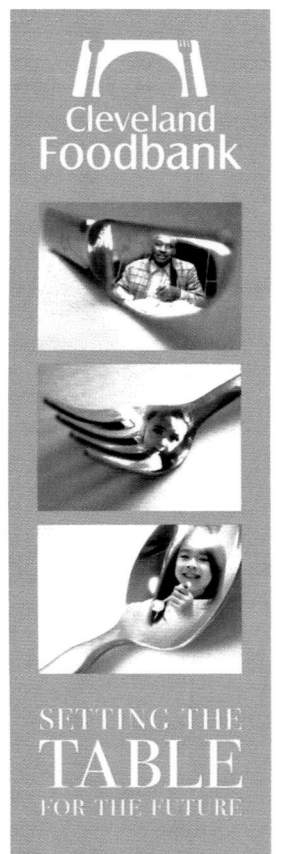

13.

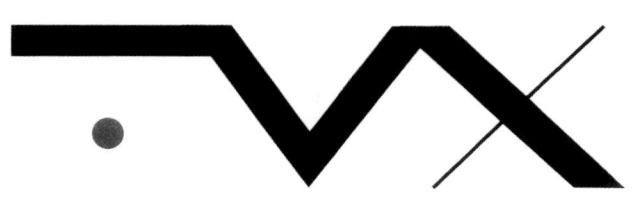

14.

1 - 8
Design Firm **Colin Magnuson Creative**
9 - 14
Design Firm **Epstein Design Partners, Inc.**

1.
Client   *J&D Printing Company*
Designer   Colin Magnuson

2, 3.
Client   *Multicare of Pierce County
& Roman Meal*
Designer   Colin Magnuson

4.
Client   *Reich Construction*
Designer   Colin Magnuson

5.
Client   *Gallery Homes, A Reich Company*
Designer   Colin Magnuson

6.
Client   *Dinner Solutions*
Designer   Colin Magnuson

7.
Client   *WestBlock Systems*
Designer   Colin Magnuson

8.
Client   *Reich Construction*
Designer   Colin Magnuson

9.
Client   *Ulmer & Berne, LLP*
Designer   John Okal

10.
Client   *Josh Gottlieb Companies*
Designer   John Okal

11.
Client   *The Nature Center at
Shaker Lakes*
Designer   Brian Jasinski

12.
Client   *Foundation Management
Services, Inc.*
Designer   Brian Jasinski

13.
Client   *Cleveland Foodbank*
Designers   John Okal, Brian Jasinski

14.
Client   *The Value Exchange*
Designer   Brian Jasinski

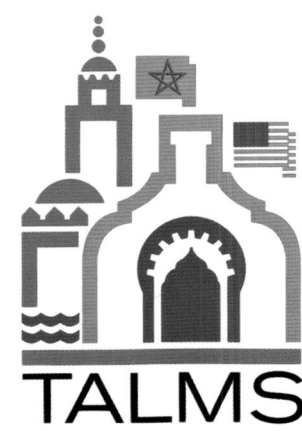

UV Solutions

1.

TALMS

2.

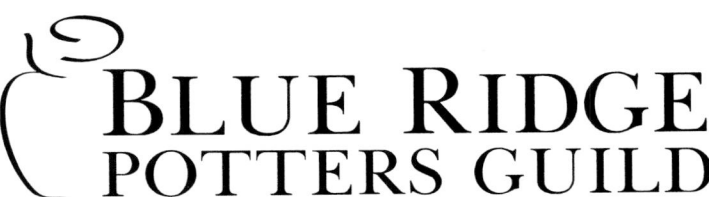

BLUE RIDGE POTTERS GUILD

3.

JEUNE LUNE

4.

3·1 Productions

5.

QC MANUFACTURING ™

6.

RCAT

REGIONAL
CONTRACT
ACADEMY
TRAINING

7.

1, 2
Design Firm **Frank D'Astolfo Design**
3
Design Firm **The Speidell Group**
4
Design Firm **Design Guys**
5
Design Firm **Purdue Student**
6
Design Firm **2g Marketing Communications, Inc.**
7
Design Firm **BBM & D**
1.
  Client   *UV Solutions Inc.*
  Designer Frank D'Astolfo
2.
  Client   *Tangier American Legation Museum Society*
  Designer Frank D'Astolfo

3.
  Client   *Blue Ridge Potters Guild*
  Designer Rebekah E.W. Hoskins
4.
  Client   *Theatre de la Jeune Lune*
  Designers Steven Sikora, Jay Theige
5.
  Client   *3-2-1 Productions*
  Designer Eric Beckner
6.
  Client   *Queen City Manufacturing*
  Designers Ken Adams, Larry Livaudais
7.
  Client   *Regional Contract Academy Training*
  Designers Ari Matson, Jon A. Leslie, Barbara Brown
(opposite)
  Client   Rocamojo
  Design Firm **Evenson Design Group**
  Designer Kera Scott

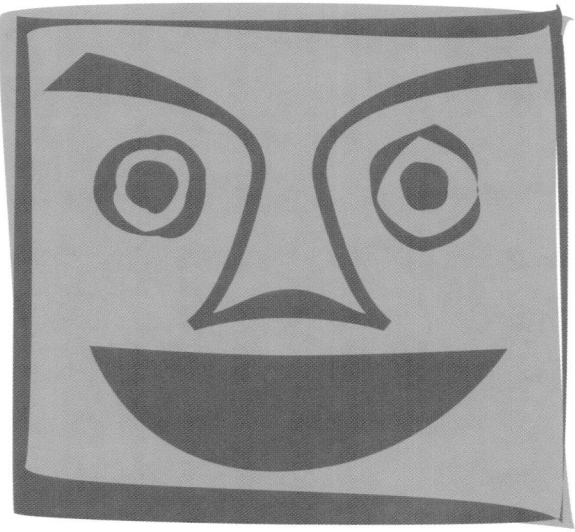

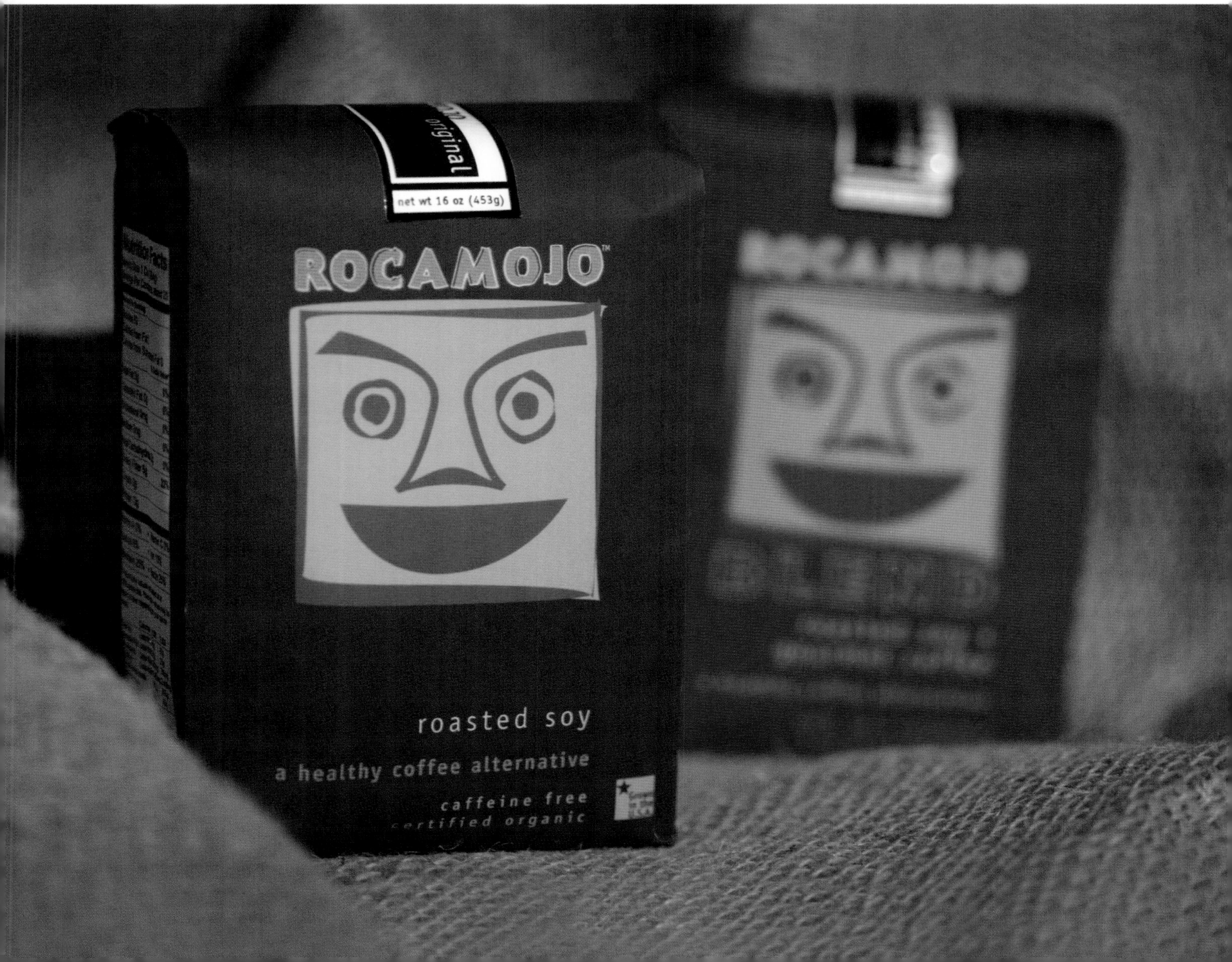

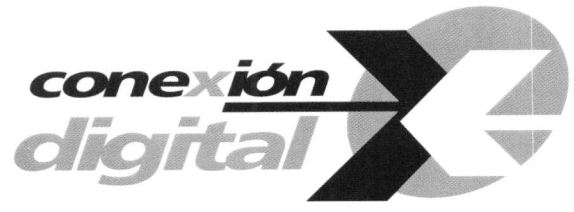

1.

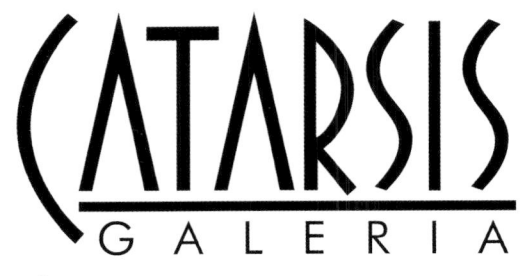

2.

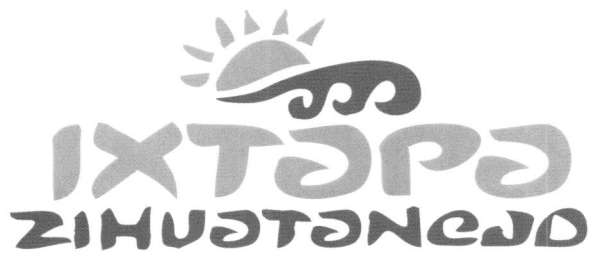

3.

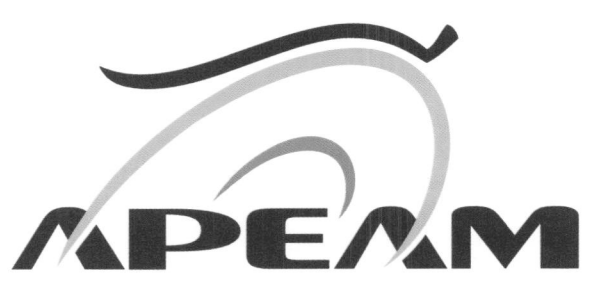

4.

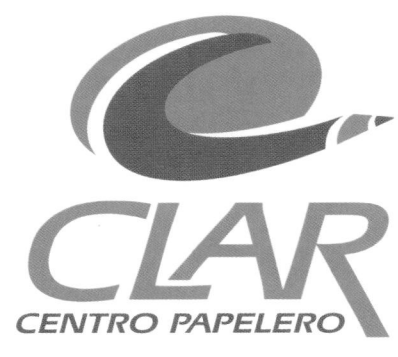

5.

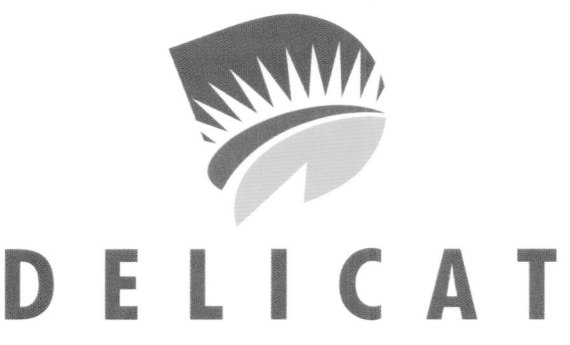

6.

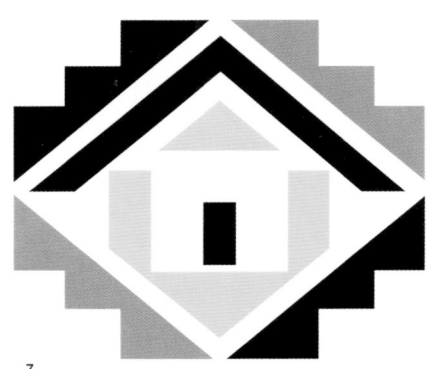

7.

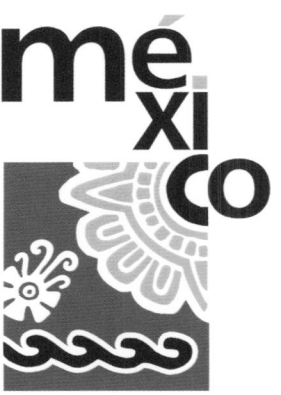

8.

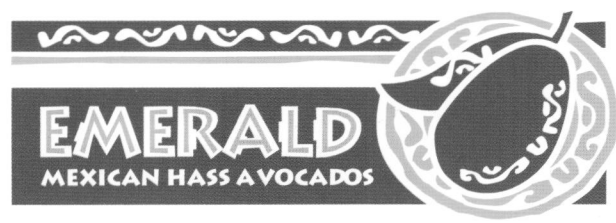

9.

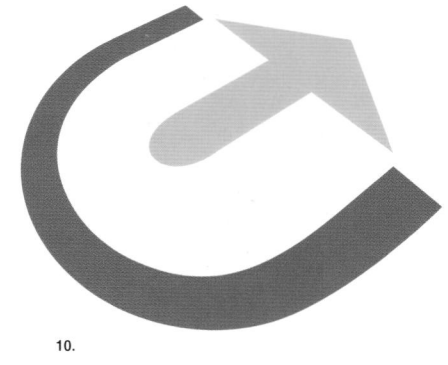

10.

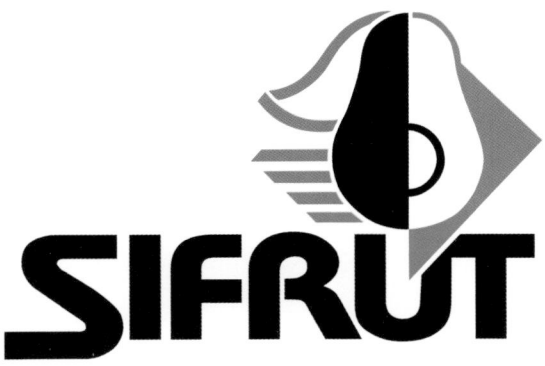

11.

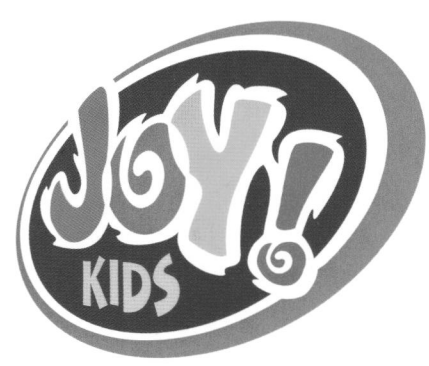

12.

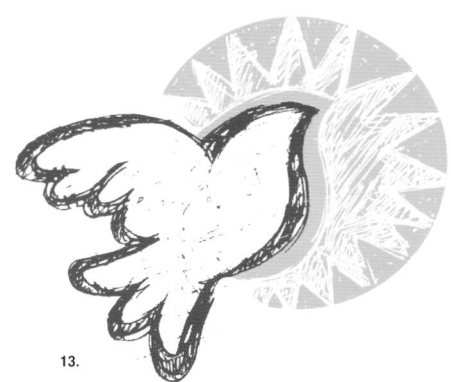

13.

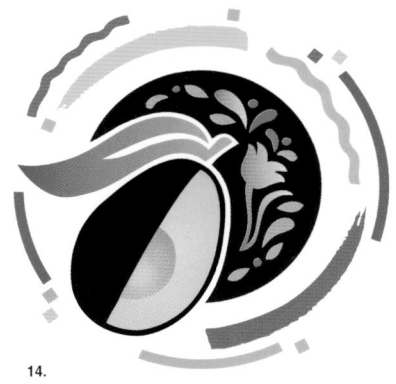

14.

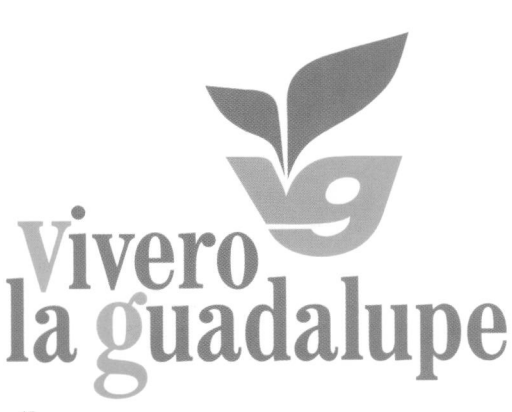

15.

1 - 15		
Design Firm	**Kenneth Diseño**	
1.		
Client	Cell Phone & Satellite TV Shop	
Designer	Kenneth Treviño	
2.		
Client	Catarsis Art Gallery	
Designers	Kenneth Treviño, Dolores Arroyo	
3.		
Client	Ixtapa Touristic Map	
Designer	Kenneth Treviño	
4.		
Client	Assoc. of Avocado Exporters Michoacan	
Designer	Kenneth Treviño	
5.		
Client	Clar Paper Store	
Designer	Kenneth Treviño	
6.		
Client	Delicat Fine Meats & Cheese	
Designer	Kenneth Treviño	
7.		
Client	Hogar Y Ceramica	
Designer	Kenneth Treviño	

8.	
Client	Playeras Michoacanas T Shirts
Designer	Kenneth Treviño
9.	
Client	Amimex
Designer	Kenneth Treviño
10.	
Client	City of Uruapan Chambers Assoc.
Designer	Kenneth Treviño
11.	
Client	Sifrut Avocado Exporters
Designer	Kenneth Treviño
12.	
Client	Joy Kids Fun Center
Designer	Kenneth Treviño
13.	
Client	Hope For A Better Future Conference
Designer	Kenneth Treviño
14.	
Client	Uruapan City Fair
Designer	Kenneth Treviño
15.	
Client	La Guadalupe Nursery
Designer	Kenneth Treviño

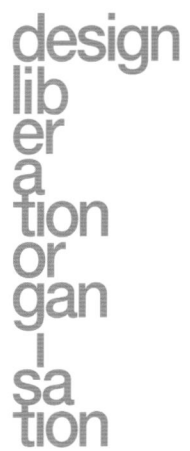

1.

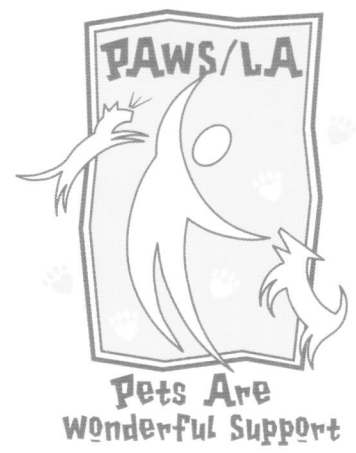

2.

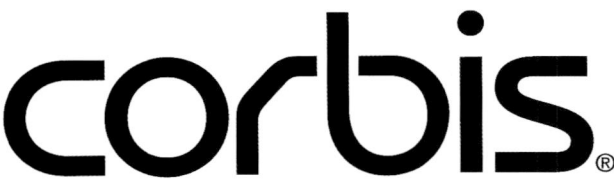

3.

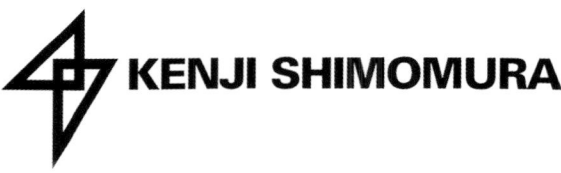

4.

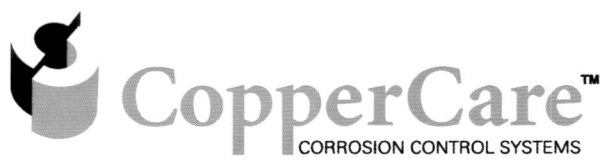

5.

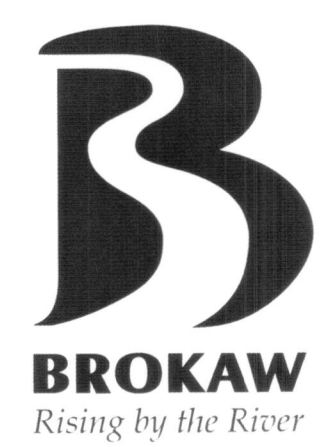

6.

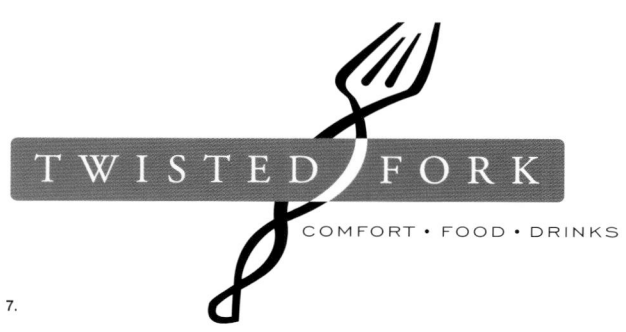

7.

1 Design Firm **Design Liberation Organisation**
2 Design Firm **Bradfield Design, Inc.**
3 Design Firm **Segura Inc.**
4 Design Firm **Kenji Shimomura**
5 Design Firm **DCG Solutions**
6 Design Firm **Foth & Van Dyke**
7 Design Firm **Becker Design**

1.
   Client   *Design Liberation Organisation*
   Designer Greg Gutbezahl
2.
   Client   *PAWS/LA*
   Designer Debra Bradfield

3.
   Client   *Corbis*
   Designer TNOP
4.
   Designer Kenji Shimomura
5.
   Client   *Copper Care, Inc.*
   Designer Marc E. Hedges
6.
   Client   *Village of Brokaw*
   Designer Daniel Green
7.
   Client   *Twisted Fork Restaurant*
   Designer Neil Becker
(opposite)
   Client   Old Orchard Brande
   Design Firm **The Bailey Group**
   Designers Steve Perry, Dave Fiedler

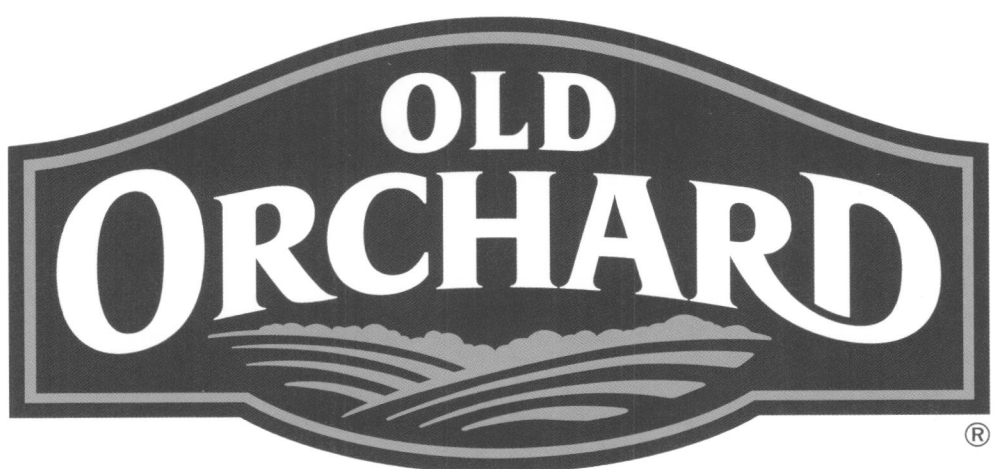

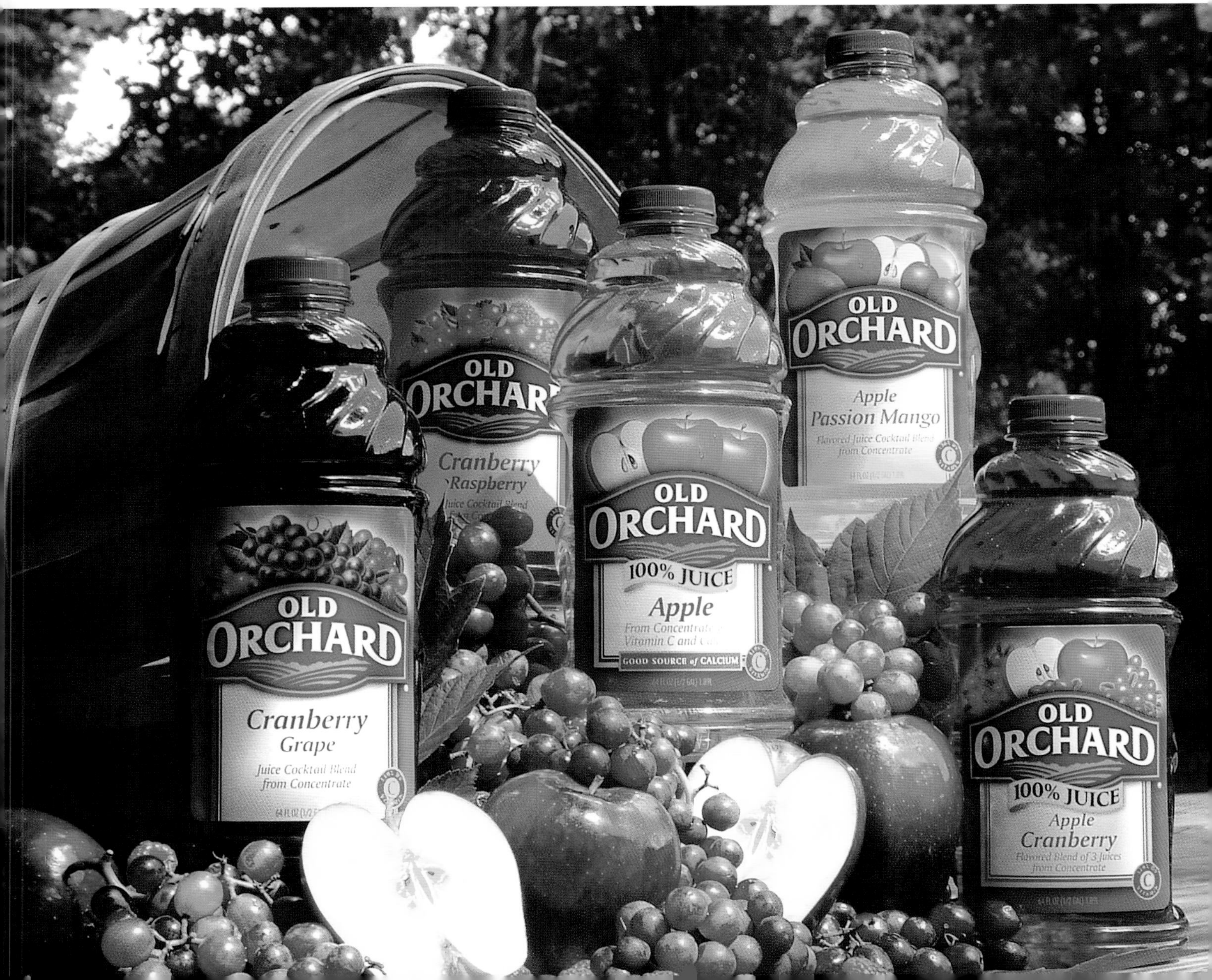

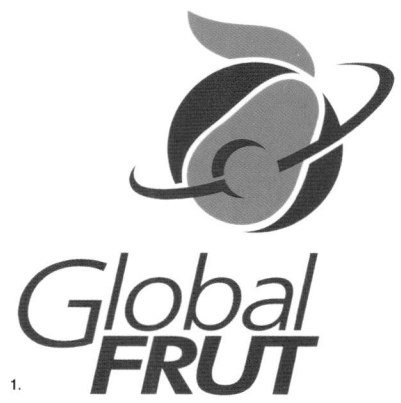

1.

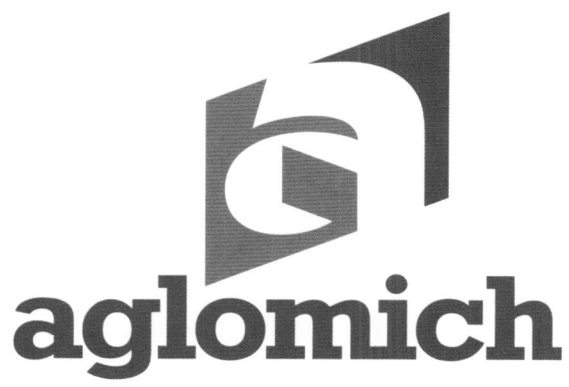

2.

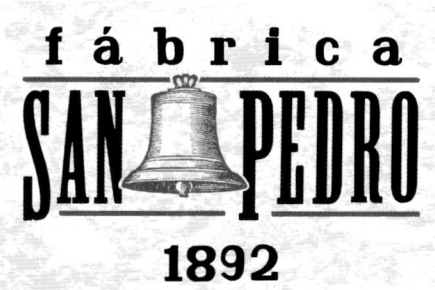

3.

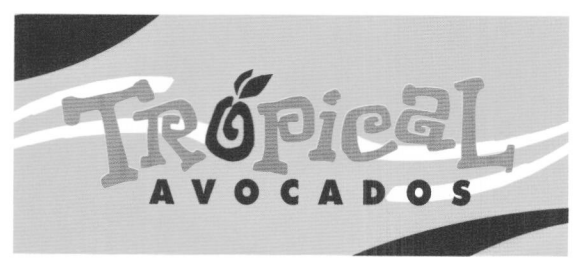

4.

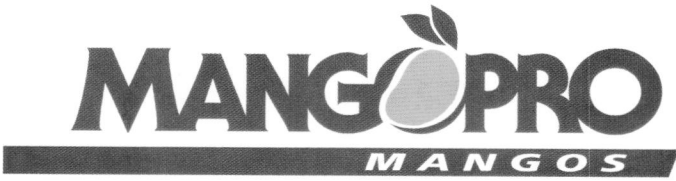

5.

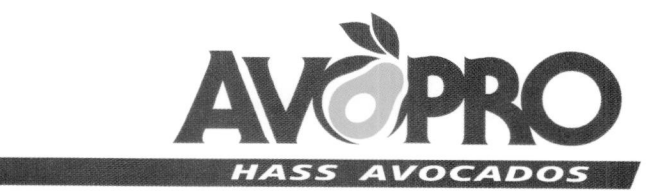

6.

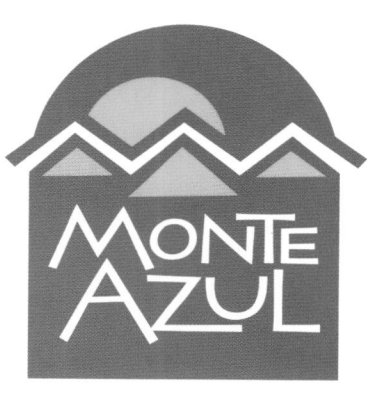

7.

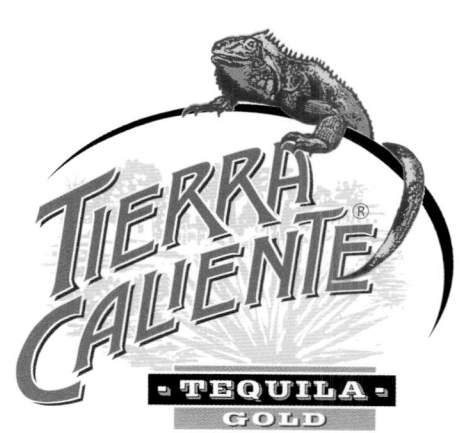

8.

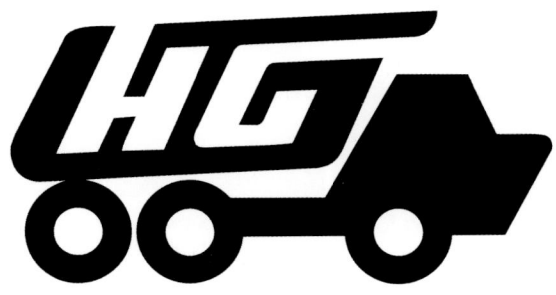

9.

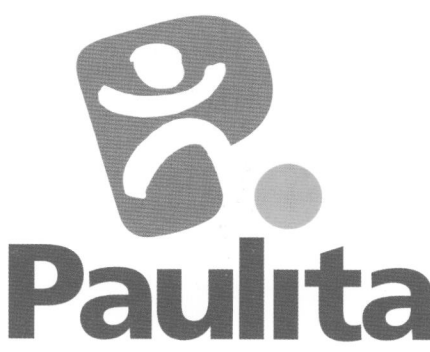

Paulíta

10.

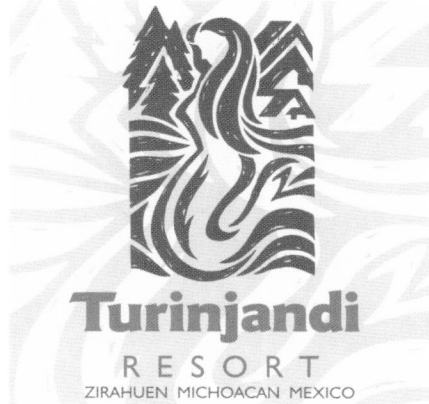

Turinjandi
RESORT
ZIRAHUEN MICHOACAN MEXICO

11.

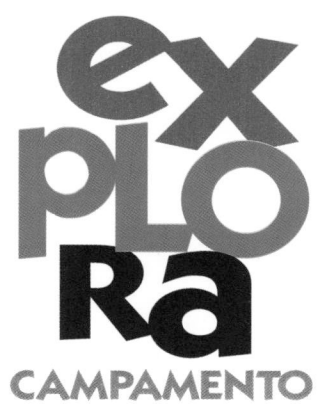

explo
Ra
CAMPAMENTO

12.

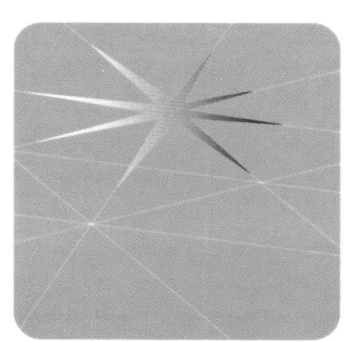

13.

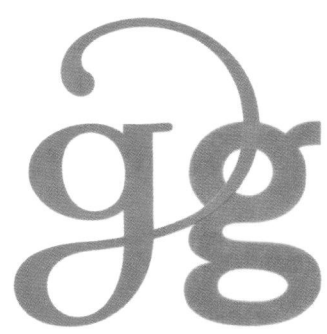

14.

The Morris Island Lighthouse · Circa 1876 · Folly Beach, S.C.

15.

1 - 12		
Design Firm	**Kenneth Diseño**	
13 - 15		
Design Firm	**Garfinkel Design**	
1.		
	Client	Global Frut Avocado Exporters
	Designer	Kenneth Treviño
2.		
	Client	Monroy Panel Factory
	Designer	Kenneth Treviño
3.		
	Client	San Pedro Old Textile Mill
	Designer	Kenneth Treviño
4.		
	Client	Fresh Directions International
	Designer	Kenneth Treviño
5, 6.		
	Client	Fresh Directions Mexicana
	Designer	Kenneth Treviño
7.		
	Client	Monte Azul Housing Development
	Designer	Kenneth Treviño

8.		
	Client	Industrial Mulsa Tequilas
	Designer	Kenneth Treviño
9.		
	Client	Hermanos Gudiño Transport
	Designer	Kenneth Treviño
10.		
	Client	Paulita Day Care Center
	Designer	Kenneth Treviño
11.		
	Client	Turinjandi Hotel-Resort
	Designer	Kenneth Treviño
12.		
	Client	Explora Summer Camp
	Designer	Kenneth Treviño
13.		
	Client	Advanced Wellness Technology
	Designer	Wendy Garfinkel-Gold
14.		
	Client	Garfinkel Design
	Designer	Wendy Garfinkel-Gold
15.		
	Client	Save the Light, Inc.
	Designer	Wendy Garfinkel-Gold

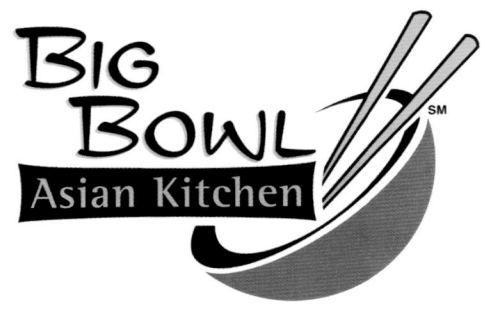

1.

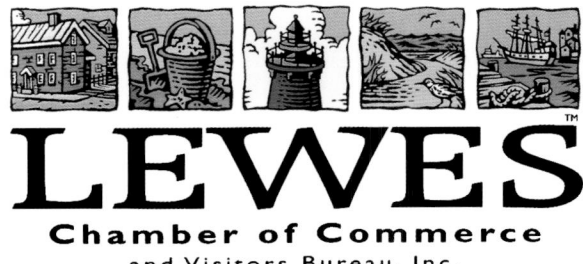

2.

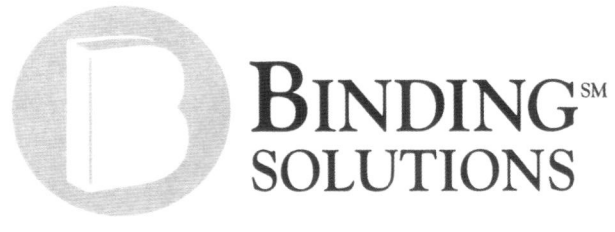

3.

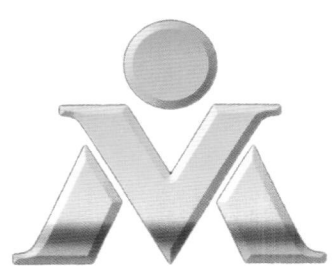

4.

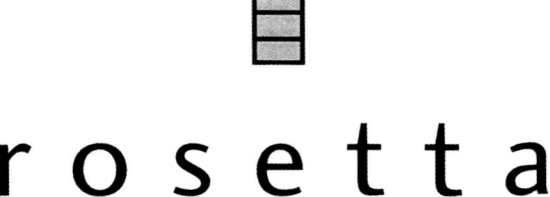

5.

6.

7.

1
Design Firm **Addison Whitney**
2
Design Firm **Dean Design/Marketing Group, Inc.**
3
Design Firm **Susan Meshberg Graphic Design**
4, 5
Design Firm **Stan Gellman Graphic Design Inc.**
6, 7
Design Firm **Dotzler Creative Arts**
1.
 Client   *Brinker International*
 Designers   Kimberlee Devis, Lisa Johnston, David Houk
2.
 Client   *Lewes Chamber of Commerce*
 Designer   Jeff Phillips
3.
 Client   *Museum of the American Piano*
 Designers   Susan Meshberg, Michele Kane

4.
 Client   *Binding Solutions*
 Designers   Teresa Thompson, Erin Goter
5.
 Client   *Rosetta Financial Advisors*
 Designers   David Kendall, Teresa Thompson
6.
 Client   *Marketplace Vision*
 Designers   Dotzler Creative Arts
7.
 Client   *Grace University*
 Designers   Dotzler Creative Arts
(opposite)
 Client   *Ameristar Casino*
 Design Firm **Visual Asylum**
 Designer   Joel Sotelo

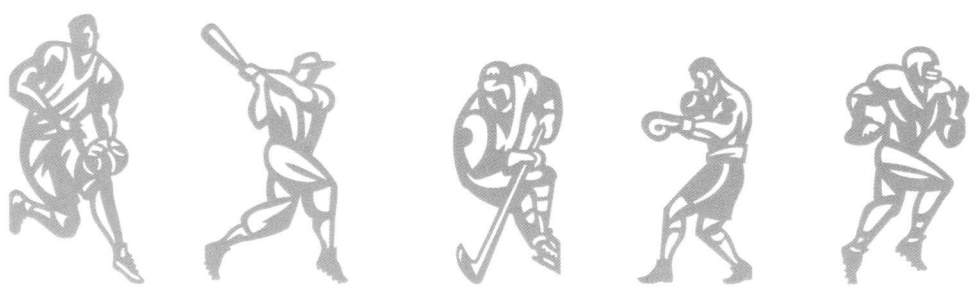

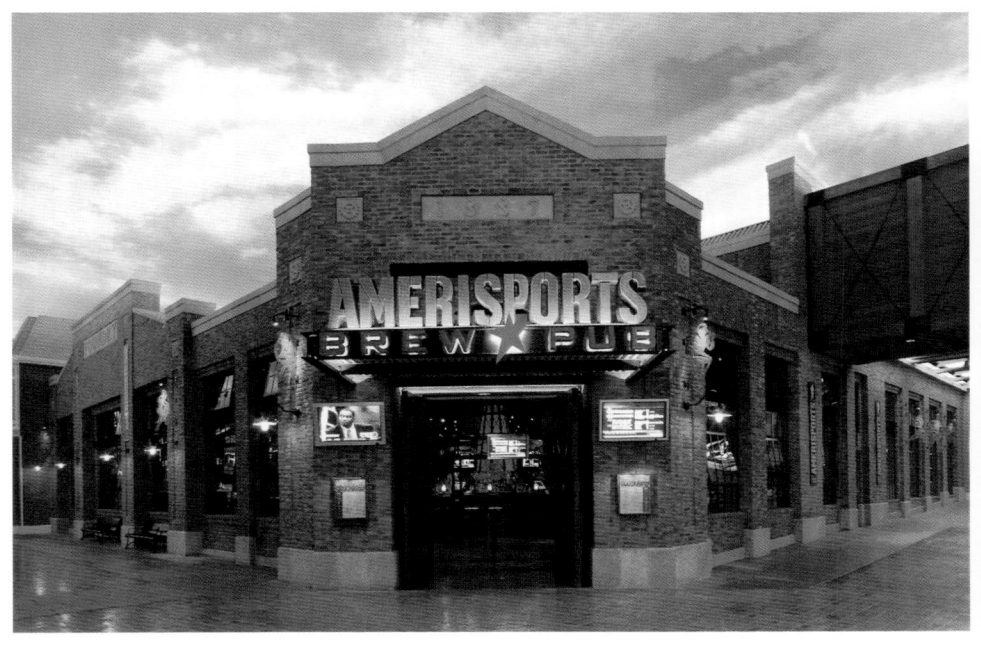

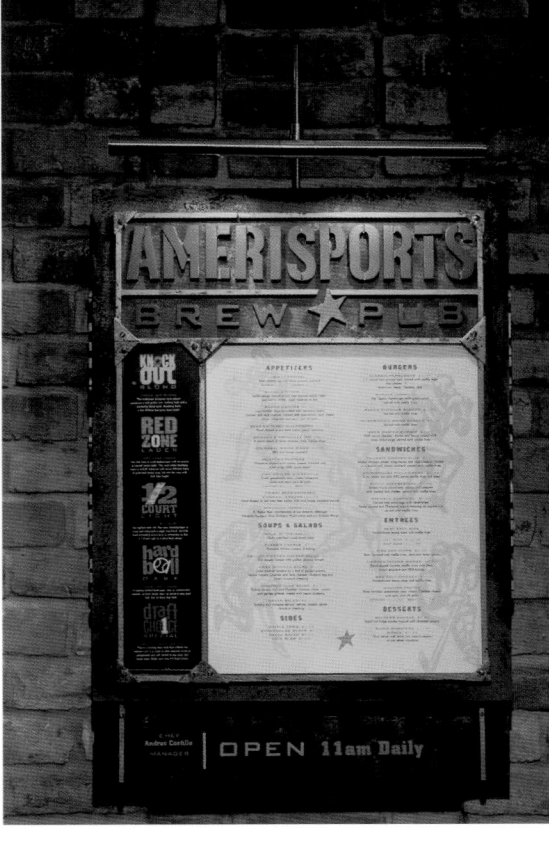

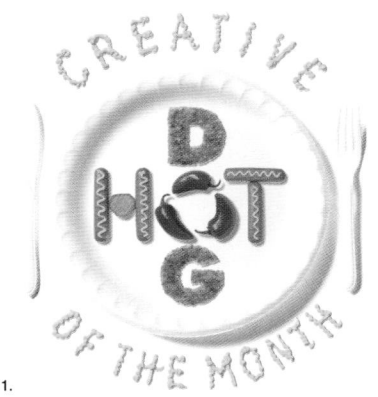

1.

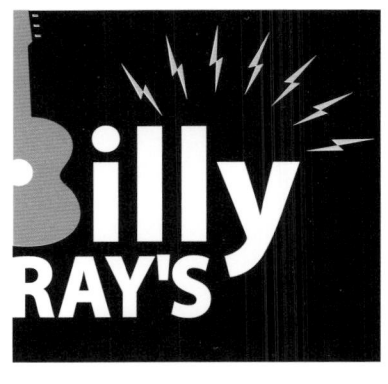

2.

3.

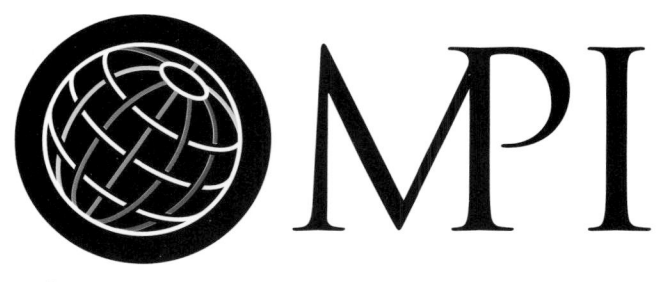

4.

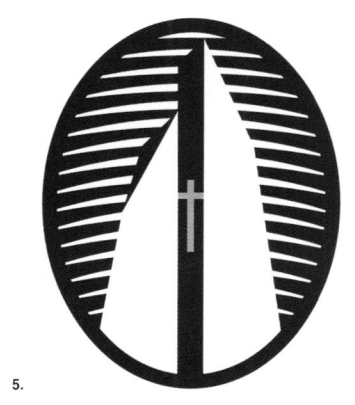

5.

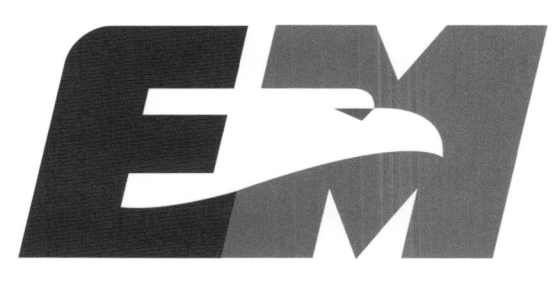

6.

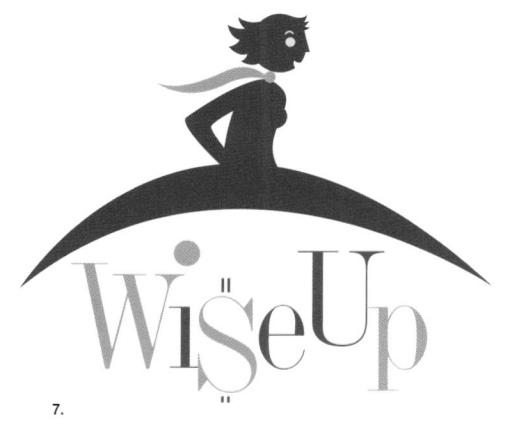

7.

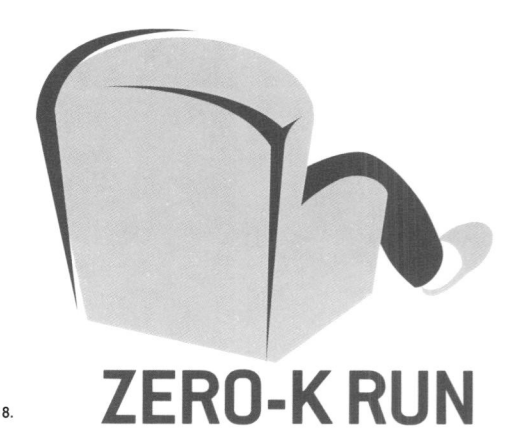

ZERO-K RUN

8.

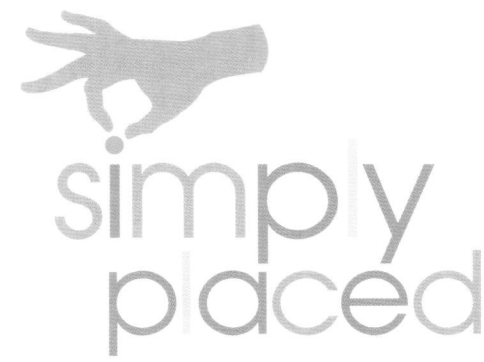

9.

10.

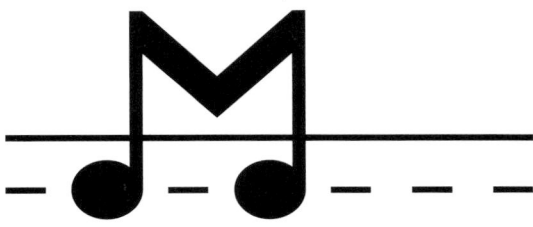

11.

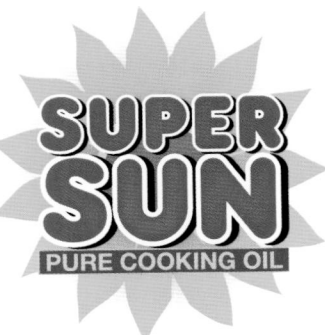

12.

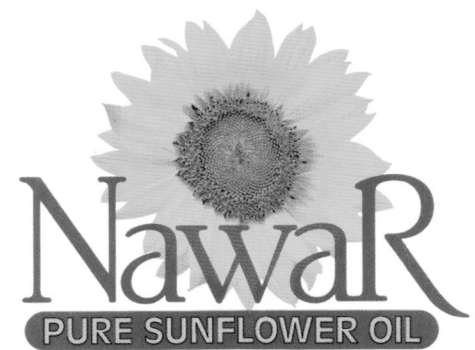

13.

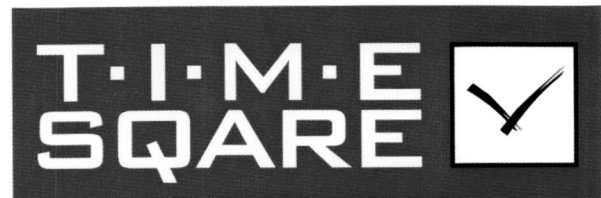

14.

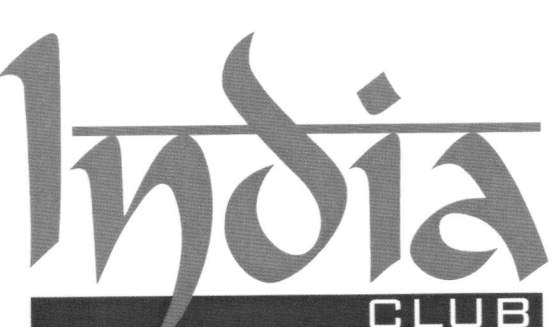

15.

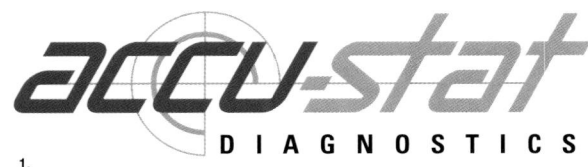

1.

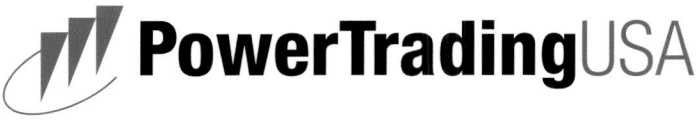

2.

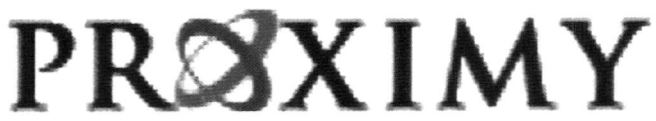

3.

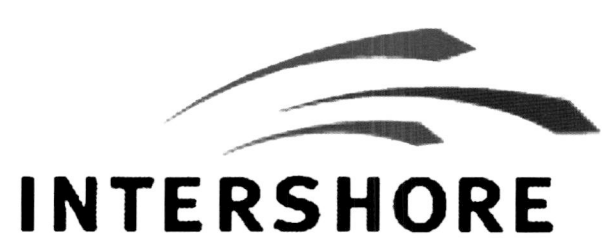

4.

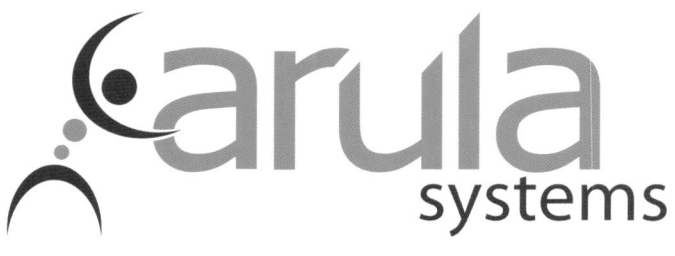

5.

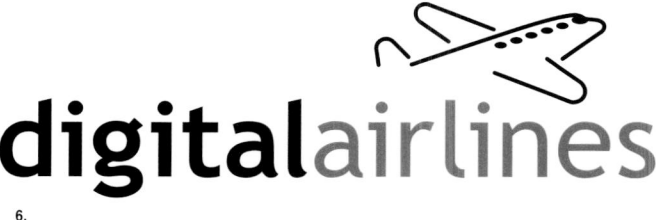

6.

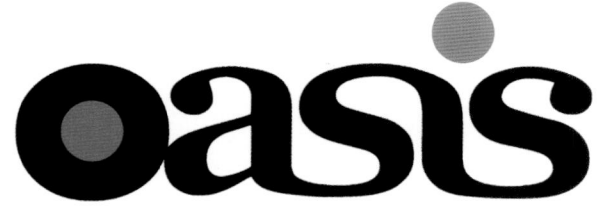

7.

1, 2
Design Firm **Vince Rini Design**
3, 4
Design Firm **Baker Brand Communications**
5, 6
Design Firm **angryporcupine_design**
7
Design Firm **Seran Design**

1.
Client   *Accu-Stat Diagnostics*
Designer   Vince Rini
2.
Client   *Power Trading USA*
Designer   Vince Rini
3.
Client   *Proximy*
Designer   Melissa Rosen
4.
Client   *Intershore*
Designer   Melissa Rosen

5.
Client   *Arula Systems, Inc.*
Designer   Cheryl Roder-Quill
6.
Client   *Novell, Inc.*
Designer   Cheryl Roder-Quill
7.
Client   *Oasis Gallery*
Designer   Sang Yoon
(opposite)
Client   Pita Products
Design Firm **Flowdesign, Inc.**
Designer   Dan Matauch

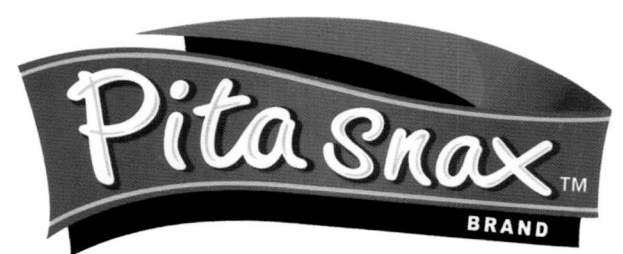

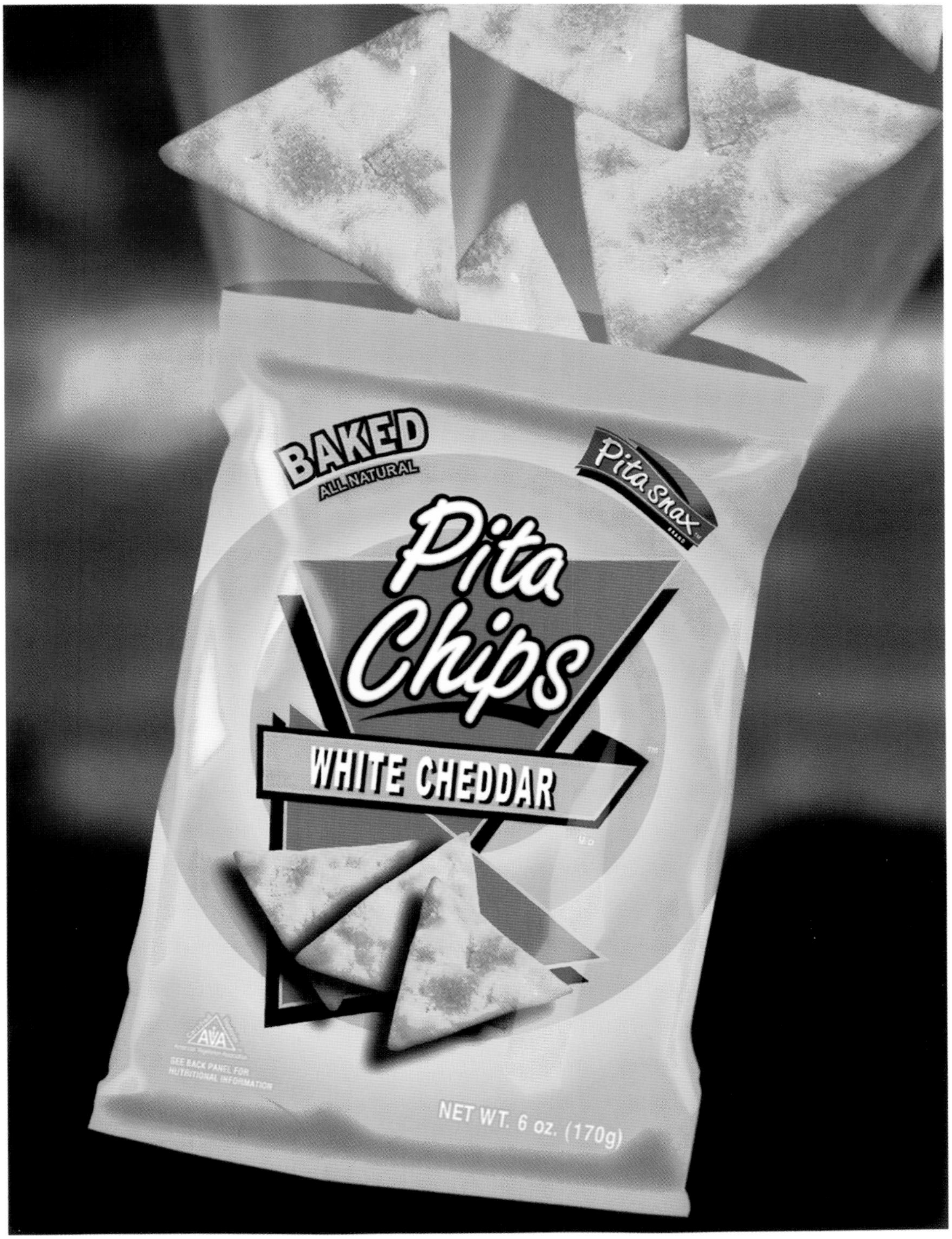

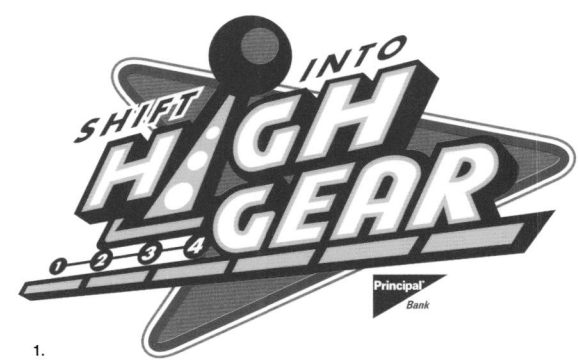

1.

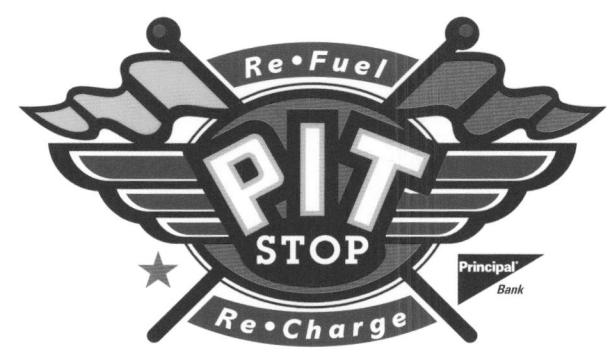

2.

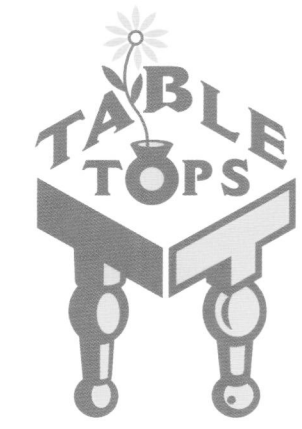

3.

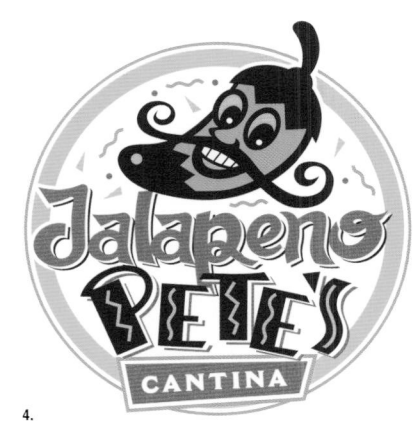

4.

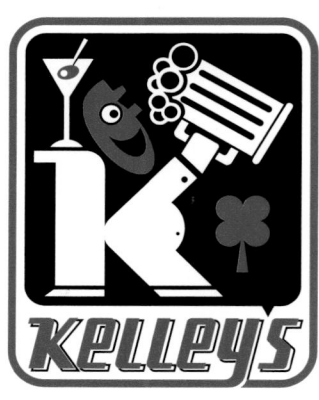

5.

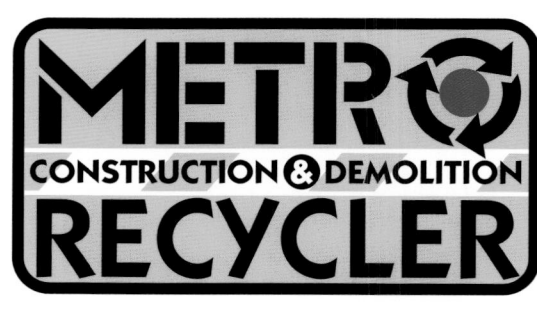

6.

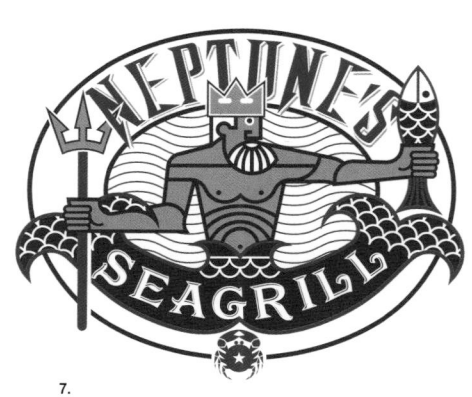

7.

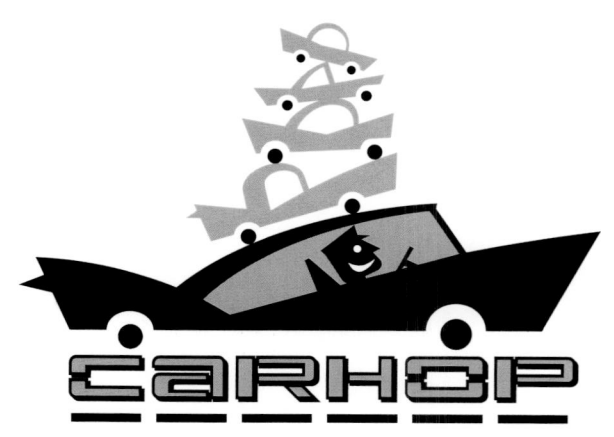

8.

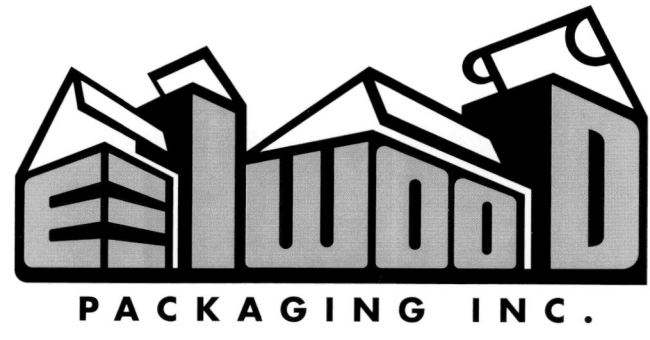

9.

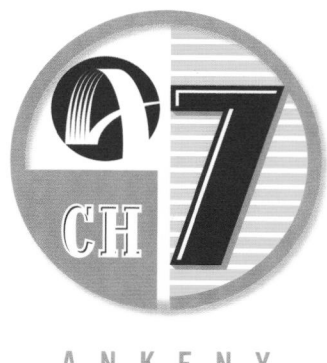

ANKENY

10.

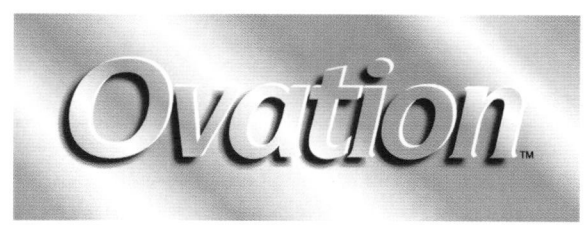

11.

LucencePhotographic

12.

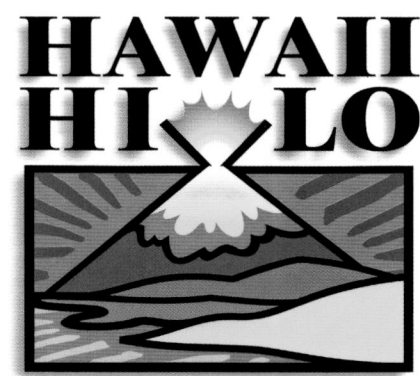

13.

Full House Gaming

14.

15.

1 - 10
Design Firm **Sayles Graphic Design, Inc.**
11 - 15
Design Firm **Lee Communciations, Inc.**
1, 2.
   Client   *Principal Bank*
   Designer John Sayles
3.
   Client   *Table Tops*
   Designer John Sayles
4.
   Client   *Kirke Financial Services*
   Designer John Sayles
5.
   Client   *Kelley's Pub and Grille*
   Designer John Sayles
6.
   Client   *Metro C&D Recycler*
   Designer John Sayles
7.
   Client   *Neptune's Seagrill*
   Designer John Sayles
8.
   Client   *Carhop*
   Designer John Sayles

9.
   Client   *Elwood Packaging*
   Designer John Sayles
10.
   Client   *City of Ankeny*
   Designer John Sayles
11.
   Client   *Essilor of America, Inc.*
   Designer Bob Lee
12.
   Client   *Lucence Photographic, Ltd.*
   Designer Bob Lee
13, 14.
   Client   *Full House Gaming, Inc.*
   Designer Bob Lee
15.
   Client   *Capitol Risk Concepts, Ltd.*
   Designer Bob Lee

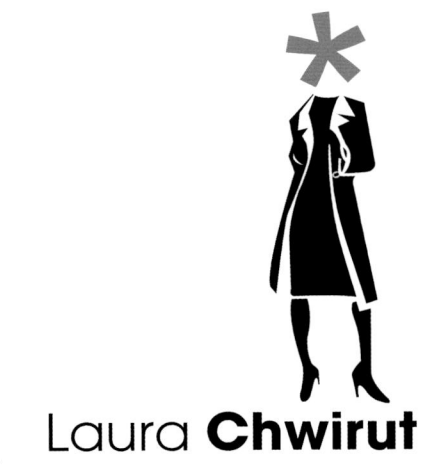

Laura **Chwirut**

1.

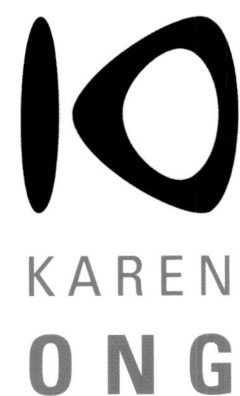

KAREN
O N G

2.

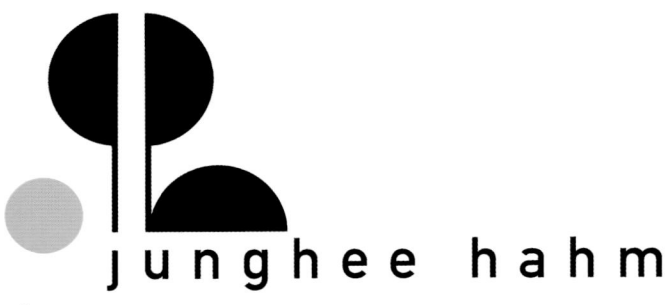

j u n g h e e   h a h m

3.

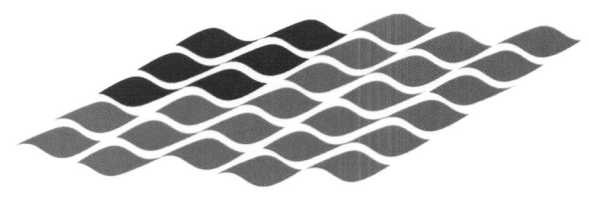

Boston ★ 2004
Nothing conventional about it.

4.

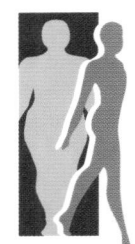

Bariatric Surgery Center
BAXTER REGIONAL MEDICAL CENTER

5.

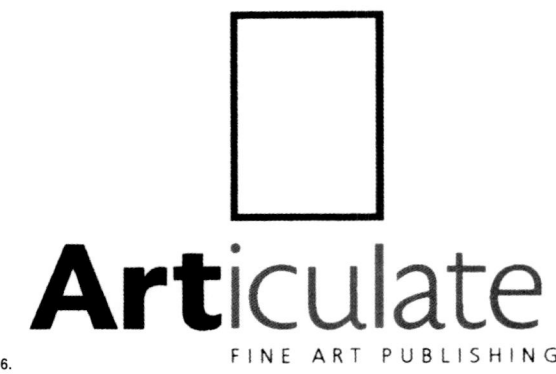

Articulate
FINE ART PUBLISHING

6.

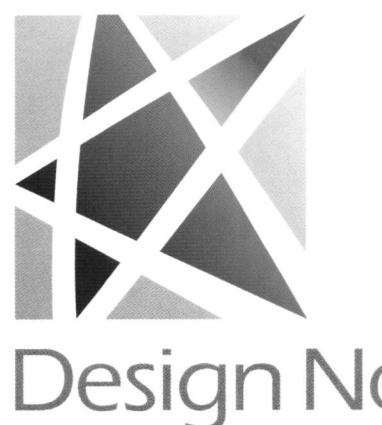

Design North

7.

1		**3.**	
Design Firm **Laura Chwirut**		Client	*Junghee Hahm*
2		Designer	Junghee Hahm
Design Firm **Karen Ong**		**4.**	
3		Client	*Democratic National Convention*
Design Firm **Junghee Hahm Design**		Designer	Vic Ceroli, Sean Westgate
4		**5.**	
Design Firm **Hill Holliday**		Client	*Bariatric Surgery Center*
5			*Baxter Regional Medical Center*
Design Firm **Brooks-Jeffrey Marketing, Inc.**		Designers	Brooks-Jeffrey Marketing
6			Creative Team
Design Firm **Robert Meyers Design**		**6.**	
7		Client	*Articulate*
Design Firm **Design North, Inc.**		Designer	Robert Meyers
1.		**7.**	
Client	*Laura Chwirut*	Client	*Design North, Inc.*
Designer	Laura Chwirut	**(opposite)**	
2.		Client	Xango
Client	*Karen Ong*	Design Firm **Flowdesign, Inc.**	
Designer	Karen Ong	Designer	Dan Matauch

194

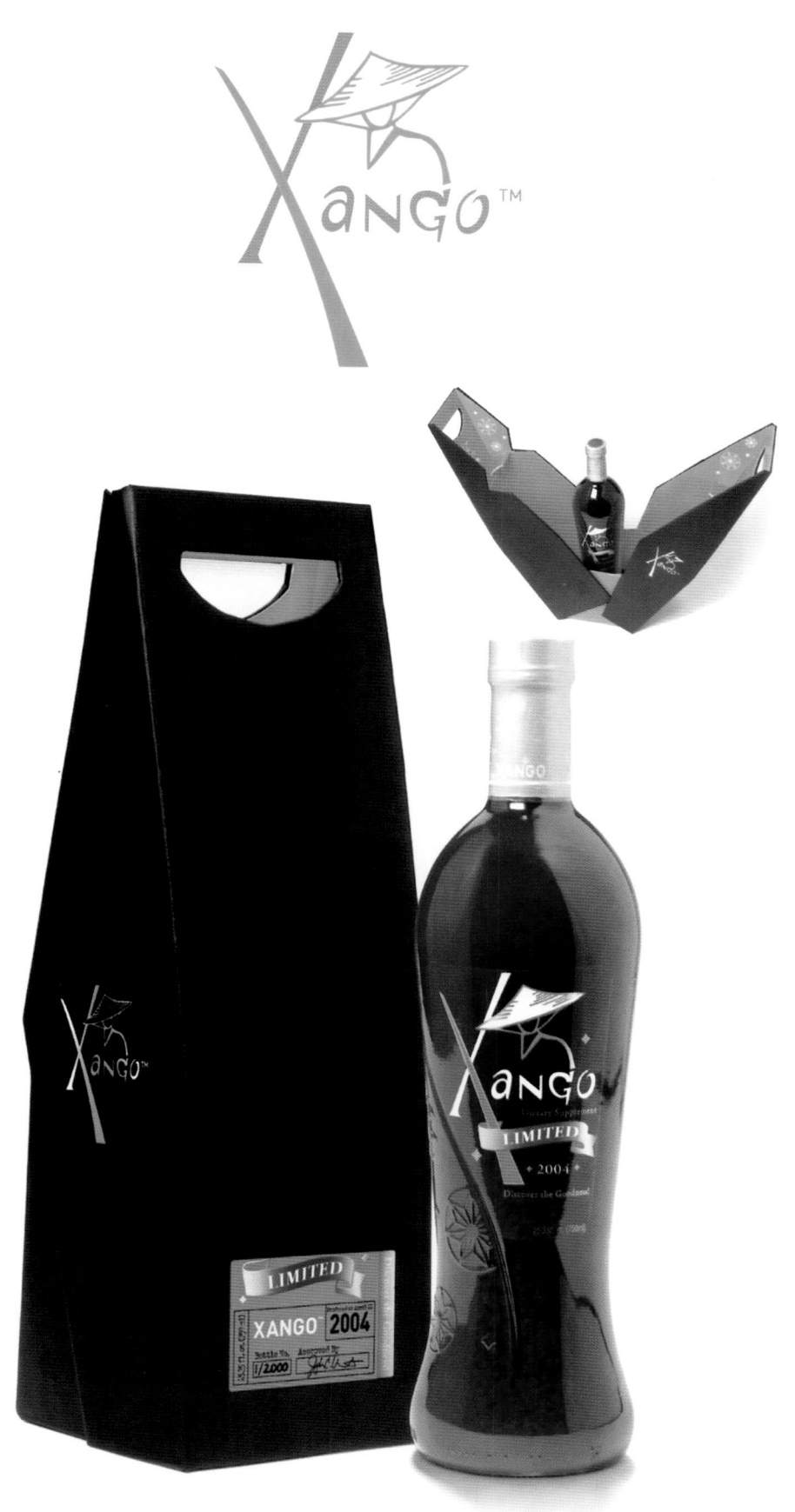

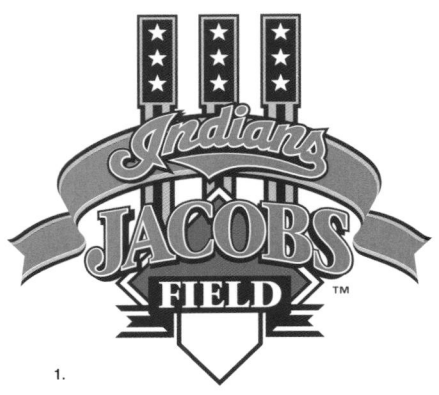

1.

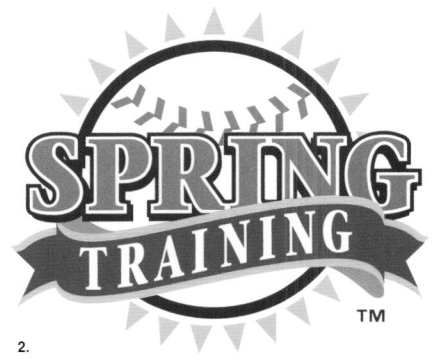

2.

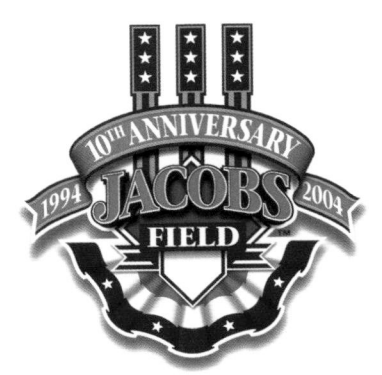

3.

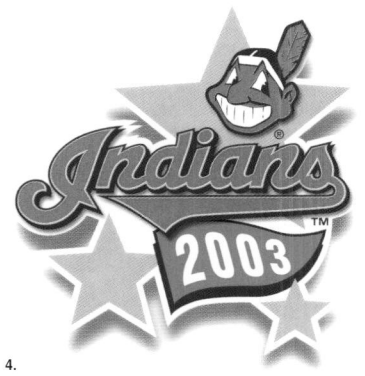

4.

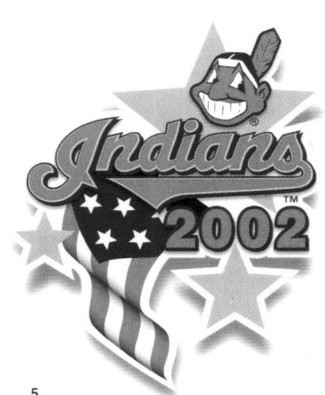

5.

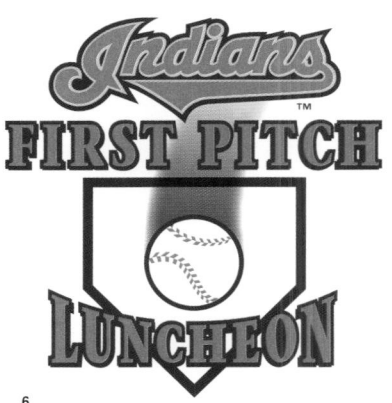

6.

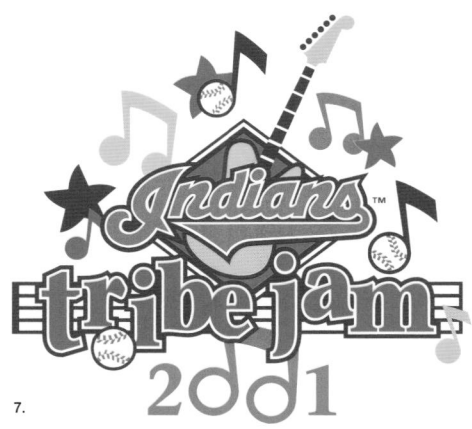

7.

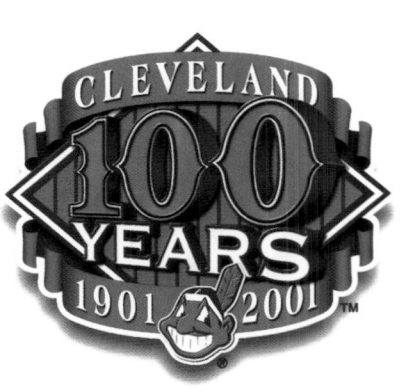

8.

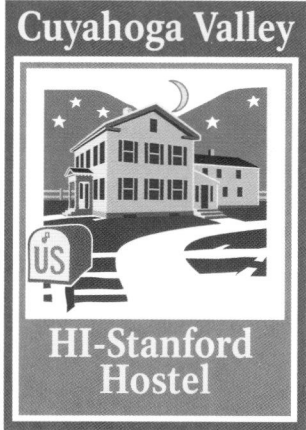

Cuyahoga Valley
HI-Stanford Hostel

9.

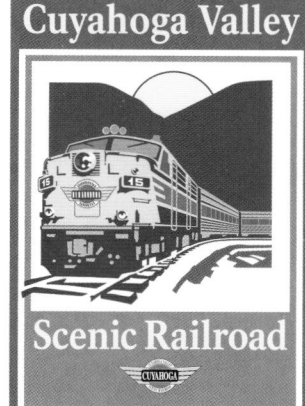

Cuyahoga Valley
Scenic Railroad

10.

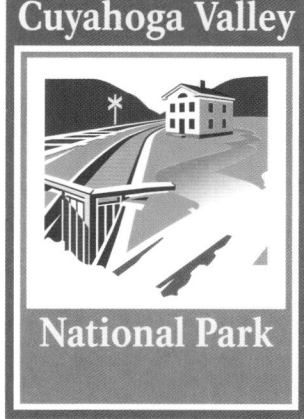

Cuyahoga Valley
National Park

11.

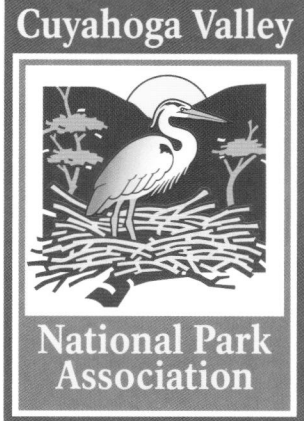

Cuyahoga Valley
National Park Association

12.

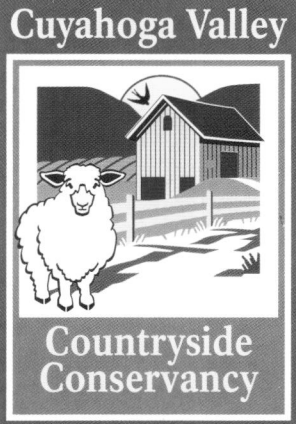

Cuyahoga Valley
Countryside Conservancy

13.

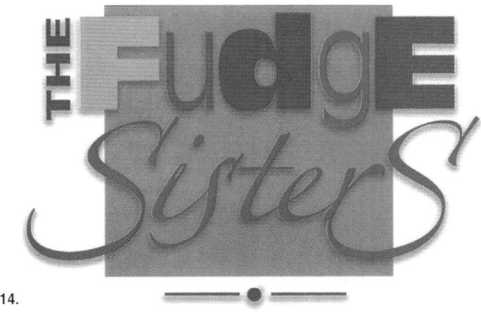

14.

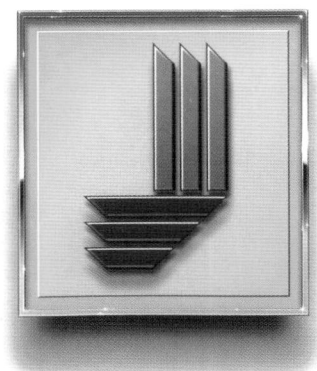

15.

1 - 15
Design Firm **Herip Design Associates, Inc.**
1 - 8.
Client *Cleveland Indians*
Designers Walter M. Herip,
John R. Menter
9 - 13.
Client *Cuyhoga Valley National Park*
Designers Walter M. Herip,
John R. Menter
14.
Client *The Fudge Sisters*
Designer Walter M. Herip
15.
Client *The Richard E. Jacobs Group, Inc.*
Designers Walter M. Herip,
John R. Menter

197

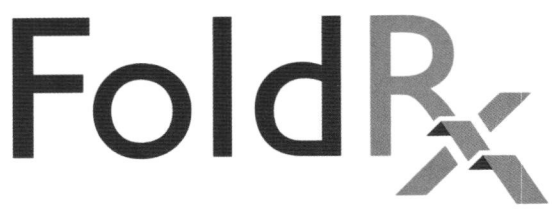

1.

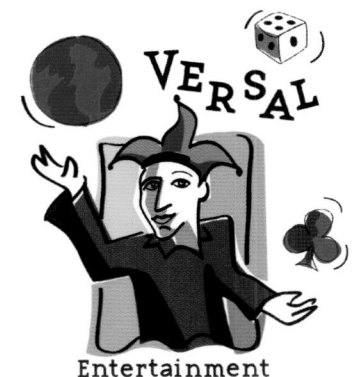

2.

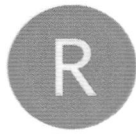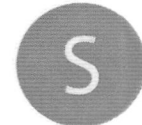

STRATEGIC | CREATIVE

3.

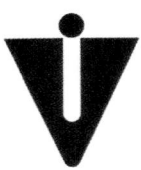

VENTURE**INVESTORS** LLC

Visionary Investments

4.

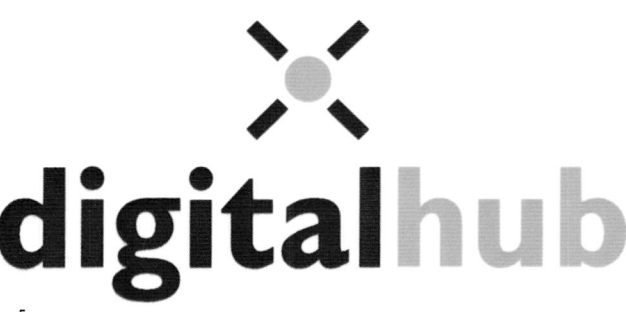

5.

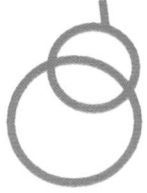

Pear Design

6.

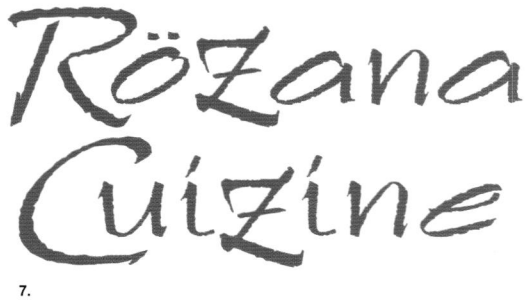

7.

1, 2
Design Firm **Fassino/Design**
3, 4
Design Firm **RS+K**
5, 6
Design Firm **Pear Design**
7
Design Firm **Walsh Design**

1.
Client   *FoldRx*
Designers   Chris Connors,
             Diane Fassino
2.
Client   *Versal Entertainment*
Designer   Angela Nannini
3.
Client   *RS+K*
Designer   Scot Kemp
4.
Client   *Venture Investors*
Designer   Kathleen Mitchell-Abendroth

5.
Client   *Digitalhub*
Designers   Linda Jackson,
             Norbert Marszalek
6.
Client   *Pear Design*
Designers   Linda Jackson,
             Norbert Marszalek
7.
Client   *Rözana Cuizine*
Designers   Miriam Lisco,
             Cathy Burnell
(opposite)
Client   ISI International
Design Firm **Walsh Design**
Designers   Miriam Lisco,
             Andrew MacDonald

PACIFIC DRAGON

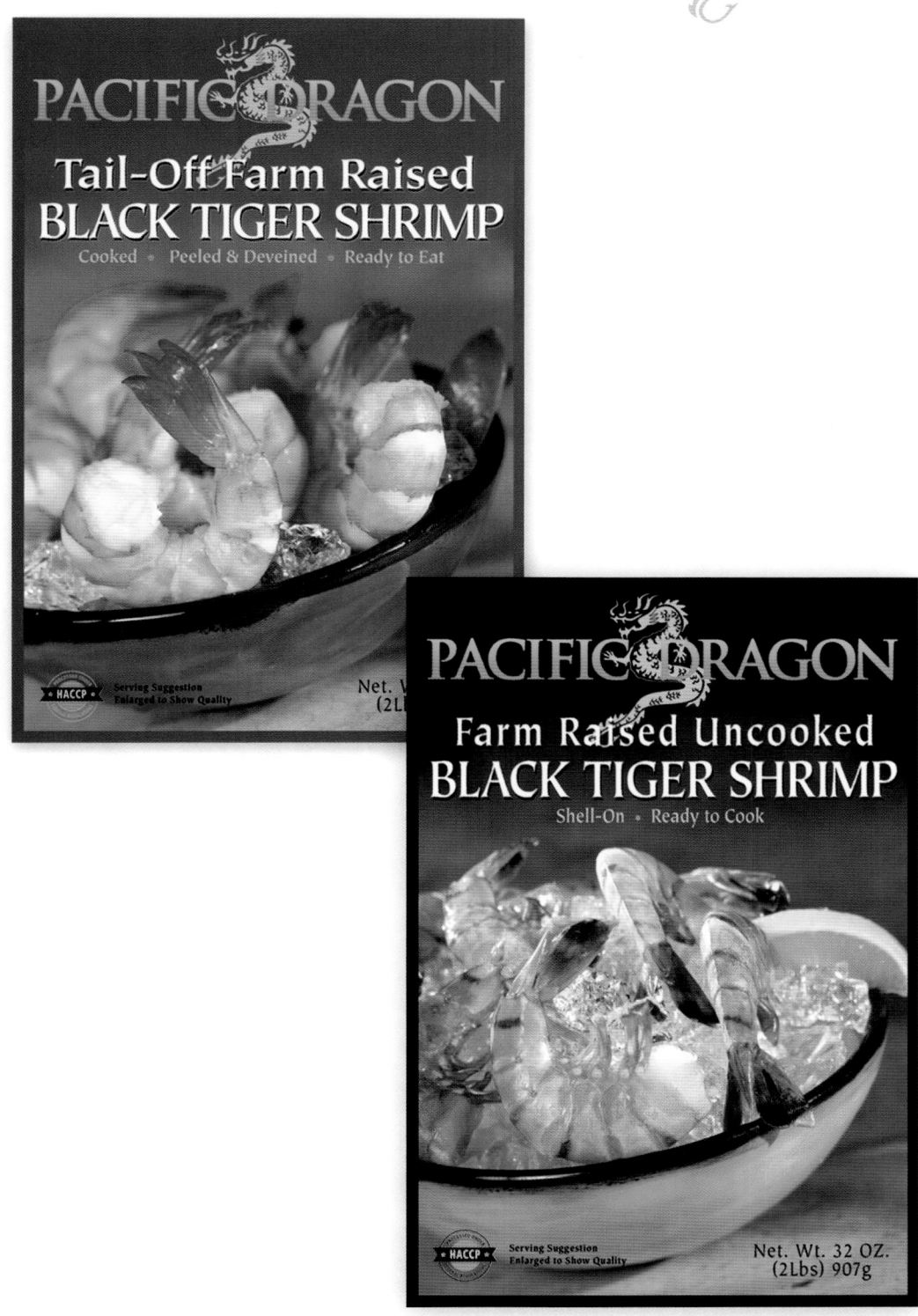

1.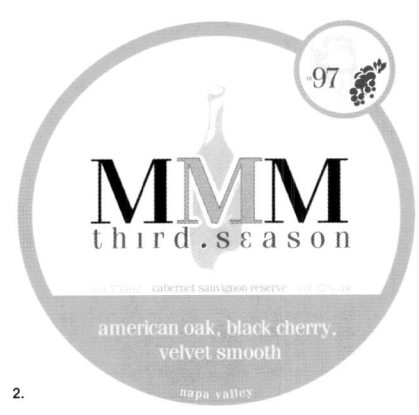
10 RED TOES

2.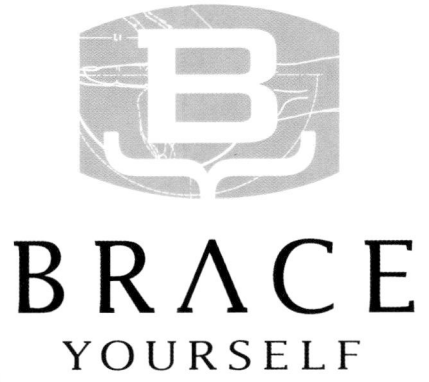
MMM
third.season
cabernet sauvignon reserve
american oak, black cherry,
velvet smooth
napa valley

3.
B
BRACE
YOURSELF

4.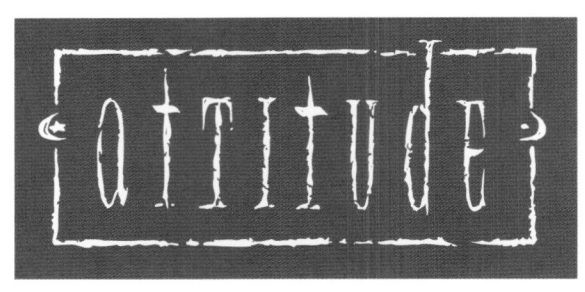
attitude

5.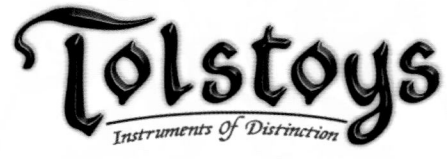
Tolstoys
Instruments Of Distinction

6.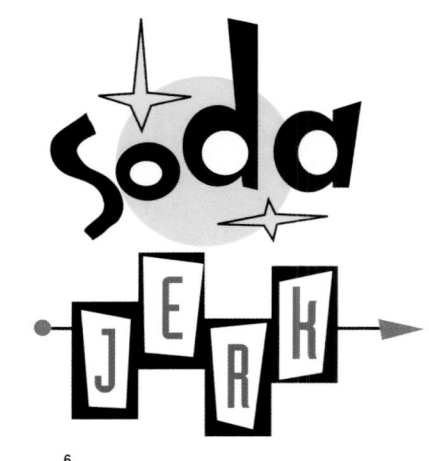
Soda
JERK

7.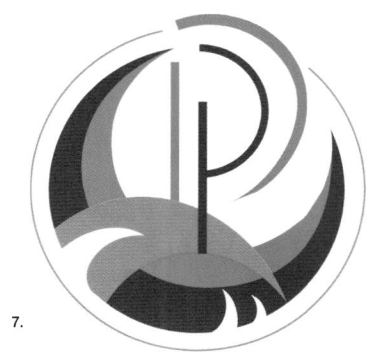

8.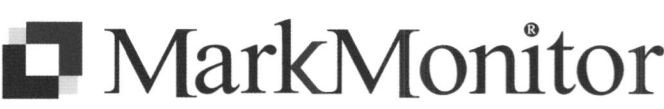
MarkMonitor®

200

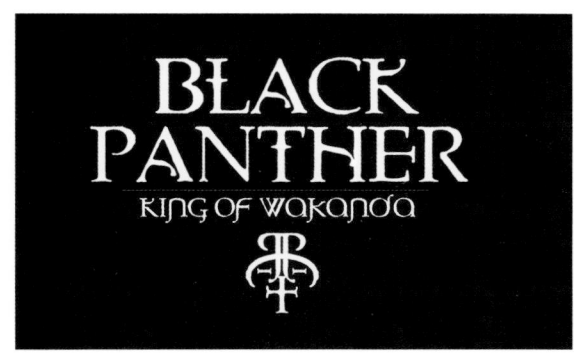

9.

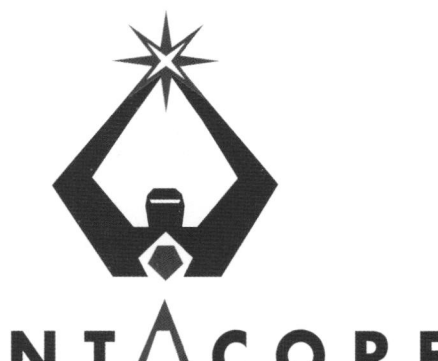

10.

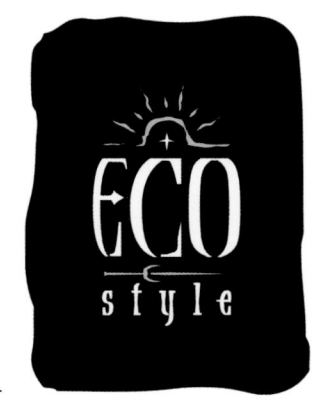

11.

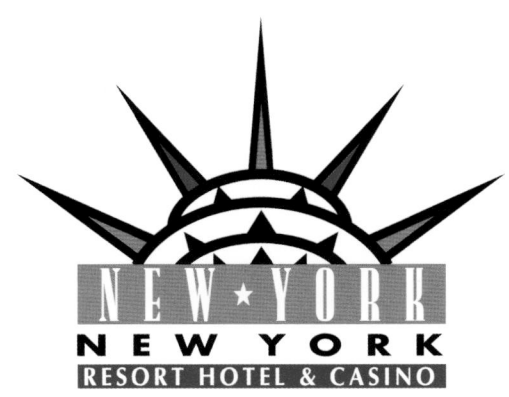

12.

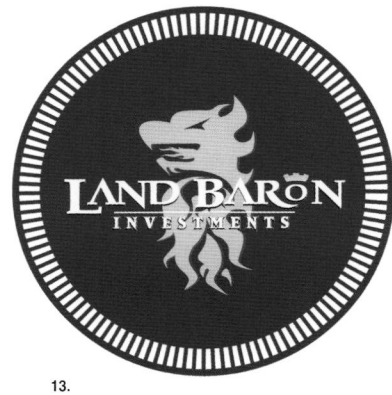

13.

LAND CAPITAL
FINANCIAL

14.

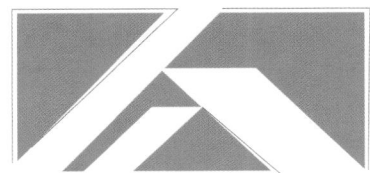

15.

1 - 15
Design Firm **M3AD.com**

1.
Client   Chronos 3
Designers   Dan McElhattan III,
             Lauren M. Brown

2.
Client   Chronos 3
Designer   Dan McElhattan III

3.
Client   Brace Yourself
Designers   Dan McElhattan III,
             Raymond Perez

4.
Client   Attitude Clothier
Designer   Dan McElhattan III

5.
Client   Navegante Group, Evolution
Designers   Dan McElhattan III,
             Raymond Perez

6.
Client   dm design lab
Designer   Dan McElhattan III

7.
Client   Paramount Professional Plaza
Designer   Dan McElhattan III

8.
Client   Elisa Cooper, Mark Monitor
Designer   Dan McElhattan III

9.
Client   M3 Advertising Design
Designer   Dan McElhattan III

10.
Client   Pentacore Engineering
Designer   Dan McElhattan III

11.
Client   Eco Style
Designer   Dan McElhattan III

12.
Client   Primm Investments
Designer   Dan McElhattan III

13.
Client   Land Baron Investments
Designer   Dan McElhattan III

14.
Client   Land Capital Financial
Designer   Dan McElhattan III

15.
Client   Luttrell Associates
Designer   Dan McElhattan III

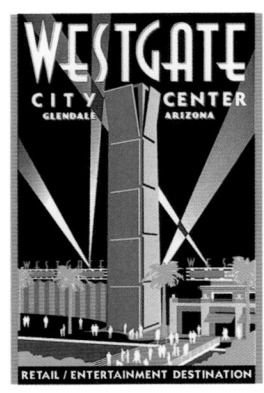

1.

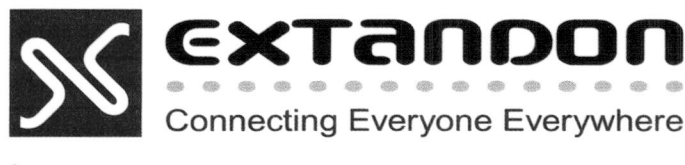

2.

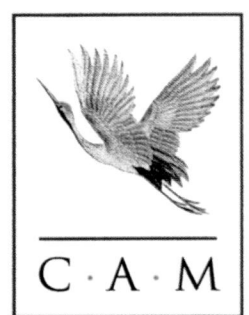

CRANE ASSET MANAGEMENT, LLC

3.

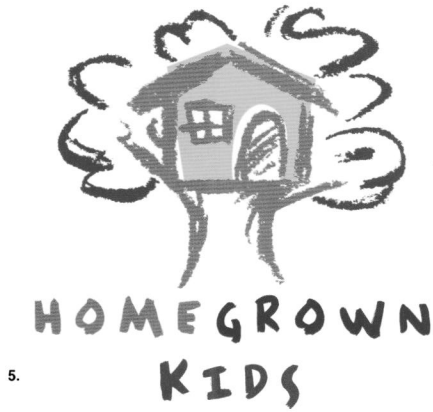

4.

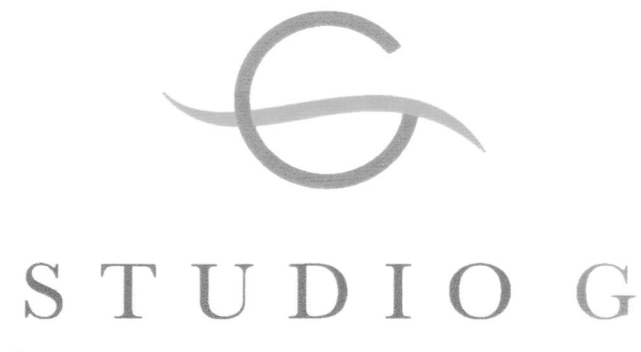

6.

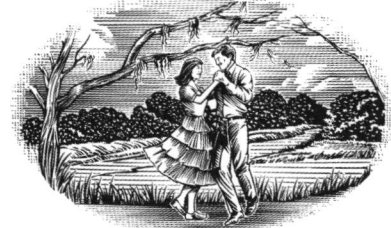

5.

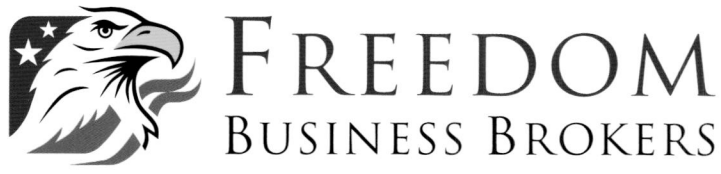

7.

1
Design Firm **Development Design Group, Inc.**
2
Design Firm **Crendo**
3
Design Firm **Bloch + Coulter Design Group**
4
Design Firm **Studio G**
5, 6
Design Firm **Vince Rini Design**
7
Design Firm **GOLD & Associates, Inc.**
1.
Client   *The Ellman Companies*
Designer   Valerie Cataffa
2.
Client   *Extandon Inc.*
Designer   Tamra Heathershaw-Hart

3.
Client   *Crane Asset Management LLC*
Designer   Ellie Young Suh
4.
Client   *Studio G*
Designer   Gretchen Wills
5.
Client   *Homegrown Kids*
Designer   Vince Rini
6.
Client   *Freedom Business Brokers*
Designer   Vince Rini
7.
Client   *Florida Folk Festival*
Designers   Keith Gold, Peter Butcavage
(opposite)
Client   *Good Humor-Breyers*
Design Firm **Smith Design**
Designer   Carol Konkowski

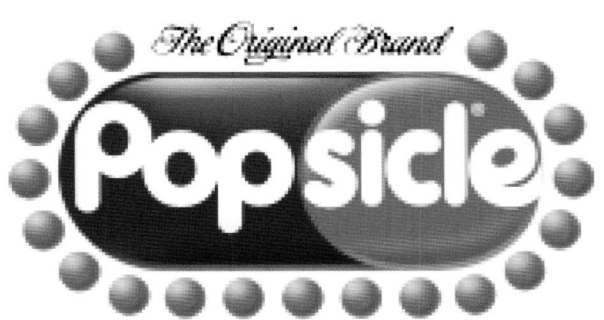

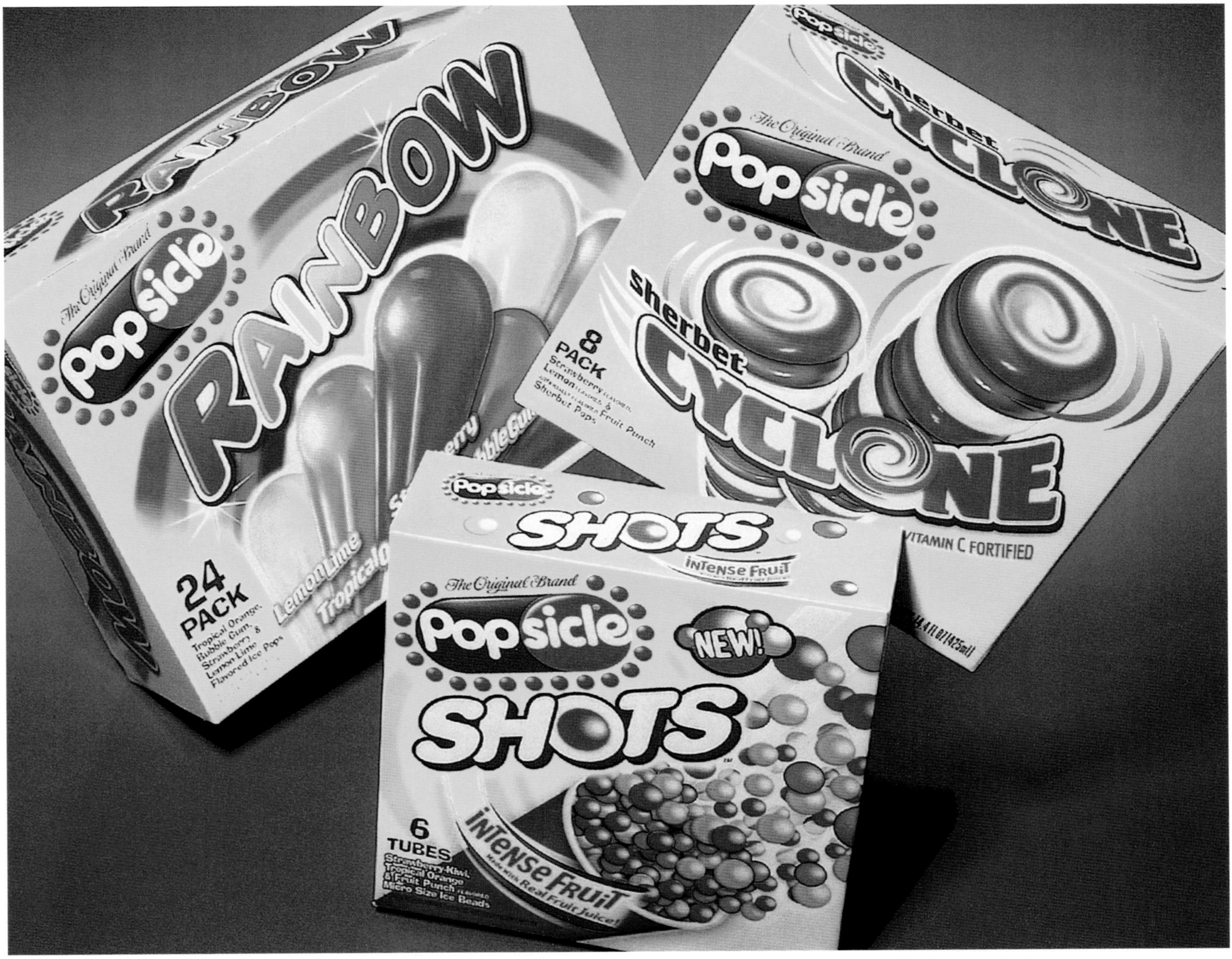

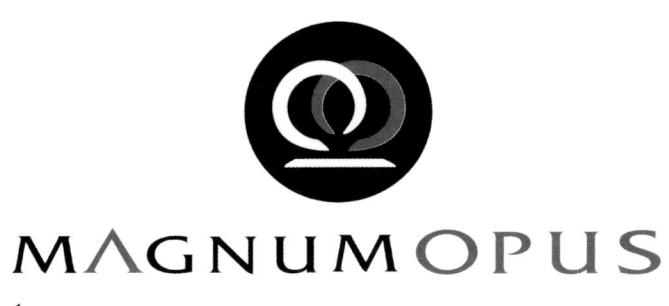

1.

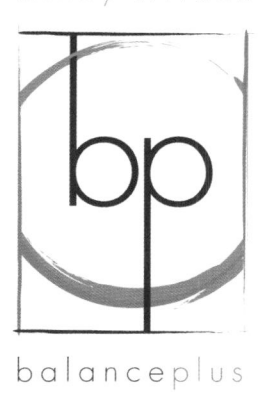

mindy l.frank

balanceplus

2.

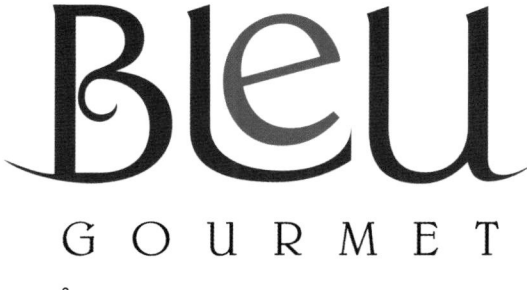

3.

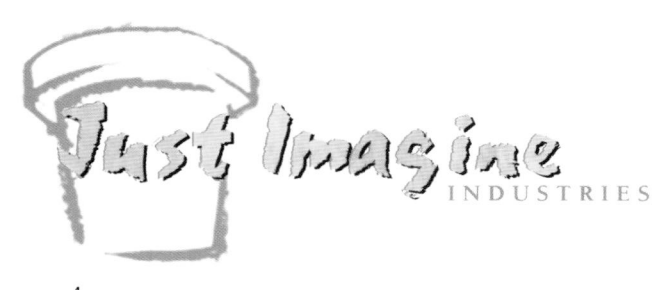

4.

C H R 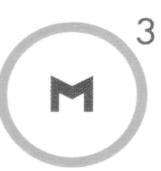 N O S

5.

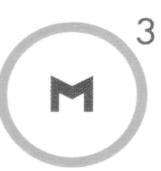

M3 ADVERTISING DESIGN

6.

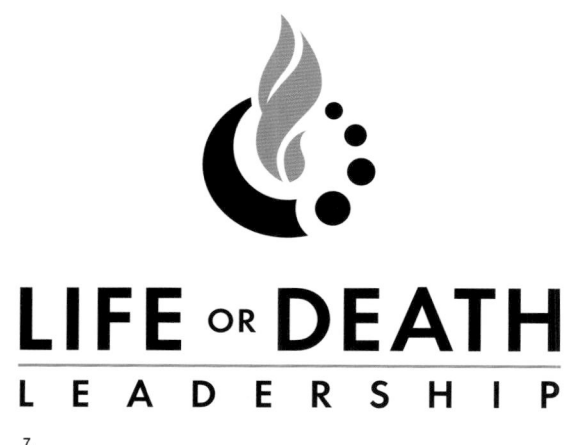

LIFE OR DEATH
LEADERSHIP

7.

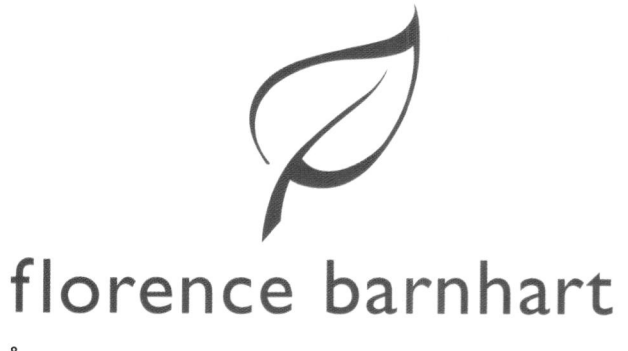

florence barnhart

8.

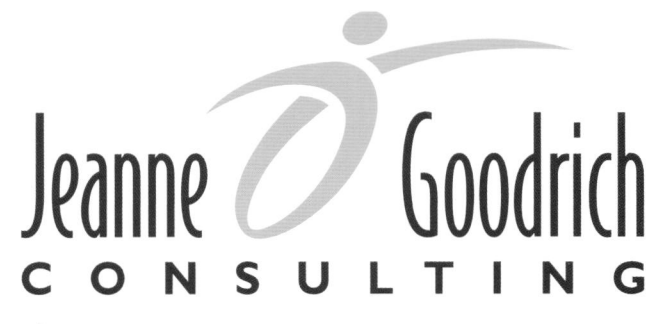

9.

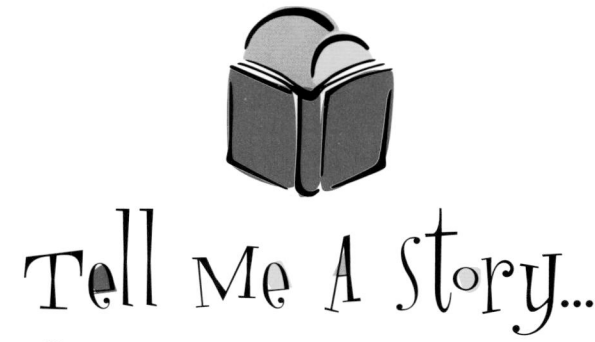

10.

VERB | creative

11.

BLACKST⊙NE

12.

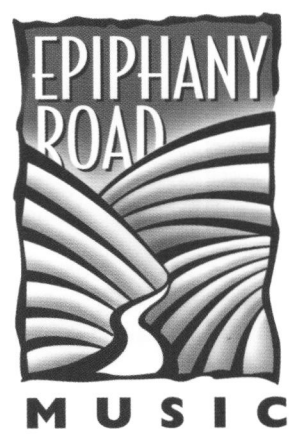

13.

PHOTON Light.COM

14.

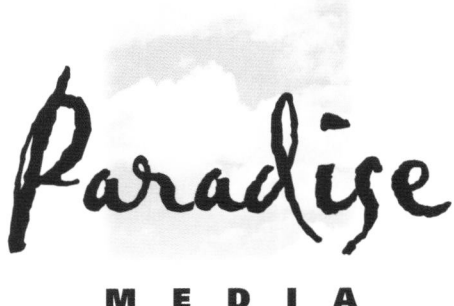

15.

1 - 6
Design Firm **M3AD.com**
7 - 15
Design Firm **Defteling Design**
1.
Client   *MagnuMOpus*
Designers   Dan McElhattan III,
   David Araujo
2.
Client   *Balance Plus*
Designer   Dan McElhattan III
3.
Client   *Sonny Ahuja*
Designers   Dan McElhattan ,
   David Araujo
4.
Client   *Just Imagine Industries*
Designer   Dan McElhattan III
5, 6.
Client   *M3 Advertising Design*
Designer   Dan McElhattan
7.
Client   *Life or Death Leadership*
Designer   Alex Wijnen

8.
Client   *Florence Barnhart*
Designer   Alex Wijnen
9.
Client   *Jeanne Goodrich Consulting*
Designer   Alex Wijnen
10.
Client   *Tell Me A Story*
Designer   Alex Wijnen
11.
Client   *Verb Creative*
Designer   Alex Wijnen
12.
Client   *Blackstone, Inc.*
Designer   Alex Wijnen
13.
Client   *Epiphany Road Music*
Designer   Alex Wijnen
14.
Client   *Photon Light*
Designer   Alex Wijnen
15.
Client   *Paradise Media, Inc.*
Designer   Alex Wijnen

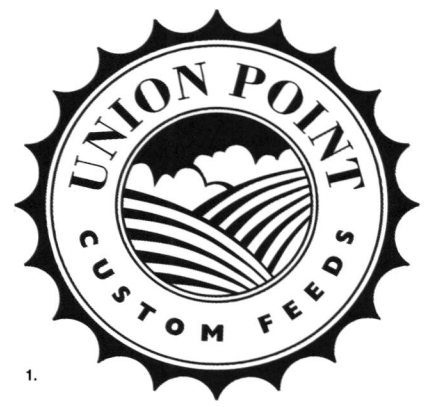

1.

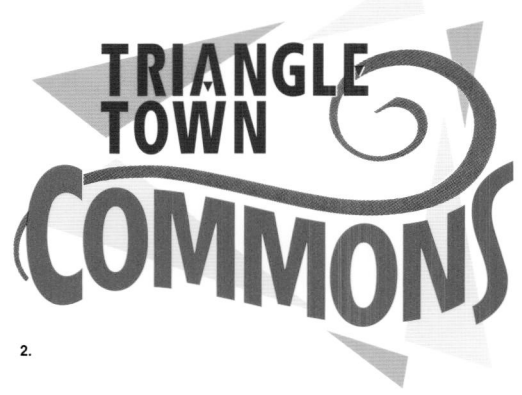

2.

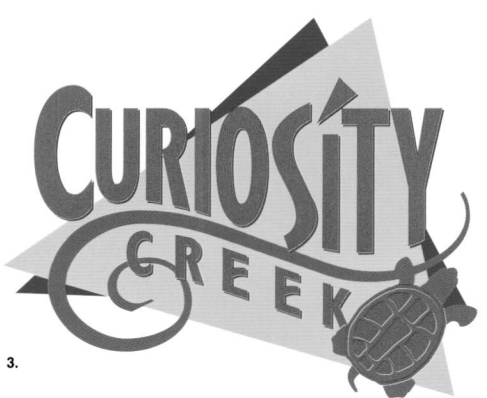

3.

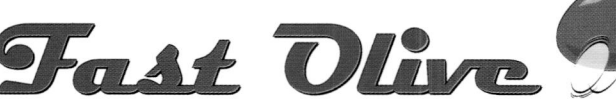

4.

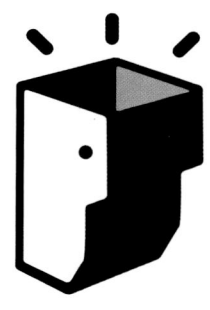

5.

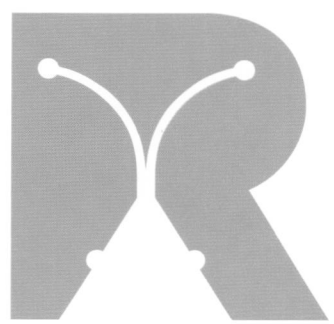

6.

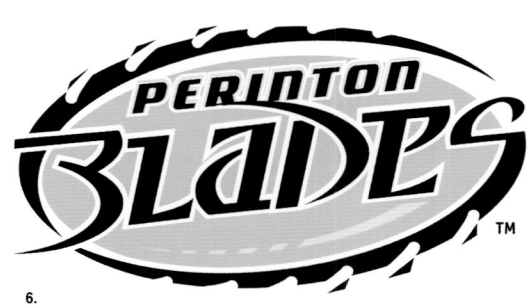

7.

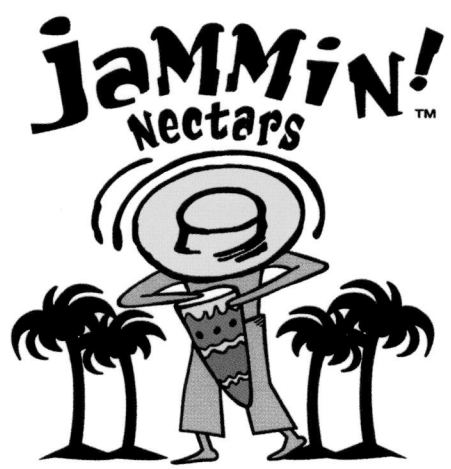

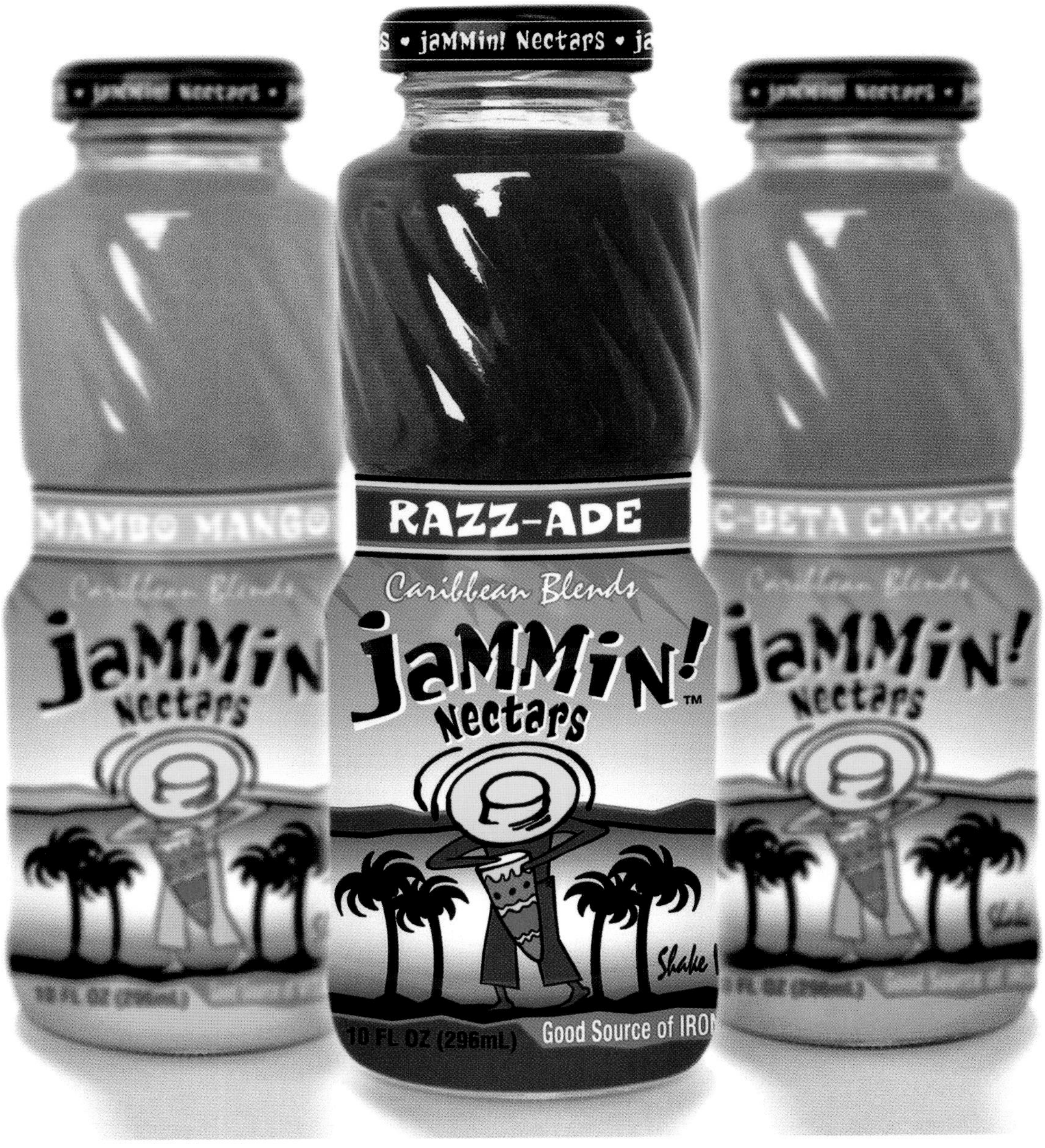

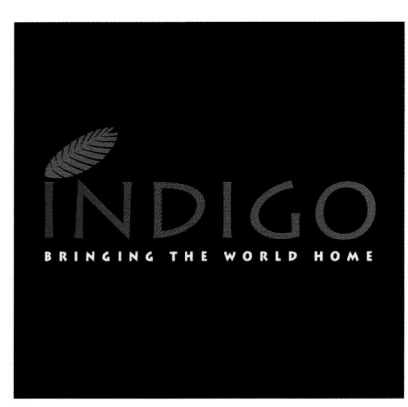

1.

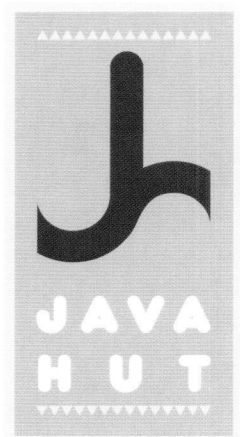

2.

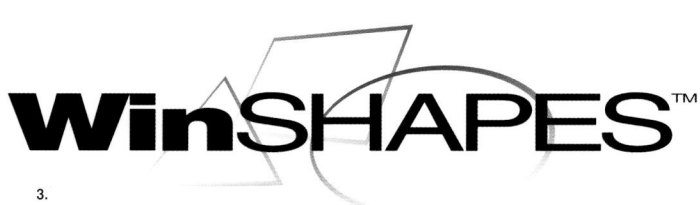

3.

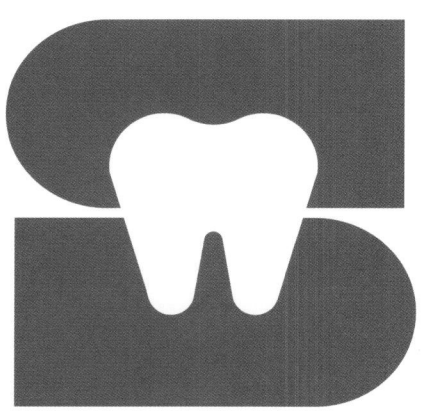

4.

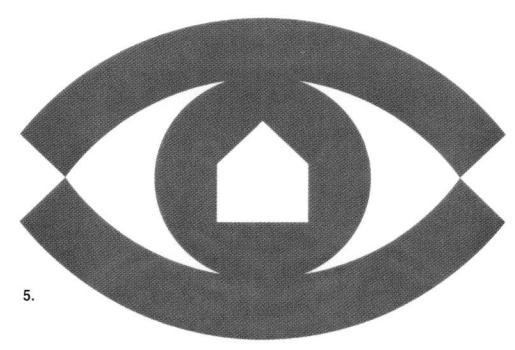

5.

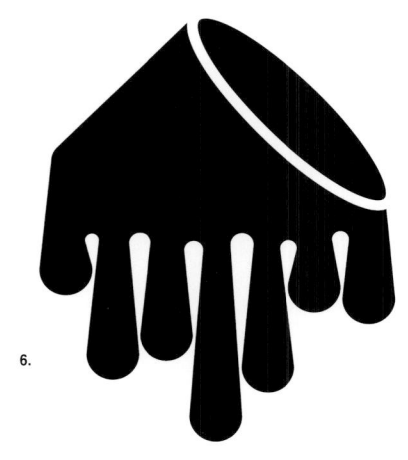

6.

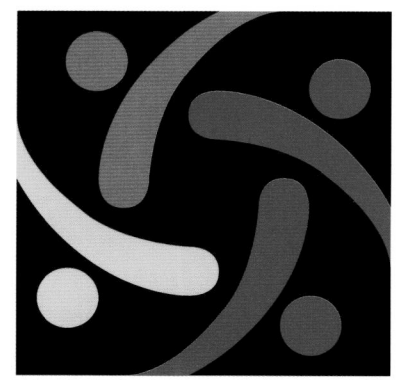

7.

8. stepxstep

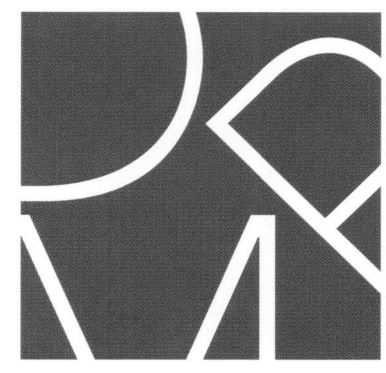

9.

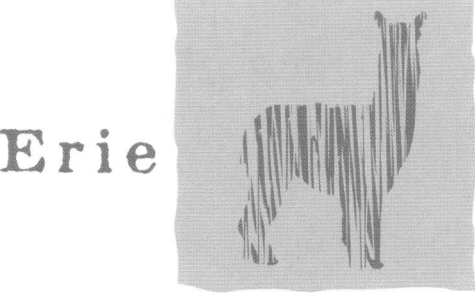

Erie Bleu

10. Alpaca Farm

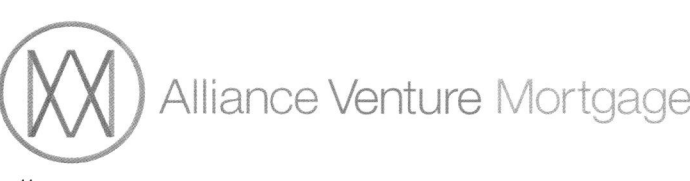

Alliance Venture Mortgage

11.

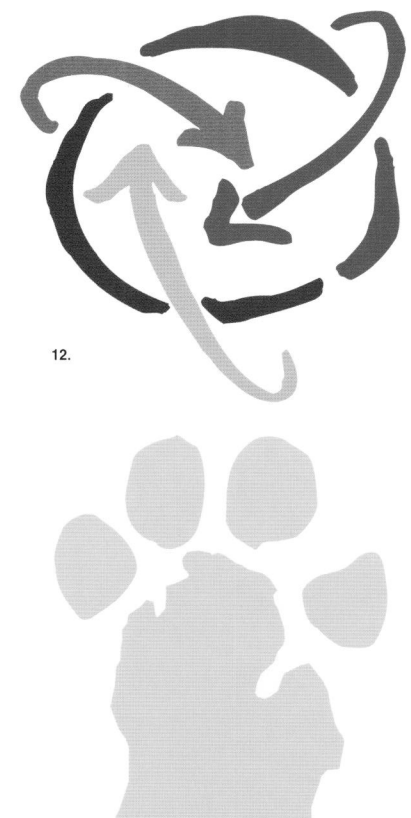

12.

ShapesSTUDIO™

13.

14.

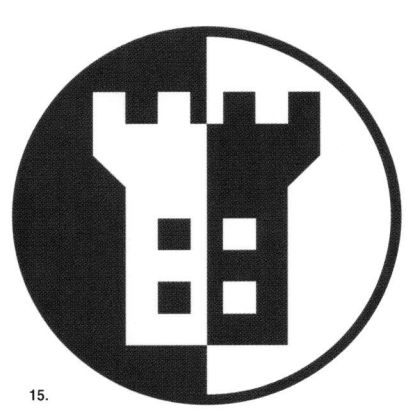

15.

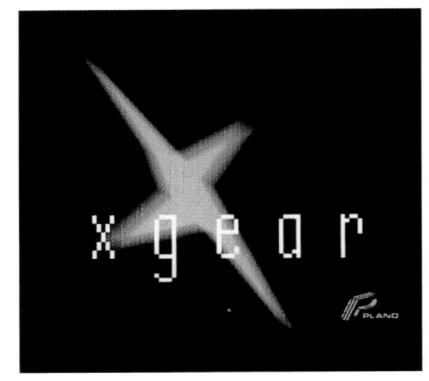

1.

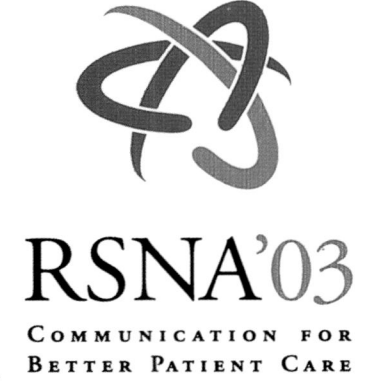

2.

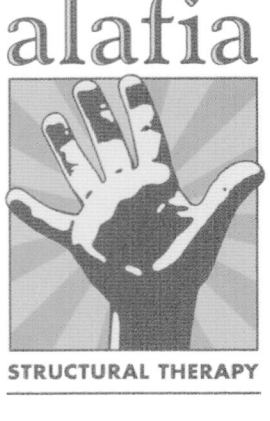

3.

4.

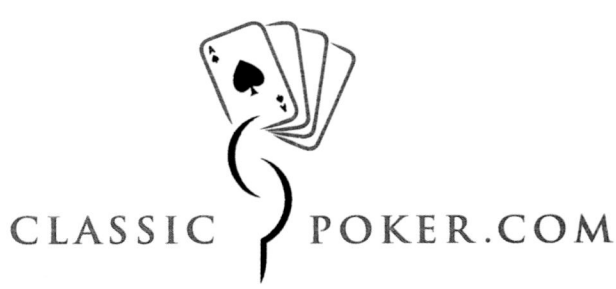

5.

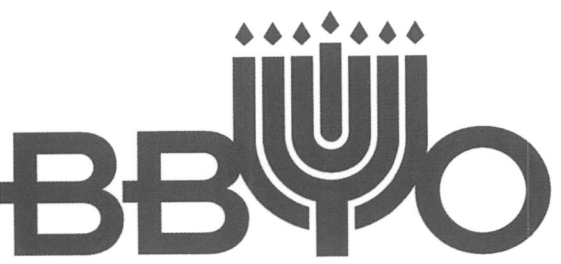

6.

BB🕎O

7.

1 - 4
Design Firm **Asylum Strategic Design**

5 - 7
Design Firm **Beth Singer Design, LLC**

1.
Client   *Plano*
Designers   Bill Current, Ron Klein

2.
Client   *Radiological*
Designers   Ron Klein, Bill Current

3.
Client   *Radiological*
Designers   Jay Vidheecharoen, Ron Klein

4.
Client   *Alafia*
Designers   Dave Bruck, Bill Current

5.
Client   *The International Commission on
            Holocaust Era Insurance Claims*
Designer   Chris Hoch

6.
Client   *Classic Poker*
Designers   Sucha Snidvongs,
            Steve Trapero

7.
Client   *B'nai B'rith Touth Organization*
Designers   Suheun Yu, Chris Hoch
(opposite)
Client   *Tom McIlhenny*
Design Firm **Performance Graphics
            of Lake Norman, Inc.**
Designer   Mitzi Mayhew

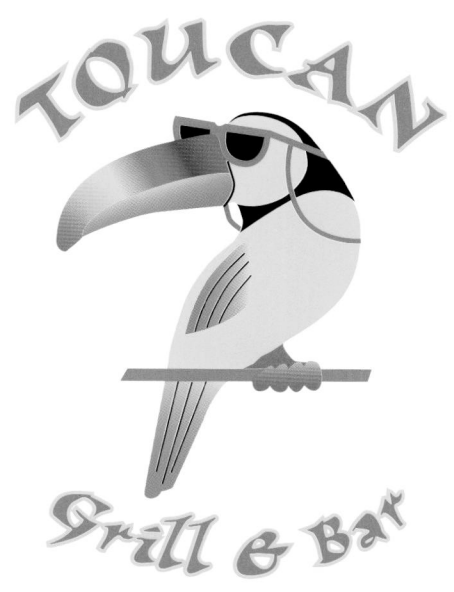

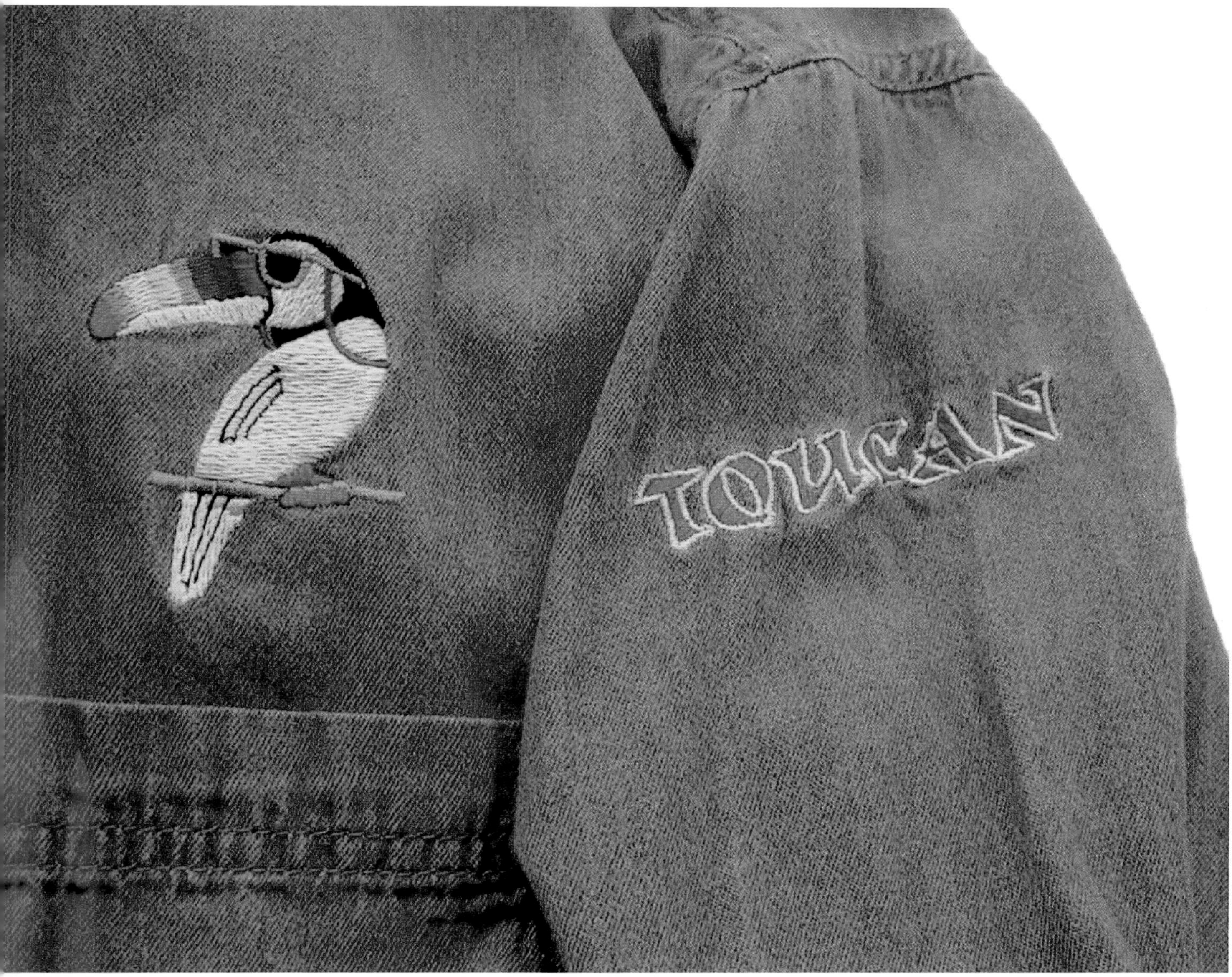

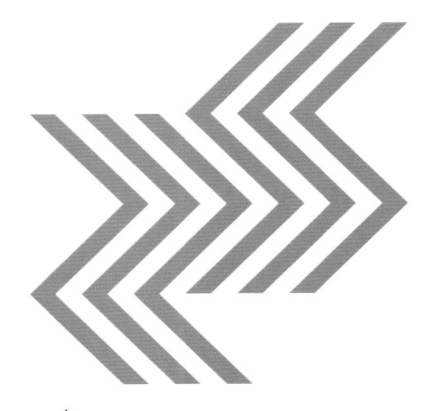

1.

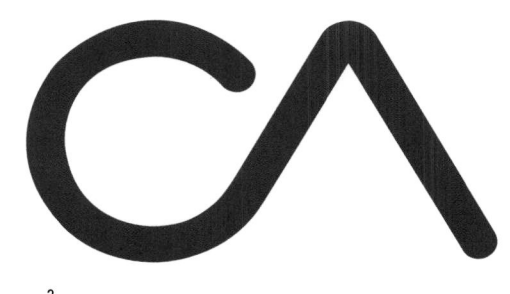

2.

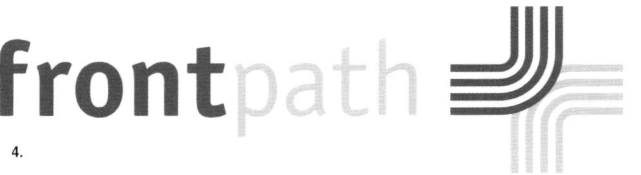

3.

frontpath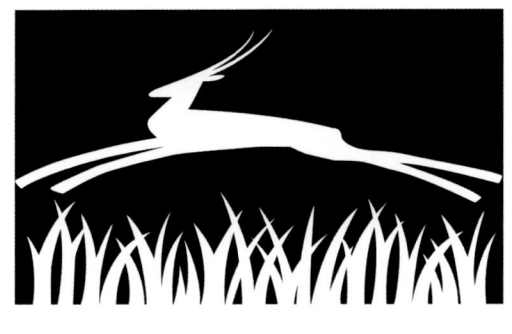

4.

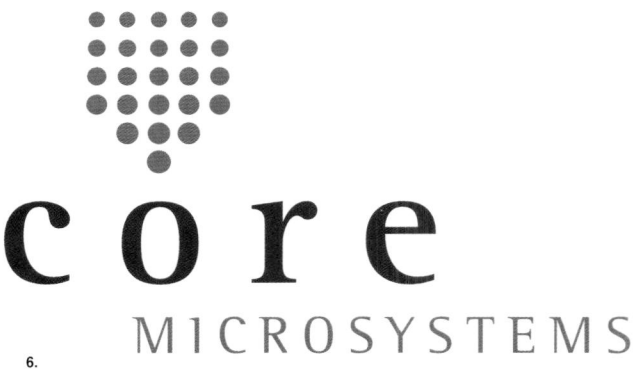

5.

core
MICROSYSTEMS

6.

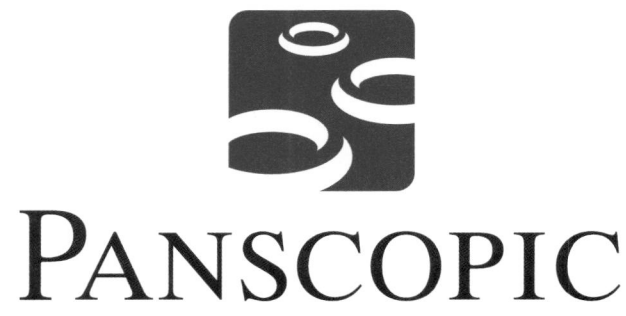

PANSCOPIC

7.

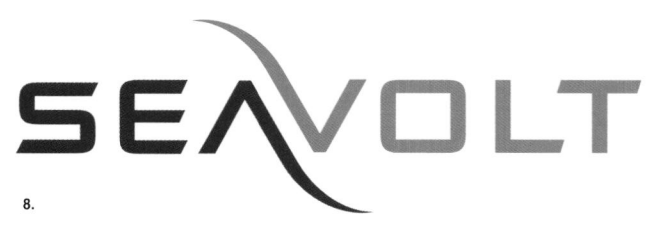

8.

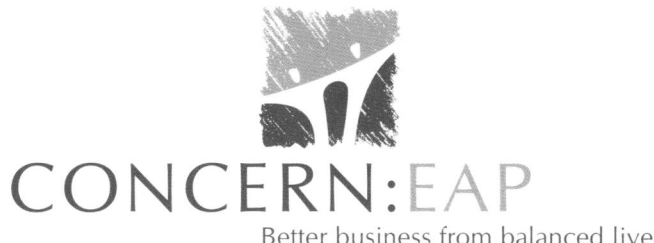

CONCERN:EAP

Better business from balanced lives

9.

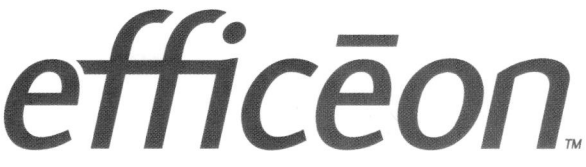

efficēon ™

10.

Transmeta

CORPORATION

11.

aftermedia ®

12.

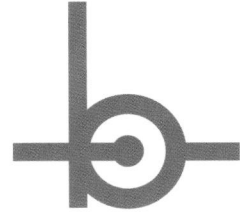

BETA BREAKERS

SOFTWARE QUALITY ASSURANCE LABS

13.

SIX ◆ DEGREES

14.

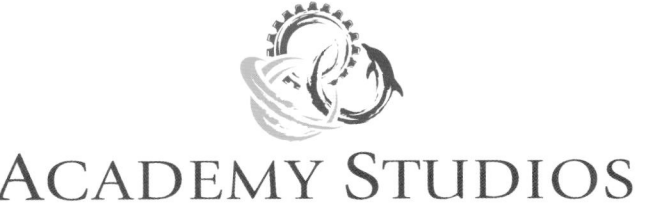

ACADEMY STUDIOS

15.

1 - 5
Design Firm **Lesniewicz Associates**
6 - 15
Design Firm **Plumbline Studios Inc.**

1.
Client *Zyndorf/Serchuk*
Designer Terry Lesniewicz

2.
Client *Construction Architects*
Designer Terry Lesniewicz

3.
Client *Racing For Recovery*
Designer Amy Lesniewicz

4.
Client *FrontPath Health Coalition*
Designer Jack Bollinger

5.
Client *Owens Corning*
Designer Jack Bollinger

6.
Client *Core Microsystems*
Designer Dom Moreci

7.
Client *Panscopic*
Designer Dom Moreci

8.
Client *Sea Volt*
Designer James Eli

9.
Client *Concern:EAP*
Designer Dom Moreci

10, 11.
Client *Transmeta Corp*
Designers James Eli, Dom Moreci

12.
Client *AfterMedia*
Designer Dom Moreci

13.
Client *Beta Breakers*
Designer Dom Moreci

14.
Client *Six Degrees*
Designer Ariel Villasol

15.
Client *Academy Studios*
Designers James Eli, Ariel Villasol, Dom Moreci, Mike Eli

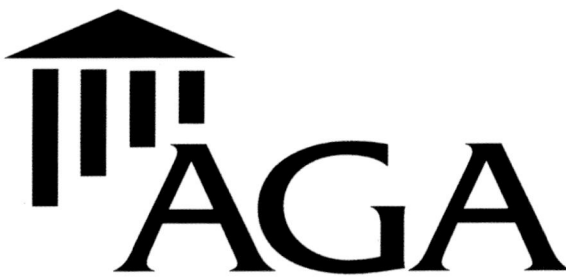

1.

GLOBAL IMPACT

2.

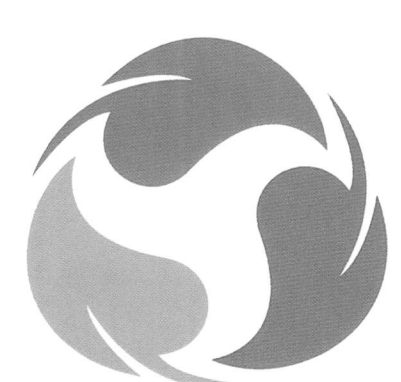

3.

SAVORY FLAVOR
M O S A I C

4.

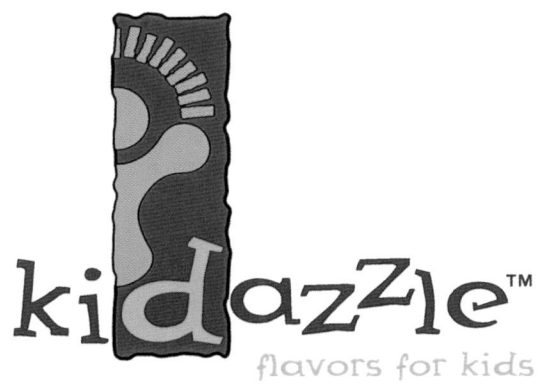

kidazzle™
flavors for kids

5.

MARIN
EDUCATION
FUND

Creating Educational Equity

6.

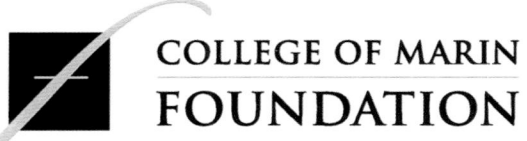

COLLEGE OF MARIN
FOUNDATION

7.

1 - 3
Design Firm **TGD Communications**
4, 5
Design Firm **AJF Marketing**
6, 7
Design Firm **Ann Hill Communications**
1.
Client *Association of Government Accountants*
Designer Jennifer Cedoz
2.
Client *Global Impact*
Designer Gloria Vestal
3.
Client *Centennial Contractors Enterprises*
Designer Gloria Vestal

4.
Client *IFF-International Flavors & Fragrances*
Designer Justin Brindisi
5.
Client *IFF-International Flavors & Fragrances*
Designer Paul Borkowski
6.
Client *Marin Education Fund*
Designer Jack Zoog
7.
Client *College of Marin Foundation*
Designer Jack Zoog
(opposite)
Client *21st Century Spirits*
Design Firm **Flowdesign, Inc.**
Designer Dan Matauch

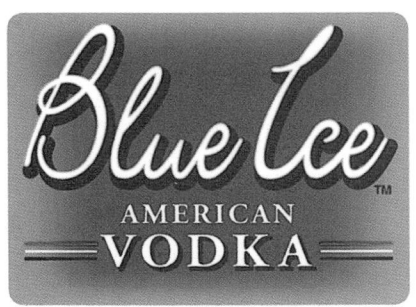

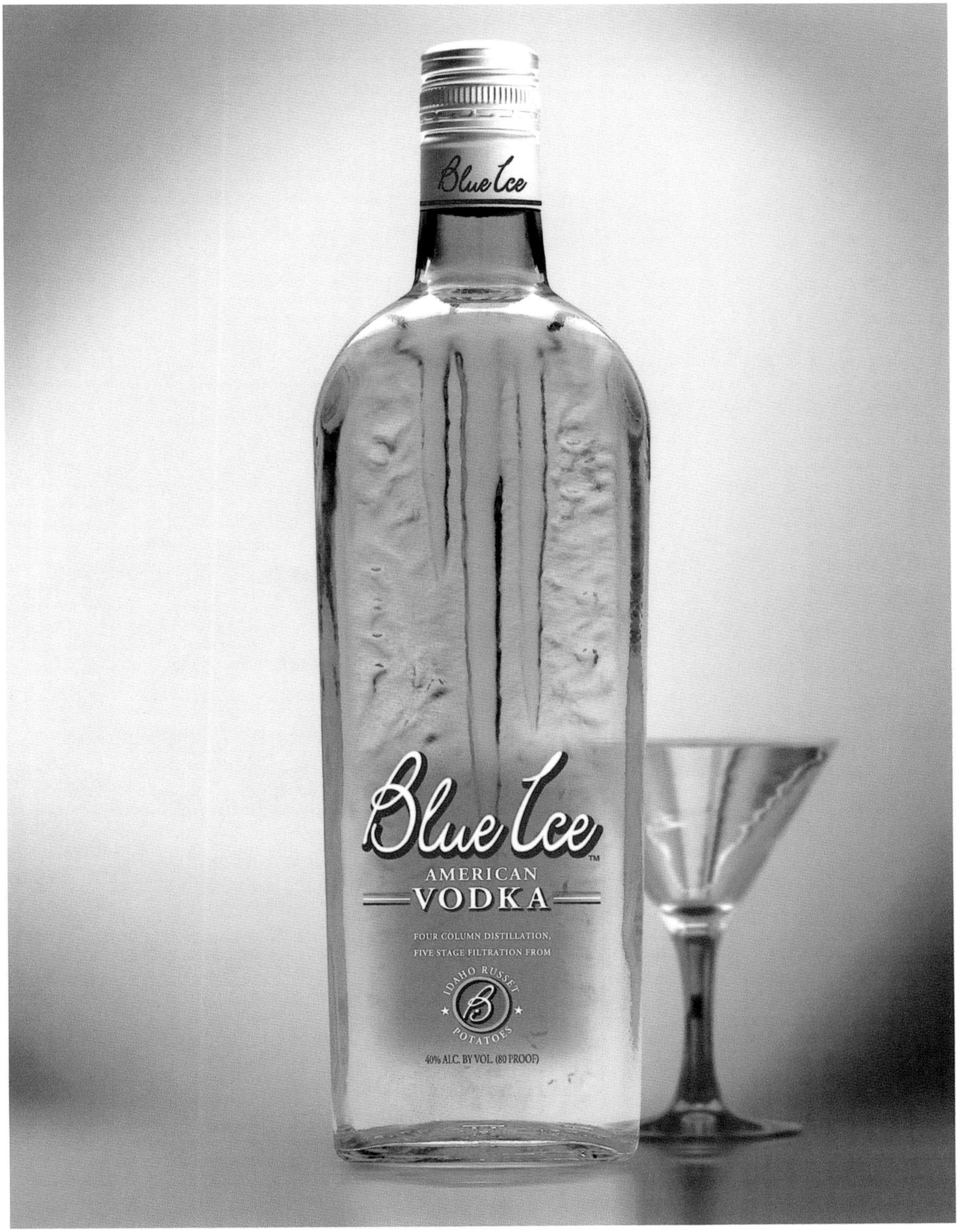

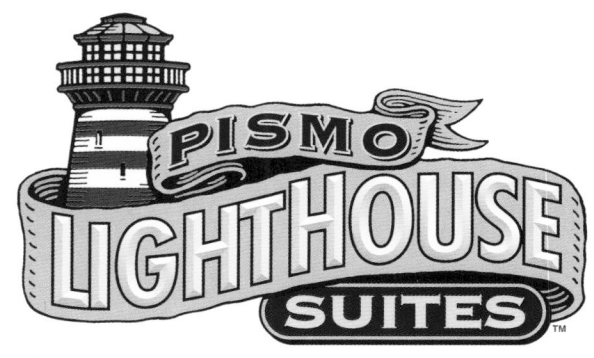

1.

OceanParkHotels

2.

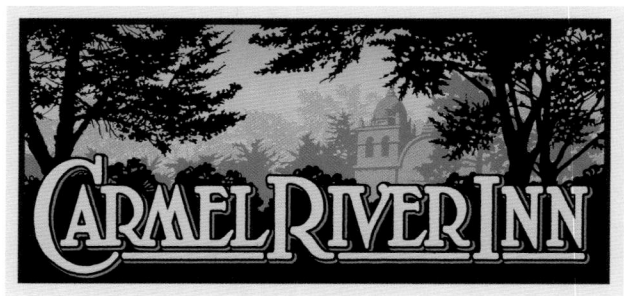

3.

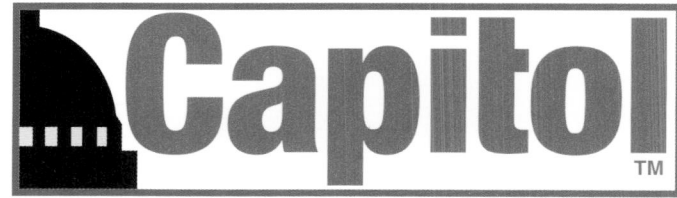

4.

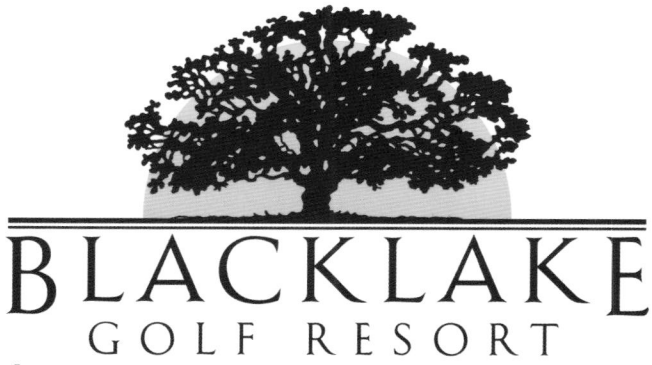

5.

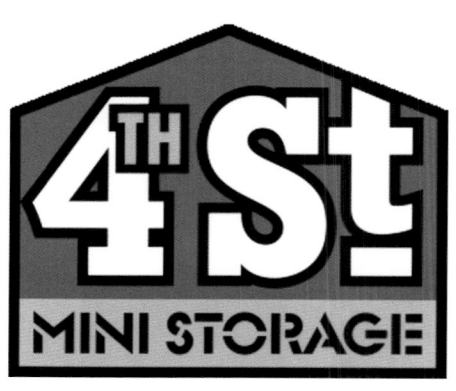

6.

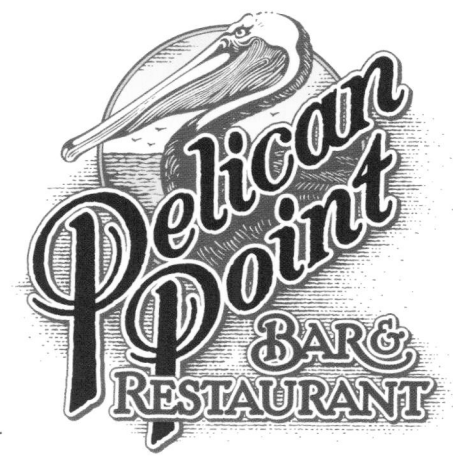

7.

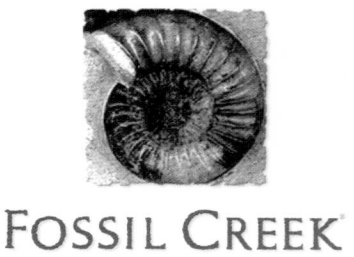

FOSSIL CREEK

8.

Petit Soleil
BED & BREAKFAST

9.

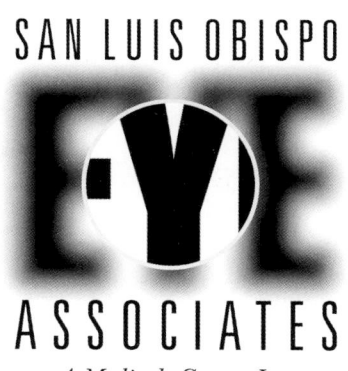

SAN LUIS OBISPO
EYE
ASSOCIATES
A Medical Group, Inc.

10.

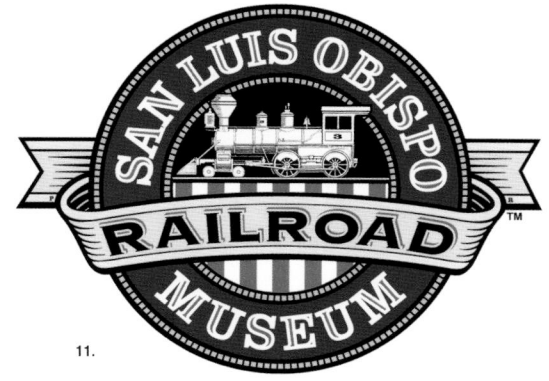

11.

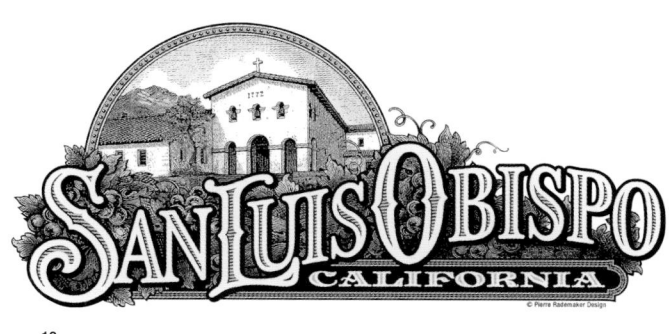

12.

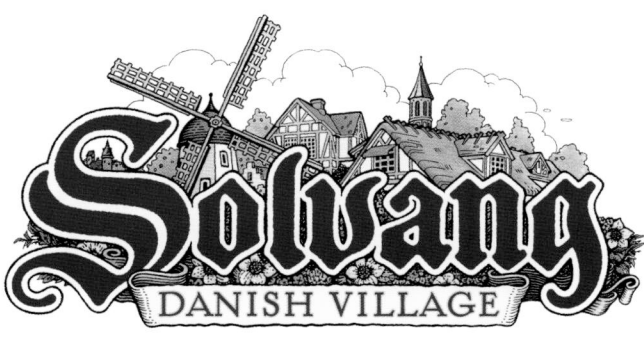

13.

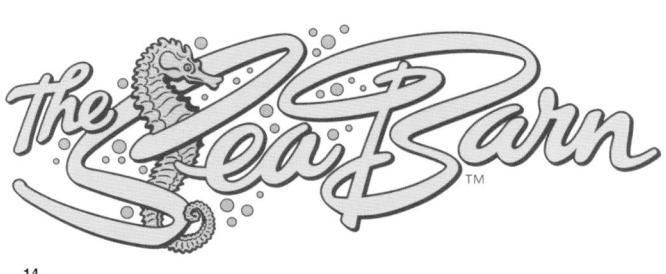

14.

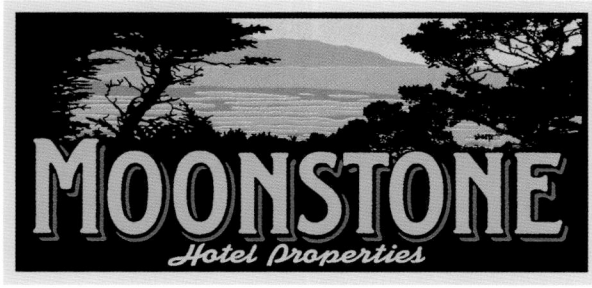

15.

1 - 15		
Design Firm	**Pierre Rademaker Design**	
1.		
	Client	Martin Resorts
	Designers	Debbie Shibata, Pierre Rademaker
2.		
	Client	Ocean Park Hotels
	Designers	Anne Bussone, Pierre Rademaker
3.		
	Client	Moonstone Hotel Properties
	Designers	Debbie Shibata, Pierre Rademaker
4.		
	Client	Capitol Outdoor
	Designers	Anne Bussone, Pierre Rademaker
5.		
	Client	Infinite Horizon's
	Designers	Debbie Shibata, Pierre Rademaker
6.		
	Client	Martin & Hobbs
	Designers	Anne Bussone, Sierra Slade, Pierre Rademaker
7.		
	Client	Martin Resorts
	Designers	Pierre Rademaker, Debbie Shibata

8.		
	Client	Fossil Creek Winery
	Designers	Anne Bussone, Pierre Rademaker
9.		
	Client	Petite Soleil
	Designers	Anne Bussone, Pierre Rademaker
10.		
	Client	San Luis Obispo Eye Associates
	Designers	Kenny B. Swete, Dusty Davis, Pierre Rademaker
11.		
	Client	San Luis Railroad Museum
	Designers	Elisa York, Anne Bussone, Pierre Rademaker
12.		
	Client	San Luis Obispo
	Designer	Pierre Rademaker
13.		
	Client	Solvang
	Designers	Pierre Rademaker, Debbie Shibata
14.		
	Client	The Sea Barn
	Designers	Elisa York, Pierre Rademaker, Debbie Shibata
15.		
	Client	Moonstone Hotel Properties
	Designers	Pierre Rademaker, Debbie Shibata

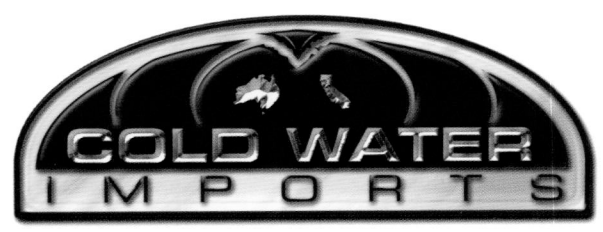

1.

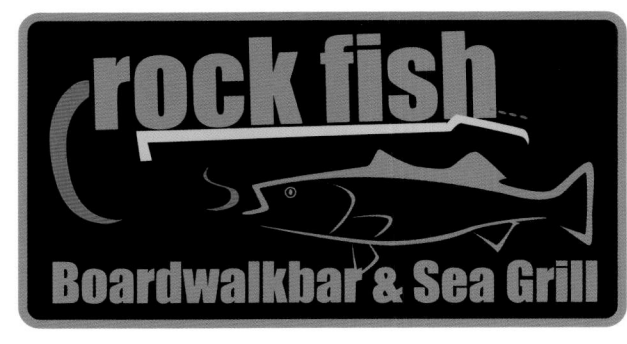

2.

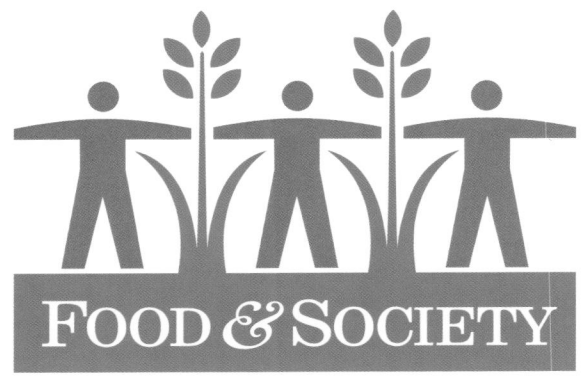

3.

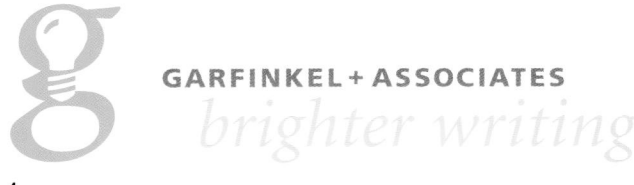

4.

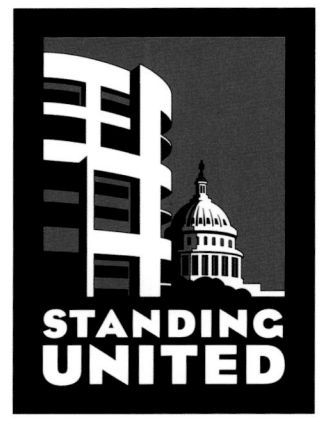

5.

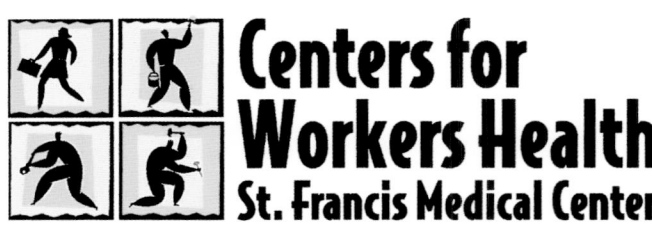

6.

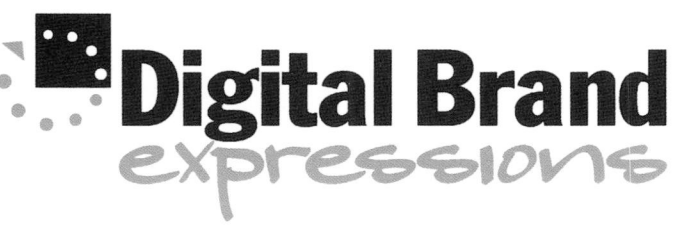

7.

1, 2
Design Firm **Medialias Creative**
3 - 5
Design Firm **Levine & Associates**
6, 7
Design Firm **Zoe Graphics**
1.
    Client   *Cold Water Imports*
    Designers Gregg Holda,
                Shaun Menestrina
2.
    Client   *Rockfish Boardwalk Bar & Sea Grill*
    Designers Gregg Holda,
                Shaun Menestrina
3.
    Client   *Kellogg Foundation*
    Designer Lena Markley
4.
    Client   *Garfinkel + Associates*
    Designer Jennie Jariel

5.
    Client   *United Brotherhood of*
                Carpenters & Joiners of America
    Designer Steve Ofner
6.
    Client   *St. Francis Medical Ctr.*
    Designers Kim Waters, Kathy Pagano
7.
    Client   *Digital Brand Expressions*
    Designers Kim Waters, Kathy Pagano
(opposite)
    Client   *American Beverage Marketers*
    Design Firm **Flowdesign, Inc.**
    Designer Dan Matauch

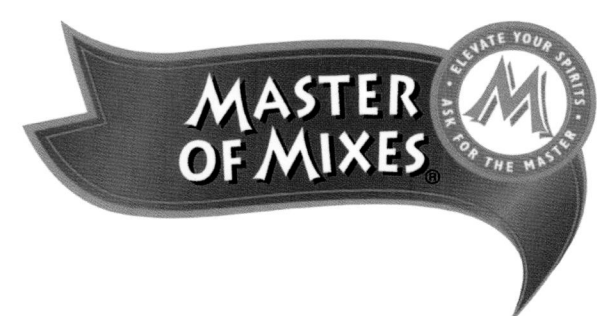

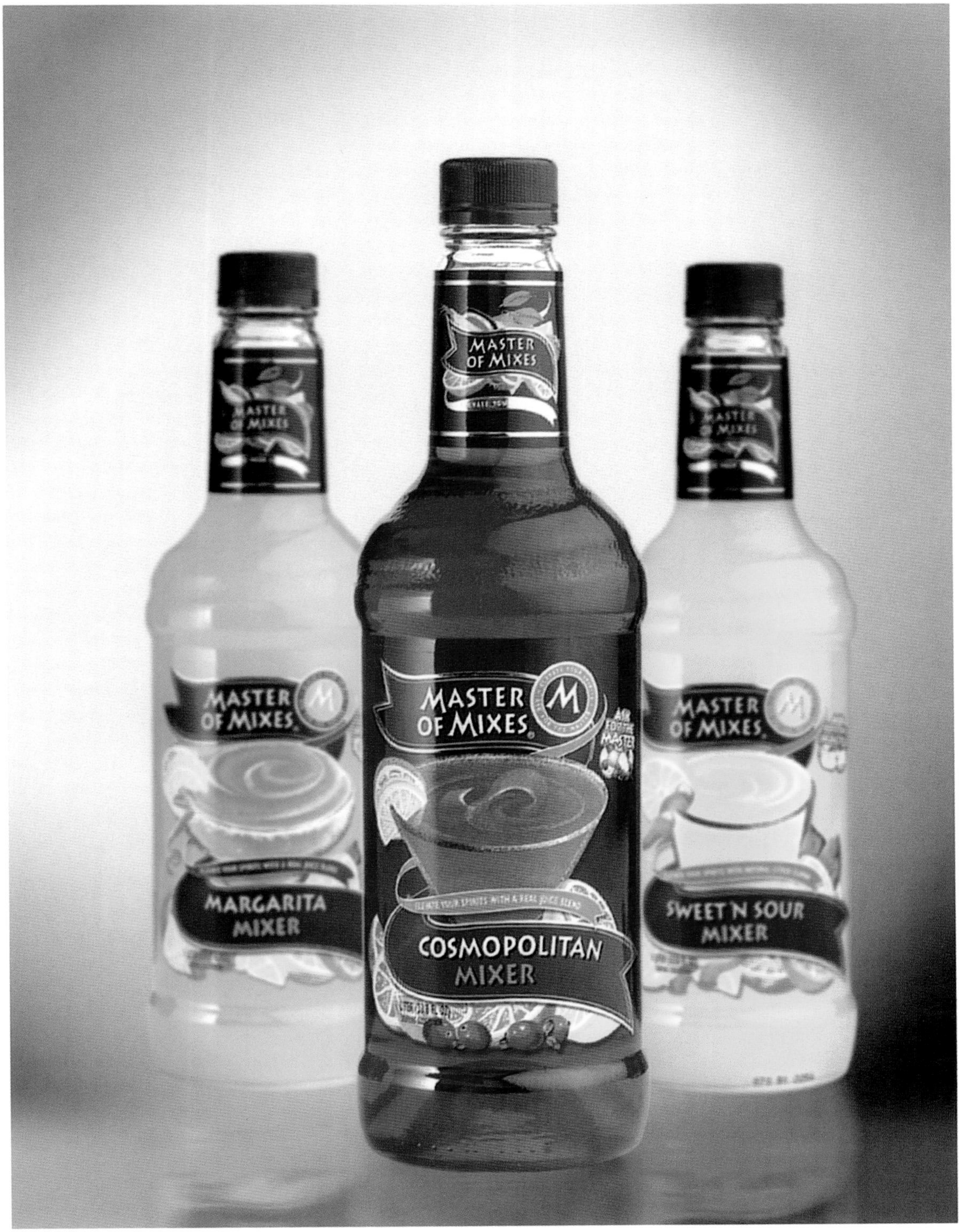

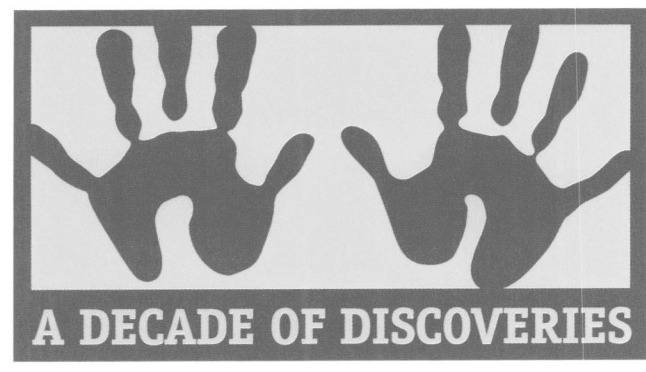

1.

eye Physicians™

2.

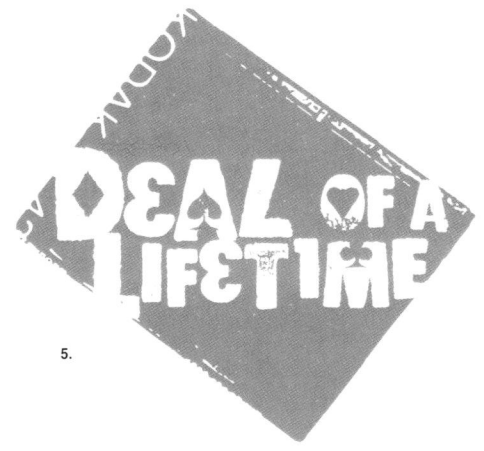

3.

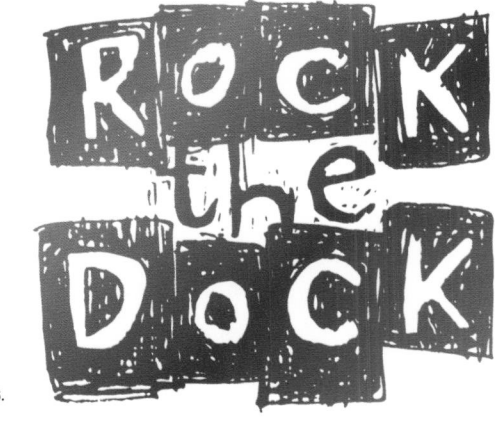

4.

5.

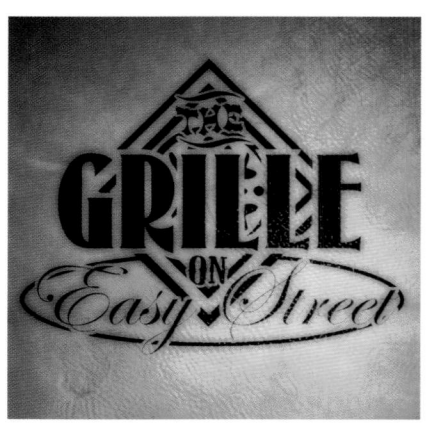

6.

YO PHILLY BLOCK PARTY

7.

8.

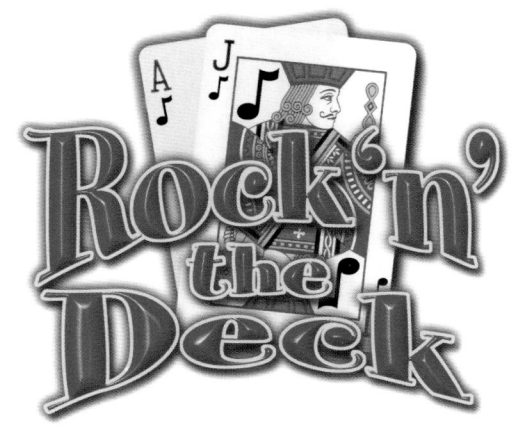

9.

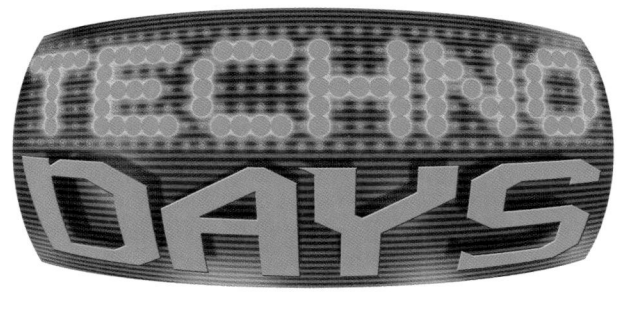

10.

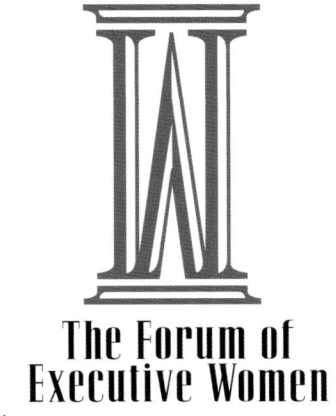

The Forum of Executive Women

11.

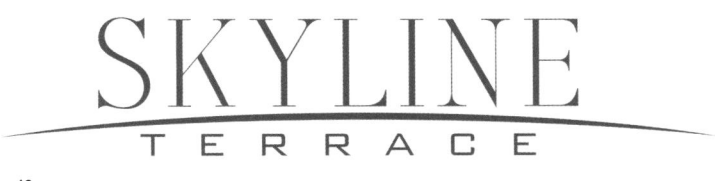

12.

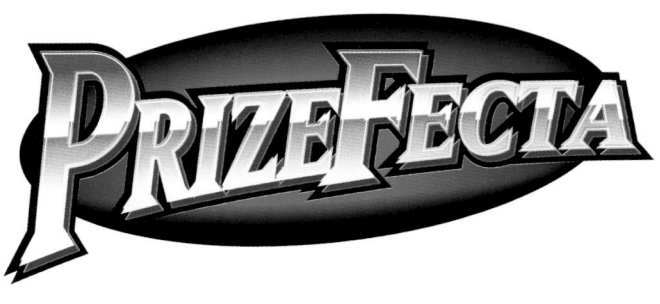

13.

WEST END

CITY APARTMENTS

14.

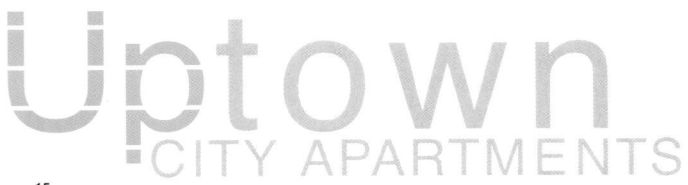

15.

1 - 13
Design Firm **The STAR Group**
14, 15
Design Firm **Skidmore Inc.**

1.
Client — *Garden State Discovery Museum*
Designer — Dave Girgenti

2.
Client — *Eye Physicians*
Designer — Dave Girgenti

3.
Client — *Design Command Center*
Designer — Dave Girgenti

4.
Client — *Pennsylvania University*
Designer — Dave Girgenti

5 - 7.
Client — *Trump Marina*
Designer — Dave Girgenti

8 - 10.
Client — *Blue Chip Casino*
Designer — Dave Girgenti

11.
Client — *The Forum For Executive Women*
Designer — Dave Girgenti

12, 13.
Client — *Charles Town Races & Slots*
Designer — Dave Girgenti

14, 15.
Client — *Village Green Companies*
Designer — Pete Nothstein

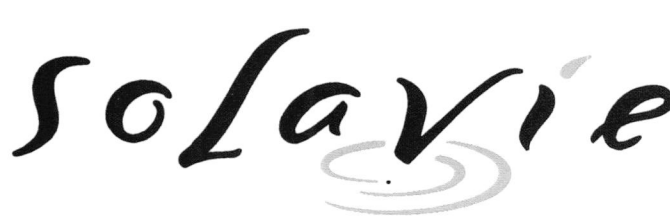

1.

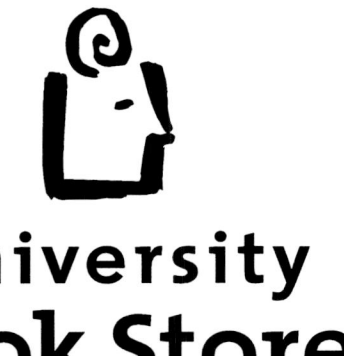

University **Book Store**

2.

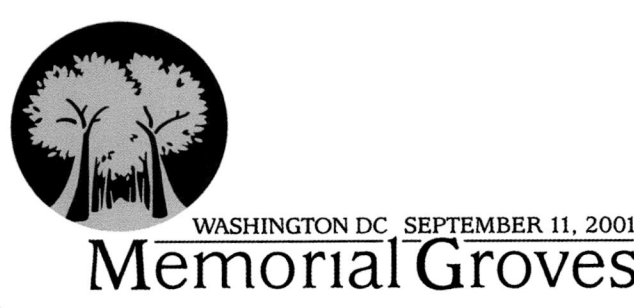

3.

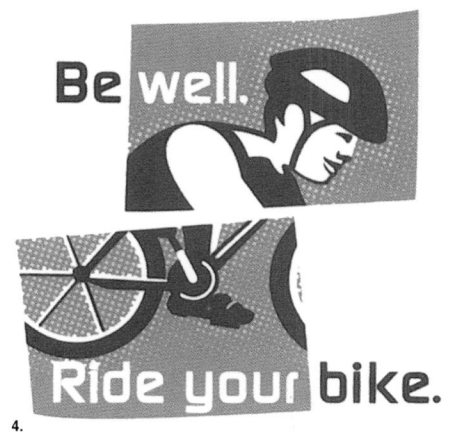

4.

5.

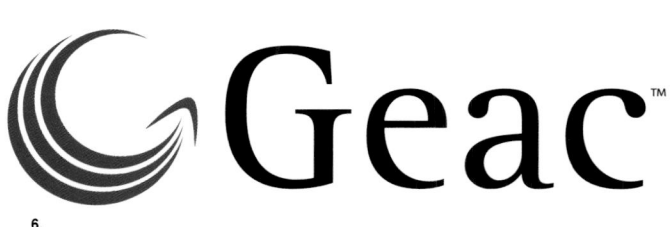

6.

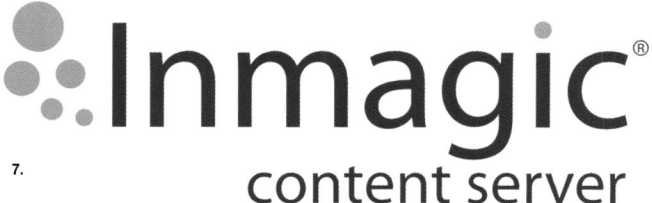

7.

1, 2
Design Firm **Hornall Anderson Design Works**
3 - 5
Design Firm **Blank Inc.**
6, 7
Design Firm **Hull Creative Group**

1.
Client *Solavie*
Designers Jack Anderson, Kathy Saito, Gretchen Cook, Sonja Max, Henry Yiu, Alan Copeland

2.
Client *University Book Store*
Designers John Hornall, Mary Hermes, Belinda Bowling, Holly Craven

3.
Client *Greenspaces for DC*
Designers Danielle Willis, Robert Kent Wilson

4.
Client *League of American Bicyclists*
Designers Robert Kent Wilson, Jay Kokernak, Christine Dzieciolowski

5.
Client *Blank Inc.*
Designers Robert Kent Wilson, Christine Dzieciolowski

6.
Client *Geac Corporation*
Designer Amy Braddock

7.
Client *Inmagic Corporation*
Designer Carolyn Colonna

(opposite)
Client *Oliver Winery*
Design Firm **Flowdesign, Inc.**
Designer Dan Matauch

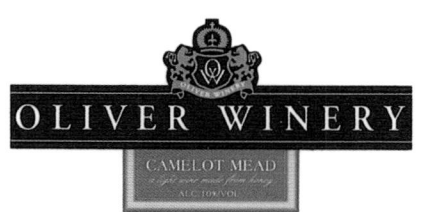

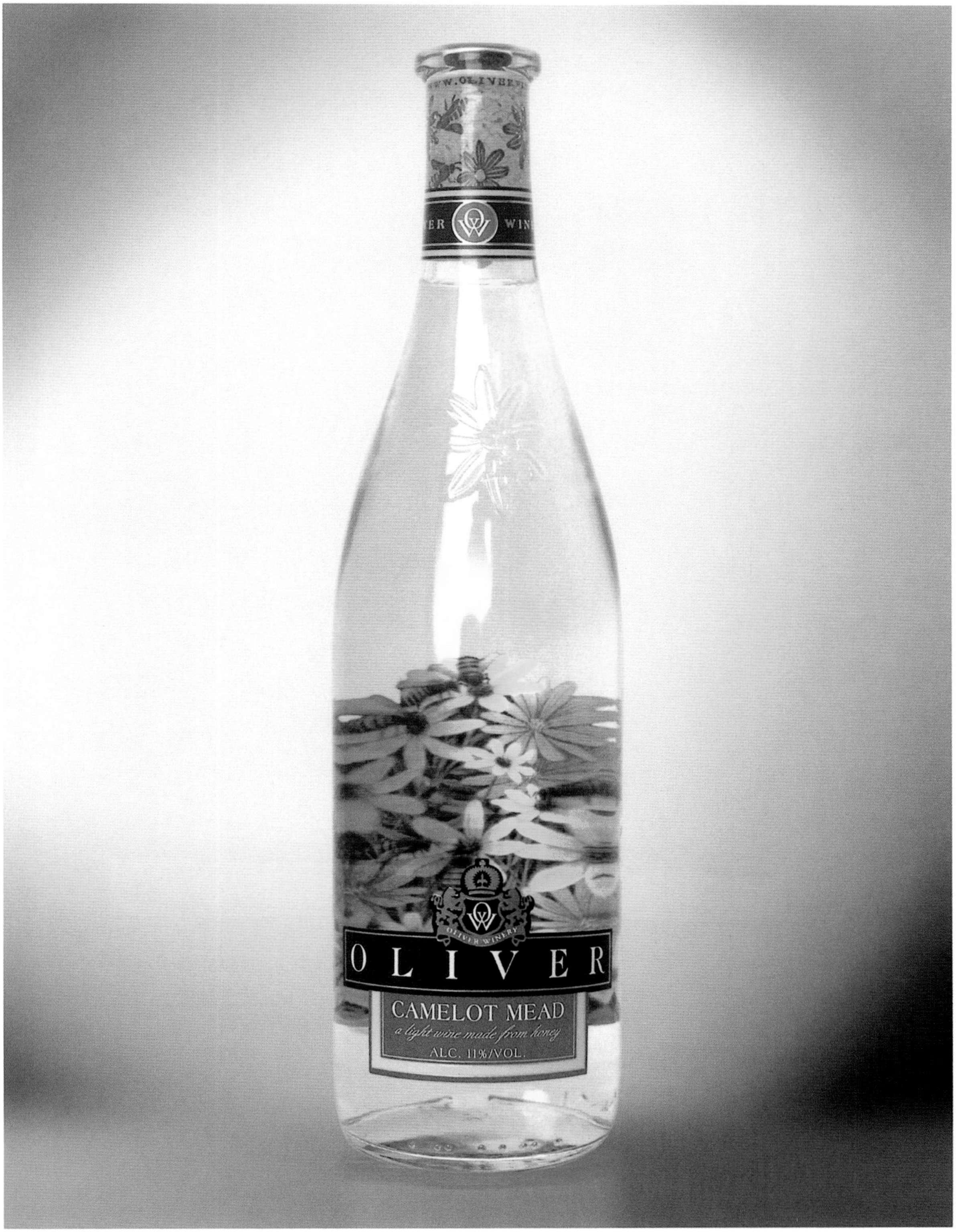

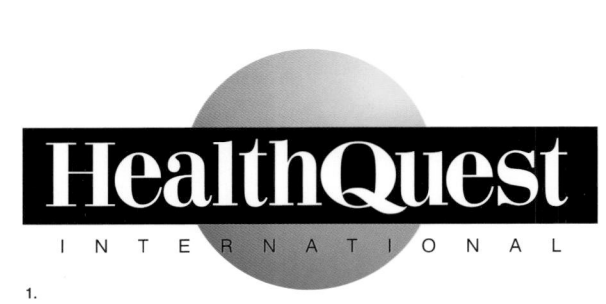

1.

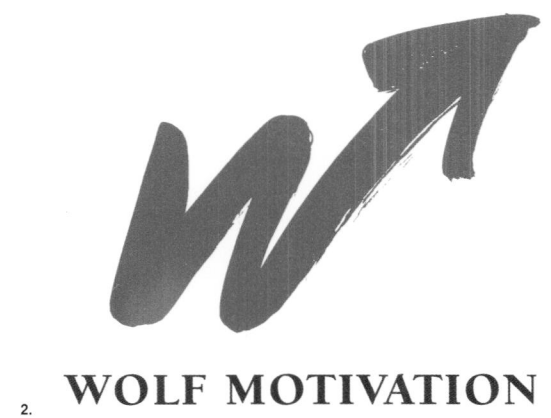

2. **WOLF MOTIVATION**

Chicago Avenue Evanston

3.

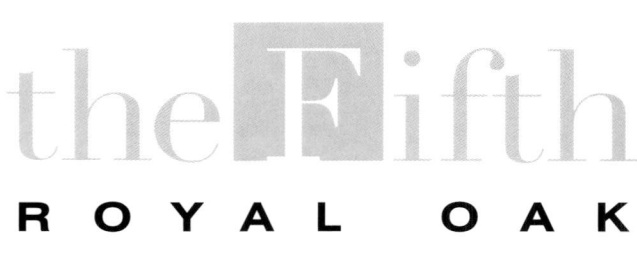

4.

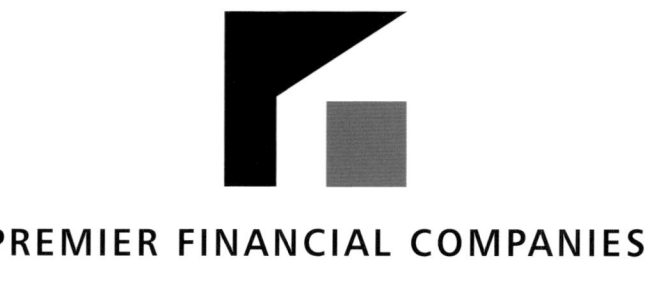

PREMIER FINANCIAL COMPANIES

5.

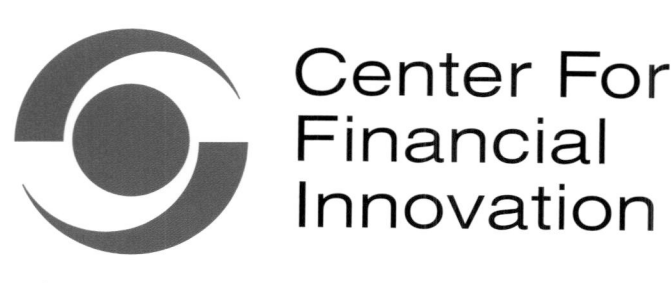

6.

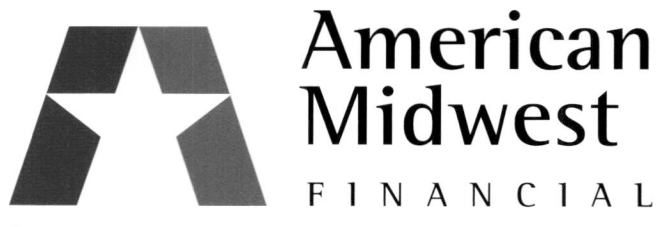

7.

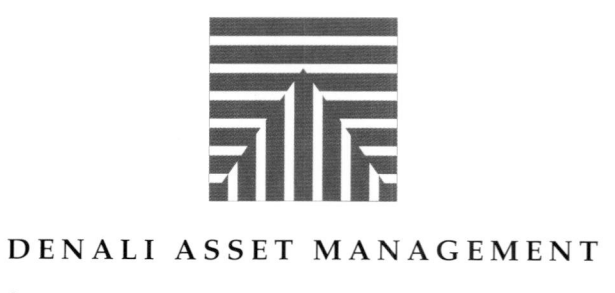

8.

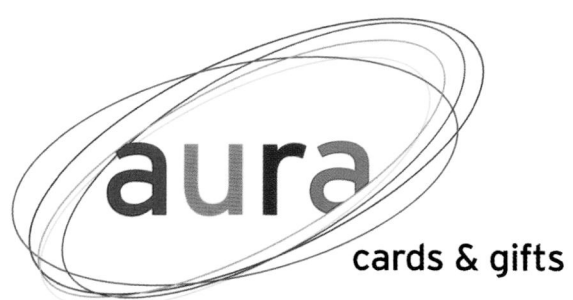

9.

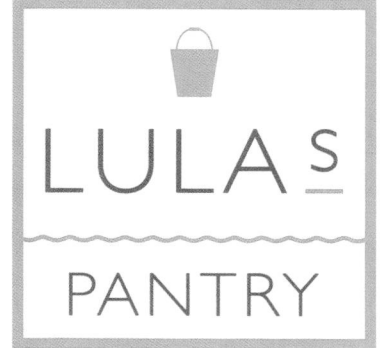

10.

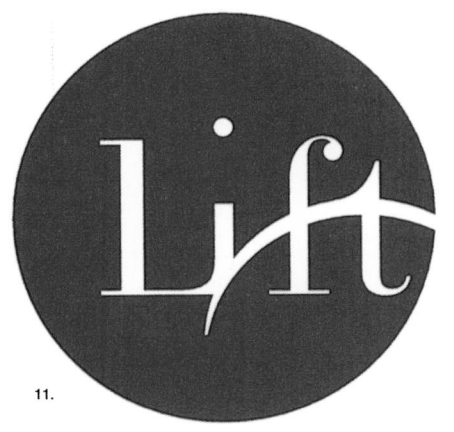

11.

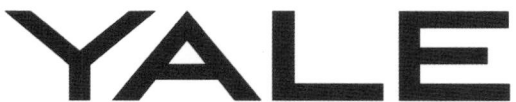

12.

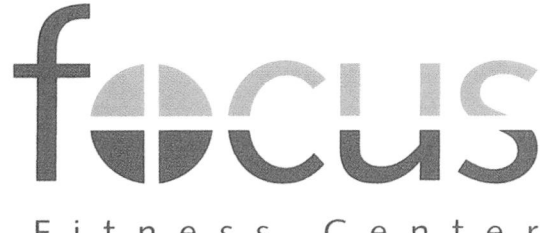

13.

SHADES

14.

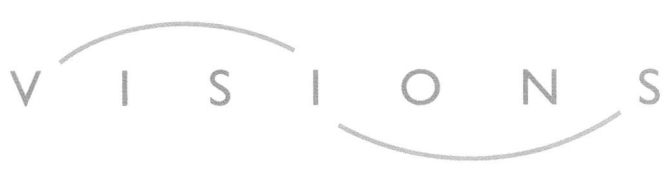

15.

1 - 8
Design Firm **Lienhart Design**
9 - 15
Design Firm **Kor Group**

1.
Client — *Healthquest International*
Designer — James Lienhart

2.
Client — *Wolf Motivation*
Designer — James Lienhart

3.
Client — *900 Chicago Avenue Evanston*
Designer — James Lienhart

4.
Client — *The Fifth Royal Oak*
Designer — James Lienhart

5.
Client — *Premier Financial Companies*
Designer — James Lienhart

6.
Client — *Center for Financial Innovation*
Designer — James Lienhart

7.
Client — *American Midwest Financial*
Designer — James Lienhart

8.
Client — *Denali Asset Management*
Designer — James Lienhart

9.
Client — *Aura Cards & Gifts*
Designers — Karen Dendy Smith, MB Jarosik, Jim Gibson

10.
Client — *Lula's Pantry*
Designers — Karen Dendy Smith, Jim Gibson, James Grady

11.
Client — *Lift*
Designers — Karen Dendy Smith, Kjerstin Westguard

12.
Client — *Yale Appliance & Lighting*
Designers — Karen Dendy Smith, Brian Azer

13 - 15.
Client — *Southbridge Hotel & Conference Center*
Designers — MB Jarosik, Sandra Meyer

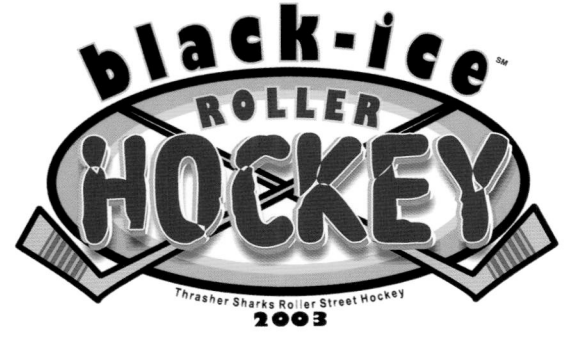

1.

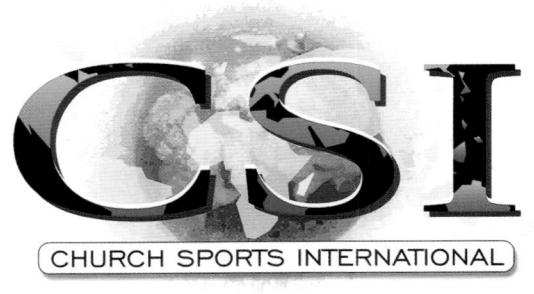

2.

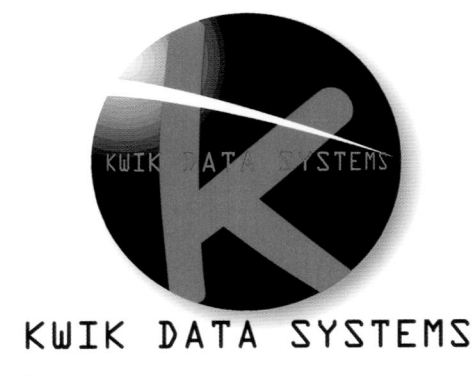

KWIK DATA SYSTEMS

3.

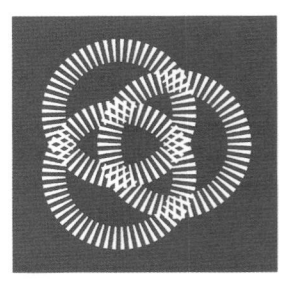

Greater Jamaica
Development
Corporation

4.

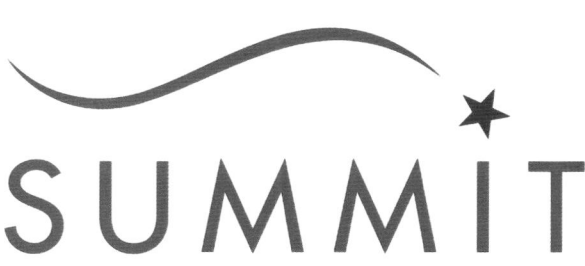

5.

AZIA
center
汇 亚 大 厦

6.

7.

1 - 3
Design Firm **imagineGrafx**
4 - 6
Design Firm **Calori & Vanden-Eynden**
7
Design Firm **FUSZION Collaborative**

1.
Client *South Valley Christian Church*
Designer Stephen Guy

2.
Client *Church Sports Int'l*
Designer Stephen Guy

3.
Client *KWIK Data Systems*
Designer Stephen Guy

4.
Client *Greater Jamaica Development Corporation*
Designers David Vanden-Eynden, Marisa Schulman

5.
Client *City of Summit, NJ*
Designers David Vanden-Eynden, Denise Funaro-Psoinos

6.
Client *Shanghai Investment Real Estate Development*
Designers David Vanden-Eynden, Chris Calori, Lindsay McCosh, Marisa Schulman

7.
Client *uReach.com*
Designer Steve Dreyer
(opposite)
Client *Morinda, Inc.*
Design Firm **Flowdesign, Inc.**
Designer Dan Matauch

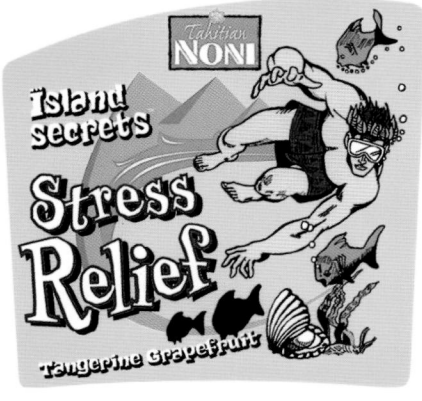

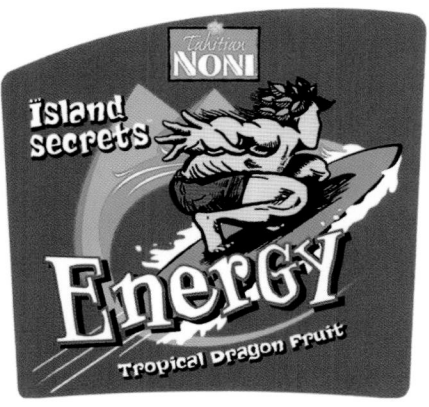

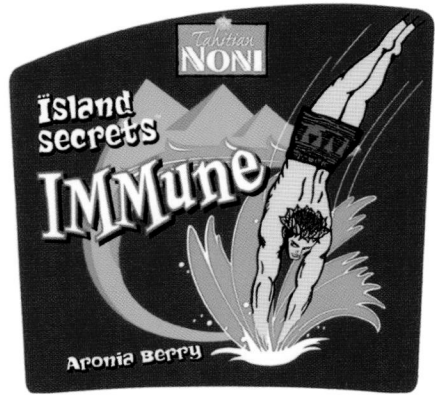

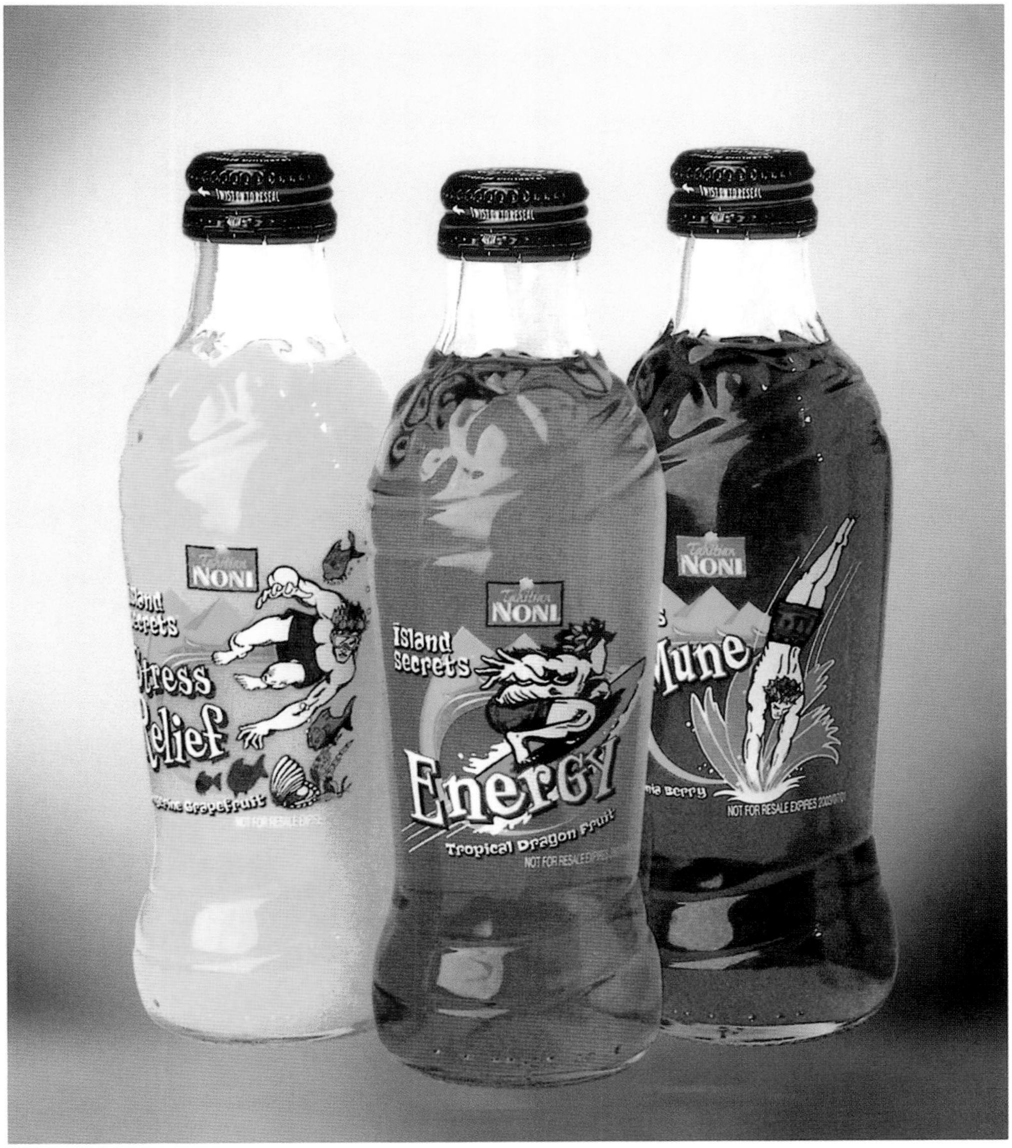

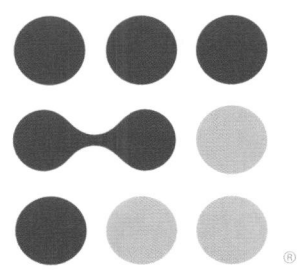

FUSZION | COLLABORATIVE

1.

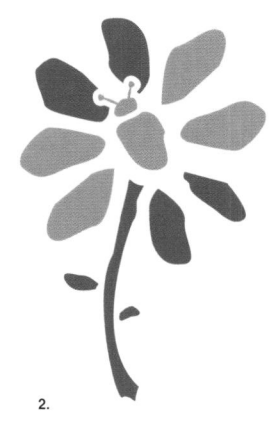

2.

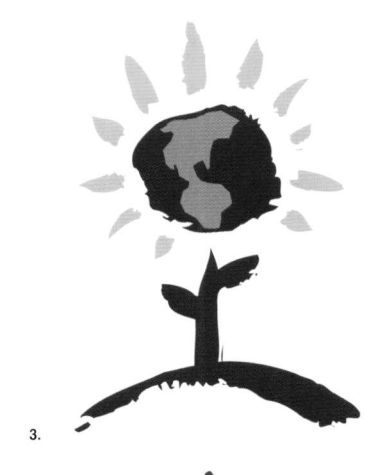

3.

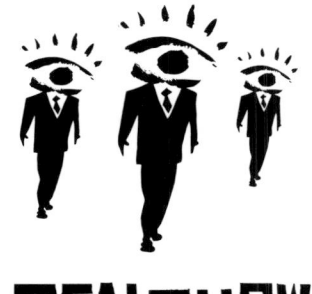

REALSHOW

4.

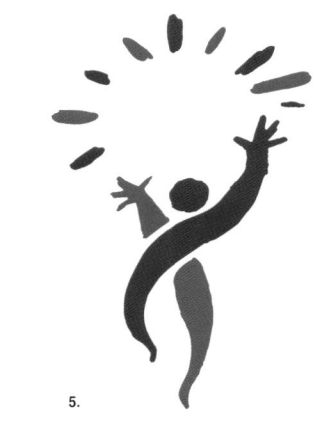

5.

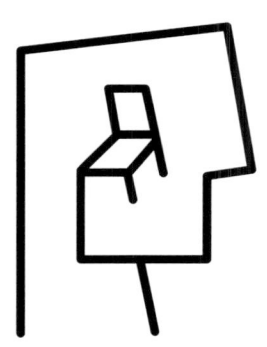

DECO THERAPY

6.

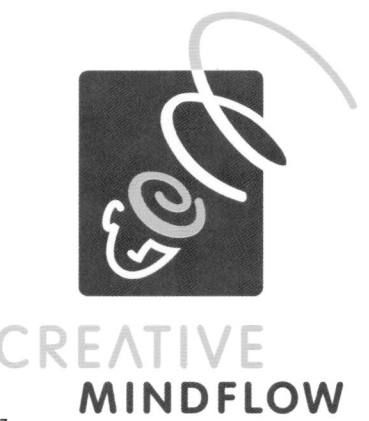

CREATIVE
MINDFLOW

7.

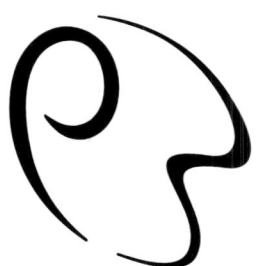

P A L E T T E

8.

9.

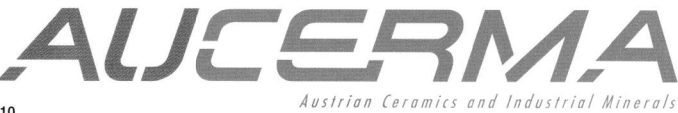

10.

AUCERMA
Austrian Ceramics and Industrial Minerals

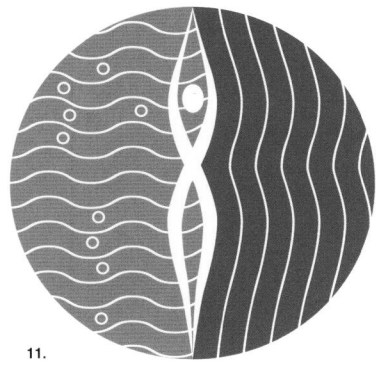

11.

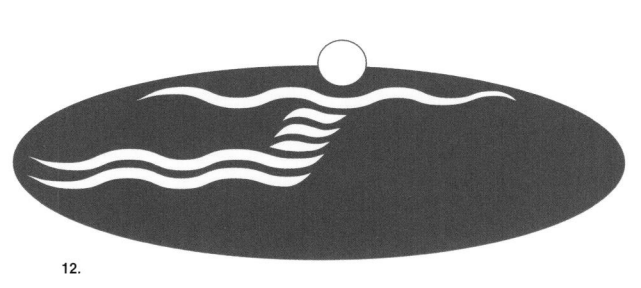

12.

ARCUTERM

14.

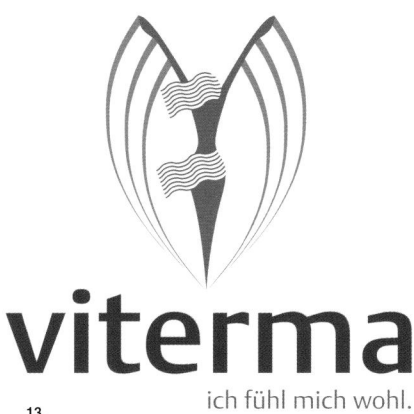

viterma
ich fühl mich wohl.

13.

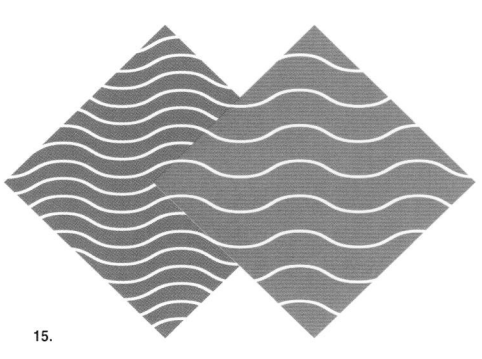

15.

1 - 8		
Design Firm	**FUSZION Collaborative**	
9 - 15		
Design Firm	**motterdesign**	
1.		
Client	*FUSZION Collaborative*	
Designers	Tony Fletcher, Rick Heffner	
2.		
Client	*Smith Fellows*	
Designer	John Foster	
3.		
Client	*Community Anti-Drug Coalitions of America*	
Designer	John Foster	
4.		
Client	*Art Director's Club of Metropolitan Washington*	
Designer	John Foster	
5.		
Client	*Americans for the Arts*	
Designer	John Foster	
6.		
Client	*Deco Therapy*	
Designers	Steve Dreyer, Rick Heffner	

7.	
Client	*Creative Mindflow*
Designer	Christian Baldo
8.	
Client	*Palette Restaurant*
Designers	Tony Fletcher, Rick Heffner
9.	
Client	*Frewein & Farr*
Designer	Siegmund Motter
10.	
Client	*Aucerma*
Designer	Siegmund Motter
11.	
Client	*Unitec*
Designer	Siegmund Motter
12.	
Client	*Ö-Bad**
Designer	Siegmund Motter
13.	
Client	*Viterma*
Designer	Siegmund Motter
14.	
Client	*Arcuterm*
Designer	Siegmund Motter
15.	
Client	*Holzmüller*
Designer	Siegmund Motter

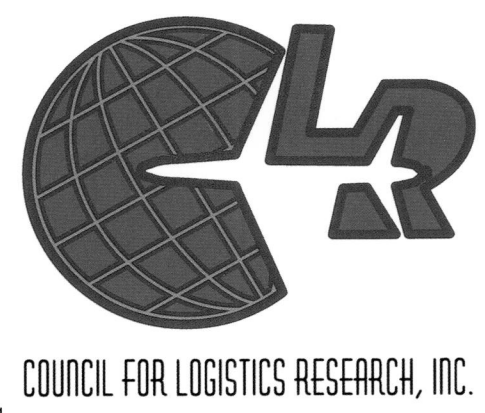

COUNCIL FOR LOGISTICS RESEARCH, INC.

1.

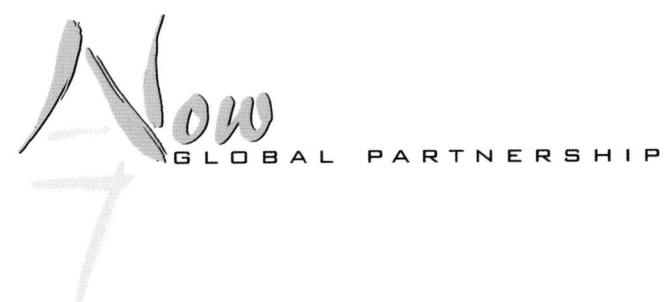

2.

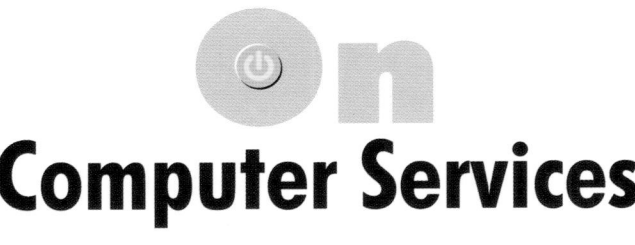

3.

Denali™

4.

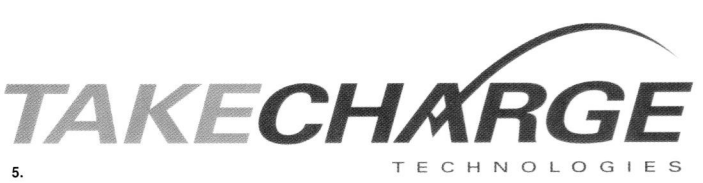

5.

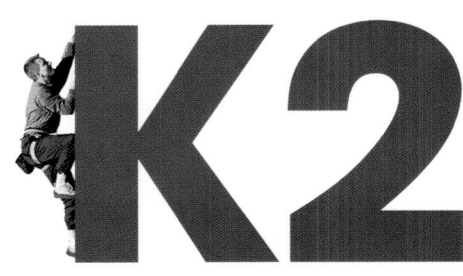

6.

Everest™

7.

1 - 3
Design Firm **MDVC Creative, Inc.**
4 - 7
Design Firm **Martin-Schaffer, Inc.**
1.
Client   *Council for Logistics Research, Inc.*
2.
Client   *Mitsui Bussan Logistics*
3.
Client   *On Computer Services*
4.
Client   *Grace Vydac*
Designers Steve Cohn,
          Tina Martin

5.
Client   *TakeCharge Technologies*
Designers Kelly Mathieu,
          Tina Martin
6, 7.
Client   *Grace Vydac*
Designers Steve Cohn,
          Tina Martin
(opposite)
Client   *Fuze Candy*
Design Firm **Out Of The Box**
Designer   Rick Schneider

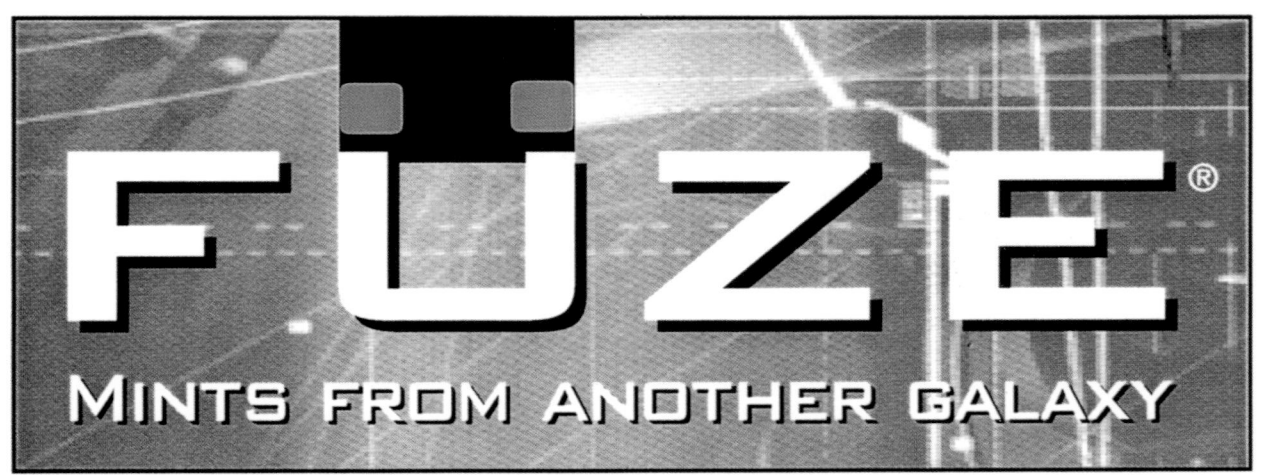

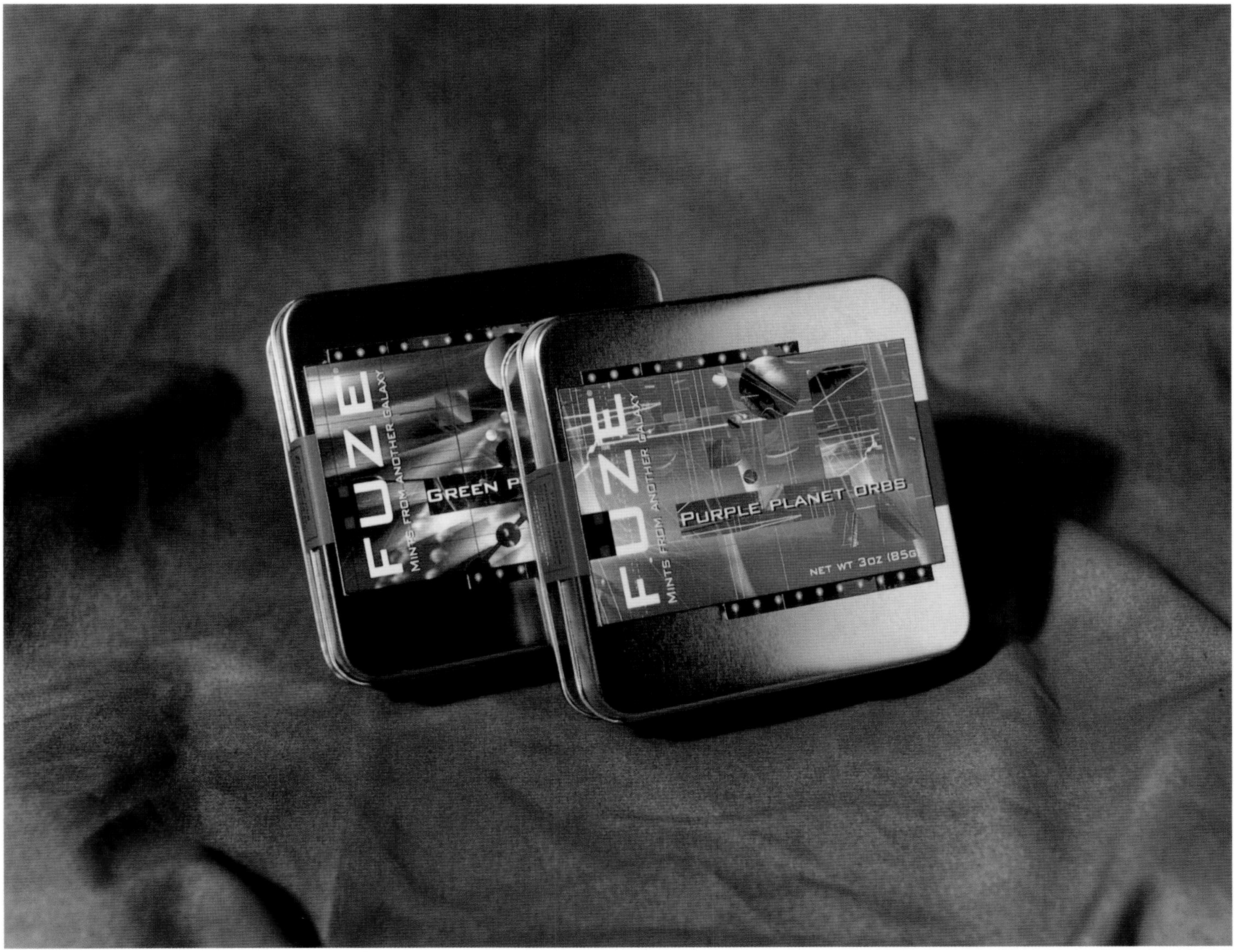

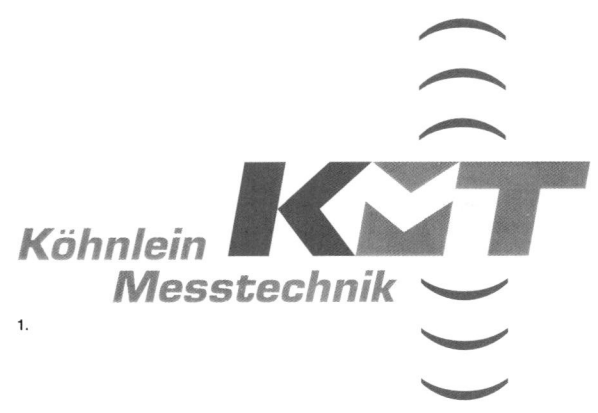

1.

KAPPLER
Bäder zum Leben

2.

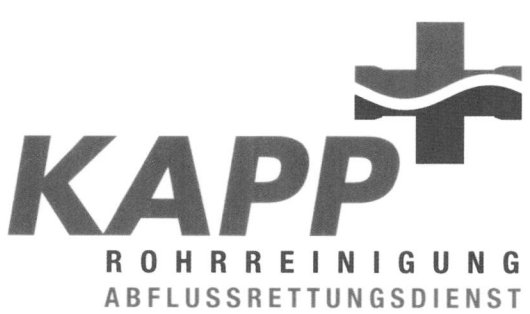

KAPP
ROHRREINIGUNG
ABFLUSSRETTUNGSDIENST

3.

EBINGER DETT

4.

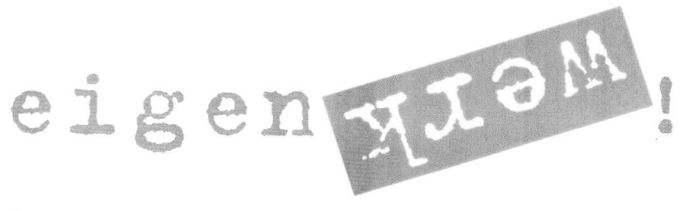

5.

Ramah Wagner
business of health

6.

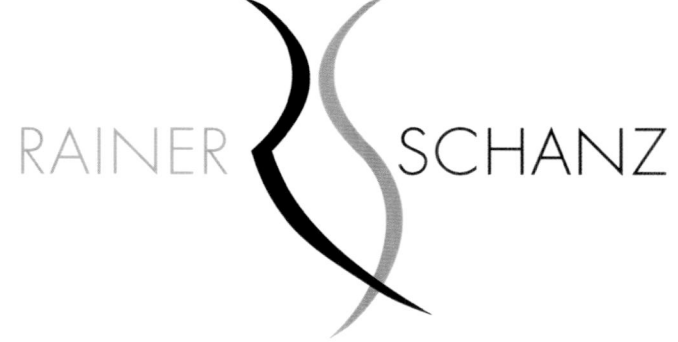

7.

RAINER SCHANZ

8.

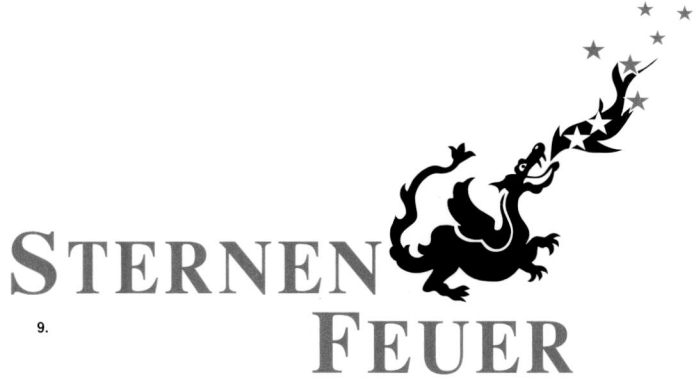

9.

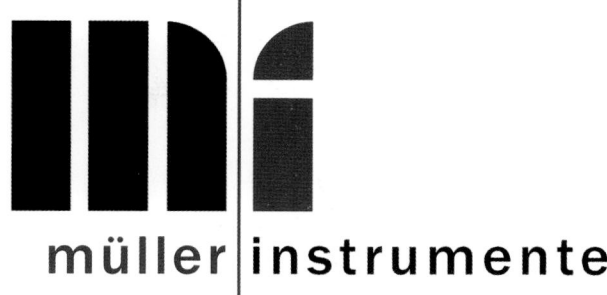

müller│instrumente

10.

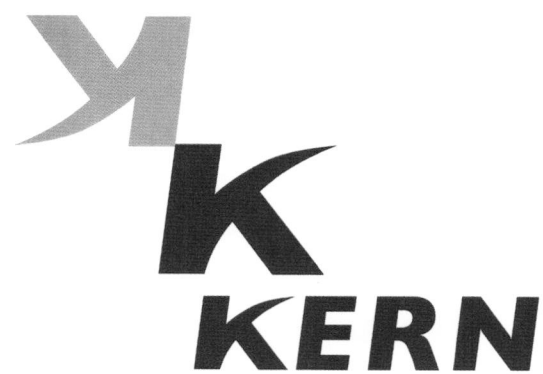

11.

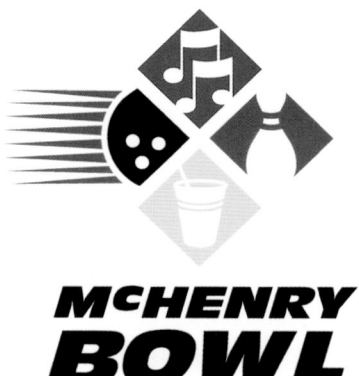

12.

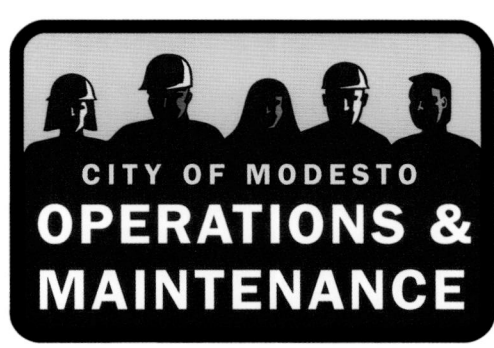

13.

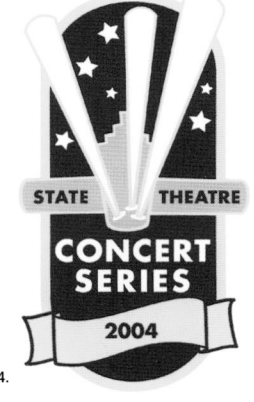

14.

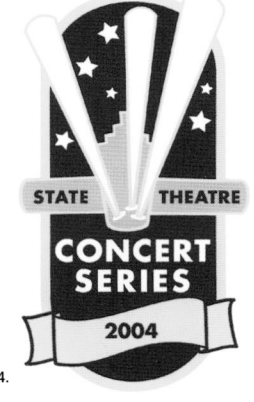

15.

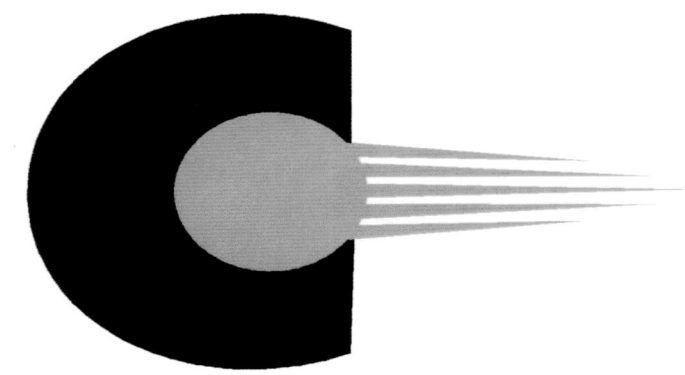

1.

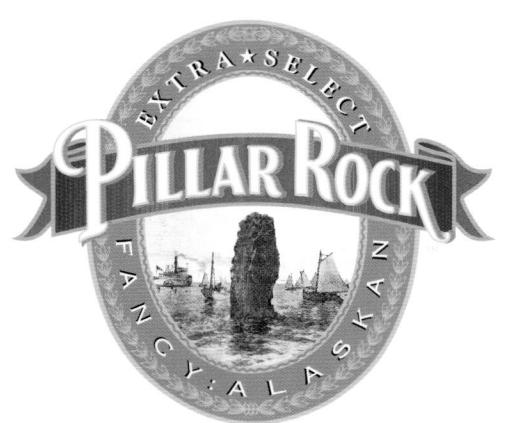

2.

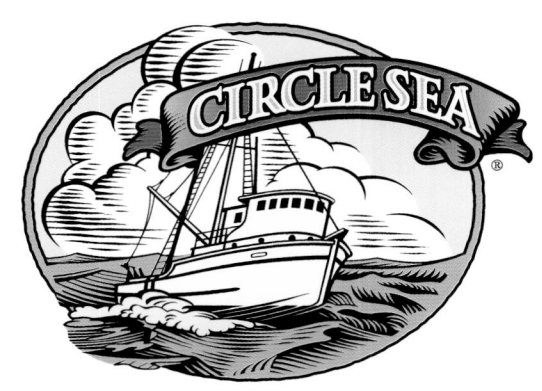

3.

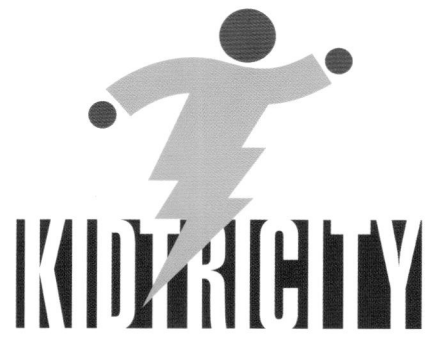

4.

5.

6.

roche salon

www.rochesalon.com

7.

1, 2
Design Firm **Michael Lee Advertising & Design, Inc.**

3, 4
Design Firm **Mark Oliver, Inc.**

5, 6
Design Firm **Redpoint Design**

7
Design Firm **Lomangino Studio, Inc.**

1.
Client   *Coastal Welding Supply*
Designers   Michael Lee, Debby Stasinopoulou

2.
Client   *Matagorda Yacht Club*
Designers   Michael Lee, Debby Stasinopoulou

3.
Client   *Ocean Beauty Seafoods*
Designers   Mark Oliver, Harry Bates

4.
Client   *Ocean Beauty Seafoods*
Designers   Mark Oliver, Tom Hennessy

5.
Client   *Kidtricity*
Designers   Clark Most, Ty Smith

6.
Client   *Heart Design*
Designer   Clark Most

7.
Client   *Roche Salon*
Designer   Kristina Bonner

(opposite)
Client   *Firenze Bread Co.*
Design Firm **Pandora**
Designer   Silvia Grossman

234

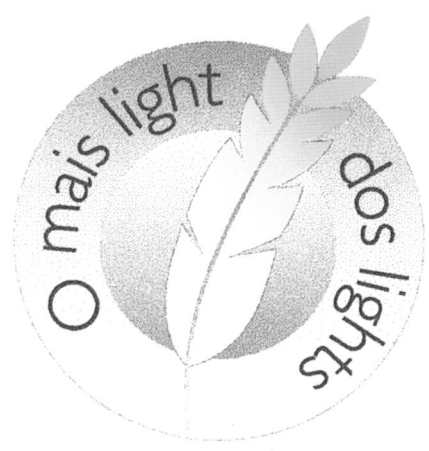

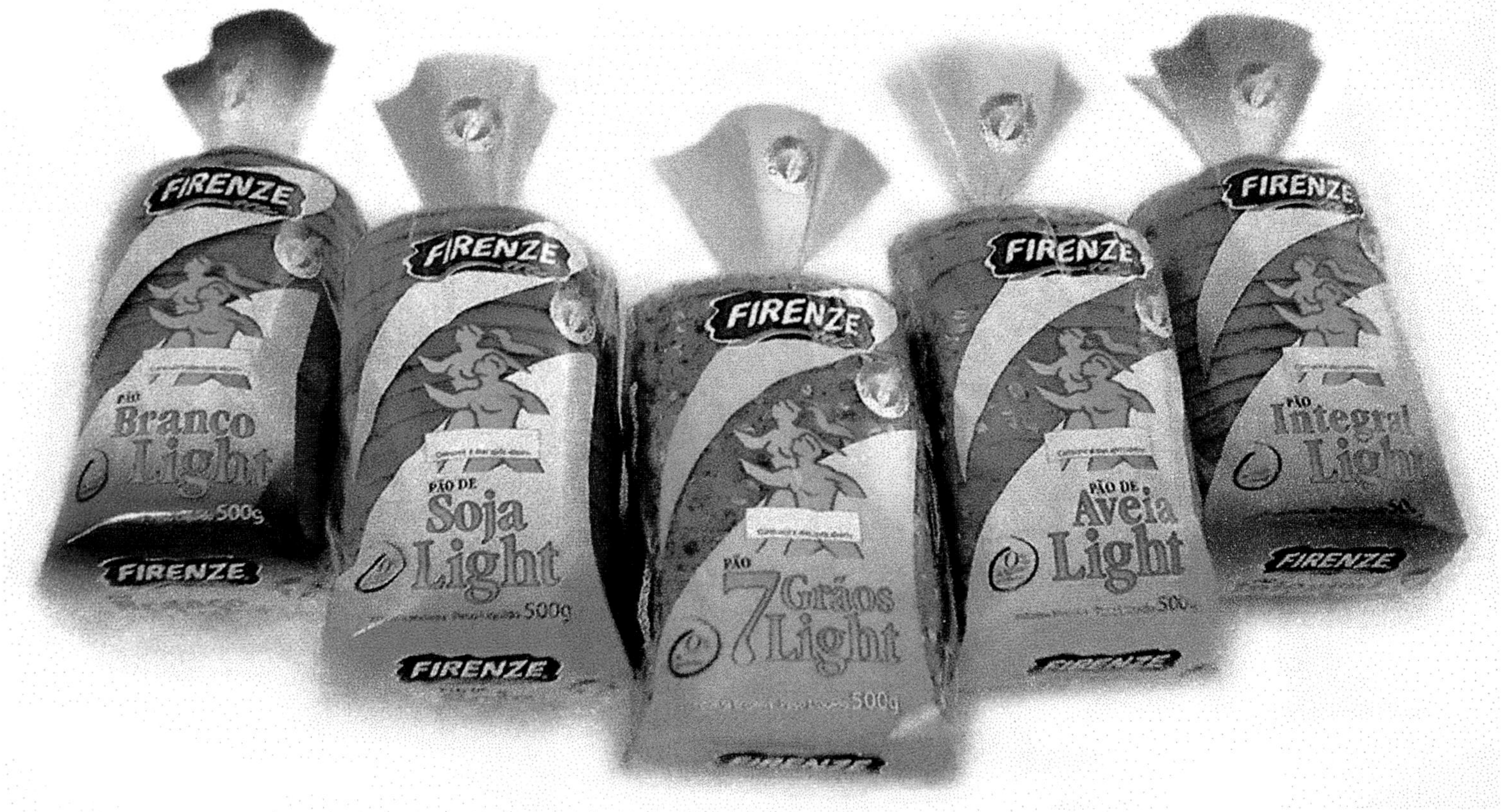

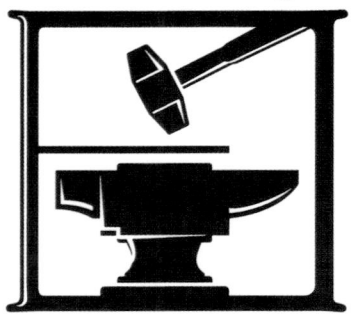

1.

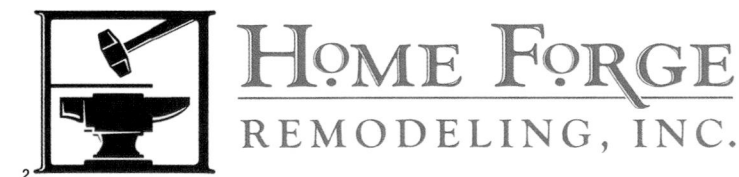

2.

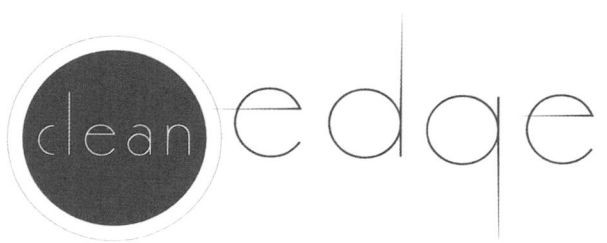

3.

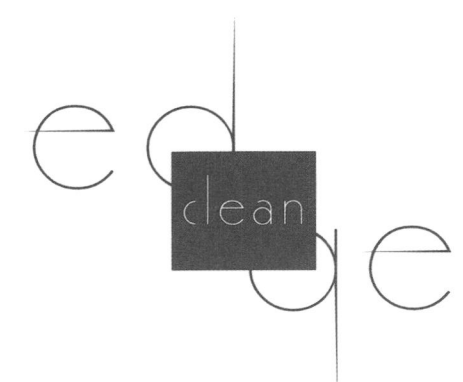

4.

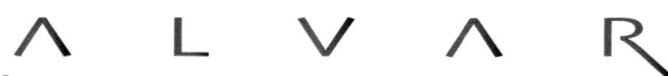

5.

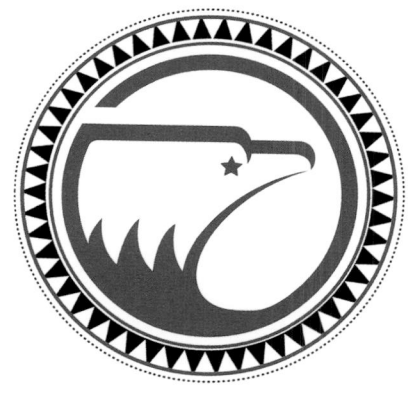

6.

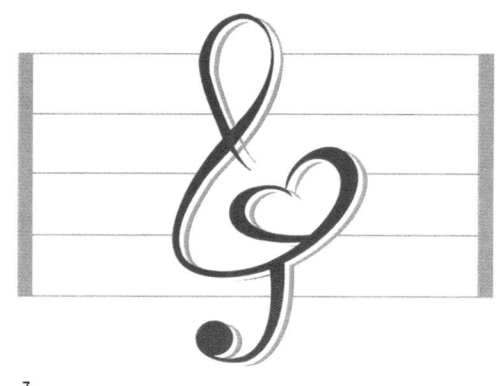

7.

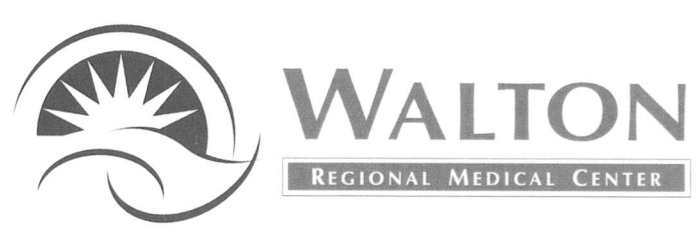

8.

236

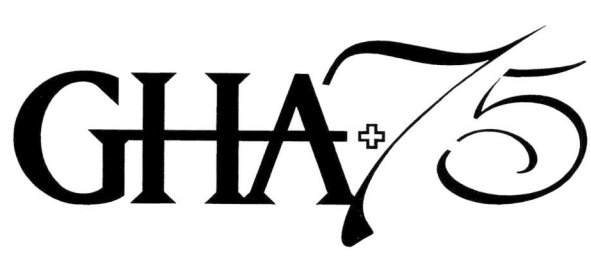

9.

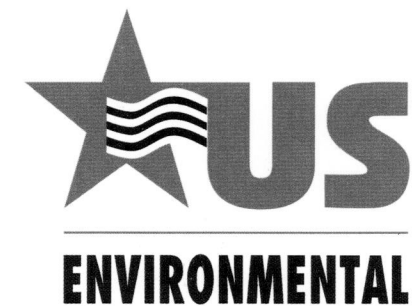

10.

11.

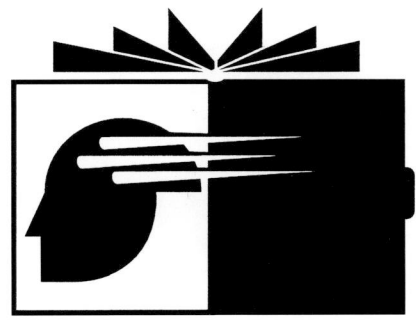

12.

13.

14.

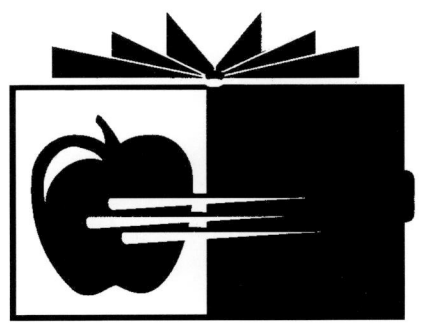

15.

1 - 15
Design Firm **WorldSTAR Design**

1, 2.
Client   *Home Forge Remodeling, Inc.*
Designer   Greg Guhl

3, 4.
Client   *Clean Edge*
         Domestic Services, Inc.
Designer   Greg Guhl

5.
Client   *Decorative Expressions, Inc.*
Designer   Greg Guhl

6.
Client   *Contingency*
         Management Group, LLC
Designer   Greg Guhl

7.
Client   *American Heart Association*
Designer   Greg Guhl

8.
Client   *Walton Regional*
         Medical Center
Designer   Greg Guhl

9.
Client   *Georgia Hospital Association*
Designer   Greg Guhl

10.
Client   *U.S. Environmental Services, Inc.*
Designer   Greg Guhl

11.
Client   *The Specialty Hospital*
Designer   Greg Guhl

12.
Client   *WellStar Health System*
Designer   Greg Guhl

13 - 15.
Client   *Georgia Hospital Association*
Designer   Greg Guhl

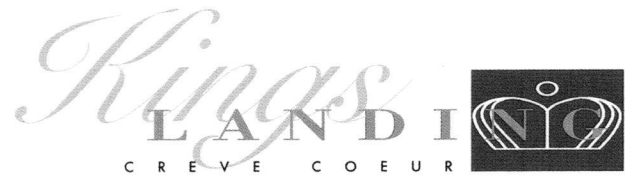

1.

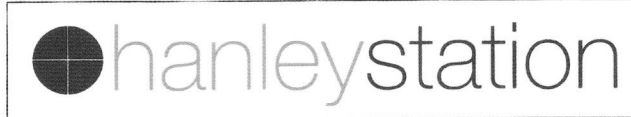

2.

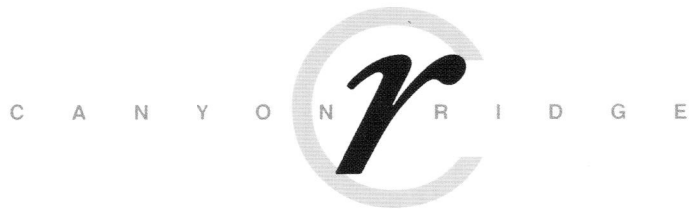

3.

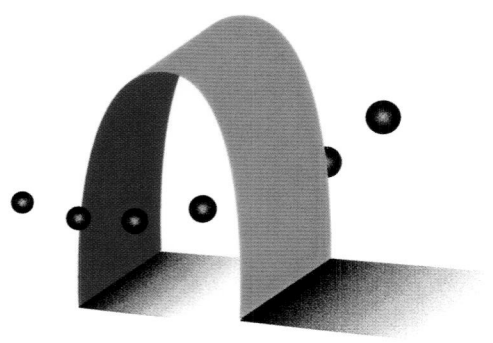

4.

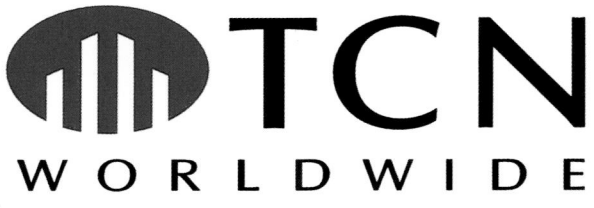

5.

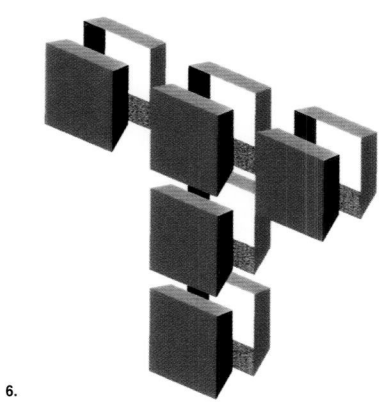

6.

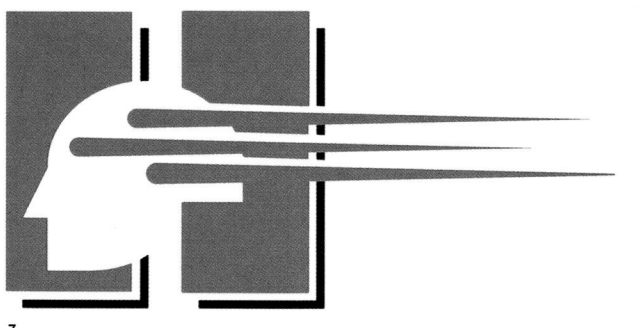

7.

1 - 3
Design Firm **Grizzell & Co.**
4 - 6
Design Firm **Lambert Design**
7
Design Firm **WorldSTAR Design**
1 - 3.
Client   *MLP*
Designer   John H. Grizzell
4.
Client   *Access HDTV*
Designer   Amy Sharp
5.
Client   *TCN Worldwide*
Designer   Christie Lambert

6.
Client   *TechLife Styles*
Designer   Christie Lambert
7.
Client   *Georgia Hospital Association*
Designer   Greg Guhl
(opposite)
Client   *Dr. Temt Laboratories
            (Cosmetics)*
Design Firm **designbuero**
Designer   Thomas Stockhammer

go**4**elements

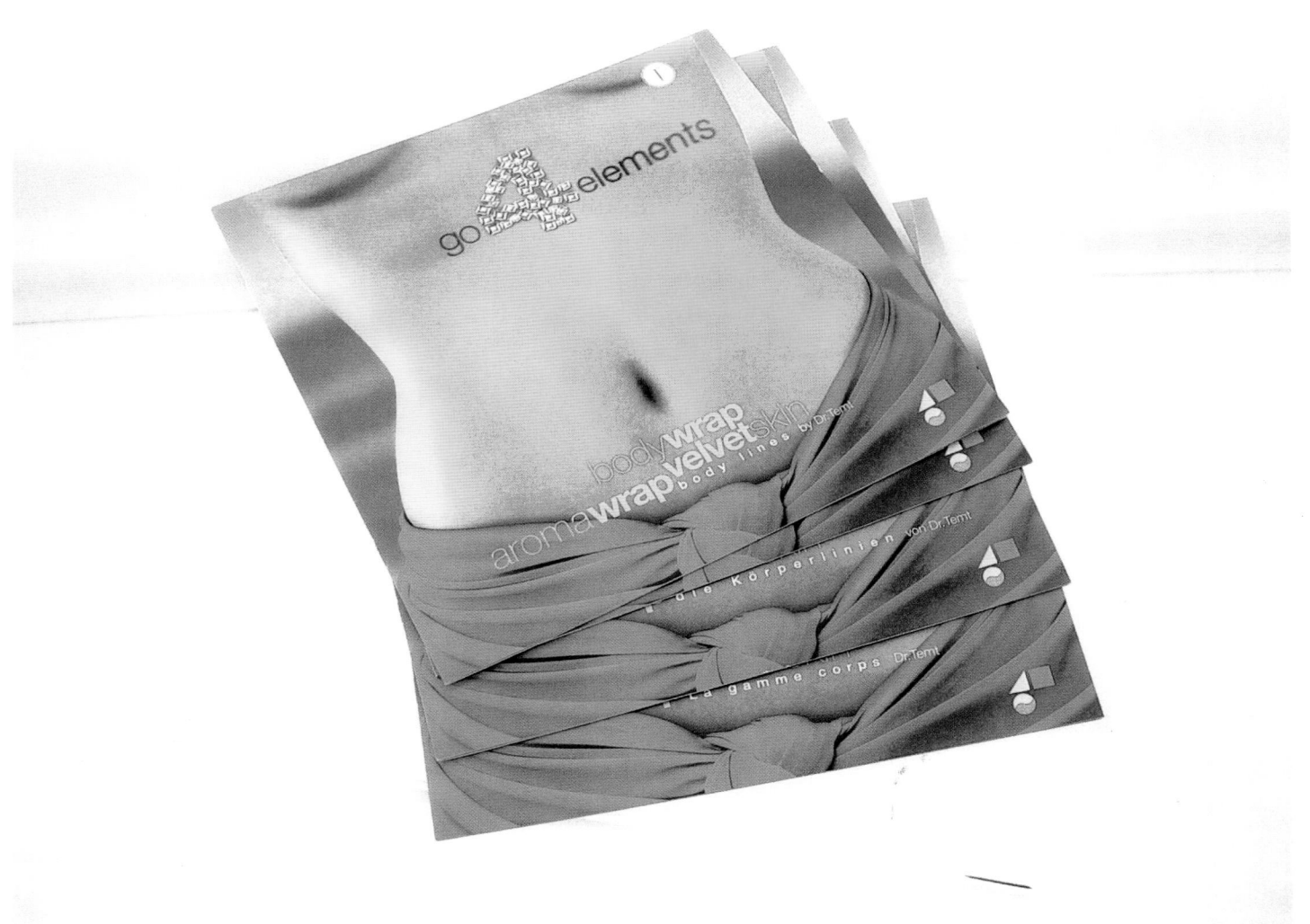

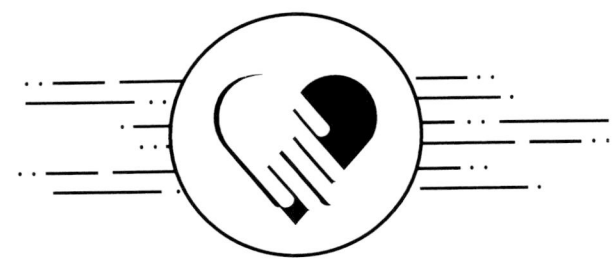

1.

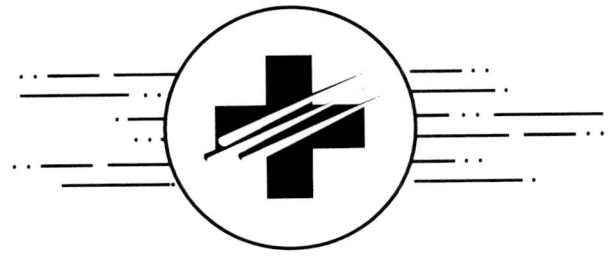

2.

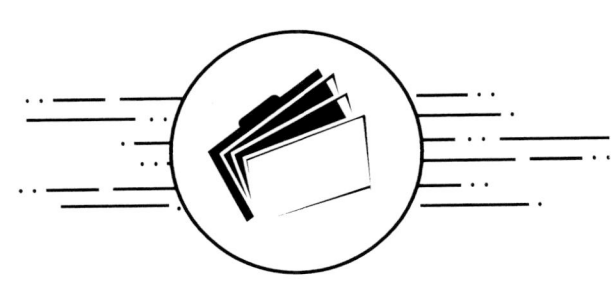

3.

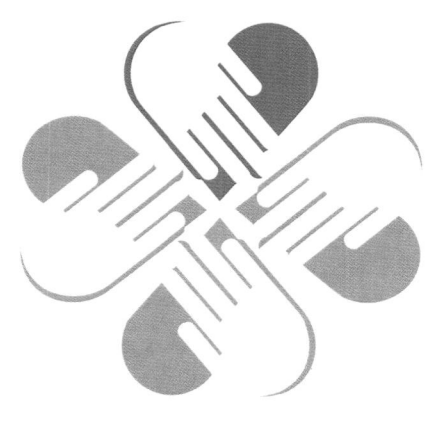

4.

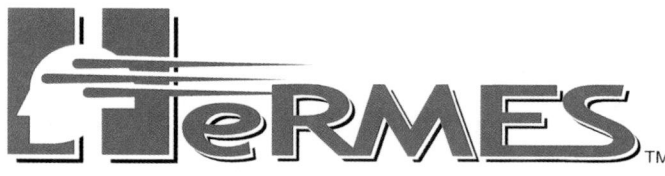

5.

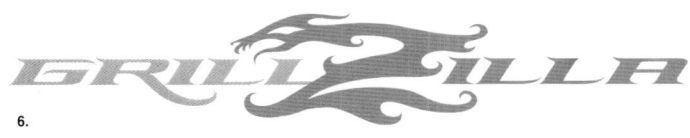

6.

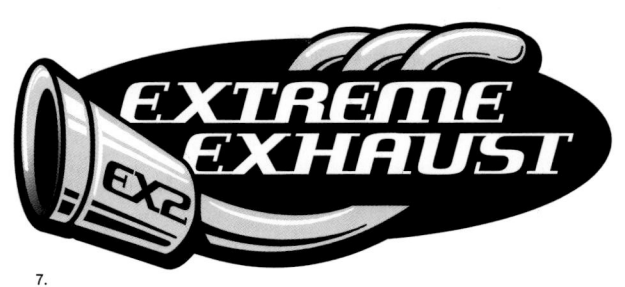

7.

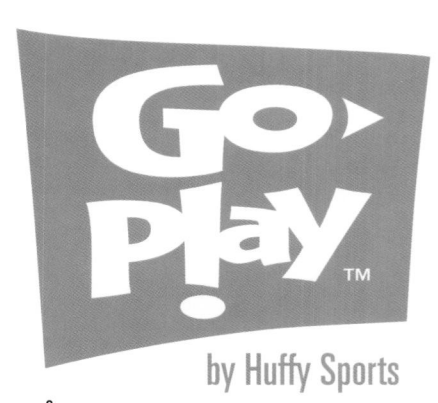

8.

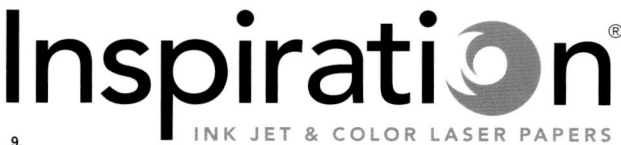

9.

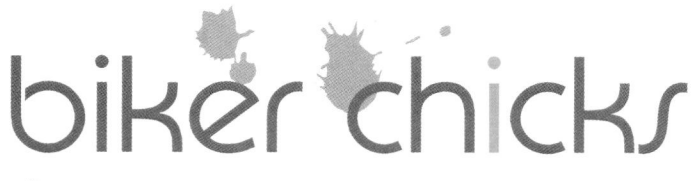

10.

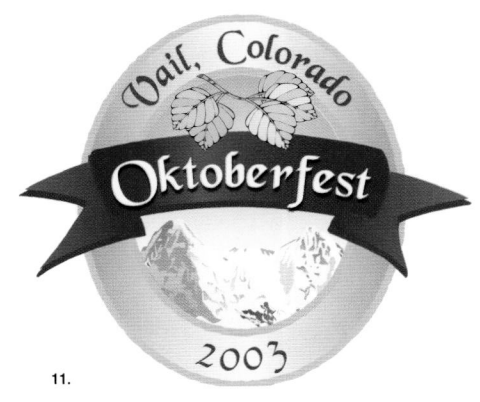

11.

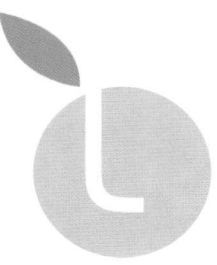

LemonAid Crutches

12.

EAGLE HILL

13.

ΛCCESSCOMPLIANCE™

A CFM Partners Program

14.

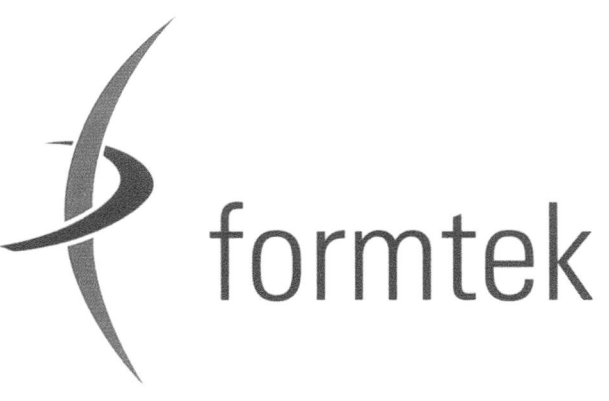

15.

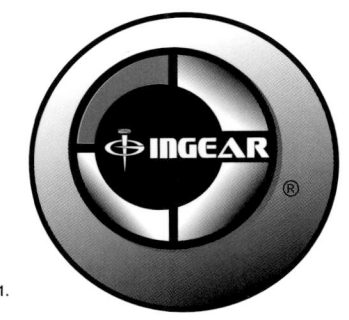

1.

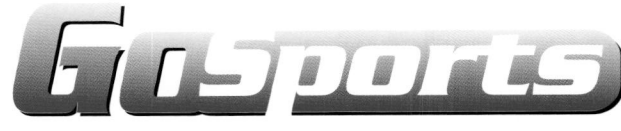

2.

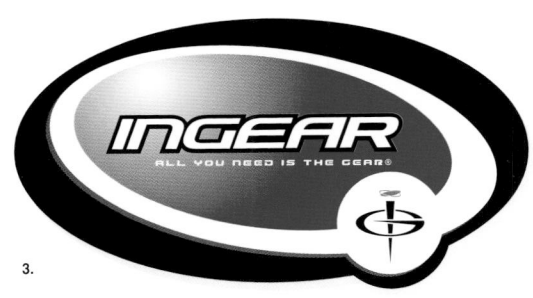

3.

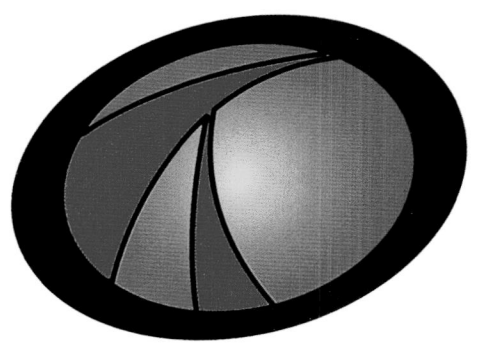

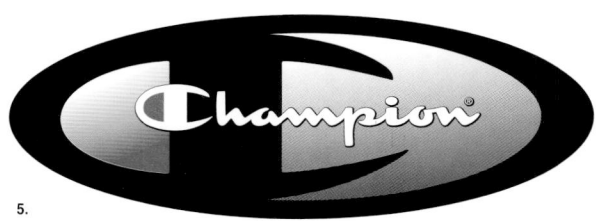

5.

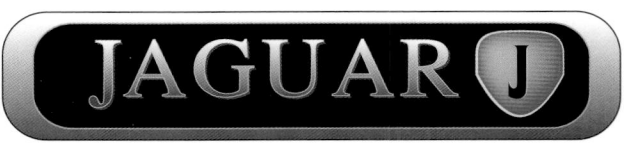

6.

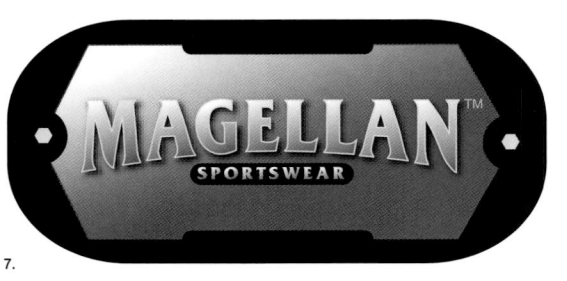

7.

1 - 7
Design Firm **InGEAR**
1.
Client   *Meijer*
Designer   Matt Hassler
2.
Client   *Target*
Designer   Matt Hassler
3.
Client   *Kmart*
Designer   Matt Hassler
4.
Client   *InGEAR Corporation*
Designer   Kurt Lichte

5, 6.
Client   *JC Penney*
Designer   Matt Hassler
7.
Client   *The Sports Authority*
Designer   Matt Hassler
(opposite)
Client   *Sony Computer*
    Entertainment America
Design Firm **CDI Studios**
Designer   Eddie Roberts

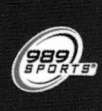

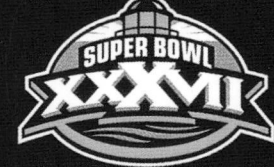
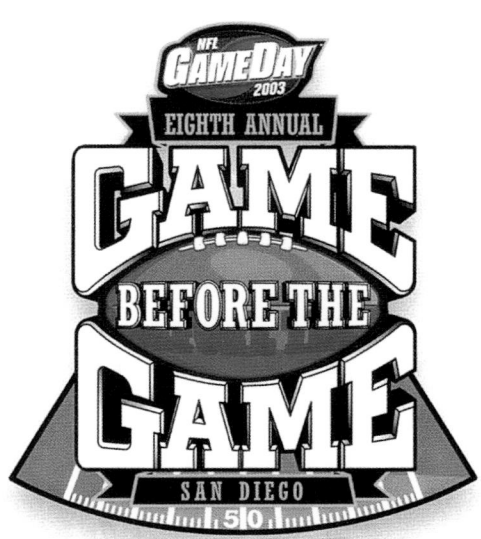
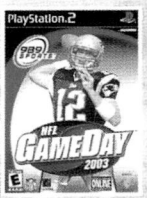

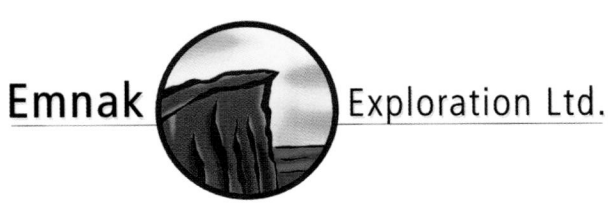

1.

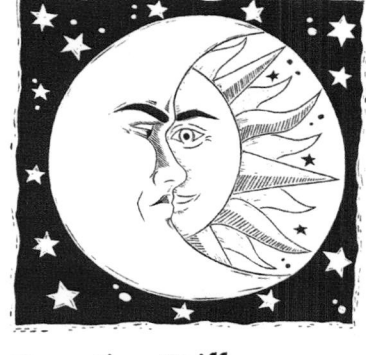

Creative Differences

2.

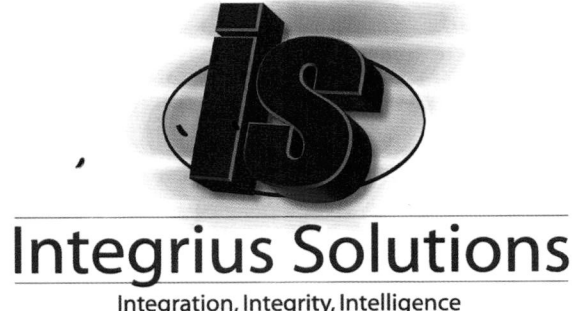

Integration, Integrity, Intelligence

3.

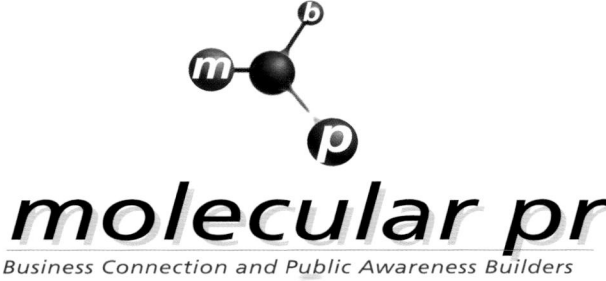

Entrepreneur to Entrepreneur

4.

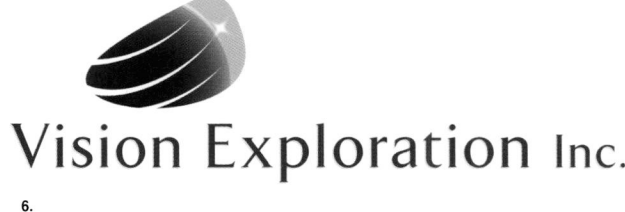

Business Connection and Public Awareness Builders

5.

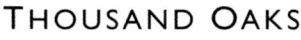

Vision Exploration Inc.

6.

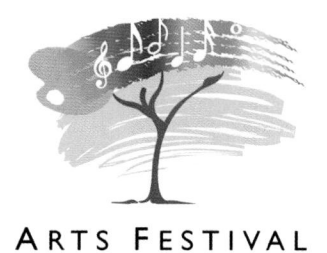

THOUSAND OAKS

ARTS FESTIVAL

7.

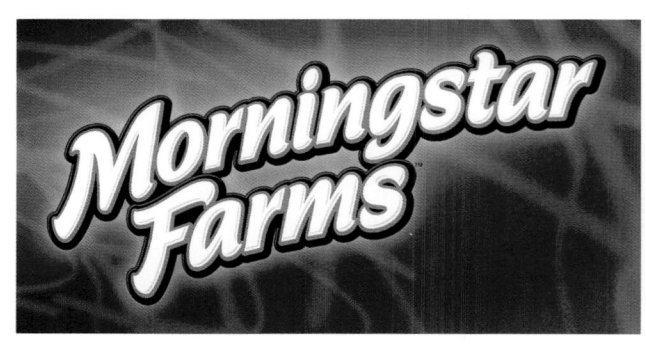

8.

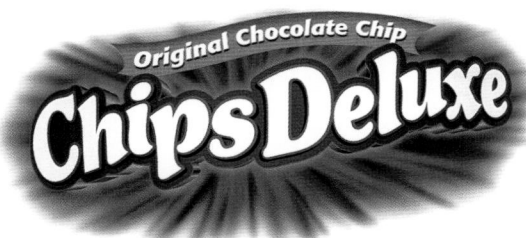

9.

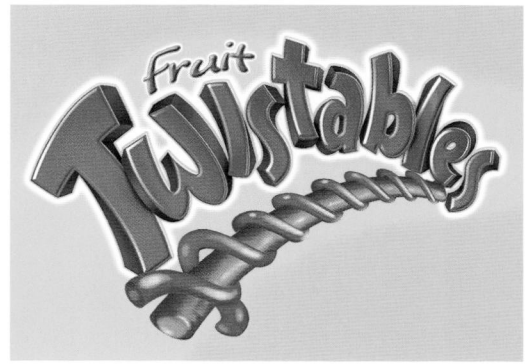

10.

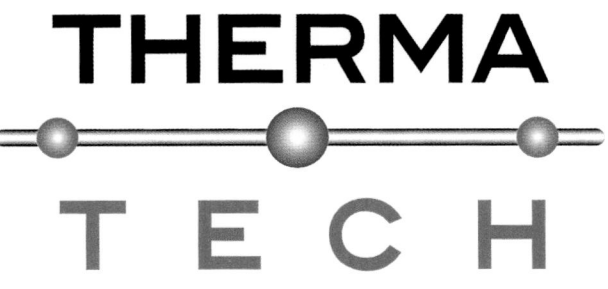

11.

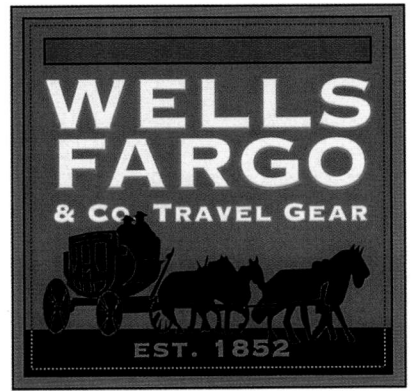

12.

THERMA

TECH

13.

WELLS FARGO & Co. TRAVEL GEAR
EST. 1852

14.

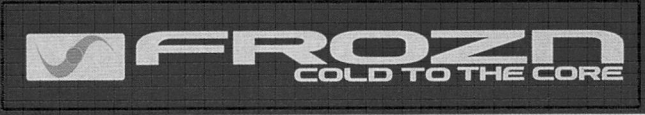

15.

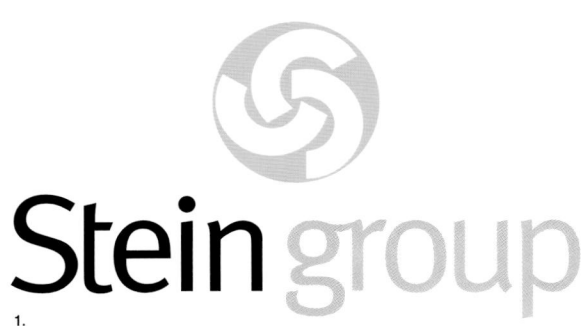

1.

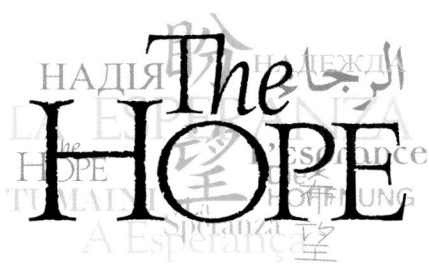

THE STORY OF GOD'S
PROMISE FOR ALL PEOPLE

2.

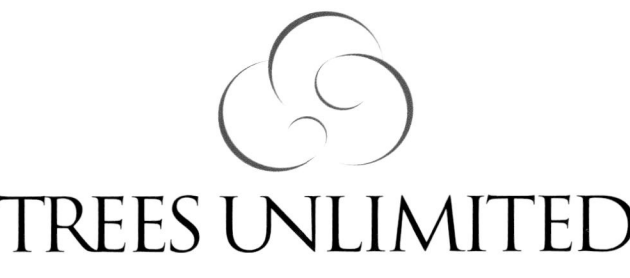

TREES UNLIMITED

3.

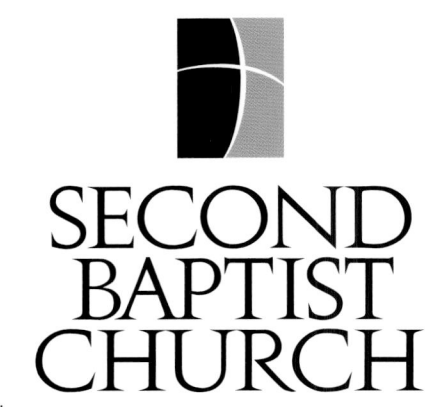

SECOND
BAPTIST
CHURCH

4.

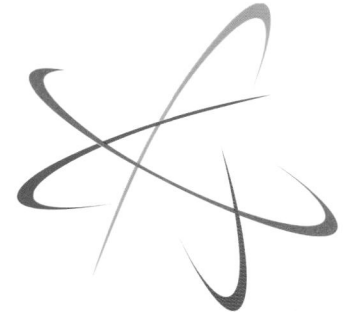

Integrated Electrical Services

5.

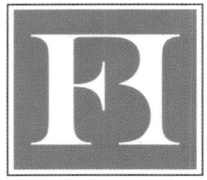

FISHER, BOYD, BROWN
BOUDREAUX & HUGUENARD LLP

6.

ATTORNEYS AT LAW

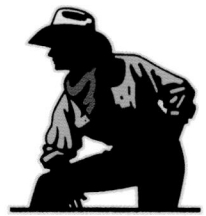

THE
TEXAN
TWO
STEP

7.

1 - 7
Design Firm **Loucks Designworks**
1.
Client	*Stein Group*
Designer	Jay Loucks
2.
Client	*Mars Hill Productions*
Designer	Jay Loucks
3.
Client	*Trees Unlimited*
Designer	Jay Loucks
4.
Client	*Second Baptist Church*
Designer	Jay Loucks

5.
Client	*Integrated Electrical Services*
Designer	Jay Loucks
6.
Client	*Fisher Boyd*
Designer	Jay Loucks
7.
Client	*Ronald McDonald House of Houston*
Designer	Jay Loucks
(opposite)
Client	*Tumak's Bar & Grill*
Design Firm	**CDI Studios**
Designer	Eddie Roberts

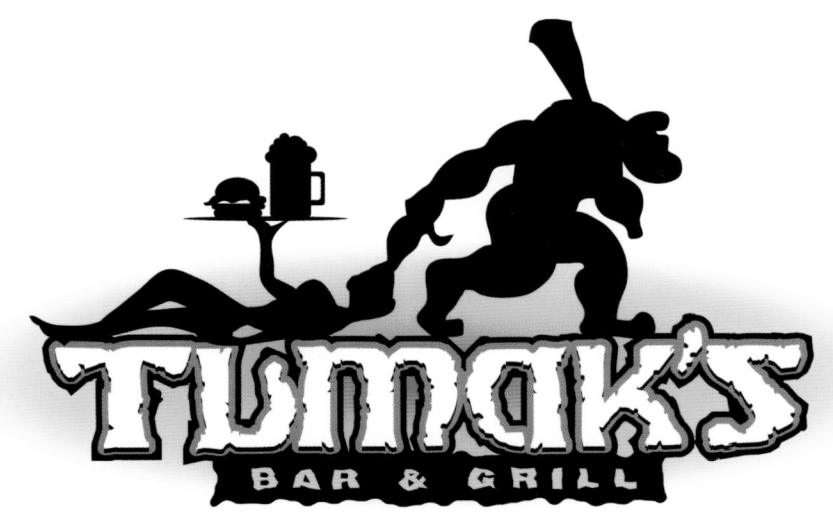

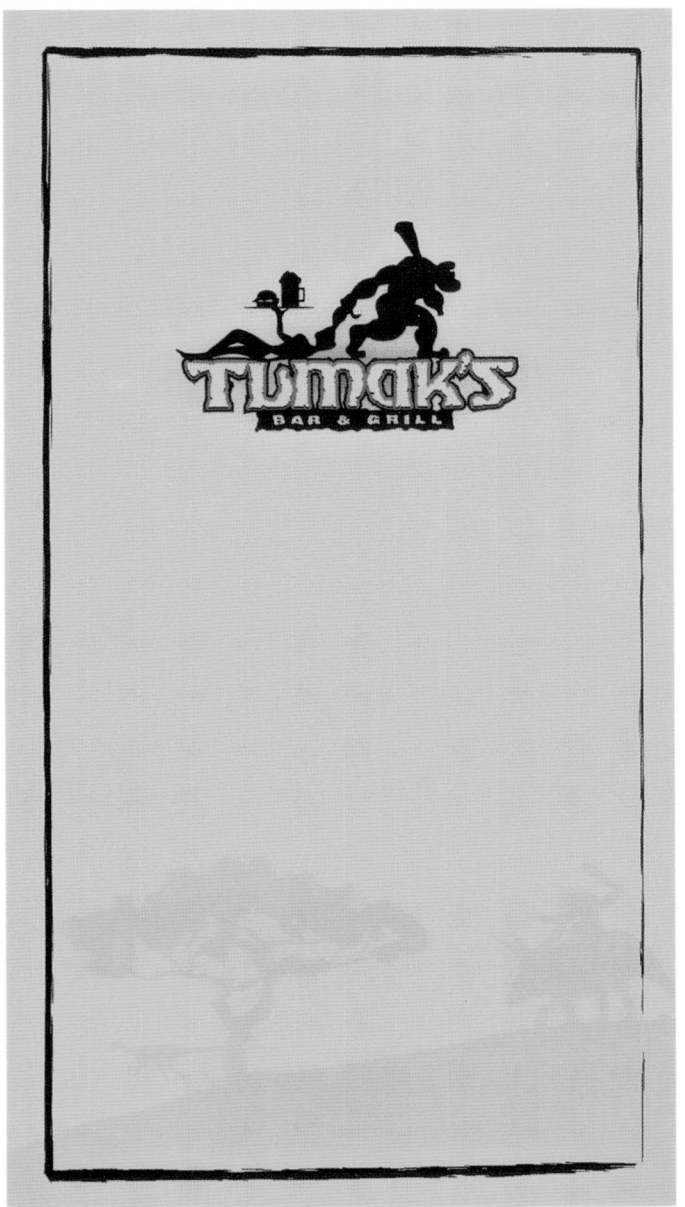

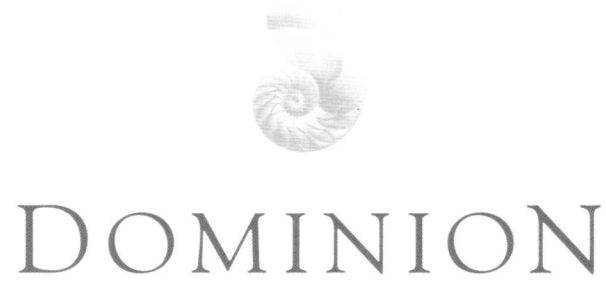

DOMINION

POST OAK

1.

firstbank

2.

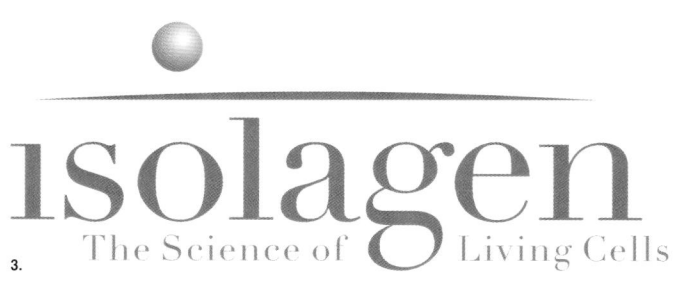

isolagen

The Science of · Living Cells

3.

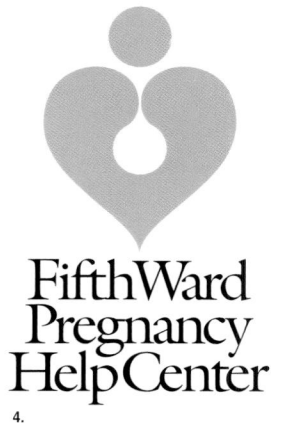

FifthWard
Pregnancy
HelpCenter

4.

Environmental
Achievement
Award

Schering-Plough

5.

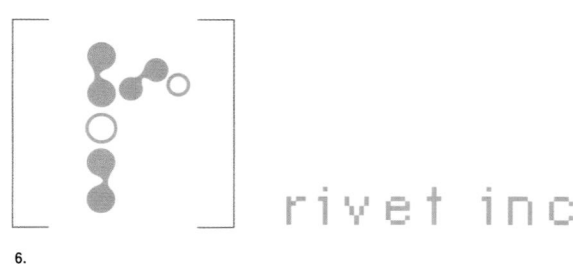

rivet inc.

6.

RED OAK
CONSULTING

A DIVISION OF MALCOLM PIRNIE

7.

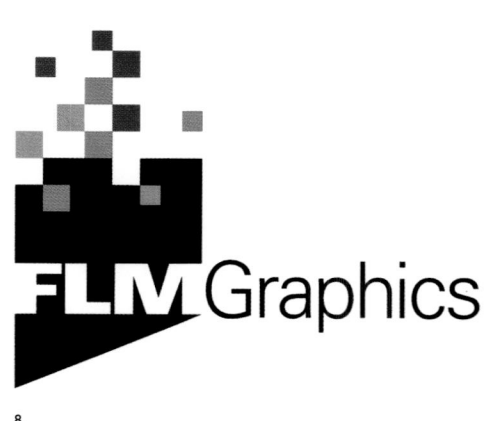

FLM Graphics

8.

elucient

dse | b®andesign

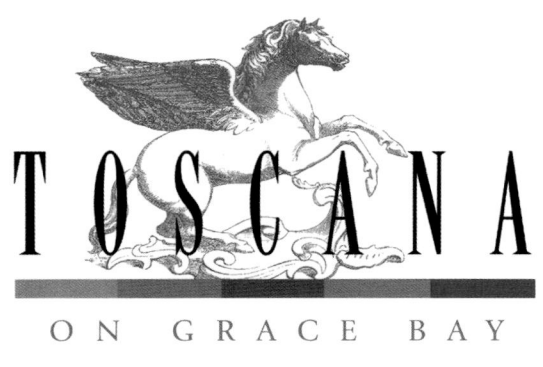

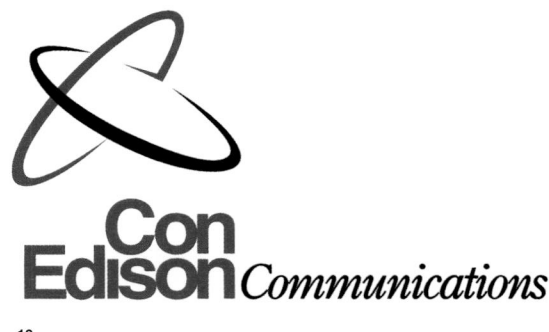

Con Edison *Communications*

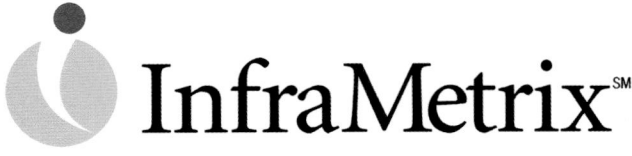

InfraMetrix℠

INFRASTRUCTURE DIAGNOSTIC SERVICES

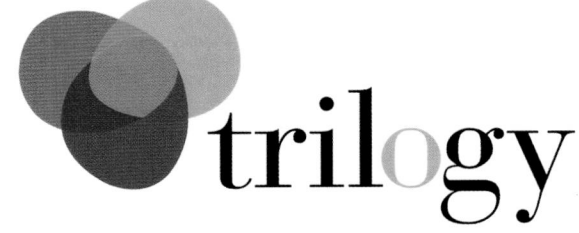

tril**o**gy

PATCHAM

1 - 4
Design Firm **Loucks Designworks**
5 - 14
Design Firm **Design Source East**
15
Design Firm **T-1 Productions**

1.
Client   *Dominion Post Oak*
Designer   Jay Loucks
2.
Client   *First Federal Bank, Texas*
Designer   Jay Loucks
3.
Client   *Isolagen*
Designer   Jay Loucks
4.
Client   *Fifth Ward Pregnancy*
Designer   Jay Loucks
5.
Client   *Schering-Plough*
Designer   H. Dean Pillion
6.
Client   *Rivet Inc.*
Designer   Mark Lo Bello

7.
Client   *Red Oak Consulting*
Designer   Mark Lo Bello
8.
Client   *FLM Graphics Corporation*
Designer   Mark Lo Bello
9.
Client   *elucient*
Designer   Mark Lo Bello
10.
Client   *Design Source East*
Designer   Mark Lo Bello
11.
Client   *Toscana USA, LLC*
Designer   Mark Lo Bello
12.
Client   *Con Edison Communications*
Designers   Mark Lo Bello, H. Dean Pillion
13.
Client   *InfraMetrix*
Designer   Mark Lo Bello
14.
Client   *Trilogy Publications LLC*
Designer   Mark Lo Bello
15.
Client   *Patcham Chemicals*
Designer   Parisa Chum

249

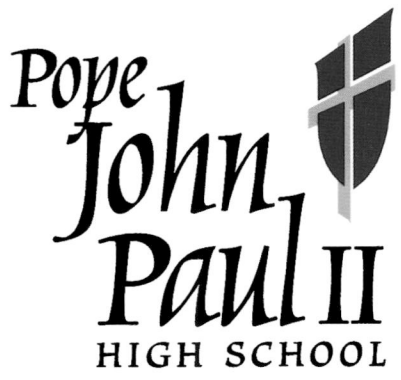

1.

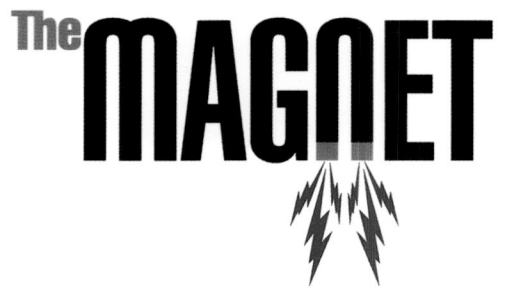

MUSIC GROUP

2.

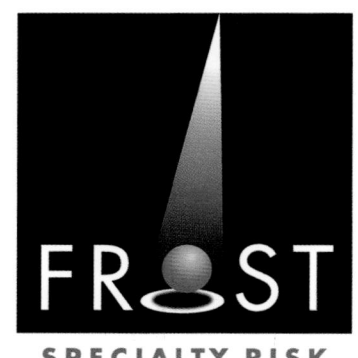

SPECIALTY RISK

3.

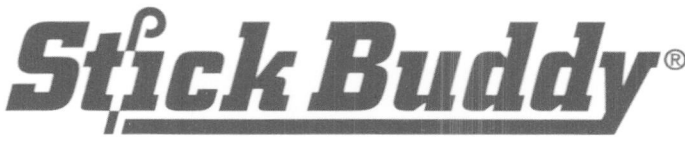

4.

THE DESIGN ACADEMY

5.

interiors·R·us

6.

D-TRAN

7.

1 - 4
Design Firm **Ventress Design Group**
5 - 7
Design Firm **T-1 Productions**

1.
Client   *Pope John Paul II High School*
Designer   Tom Ventress

2.
Client   *The Magnet Music Group*
Designer   Tom Ventress

3.
Client   *Frost Specialty Risk*
Designer   Tom Ventress

4.
Client   *T.A.C.K. Inc.*
Designer   Tom Ventress

5.
Client   *The Design Academy*
Designers   Pallav Patel, Parisa Chum

6.
Client   *Interiors R Us*
Designers   Parisa Chum, Pallav Patel

7.
Client   *D-TRAN.com*
Designer   Pallav Patel

(opposite)
Client   *Ambiance design group*
Design Firm **CDI Studios**
Designer   Michelle Georgilas

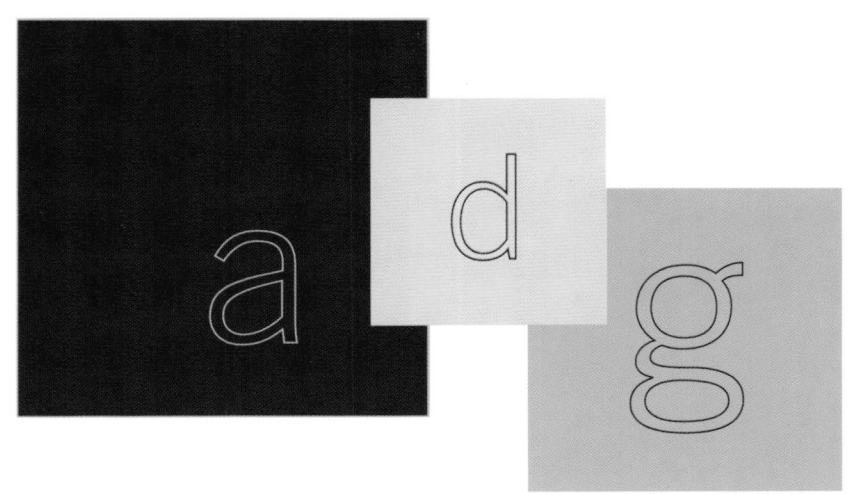

AMBIANCE design group*

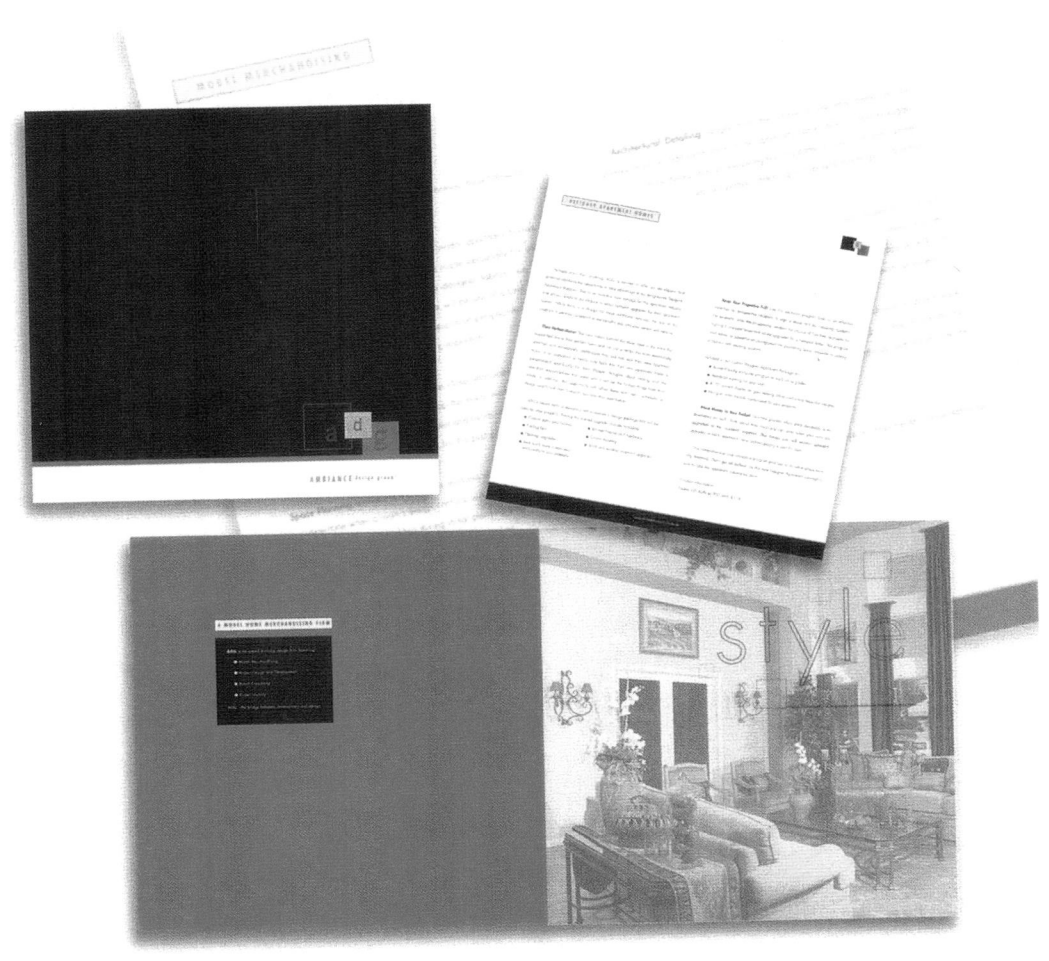

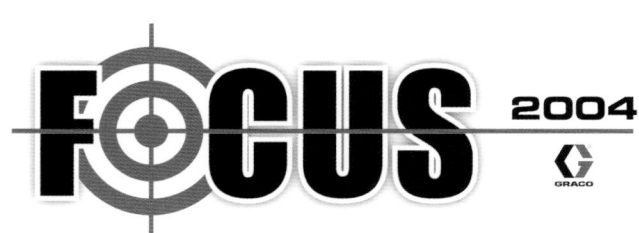

1.

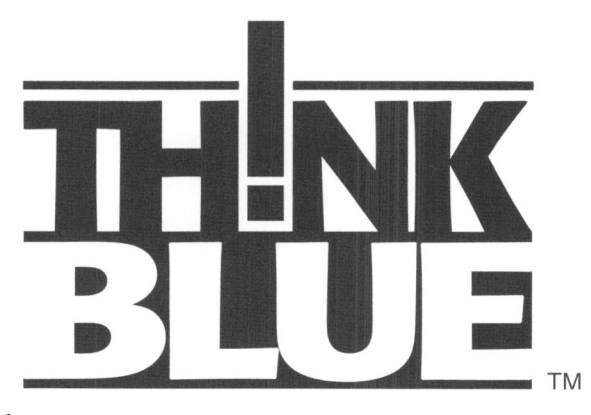

2.

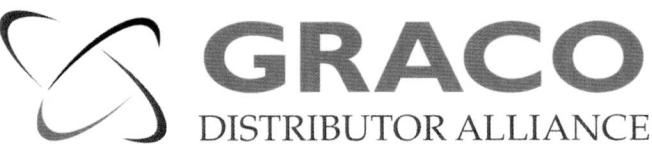

3.

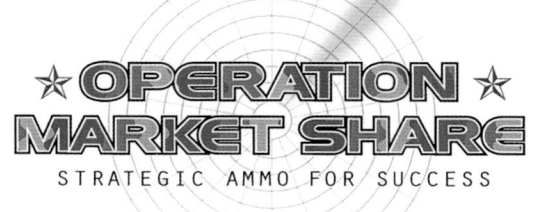

4.

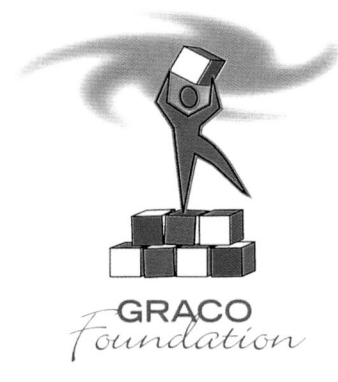

5.

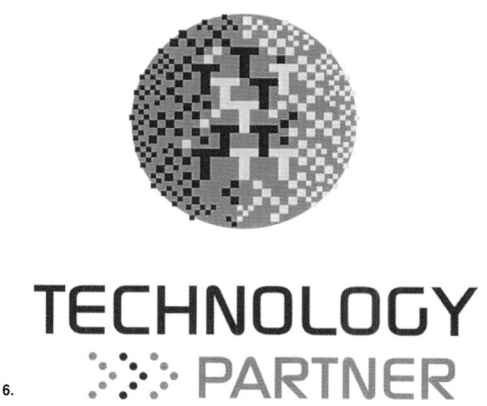

6.

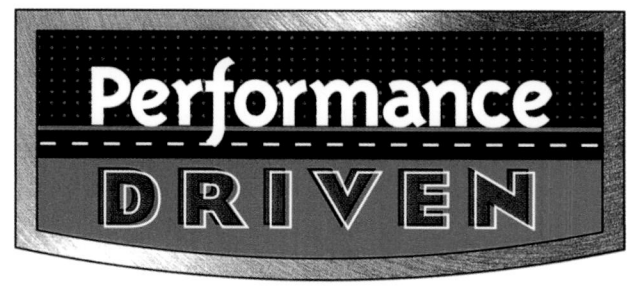

7.

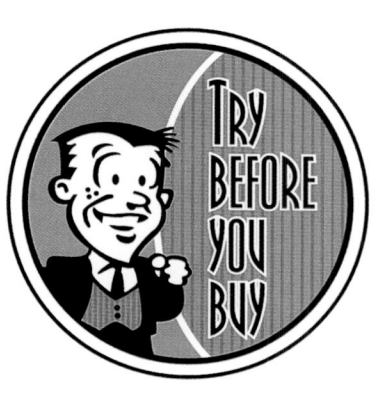

8.

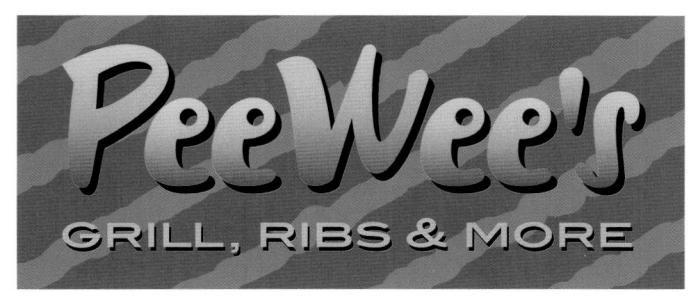

9.

Autoridad de Acueductos y Alcantarillados

10.

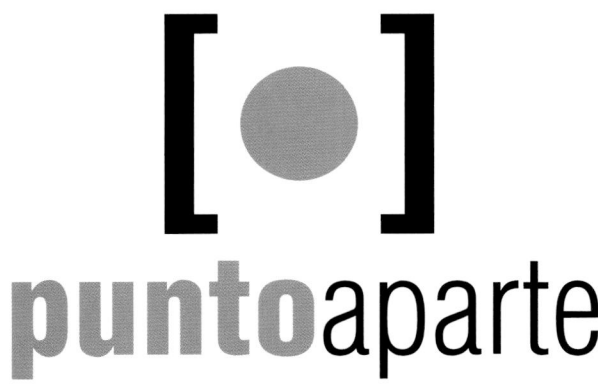

puntoaparte

11.

FUNDACIÓN COMUNITARIA
DE PUERTO RICO

12.

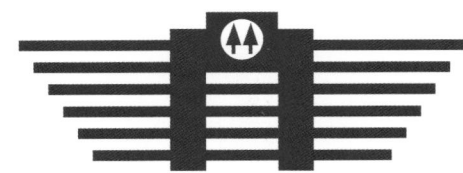

COOPERATIVA DE
SEGUROS MULTIPLES
DE PUERTO RICO

13.

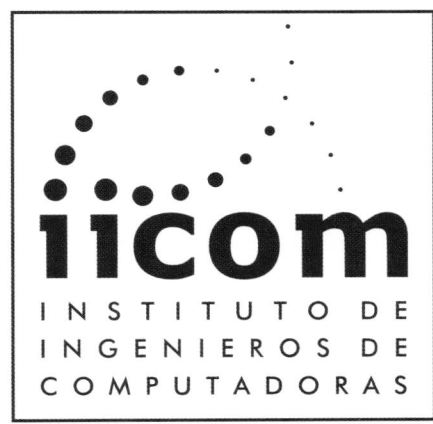

14.

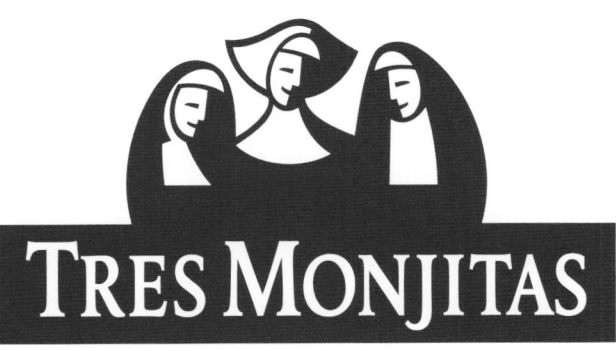

15.

1 - 8
Design Firm **Graco Inc.**
9 - 15
Design Firm **ID Group**
1.
Client *Contractor Division*
Designer Todd Safgren
2.
Client *Contractor Division*
Designer David Orwoll
3 - 7.
Client *Industrial Division*
Designer Gary Schmidt
8.
Client *Corporate*
Designer Gary Schmidt
9.
Client *PeeWee's Grill*
Designers Carolina Carezis,
Abner Gutiertuez

10.
Client *Autoridad de Acueductos*
y Alcantarillados
Designers Jorge Colon,
Abner Gutierrez
11.
Client *Punto Aparte Publicidad*
Designers Sofiá Saenz,
Abner Gutierrez
12.
Client *Fundacion Comunitaria De PR*
Designer Mayra Maldonado
13.
Client *Cooperativa Seguros*
Multiples PR
Designers Mayra Maldonado,
Abner Gutierrez
14.
Client *Instituto Ingenieros*
De Computadoras
Designer Mayra Maldonado
15.
Client *Tres Monjitas Dairy*
Designers Abner Gutierrez,
Mayra Maldonado

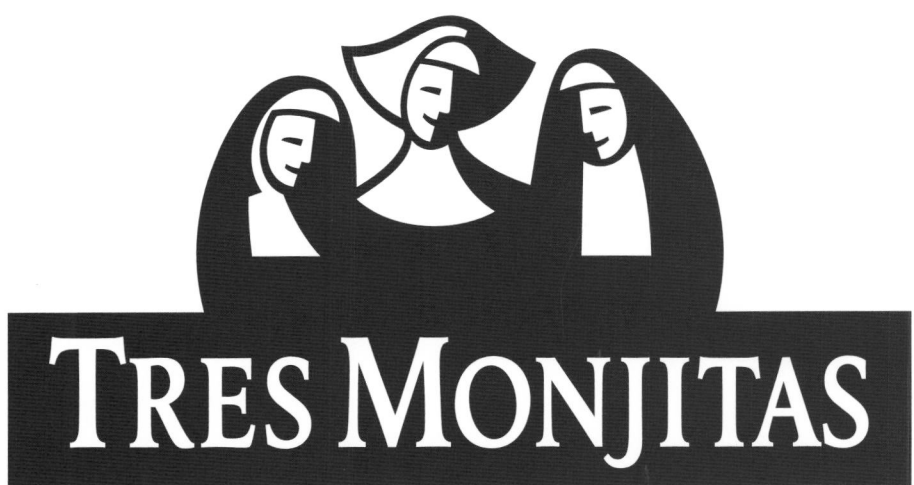

Design Firm **ID Group**
Client   *Tres Monjitas Dairy*
Designers Abner Gutierrez,
           Mayra Maldonado

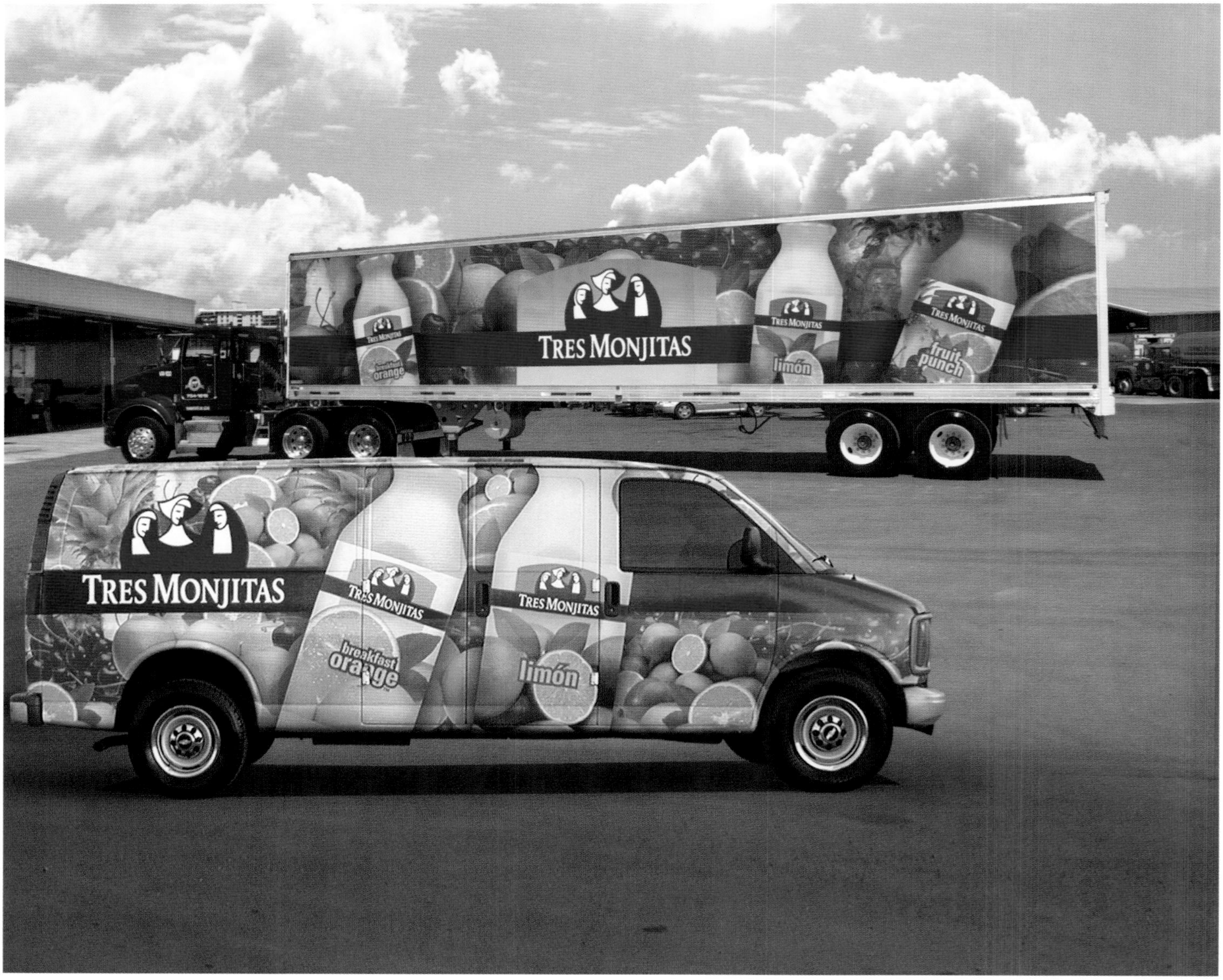

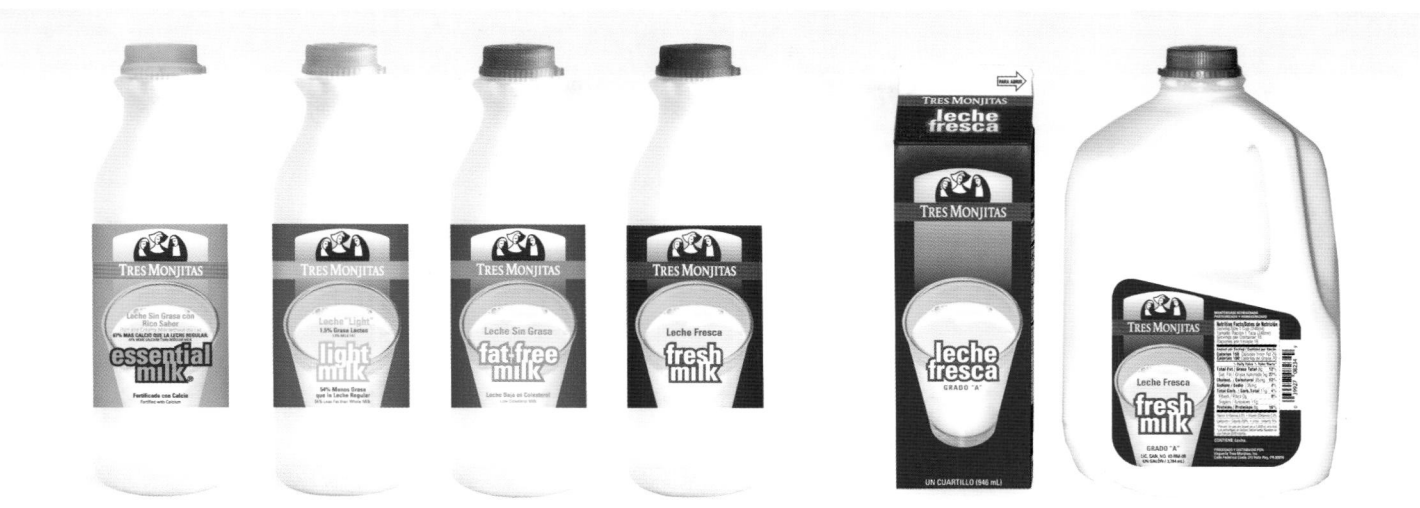

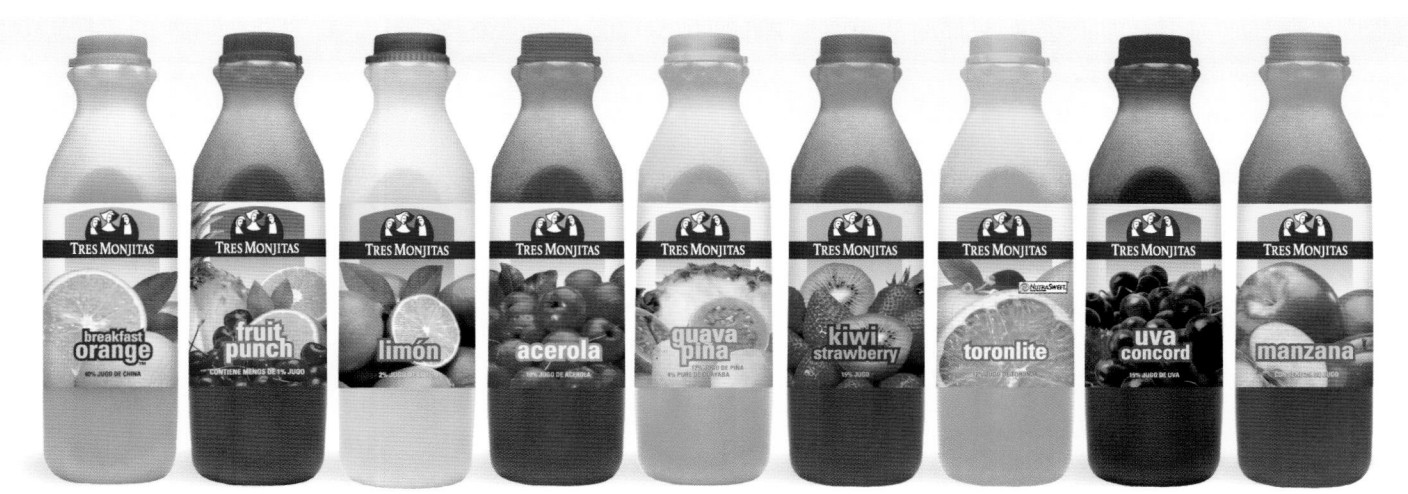

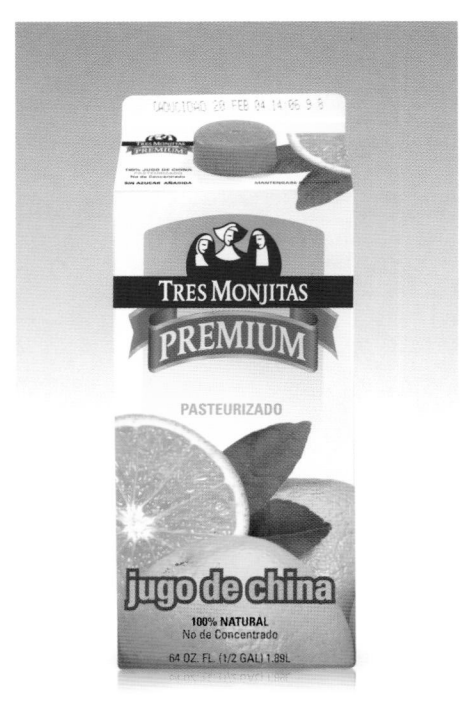

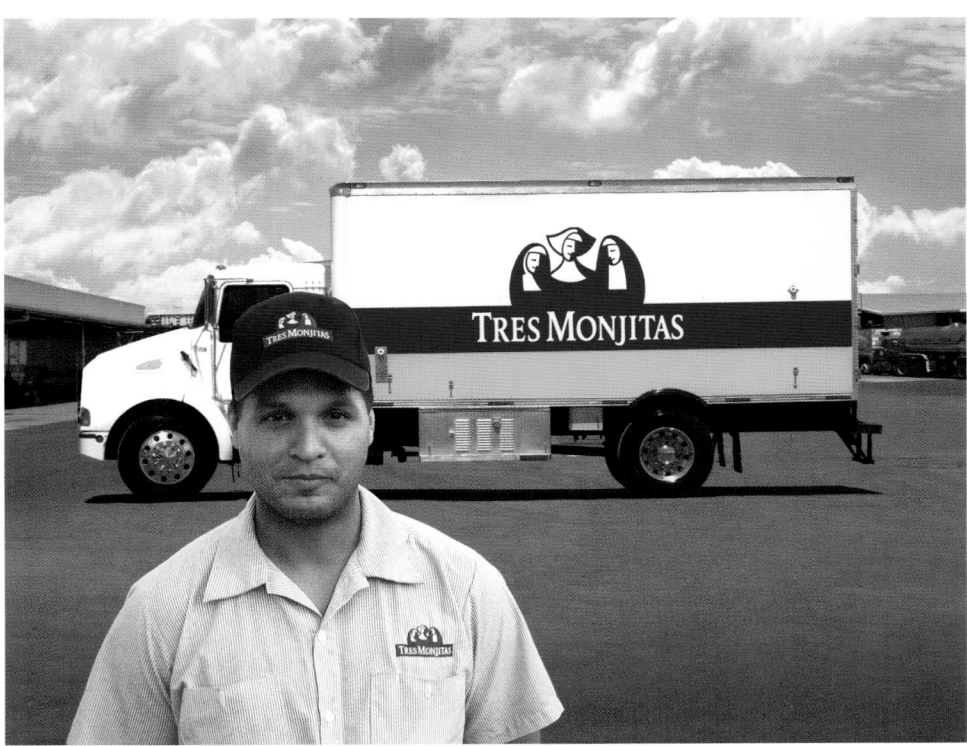

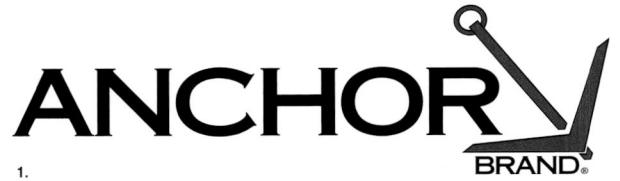

1.

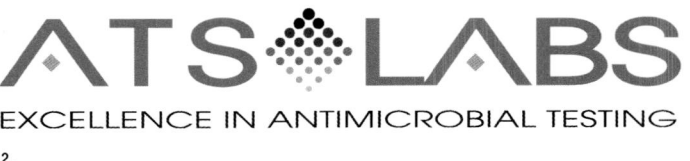

2.

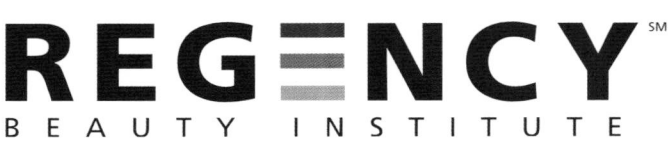

3.

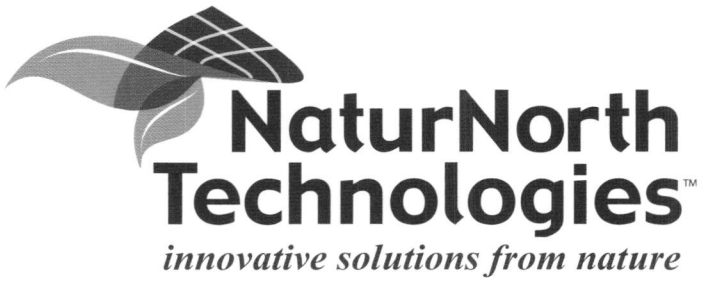

4.

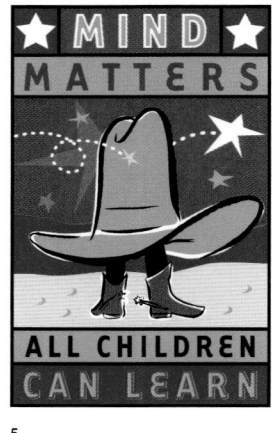

5.

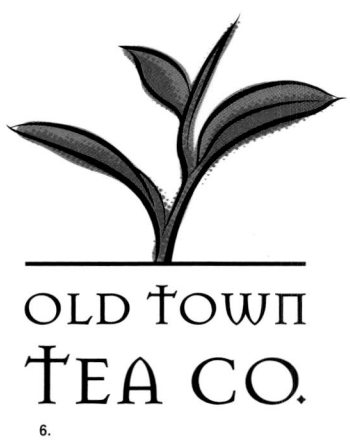

6.

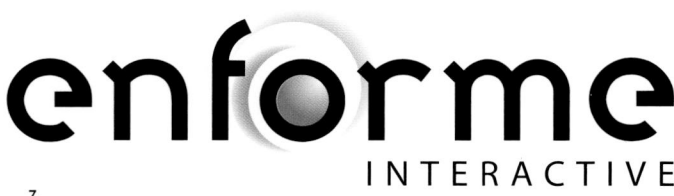

7.

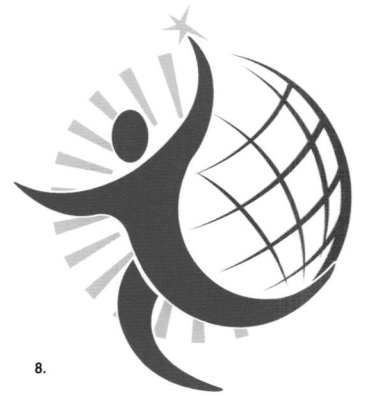

8.

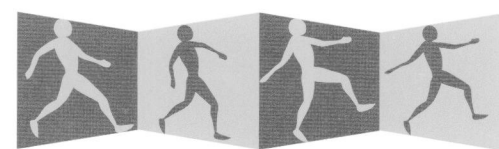

STRUT YOUR STUFF
Displays & Exhibits

9.

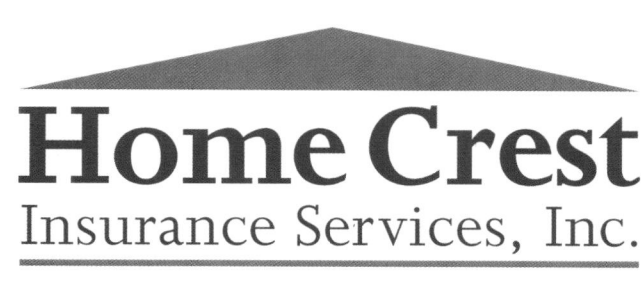

10.

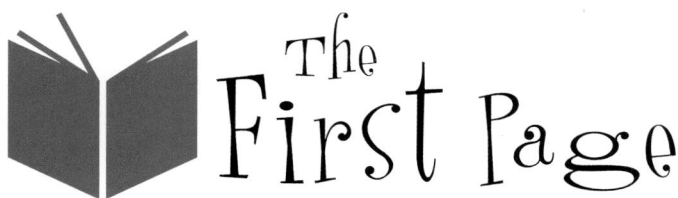

11.

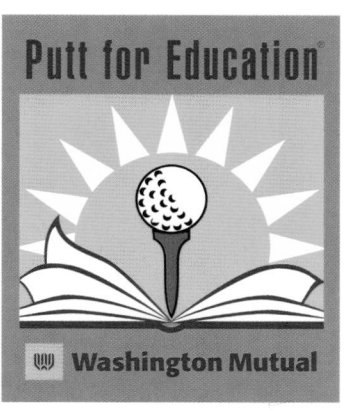

12.

tax**homme**
www.taxhomme.com

13.

medicalalumniassociation

14.

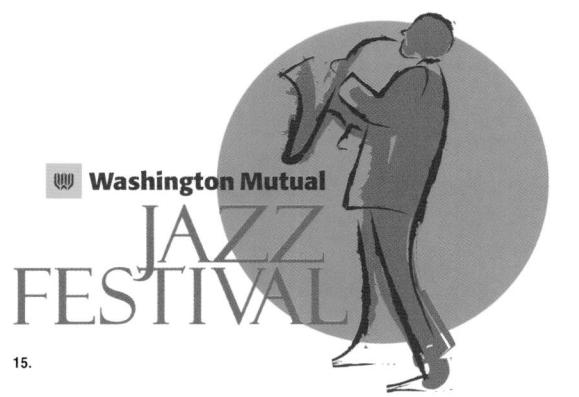

15.

1 - 4
Design Firm **MVP Marketing & Design, Inc.**
5 - 9
Design Firm **Octavo Designs**
10 - 15
Design Firm **Tajima Creative**

1.
Client *ORS Nasco*
Designer Alex Watkins
2.
Client *ATS Labs*
Designer Greg Schultz
3.
Client *Regency Beauty Institute*
Designer Greg Schultz
4.
Client *NaturNorth Technologies*
Designer Mike Esson
5.
Client *National Association
of School Psychologists*
Designers Sue Hough, Mark Burrier
6.
Client *Old Town Tea Co.*
Designers Sue Hough, Mark Burrier

7.
Client *Enforme Interactive*
Designers Sue Hough, Mark Burrier
8.
Client *Caribbean Latin American Action*
Designer Mark Burrier
9.
Client *Strut Your Stuff Displays & Exhibits*
Designer Mark Burrier
10.
Client *Home Crest
Insurance Services, Inc.*
Designer Ximena
11.
Client *First Page Books*
12.
Client *Washington Mutual, Inc.*
Designer Chris Lena
13.
Client *Tax Homme*
14.
Client *University of California
San Francisco Medical School*
Designer Komal Dedhia
15.
Client *Washington Mutual, Inc.*
Designer Roz Roos

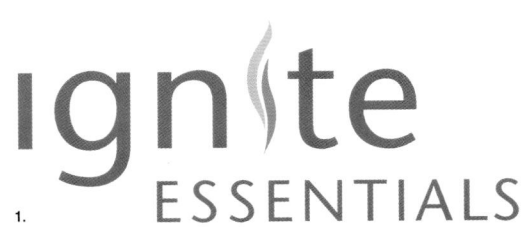

1.

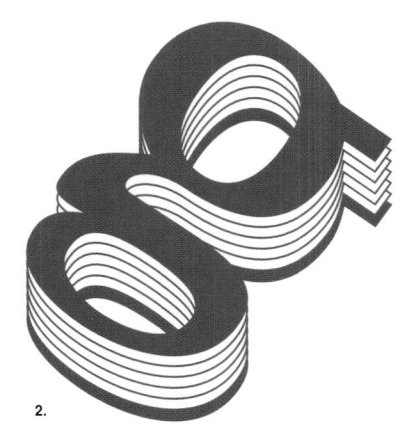

2.

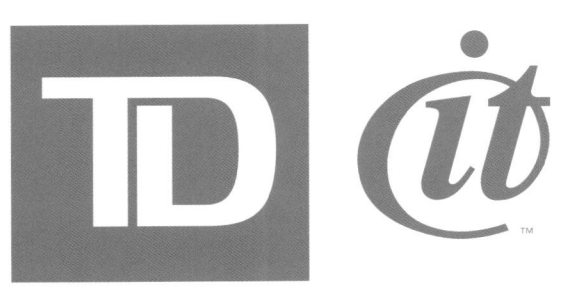

IT's different here.™

3.

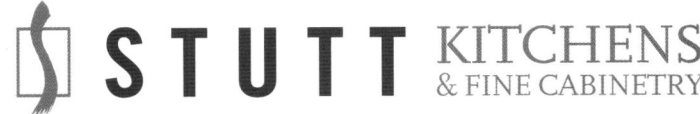

4.

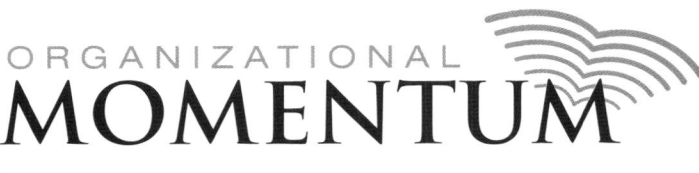

skule alumni

5.

ORGANIZATIONAL
MOMENTUM

6.

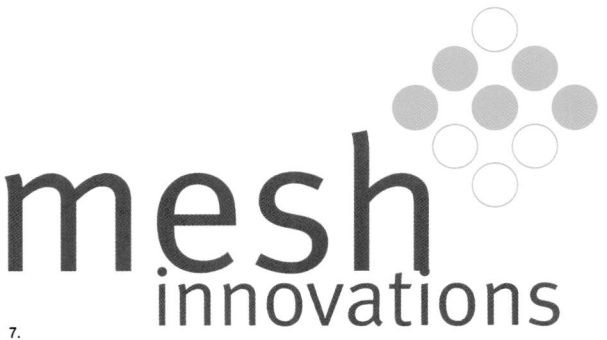

mesh innovations

7.

1 - 7
Design Firm **Provoq Inc.**

1.
Client — *Ignite Essentials Leadership Development*
Designer — Jeffrey Chow

2.
Client — *The Gallanough Resource Centre*
Designer — Jeffrey Chow

3.
Client — *TD Bank Financial Group*
Designer — Jeffrey Chow

4.
Client — *Stutt Kitchens & Fine Cabinetry*
Designer — Jeffrey Chow

5.
Client — *University of Toronto Engineering Alumni Association*
Designer — Jeffrey Chow

6.
Client — *Organizational Momentum*
Designer — Jeffrey Chow

7.
Client — *Mesh Innovations Inc.*
Designer — Jeffrey Chow

(opposite)
Client — *Sony Computer Entertainment America*
Design Firm **CDI Studios**
Designer — Eddie Roberts

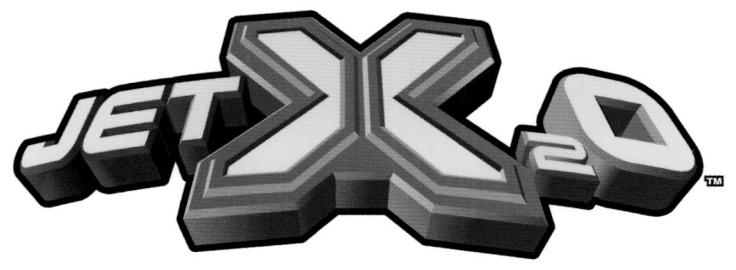

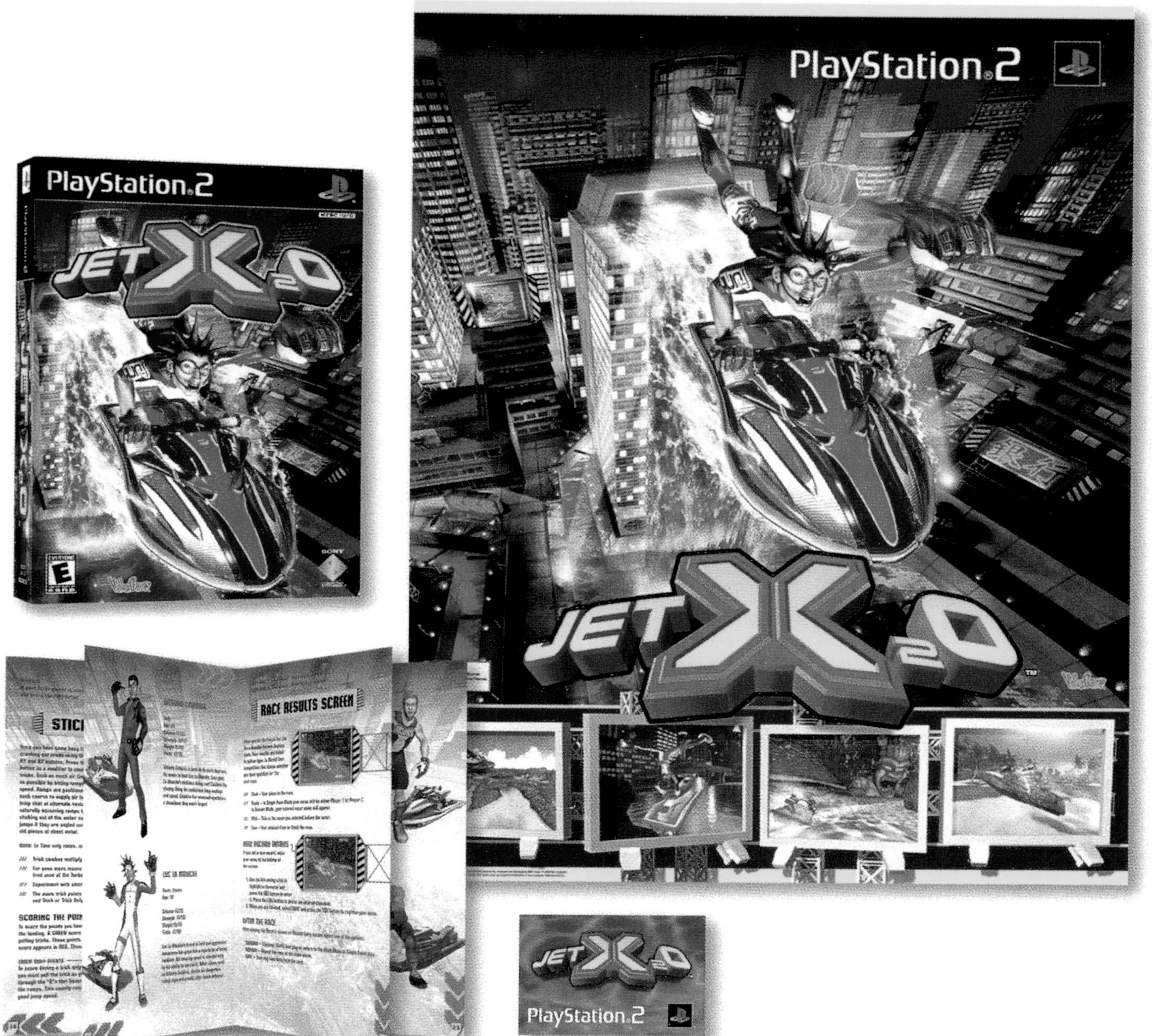

icon style guide

To maintain the CHOC brand image, any icon created and used to represent the hospital or its affiliates follows the same visual style as that established by the masterbrand signature, the mascot, and the affiliate icons. The examples below show various icons created for use in conjunction with newsletters and other collateral materials. Their shared characteristics include energetic, gestural pen strokes and simplified graphic treatments. Extend this same illustrative style when creating new iconic artwork.

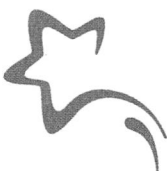

CHOC Institute

CHOC Foundation
for Children

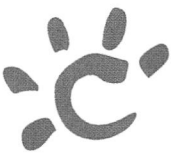

Kids Health: Calendar

Literacy

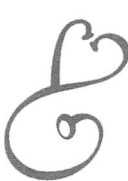

Physician Connection Logo

P.C: CME Lectures/Dinners

P.C: This & That

P.C: Case Study

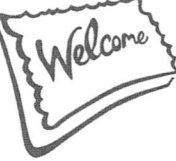

P.C: Welcome

15

choc affiliates

ICON USAGE

Our affiliates are fund-raising groups that support our organization and are an integral part of CHOC. Each has an icon that visually ties into the brand image. These icons are used to represent Guild activities that promote our hospital. It is important that these icons be used with as much respect and care as the CHOC Mascot. Like the mascot, these icons may be cropped and screened in their specified color, as long as they maintain their unique characteristics and recognizability. Be sure to leave a clear space of at least $\frac{1}{2}$" around each icon when used as a logo. Each icon prints in one color, using the specified color, in black, or reversed to white.

Mad Hatter Guild
PMS 347

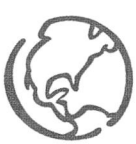

Small World Guild
PMS 660

Little Red Wagon Guild
PMS 200

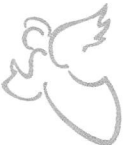

Littlest Angel Guild
PMS 310

Lamp Lighter Guild
PMS 129

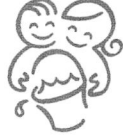

Jack & Jill Guild
PMS 660

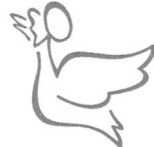

Mother Goose Guild
PMS 200

11

Design Firm **Hornall Anderson Design Works**
Client *CHOC (Children's Hospital of Orange County)*
Designers Jack Anderson, Lisa Cerveny, Debra McCloskey, Steffanie Lorig, Jana Wilson Esser, Gretchen Cook, Jana Nishi, Darlin Gray

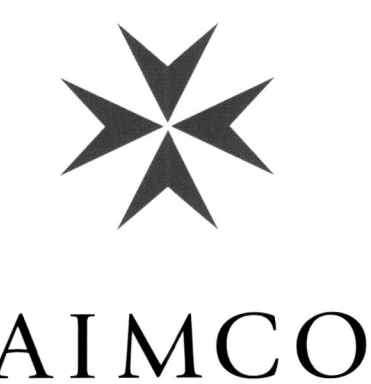

AIMCO

1.

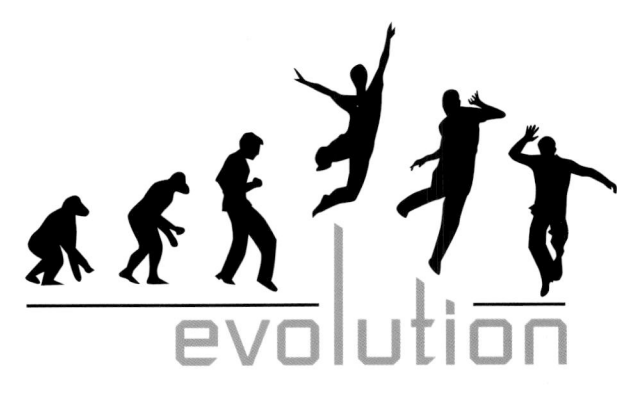

evolution

sports & music

2.

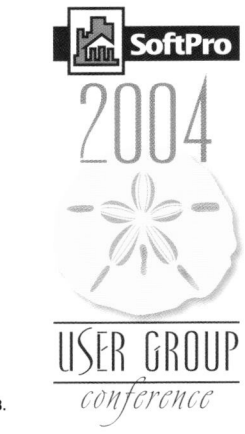

SoftPro

2004

USER GROUP
conference

3.

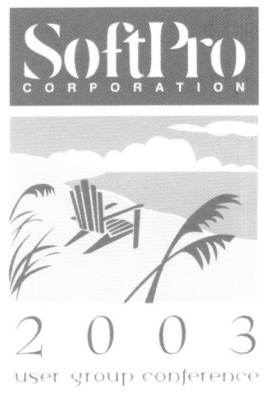

SoftPro
CORPORATION

2 0 0 3

user group conference

4.

3 v CAPITAL

5.

MONTAGGIO

european style for the american lifestyle

6.

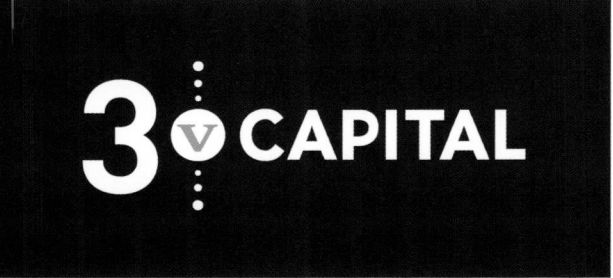

7.

1 - 4
Design Firm **CAI Communications**
5, 6
Design Firm **OrangeSeed Design**
7
Design Firm **Rickabaugh Graphics**
1.
Client   *Key Risk*
Designer Steve McCulloch
2.
Client   *Evolution Technologies*
Designer Beth Greene
3, 4.
Client   *SoftPro*
Designer Beth Greene

5.
Client   *3v Capital*
Designers Damien Wolf, Phil Hoch
6.
Client   *Montaggio*
Designers Damien Wolf, Phil Hoch
7.
Client   *Run for Christ*
Designer Eric Rickabaugh
(opposite)
Client   *AIGA Las Vegas*
Design Firm **CDI Studios**
Designers Michelle Georgilas,
          MacKenzie Walsh

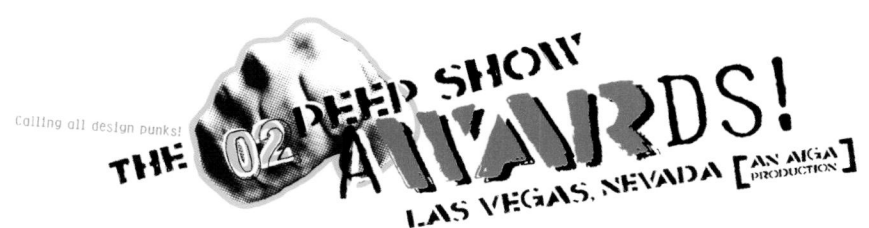

Calling all design punks!
THE 02 PEEP SHOW AWARDS!
LAS VEGAS, NEVADA [AN AIGA PRODUCTION]

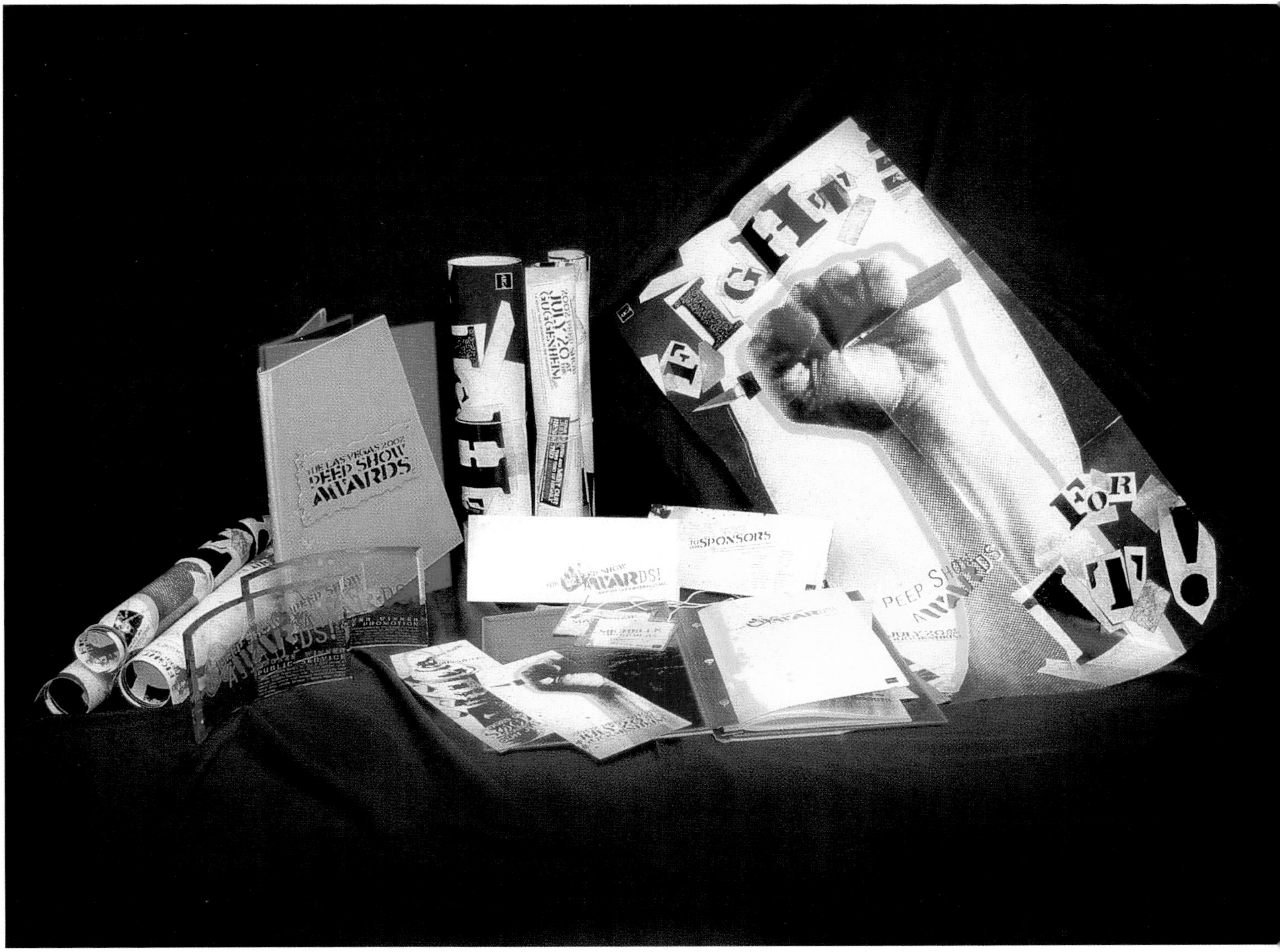

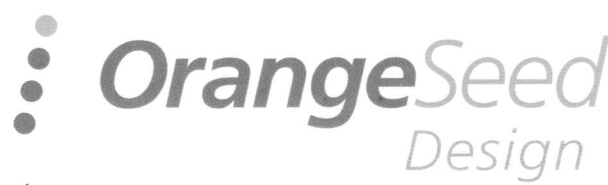

1.

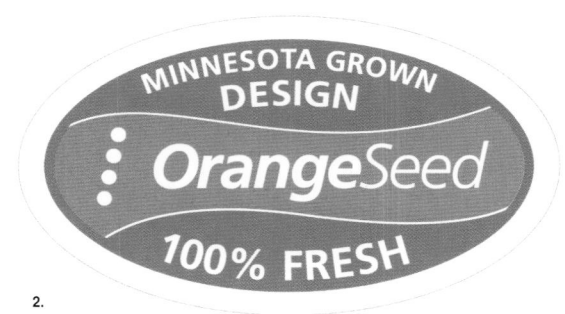

2.

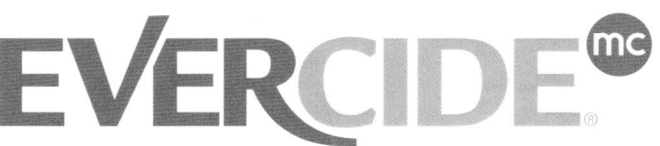

3.

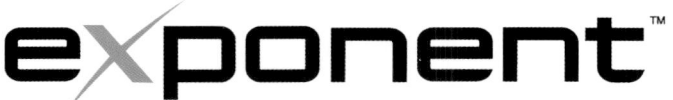

4.

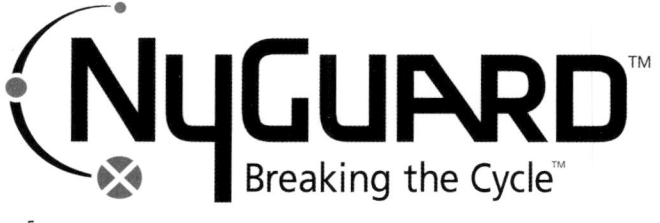

5.

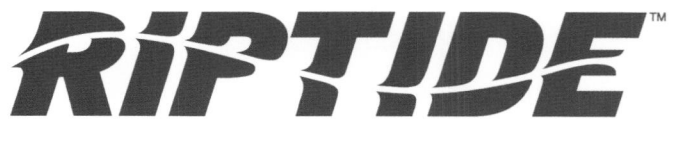

6.

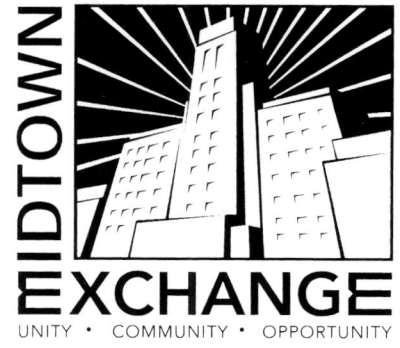

7.

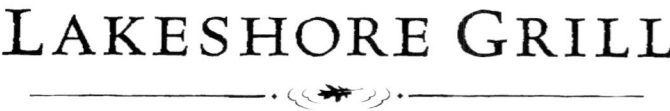

8.

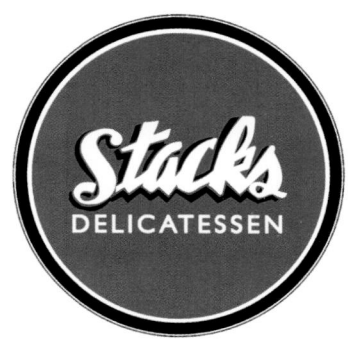

9.

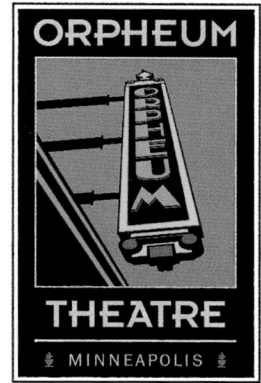

10.

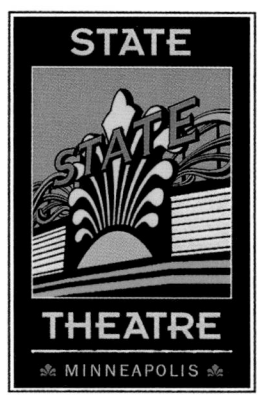

11.

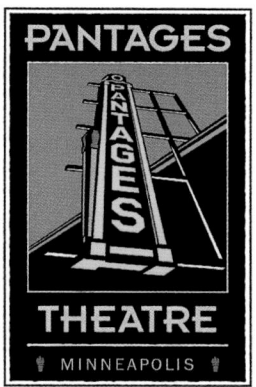

12.

13.

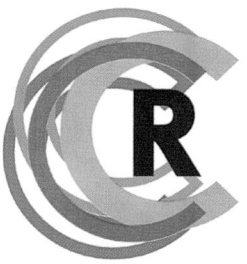

CENTER ROKODELSTVA LJUBLJANA

14.

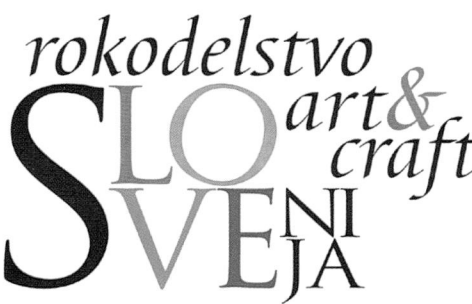

15.

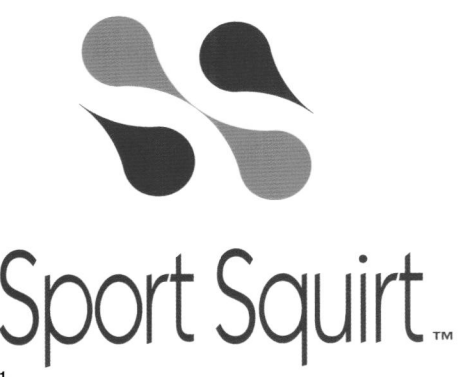

Sport Squirt™

1.

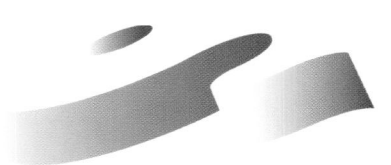

Flexo Impressions, Inc.

2.

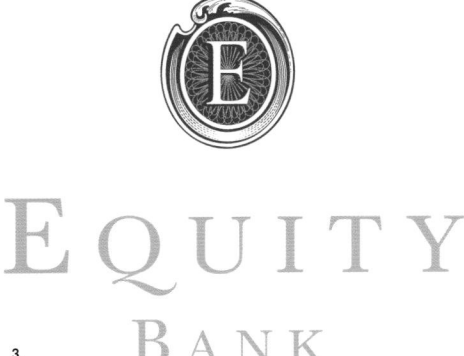

EQUITY BANK

3.

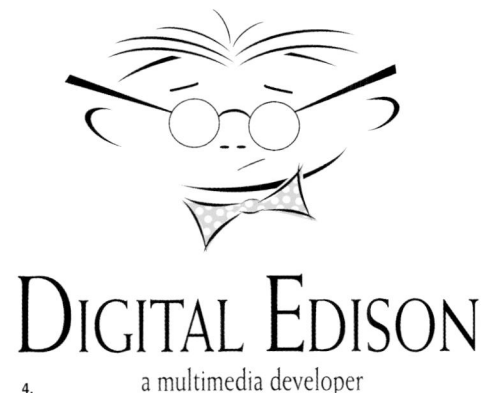

DIGITAL EDISON
a multimedia developer

4.

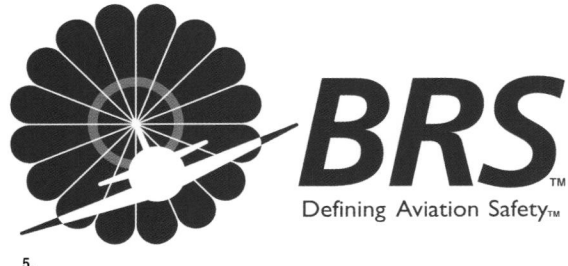

BRS™
Defining Aviation Safety™

5.

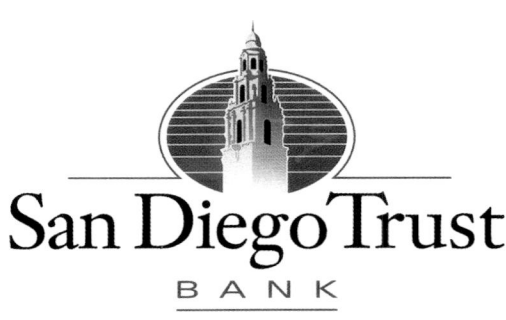

San Diego Trust
BANK

6.

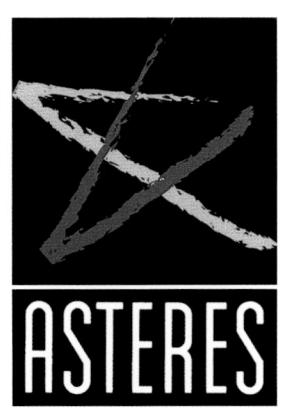

7.

1 - 5		
Design Firm	**Hendler-Johnston**	
6, 7		
Design Firm	**Crouch and Naegeli/ Design Group West**	
1.		
	Client	*Sport Squirt*
	Designer	Chris Hendler
2.		
	Client	*Flexo Impressions, Inc.*
	Designer	Chris Hendler
3.		
	Client	*Equity Bank*
	Designer	Chris Hendler

4.		
	Client	*Digital Edison*
	Designer	Chris Hendler
5.		
	Client	*BRS*
	Designer	Chris Hendler
6.		
	Client	*San Diego Trust Bank*
	Designer	Jim Naegeli
7.		
	Client	*Asteres*
	Designer	Jim Naegeli
(opposite)		
	Client	*Project Sunshine*
	Design Firm	**CDI Studios**
	Designer	Michelle Georgilas

RED HOT 02°

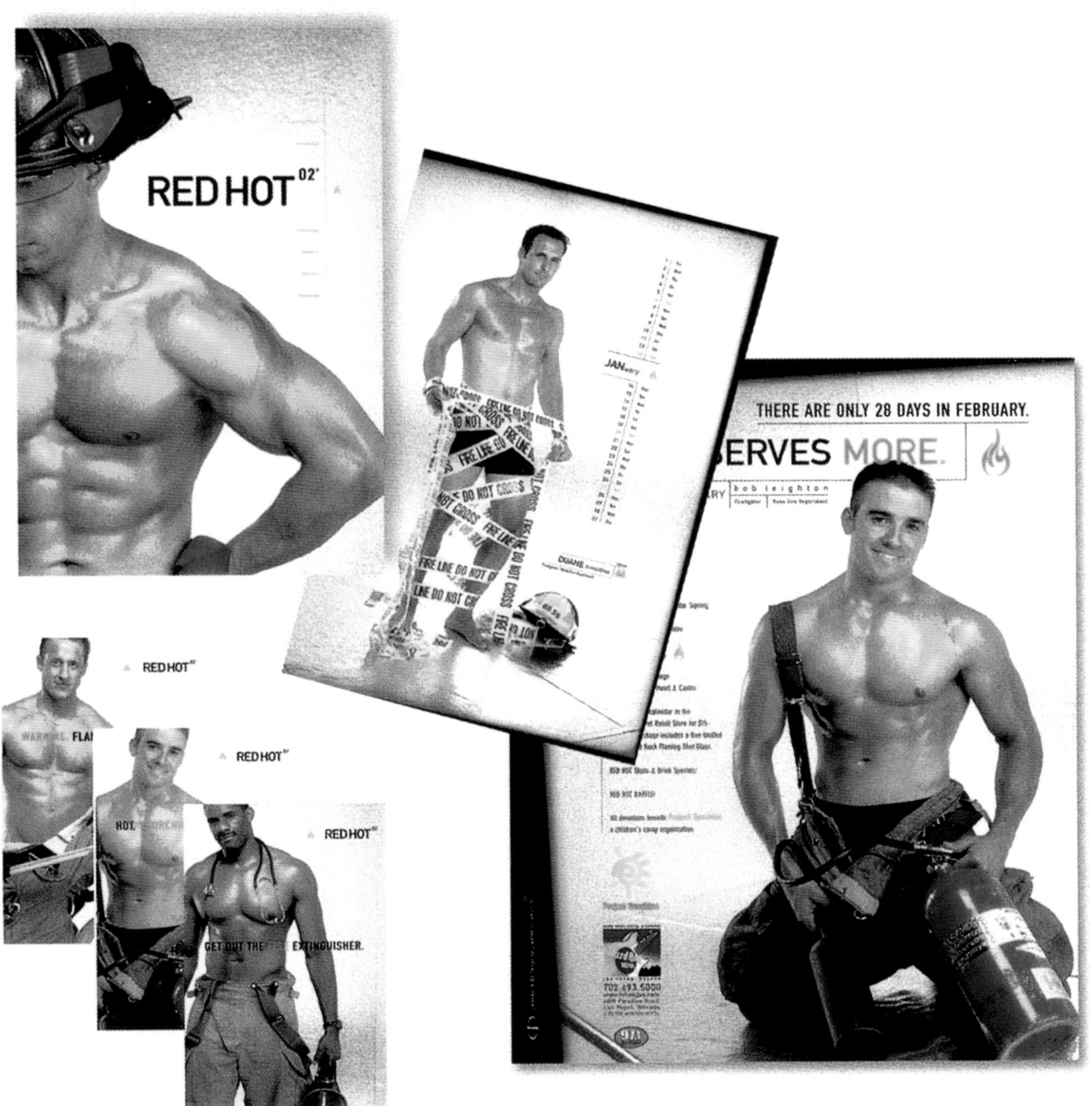

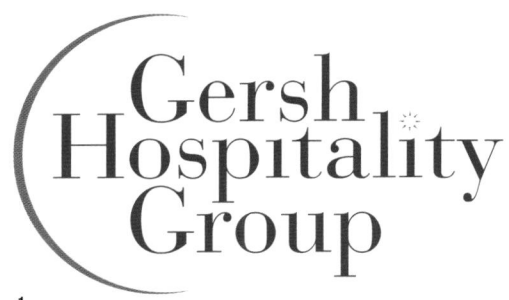

1.

Sole Indulgence™

2.

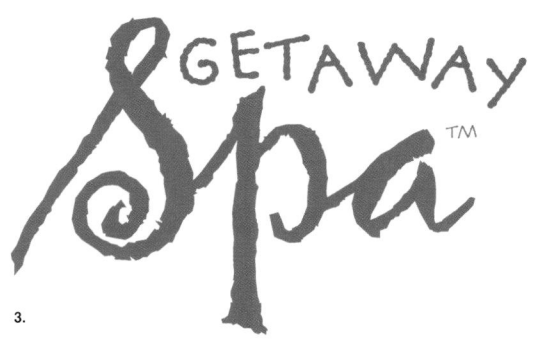

3.

水 WATER

4.

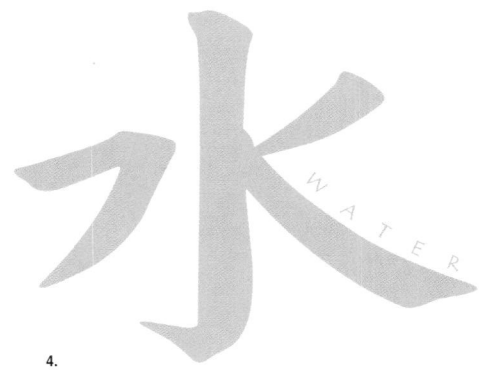

5.

advantix

6.

Venus™

7.

NECKY KAYAKS

8.

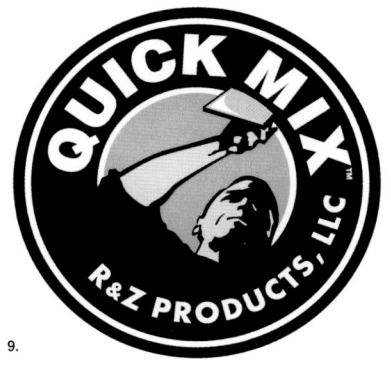

9.

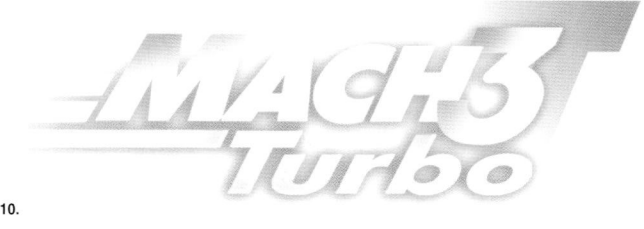

10.

 **Lowe**Associates

11.

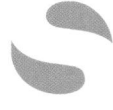 stress**design**

12.

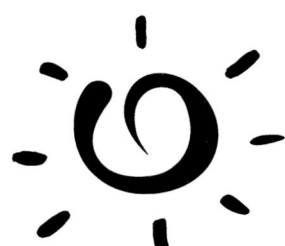

Unwin Development
Support for Public Broadcasting

13.

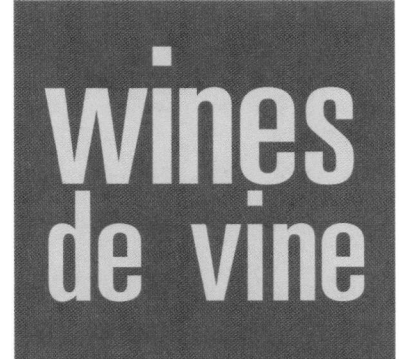

14.

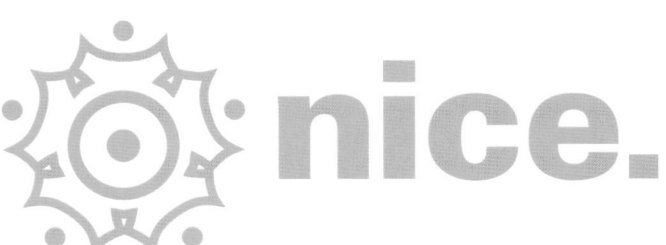

15.

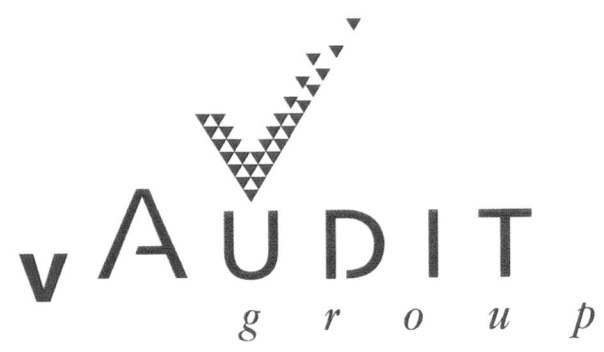

1.

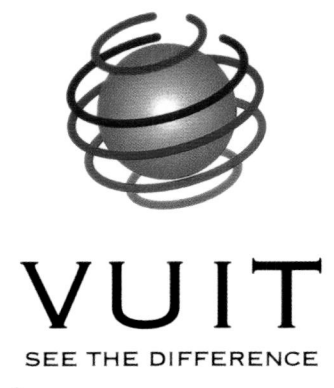

2.

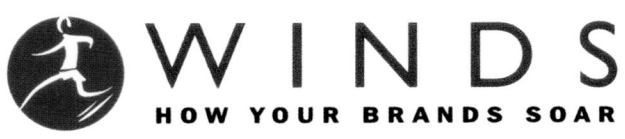

3.

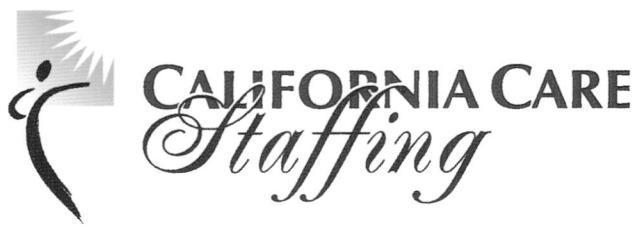

4.

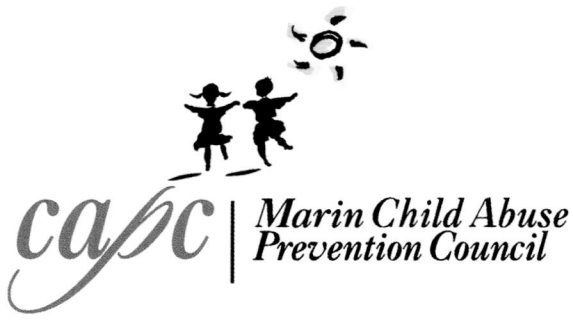

5.

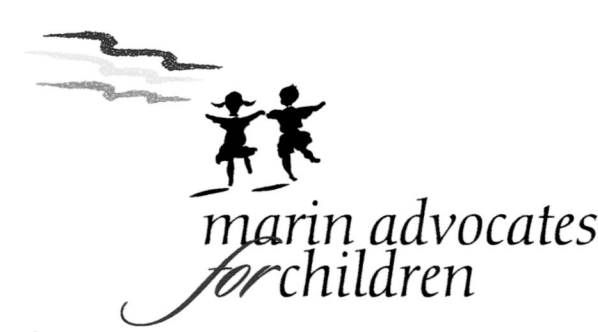

6.

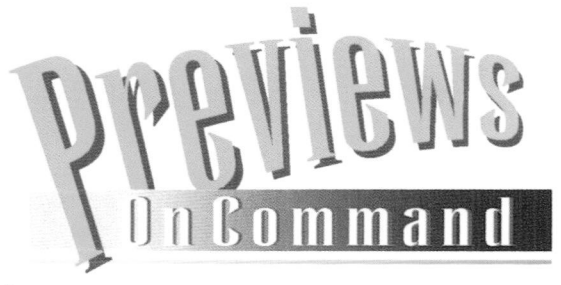

7.

1 - 3
Design Firm **Crouch and Naegeli/**
Design Group West
4 - 7
Design Firm **Dan Liew Design**

1.
Client — *Vaudit*
Designer — Jim Naegeli
2.
Client — *Vuit*
Designer — Jim Naegeli
3.
Client — *Winds*
Designers — Megan Boyer,
Jim Naegeli
4.
Client — *California Care Staffing*
Designers — Dan Liew, Chris Ardito

5.
Client — *Marin Child Abuse*
Prevention Center
Designer — Dan Liew
6.
Client — *Marin Advocates for Children*
Designer — Dan Liew
7.
Client — *OnCommand*
Designers — Dan Liew, Phorest Bateson
(opposite)
Client — *Sony Computer*
Entertainment America
Design Firm **CDI Studios**
Designer — Eddie Roberts

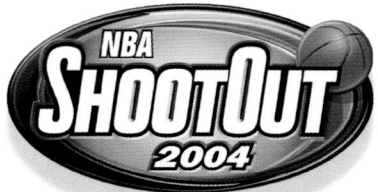

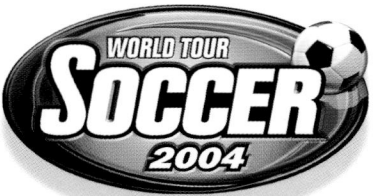

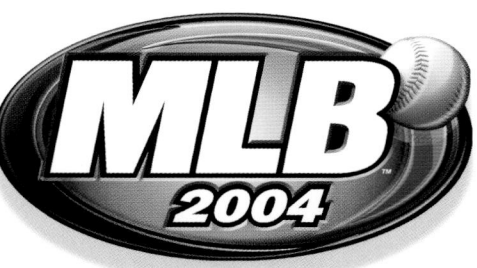

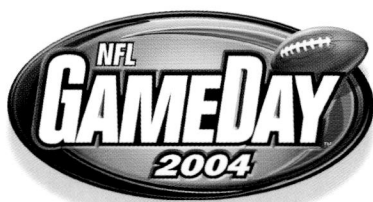

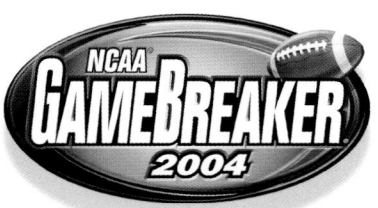

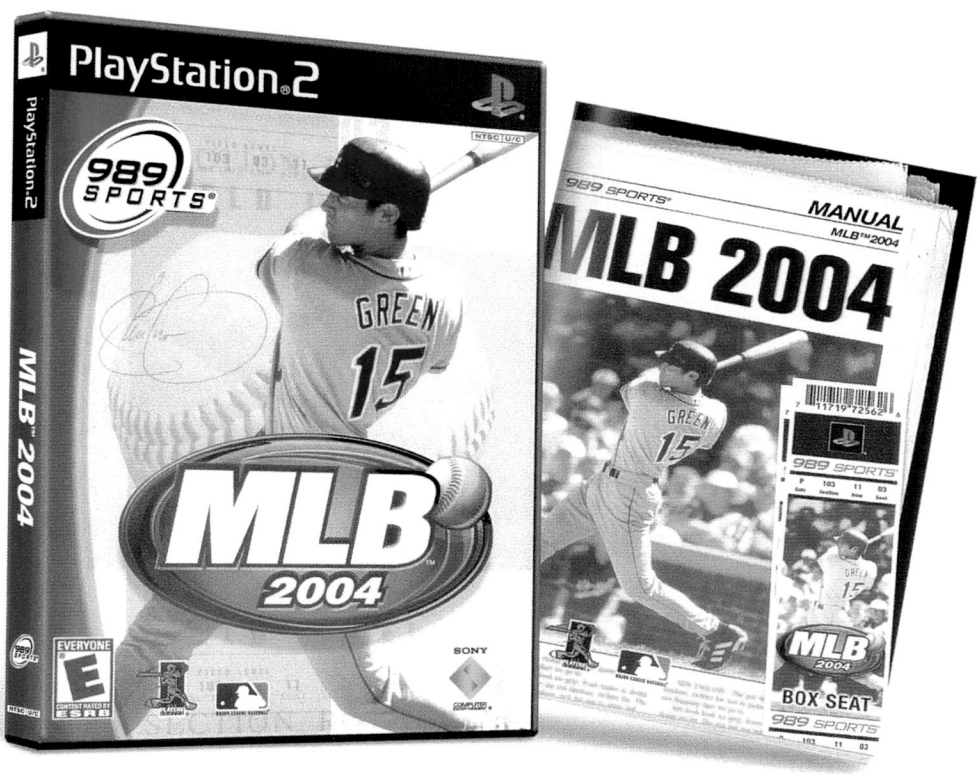

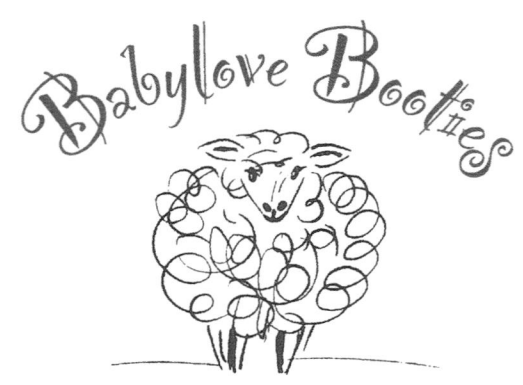

1.

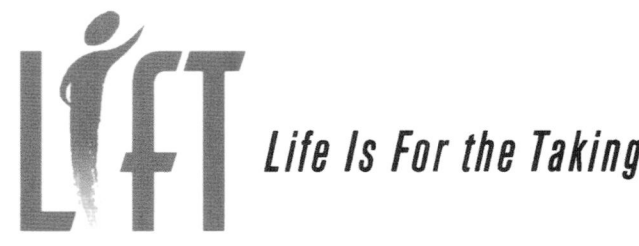

LIFT **Life Is For the Taking**

2.

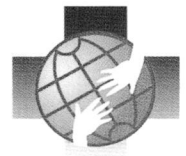

GLOBAL CARE STAFFING

3.

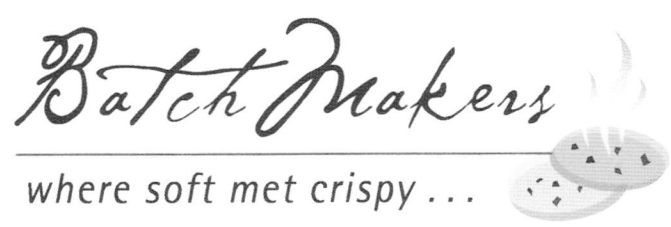

4.

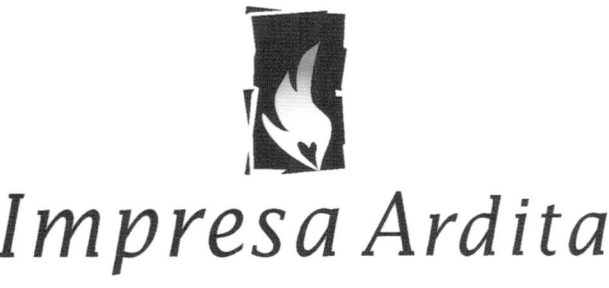

5.

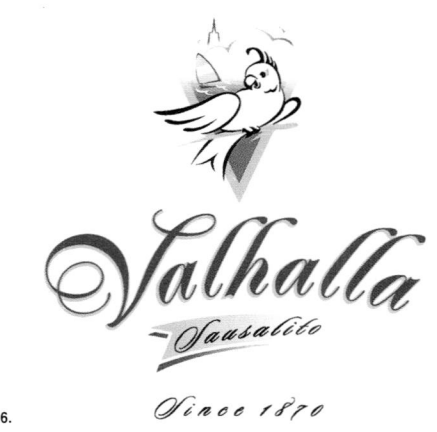

6.

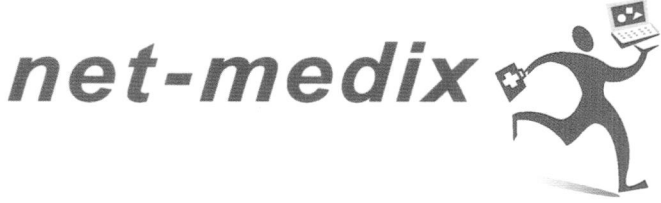

7.

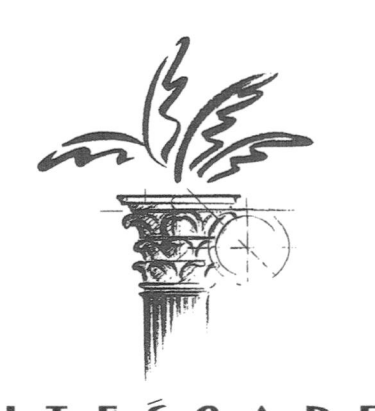

8. SITESCAPES

ibrain

9.

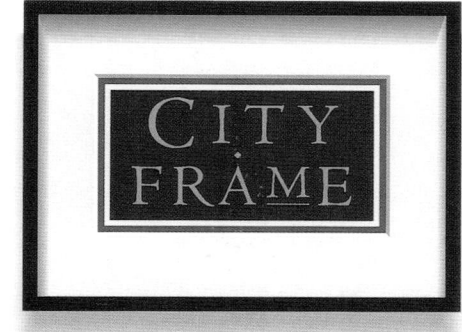

10.

Z zaphers®

11.

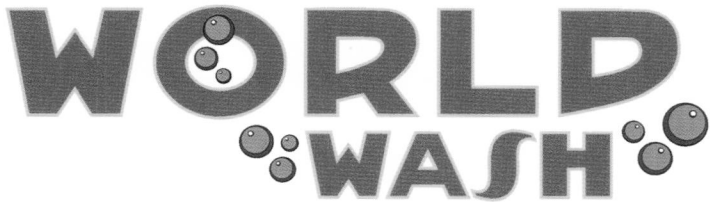

12.

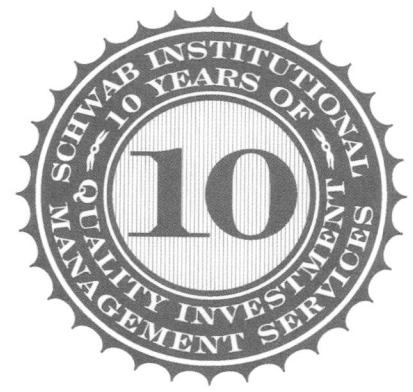

13.

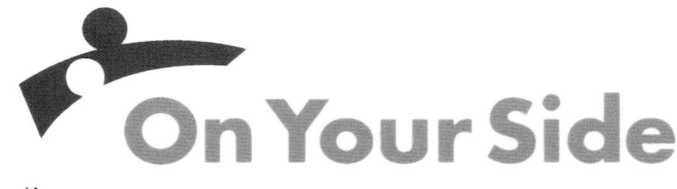

14.

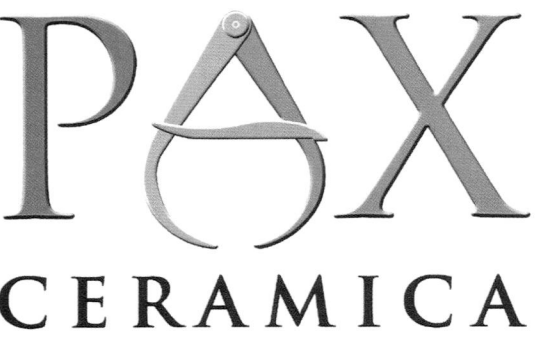

15.

1 - 8
Design Firm **Dan Liew Design**
9 - 15
Design Firm **Mitten Design**

1.
Client   *Margurite Holloway*
Designer   Dan Liew
2.
Client   *Lift*
Designers   Dan Liew, Chris Ardito
3.
Client   *Global Care Staffing*
Designers   Dan Liew, Chris Ardito
4.
Client   *BatchMakers*
Designer   Dan Liew
5.
Client   *Chris Ardito/Impresa Ardita*
Designers   Dan Liew, Chris Ardito
6.
Client   *Valhalla Restaurant*
Designers   Dan Liew, Linda Kelly, Jet Lim

7.
Client   *Net Medix*
Designers   Dan Liew, Chris Ardito
8.
Client   *Sitescapes*
Designers   Dan Liew, Linda Kelly
9.
Client   *Ibrain, Inc.*
Designer   Marianne Mitten
10.
Client   *City Frame*
Designer   Marianne Mitten
11.
Client   *Hingston Consulting Group*
Designers   Marianne Mitten, Audrey Dufresne
12.
Client   *World Wash*
Designers   Marianne Mitten, Audrey Dufresne
13.
Client   *Schwab Institutional*
Designer   Marianne Mitten
14.
Client   *On Your Side*
Designers   Marianne Mitten, Baykal Askar
15.
Client   *Pax Ceramica*
Designer   Marianne Mitten

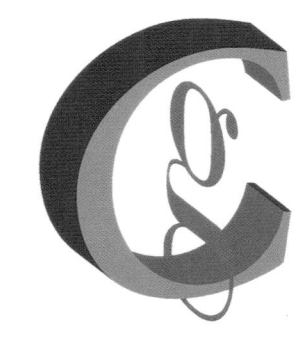

The Cata*lyst* Group, Inc.

1.

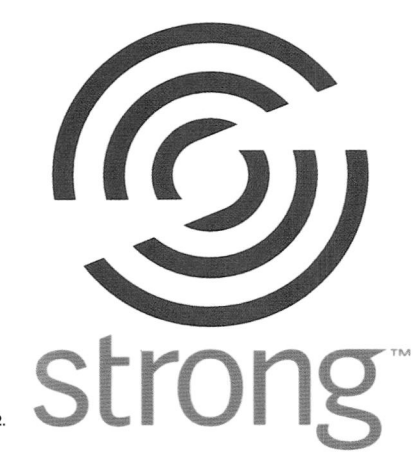

strong™

2.

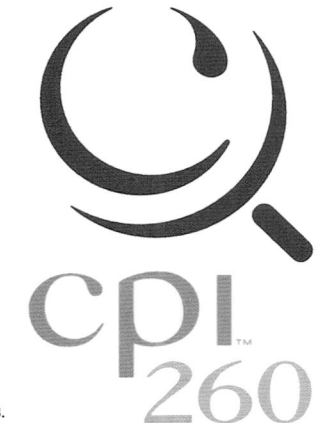

CP**I**™
260

3.

Circle
BANK

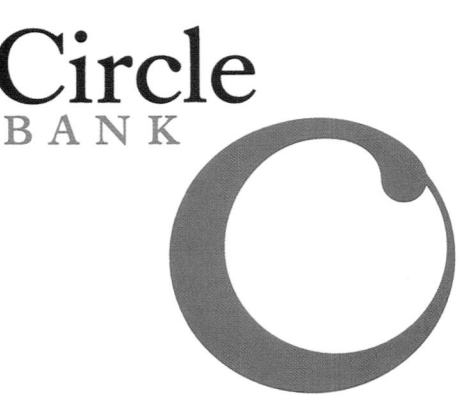

4.

5
FIVEPOINT
CREDIT UNION

5.

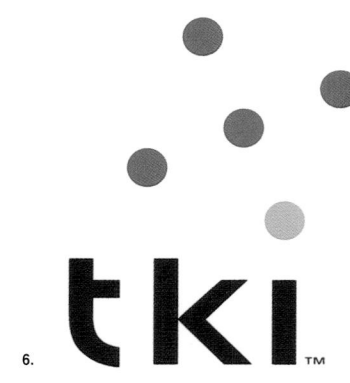

tki™

6.

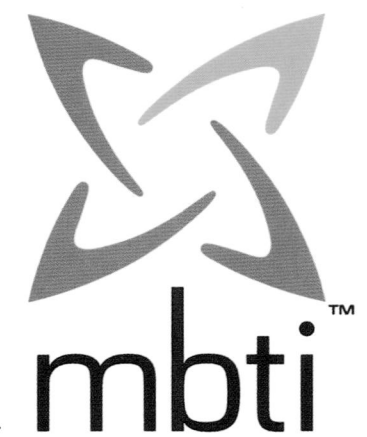

mbti™

7.

1
Design Firm **Mitten Design**
2 - 7
Design Firm **Mortensen Design Inc.**
1.
Client — *The Catalyst Group*
Designer — Marianne Mitten
2, 3.
Client — *CPP Inc.*
Designers — Helena Seo,
Gordon Mortensen
4.
Client — *Circle Bank*
Designers — Ann Jordan,
Gordon Mortensen

5.
Client — *FivePoint Credit Union*
Designers — Helena Seo,
Gordon Mortensen
6, 7.
Client — *Cpp Inc.*
Designers — Helena Seo,
Gordon Mortensen
(opposite)
Client — *Sony Computer
Entertainment America*
Design Firm **CDI Studios**
Designers — Eddie Roberts,
Casey Corcoran

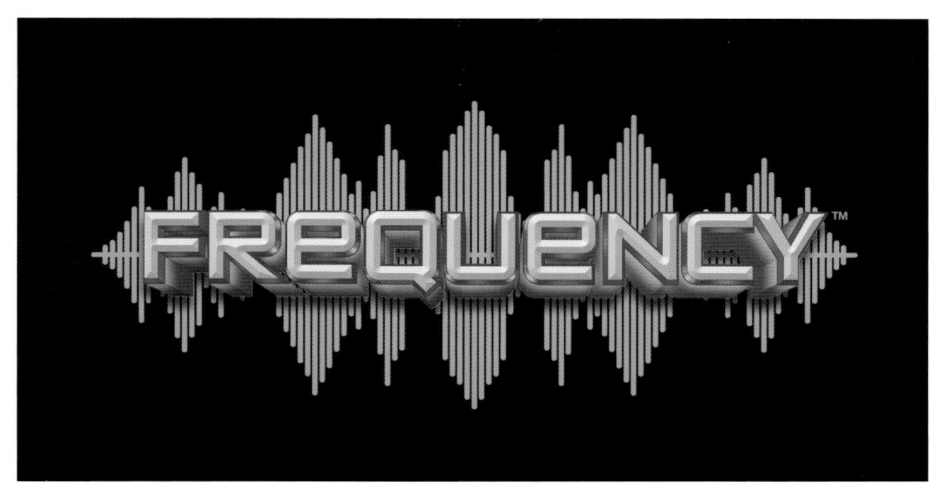

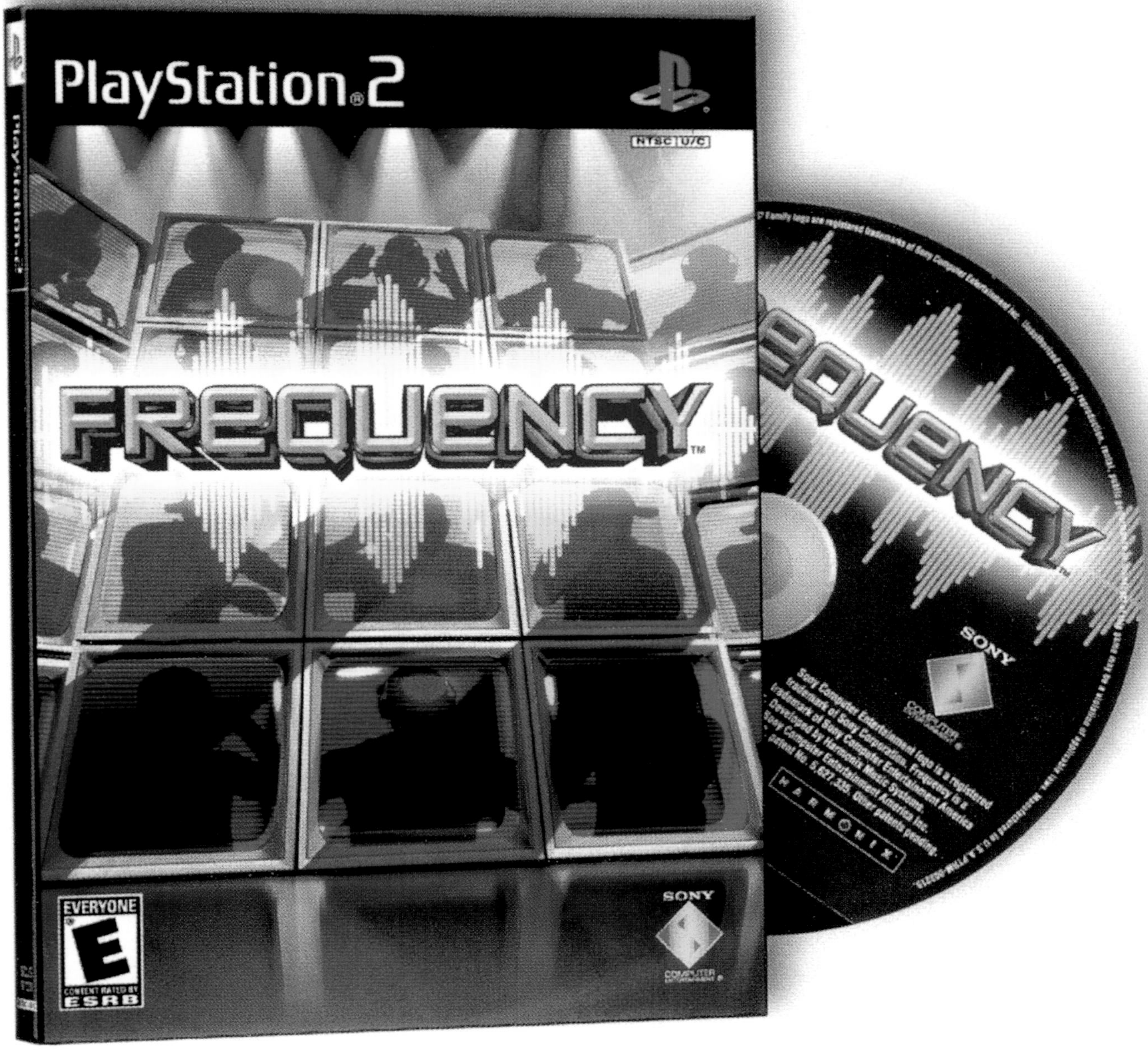

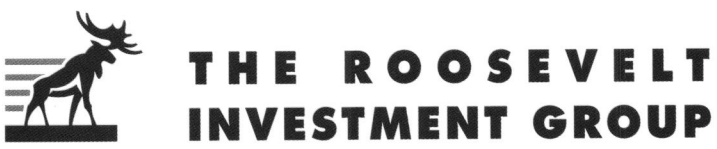

1.

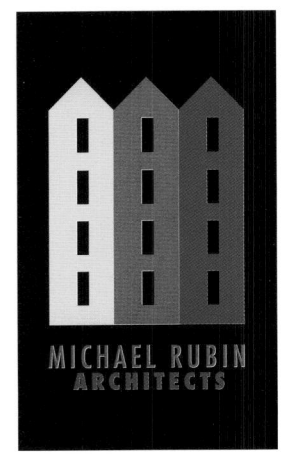

2.

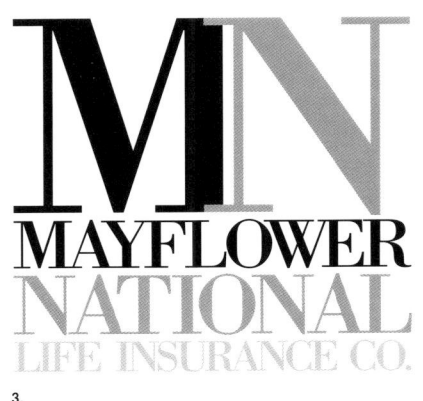

3.

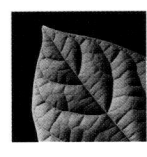

DIRTWORKS, PC

LANDSCAPE ARCHITECTURE

4.

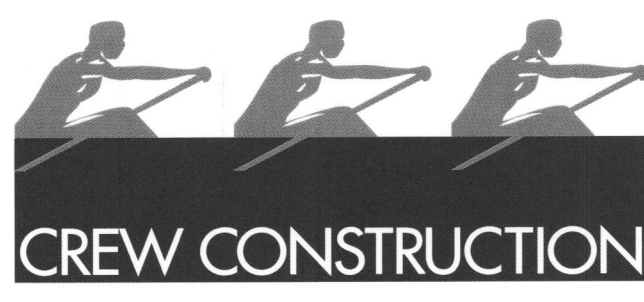

5.

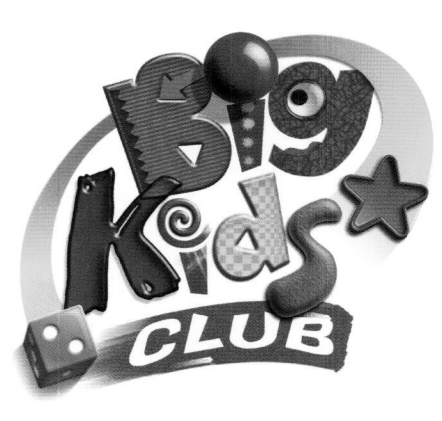

6.

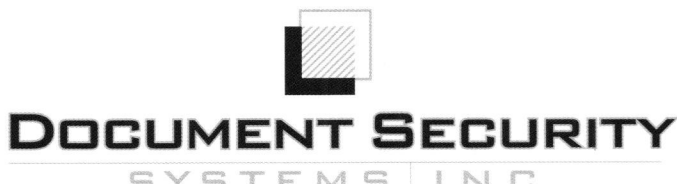

7.

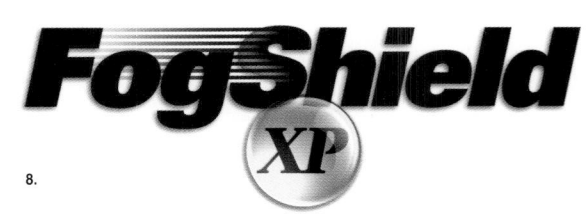

8.

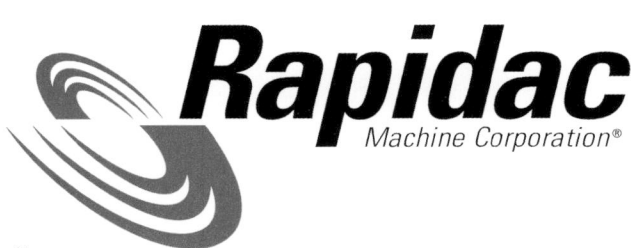

9.

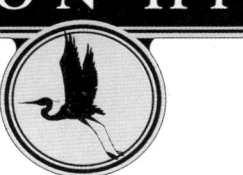

10.

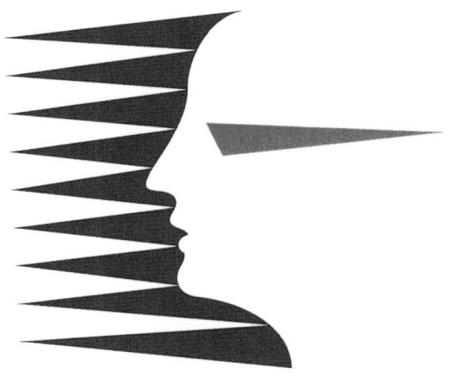

11.

12.

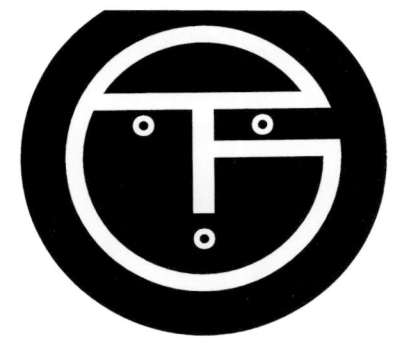

13.

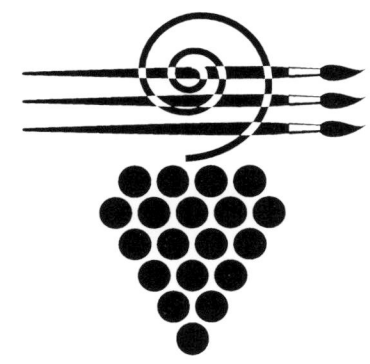

14.

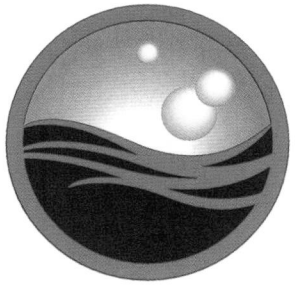

GLOBAL LIQUIDS TEAM

15.

1 - 5
Design Firm **Acme Communications, Inc.**
6 - 11
Design Firm **McElveney & Palozzi Design Group Inc.**
12 - 15
Design Firm **Tom Fowler, Inc.**

1.
Client	*The Roosevelt Investment Group*
Designers	Kiki Boucher, Jon Livingston

2.
Client	*Michael Rubin Architects*
Designer	Kiki Boucher

3.
Client	*Mayflower National Life Insurance Co.*
Designers	Andrea Ross Boyle, Kiki Boucher

4.
Client	*Dirtworks, PC*
Designers	Kiki Boucher, Jon Livingston

5.
Client	*Crew Construction Corp.*
Designer	Kiki Boucher

6.
Client	*McElveney & Palozzi Design Group Inc.*
Designers	Gloria Kreitzberg, Steve Palozzi, William McElveney

7.
Client	*Document Security Systems Inc.*
Designers	William McElveney, Lisa Gates

8.
Client	*Bausch & Lomb*
Designer	Steve Palozzi

9.
Client	*Gravure Magazine*
Designers	William McElveney, Lisa Gates

10.
Client	*Heron Hill Winery*
Designers	Steve Palozzi, William McElveney

11.
Client	*Rapidac Machine Corporation*
Designers	Matt Nowicki, Lisa Gates

12.
Client	*CPS Communications*
Designer	Thomas G. Fowler

13.
Client	*Inua Gallery*
Designer	Thomas G. Fowler

14.
Client	*Table to Table*
Designer	Thomas G. Fowler

15.
Client	*Unilever HPC NA*
Designers	Mary Ellen Butkus, Jennifer Lipsett

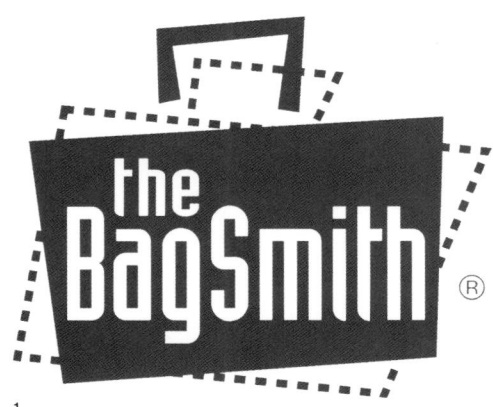

1.

2.

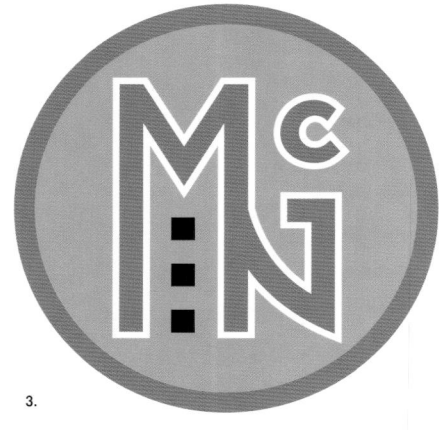

3.

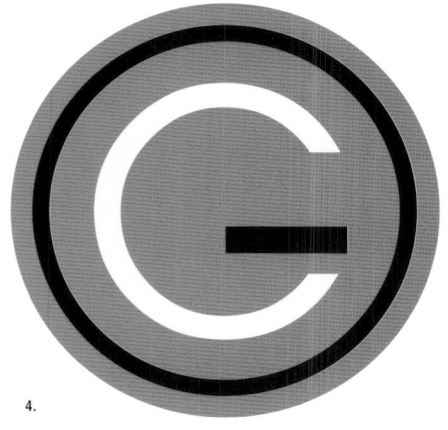

4.

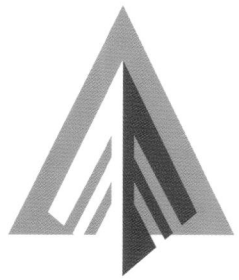

Northamerican
Financial
Corporation

5.

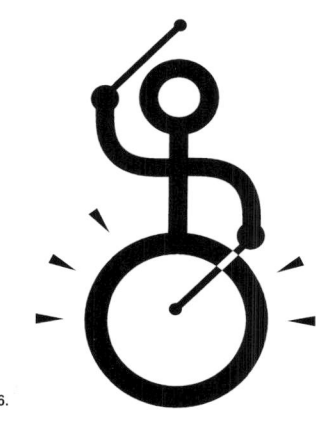

6.

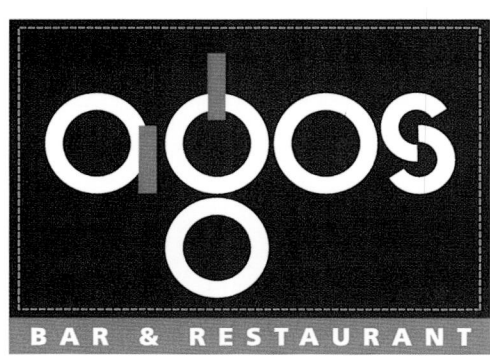

7.

1
   Design Firm **Karen Skunta & Company**
2
   Design Firm **Kellum McClain Inc.**
3 - 5
   Design Firm **McGaughy Design**
6, 7
   Design Firm **Tom Fowler, Inc.**
1.
   Client   *Smith International*
   Designers   Karen A. Skunta,
               Christopher Suster,
               Barbara Chin

2.
   Client   *Primedia*
   Designers   Beverly McClain,
               Ron Kellum

3.
   Client   *McGaughy Design*
   Designer   Malcolm McGaughy
4.
   Client   *Carole Goeas*
   Designer   Malcolm McGaughy
5.
   Client   *Northamerican Financial Corp*
   Designers   McGaughy Design
6.
   Client   *Gideon Cardozo
               Communications*
   Designer   Thomas G. Fowler
7.
   Client   *Agos Bar and Restaurant*
   Designer   Thomas G. Fowler
(opposite)
   Client   *Westwood Studios*
   Design Firm **CDI Studios**
   Designer   Victoria Hart

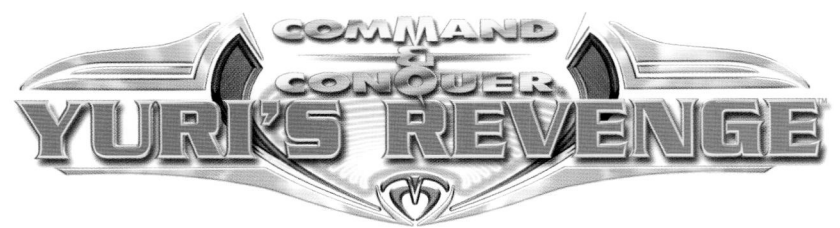

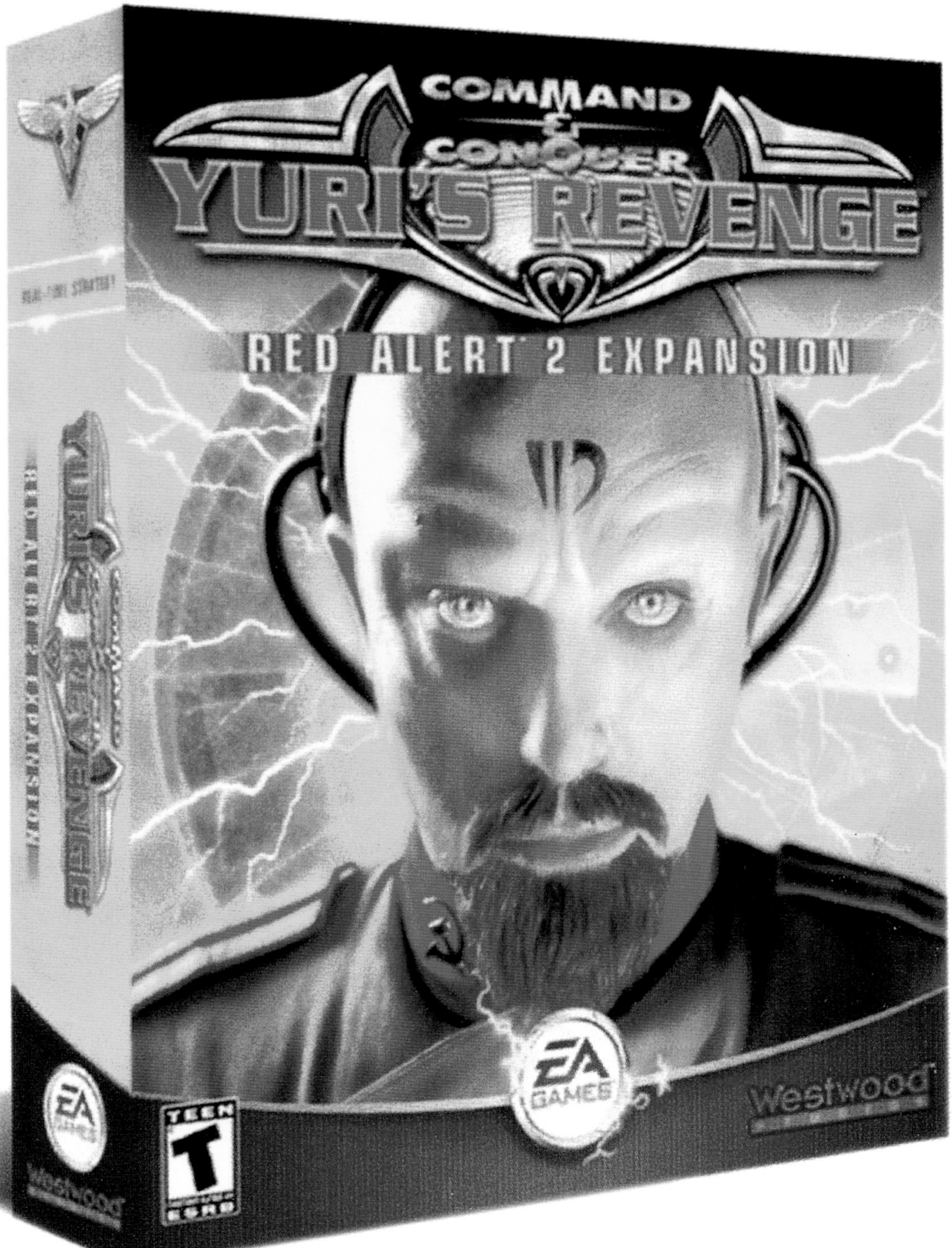

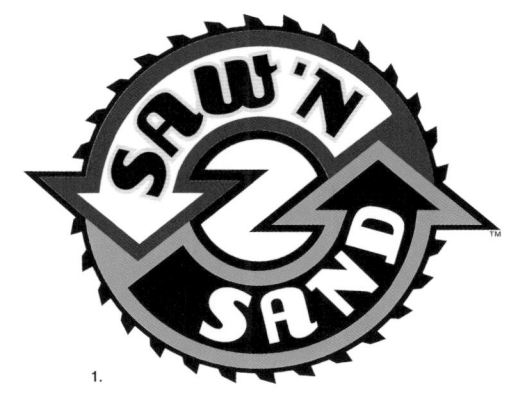

1.

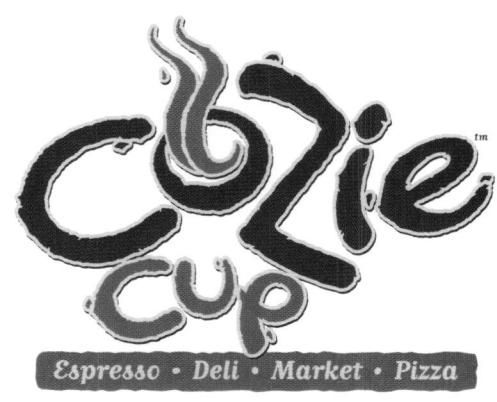

2.

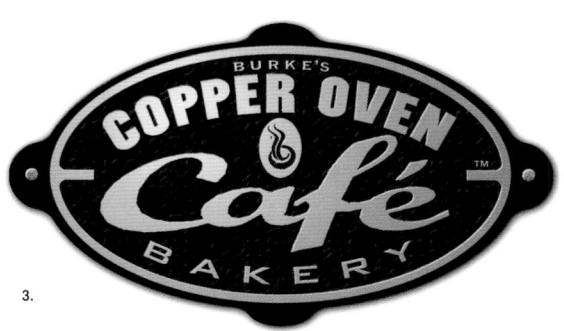

3.

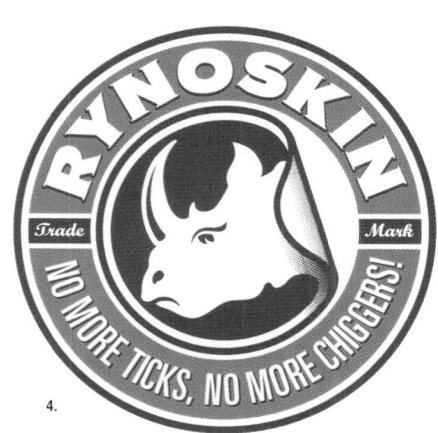

4.

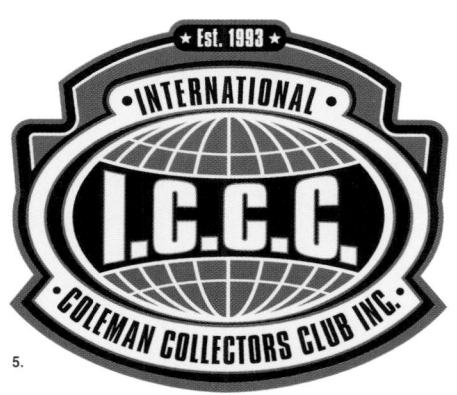

5.

6.

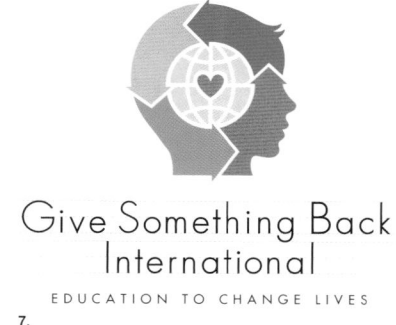

7.

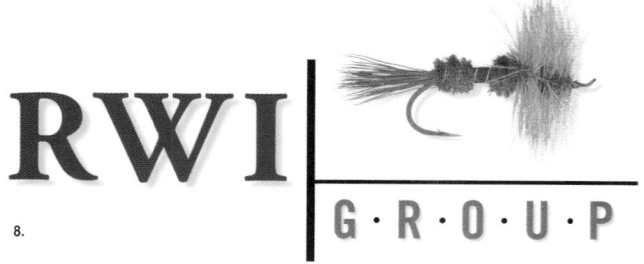

8.

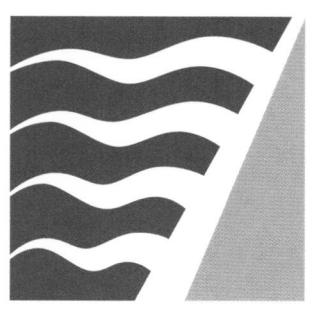

BAY AREA
AIR QUALITY
MANAGEMENT
DISTRICT

9.

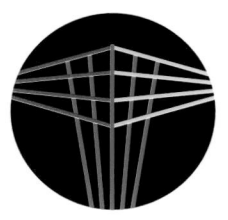

TELEPLACE

10.

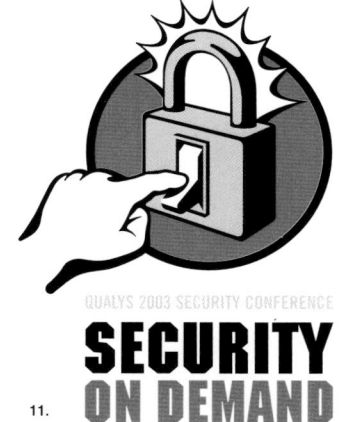

QUALYS 2003 SECURITY CONFERENCE
SECURITY
ON DEMAND

11.

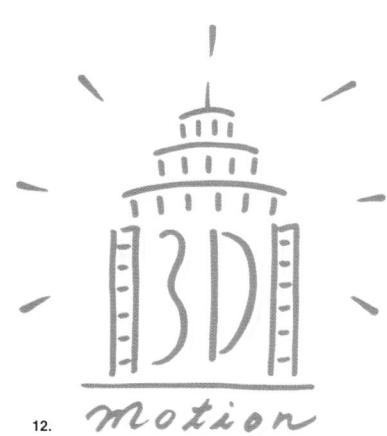

motion

12.

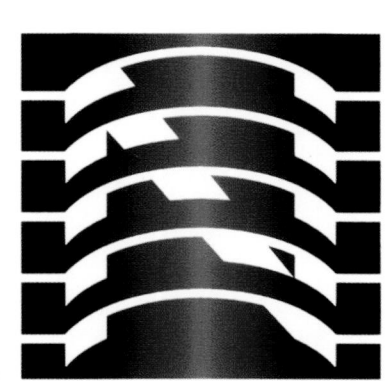

13.

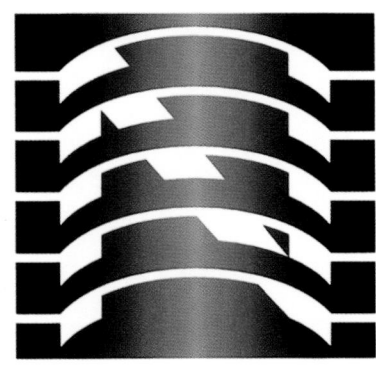

14.

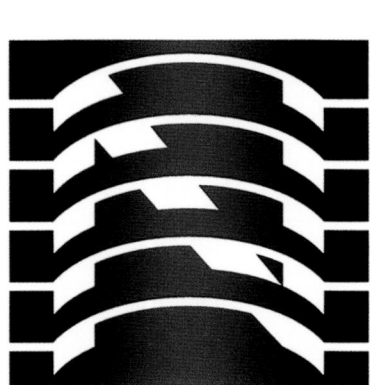

15.

1 - 6
Design Firm **LPG Design**
7 - 15
Design Firm **Gee + Chung Design**
1.
  Client   *B-H Innovations*
  Designer   Dustin Commer
2, 3.
  Client   *Burke Enterprise*
  Designer   Dustin Commer
4.
  Client   *Har-son Inc.*
  Designer   Dustin Commer
5.
  Client   *International Coleman
              Collectors Club Inc.*
  Designer   Dustin Commer
6.
  Client   *Love Packaging Group*
  Designer   Rick Gimlin

7.
  Client   *Give Something Back
              International Foundation*
  Designer   Earl Gee
8.
  Client   *RWI Group, LLP*
  Designer   Earl Gee
9.
  Client   *Bay Area Air Quality
              Management District*
  Designer   Earl Gee
10.
  Client   *TelePlace*
  Designer   Earl Gee
11.
  Client   *Qualys, Inc.*
  Designer   Earl Gee
12.
  Client   *3-D Motion*
  Designer   Fani Chung
13 - 15.
  Client   *Nanocosm Technologies, Inc.*
  Designer   Fani Chung

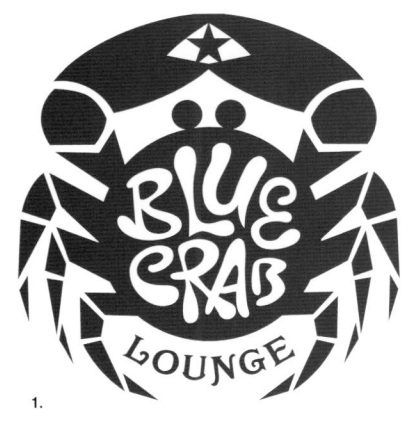

1.

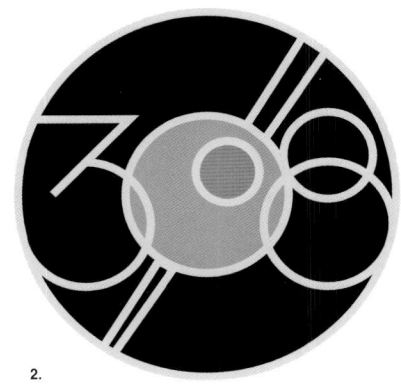

2.

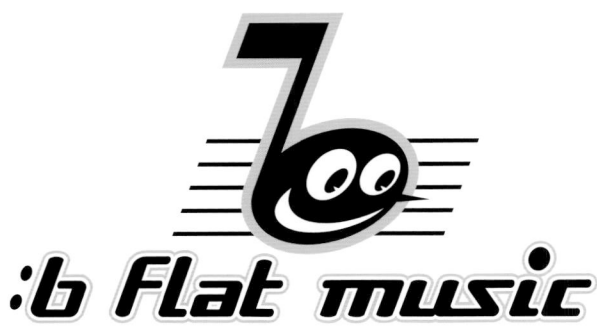

3.

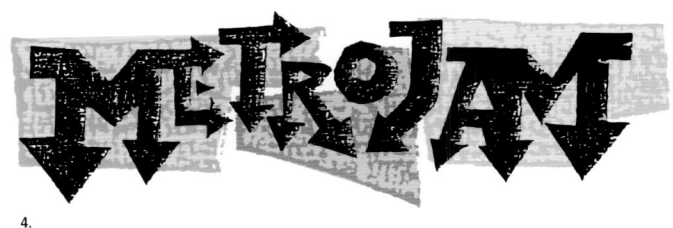

4.

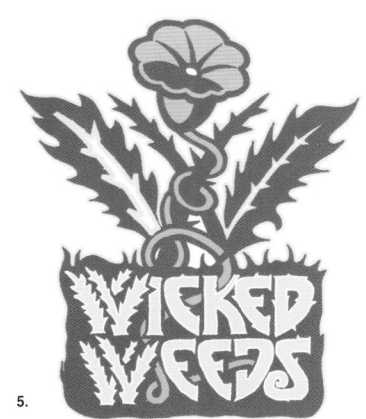

5.

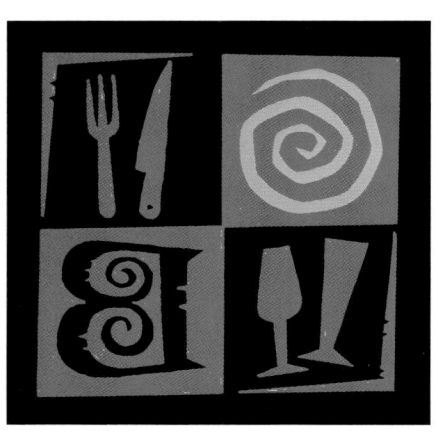

6.

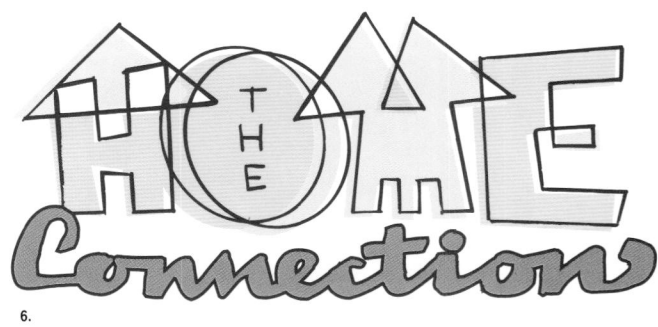

7.

1 - 7
Design Firm **Sayles Graphic Design, Inc.**
1.
   Client   *Blue Crab Lounge*
   Designer   John Sayles
2.
   Client   *308 Martini Bar*
   Designer   John Sayles
3.
   Client   *B-Flat Music*
   Designer   John Sayles
4.
   Client   *MetroJam*
   Designer   John Sayles
5.
   Client   *Meredith Corporation*
   Designer   John Sayles

6.
   Client   *Home Connection*
   Designer   John Sayles
7.
   Client   *Backburner Grille and Cafe*
   Designer   John Sayles
(opposite)
   Client   *Westwood Studios*
   Design Firm **CDI Studios**
   Designer   Victoria Hart

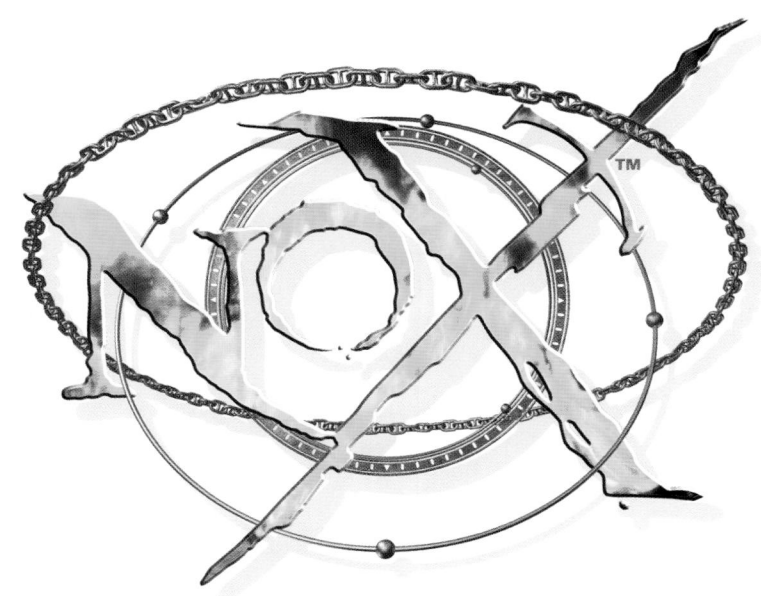

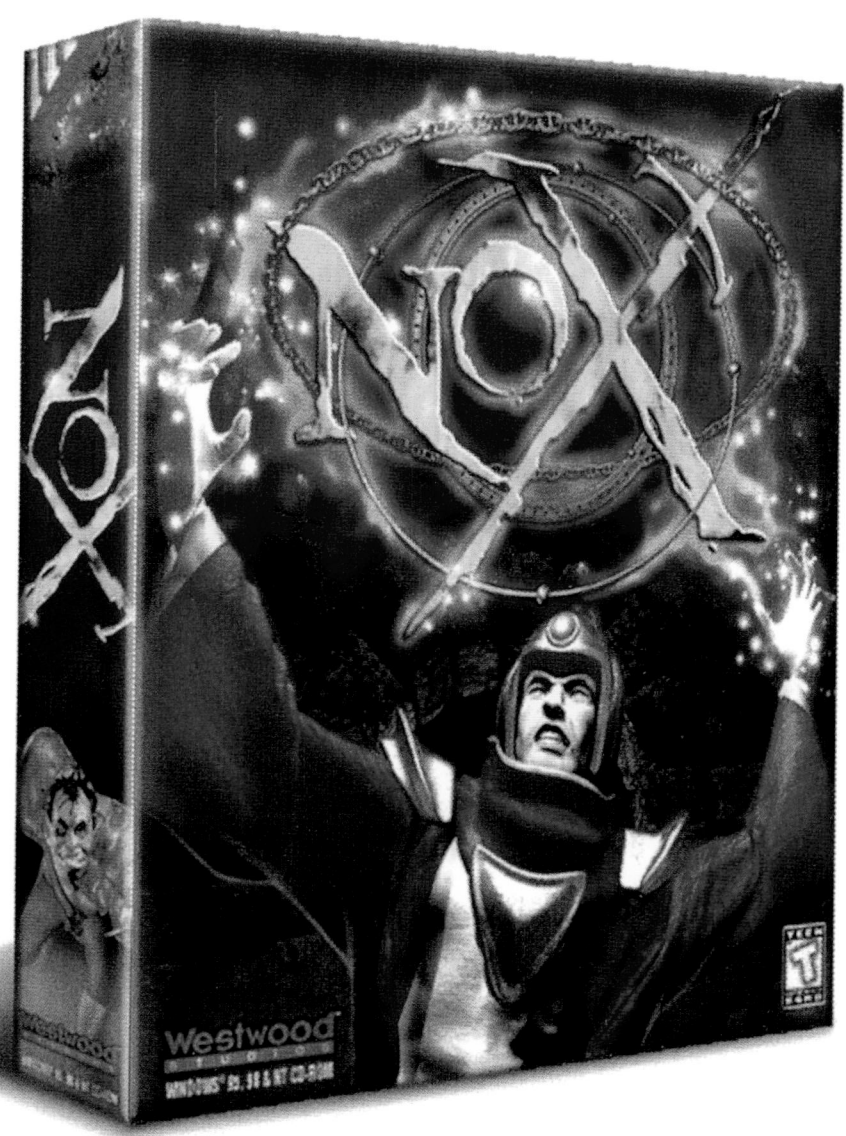

The corporate logo can be reversed out (appear all in white) of a virtually unlimited variety of bold and bright background colors. The key is to make sure there is adequate contrast between the logo and background. Background options range from our corporate colors (shown here) to Pantone cool and warm grays, four and darker, to any other color with appropriate contrast. Steer clear of pale, washed out, and neutral background colors.

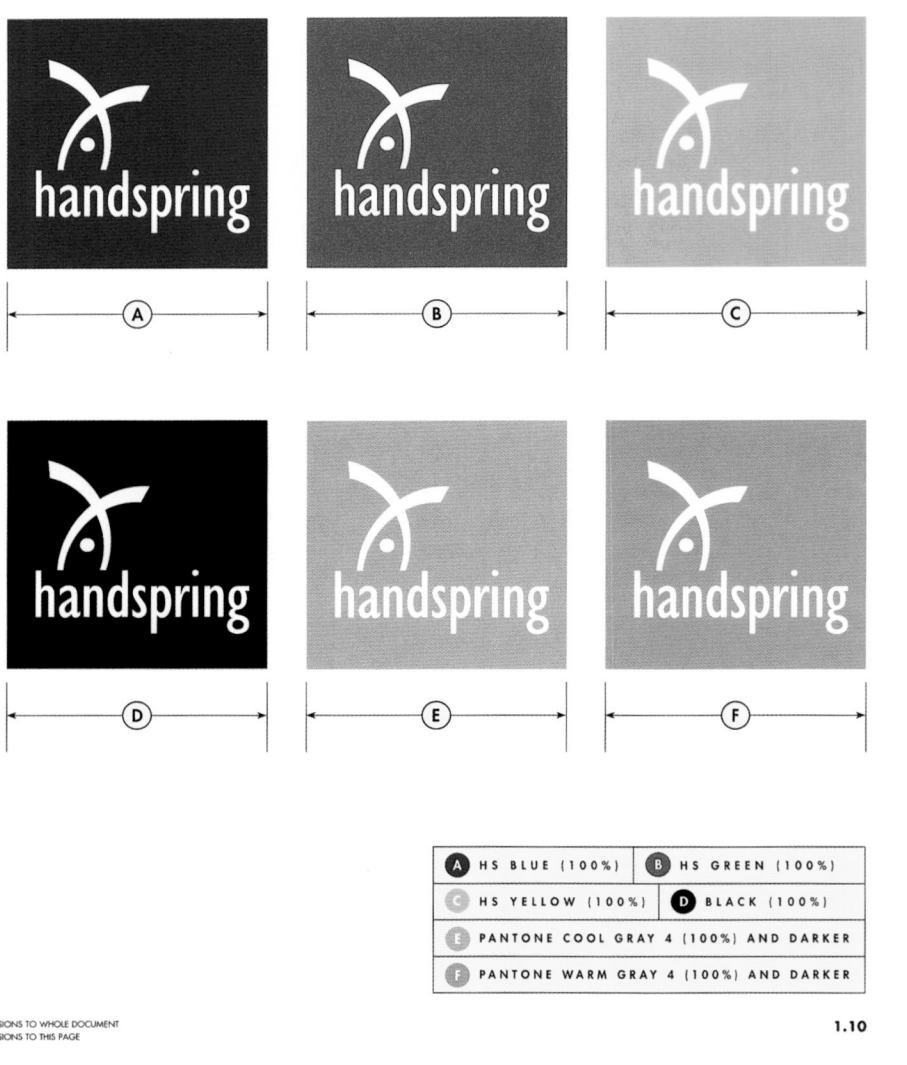

A	HS BLUE (100%)	B	HS GREEN (100%)
C	HS YELLOW (100%)	D	BLACK (100%)
E	PANTONE COOL GRAY 4 (100%) AND DARKER		
F	PANTONE WARM GRAY 4 (100%) AND DARKER		

7/99 DATE OF LAST REVISIONS TO WHOLE DOCUMENT
7/99 DATE OF LAST REVISIONS TO THIS PAGE

1.10

Design Firm **Mortensen Design**
Client   *Handspring*
Designers   Gorden Mortensen,
             PJ Nidecker

A good background treatment can make the corporate symbol and/or signature pop off the page. After testing scores of options, we've determined the symbol is most compelling against a white background. If white isn't appropriate, Pantone's cool gray colors—one through eight—provide a complementary contrast without overshadowing the dynamics of the symbol. Use the following sample treatments to get a feel for effective background color usage.

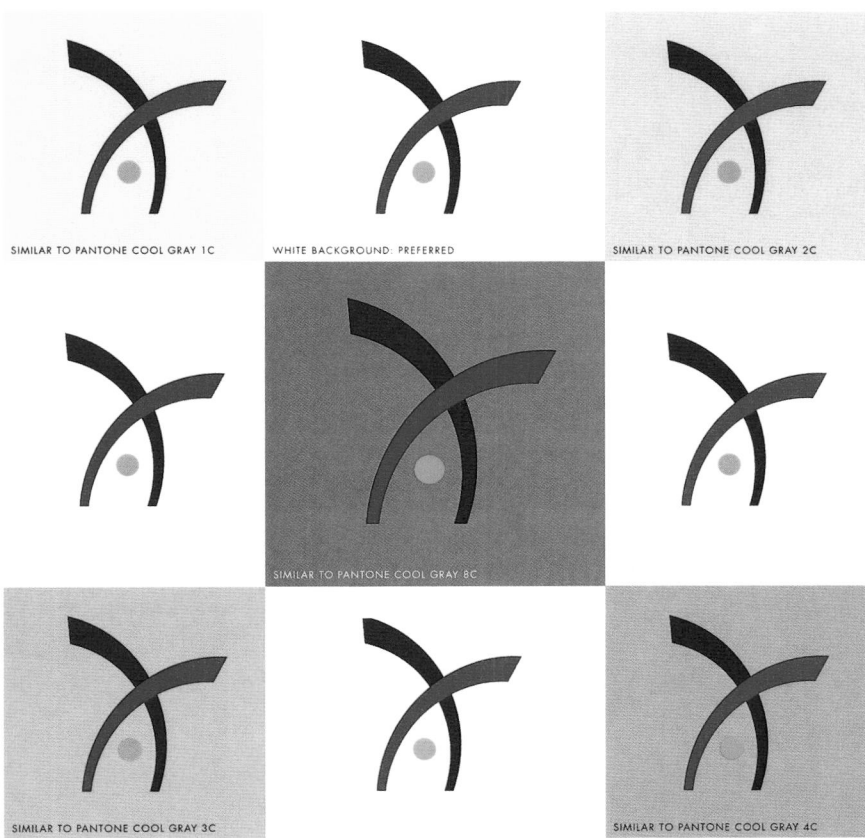

SIMILAR TO PANTONE COOL GRAY 1C

WHITE BACKGROUND: PREFERRED

SIMILAR TO PANTONE COOL GRAY 2C

SIMILAR TO PANTONE COOL GRAY 8C

SIMILAR TO PANTONE COOL GRAY 3C

SIMILAR TO PANTONE COOL GRAY 4C

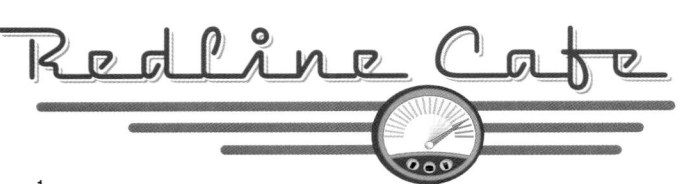

1.

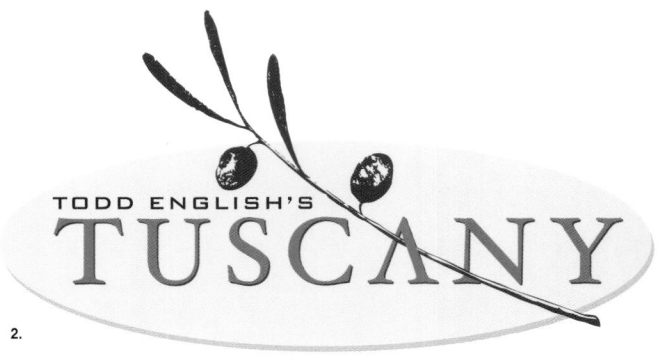

2.

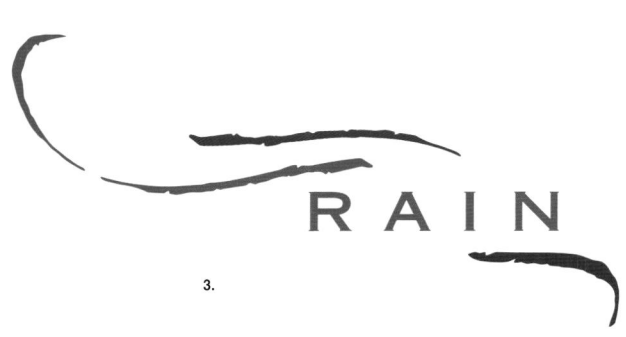

3.

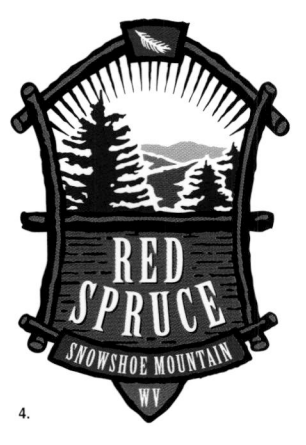

4.

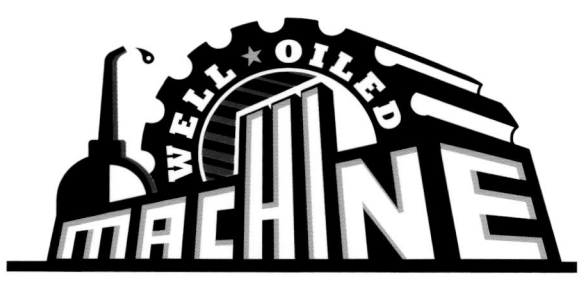

5.

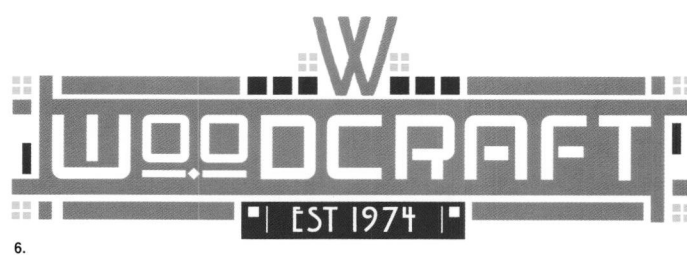

6.

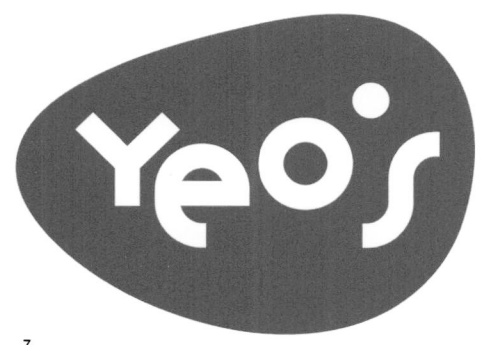

7.

1 - 4
Design Firm **Sonalysts, Inc.**
5, 6
Design Firm **Sayles Graphic Design, Inc.**
7
Design Firm **Ukulele Brand
Consultants Pte Ltd**

1.
Client   *Southern Auto Auction*
Designers   Stephen Freitas, Rob King,
              Carol Hoyem, Rena DeBortoli

2.
Client   *Todd English's Tuscany*
Designers   Kathee Speranza-Ryan,
              Tracy Sainte Marie,
              John Visgilio

3.
Client   *Mohegan Sun*
Designers   Kathee Speranza-Ryan,
              Shannon Brenek,
              John Visgilio

4.
Client   *Intrawest*
Designers   Mike Skiles,
              Tracy Sainte Marie,
              John Visgilio

5.
Client   *Well-Oiled Machine*
Designer   John Sayles

6.
Client   *WoodCraft Architectural Millwork*
Designer   John Sayles

7.
Client   *Yeo Hiap Seng
              (Singapore) Pte Ltd*
Designers   Kim Chun-wei,
              Cheng Tze Tzuen

(opposite)
Client   *Herbal Philosophy Pte Ltd*
Design Firm **Ukulele Brand
              Consultants Pte Ltd**
Designers   Kim Chun-wei,
              Yvonne Lee

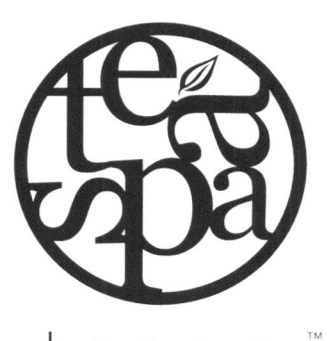

teaspa™

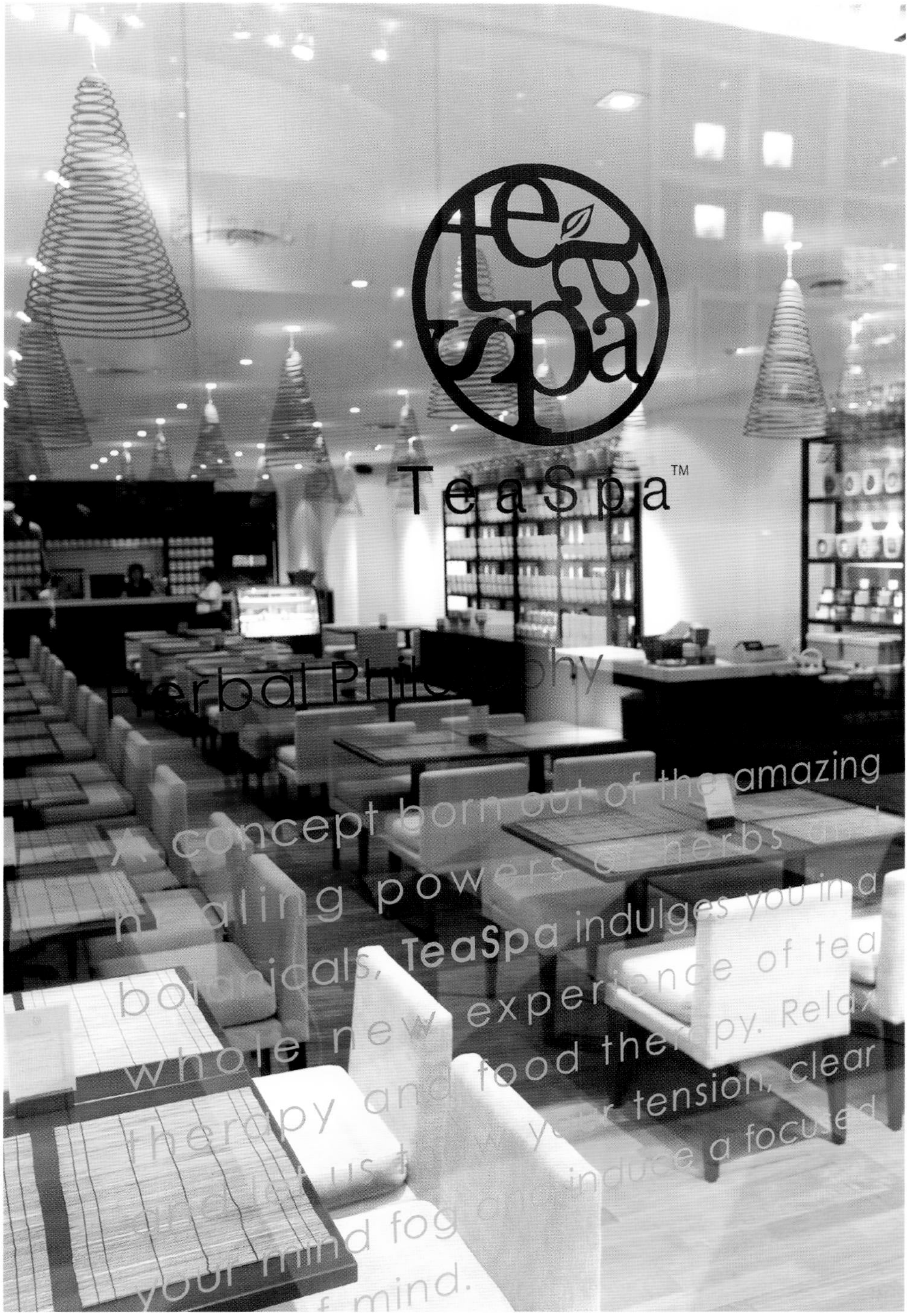

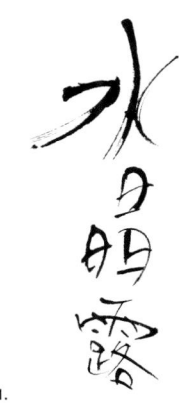

1.

2.

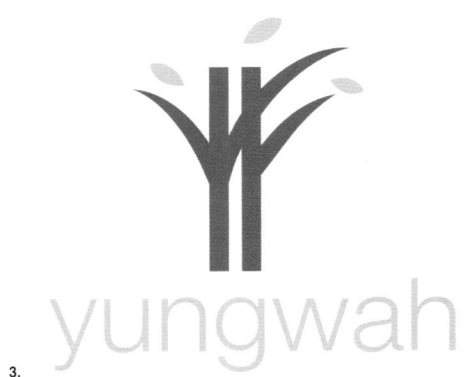

ONEFORT

3.

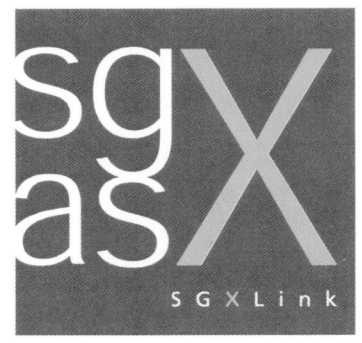

yungwah

4.

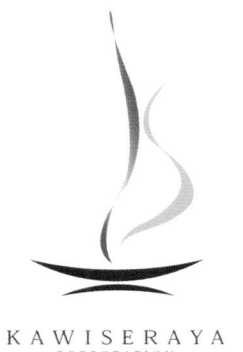

n e x u s

Connecting Ideas

5.

sg as X

SGXLink

6.

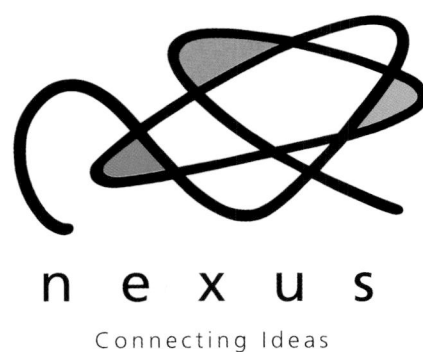

7.

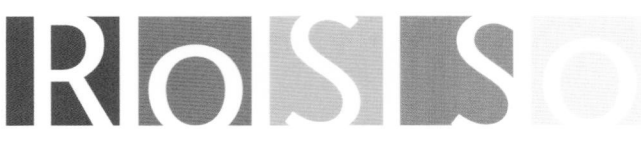

KAWISERAYA
CORPORATION

8.

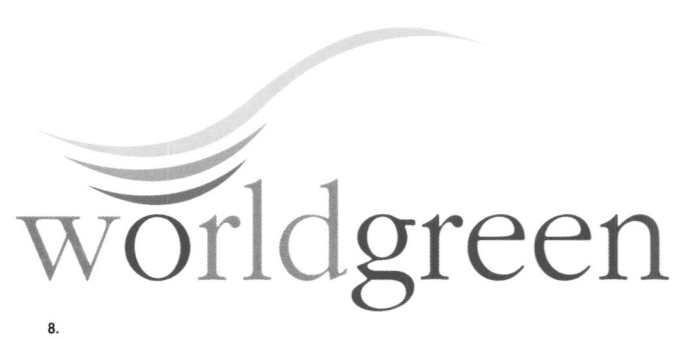

worldgreen

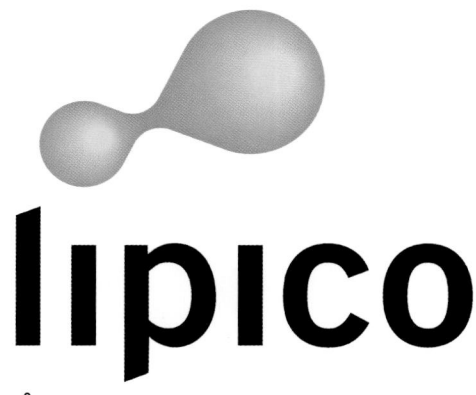

9.

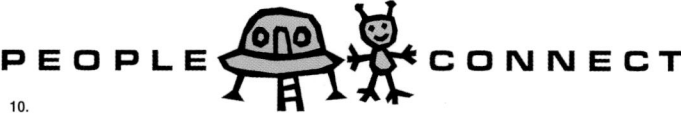

10.

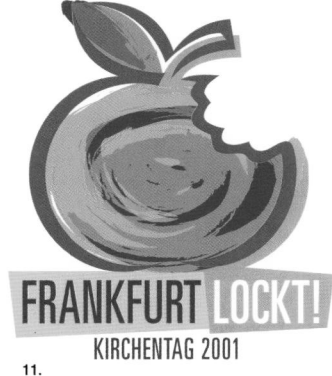

FRANKFURT LOCKT!

KIRCHENTAG 2001

11.

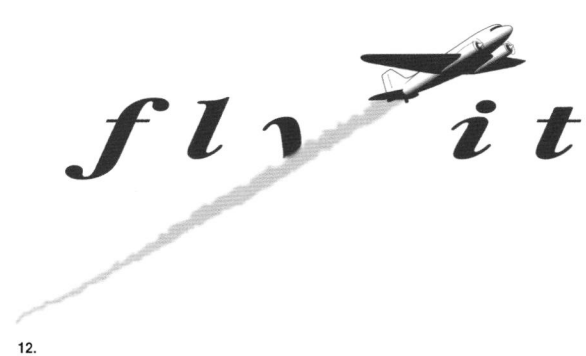

12.

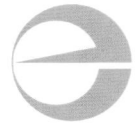 ERACON

13.

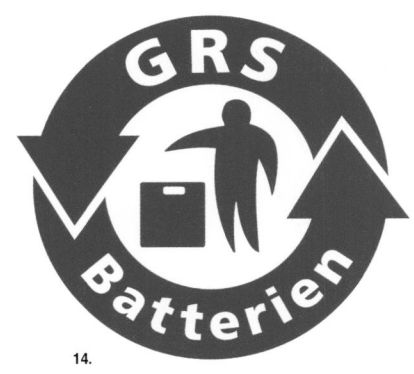

14.

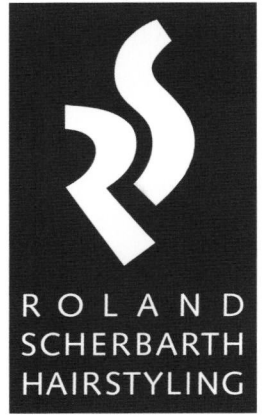

ROLAND
SCHERBARTH
HAIRSTYLING

15.

1 - 9			7.		
Design Firm	**Ukulele Brand**			Client	*Kawiseraya Corporation*
	Consultants Pte Ltd			Designers	Kim Chun-wei, Daphne Chan
10 - 15			8.		
Design Firm	**Aufgeweckte Werbung**			Client	*Worldgreen Pte Ltd*
1.				Designers	Kim Chun-wei, Lynn Lim
	Client	*Yeo Hiap Seng (Singapore) Pte Ltd*	9.		
	Designers	Kim Chun-wei, Stephanie Tan		Client	*Lipico Technologies Pte Ltd*
2.				Designers	Kim Chun-wei, Cheng Tze Tzuen
	Client	*Chip Eng Seng Corporation Ltd*	10.		
	Designers	Kim Chun-wei, Cheng Tze Tzuen		Client	*People-Connect*
3.				Designer	Georg Hahn, Fout Simbolico
	Client	*Yung Wah Industrial Co. (Pte) Ltd*	11.		
	Designers	Kim Chun-wei, Jessica Ang		Client	*Sound of Frankfurt*
4.				Designer	Georg Hahn, Thomas Maritsdike
	Client	*Ministry of Manpower*	12.		
	Designers	Kim Chun-wei, Jessica Ang		Client	*fly-it*
5.				Designers	Georg Hahn, Sonja Bader
	Client	*Singapore Exchange*	13.		
	Designers	Kim Chun-wei, Yvonne Lee		Client	*Eracon*
6.				Designer	Georg Hahn
	Client	*Office Libre Pte Ltd*	14.		
	Designers	Kim Chun-wei, Kok Yu Kim		Client	*GRS*
				Designer	Georg Hahn
			15.		
				Client	*Roland Scherbarth*
				Designer	Georg Hahn

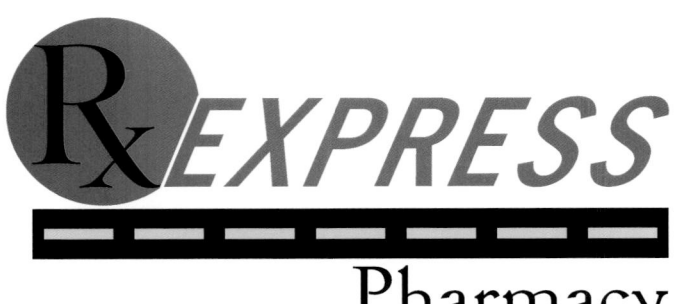

1.

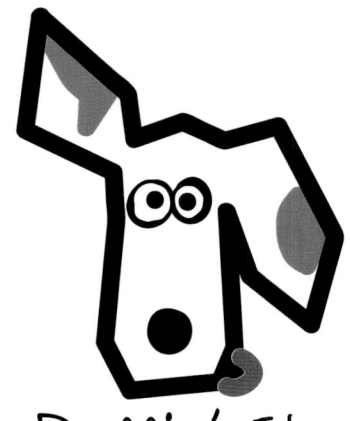

2. Ruffin' It

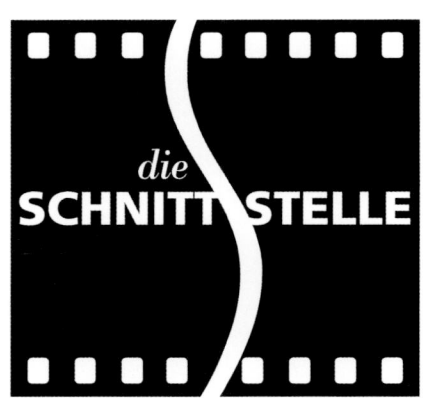

3.

4.

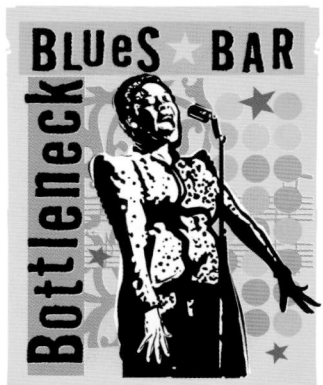

5.

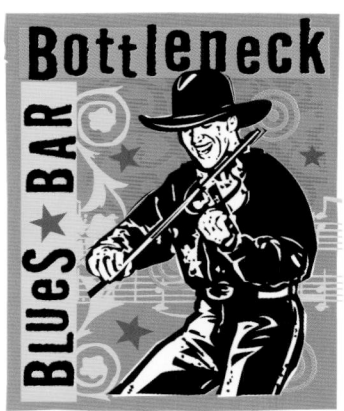

6.

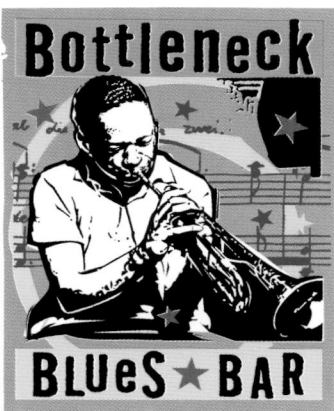

7.

1, 2
Design Firm **Designs on You!**
3
Design Firm **Aufgeweckte Werbung**
4 - 7
Design Firm **Visual Asylum**
1.
   Client   *Rx Express*
   Designers Suzanna Stephens,
                Anthony B. Stephens
2.
   Client   *Ruffin' It*
   Designers Anthony B. Stephens,
                Suzanna Stephens
3.
   Client   *die Schnittstelle*
   Designer   George Hahn

4 - 7.
   Client   *Ameristar Casinos*
   Designer   Joel Sotelo
(opposite)
   Client   *O-Ton*
   Design Firm **Aufgeweckte Werbung**
   Designer   Georg Hahn

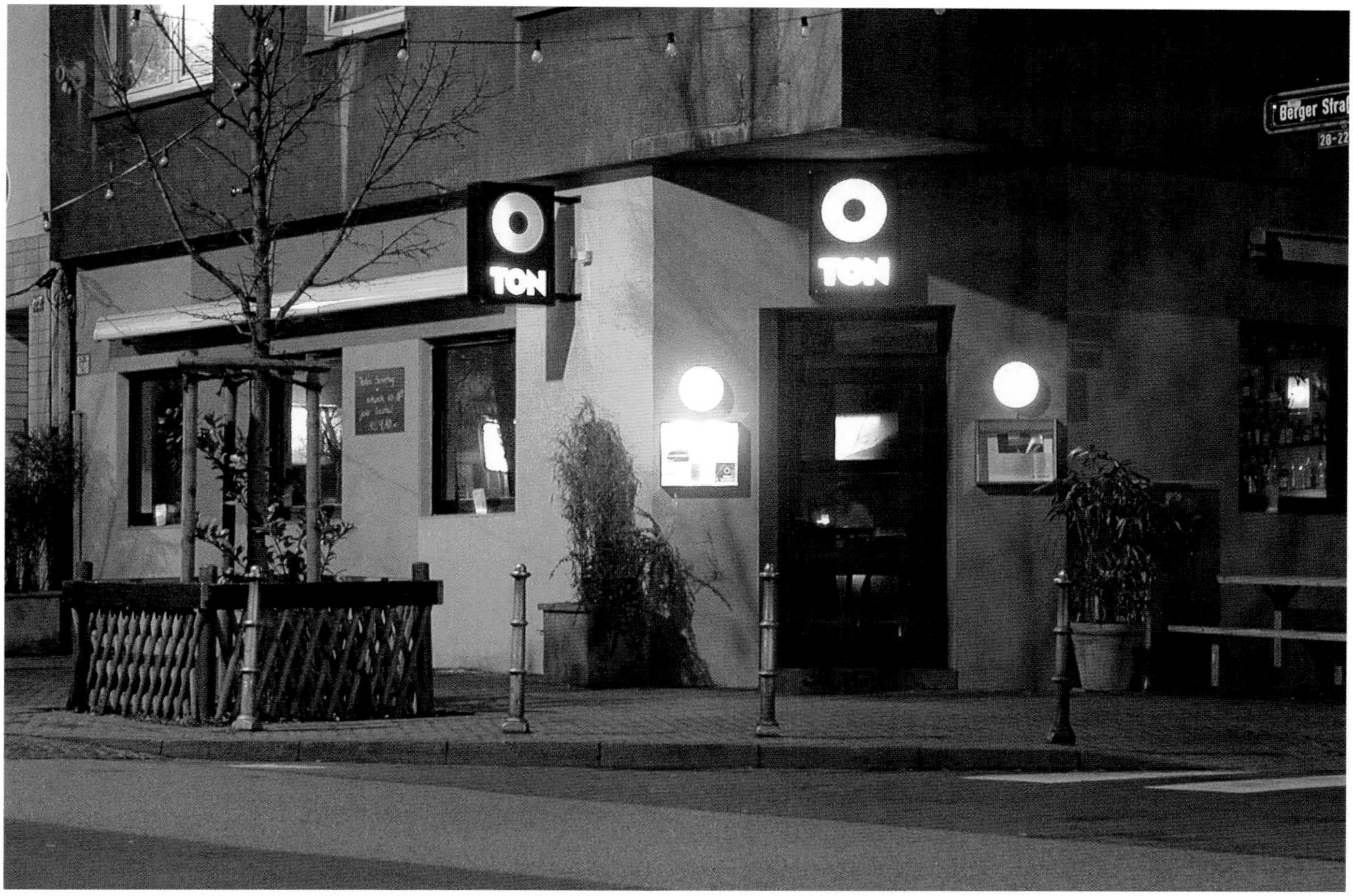

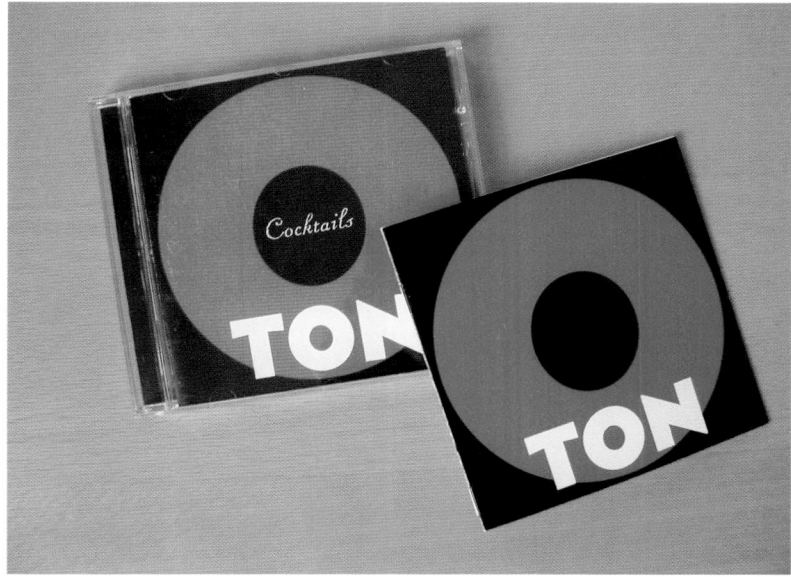

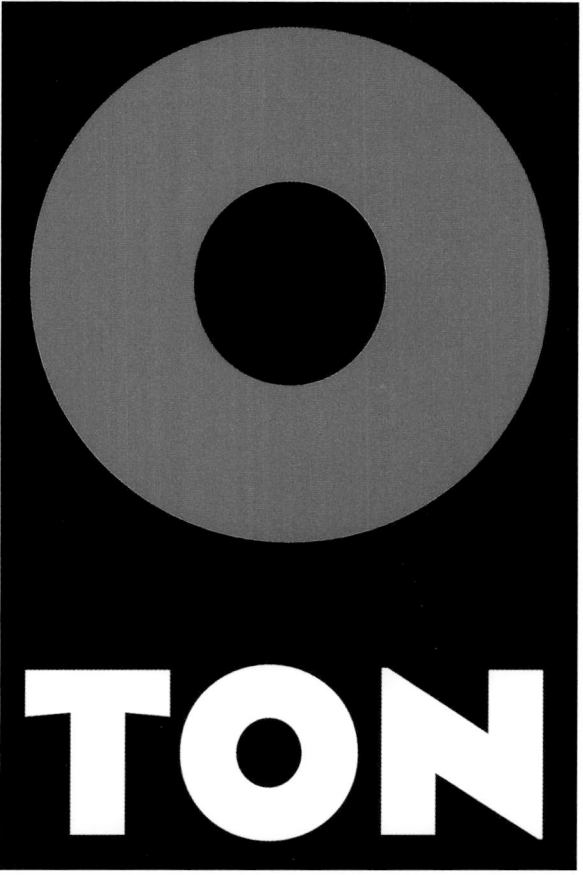

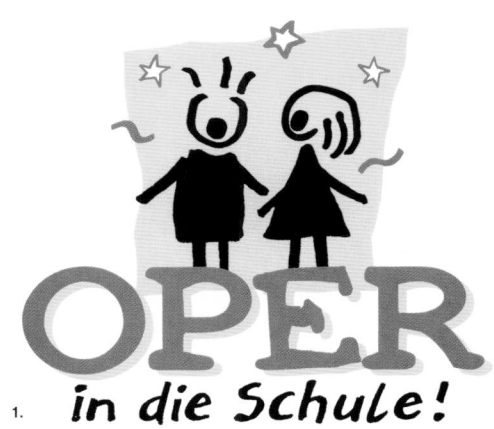

1. OPER in die Schule!

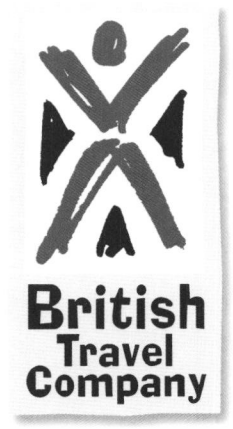

2. British Travel Company

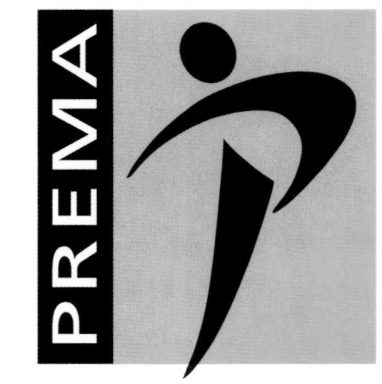

3. PREMA

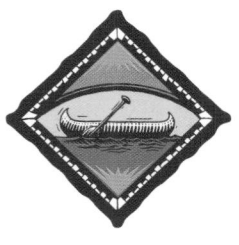

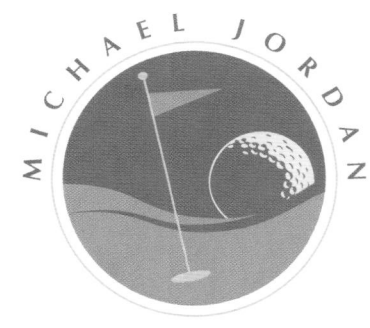

4. LEFFINGWELLS

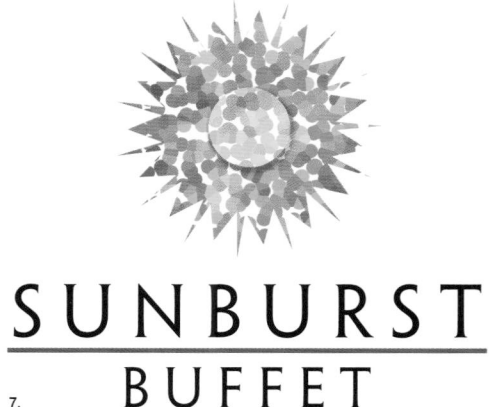

5. MICHAEL JORDAN CELEBRITY INVITATIONAL

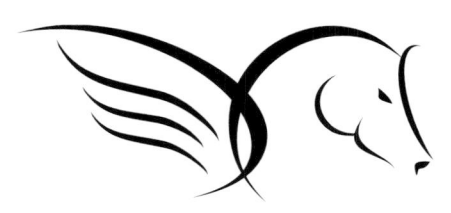

6. PEGASUS RACE & SPORTS BOOK

SUNBURST BUFFET

7.

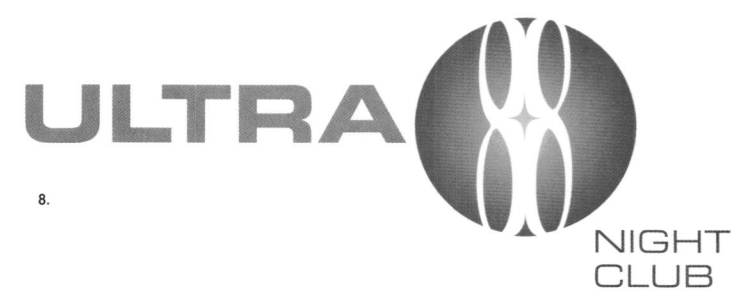

8. ULTRA NIGHT CLUB

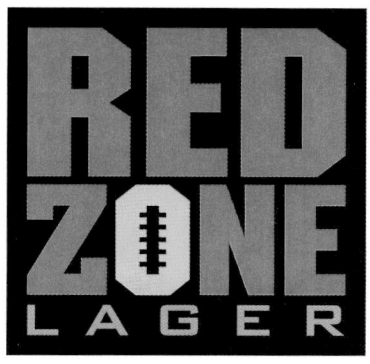

9.

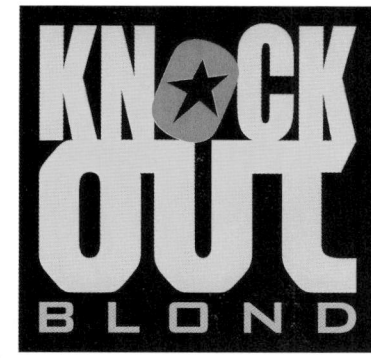

10.

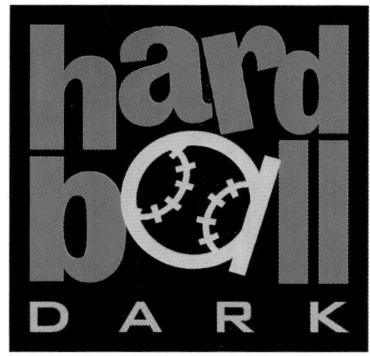

11.

12.

13.

14.

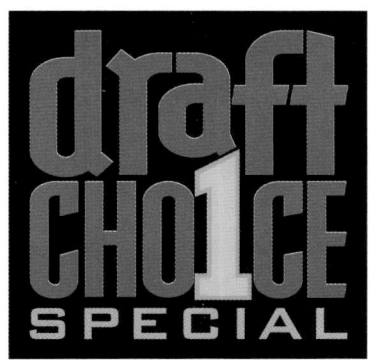

15.

1 - 3
Design Firm **Aufgeweckte Werbung**
4 - 8
Design Firm **Sonalysts, Inc.**
9 - 15
Design Firm **Visual Asylum**

1.
  Client   *Oper in die Schule*
  Designer   Georg Hahn
2.
  Client   *British Travel Company*
  Designer   Georg Hahn
3.
  Client   *Prema Show Productions Ltd.*
  Designer   Georg Hahn
4.
  Client   *Mohegun Sun*
  Designers   Kathee Speranza-Ryan,
                Carol Hoyem
5.
  Client   *Atlantis*
  Designer   Kathleen Damiata

6.
  Client   *Atlantis*
  Designers   Kathleen Damiata,
                Rena DeBortoli
7.
  Client   *Mohegan Sun*
  Designer   Rena DeBortoli
8.
  Client   *Patrick Lyon*
  Designer   Rena DeBortoli
9 - 13.
  Client   *Ameristar Casino*
  Designers   Visual Asylum
14.
  Client   *San Diego City College*
                Graphic Design
  Designer   Joel Sotelo
15.
  Client   *3 Squares "gourmet on the go"*
  Designer   Joel Sotelo

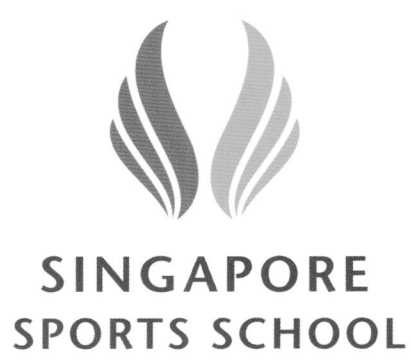

SINGAPORE SPORTS SCHOOL

1.

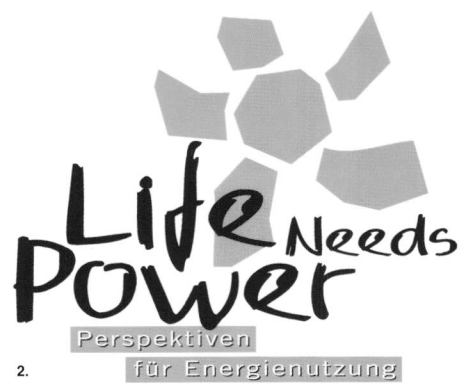

2.

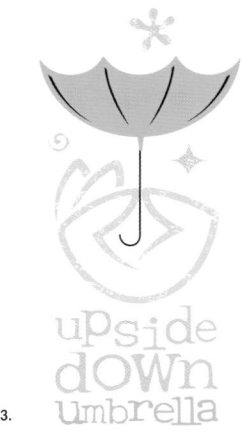

uPside dOWn umbrella

3.

mârketing

REÑOVATION

4.

bondepus
GRAPHIC
DESIGN

5.

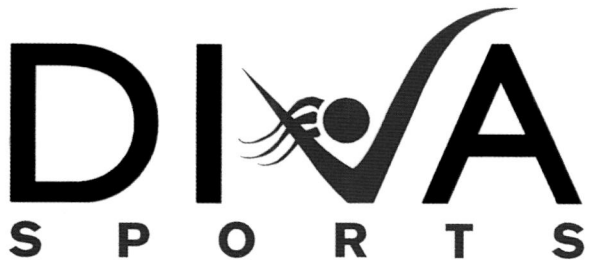

J&B PROPERTIES

6.

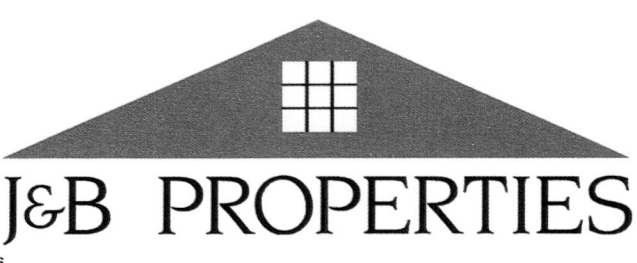

DI\A
SPORTS

7.

1
Design Firm **Ukulele Brand Consultants Pte Ltd**
2
Design Firm **Aufgeweckte Werbung**
3, 4
Design Firm **Visual Asylum**
5 - 7
Design Firm **Bondepus Graphic Design**
1.
Client *Singapore Sports School*
Designers Kim Chun-wei, Cheng Tze Tzuen
2.
Client *ZVEI (Zentralverband Elektrotechnik und Elektronikindustrie*
Designer Georg Hahn
3.
Client *Upside Down Umbrella*
Designers Visual Asylum

4.
Client *Meg Joseph*
Designer Long Lé
5.
Client *Bondepus Graphic Design*
Designers Gary Epis, Amy Bond
6.
Client *J+B Properties*
Designers Gary Epis, Amy Bond
7.
Client *DIVA Sports*
Designers Gary Epis, Amy Bond
(opposite)
Client *Protegrity Incorporated*
Design Firm **Resendesign**
Designer Ken Resen

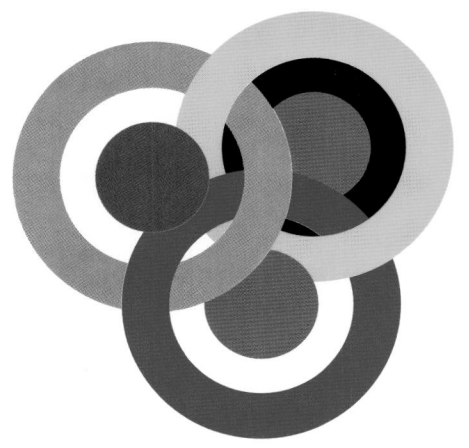

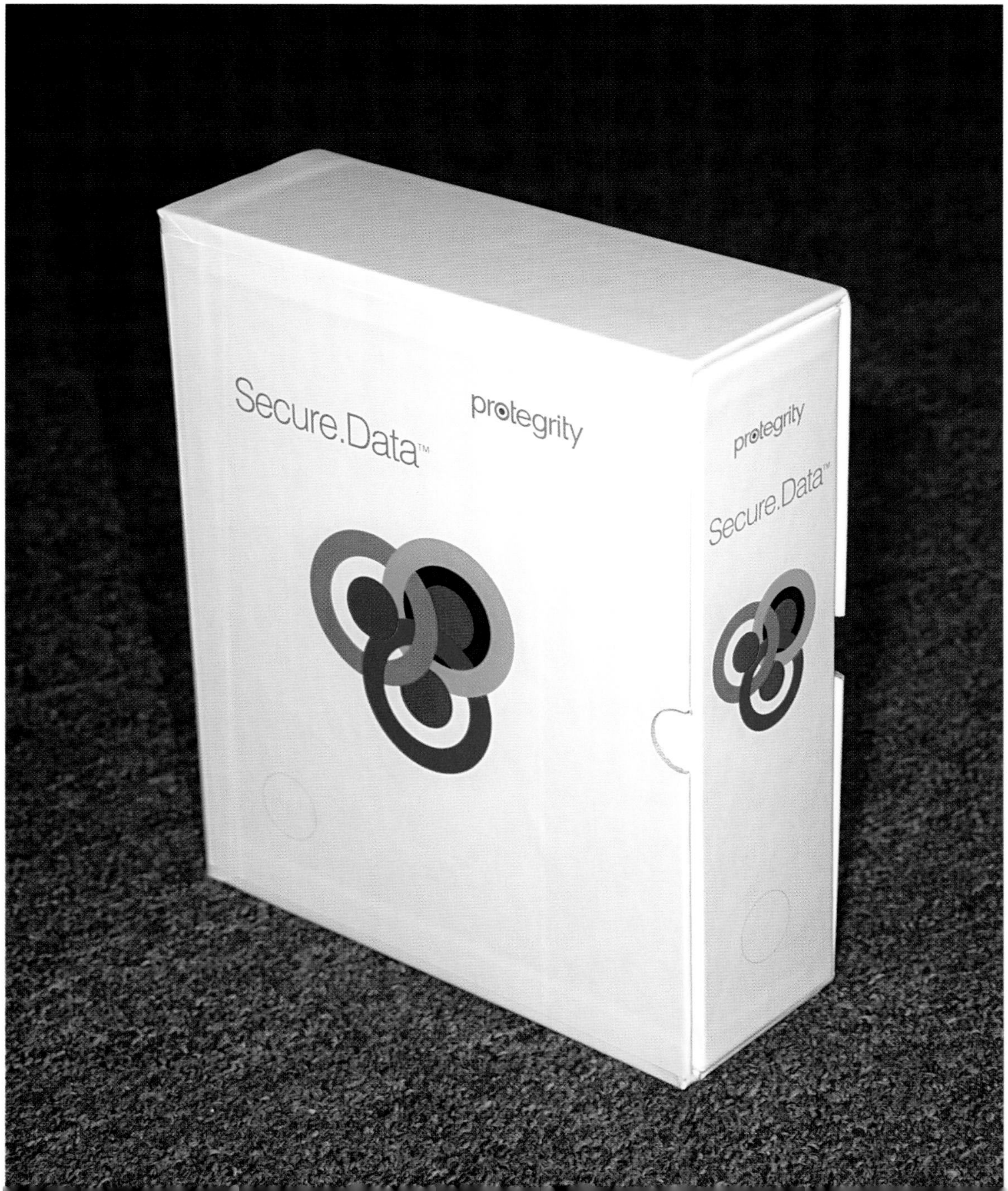

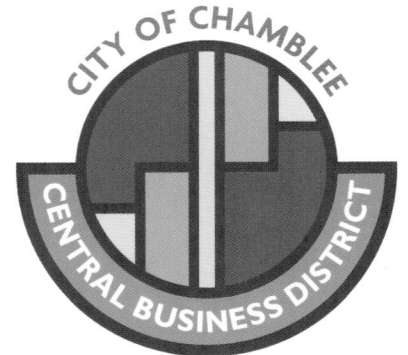

CITY OF CHAMBLEE
CENTRAL BUSINESS DISTRICT

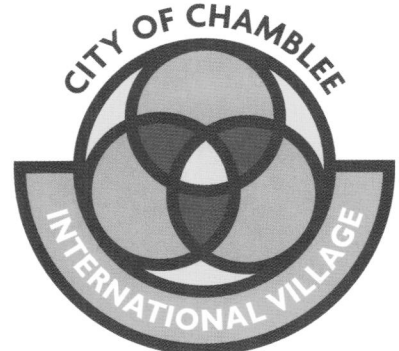

CITY OF CHAMBLEE
INTERNATIONAL VILLAGE

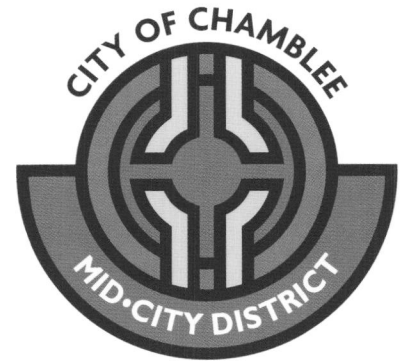

CITY OF CHAMBLEE
MID·CITY DISTRICT

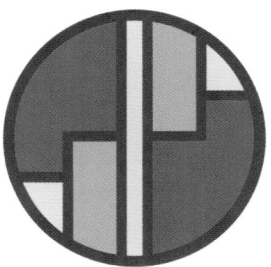

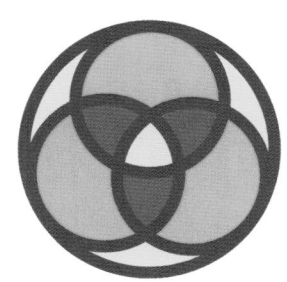

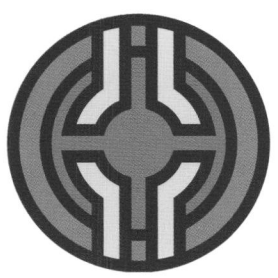

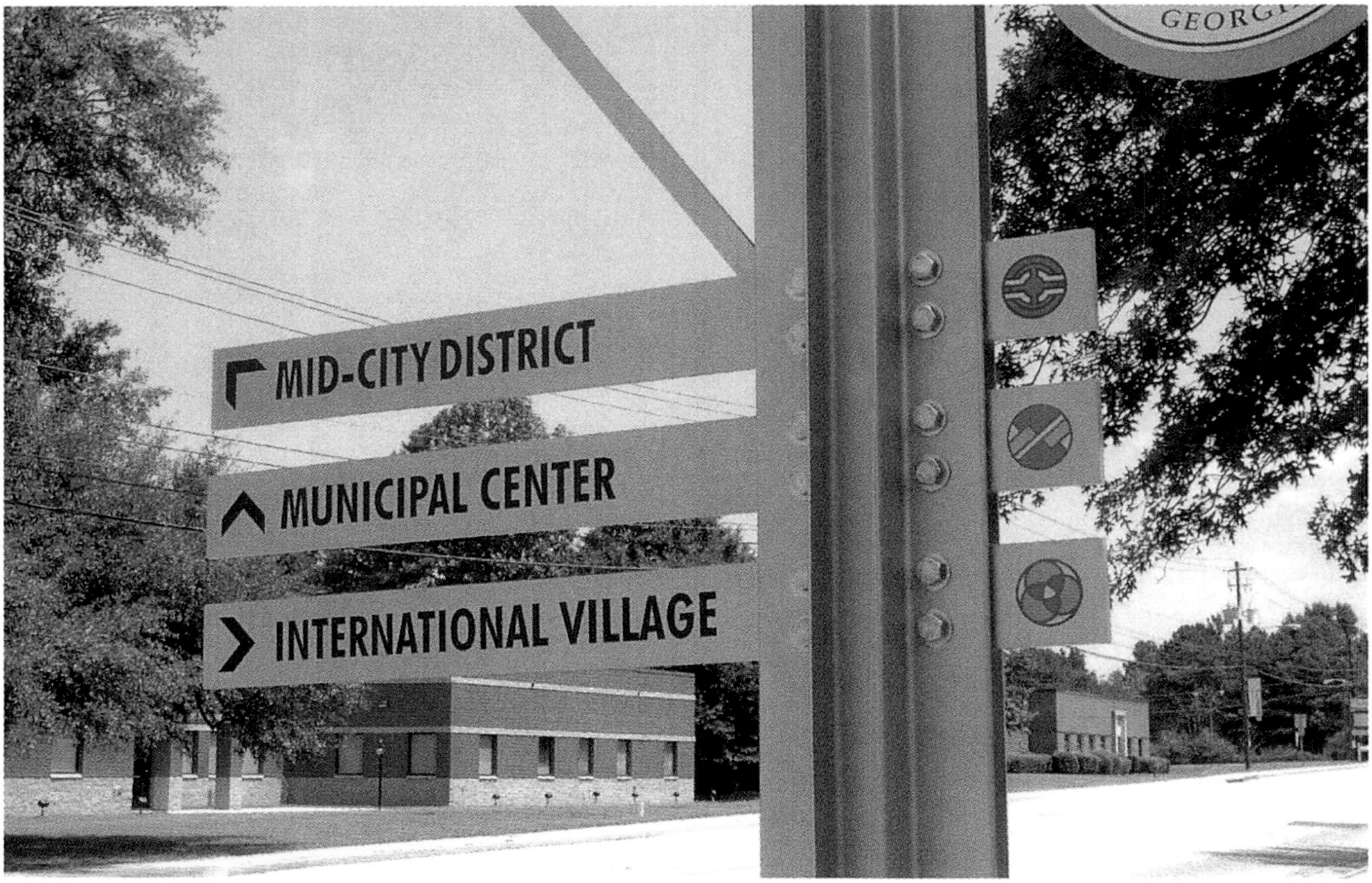

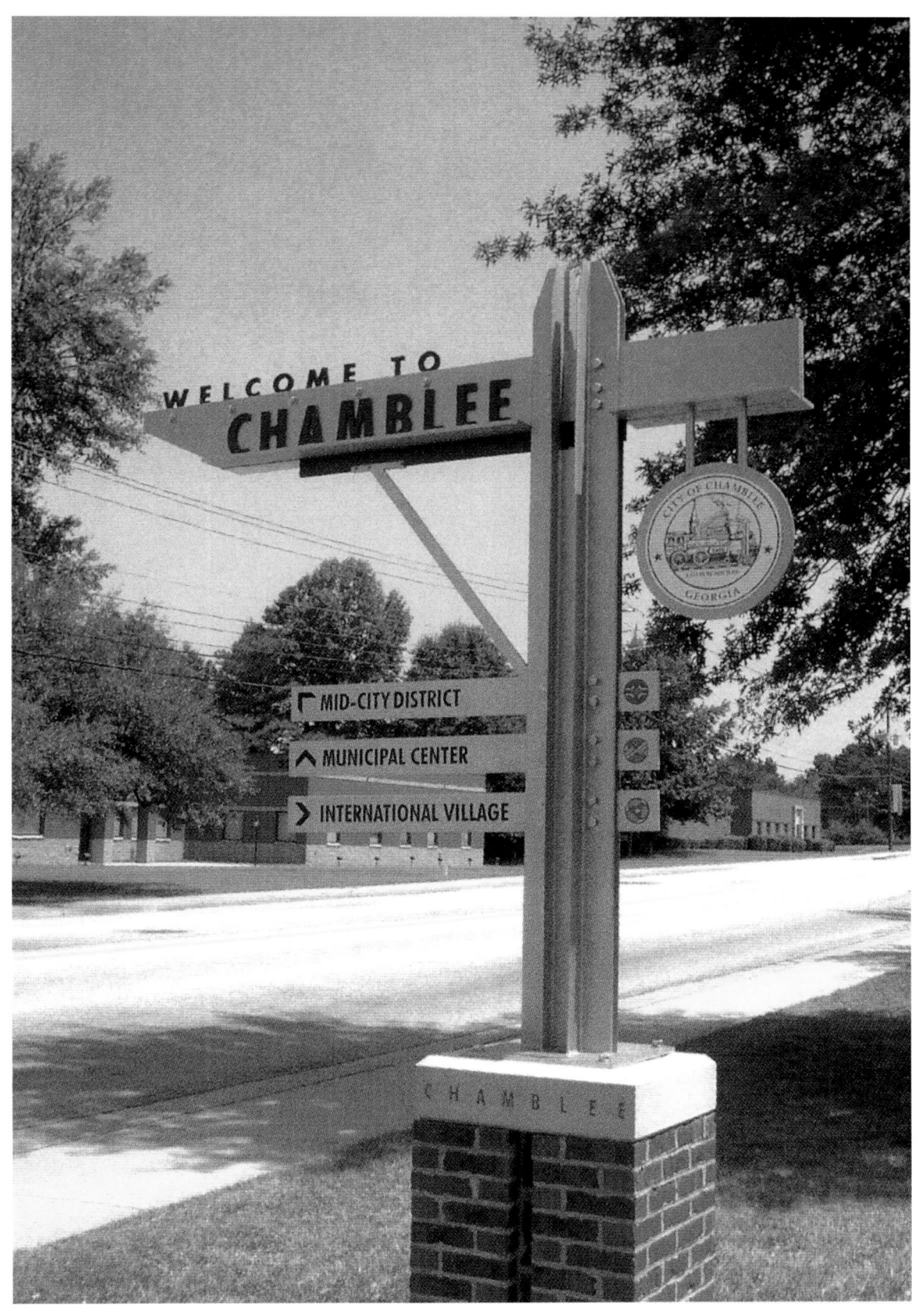

Design Firm **Sky Design**
Client   *City Of Chamblee, Ga.*
Designers   W. Todd Vaught,
            Carrie Brown

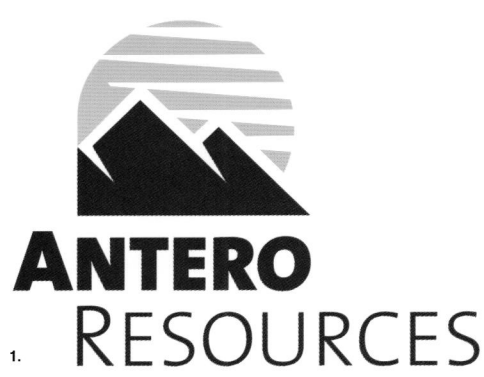

ANTERO
1. RESOURCES

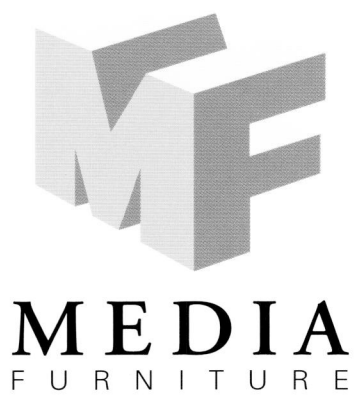

MEDIA
FURNITURE
2.

ÂPEX
DERMATOLOGY
3. GROUP

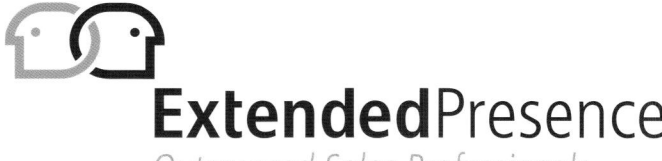

ExtendedPresence
4. *Outsourced Sales Professionals*

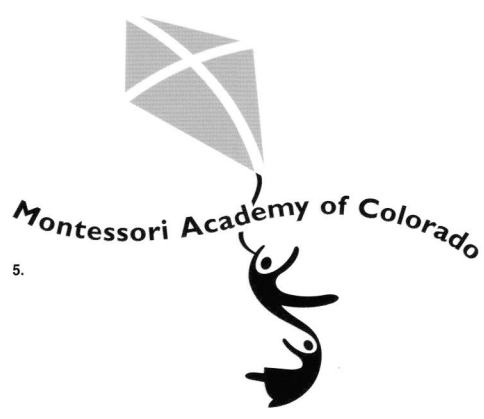

Montessori Academy of Colorado
5.

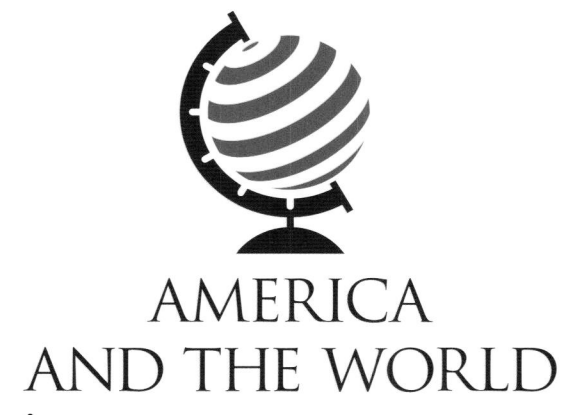

AMERICA
AND THE WORLD
6.

eBoard
7.

1 - 7
Design Firm **Convexus Consulting, Inc.**
1.
    Client   *Antero Resources*
    Designers Karl Peters,
             David Warren
2.
    Client   *Media Furniture*
    Designer Karl Peters
3.
    Client   *Apex Dermatology Group*
    Designers Karl Peters,
             David Warren
4.
    Client   *Extended Presence*
    Designers Karl Peters,
             David Warren
5.
    Client   *Montessori Academy of Colorado*
    Designers Karl Peters,
             David Warren

6.
    Client   *America and the World*
    Designers Karl Peters,
             David Warren
7.
    Client   *eBoard.com*
    Designer Karl Peters
(opposite)
    Client   *Aga Khan Foundation USA*
    Design Firm **Poonja Design, Inc.**
    Designer Suleman Poonja

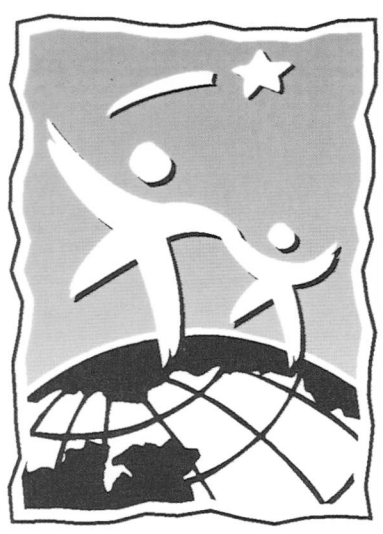

Partnership*Walk*

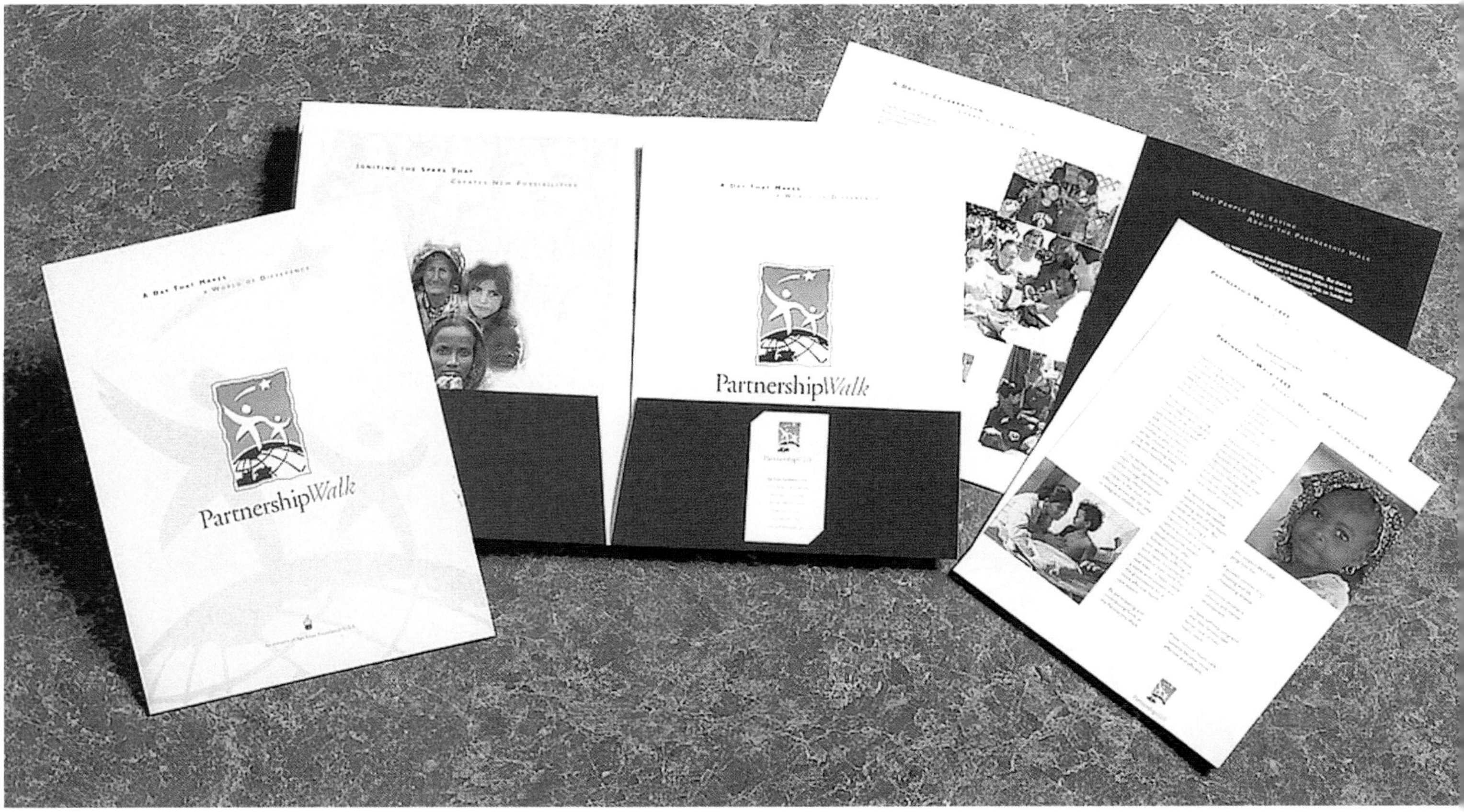

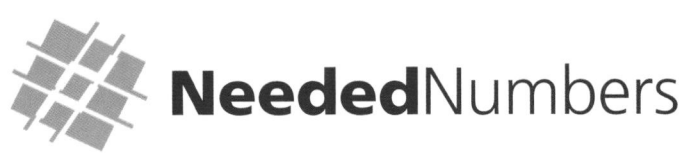

1.

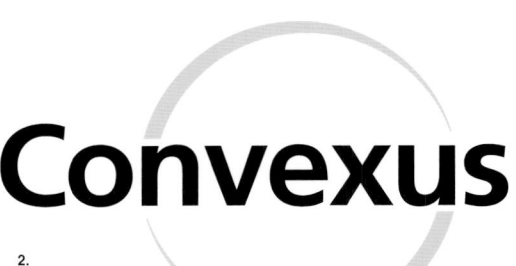

2.

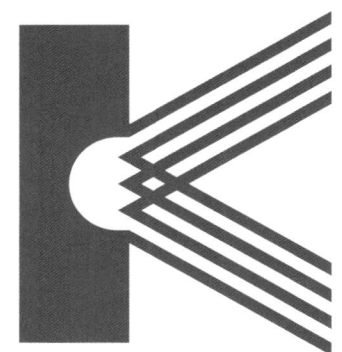

3.

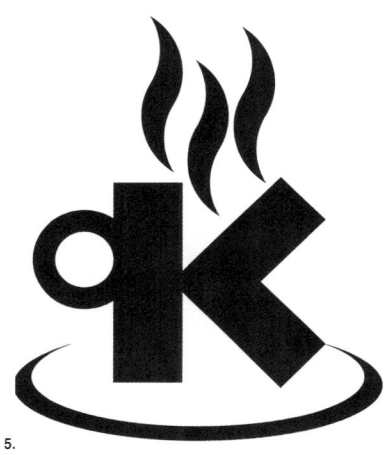

4.

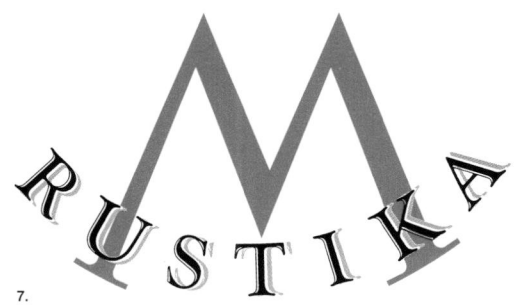

5.

6.

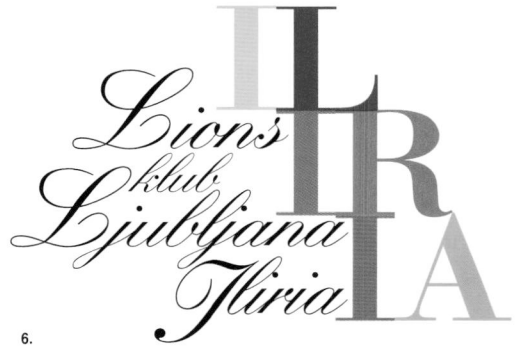

7.

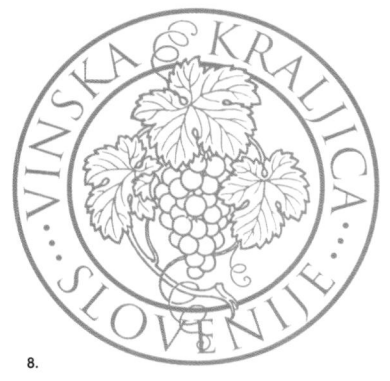

8.

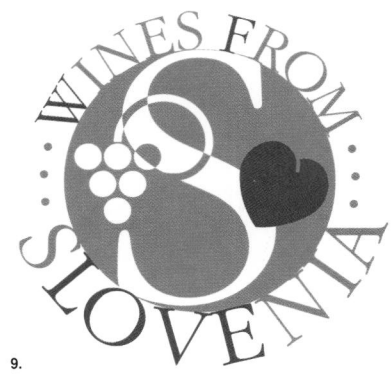

9.

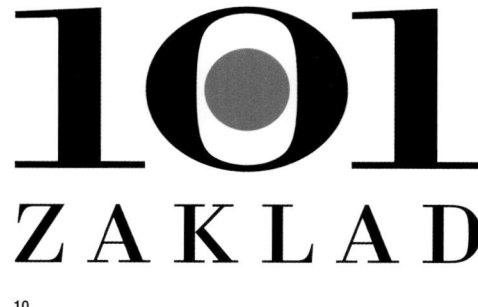

10.

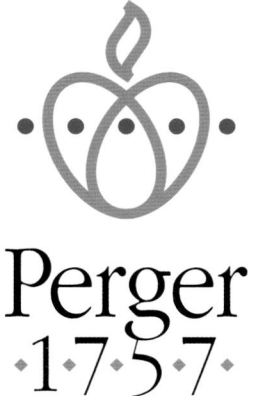

Perger
·1·7·5·7·

11.

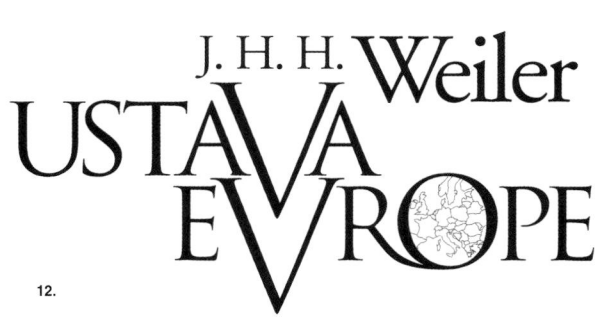

12.

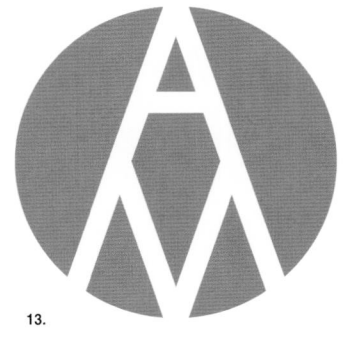

13.

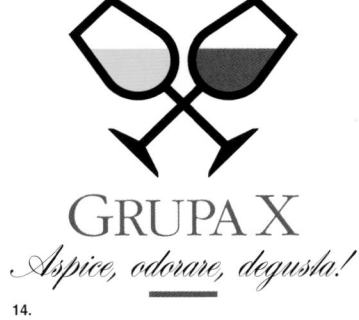

GRUPA X

Aspice, odorare, degusta!

14.

LITTERA·SCRIPTA·MANET

15.

1, 2
Design Firm **Convexus Consulting, Inc.**
3 - 15
Design Firm **KROG**

1.
Client *Optima Marketing*
Designer Karl Peters

2.
Client *Convexus Consulting, Inc.*
Designers Karl Peters, David Warren

3, 4.
Client *Presernova druzba, Ljubljana*
Designer Edi Berk

5.
Client *Mladinska knjiga, Ljubljana*
Designer Edi Berk

6.
Client *Lions klub Ljubljana Iliria*
Designer Edi Berk

7.
Client *Janko in Zdena Mlakar, Ljubljana*
Designer Edi Berk

8.
Client *Pomurski sejem, Gornja Radgona*
Designer Edi Berk

9.
Client *Ministry of Agriculture of the Republic of Slovenia, Ljubljana*
Designer Edi Berk

10.
Client *Kmecki glas, Ljubljana*
Designer Edi Berk

11.
Client *Hrabroslav Perger, Slovenj Gradec*
Designer Edi Berk

12.
Client *Pravna fakulteta, Ljubljana*
Designer Edi Berk

13.
Client *Andrej Mlakar, Ljubljana*
Designer Edi Berk

14.
Client *Grupa X, Ljubljana*
Designer Edi Berk

15.
Client *Pravna fakulteta, Ljubljana*
Designer Edi Berk

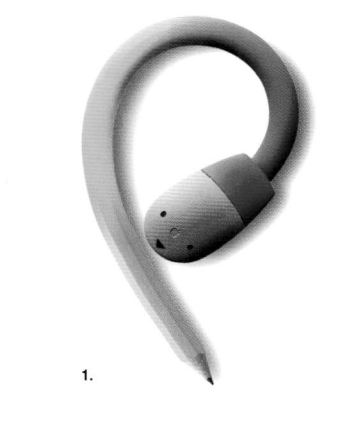

1.

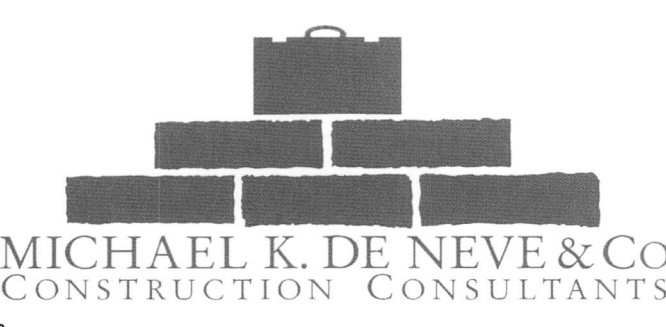

MICHAEL K. DE NEVE & CO
CONSTRUCTION CONSULTANTS

2.

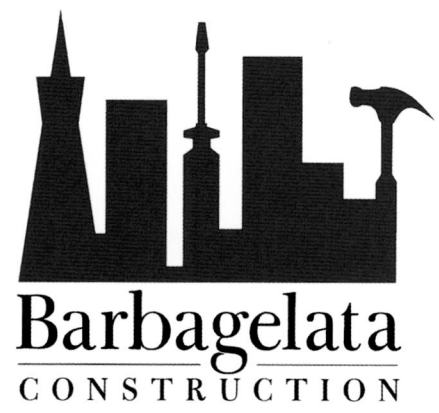

Barbagelata
CONSTRUCTION

3.

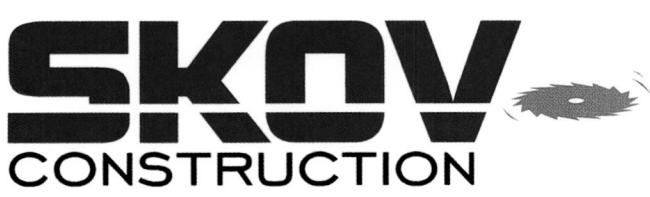

4.

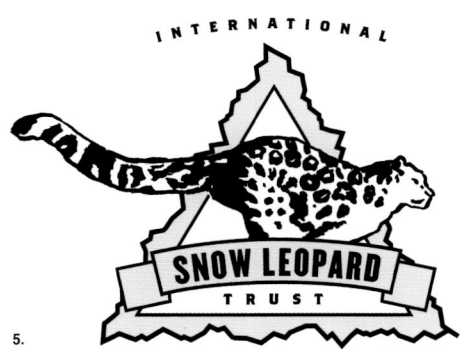

5.

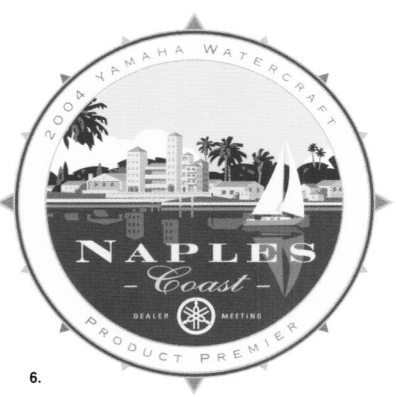

6.

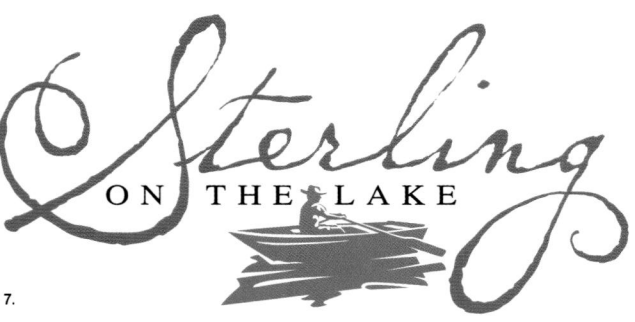

7.

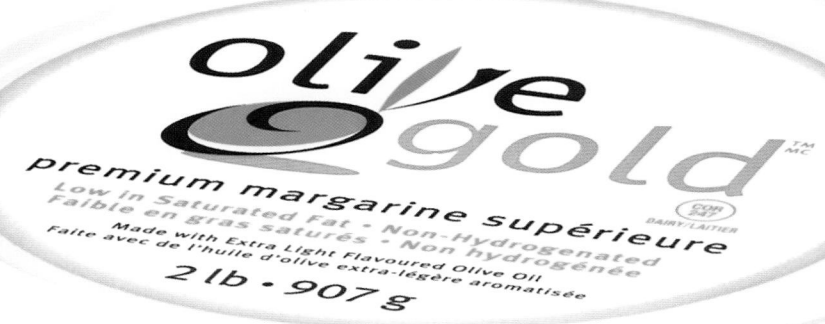

olive gold™
premium margarine supérieure
Low in Saturated Fat · Non-Hydrogenated
Faible en gras saturés · Non hydrogénée
Made with Extra Light Flavoured Olive Oil
Faite avec de l'huile d'olive extra-légère aromatisée

2 lb · 907 g

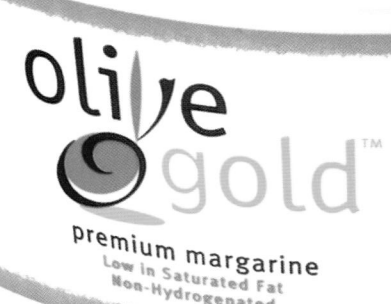

olive gold™
premium margarine
Low in Saturated Fat
Non-Hydrogenated

INGREDIENTS: CANOLA OIL AND EXTRA LIGHT OLIVE OIL 69.5%, WATER 16%, MODIFIED PALM OIL 10.5%, SALT 1.8%, WHEY POWDER 1.4%, VEGETABLE MONO AND DIGLYCERIDES 0.4% SOY LECITHIN 0.2%, POTASSIUM SORBATE 0.1%, ARTIFICIAL FLAVOUR, ALPHA TOCOPHEROL, VITAMIN A PALMITATE, VITAMIN D3, BETA CAROTENE, CITRIC ACID. KEEP REFRIGERATED. GOOD FOR COOKING AND BAKING. ONE ASPECT OF A HEALTHY DIET IS TO HAVE NOT MORE THAN 10% OF ENERGY FROM SATURATED FAT.

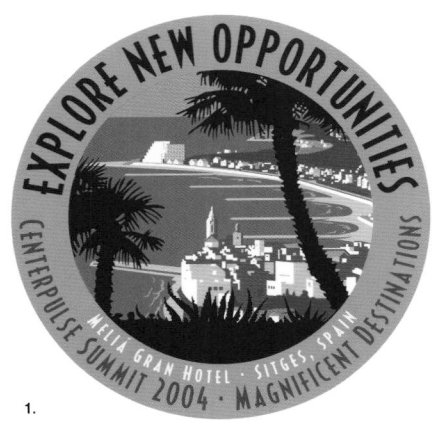

1.

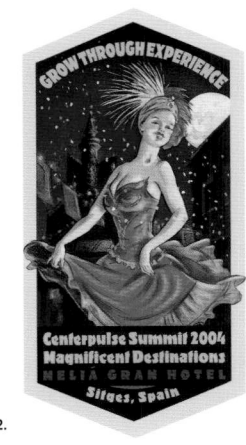

2.

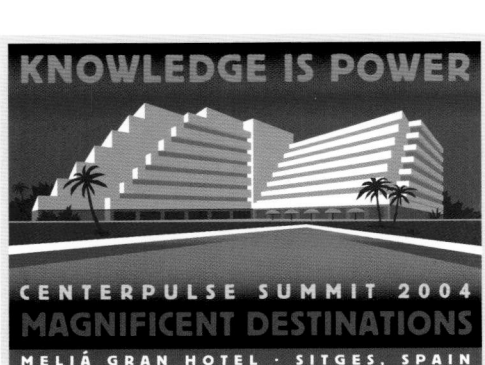

3.

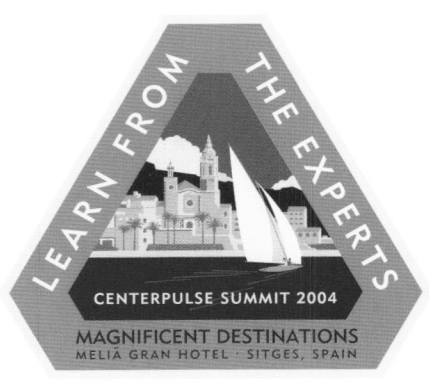

4.

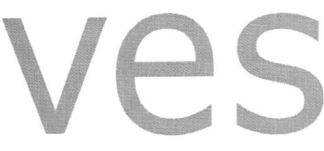

5.

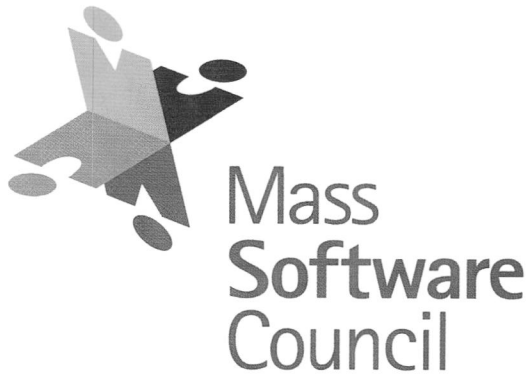

6.

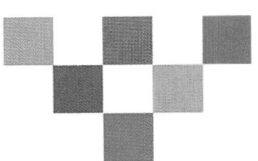

7.

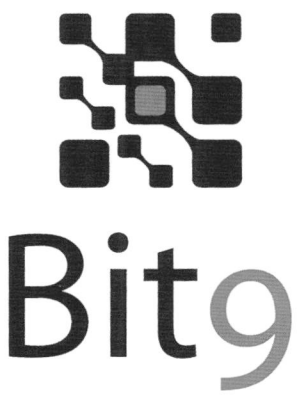

8.

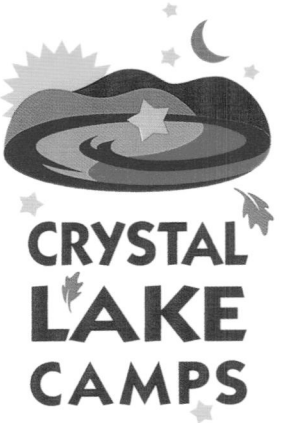

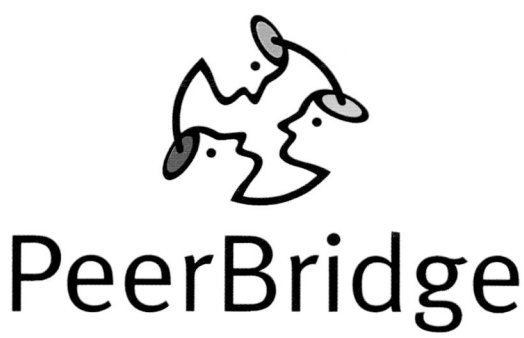

PeerBridge

9.

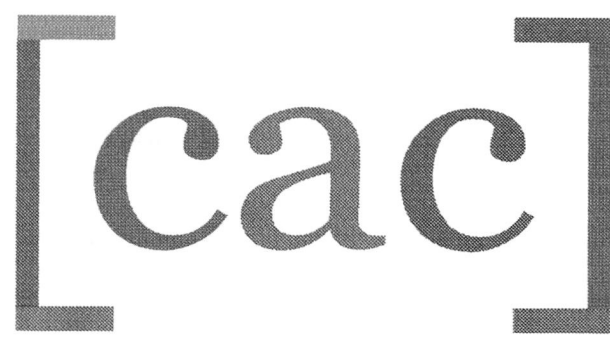

[cac]

10.

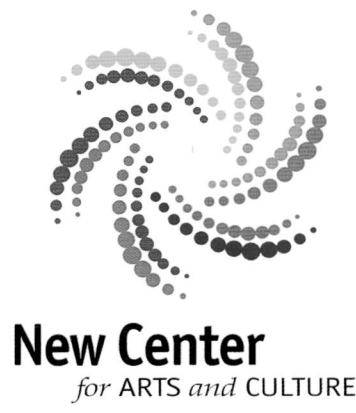

New Center
for ARTS *and* CULTURE

11.

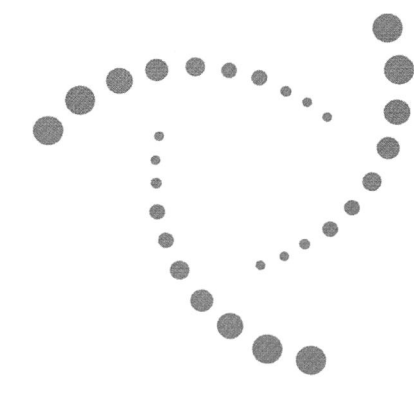

12.

Taralon

13.

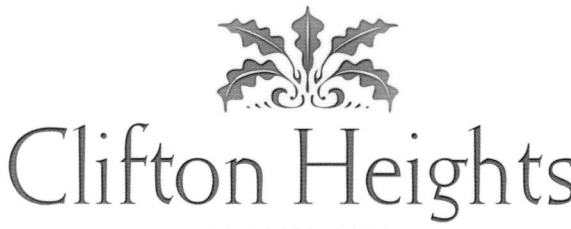

Clifton Heights

LA COSTA OAKS

14.

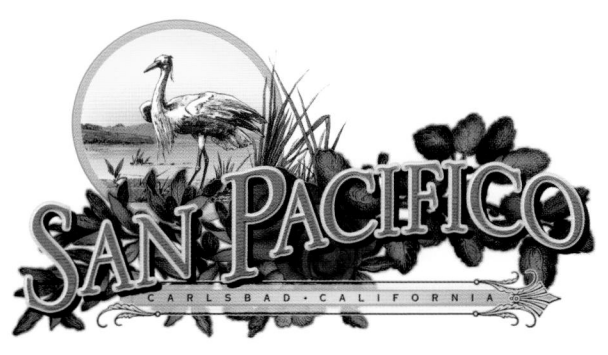

15.

1 - 4	
Design Firm	**Parker/White**
5 - 12	
Design Firm	**Gill Fishman Associates**
13, 14	
Design Firm	**Roni Hicks & Associates**
15	
Design Firm	**Sabingrafik, Inc.**
1 - 4.	
Client	*Centerpulse*
Designers	Tracy Sabin, Dylan Jones
5.	
Client	*Harvard VES*
Designer	Alicia Ozyjowski
6.	
Client	*Mass Software Council*
Designers	Alicia Ozyjowski,
	Michael Persons
7.	
Client	*Bit9 Inc.*
Designer	Alicia Ozyjowski

8.	
Client	*Crystal Lake Camps*
Designer	Michael Persons
9.	
Client	*Peerbridge Group*
Designer	Michael Persons
10.	
Client	*Brown University*
Designer	Gill Fishman
11.	
Client	*New Jewish Center for Arts*
Designer	Alicia Ozyjowski
12.	
Client	*Trine Pharmaceuticals*
13.	
Client	*Taralon*
Designers	Tracy Sabin, Stephen Sharp
14.	
Client	*Clifton Heights*
Designers	Tracy Sabin, Stephen Sharp
15.	
Client	*San Pacifico*
Designer	Tracy Sabin

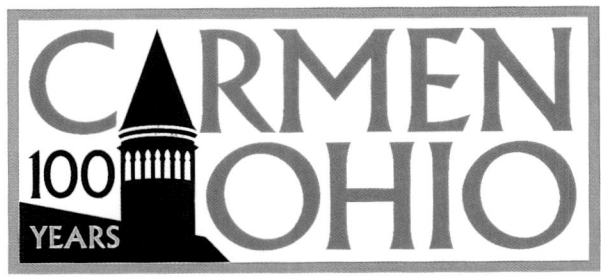

1.

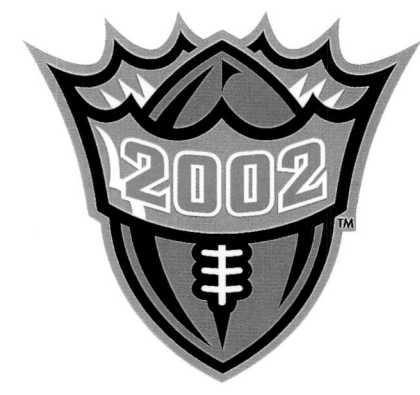

2.

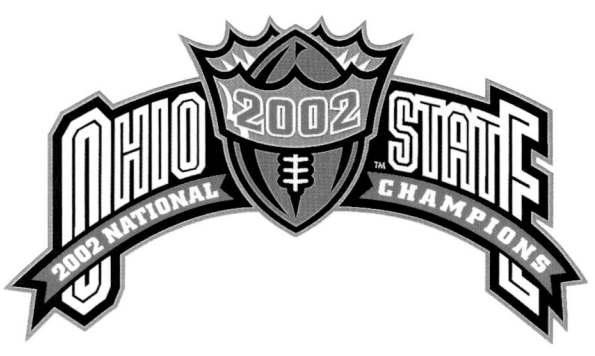

3.

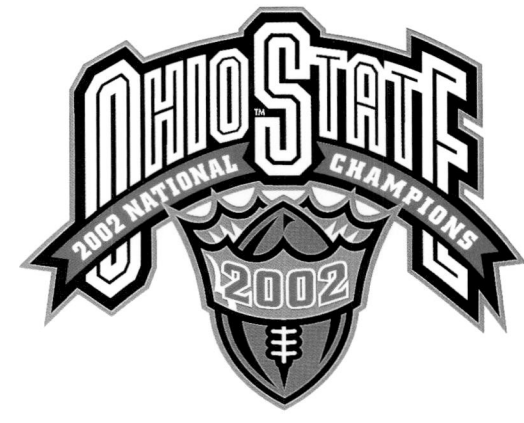

4.

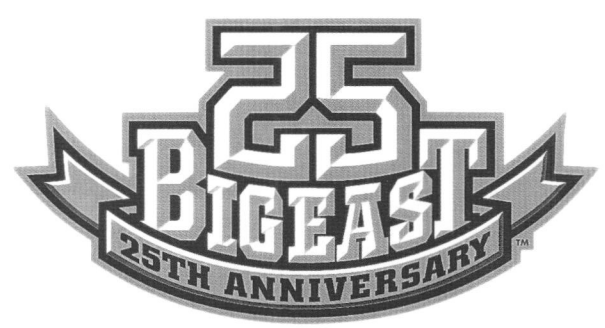

5.

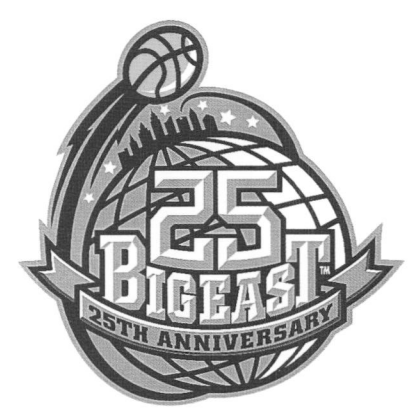

6.

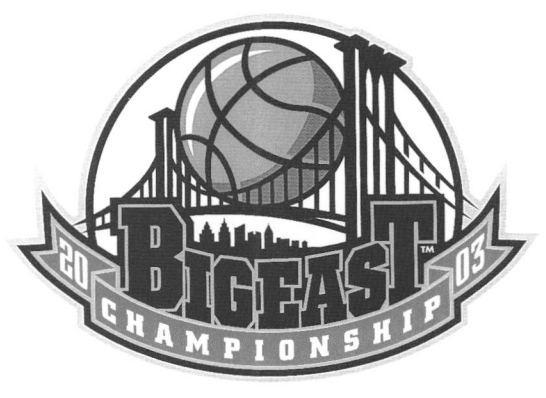

7.

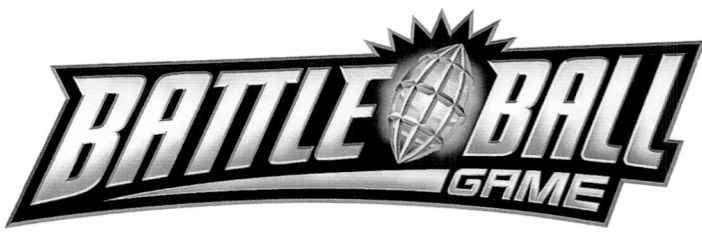

8.

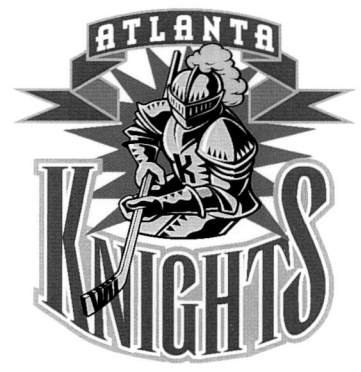

9.

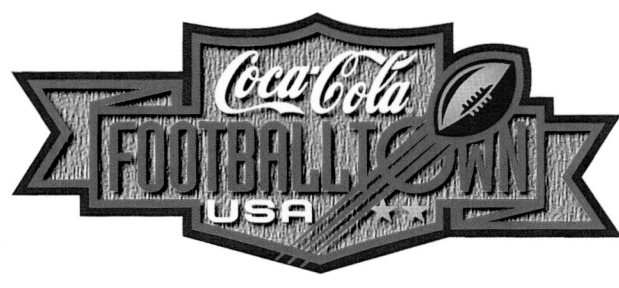

10.

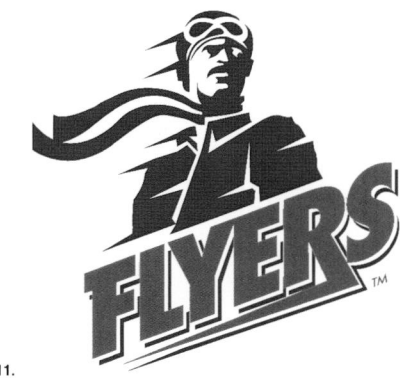

11.

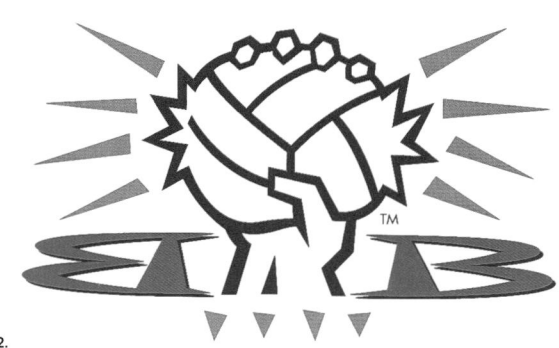

12.

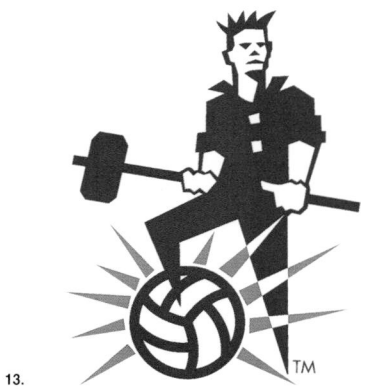

13.

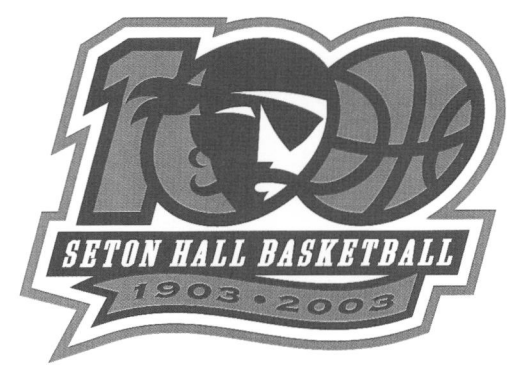

14.

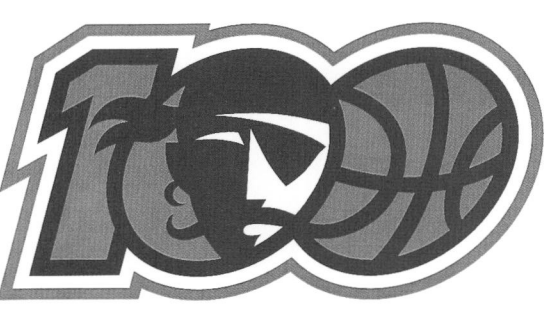

15.

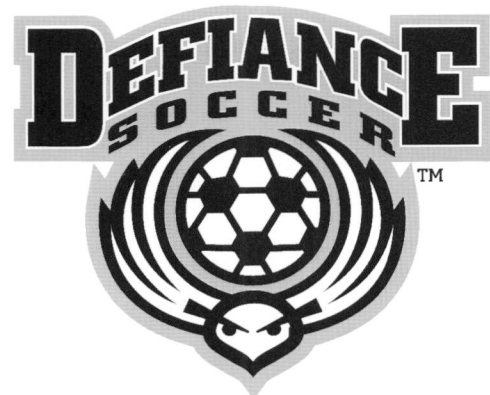

1.

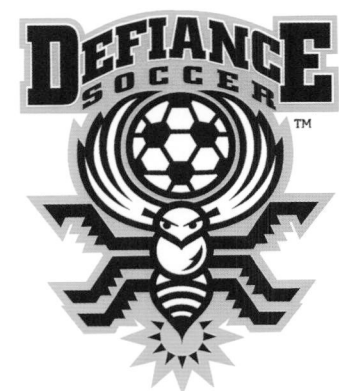

2.

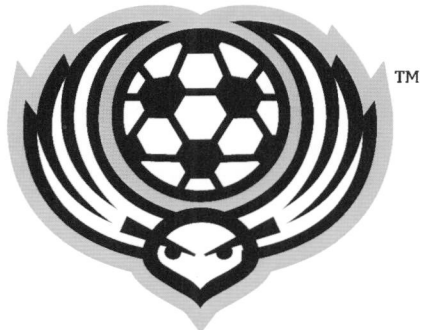

3.

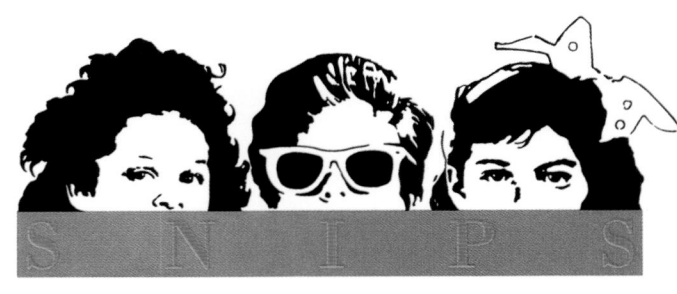

4.

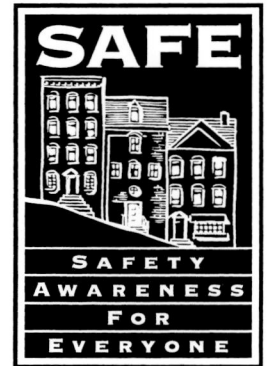

5.

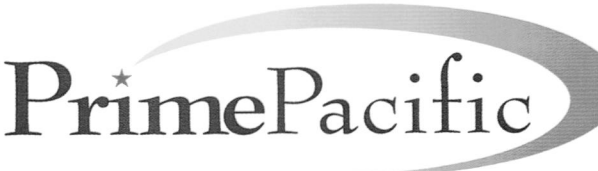

6.

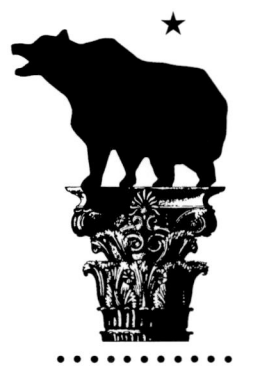

Northern California Investments

7.

1 - 3
Design Firm **Rickabaugh Graphics**
4 - 7
Design Firm **Steven Lee Design**
1 - 3.
Client   *Defiance College*
Designer   Eric Rickabaugh
4.
Client   *SNIPS*
Designer   Steven Lee
5.
Client   *Safety Awareness for Everyone*
Designer   Steven Lee
6.
Client   *Prime Pacific Global Management Corporation*
Designer   Steven Lee

7.
Client   *Northern California Investments*
Designer   Steven Lee
(opposite)
Client   *Saint John's Health Center*
Design Firm **Poonja Design, Inc.**
Designer   Suleman Poonja

JIMMY STEWART
RELAY MARATHON
2001

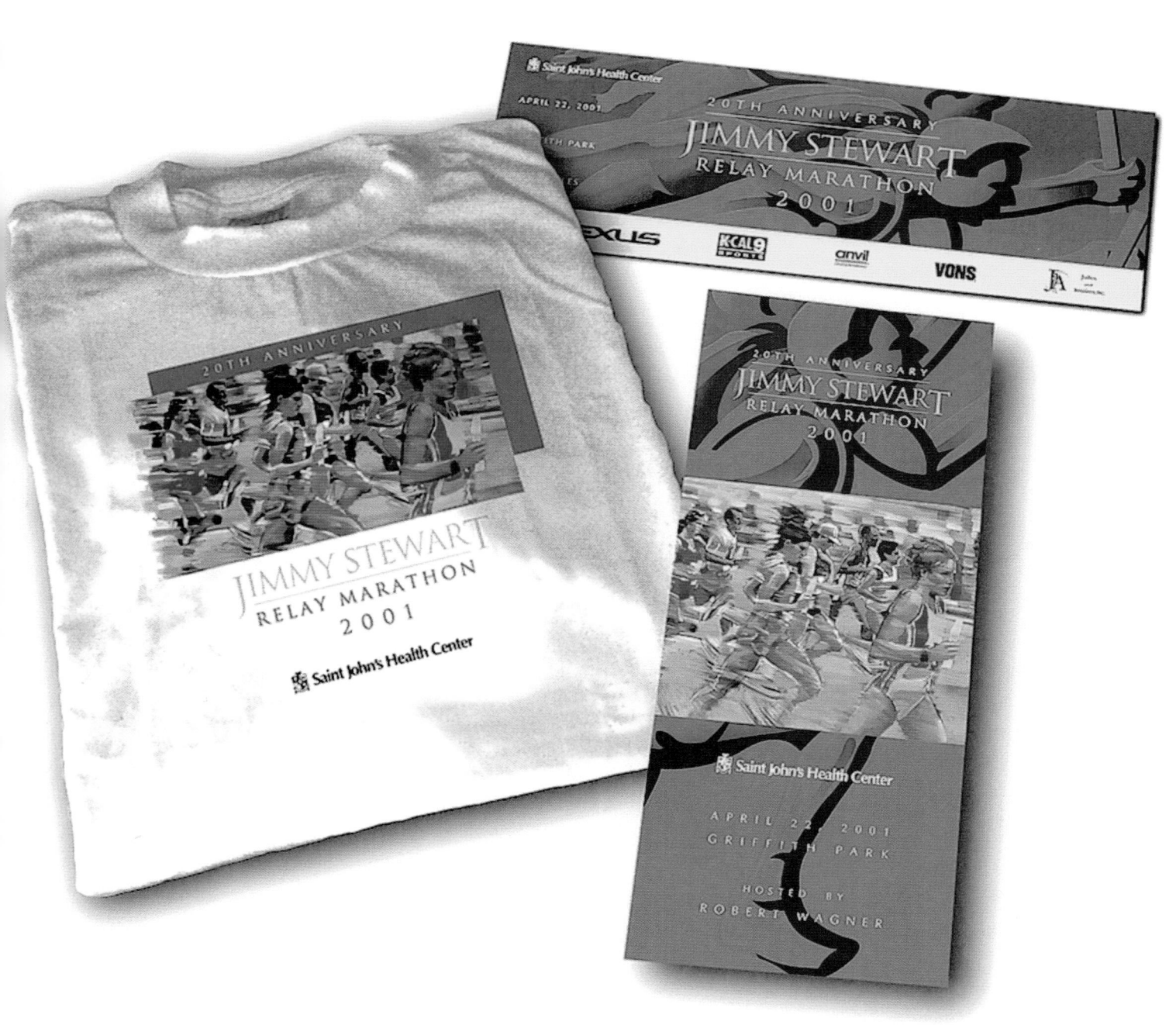

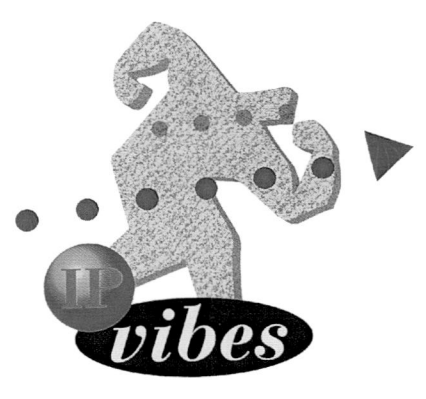

1.

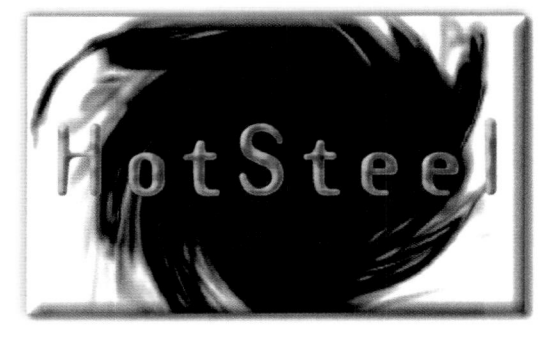

2.

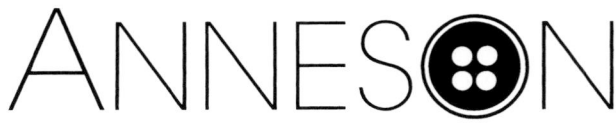

3.

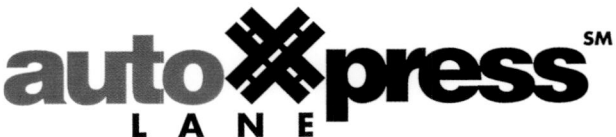

4.

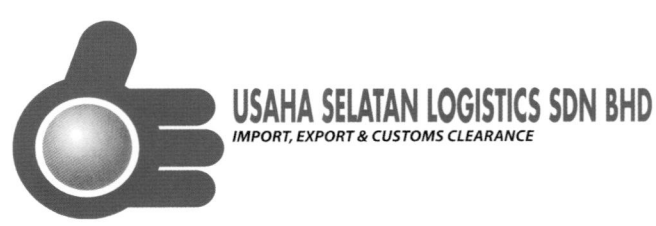

5.

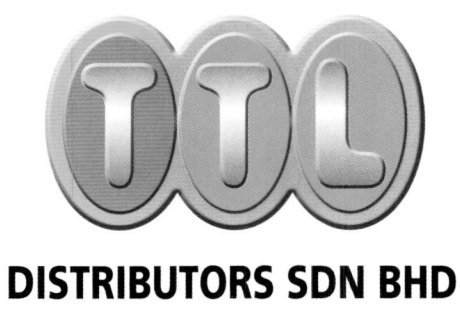

6.

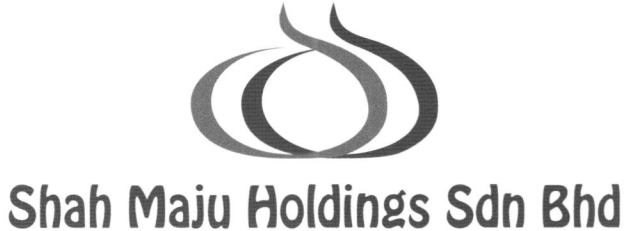

7.

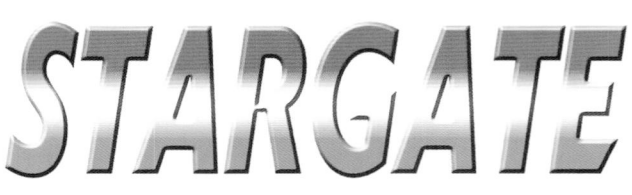

8.

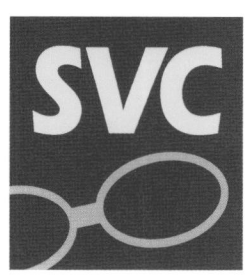

STANDARD VISION CARE SDN BHD

9.

TCL PLASTIC INDUSTRIES SDN. BHD.

10.

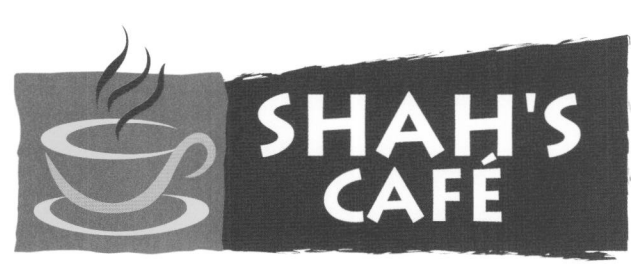

11.

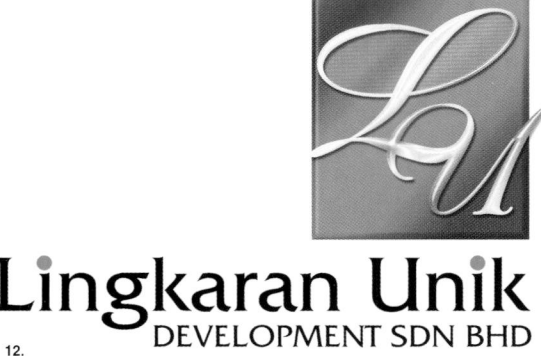

Lingkaran Unik
DEVELOPMENT SDN BHD

12.

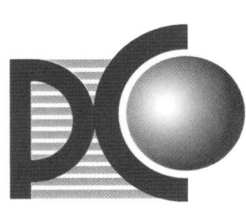 **PLANO-COMP**

13.

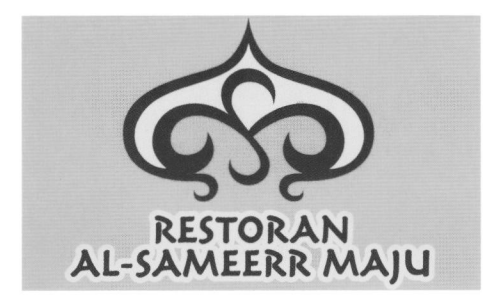

14.

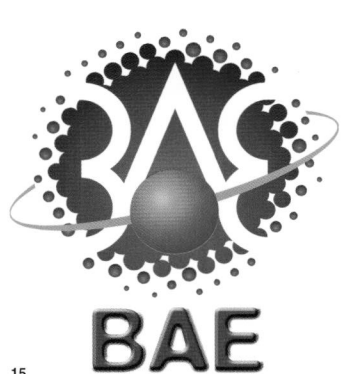

15.

PROMOTIONAL TRADESHOW MATERIALS:

- The examples at the right demonstrate several approved executions of the Promotional template in vertical and horizontal applications. Be sure to mix and match the Figure Photography supplied in the Photography Library and NOT focus on a single visual per promotion. The Photography Library was created to reinforce the brand and is not product or Category-specific.

- When creating banners, posters, or any other large format pieces for special events and tradeshows, you may flood with the medium color of the Color Banding System for general corporate. You may also use a Service Category color. Remember that it is NOT necessary to flood the live area with a color all the time, Novell has ownership in large, bold fields of white.

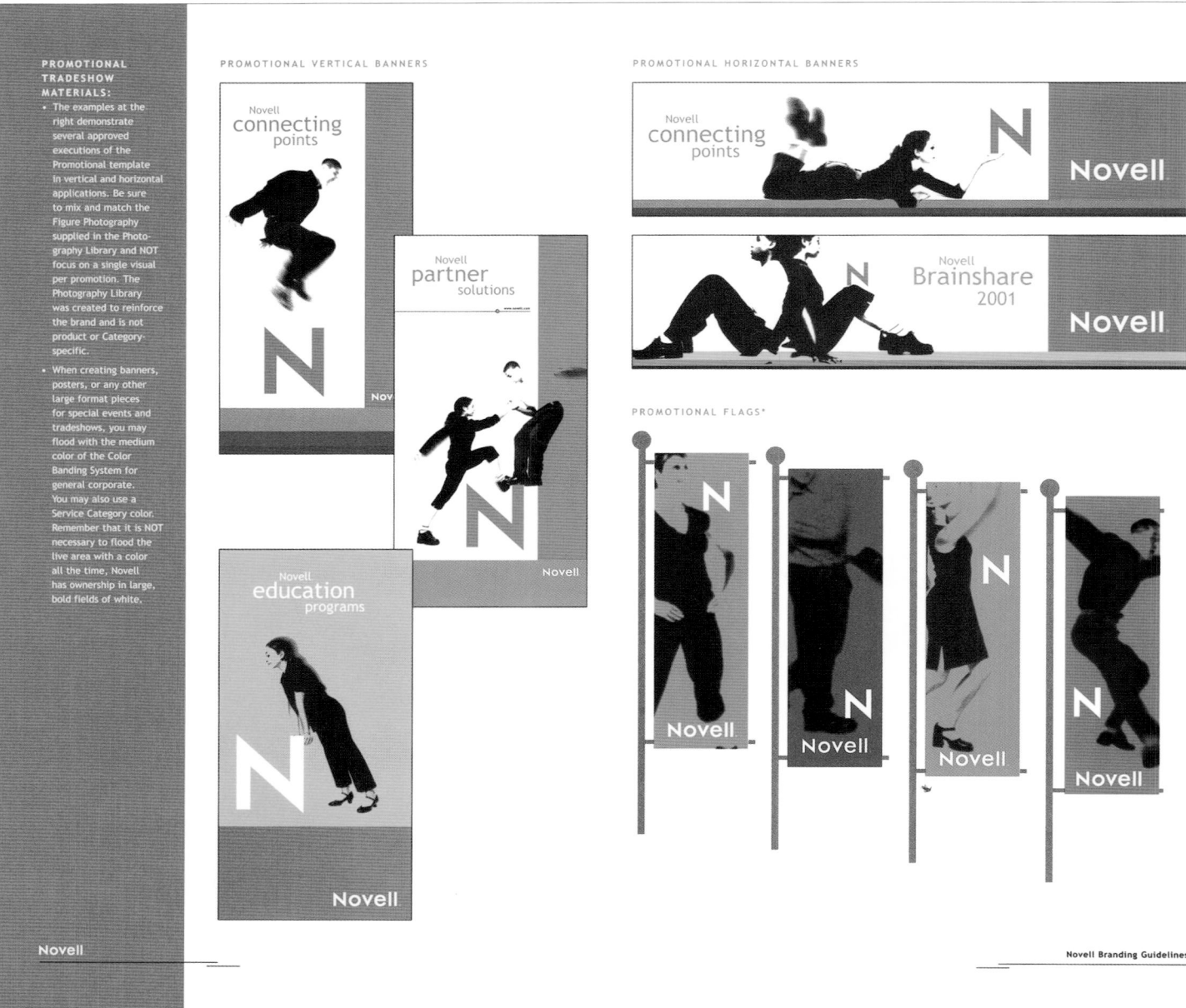

PROMOTIONAL FLAGS*

Novell

Novell Branding Guidelines

Design Firm **Hornall Anderson Design Works, Inc.**
Client   *Novell, Inc.*
Designers   Larry Anderson, Jack Anderson, James Tee, Holly Craven, Michael Brugman, Kaye Farmer, Taro Suzuki, Jay Hilburn, Belinda Bowling

MERCHANDISE:

- Using a sparse look to build brand equity is a mandate from Novell Corporate Marketing.

- All Corporate Merchandise should include the Novell Logo, preferably in Novell Red.

- All Corporate T-shirts should ONLY have the Novell Logo on the front of the shirt. Any deviation from this must be approved by Novell Corporate Marketing.

- The N Graphic and Figure Photography should appear on the back of the T-shirt. (You can use any of the images included on the CD.)

- Corporate Hats should have the N Graphic on the front and the Novell Logo on the back. The Logo appears in Novell Red on a white or light colored hat or white on a red hat.

T-SHIRT

HAT

MOUSEPAD

BUTTON

NAMETAG

Susan C.
Rockefeller-Jones

www.novell.com

- All Corporate Mousepads should be red with a white Novell Logo and the N Graphic and Figure Photography. (You can use any of the images included on the CD)

- For the Corporate Button, the Novell Logo should be set in Novell Red on a white field and sit on a red field that includes the N Graphic and Figure Photography. (You can use any of the images included on the CD.)

- The Corporate Name Tag should follow the Corporate Materials grid. Divide it into 16 equal parts width by height. Fill 9 x 16 parts Novell Red. Fill 16 x 1 part with the Color Banding System. Add the Novell Logo to the white field. Add the Information Matrix and "name" text.

Novell

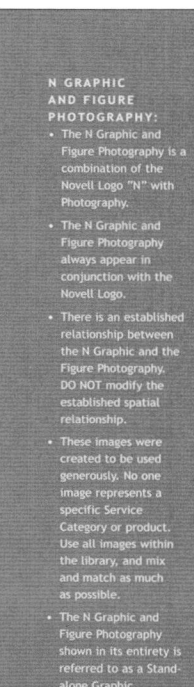

- The N Graphic and Figure Photography is a combination of the Novell Logo "N" with Photography.

- The N Graphic and Figure Photography always appear in conjunction with the Novell Logo.

- There is an established relationship between the N Graphic and the Figure Photography. DO NOT modify the established spatial relationship.

- These images were created to be used generously. No one image represents a specific Service Category or product. Use all images within the library, and mix and match as much as possible.

- The N Graphic and Figure Photography shown in its entirety is referred to as a Stand-alone Graphic.

- Stand-alone Graphics are used on all Corporate materials.

- A Supergraphic is an enlarged, close crop of the Figure Photography. The N Graphic may be removed from its locked position and placed in general proximity of the figure.

- Supergraphics are used for Promotional materials only.

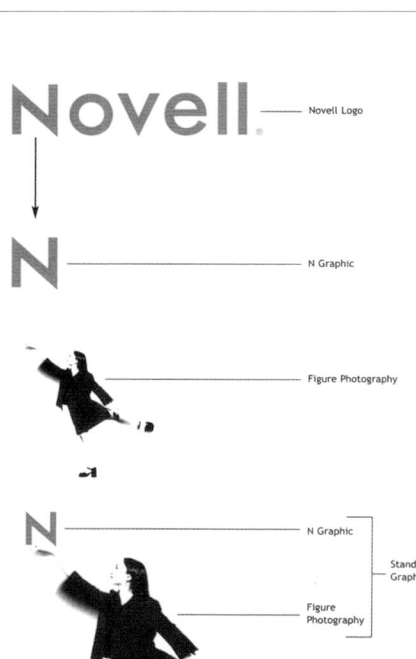

Novell® — Novell Logo

N — N Graphic

Figure Photography

N — N Graphic

Stand-alone Graphic

Figure Photography

ON WHITE BACKGROUND

ON NOVELL RED

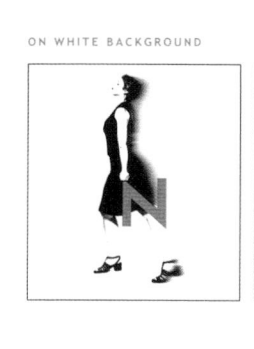

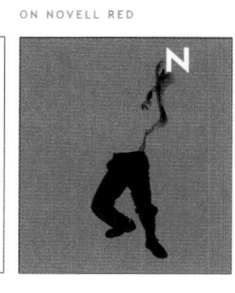

ON LIGHT BACKGROUND

ON DARK COLORS

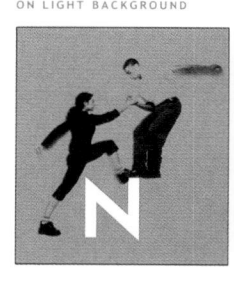

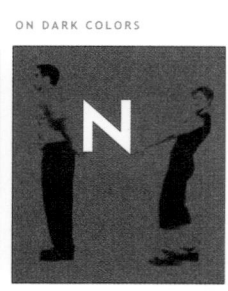

STAND-ALONE GRAPHIC

SUPERGRAPHIC

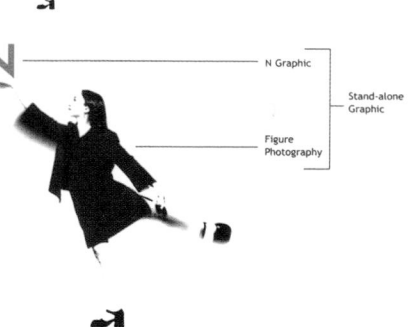

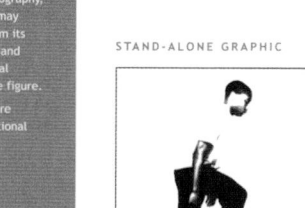

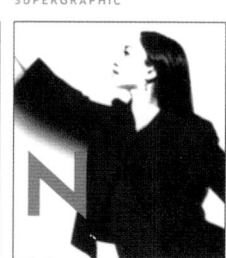

ONE COLOR ("N" IS 30% SCREEN OF BLACK)

ON COLOR BANDING SYSTEM

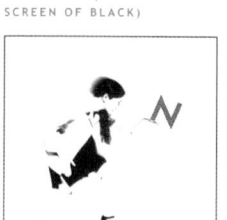

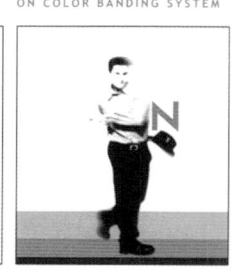

COLOR USAGE:

- The Figure Photography always appears as black on a white background OR black on one of the Novell Colors.

- The N Graphic is always Novell Red on a white background OR white on a colored background.

- If only one color is available, the N graphic prints 30% screen of black on a white background. DO NOT place the Figure Photography on a black background.

- For Promotional materials, the Figure Photography can overlap the Color Banding System.

- The images were created to be used as they are. Do NOT manipulate or distort the images found in the Figure Photography Library.

- Figure Photography is always used in conjunction with the N Graphic— never without.

NOTE: The complete directory of the Figure Photography can be found in the Reference section of these Guidelines. Figure Photography images are provided on the Branding Guidelines CDs as 1) high resolution Photoshop tiff files, 2) Illustrator eps files with the N Graphic and 3) as a combined lock-up saved as a 4-color process tiff file. A "How To" Photoshop file has been included to help guide in adding back-ground colors to the Figure Photography.

CORPORATE
PACKAGING:
All packaging products
are accompanied by
an assortment of
standardized pieces.
Typical in-box components
include registration cards,
reference guides and
license agreements.

Product packaging is
always developed in
concert with Novell
Corporate Marketing
Communication and a
Product Operations
Manager.

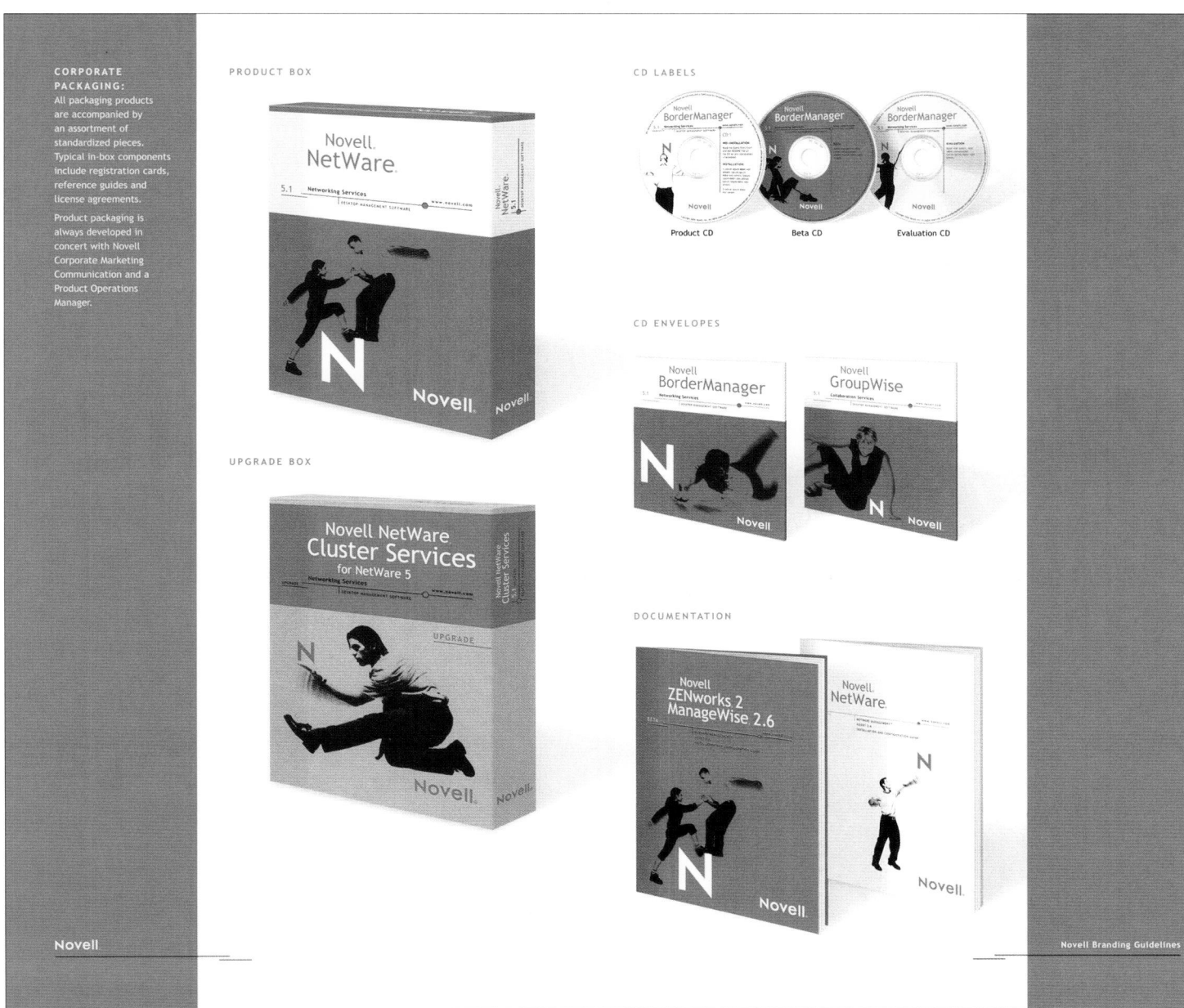

PRODUCT BOX

CD LABELS

Product CD   Beta CD   Evaluation CD

UPGRADE BOX

CD ENVELOPES

DOCUMENTATION

Novell

Novell Branding Guidelines

(continued)
Design Firm **Hornall Anderson Design Works**
Client   *Novell, Inc.*

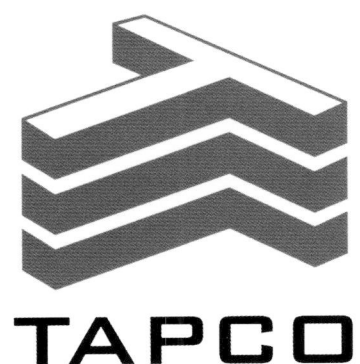

1. TAPCO

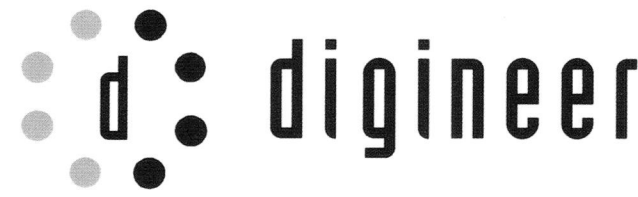

2. digineer

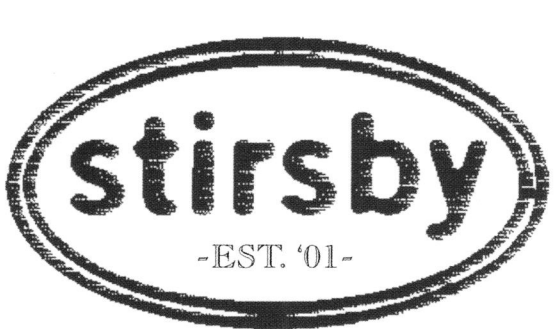

stirsby -EST. '01-

3.

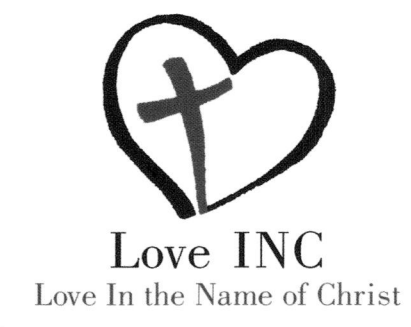

Love INC
Love In the Name of Christ

4.

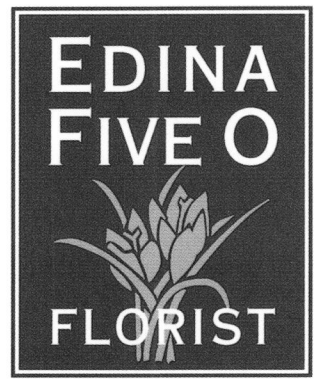

EDINA FIVE O FLORIST

5.

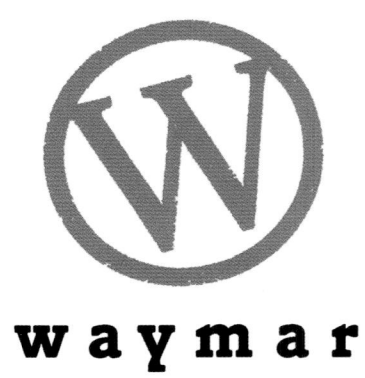

6. waymar

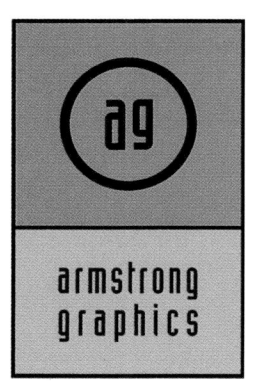

ag armstrong graphics

7.

1 - 7
Design Firm **Armstrong Graphics**
1.
Client *Tapco*
Designer R. Bruce Armstrong
2.
Client *Digineer*
Designer R. Bruce Armstrong
3.
Client *John Danicic*
Designer R. Bruce Armstrong
4.
Client *Love Inc.*
Designer R. Bruce Armstrong
5.
Client *Edina Five-O Florist*
Designer R. Bruce Armstrong

6.
Client *Waymar Restaurant Furniture*
Designer R. Bruce Armstrong
7.
Client *Armstrong Graphics*
Designer R. Bruce Armstrong
(opposite)
Client *Malaysian Institute of Baking*
Design Firm **FGA**
Designers FGA Creative Team

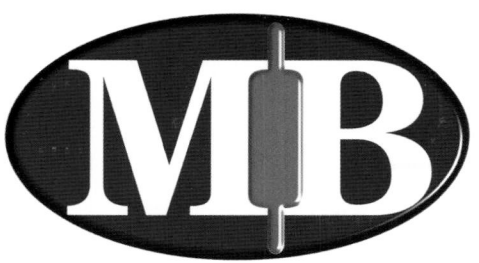

MALAYSIAN INSTITUTE OF BAKING

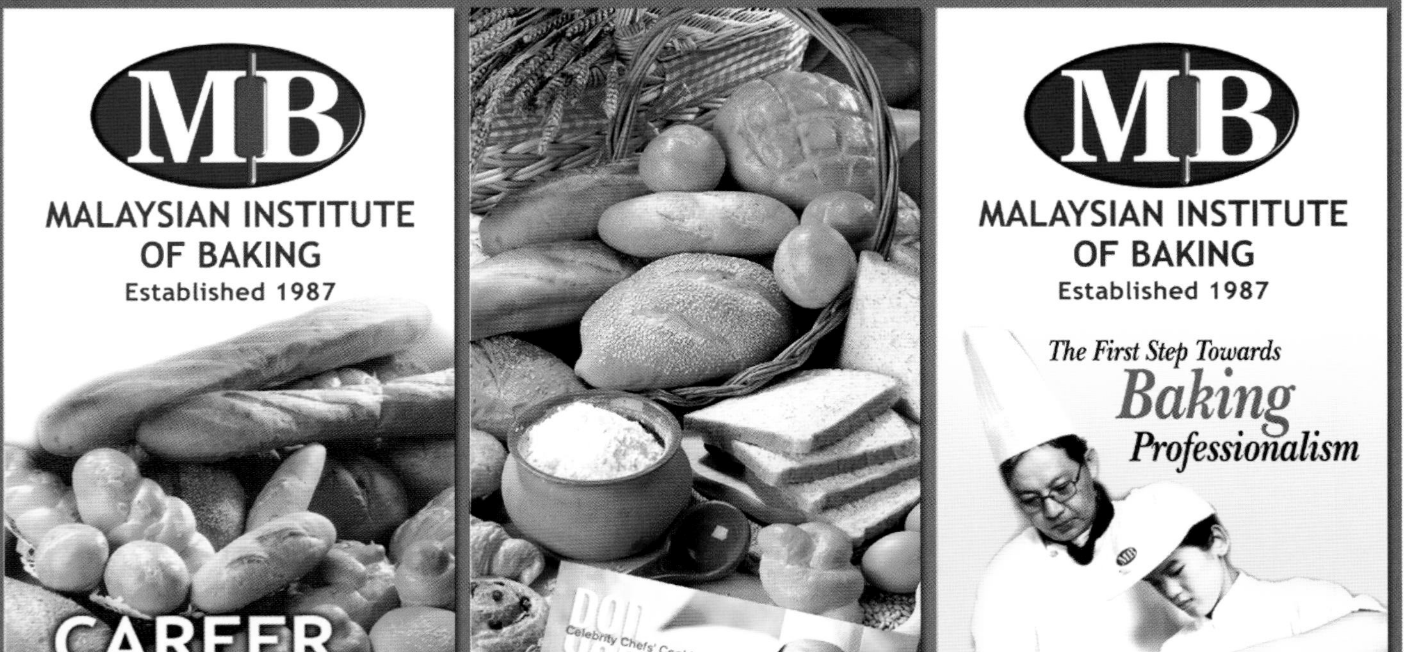

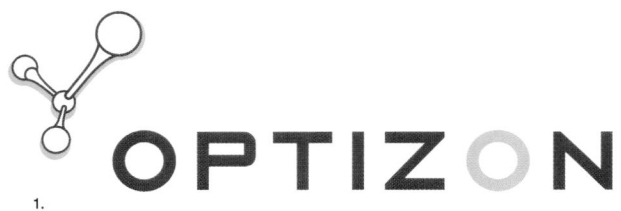

1.

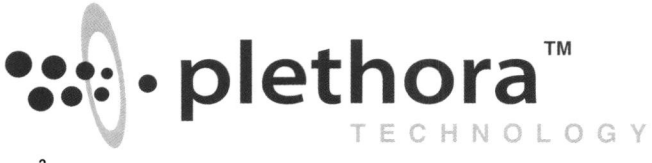

2.

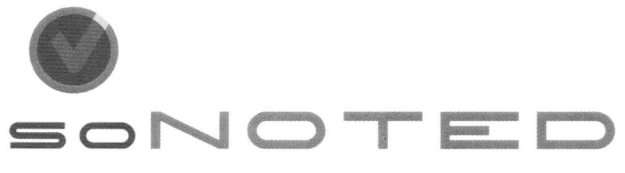

3.

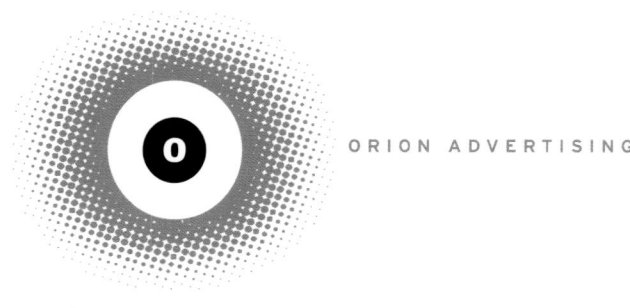

4.

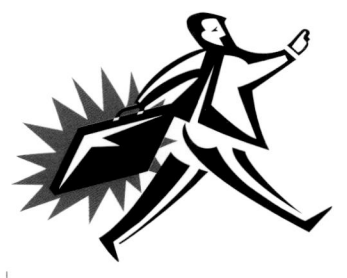

5.

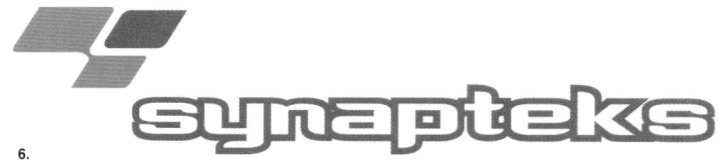

6.

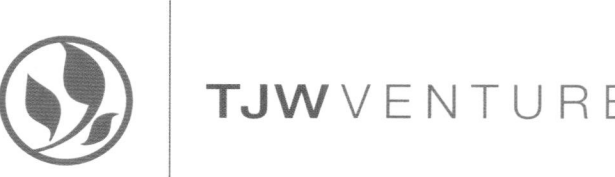

7.

8.

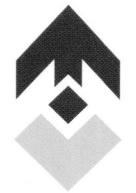

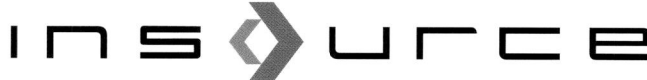

10.

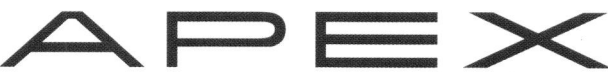

9.

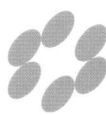

MiND INVENTIONS

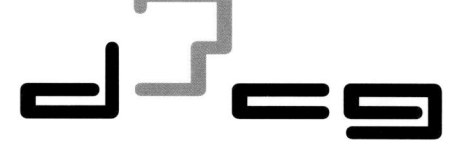

11.

12.

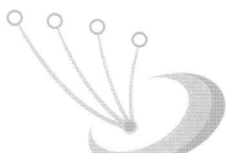

digiVILLage

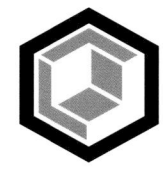 alphainsight

13.

14.

LITECAST

15.

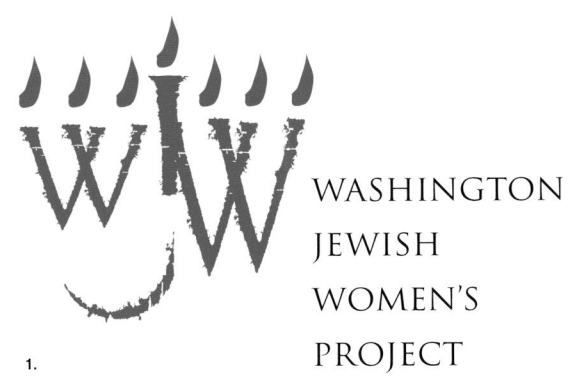

WASHINGTON
JEWISH
WOMEN'S
PROJECT

1.

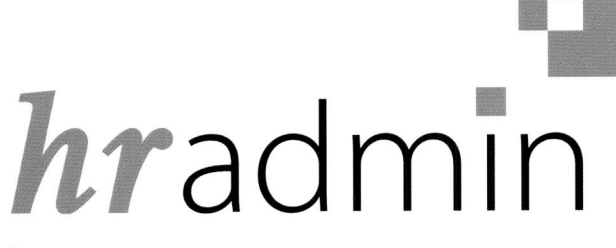

2.

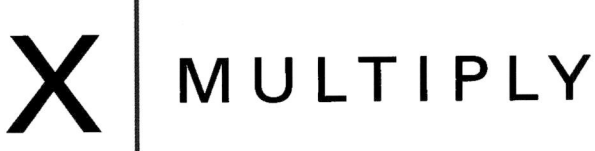

3.

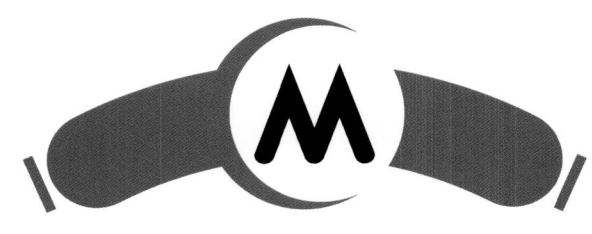

4.

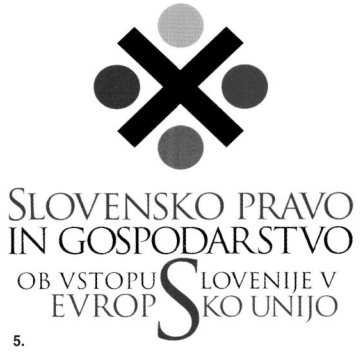

5.

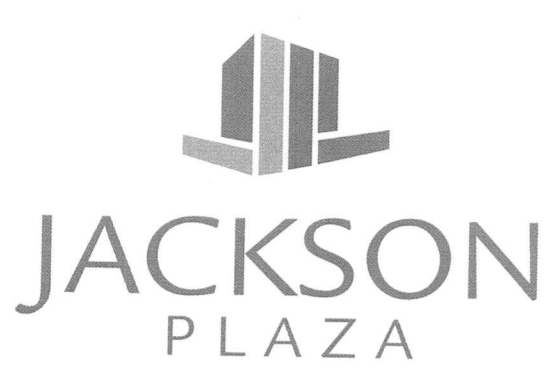

6.

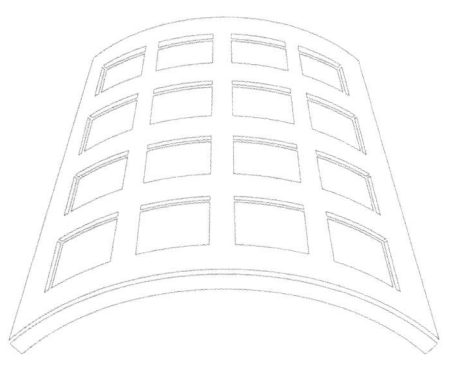

7. MERIDIAN

320

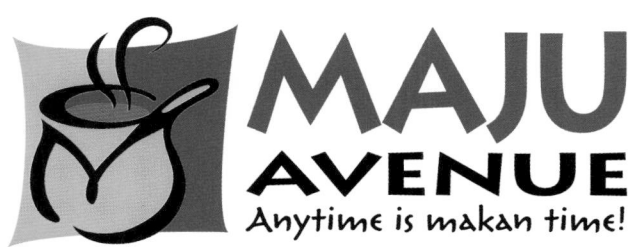

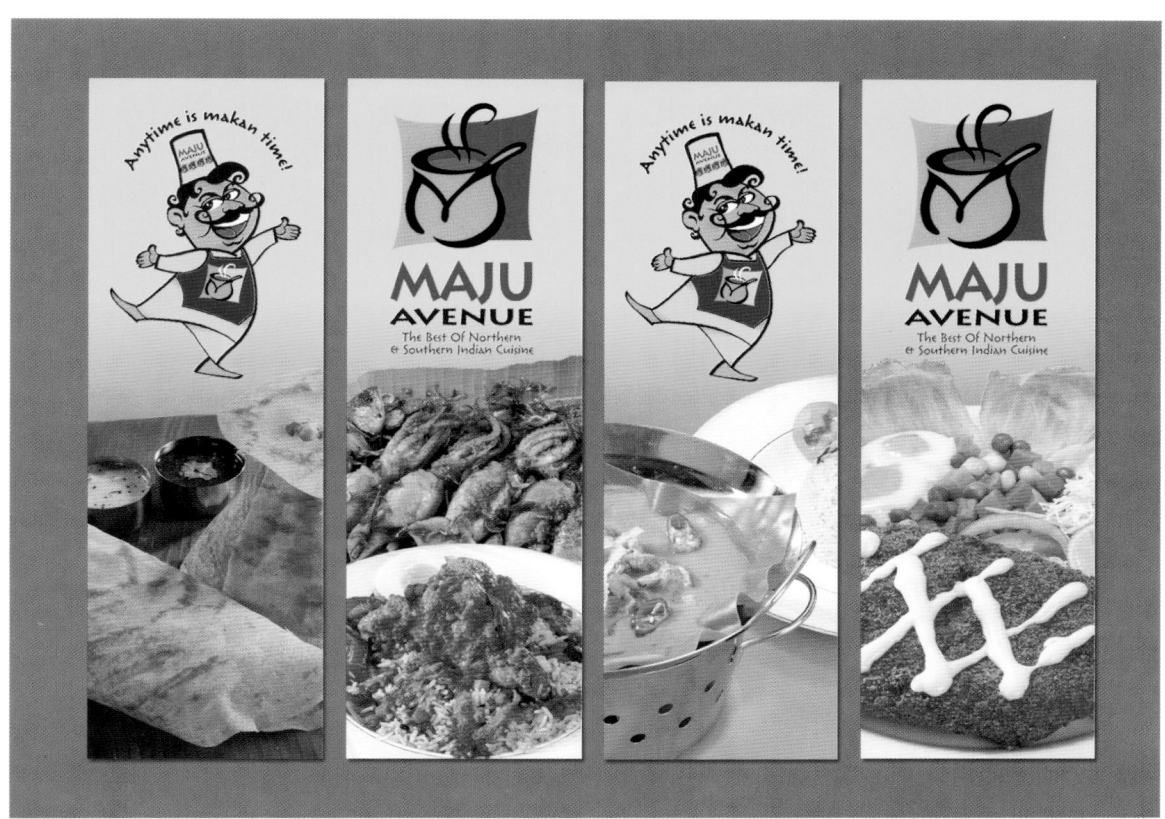

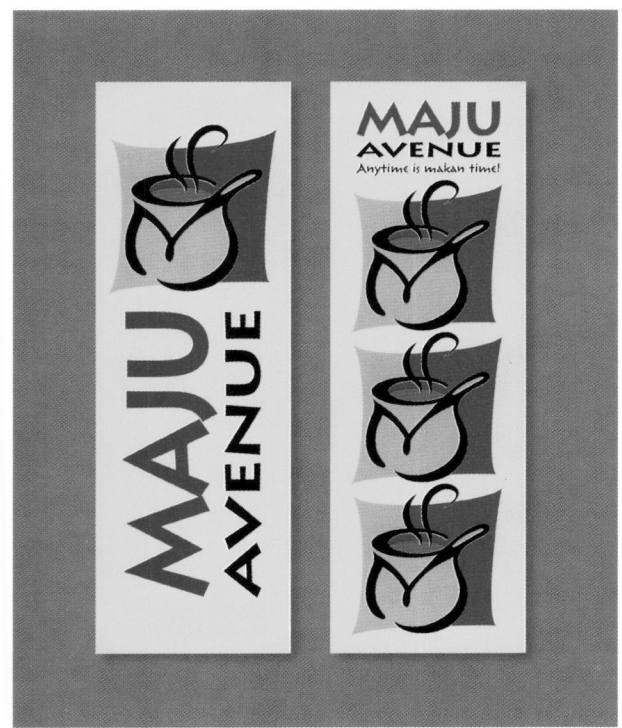

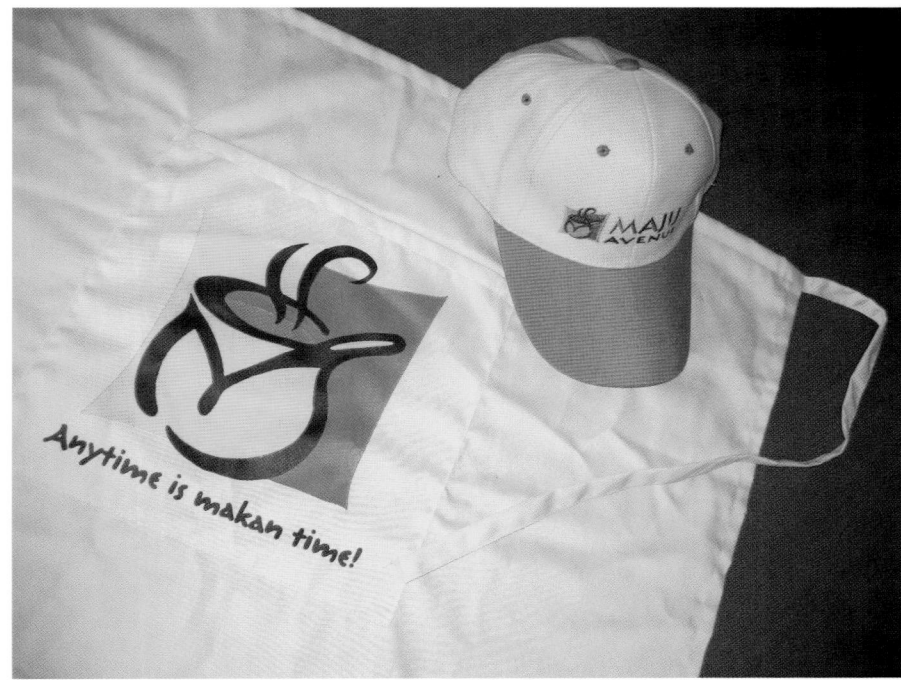

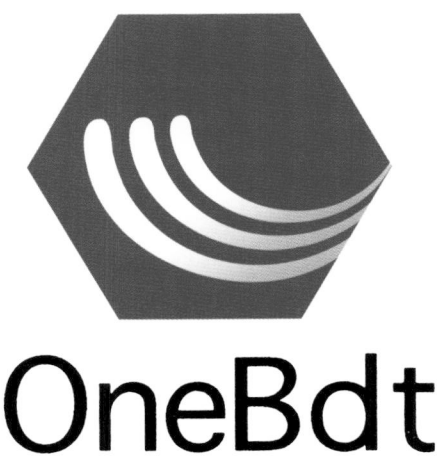

OneBdt

Design Firm **Longwater & Co., Inc.**
Client *One Bolt, Inc.*
Designers Kathryn Strozier,
Elaine Longwater,
Anastasia Kontos

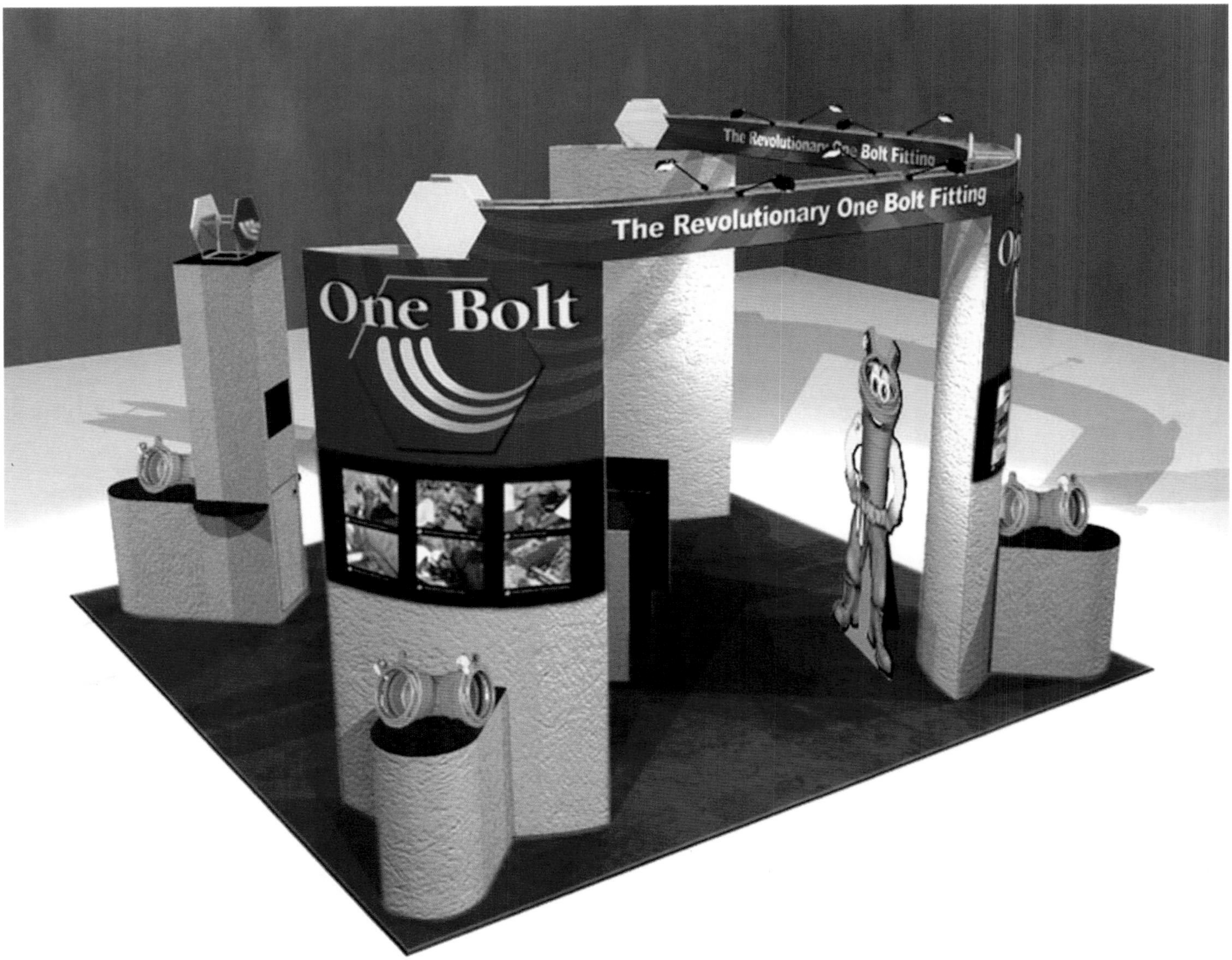

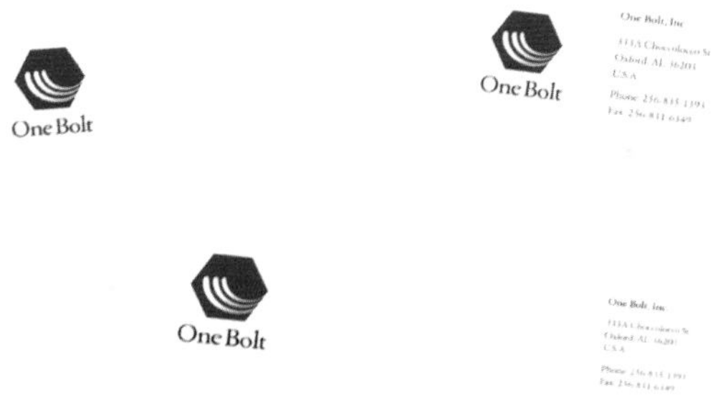

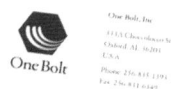

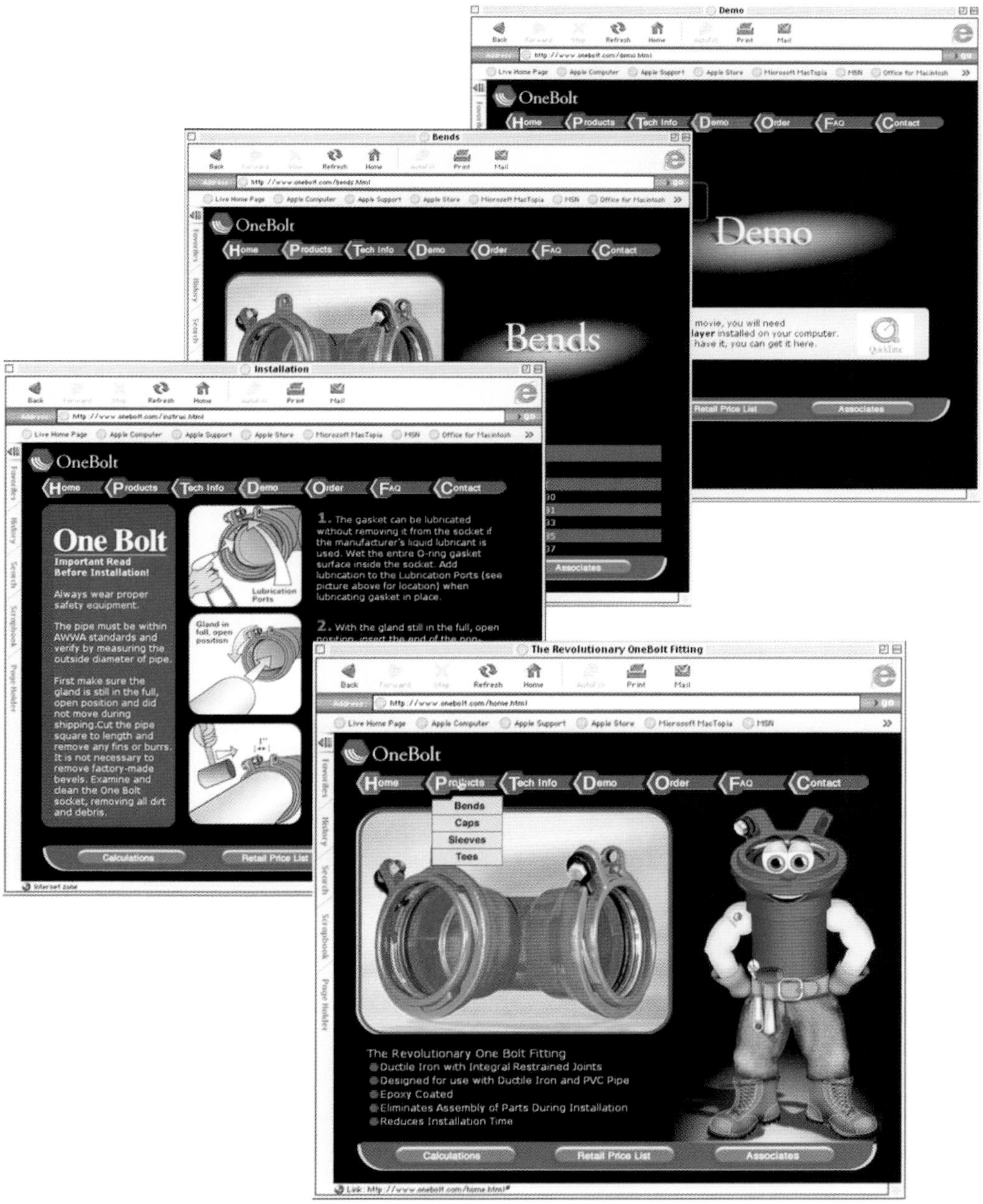

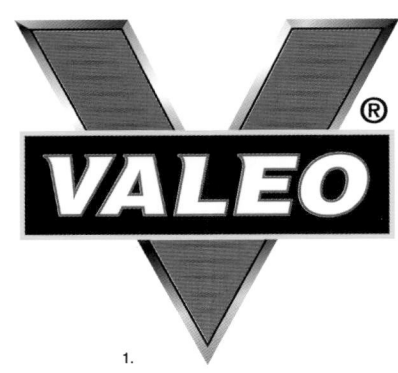

1.

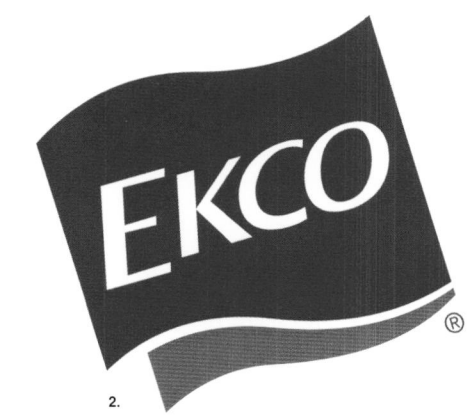

2.

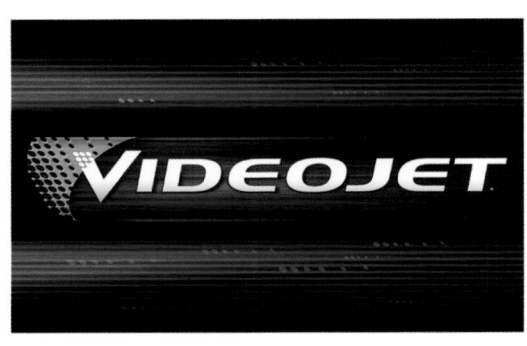

3.

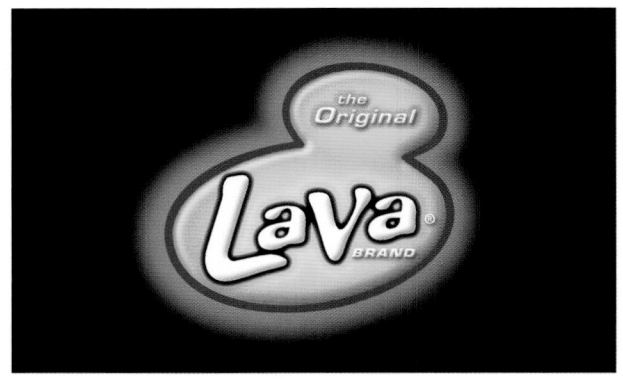

4.

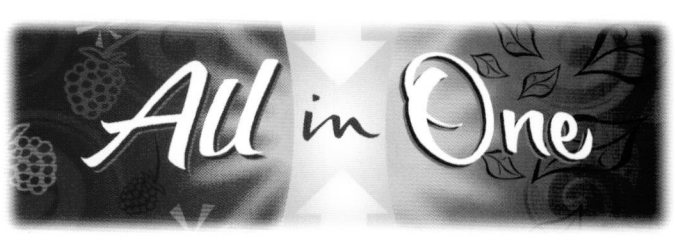

5.

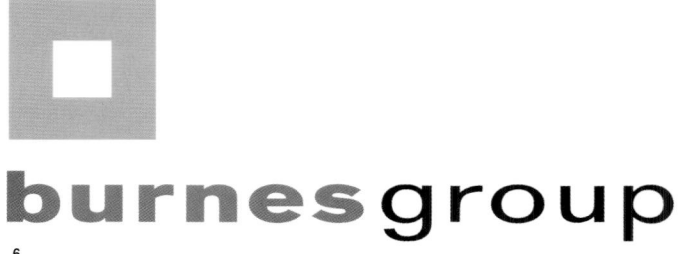

6.

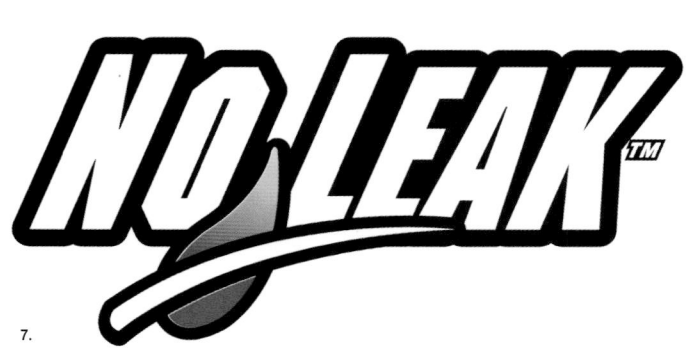

7.

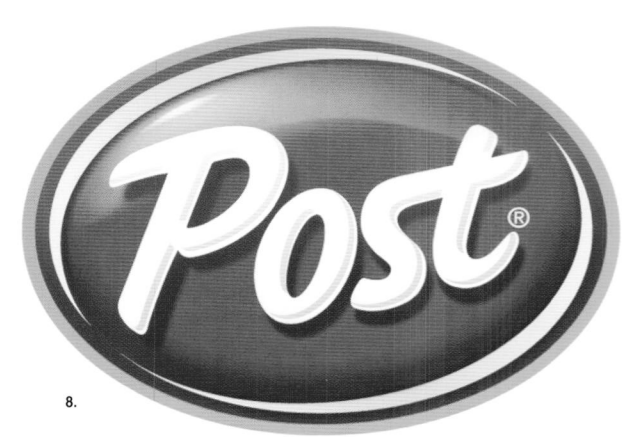

8.

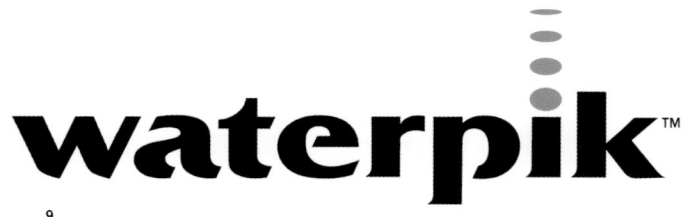

9.

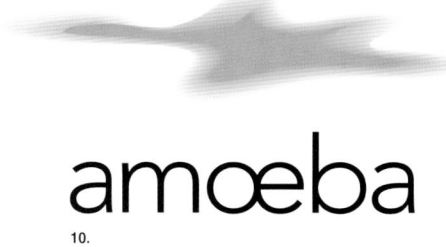

10.

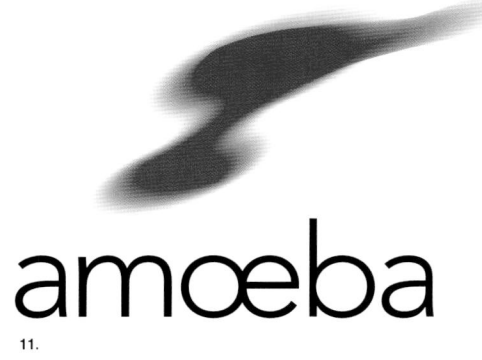

11.

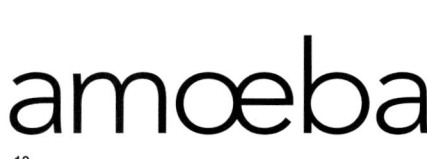

12.

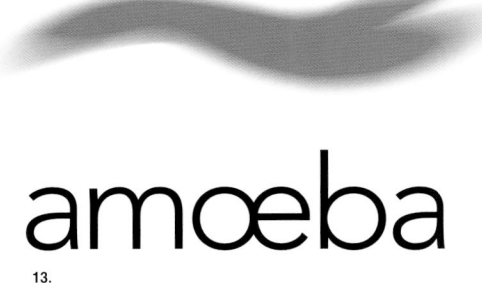

13.

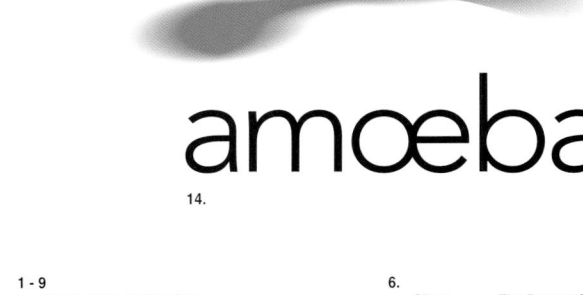

14.

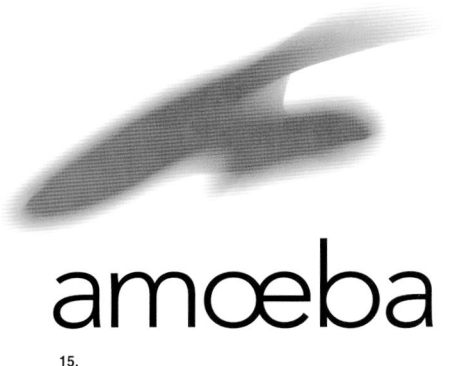

15.

1 - 9
Design Firm **Source/Inc.**
10 - 15
Design Firm **Bright Strategic Design**

1.
   Client   *Valeo, Inc.*
   Designers Susan Hartline, Sarrah Trembley, Bernie Dolph, Mike Nicholson

2.
   Client   *World Kitchen Inc.*
   Designers Sabrina Chan, Adrienne Nole, Mike Nicholson

3.
   Client   *Videojet Technologies*
   Designers Scott Burns, Mike Nicholson

4.
   Client   *Haggerty Enterprises*
   Designers Sabrina Chan, Adrienne Nole, Mike Nicholson

5.
   Client   *Chatlem, Inc.*
   Designers Mike Nicholson, Bernie Dolph

6.
   Client   *The Burnes Group*
   Designers Adrienne Nole, Mike Nicholson

7.
   Client   *Gold Eagle Co.*
   Designers Scott Burns, Mike Nicholson

8.
   Client   *Kraft Foods Inc.*
   Designers Scott Burns, Adam Ferguson, Mike Nicholson, Michael Bast

9.
   Client   *Waterpik Technologies*
   Designers Sabrina Chan, Adrienne Nole, Mike Nicholson

10 - 15.
   Client   *Amoeba*
   Designers Keith Bright, Glenn Sakamoto

1.

Adaptis

2.

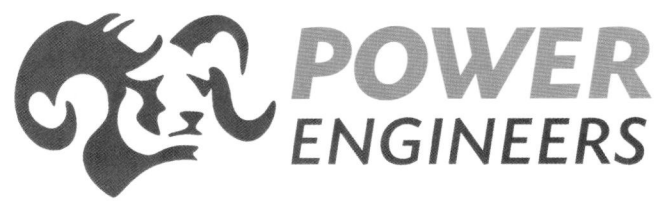

POWER
ENGINEERS

3.

Nesting Bird

4.

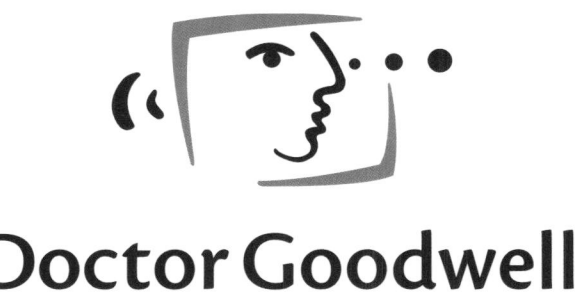

Doctor Goodwell

5.

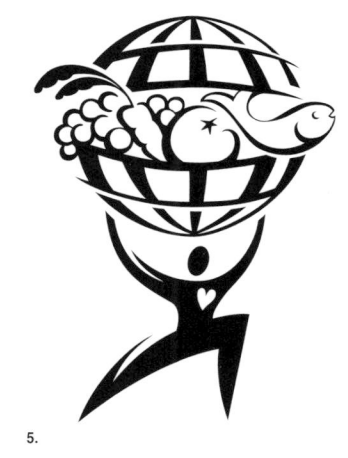

6.

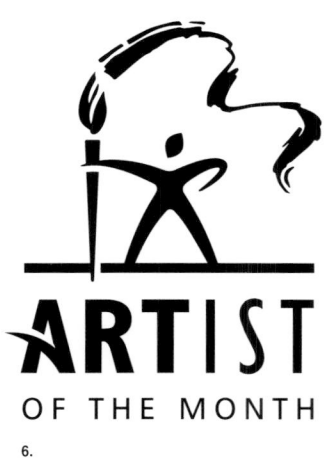

ARTIST
OF THE MONTH

7.

Captaris

8.

VERITY
CREDIT UNION

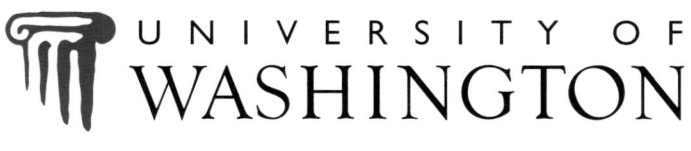

9.

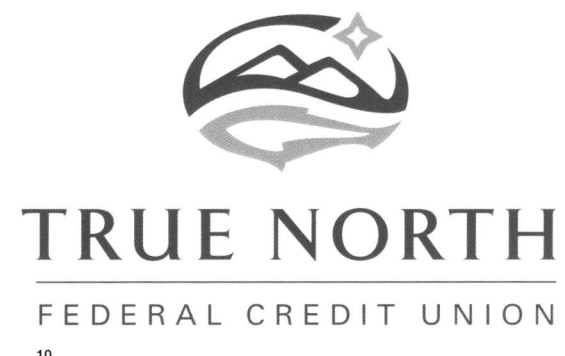

10.

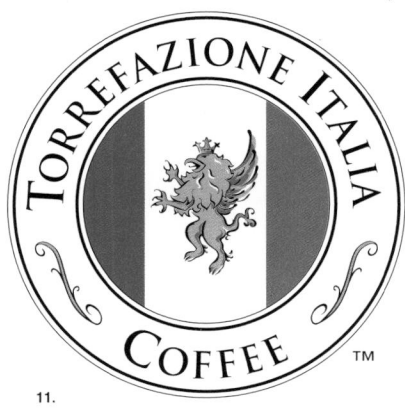

11.

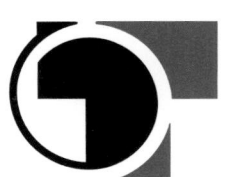

12.

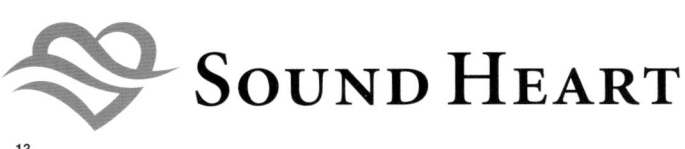

13.

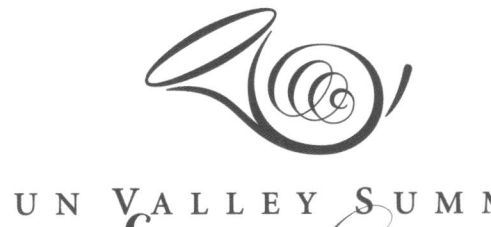

14.

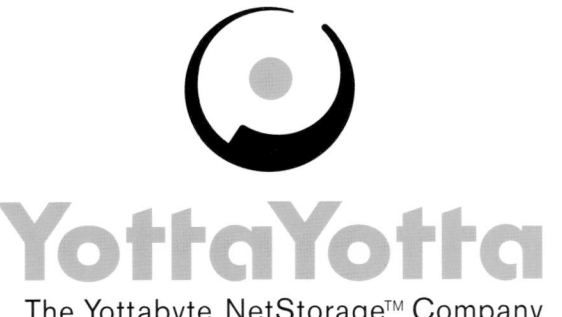

15.

1 - 15
Design Firm **Phinney/Bischoff Design House**
1.
   Client   *Adaptis*
   Designer   Brian Buckner
2.
   Client   *Power Engineers, Inc.*
   Designer   Cody Rasmussen
3.
   Client   *Nesting Bird*
   Designer   Dean Hart
4.
   Client   *Doctor Goodwell*
   Designers   Dean Hart, Lorie Ransom
5.
   Client   *Children's Hospital Seattle*
   Designer   Cody Rasmussen
6.
   Client   *Children's Hospital Seattle*
   Designer   Lorie Ransom
7.
   Client   *Captaris*
   Designer   Dean Hart

8.
   Client   *Verity Credit Union*
   Designer   Cody Rasmussen
9.
   Client   *University of Washington*
   Designer   Lorie Ransom
10.
   Client   *True North Federal Credit Union*
   Designer   Lorie Ransom
11.
   Client   *Torrefazione Italia*
   Designers   Dean Hart, Brian Buckner
12.
   Client   *Tela*
   Designer   Lorie Ransom
13.
   Client   *Sound Heart*
   Designer   Dean Hart
14.
   Client   *Sun Valley Summer Symphony*
   Designer   Dean Hart
15.
   Client   *Yotta Yotta*
   Designer   Cody Rasmussen

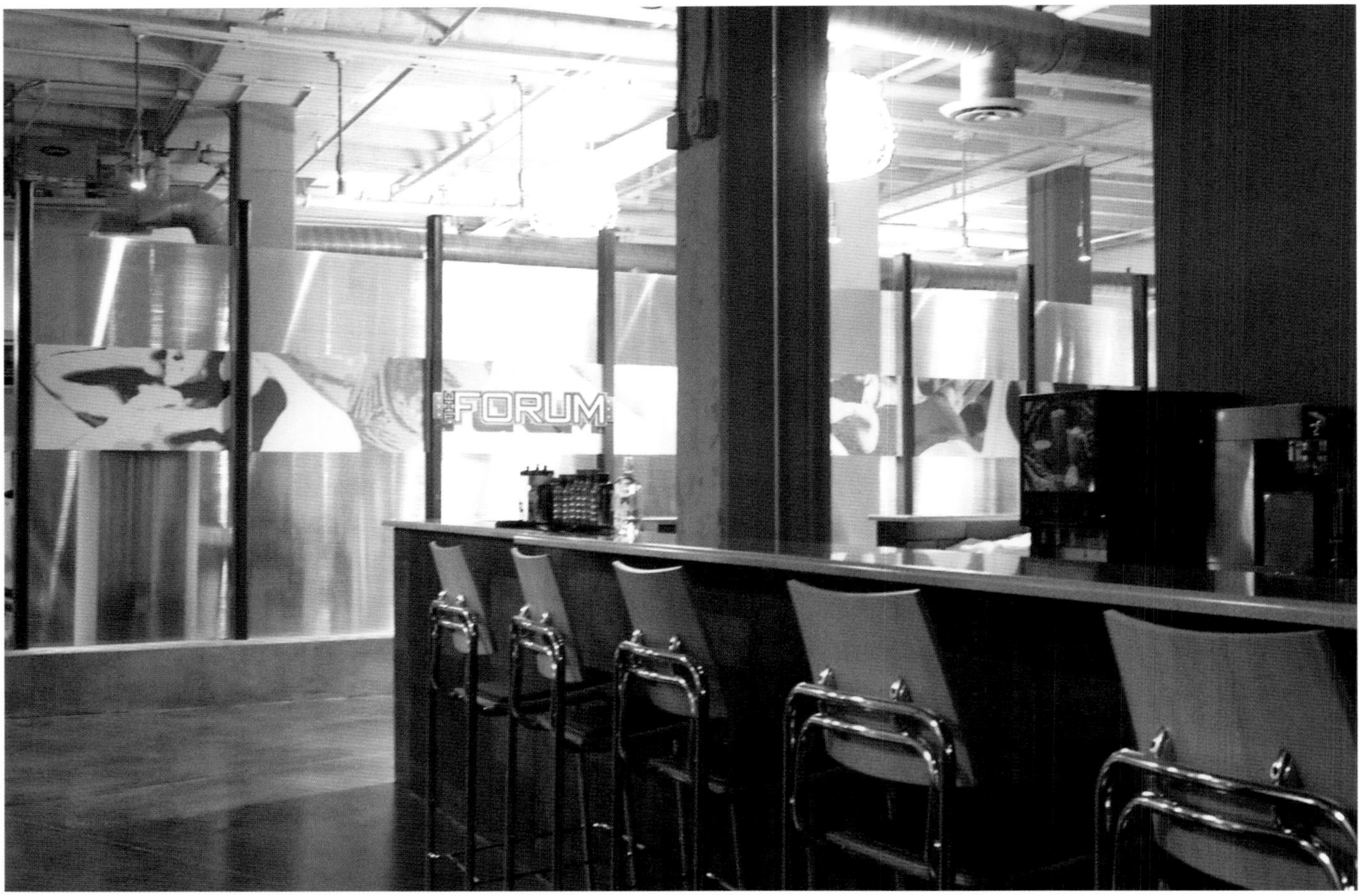
FORUM
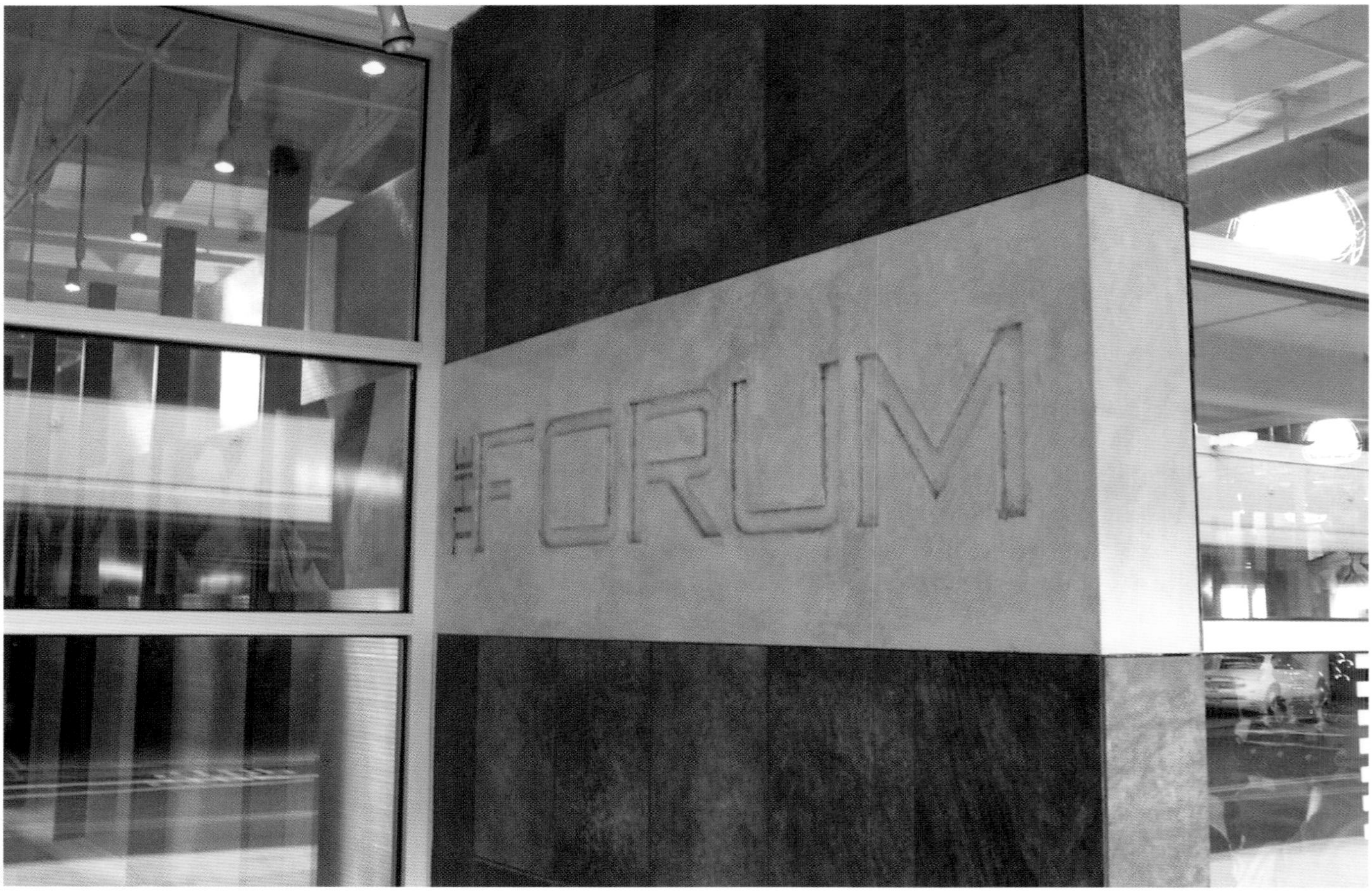
THE FORUM

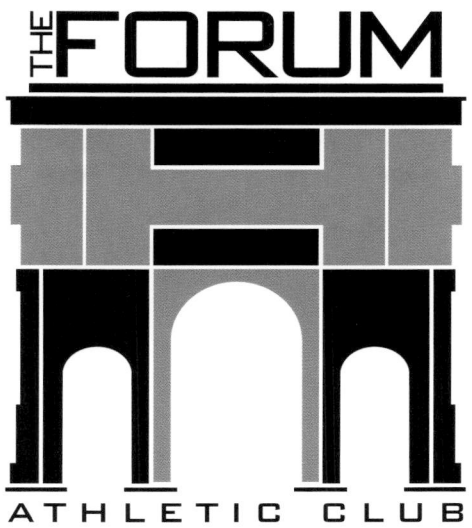

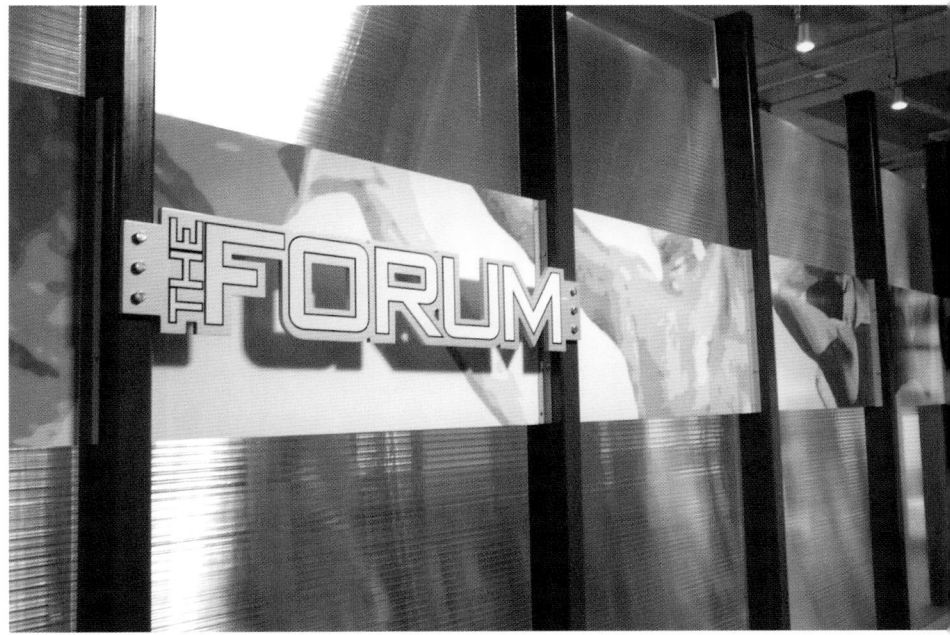

Design Firm **Sky Design**
Client *The Forum*
Designers W. Todd Vaught,
Celie Goforth

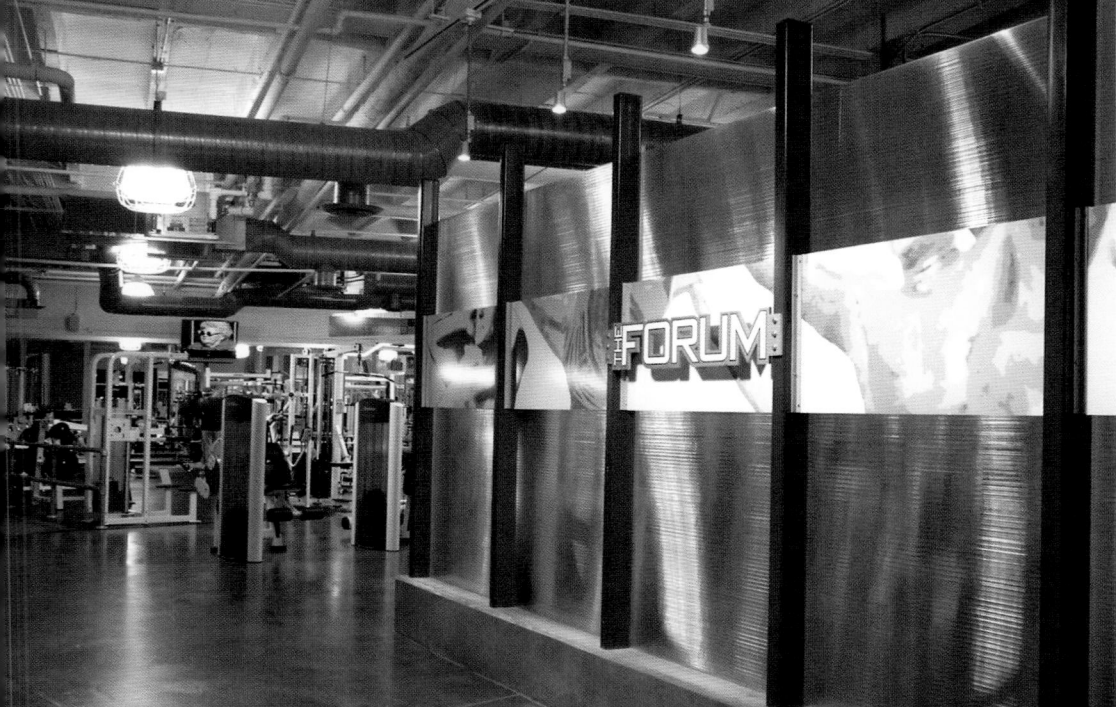

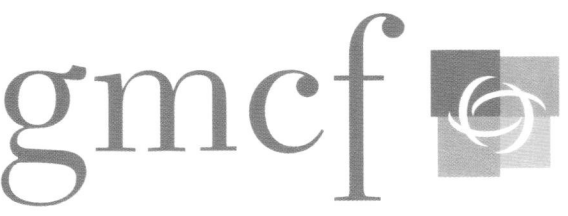

1.

MEADOWS, ICHTER & BOWERS
ATTORNEYS AT LAW

2.

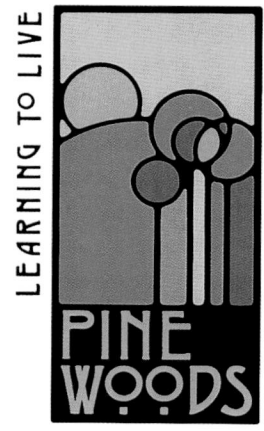

3.

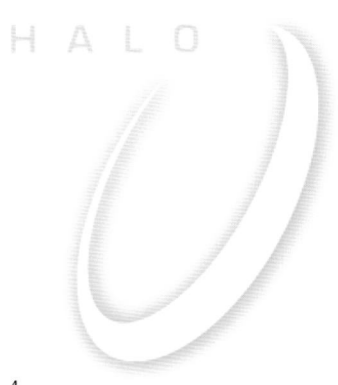

4.

greenHOUSE

5.

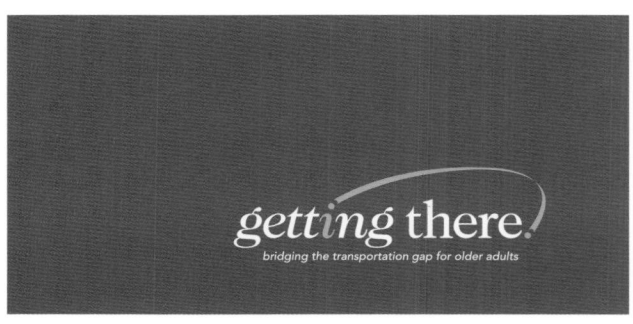

6.

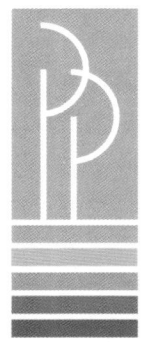

PENTERRA PLAZA

7.

1 - 4
Design Firm **Sky Design**
5 - 7
Design Firm **Noble Erickson Inc.**
1.
 Client *Georgia Medical Care Foundation*
 Designers Celie Goforth, W. Todd Vaught,
     Carrie Brown
2.
 Client *Meadows, Ichter & Bowers*
 Designers W. Todd Vaught, Matt Worsham
3.
 Client *Pinewoods*
 Designers W. Todd Vaught,
     Carrie Brown
4.
 Client *Halo*
 Designers W. Todd Vaught,
     Thom Williams

5.
 Client *Zeppelin Development*
 Designer Jackie Noble
6.
 Client *The Rose Foundation*
 Designer Robin Ridley
7.
 Client *Simpson Housing*
 Designers Steven Erickson, Jackie Noble,
     Robin Ridley
(opposite)
 Client *DataPeer, Inc.*
 Design Firm **Design Source East**
 Designer Mark Lo Bello

power^{2}sync

Powered by DataPeer, Inc.

power^{2}share

Powered by DataPeer, Inc.

power^{2}search

Powered by DataPeer, Inc.

power^{2}network

Powered by DataPeer, Inc.

power^{2}store

Powered by DataPeer, Inc.

power^{2}host

Powered by DataPeer, Inc.

power^{2}protect

Powered by DataPeer, Inc.

power^{2}govern

Powered by DataPeer, Inc.

power^{2}educate

Powered by DataPeer, Inc.

power^{2}profit

Powered by DataPeer, Inc.

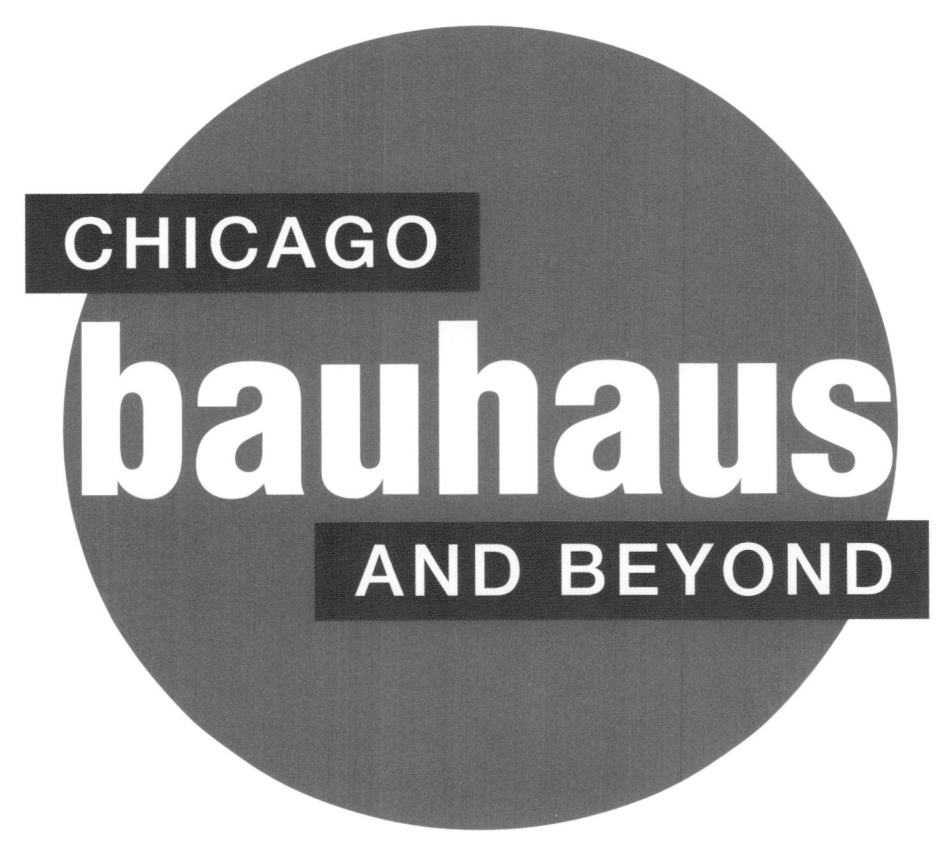

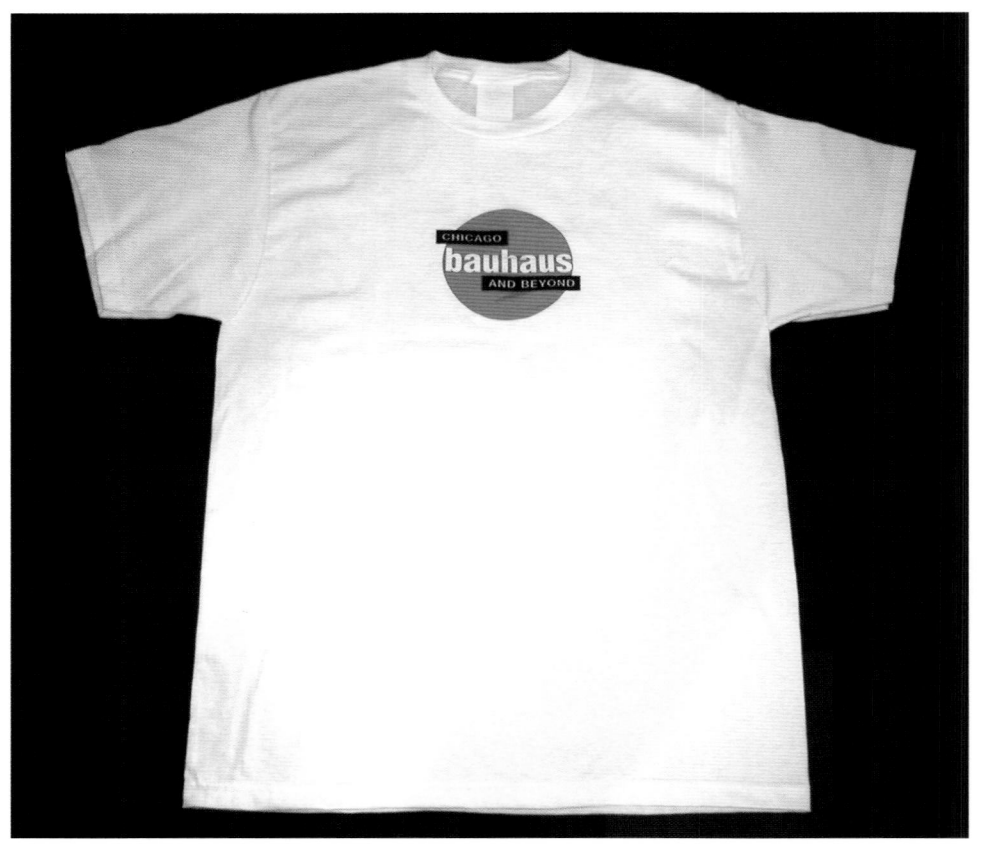

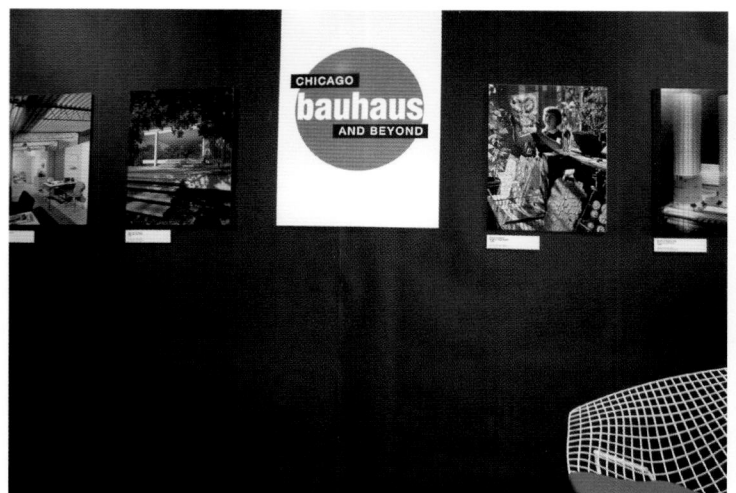

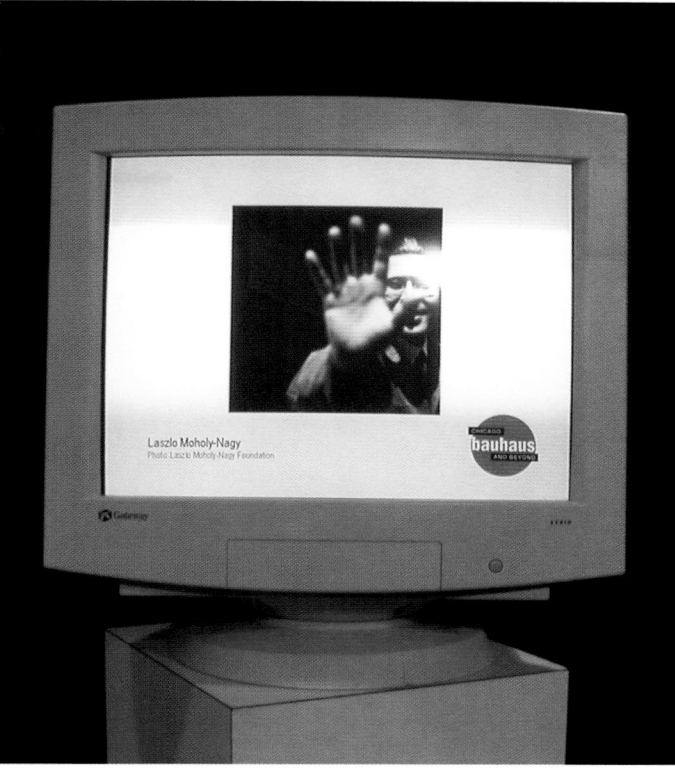

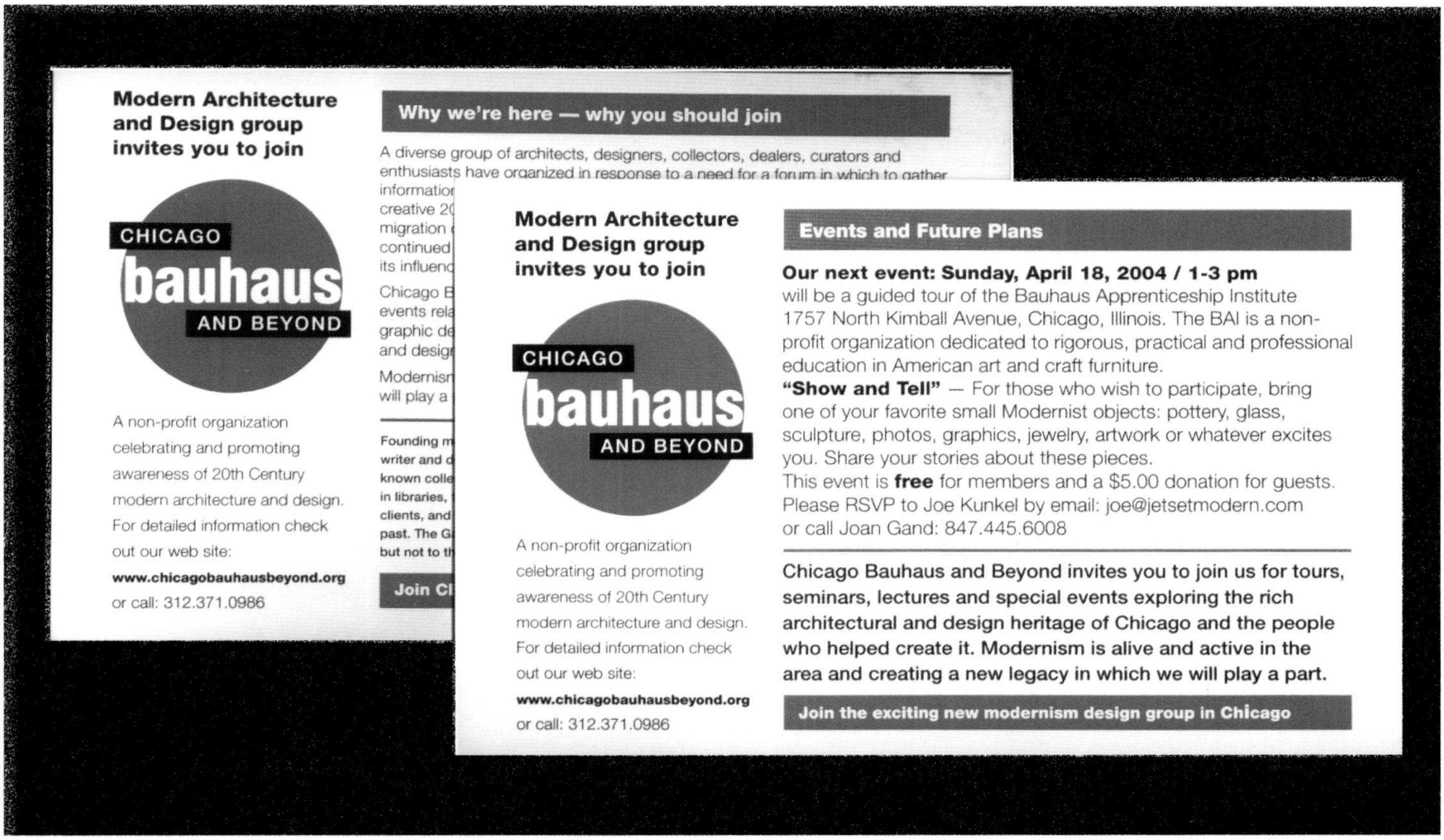

Modern Architecture and Design group invites you to join

Why we're here — why you should join

A diverse group of architects, designers, collectors, dealers, curators and enthusiasts have organized in response to a need for a forum in which to gather information...
creative 20...
migration...
continued...
its influenc...

Chicago B...
events rel...
graphic de...
and desig...

Modernism...
will play a...

Founding m...
writer and d...
known colle...
in libraries,...
clients, and...
past. The G...
but not to th...

Join Cl...

A non-profit organization celebrating and promoting awareness of 20th Century modern architecture and design. For detailed information check out our web site:

www.chicagobauhausbeyond.org
or call: 312.371.0986

Modern Architecture and Design group invites you to join

A non-profit organization celebrating and promoting awareness of 20th Century modern architecture and design. For detailed information check out our web site:

www.chicagobauhausbeyond.org
or call: 312.371.0986

Events and Future Plans

Our next event: Sunday, April 18, 2004 / 1-3 pm
will be a guided tour of the Bauhaus Apprenticeship Institute 1757 North Kimball Avenue, Chicago, Illinois. The BAI is a non-profit organization dedicated to rigorous, practical and professional education in American art and craft furniture.
"Show and Tell" — For those who wish to participate, bring one of your favorite small Modernist objects: pottery, glass, sculpture, photos, graphics, jewelry, artwork or whatever excites you. Share your stories about these pieces.
This event is **free** for members and a $5.00 donation for guests. Please RSVP to Joe Kunkel by email: joe@jetsetmodern.com or call Joan Gand: 847.445.6008

Chicago Bauhaus and Beyond invites you to join us for tours, seminars, lectures and special events exploring the rich architectural and design heritage of Chicago and the people who helped create it. Modernism is alive and active in the area and creating a new legacy in which we will play a part.

Join the exciting new modernism design group in Chicago

Design Firm **Allen Porter Design**
Client   *Chicago Bauhaus*
           and Beyond
Designer   Allen Porter

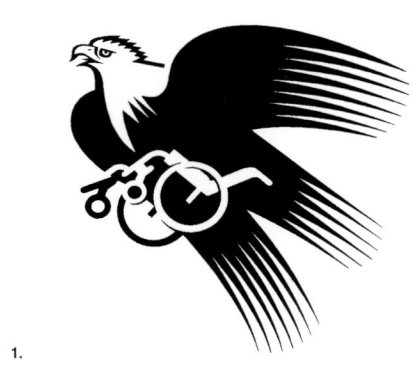

1.

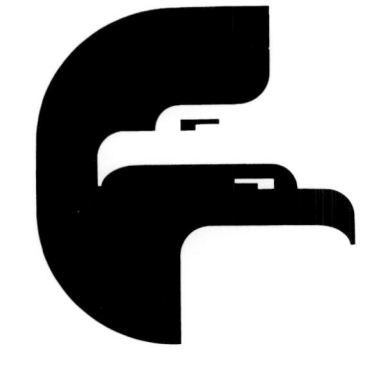

2.

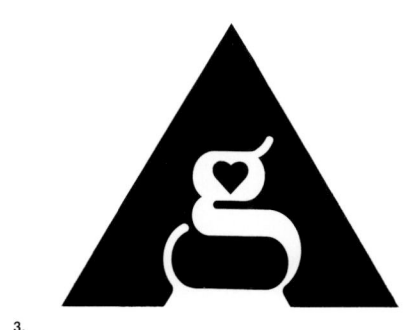

3.

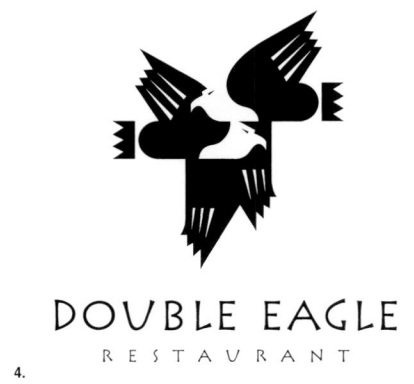

DOUBLE EAGLE
RESTAURANT

4.

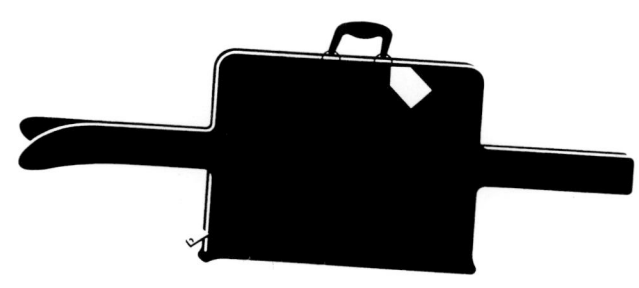

5.

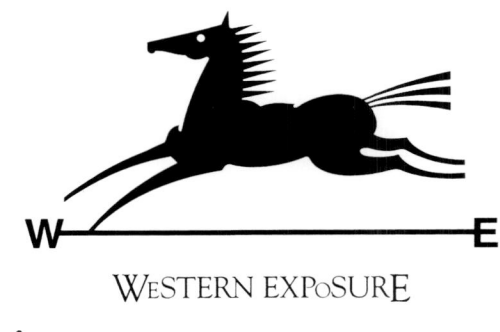

W————————E

WESTERN EXPOSURE

6.

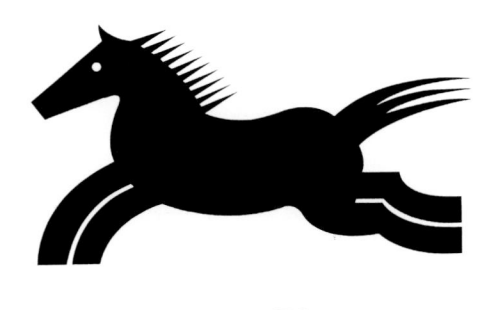

Polo Ridge
F A R M S

7.

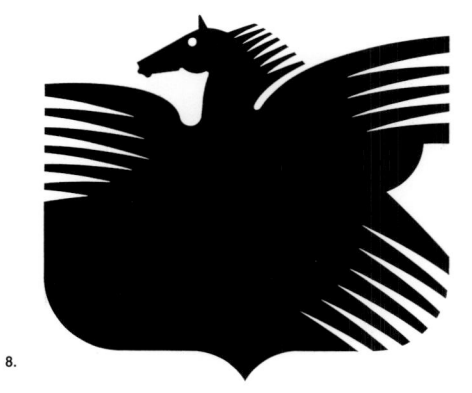

8.

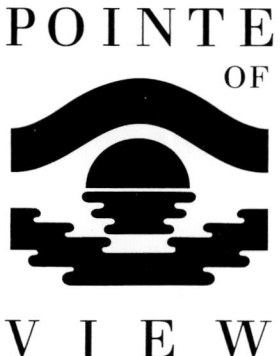

POINTE

OF

VIEW

9.

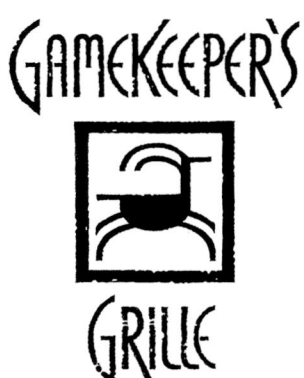

GAMEKEEPER'S

GRILLE

10.

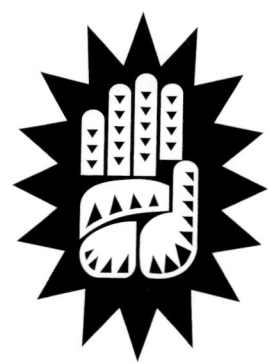

11.

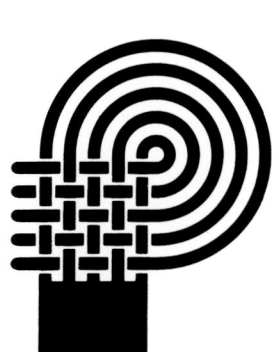

12.

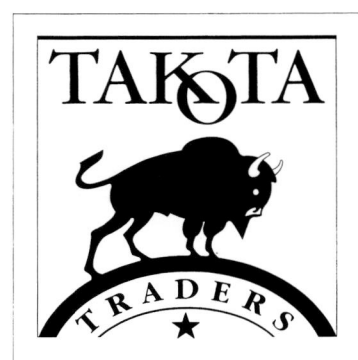

TAKOTA

TRADERS

13.

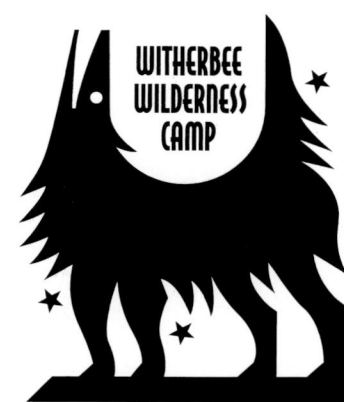

WITHERBEE WILDERNESS CAMP

15.

14. **ROCKY MOUNTAIN BAIL BONDS**

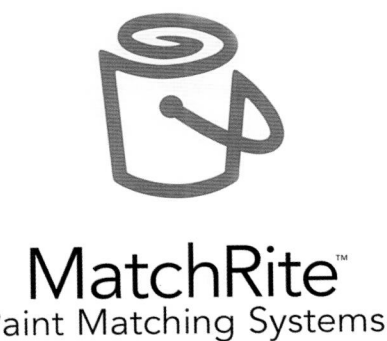

MatchRite™
Paint Matching Systems

1.

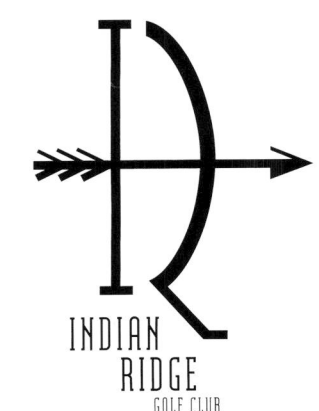

INDIAN RIDGE
GOLF CLUB

2.

Partner

3.

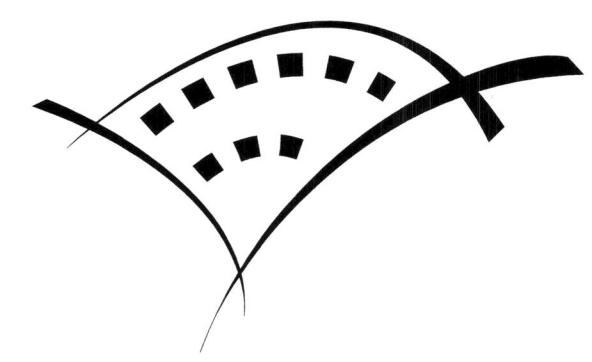

4.

Jewelry

5.

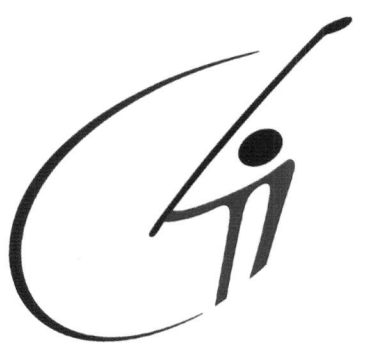

6.

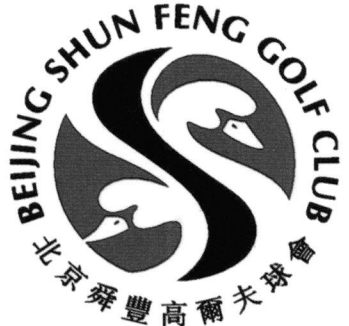

7.

1			**3.**	
Design Firm	**Square One Design**		Client	*Slovenska Knjiga, Ljubljana*
2			Designer	Edi Berk
Design Firm	**Peg Faimon Design**		**4.**	
3			Client	*The Asian American Institute*
Design Firm	**KROG**		Designer	Andrea Polli
4			**5.**	
Design Firm	**Robert Morris College Institute**		Client	*Joanna Jewelry, Inc.*
	of Art and Design		Designer	David Chiow
5			**6.**	
Design Firm	**Cube Advertising & Design**		Client	*Alfred Dunhill*
6, 7			Designer	William C.K. Ho
Design Firm	**William Ho Design Associates**		**7.**	
	Ltd.		Client	*Shun Feng Golf Club*
1.			Designer	William C.K. Ho
Client	*X-Rite*		**(opposite)**	
Designers	Yolanda Gonzaez,		Client	*Johnny Rockets*
	Lin Ver Meulen		Design Firm	**Northten, Inc.**
2.			Designers	Sandi Ciz,
Client	*Indian Ridge Golf Club*			Kevin Favell
Designer	Peg Faimon			

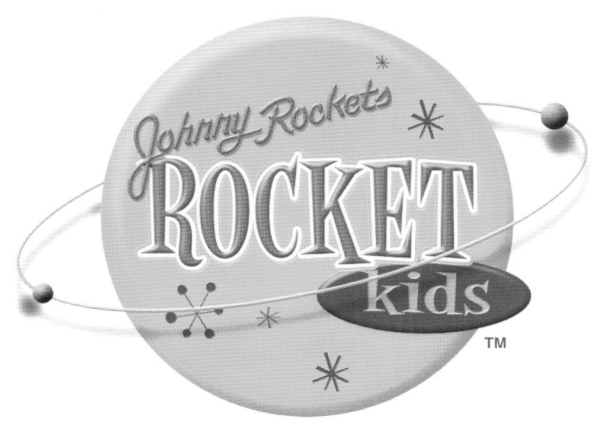

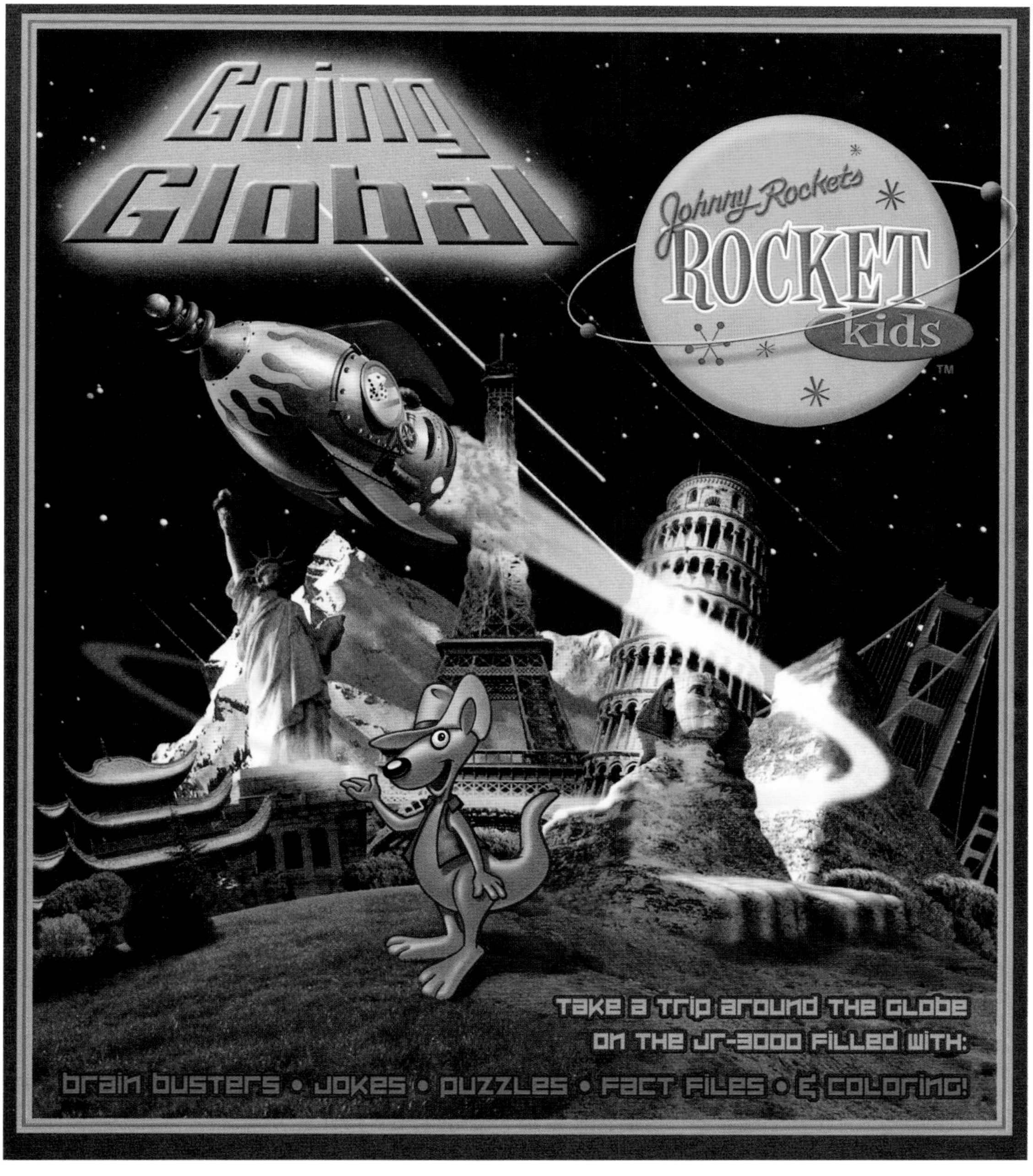

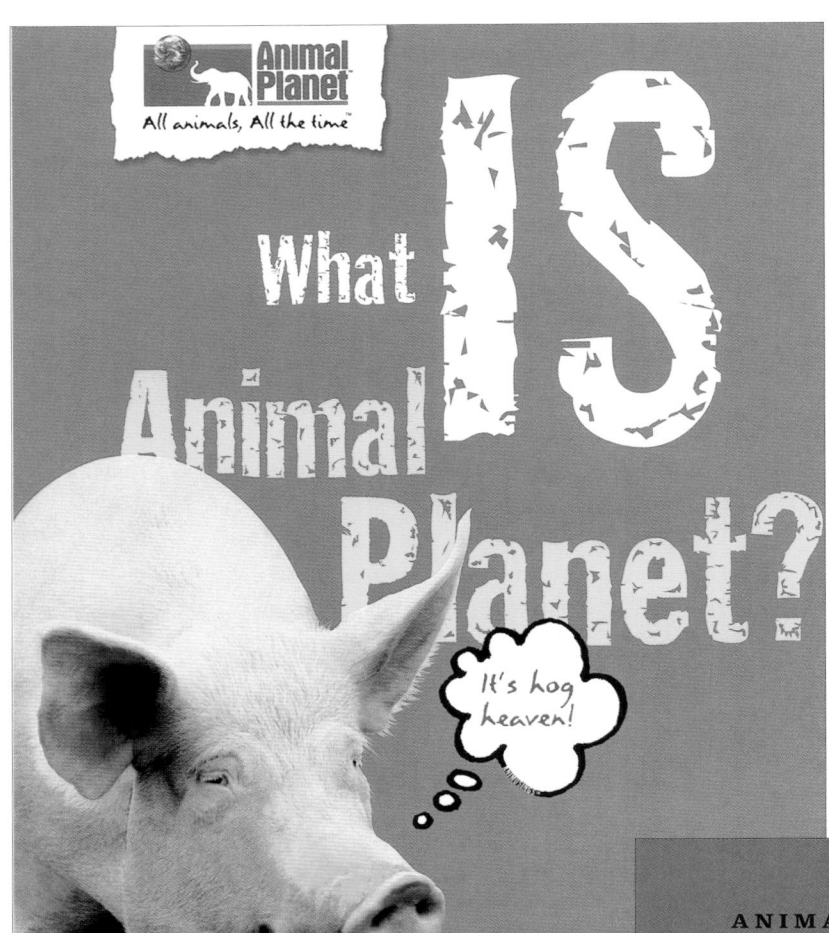

Client   *Animal Planet*
Design Firm   **Animal Planet**

Patterns

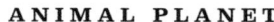

The most striking

artistic patterns

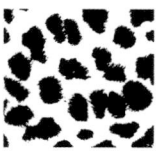 DALMATIAN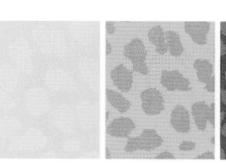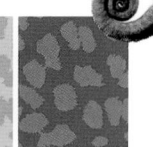

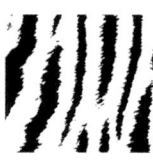 TIGER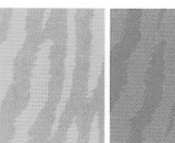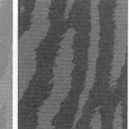

 CHEETAH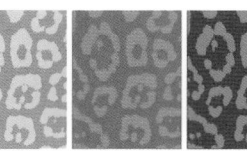

GIRAFFE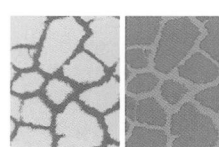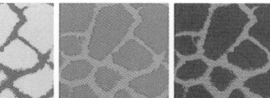

Silhouetting

To focus attention on the animal rather than its habitat, remove the backgrounds from photographs whenever practical.

Use sharp, crisp photographs that silhouette cleanly.

Do it right—or there will be consequences. Trust me!

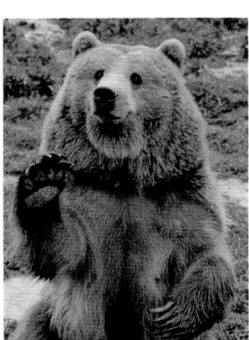

Before:
The background distracts from the star of the show.

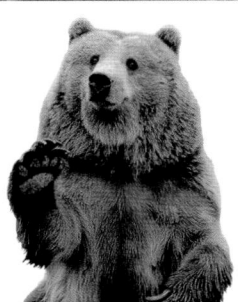

After:
By removing the background, attention is focused on the animal.

IMAGE DON'TS

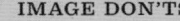

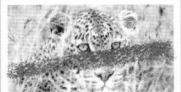
Don't use complicated images. They should be well defined and easy to silhouette. If you must include a background, keep it simple.

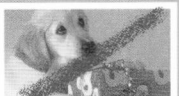
Don't use images that look posed or premeditated. Animal Planet images should be full of character and expression.

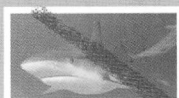
Don't use images of expressionless animals. It's difficult, for example, to get a good sense of the personality of a shark.

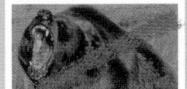
Don't use aggressive or ferocious images.

3.5

Mix and match colors and patterns to produce interesting combinations beyond what is found in nature. Be sure to use stylized colors to avoid anything looking like actual fur.

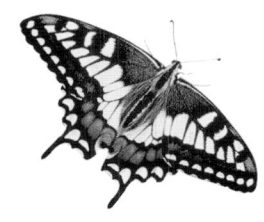

are inspired by animals

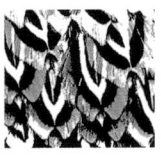

BIRD

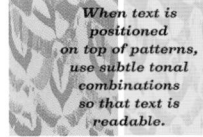

When text is positioned on top of patterns, use subtle tonal combinations so that text is readable.

COW

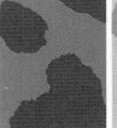 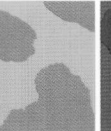 

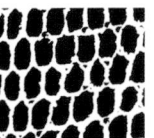

REPTILE

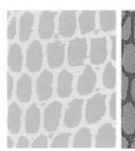 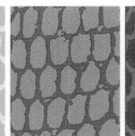 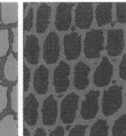

ZEBRA

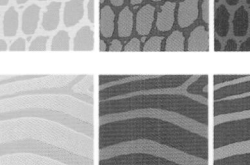

3.9

(continued)
Client   *Animal Planet*
Design Firm **Animal Planet**

ANIMAL PLANET Animusings™

Thought balloons containing Animusings™ should be drawn to resemble soft, puffy clouds with a trail of three bubbles, descending in size, leading to the animal.

And remember, these are thought balloons...animals don't speak.

The use of these thought balloons helps humans to better understand OUR way of thinking.

ANIMUSINGS™

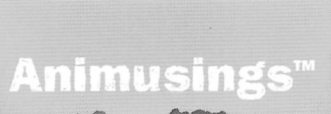

Samples of Animusings artwork can be downloaded from the Virtual Library.

3.11

(opposite)
Client   *TrueFACES*
Design Firm **TrueFACES Creation**
Designer   Allen Tan

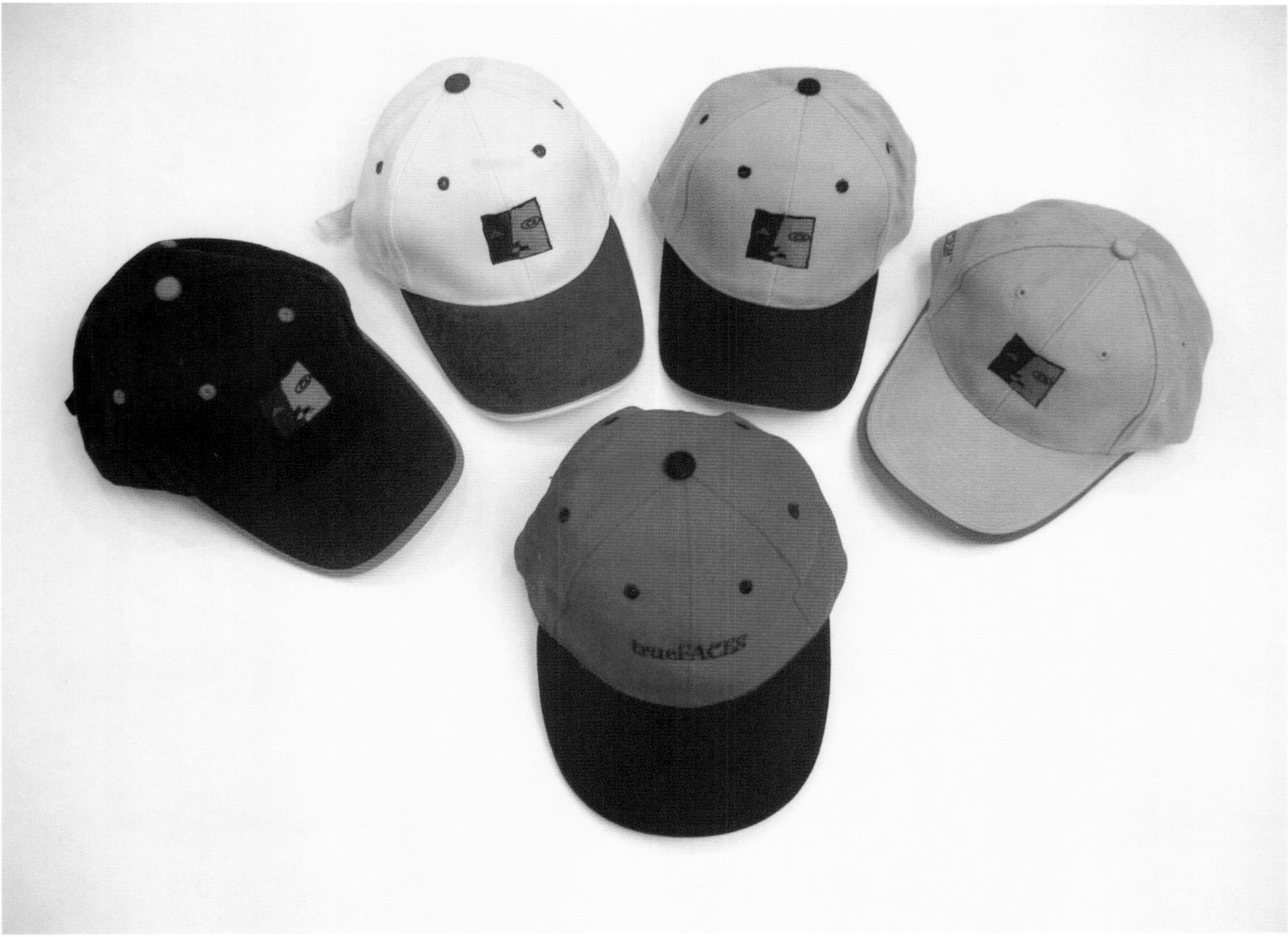

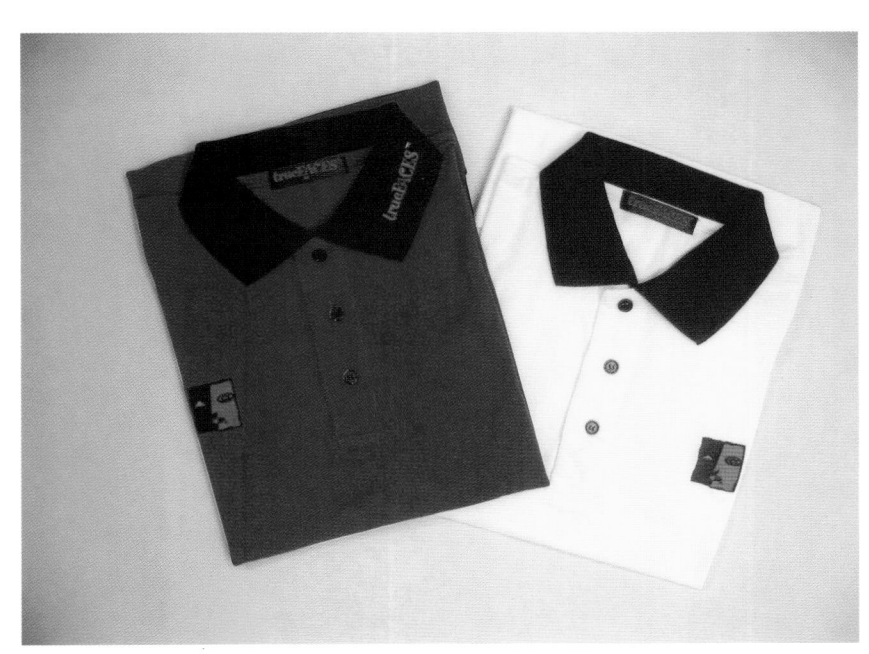

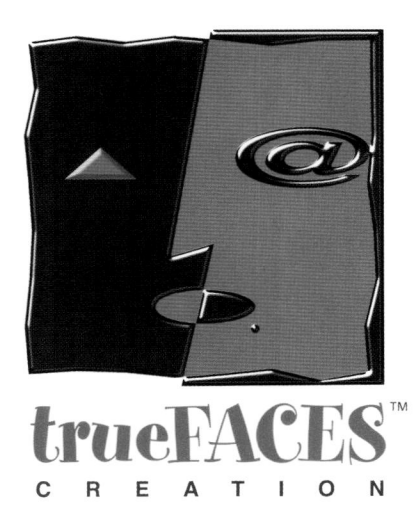

trueFACES™
CREATION

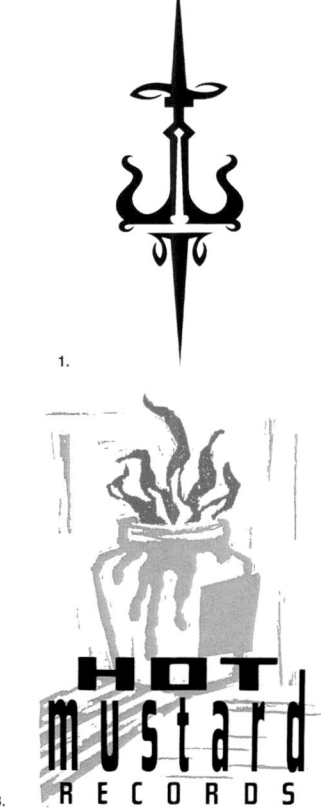

1.

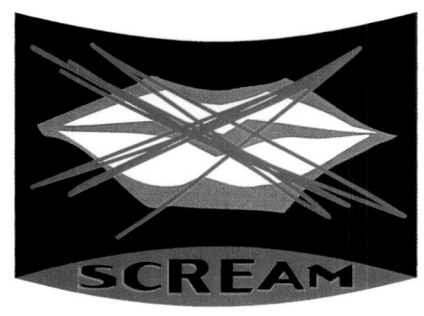

2.

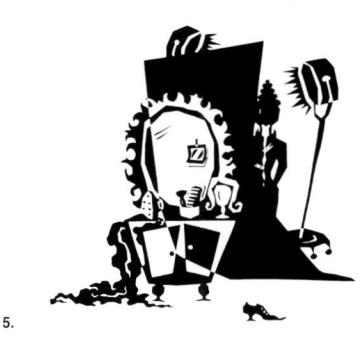

3.

4.

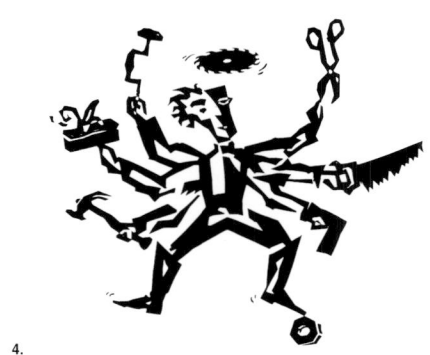

5.

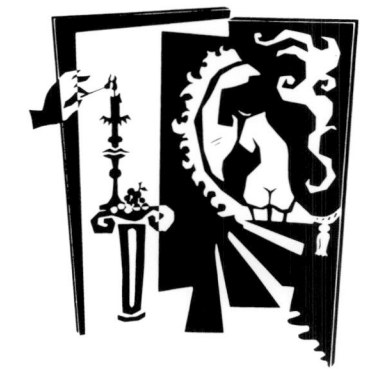

6.

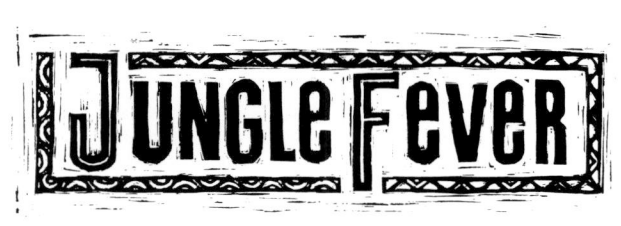

7.

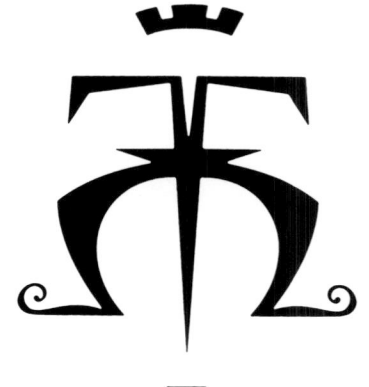

8.

9.

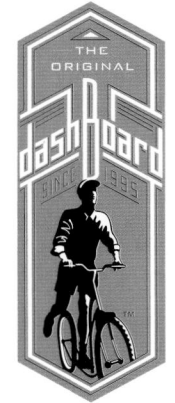

10.

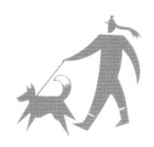 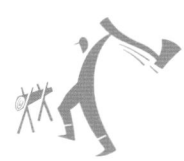 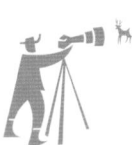

11.

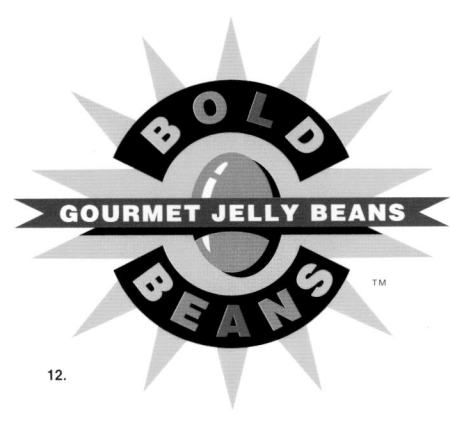

12.

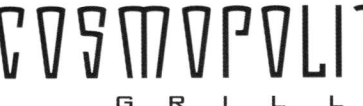

AMERICAN

MUSEUM OF QUILTS

& TEXTILES

13.

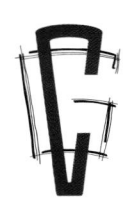

14.

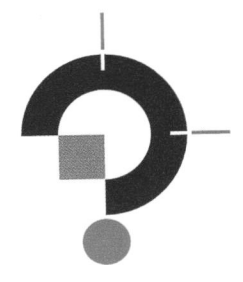

Media-
Network

15.

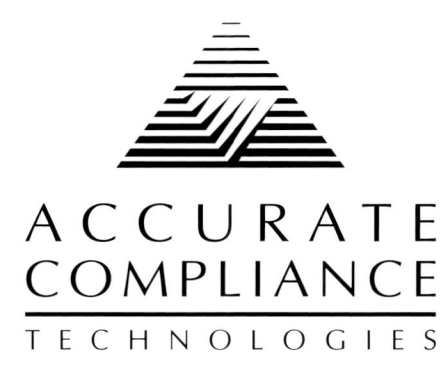

1.

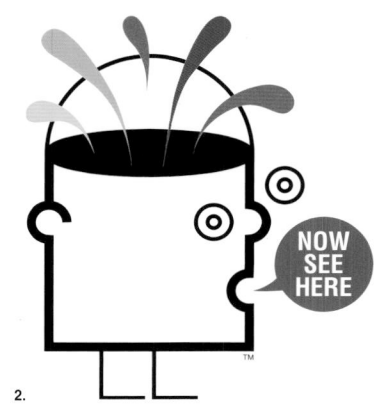

2.

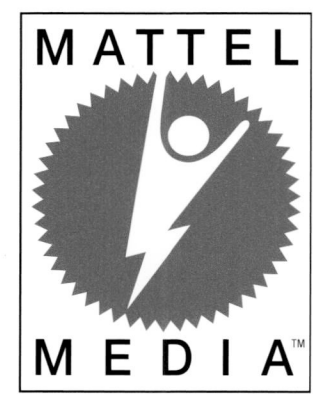

3.

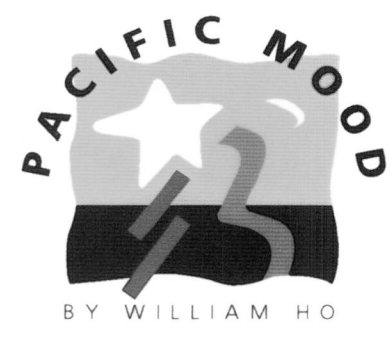

4.

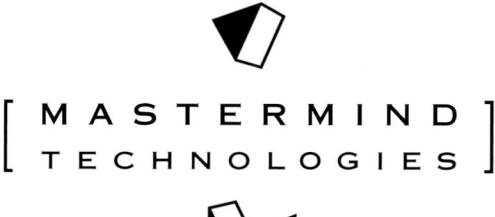

5.

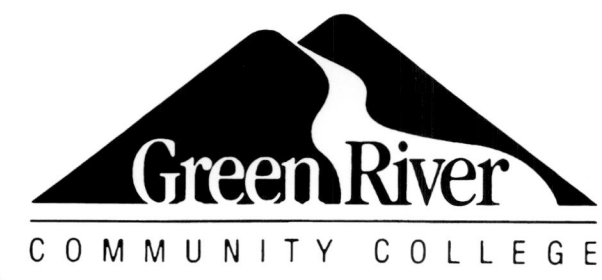

6.

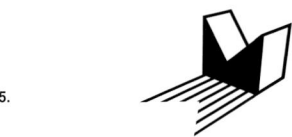

7.

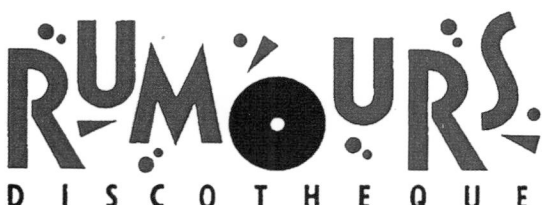

1
  Design Firm **GOLD & Associates**
2
  Design Firm **Fairly Painless Advertising**
3
  Design Firm **B.D. Fox & Friends, Advertising**
4
  Design Firm **William Ho Design
    Associates Ltd.**
5
  Design Firm **Lomangino Studio Inc.**
6, 7
  Design Firm **Hansen Design Company**
1.
  Client   *Accurate Compliance Technologies*
  Designer Keith Gold
2.
  Client   *Miller SQA*
  Designers Steve Frykholm,
    Brian Hauch

3.
  Client   *Mattel*
  Designer Garrett Burke
4.
  Client   *Pacific Mood*
  Designer William C.K. Ho
5.
  Client   *Mastermind Technologies*
  Designer Arthur Hsu
6.
  Client   *Green River
    Community College*
  Designers Pat Hansen, Jesse Doquilo
7.
  Client   *Rumours Discotheque*
  Designers Pat Hansen, Sheila Schimpf
(opposite)
  Client   *jstar Brands*
  Design Firm **Cahan & Associates**
  Designers Michael Braley, Bill Cahan,
    Todd Simmons

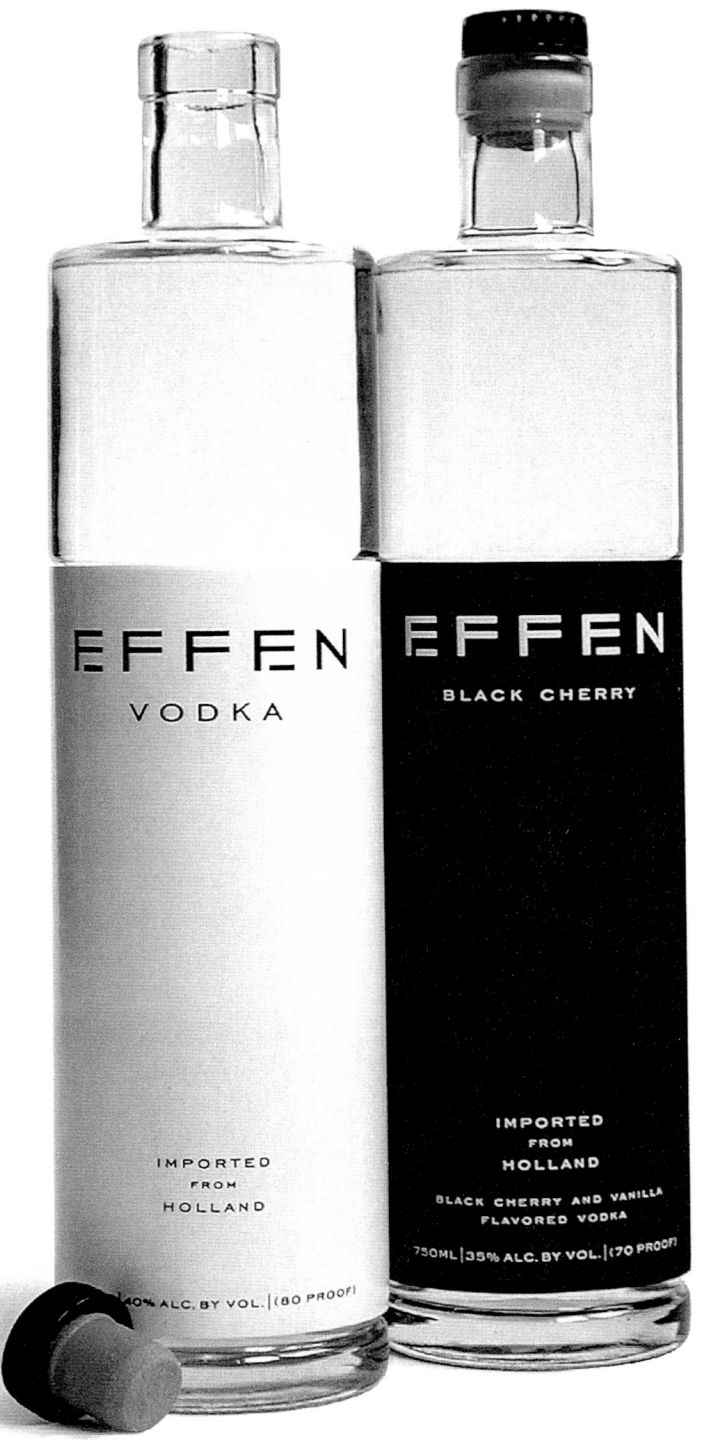

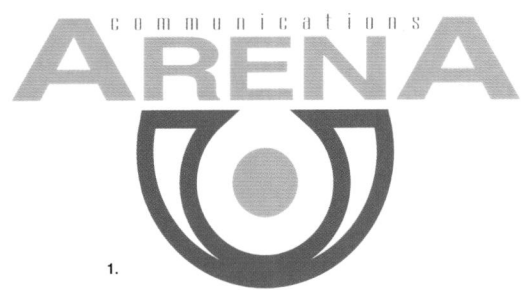

1.

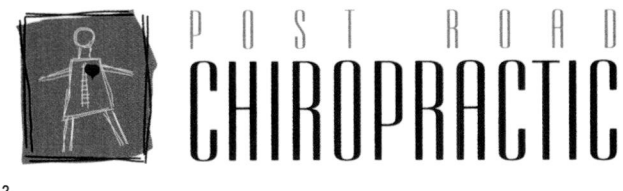

2.

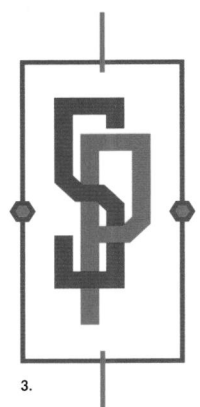

3.

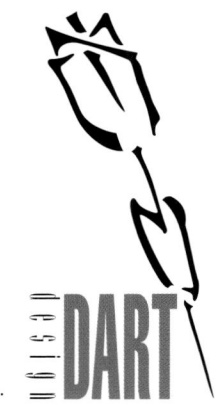

4.

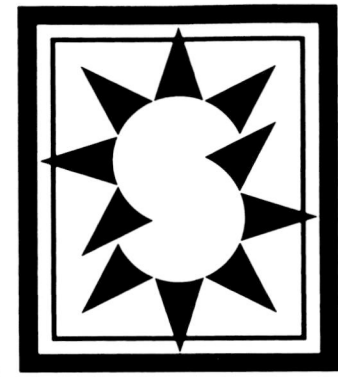

5.

6.

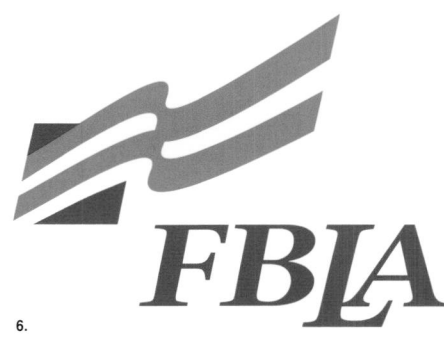

7.

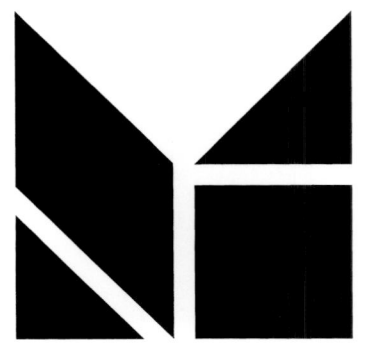

8.

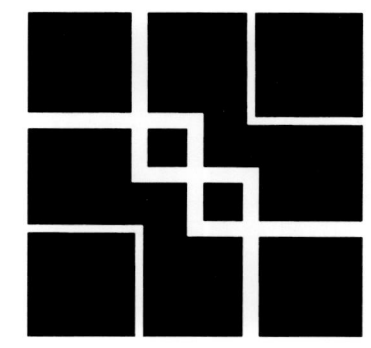

9.

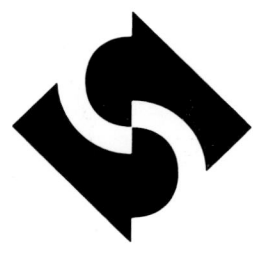

STRATEGIC CONCEPTS

10. **I N C O R P O R A T E D**

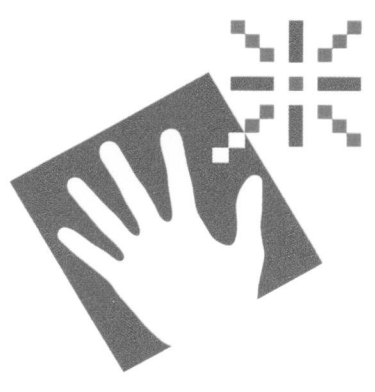

11. **PsyTrust**

12.

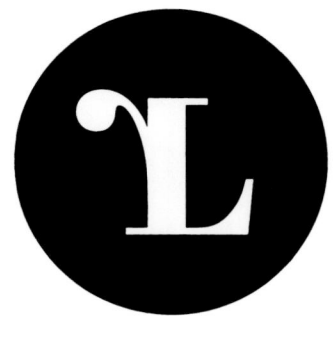

14.

I R S
SERVICE TEAM

13.

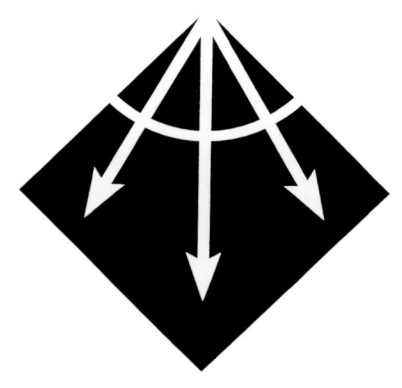

15.

1 - 3, 5
Design Firm **Dart Design**
4
Design Firm **Kendrew Group**
6 - 15
Design Firm **Fuller Designs, Inc.**
1.
Client   *Arena Communications*
Designer David Anderson
2.
Client   *Post Road Chiropractic*
Designer David Anderson
3.
Client   *Success Printing*
Designer David Anderson
4.
Client   *HBO*
Designer David Anderson-Dart Design
5.
Client   *Dart Design*
Designer David Anderson
6.
Client   *Future Business Leaders of America*
Designer Doug Fuller

7.
Client   *Sharp Building Corp.*
Designer Doug Fuller
8.
Client   *McDonald Management Solutions*
Designer Doug Fuller
9.
Client   *Integrated Healthcare*
          Arlington Hospital
Designer Doug Fuller
10.
Client   *Strategic Concepts, Inc.*
Designer Doug Fuller
11.
Client   *PsyTrust, LLC*
Designer Doug Fuller
12.
Client   *Florida Entech Corporation*
Designer Doug Fuller
13.
Client   *Price Waterhouse*
Designer Doug Fuller
14.
Client   *Regis Lefebure Photography*
Designers Doug Fuller, Aaron Taylor
15.
Client   *Active Adventures*
Designer Doug Fuller

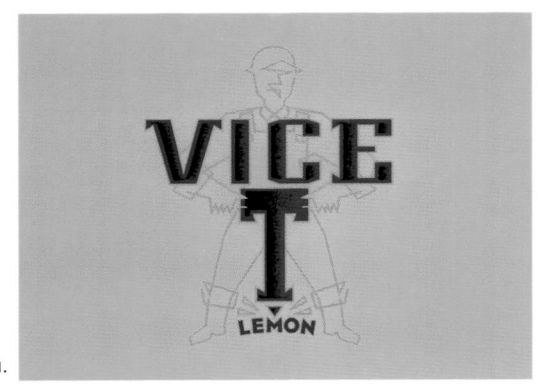

1.

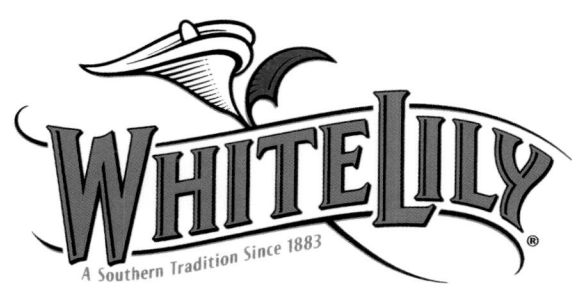

2.

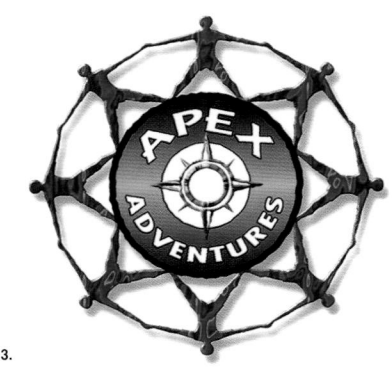

3.

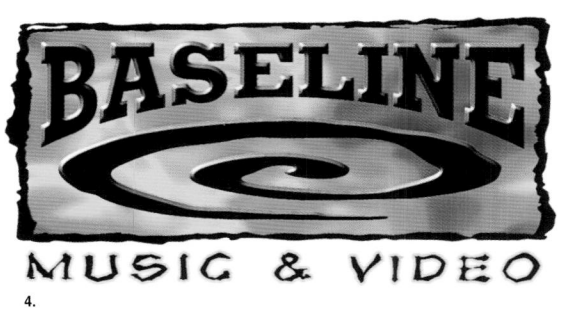

4.

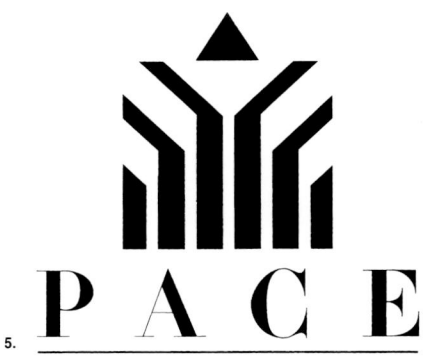

5.

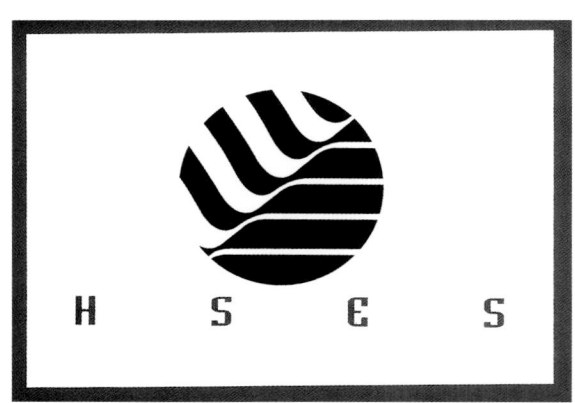

6.

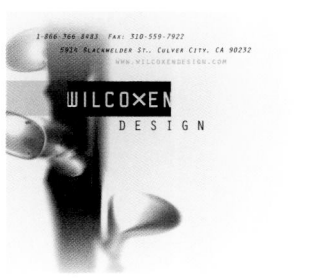

7.

GTA

GOLDEN TRIANGLE

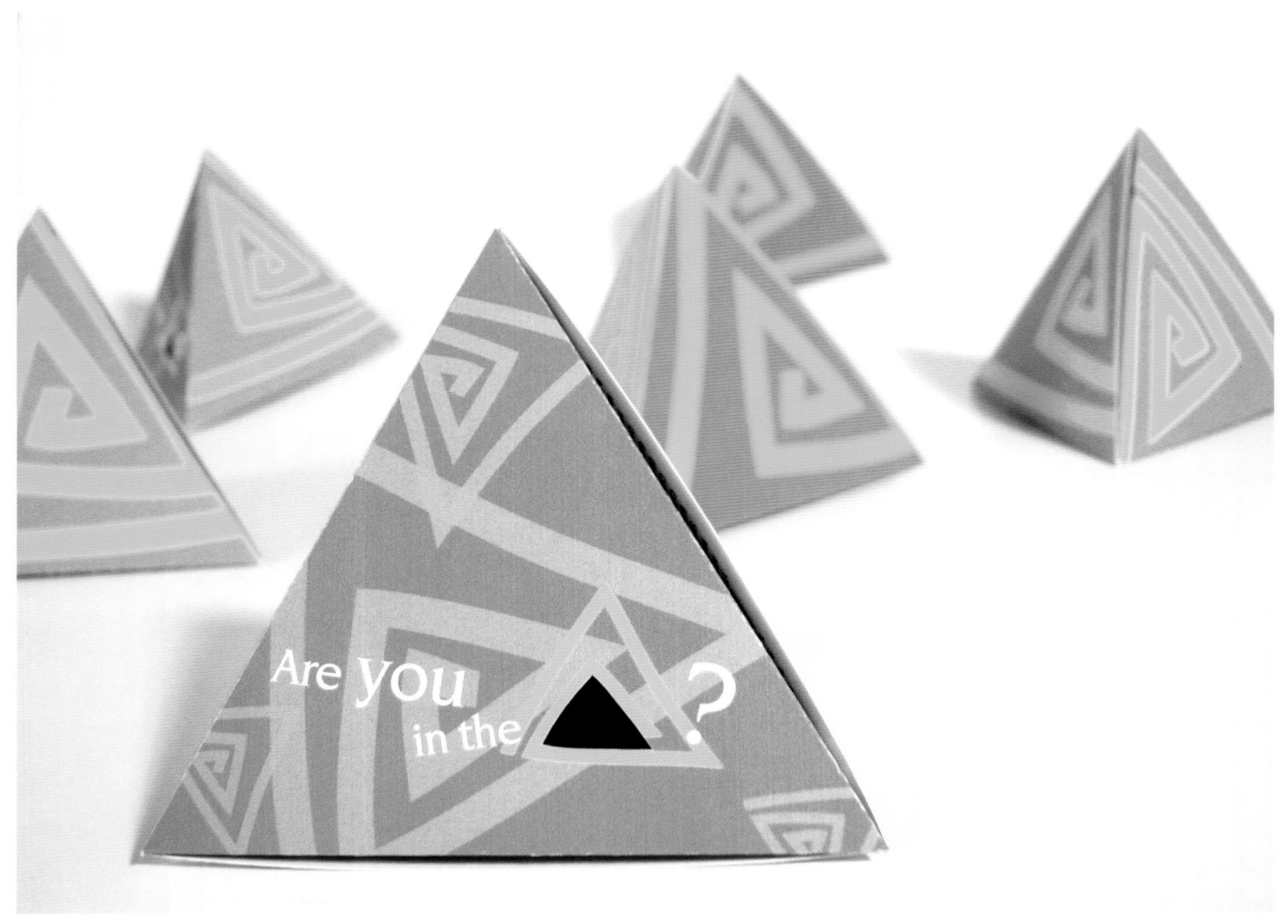

Are **you** in the ▲?

HEY ARNOLD! LOGO

Show Logos

Standard Full Color Logo

black
C= 40 M= 40
Y= 40 K= 100

PMS 122c
C= 0 M= 15
Y= 100 K= 0

Black & White Logo

black
C= 40 M= 40
Y= 40 K= 100

white

Full Color Logo on Dark Background

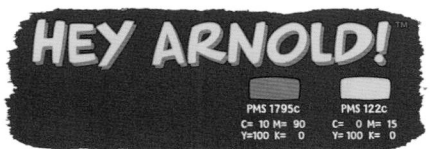

PMS 1795c
C= 10 M= 90
Y=100 K= 0

PMS 122c
C= 0 M= 15
Y= 100 K= 0

Full Color Packaging Logo with Nickelodeon Logo

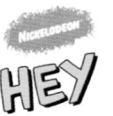
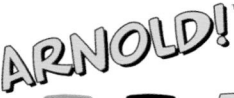

PMS 021c

black
C= 40 M= 40
Y= 40 K= 100

PMS 122c
C= 0 M= 15
Y= 100 K= 0

©

Design Firm **Nickelodeon**
Client *Nickelodeon*

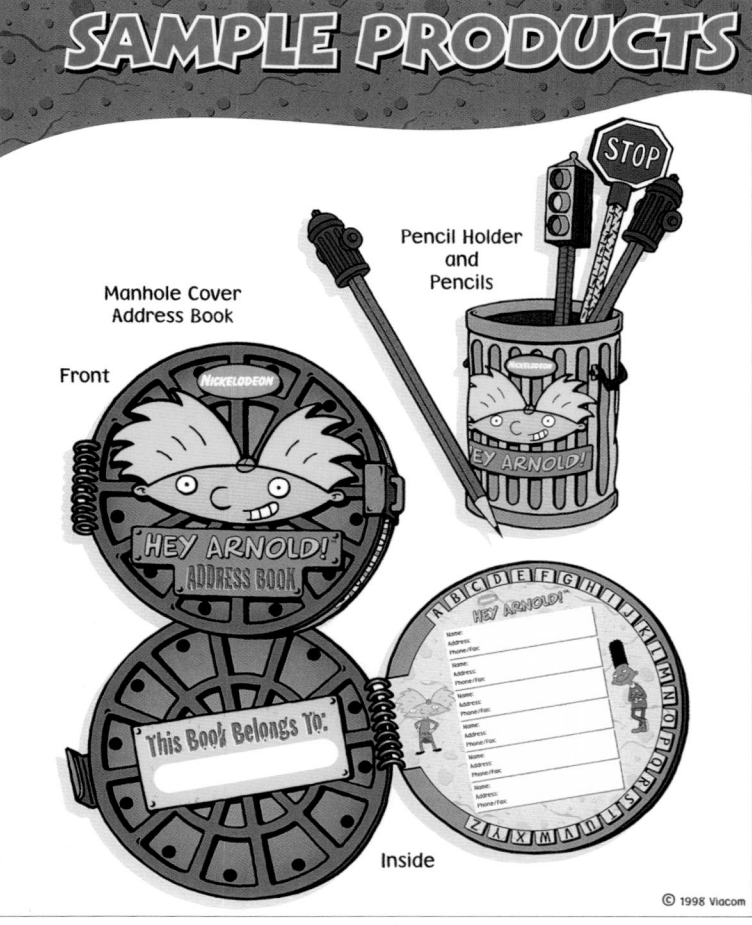

© 1998 Viacom

350

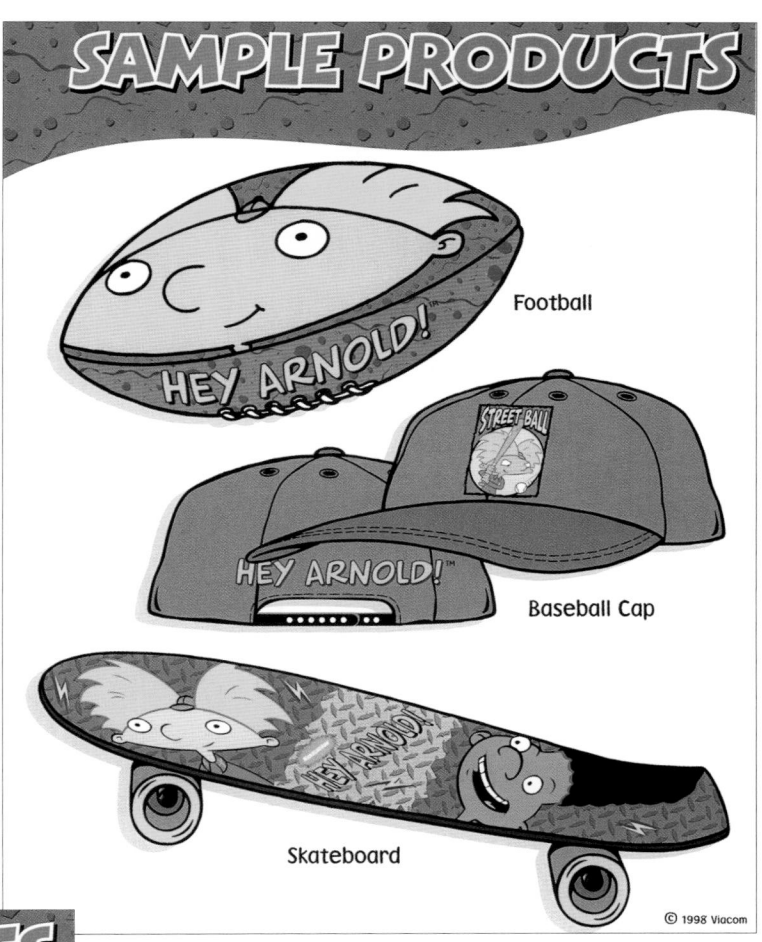

SAMPLE PRODUCTS

Football

Baseball Cap

Skateboard

© 1998 Viacom

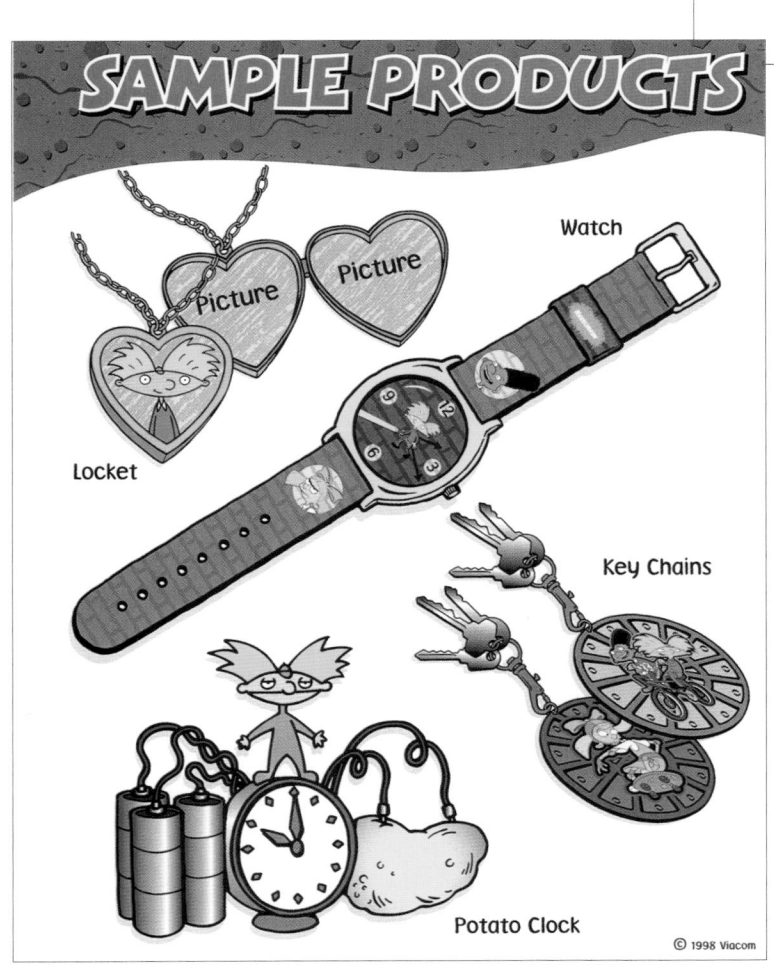

SAMPLE PRODUCTS

Watch

Picture Picture

Locket

Key Chains

Potato Clock

© 1998 Viacom

(continued)
Design Firm **Nickelodeon**
Client *Nickelodeon*

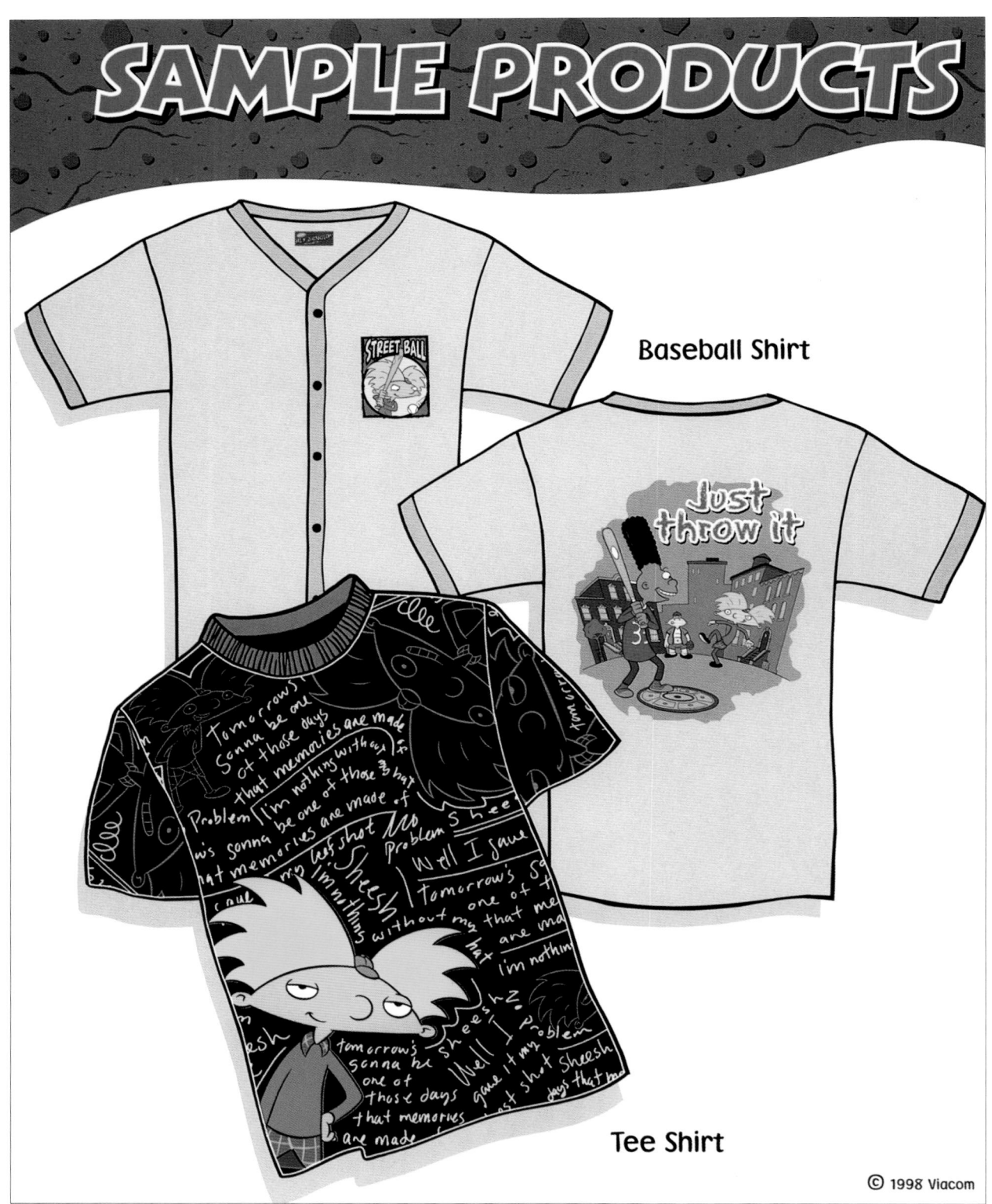

SAMPLE PRODUCTS

Baseball Shirt

Tee Shirt

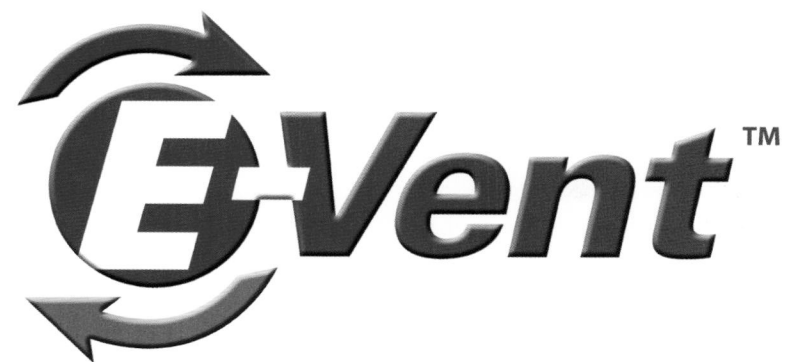

Design Firm **FGA**
Client   *Ecotint (M) Sdn Bhd*
Designers   FGA Creative Team

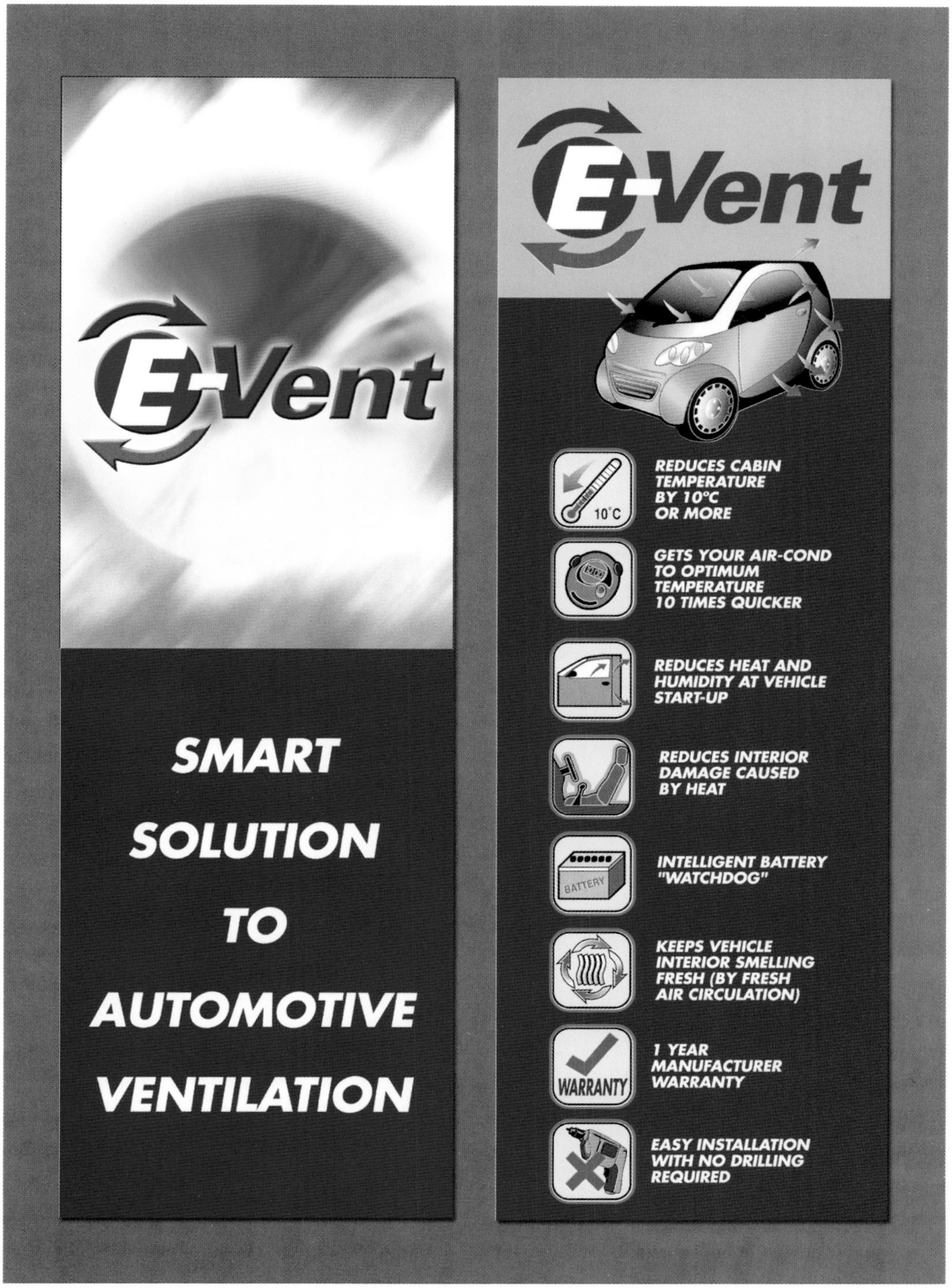

E-Vent

SMART

SOLUTION

TO

AUTOMOTIVE

VENTILATION

REDUCES CABIN
TEMPERATURE
BY 10°C
OR MORE

GETS YOUR AIR-COND
TO OPTIMUM
TEMPERATURE
10 TIMES QUICKER

REDUCES HEAT AND
HUMIDITY AT VEHICLE
START-UP

REDUCES INTERIOR
DAMAGE CAUSED
BY HEAT

INTELLIGENT BATTERY
"WATCHDOG"

KEEPS VEHICLE
INTERIOR SMELLING
FRESH (BY FRESH
AIR CIRCULATION)

1 YEAR
MANUFACTURER
WARRANTY

EASY INSTALLATION
WITH NO DRILLING
REQUIRED

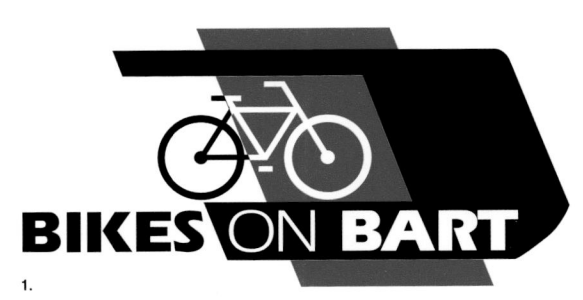

1.

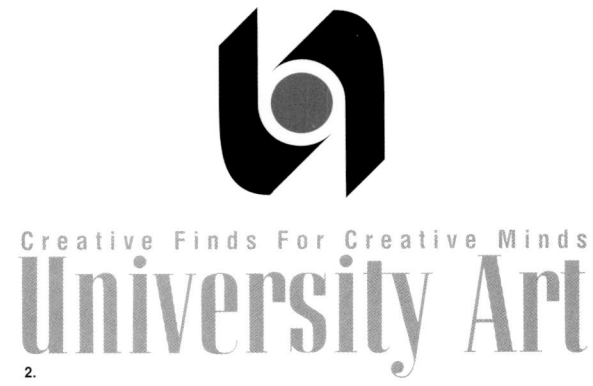

Creative Finds For Creative Minds
University Art

2.

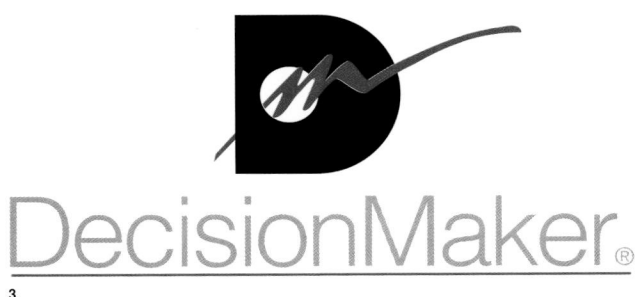

DecisionMaker®

3.

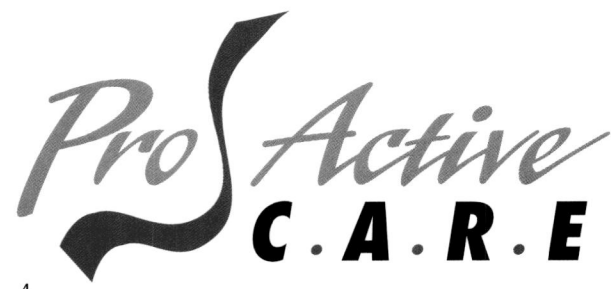

4.

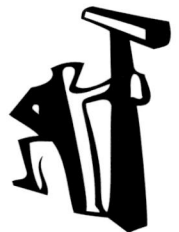

THORENFELDT CONSTRUCTION, INC.

5.

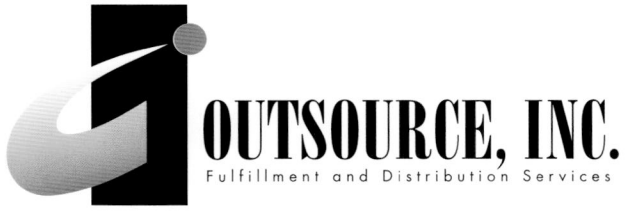

OUTSOURCE, INC.
Fulfillment and Distribution Services

6.

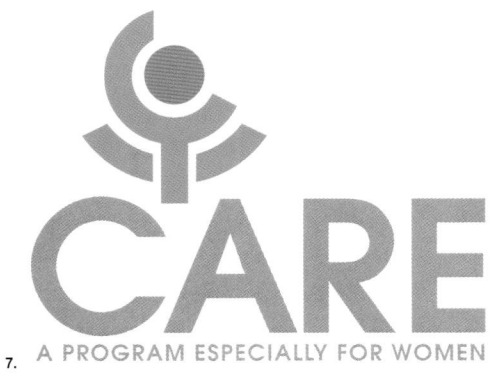

CARE
7. A PROGRAM ESPECIALLY FOR WOMEN

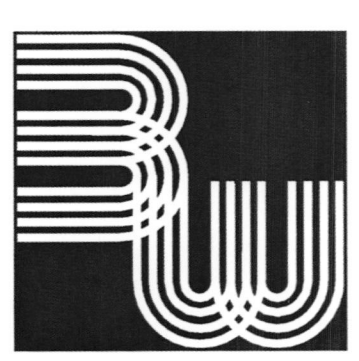

8.

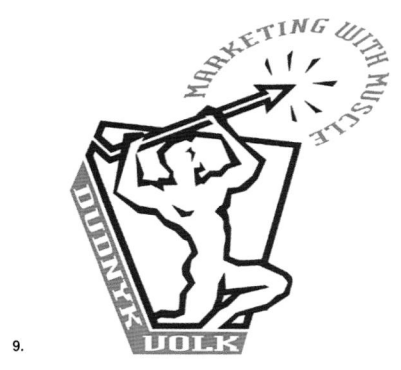

9.

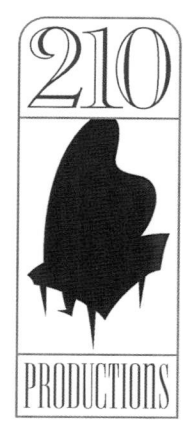

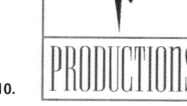

10.

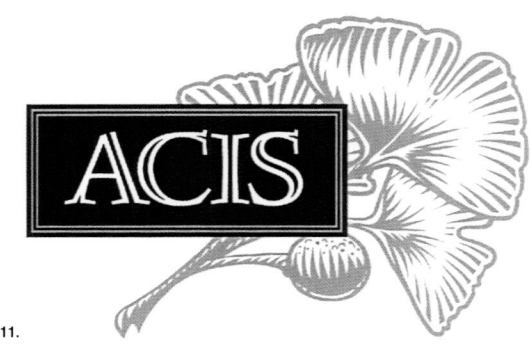

11.

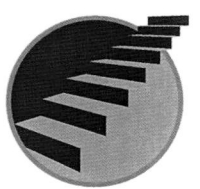

PENNSYLVANIA
EARLY STAGE PARTNERS

12.

INTERNATIONAL
DESIGN
PARTNERSHIP **idp** sm

13.

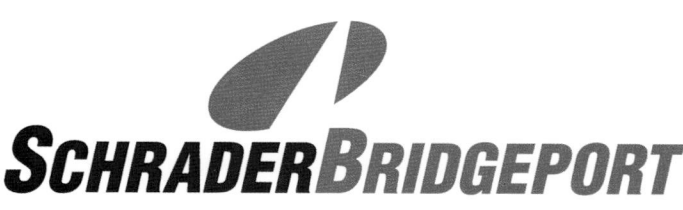

14.

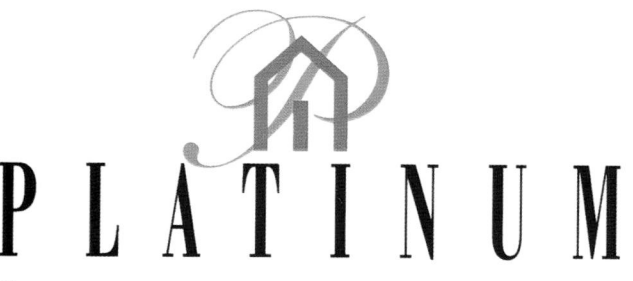

PLATINUM

15.

1 - 7
Design Firm **Imtech Communications**
8 - 12
Design Firm **NDW Communications**
13 - 15
Design Firm **Lipson, Alport,**
Glass & Associates

1.
Client *BART (SF Bay Area Rapid Transit)*
Designer Robert Keng
2.
Client *University Art*
Designer Robert Keng
3.
Client *Ma Labs*
Designer Robert Keng
4.
Client *ProActive CARE*
Designer Robert Keng
5.
Client *Thorenfeldt Construction, Inc.*
Designer Robert Keng
6.
Client *Outsource, Inc.*
Designer Robert Keng

7.
Client *CARE (Cancer Awareness*
Research & Education)
Designer Robert Keng
8.
Client *Barclay White, Inc.*
Designer Bill Healey
9.
Client *Dudnyk & Volk Advertising*
Designer Bill Healey
10.
Client *210 Productions, Inc.*
Designer Bill Healey
11.
Client *Acis, Inc.*
Designer Bill Healey
12.
Client *PA Early Stage Partners*
Designer Tom Brill
13.
Client *International Design Partnership*
Designers Lipson, Alport, Glass, & Associates
14.
Client *Schrader Bridgeport*
Designer Keith Shure
15.
Client *Platinum Home Mortgage*
Designer Katherine Holderfled

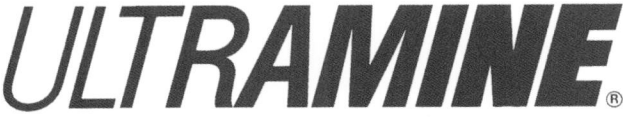

1.

TOWNPARK

2.

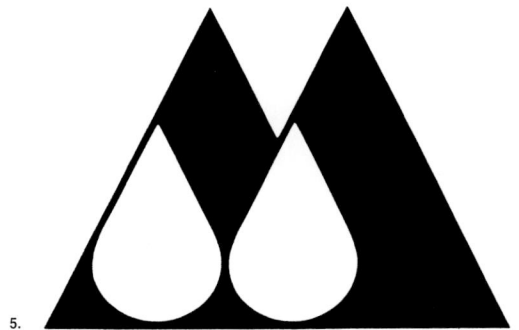

3.

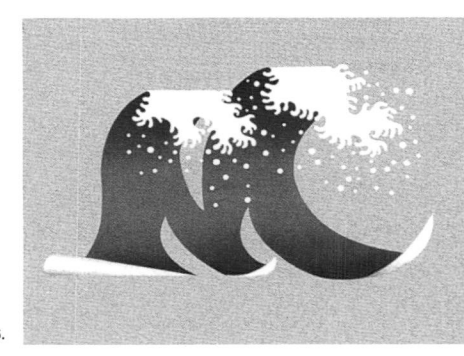

4.

5.

6.

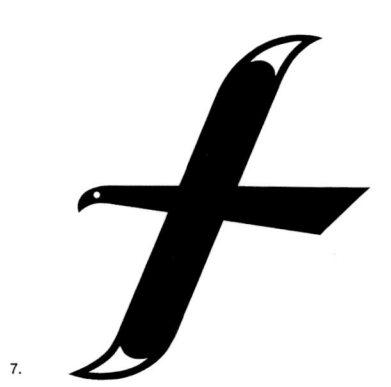

7.

1, 2
Design Firm **Rousso+Associates, Inc.**
3, 4
Design Firm **Torrisi Design Associates, Inc.**
5 - 7
Design Firm **Minoru Morita Graphic Design**
1.
Client   *The Melamine Corporation*
Designer   Steven B. Rousso
2.
Client   *Taylor Mathis*
Designer   Steven B. Rousso
3.
Client   *PCS Connect*
4.
Client   *Primary Consulting Services*

5.
Client   *Design M*
Designer   Minoru Morita
6.
Client   *M Studio*
Designer   Minoru Morita
7.
Client   *Forgerty Family*
Designer   Minoru Morita
(opposite)
Client   *Retina Consultants of Southwest Florida*
Design Firm **Cave**
Designers   David Edmundson, Matt Cave

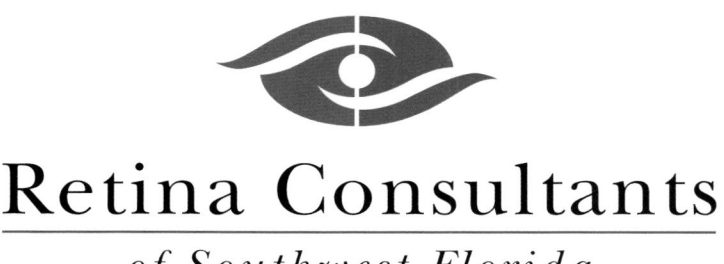

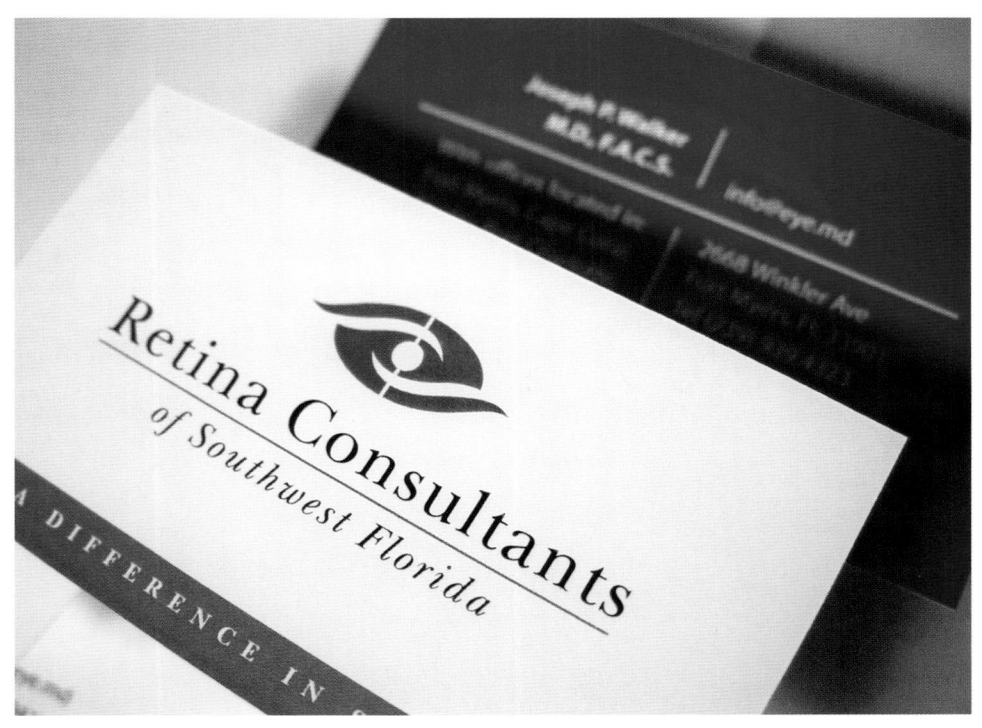

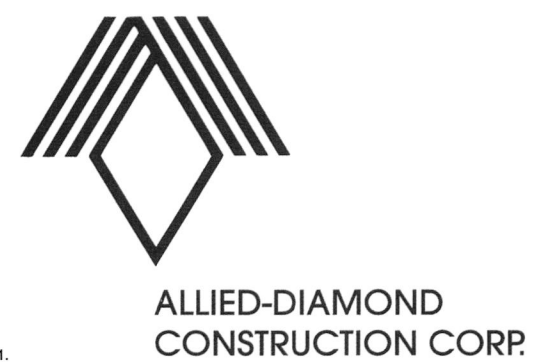

ALLIED-DIAMOND
CONSTRUCTION CORP.

1.

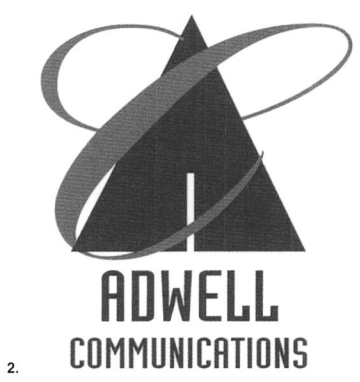

ADWELL
COMMUNICATIONS

2.

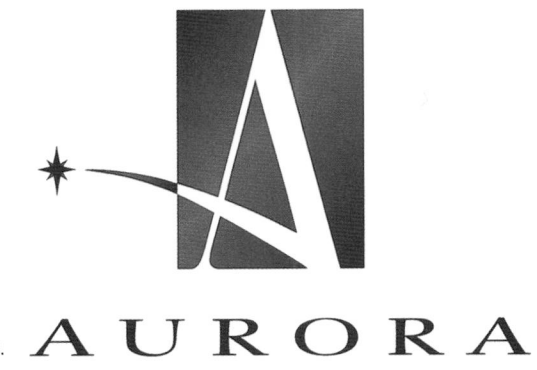

AURORA

3.

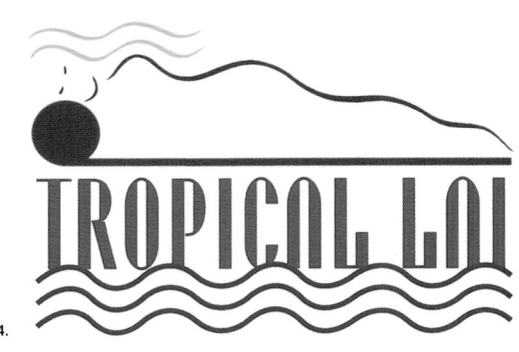

TROPICAL LOI

4.

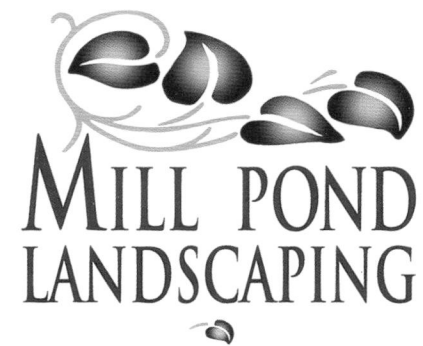

MILL POND
LANDSCAPING

5.

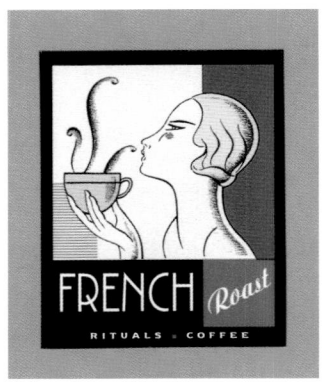

FRENCH Roast
RITUALS · COFFEE

6.

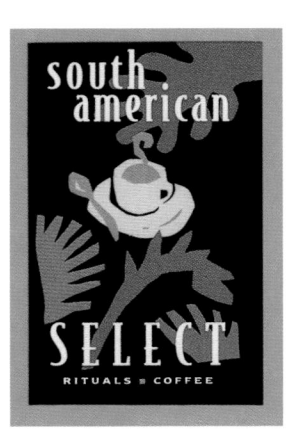

south american
SELECT
RITUALS · COFFEE

7.

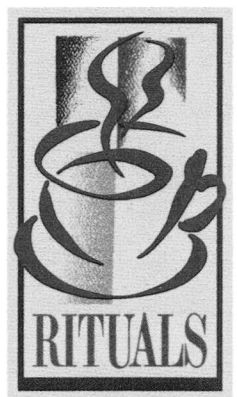

RITUALS

8.

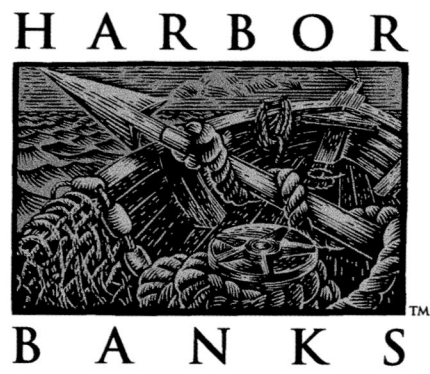

9.

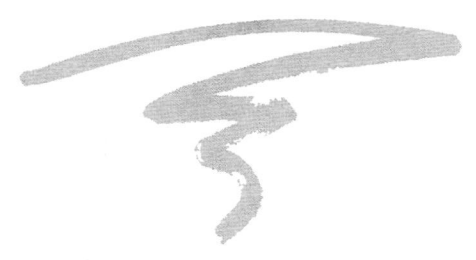

10. TectonArchitects│pc

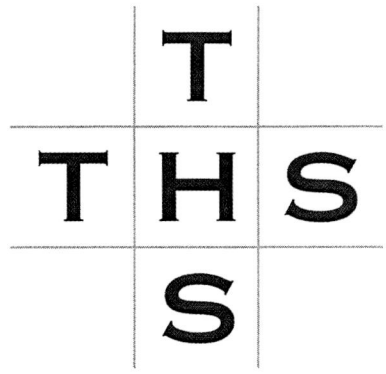

11.

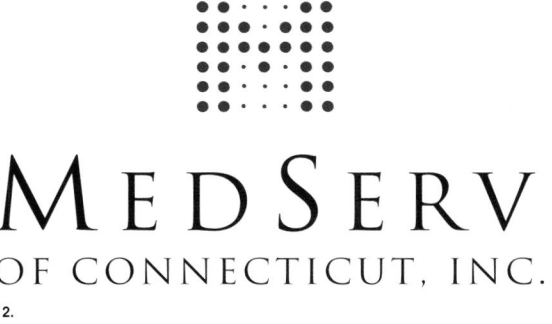

12.

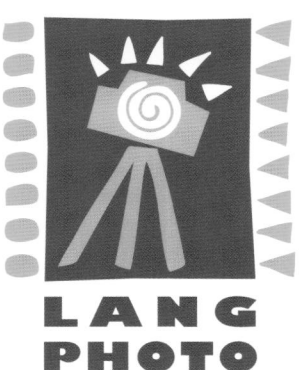

13.

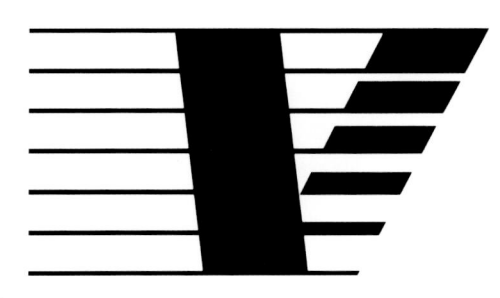

14.

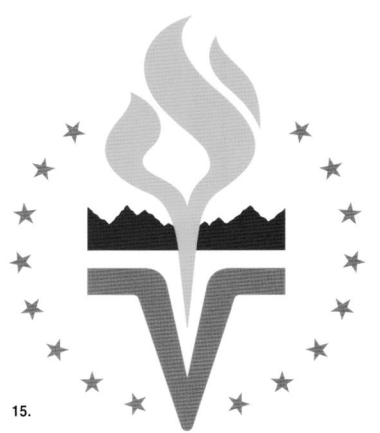

15.

1 - 5
 Design Firm **Guarino Graphics, Ltd.**
6 - 9
 Design Firm **Callahan and Company**
10 - 13
 Design Firm **Ritz Henton Design Group**
14, 15
 Design Firm **Robert W. Taylor Design, Inc.**

1.
 Client *Allied Diamond Construction*
 Designer Jan Guarino
2.
 Client *Adwell Communications*
 Designer Jan Guarino
3.
 Client *Aurora Productions*
 Designer Jan Guarino
4.
 Client *The Three Musketeers*
 Designer Jan Guarino

5.
 Client *Mill Pond Landscaping*
 Designer Jan Guarino
6, 7.
 Client *Rituals Coffee*
 Designers Paula Sloane, Jonathan Carlson
8, 9.
 Client *JP Foodservice*
 Designer Paula Sloane
10.
 Client *Tecton Architects, P.C.*
11.
 Client *Total Healthcare Solutions, Inc.*
12.
 Client *MedServ of Connecticut, Inc.*
13.
 Client *Lang Photography*
14.
 Client *Valleylab, Inc.*
 Designer Robert W. Taylor
15.
 Client *Colorado Sports Hall of Fame*
 Designers Robert W. Taylor,
 Gwyn VanderVorste

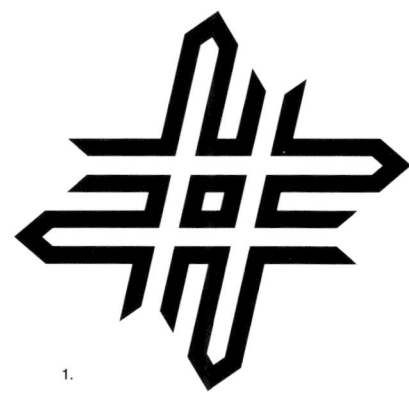

1.

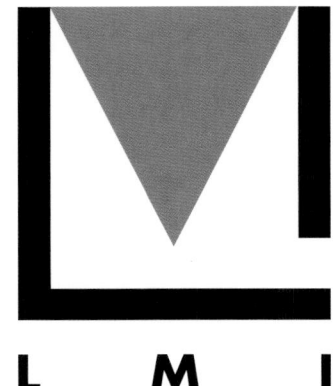

2. **L M I**

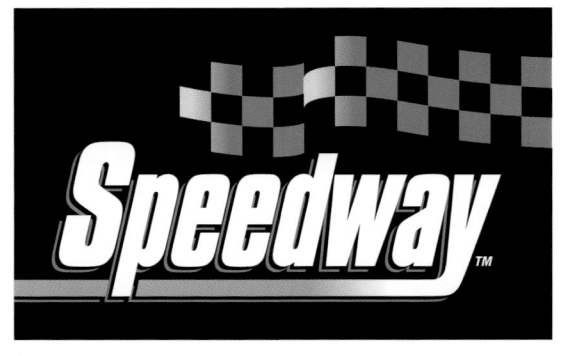

3.

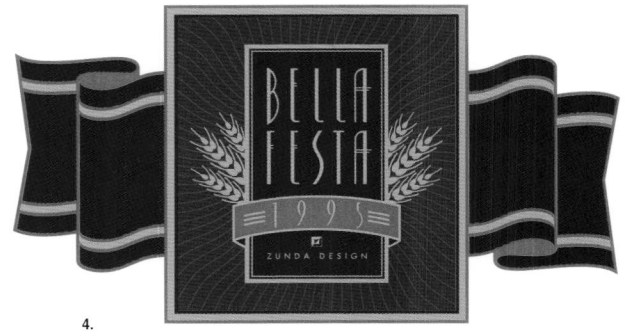

4.

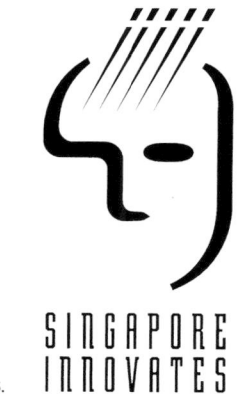

SINGAPORE INNOVATES

5.

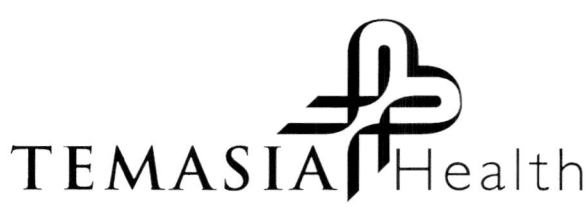

TEMASIA Health

6.

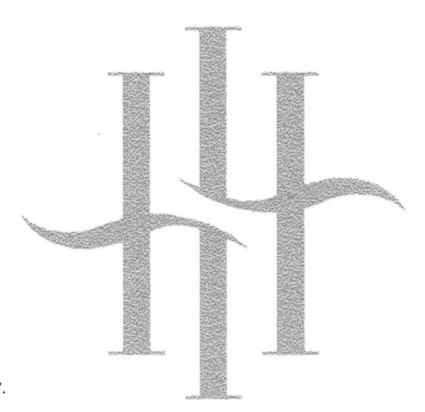

7.

1
Design Firm **Robert W. Taylor Design, Inc.**
2 - 4
Design Firm **Zunda Design Group**
5 - 7
Design Firm **Design Objectives Pte Ltd**

1.
Client   *Center for International Trade Development*
Designer   Robert W. Taylor
2.
Client   *Liebhardt Mills, Inc.*
Designer   Charles Zunda
3.
Client   *USA Detergents*
Designer   Todd Nickel

4.
Client   *Zunda Design Group*
Designers   Todd Nickel, Charles Zunda
5.
Client   *Singapore Economic Development Board*
Designer   Ronnie S C Tan
6.
Client   *Temasia Health Pte Ltd*
Designer   Ronnie S C Tan
7.
Client   *Lee Hwa Jewellery Pte Ltd*
Designer   Ronnie S C Tan
(opposite)
Client   *Southern Specialties*
Design Firm **Cave**
Designers   David Edmundson, Matt Cave

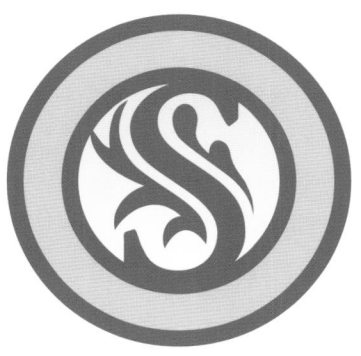

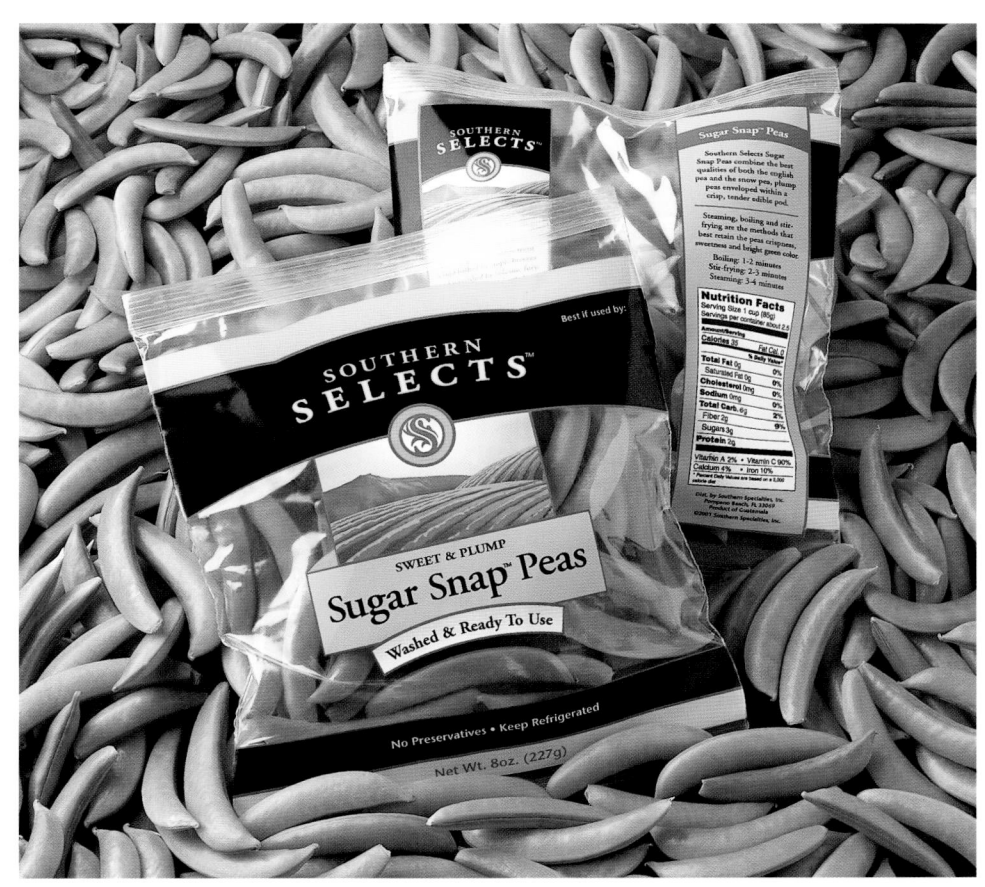

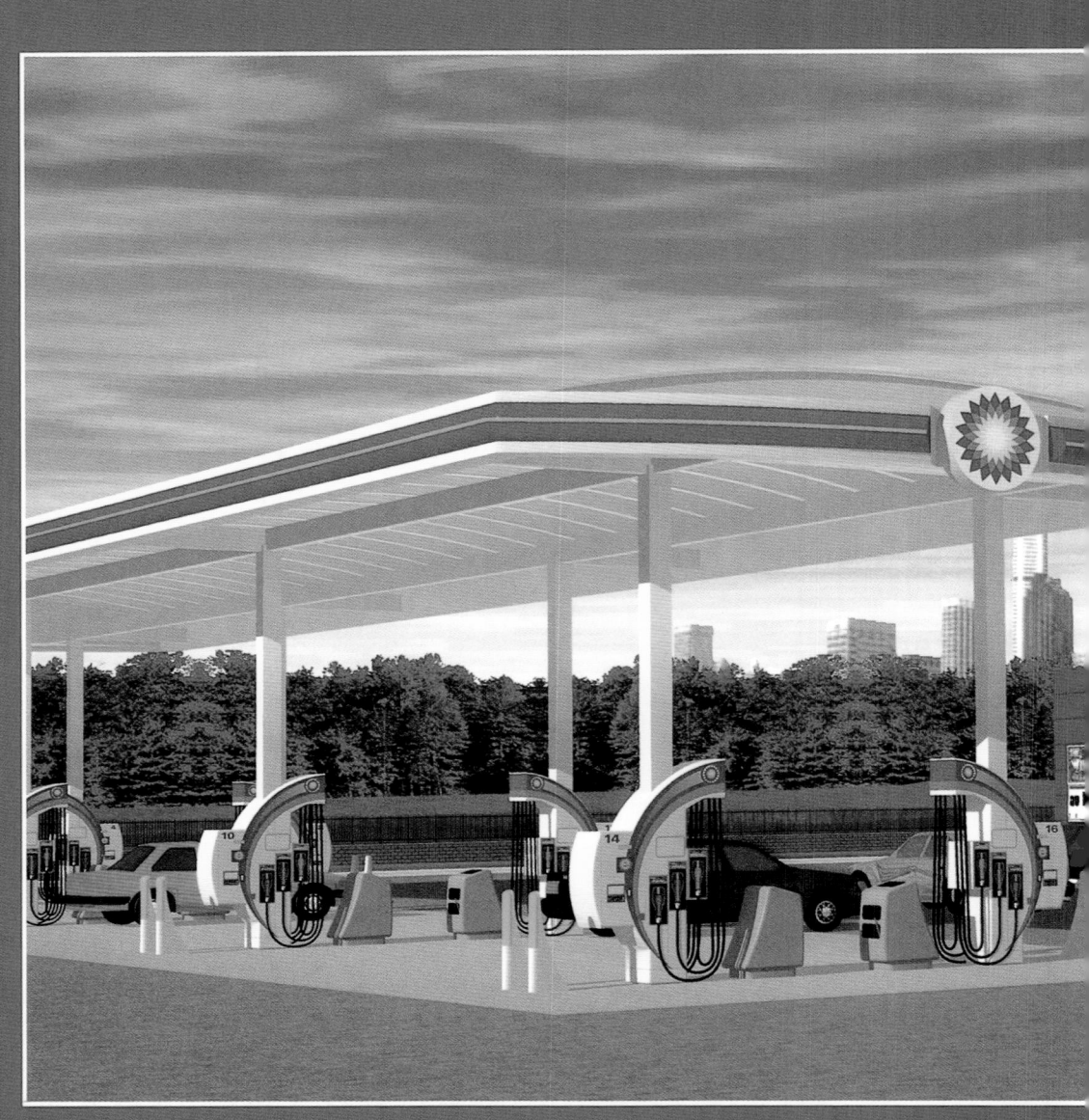

our new look

Our new identity stands for the essence of our company – it is a graphic representation of our core values. In a sense, our identity is a promise to customers, investors, competitors and the rest of our worldwide audience. It pledges that we will strive to act and communicate in an energetic, forthright and forward-thinking way in everything we do. As we show this new face to the world, we send a clear message: BP is leading the changes taking place in our industry. Our striking new look reflects the bold steps we're taking in every area, from technology to exploration to environmental protection. And this is just the beginning.

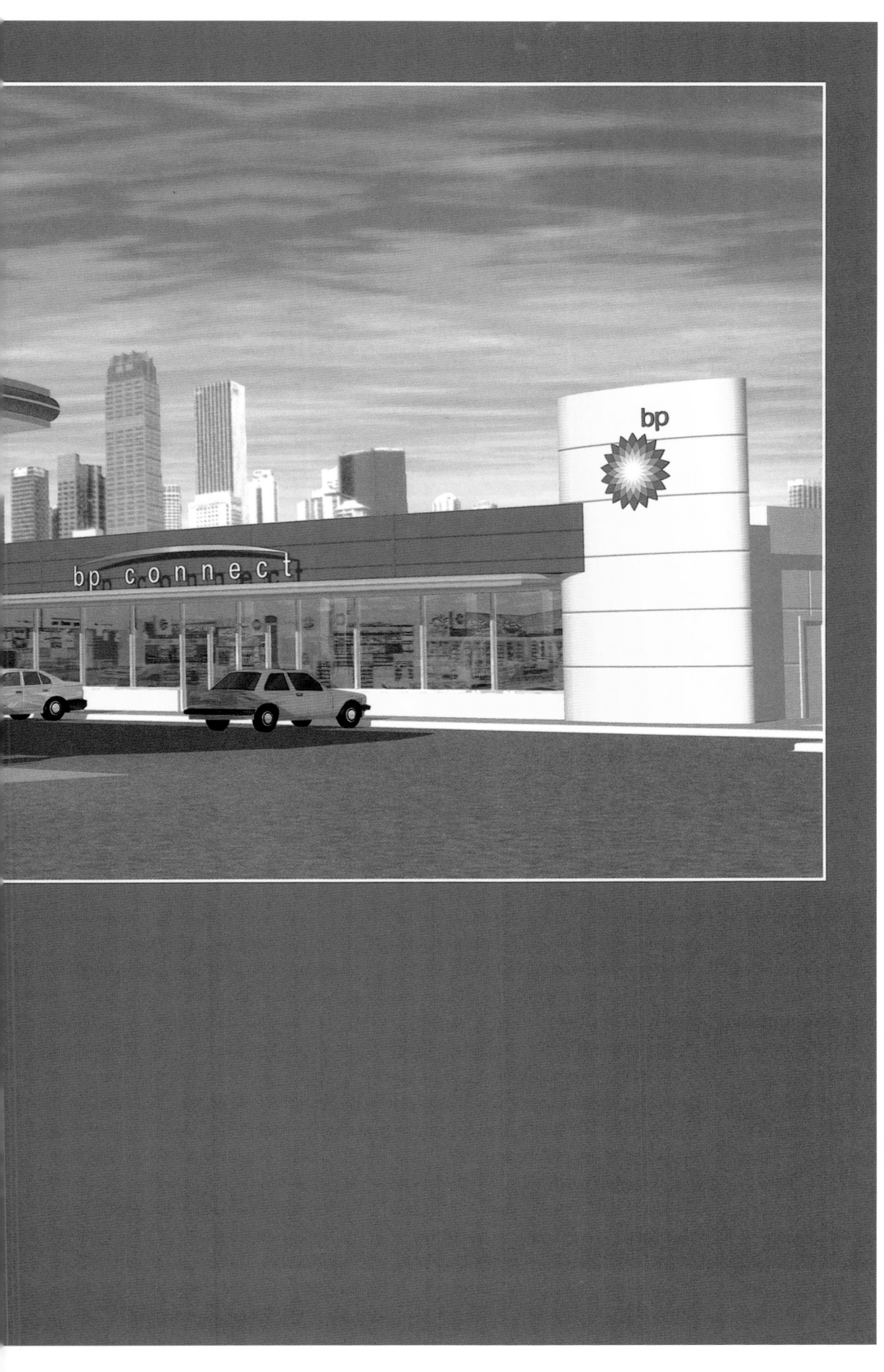

Design Firm **Landor Associates**
Client   *BP Amoco*
Designers   Margaret Youngblood,
            Nancy Hoefig,
            Courtney Reeser,
            Peter Harleman,
            David Zapata,
            Brad Scott,
            Cynthia Murnane,
            Todd True,
            Frank Mueller,
            Michele Berry,
            Cameron Imani,
            Ivan Thelin,
            Ladd Woodland,
            Maria Wenzel,
            Jane Bailey,
            Susan Manning,
            Wendy Gold,
            Greg Barnell,
            Stephen Lapaz,
            Bryan Vincent,
            Russell DeHaven

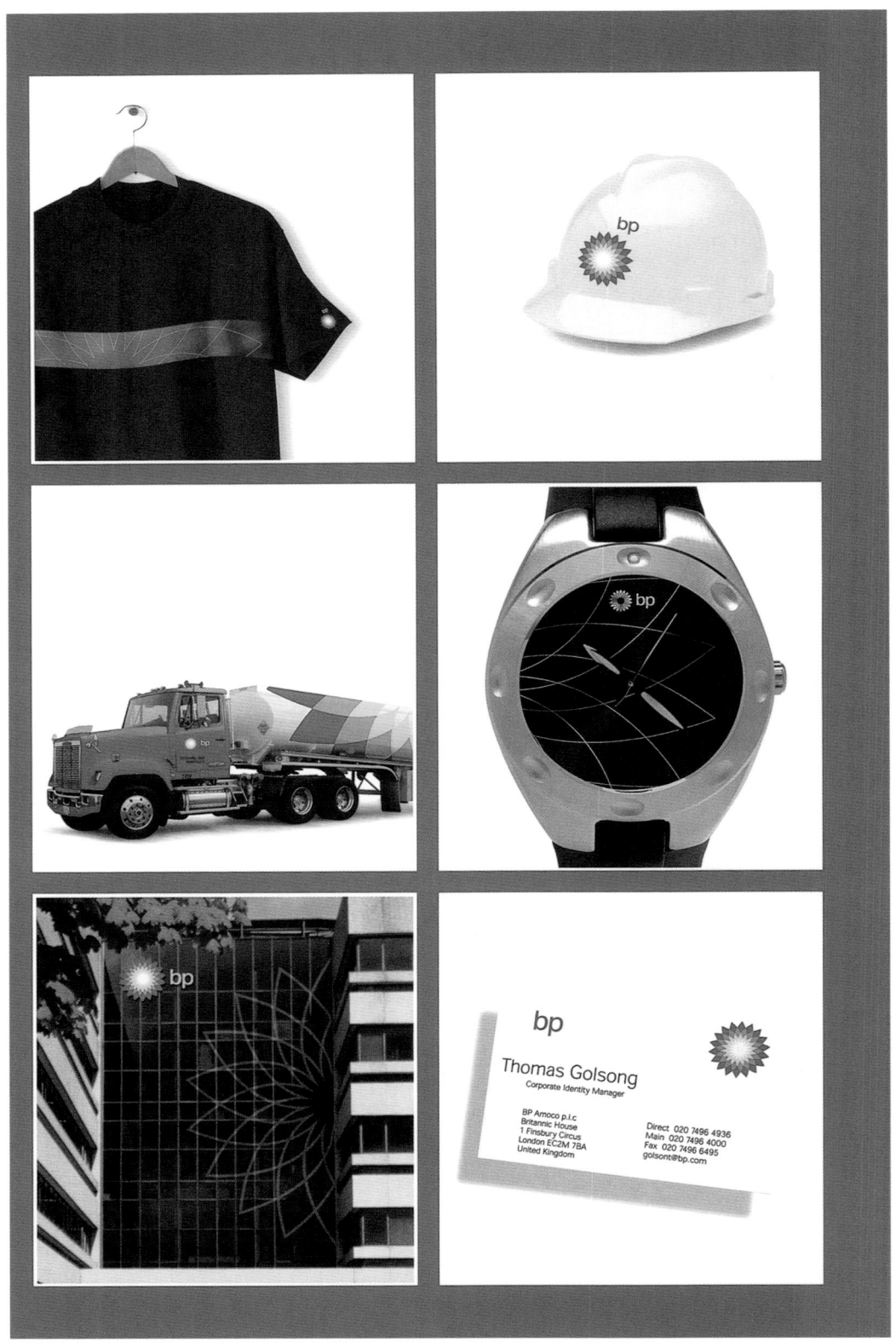

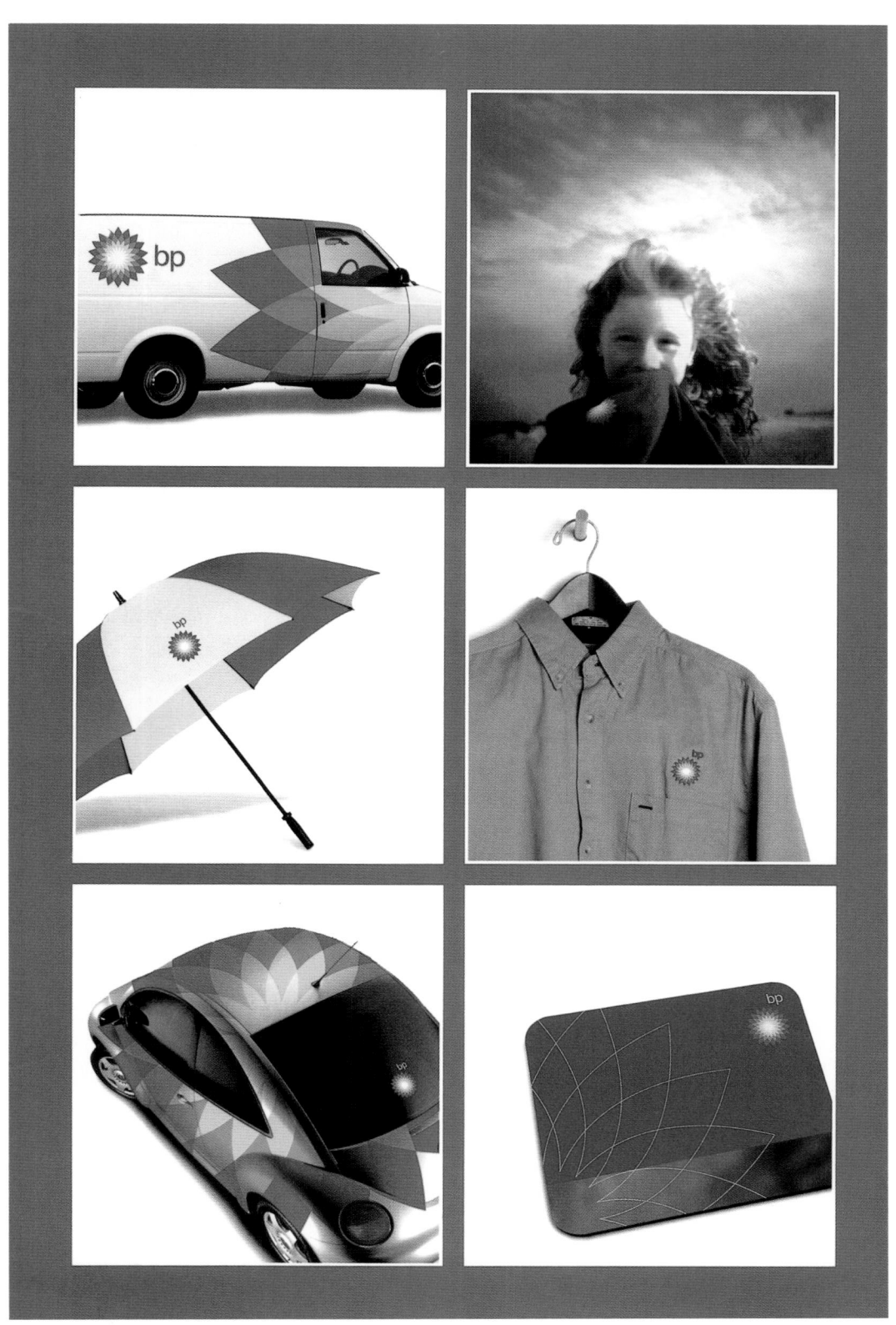

(continued)
Design Firm **Landor Associates**
Client *BP Amoco*

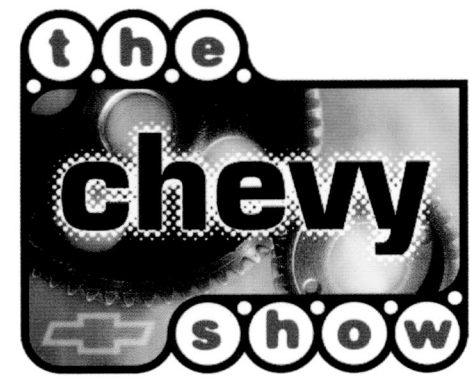

1.

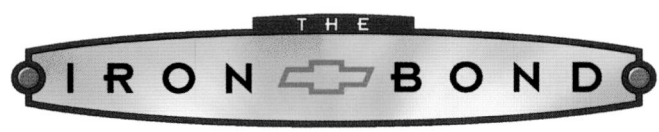

2.

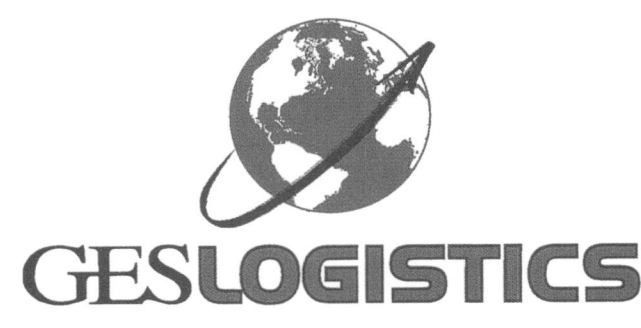

3.

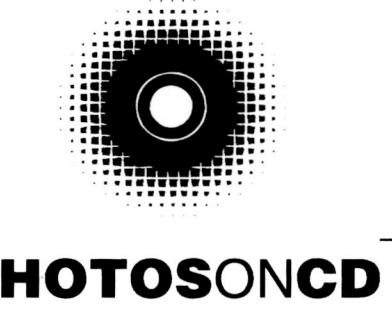

4.

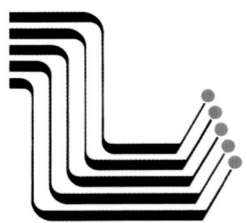

5.

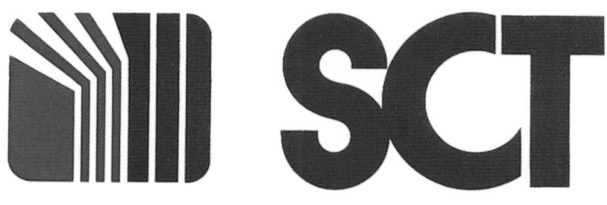

6. LITESOM CORPORATION

7.

SCT

1 - 5
Design Firm **Tieken Design
& Creative Services**

6, 7
Design Firm **The Corporate Identity People**

1.
Client   *Graham Associated Advertising*
Designers Fred E. Tieken,
          Rik Boberg

2.
Client   *Graham Associated Advertising*
Designers Fred E. Tieken,
          Sarah Spencer

3.
Client   *GES Exposition Services*
Designers Fred E. Tieken

4.
Client   *GES Exposition Services*
Designers Fred E. Tieken,
          Sarah Spencer

5.
Client   *PhotosOnCD*
Designers Fred E. Tieken

6.
Client   *Litesom Corporation*
Designer Joseph Finisdore

7.
Client   *SCT-Systems
              & Computer Technology*
Designer Joseph Finisdore
(opposite)
Client   *Palermo's*
Design Firm **Design North, Inc.**

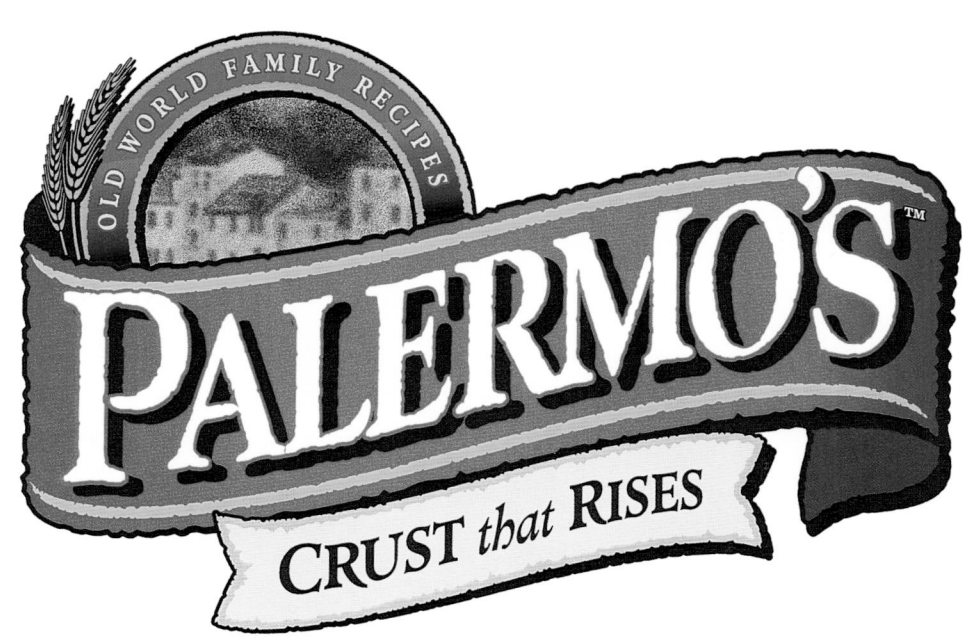

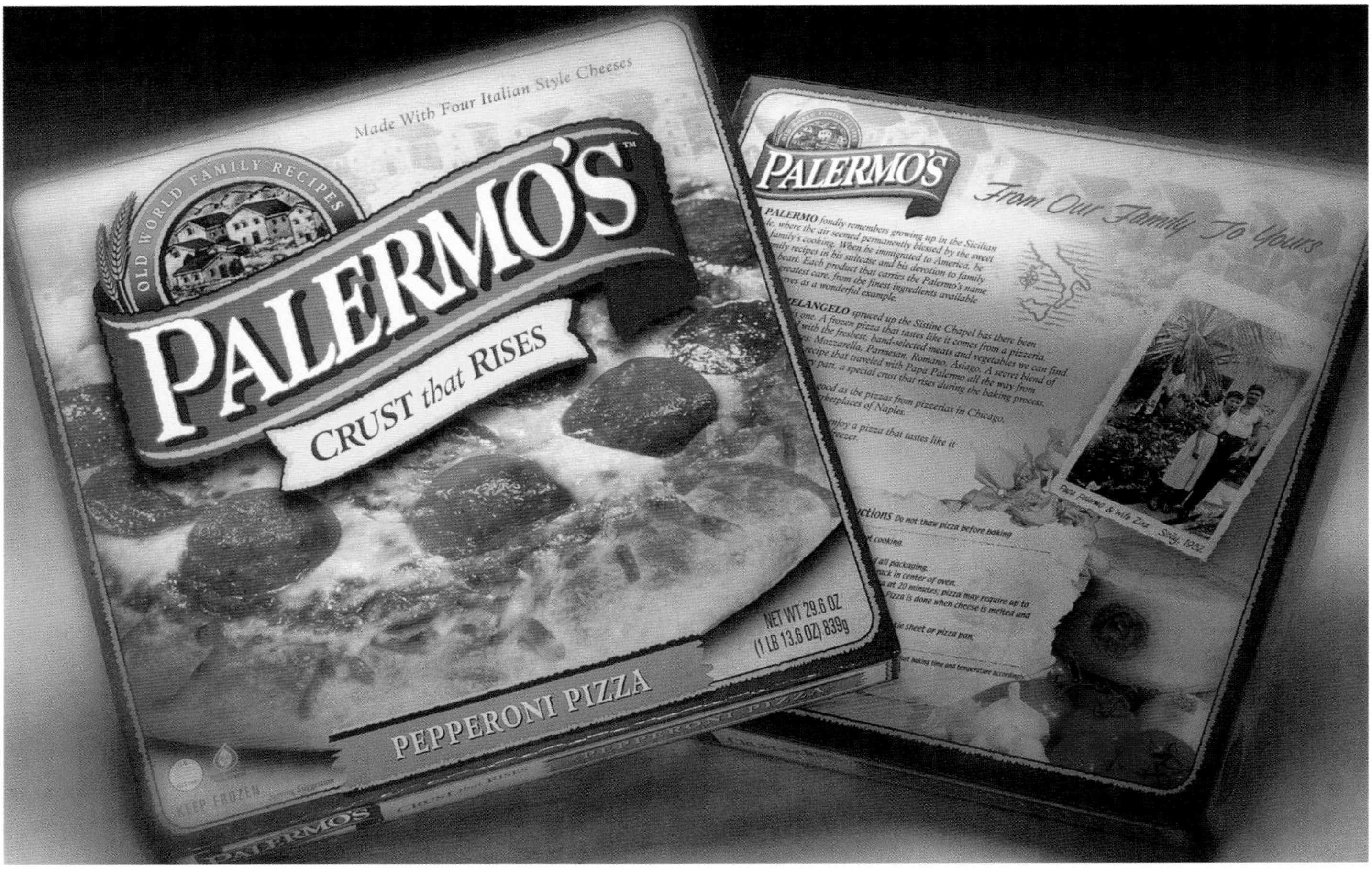

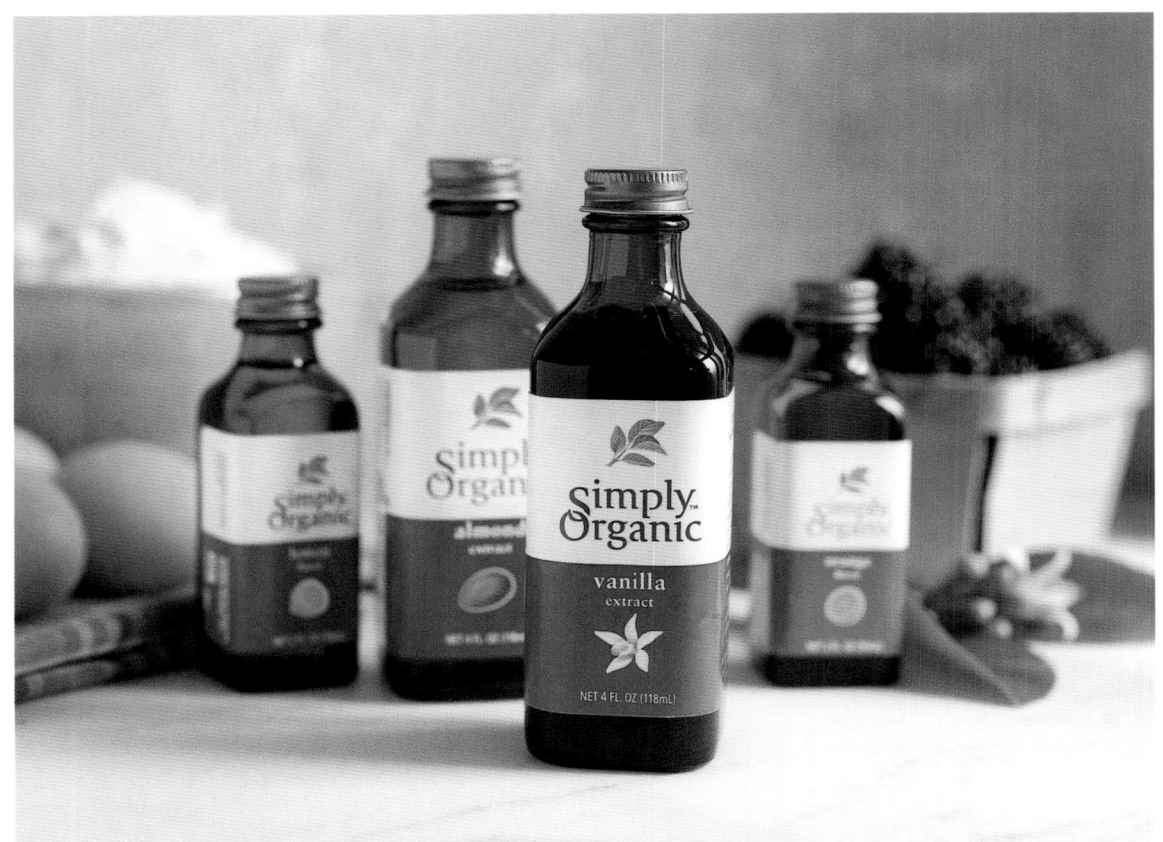

Design Firm **Be Design**
Client   *Frontier Natural Products*
Designers Eric Read,
              Suzanne Hadden,
              Monica Vallejos,
              Will Burke

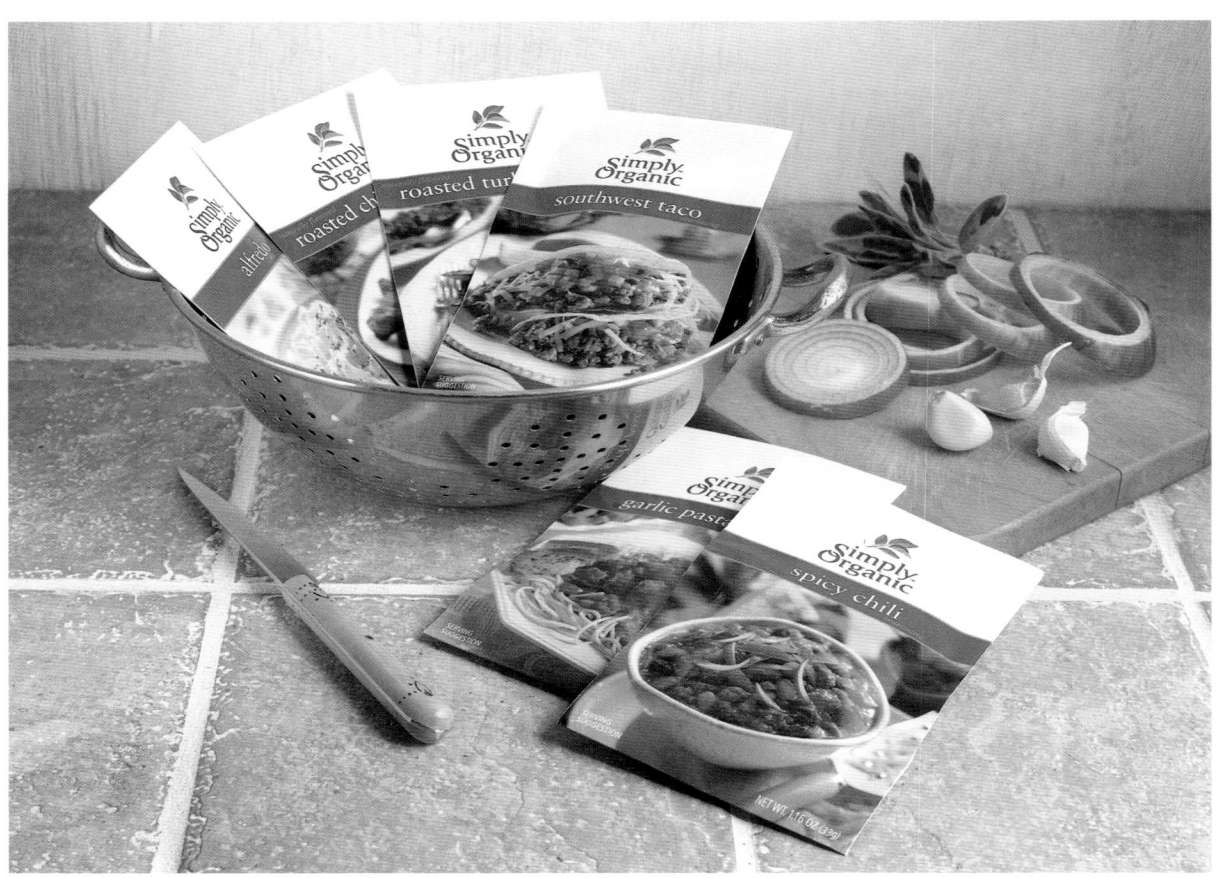

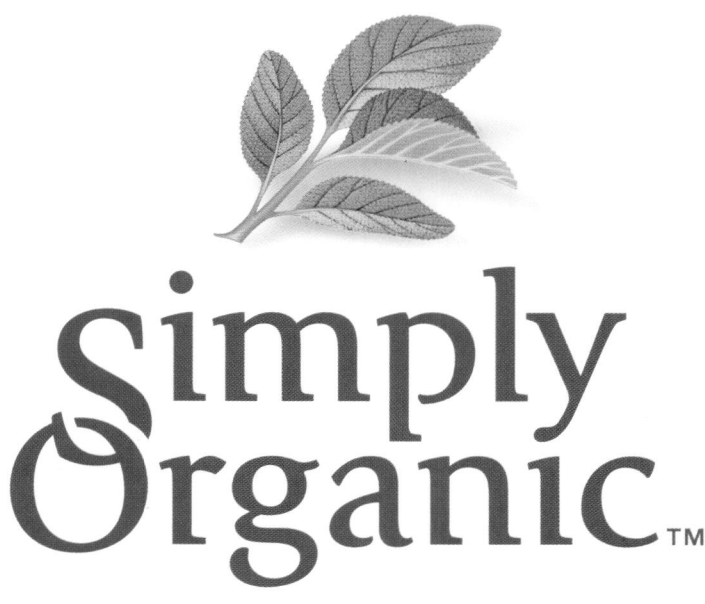

Simply Organic™

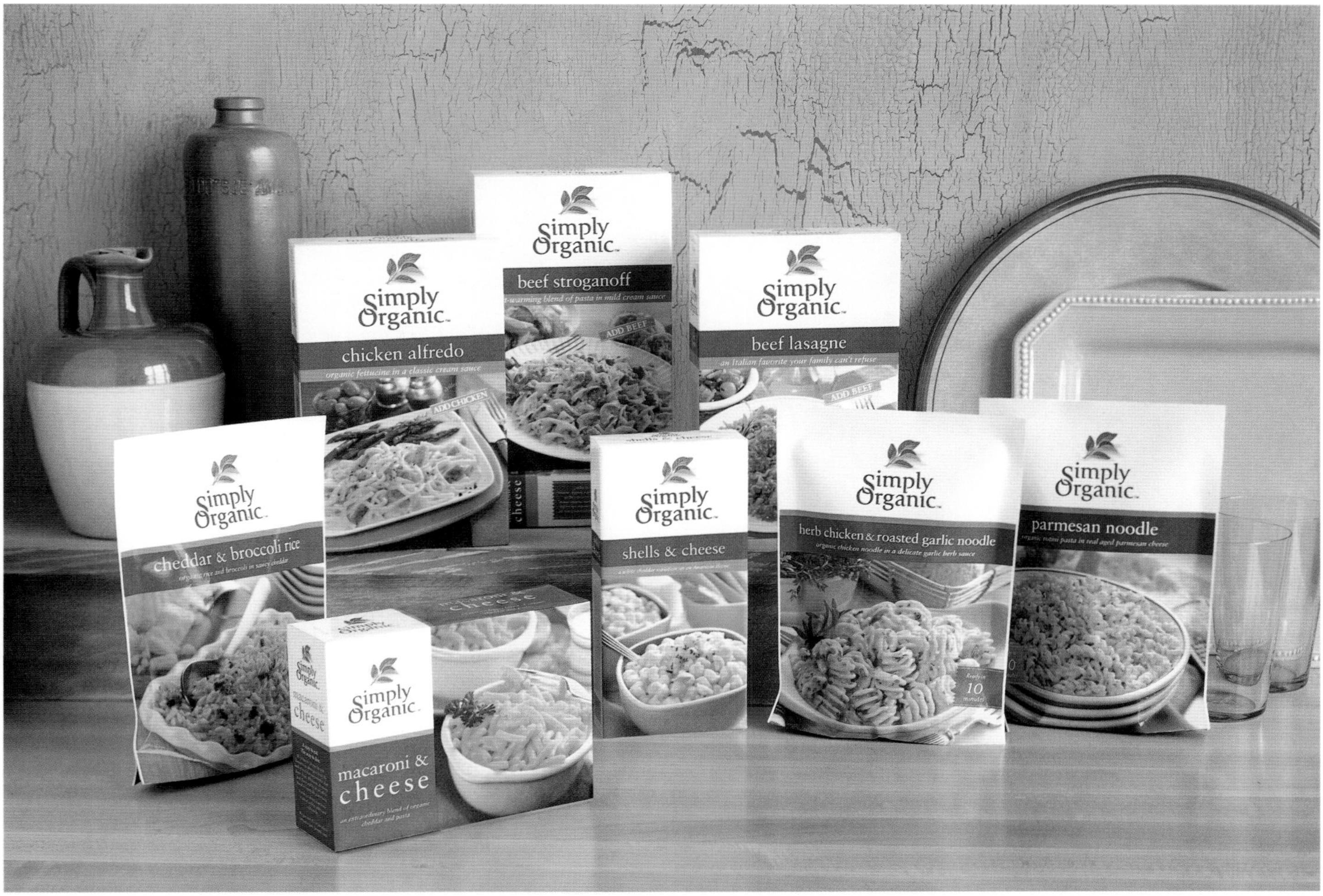

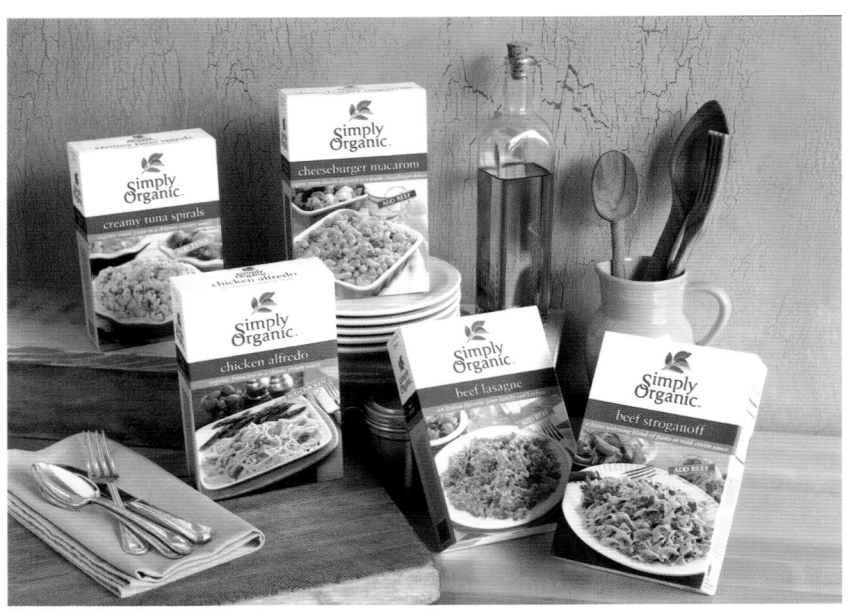

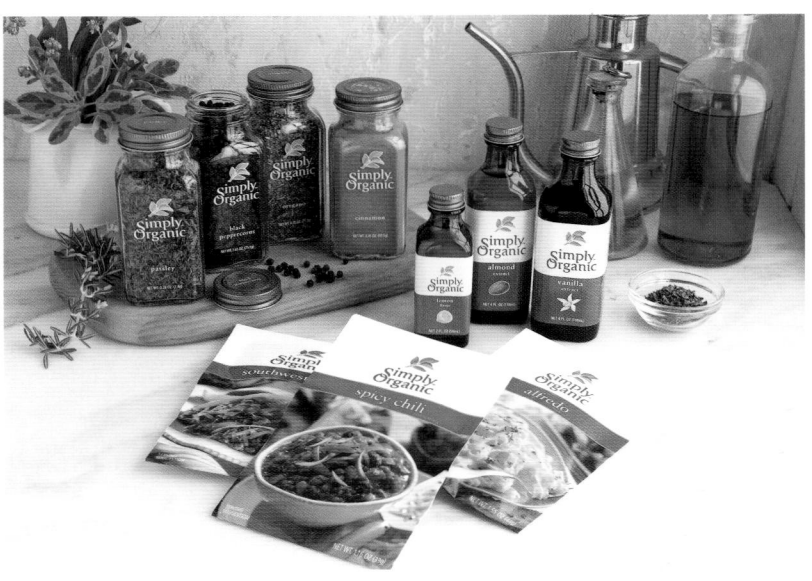

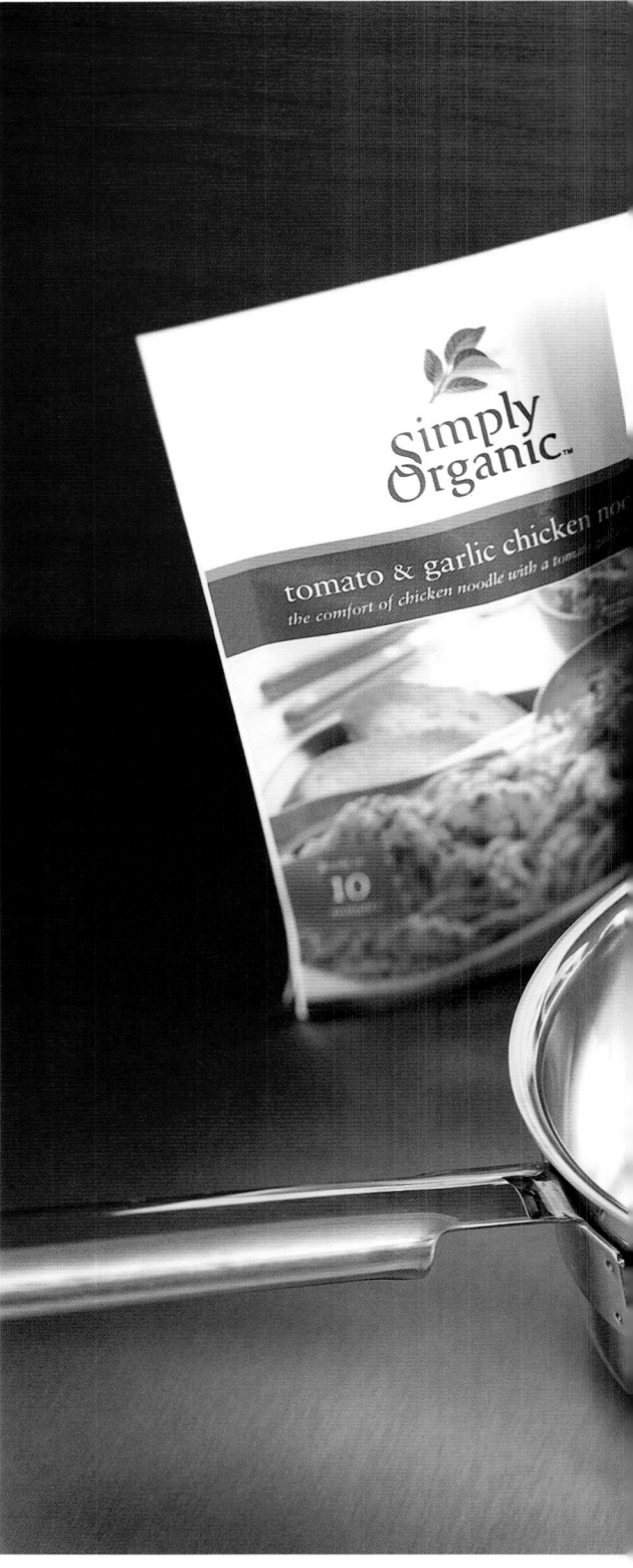

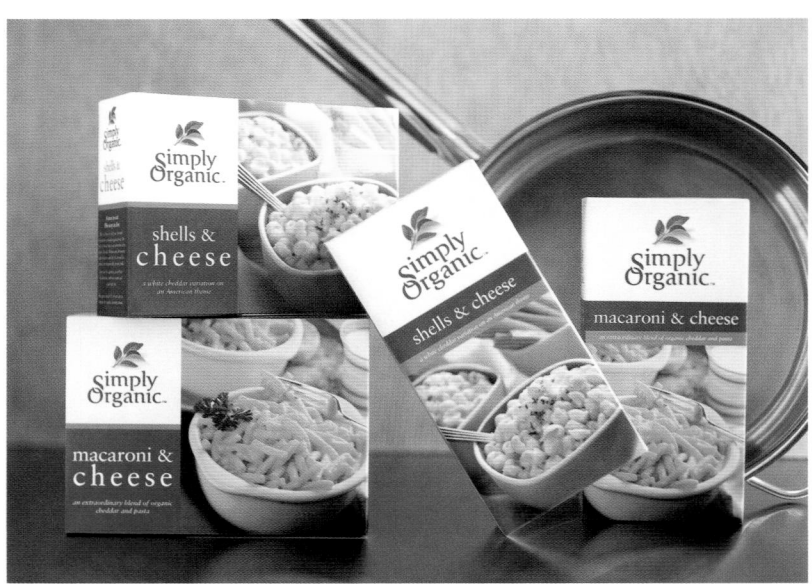

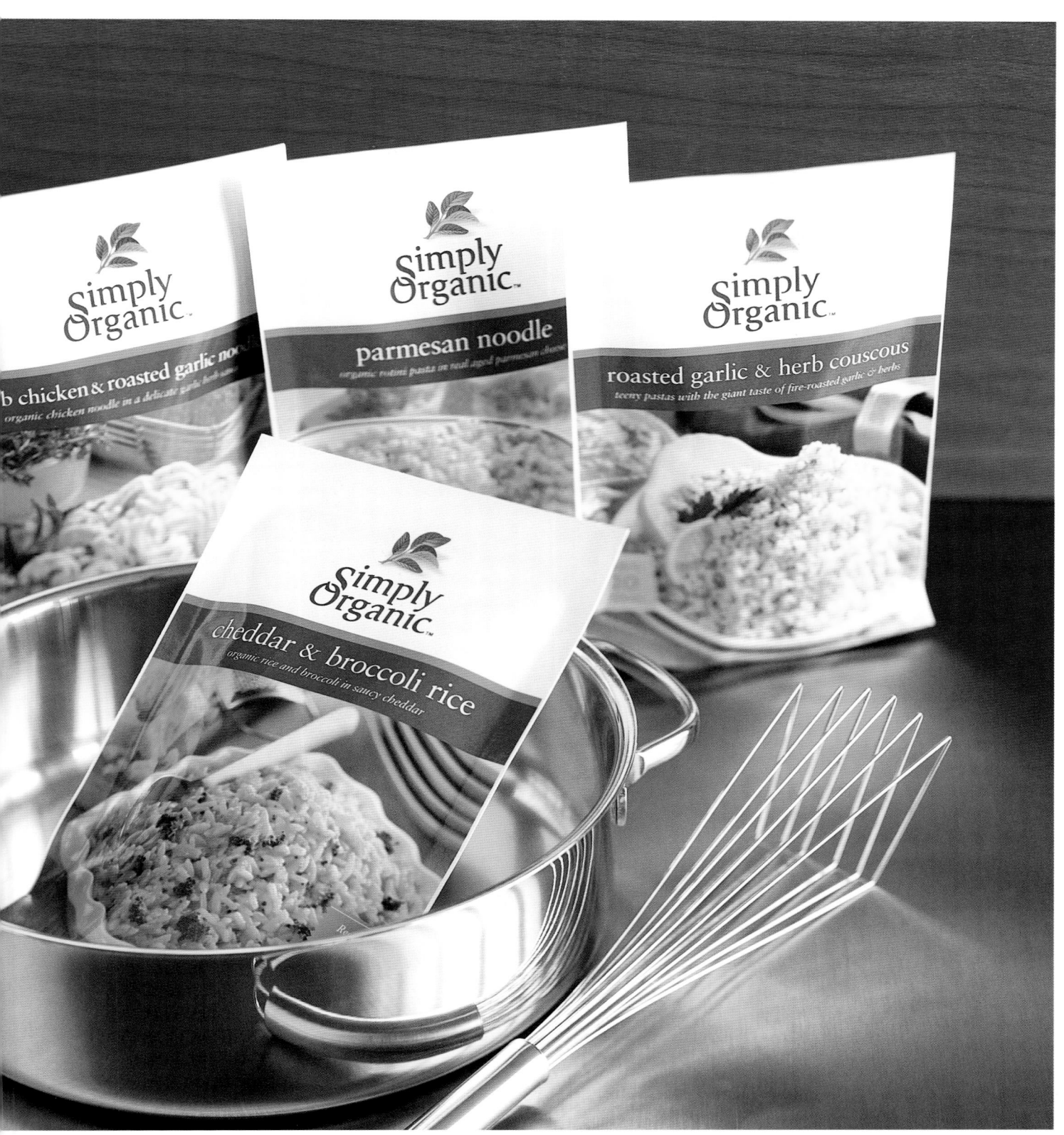

(continued)
Design Firm **Be Design**
Client   *Frontier Natural Products*

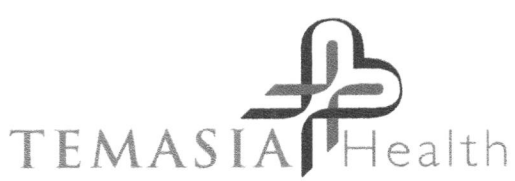

1.

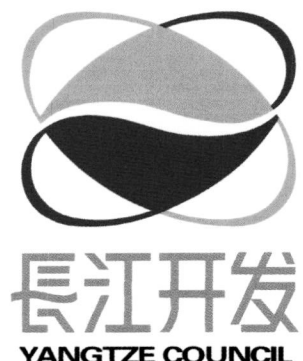

2.

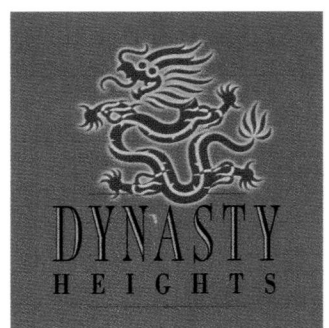

3.

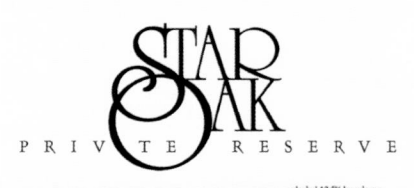

4.

5.

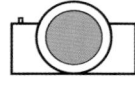

6.

7.

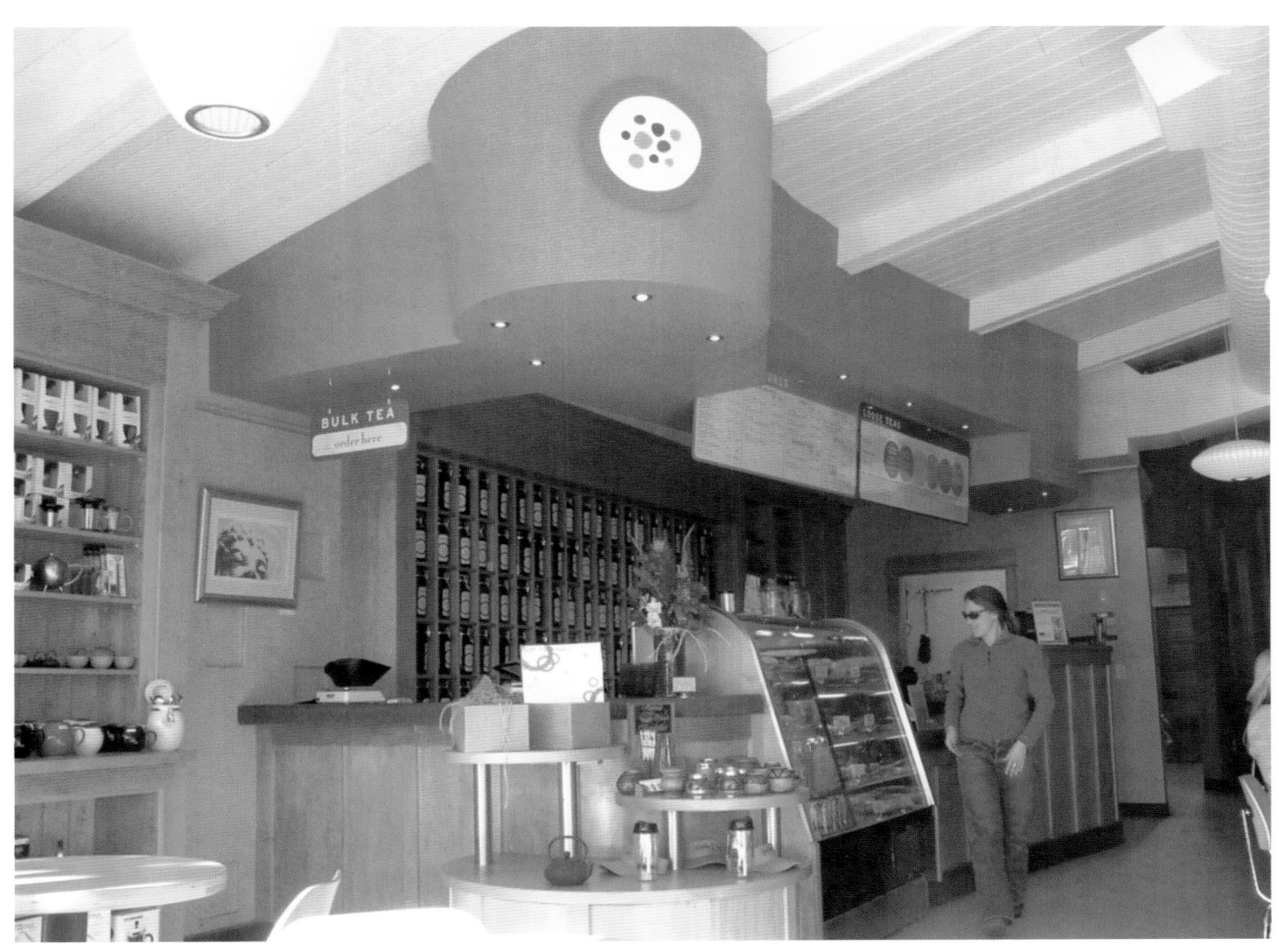

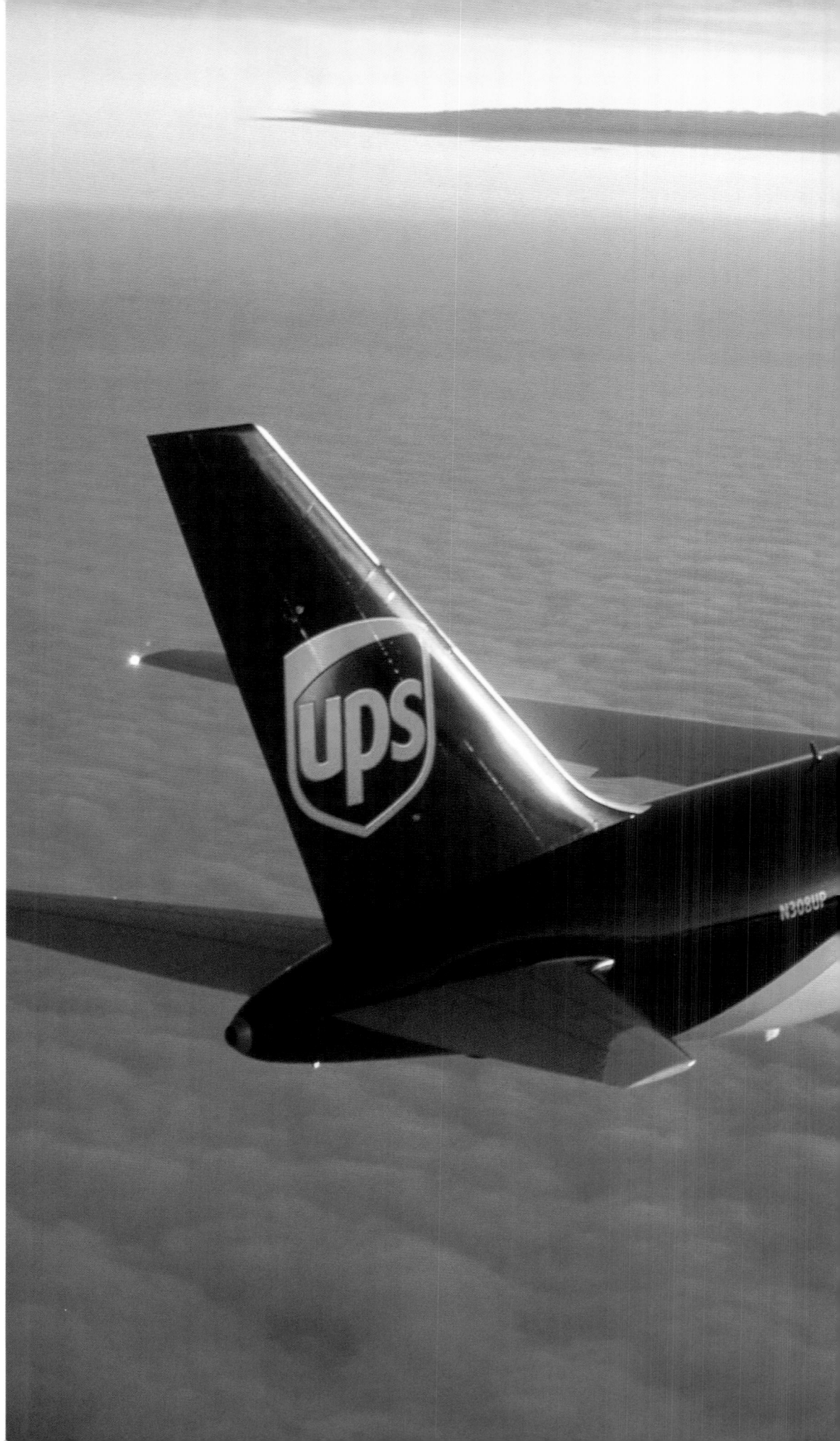

Design Firm **FutureBrand**
Client   *UPS*
Designers   Claude Salzberger,
            Sven Seger,
            Diego Kolsky,
            Michael Thibodeau,
            Alan Campbell,
            Marco Acevedo,
            Michael Matthews,
            Marie Schabenbeck,
            Mike Sheehan,
            Phil Rojas,
            Tom Li

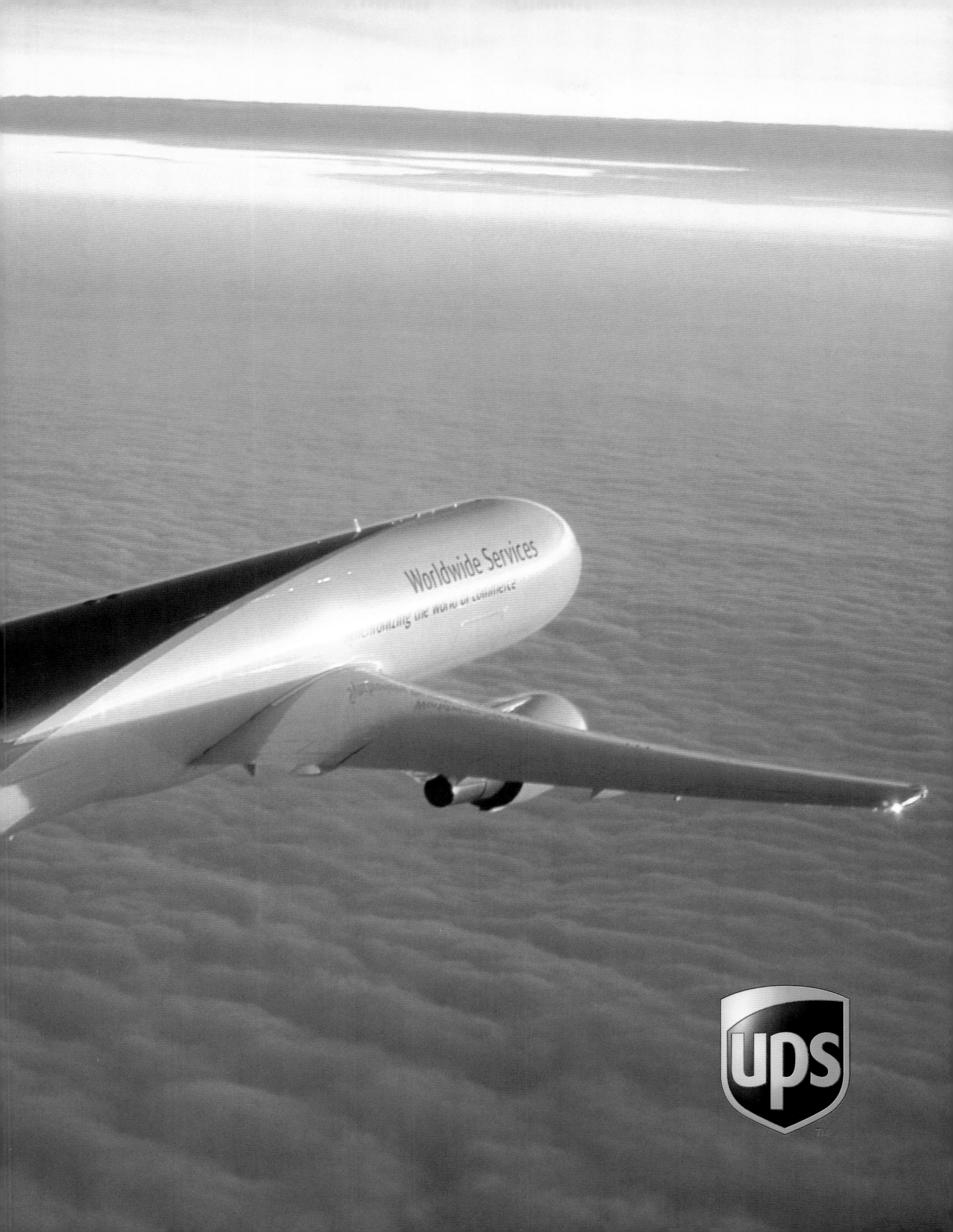

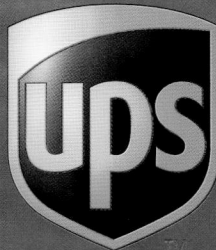

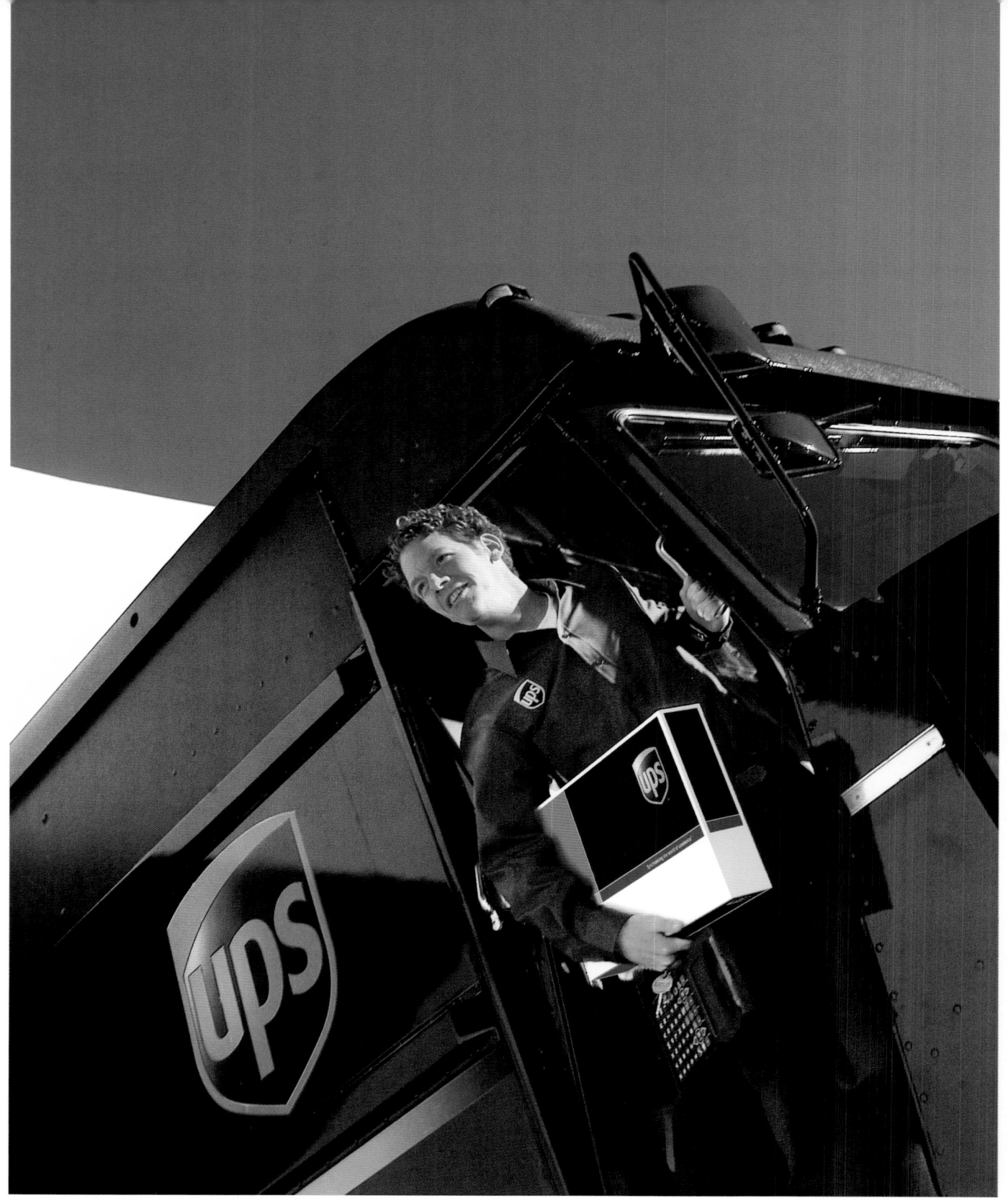

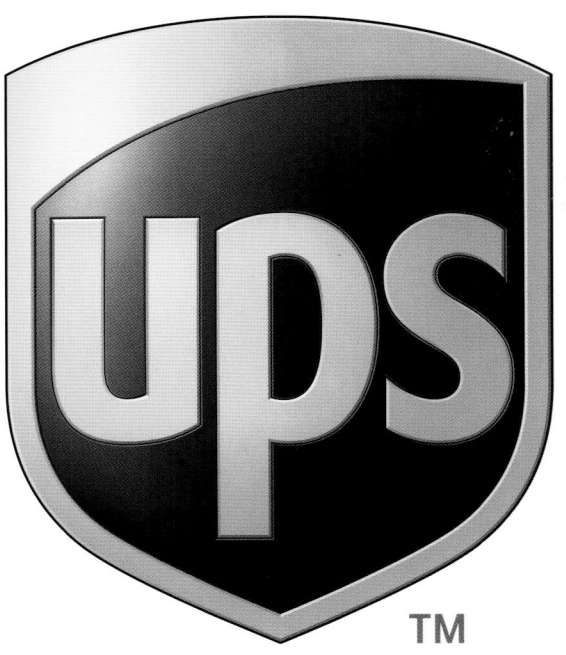

TM

(continued)
Design Firm **FutureBrand**
Client *UPS*

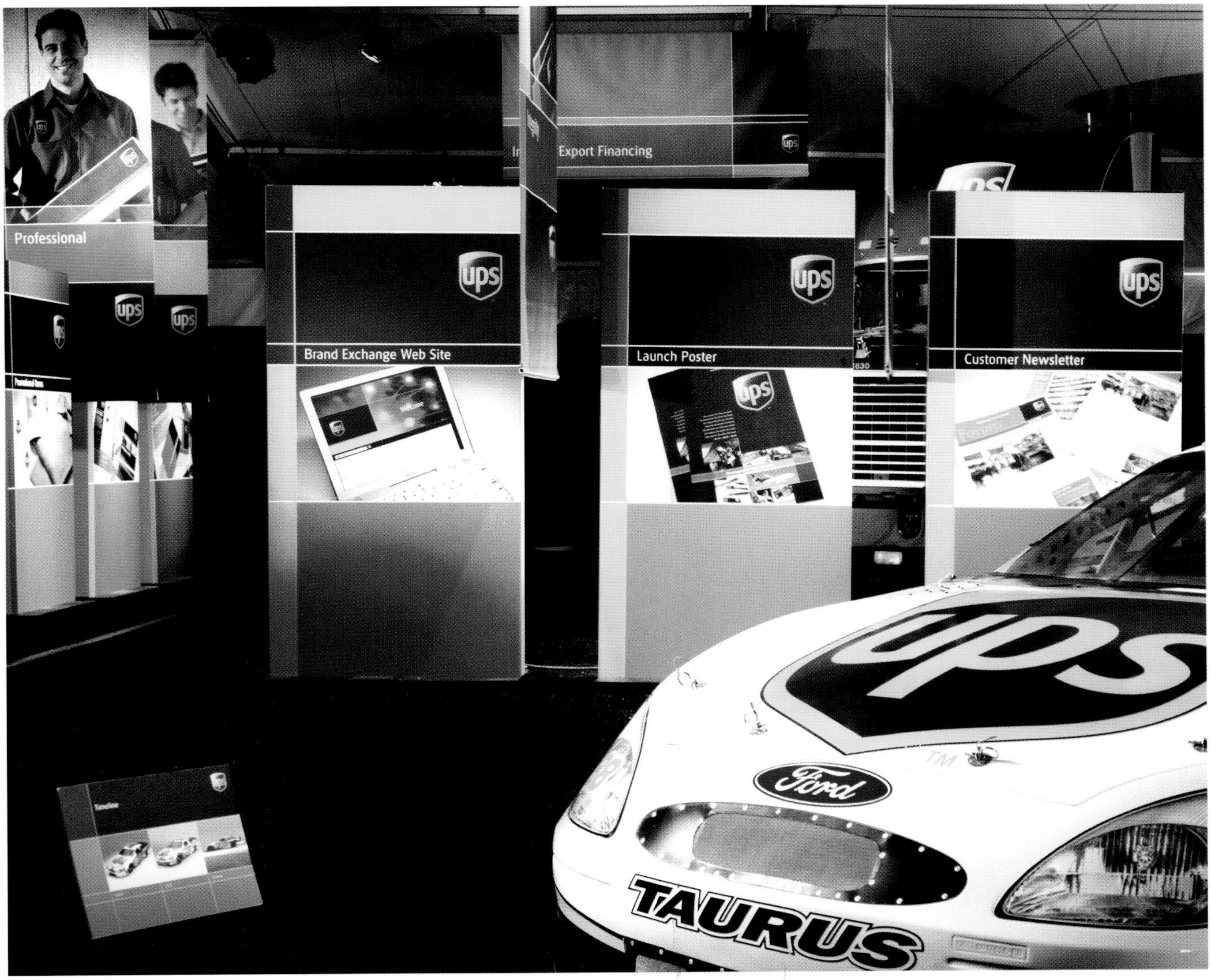

Professional

Export Financing

Brand Exchange Web Site

Launch Poster

Customer Newsletter

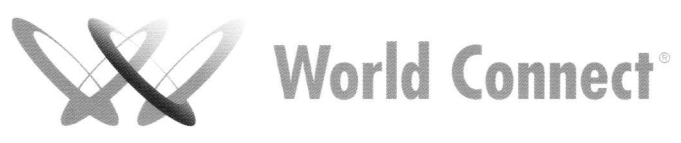

1.

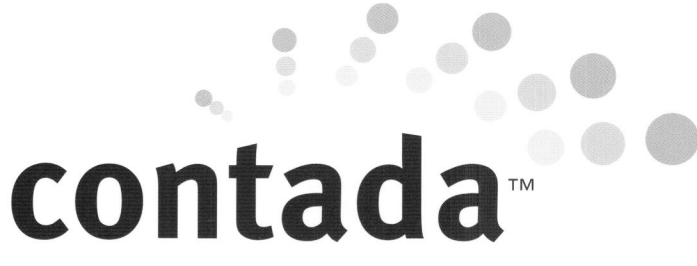

2.

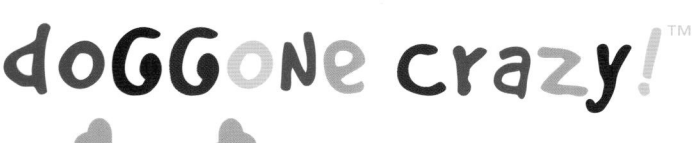

3.

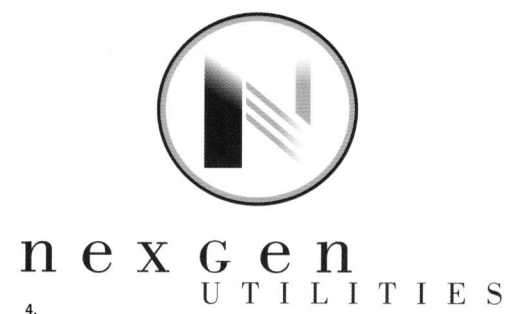

4.

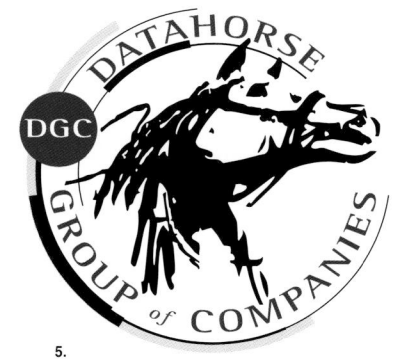

5.

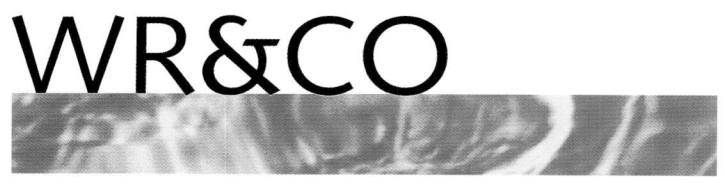

6.

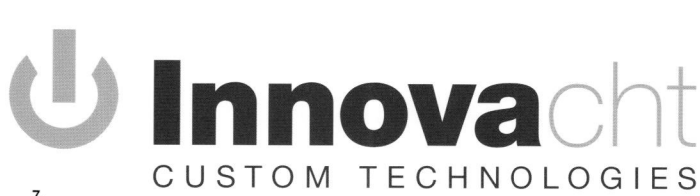

7.

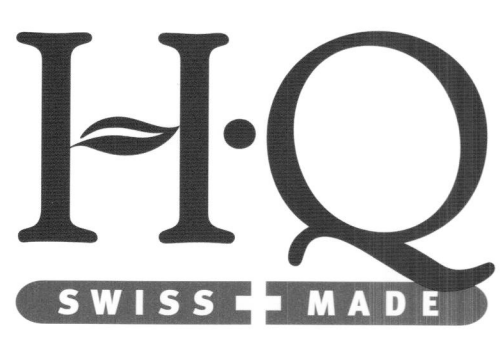

8.

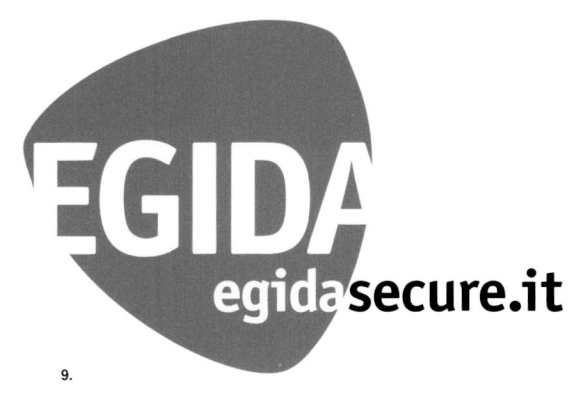

9.

CAMERA DI COMMERCIO
INDUSTRIA ARTIGIANATO AGRICOLTURA
DI VICENZA

10.

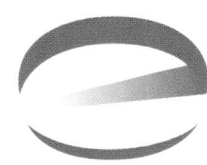

11.

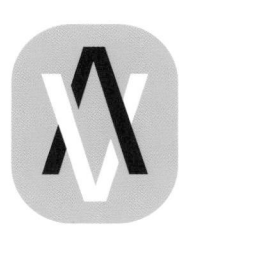

12.

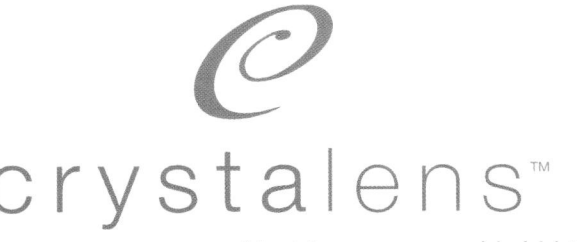

13.

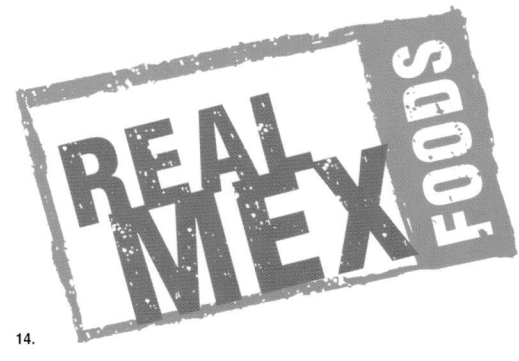

14.

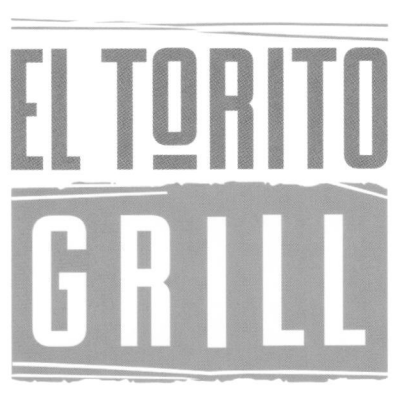

15.

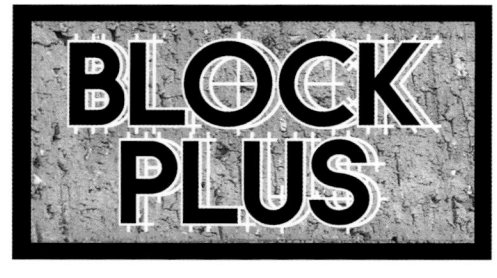

BLOCK PLUS (M) SDN. BHD.

1.

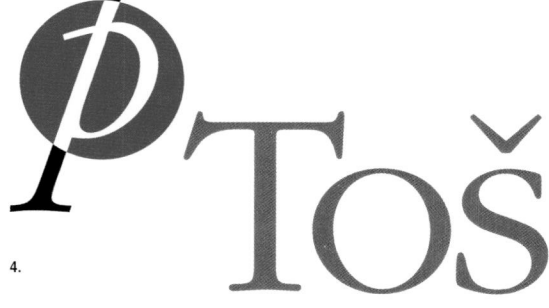

2.

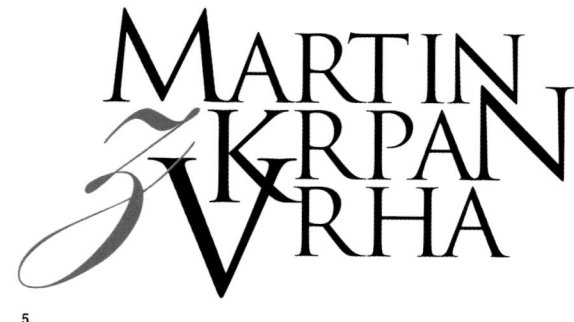

3.

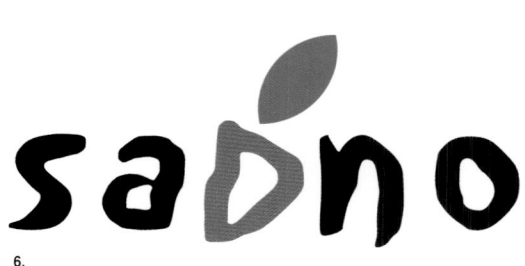

4.

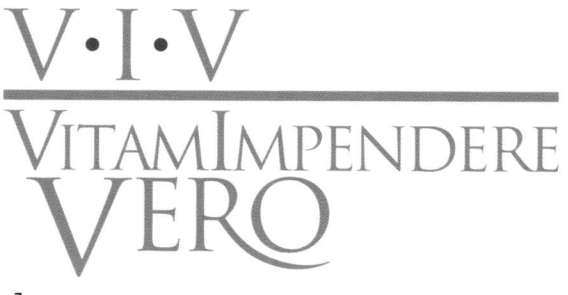

5.

6.

V · I · V

VitamImpendere Vero

7.

1
  Design Firm **FIXGO ADVERTISING (M) SDN BHD**
2 - 7
  Design Firm **KROG**
1.
  Client   *Block Plus (M) Sdn Bhd*
  Designers FGA Creative Team
2.
  Client   *Institut za javno upravo, Ljubljana*
  Designer   Edi Berk
3.
  Client   *Institut za primerjalno pravo, Ljubljana*
  Designer   Edi Berk
4.
  Client   *Peter Tos, Ljubljana*
  Designer   Edi Berk

5.
  Client   *Presernova druzba, Ljubljana*
  Designer   Edi Berk
6.
  Client   *Zlati gric, Slovenske Konjice*
  Designer   Edi Berk
7.
  Client   *Pravna fakulteta, Ljubljana*
  Designer   Edi Berk
(opposite)
  Client   *A&P Canada*
  Design Firm **LogosBrands**
  Designers Gabriella Sousa, Sunny Chan

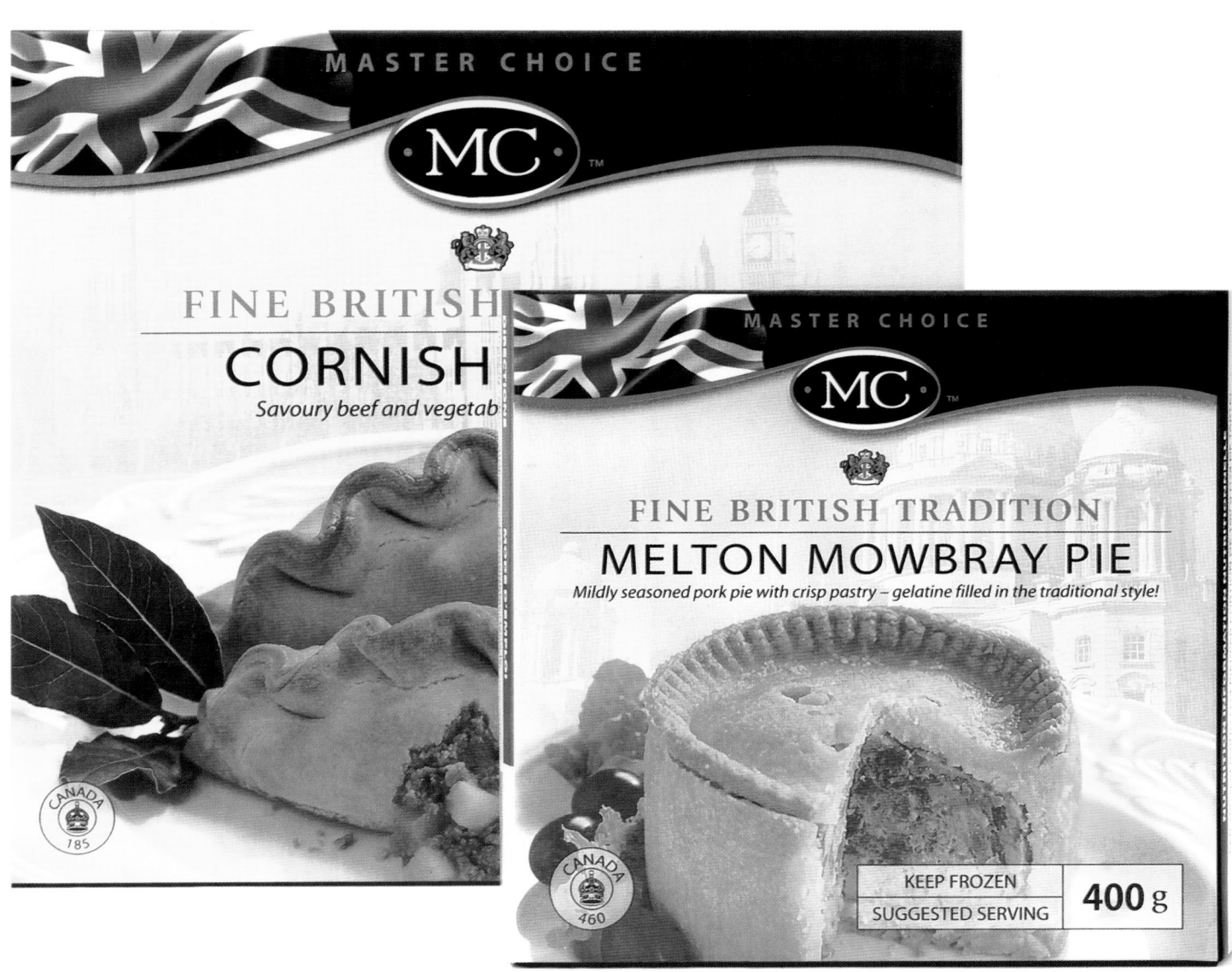

OHANA
FARM

1.

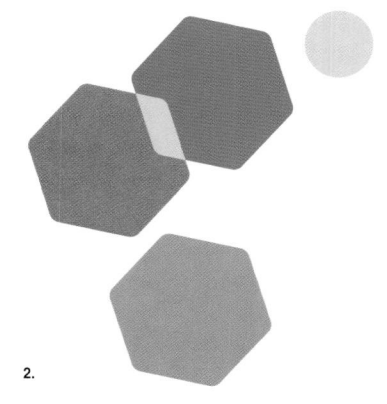

2.

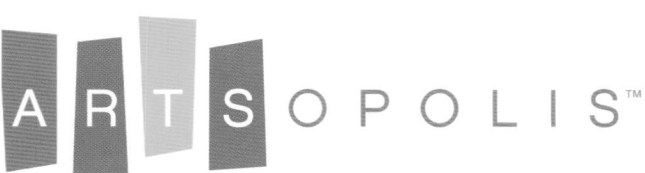

3.

JAMES
PHILLIP
WRIGHT

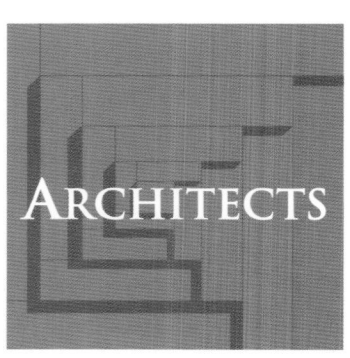

4.

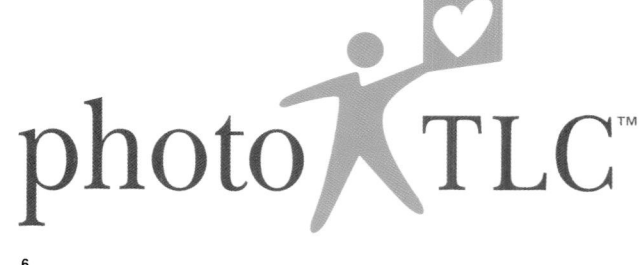 CMG FOUNDATIONS

5.

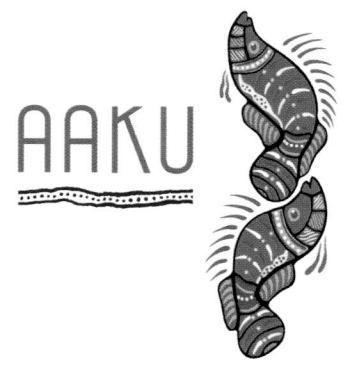 photo TLC™

6.

AAKU

7.

AAKU

8.

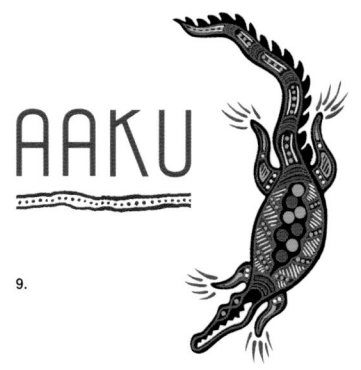

9.

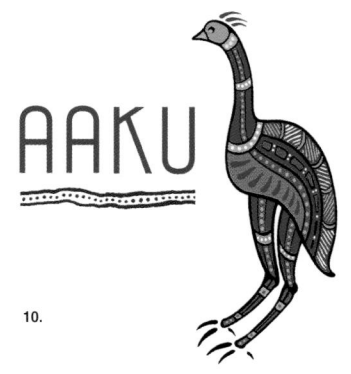

10.

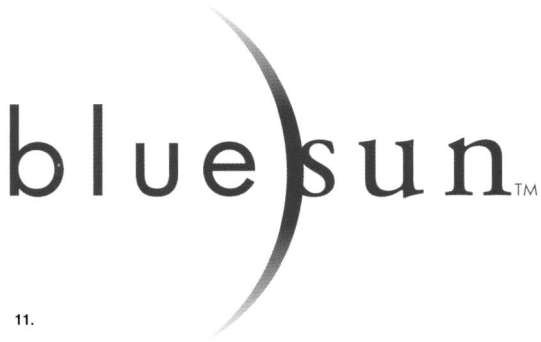

11.

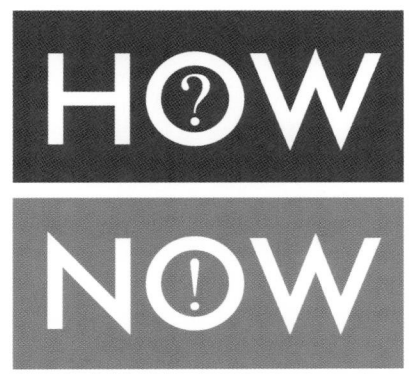

12.

S K Y L A R
+
H A L E Y

13.

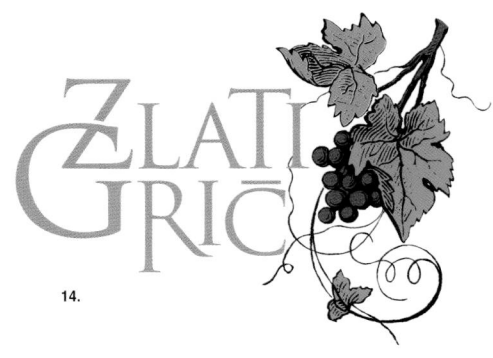

14.

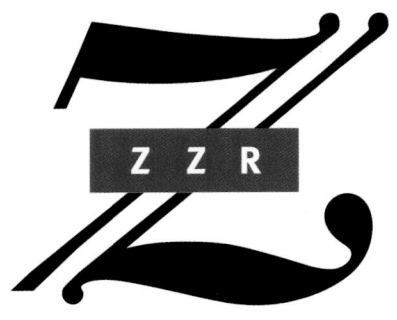

15.

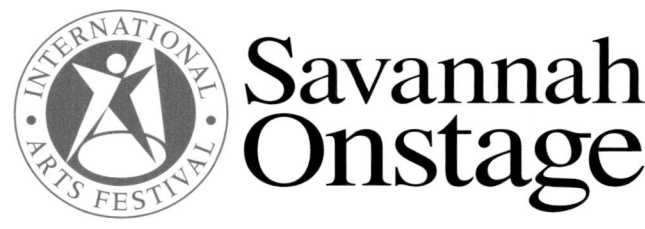

1.

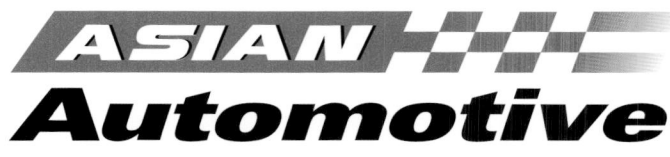

2.

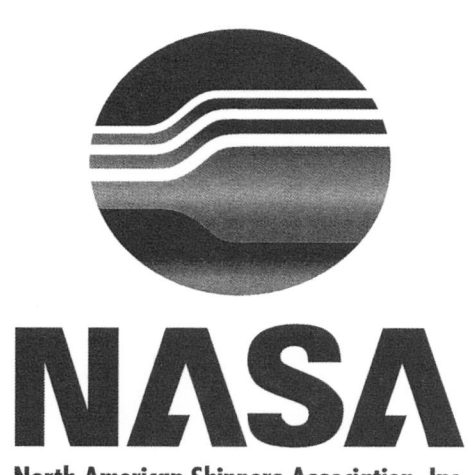

3.

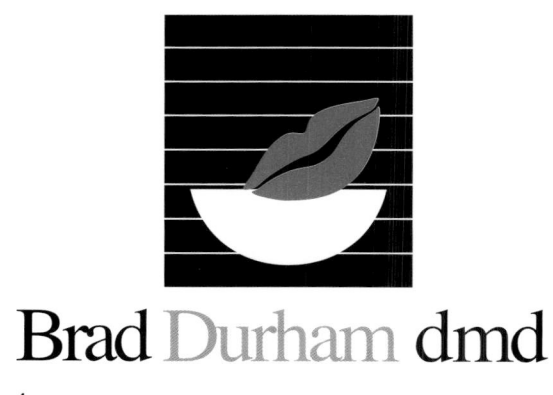

4.

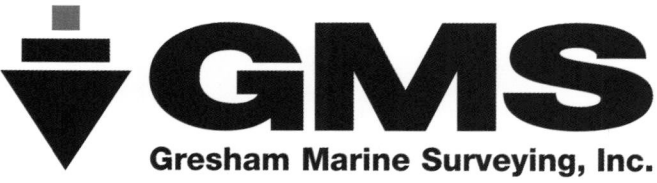

5.

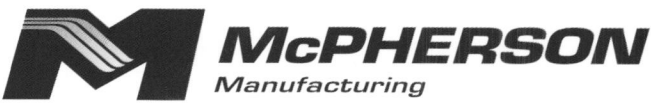

6.

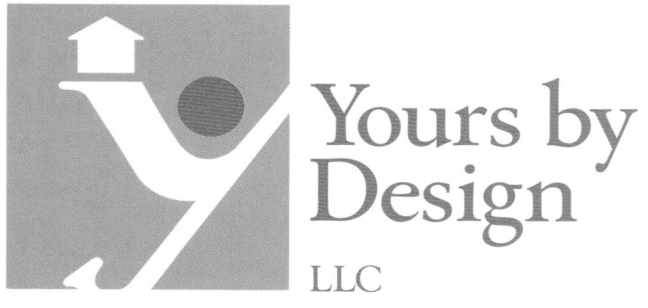

7.

1 - 7
Design Firm **Longwater & Co., Inc.**
1.
Client   *Savannah Onstage*
Designers   Kathryn Strozier,
       Elaine Longwater,
       Anastasia Kontos

2.
Client   *Asian Automotive*
Designers   Kathryn Strozier,
       Elaine Longwater,
       Anastasia Kontos

3.
Client   *North American*
       Shippers Association
Designers   Kathryn Strozier,
       Elaine Longwater,
       Anastasia Kontos

4.
Client   *Brad Durham, DMD*
Designers   Kathryn Strozier,
       Elaine Longwater,
       Anastasia Kontos

5.
Client   *Gresham Marine*
       Surveying, Inc.
Designers   Kathryn Strozier,
       Elaine Longwater,
       Anastasia Kontos

6.
Client   *McPherson Manufacturing*
Designers   Kathryn Strozier,
       Elaine Longwater,
       Anastasia Kontos

7.
Client   *Yours By Design, LLC*
Designers   Kathryn Strozier,
       Elaine Longwater,
       Anastasia Kontos

(opposite)
Client   *Ruffin' It Pet Supplies*
Design Firm **Designs On You!**
Designers   Anthony B. Stephens,
       Suzanna Stephens,

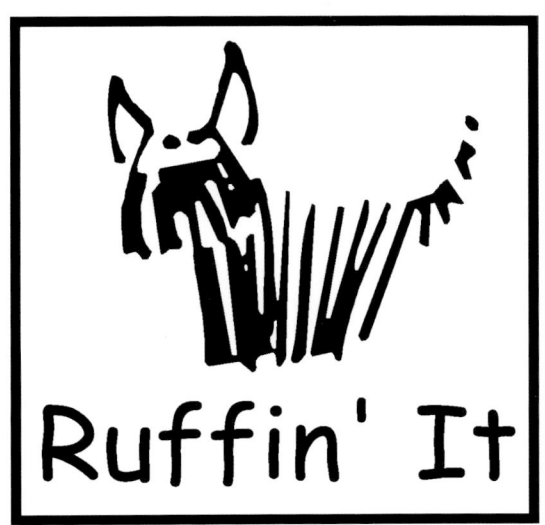

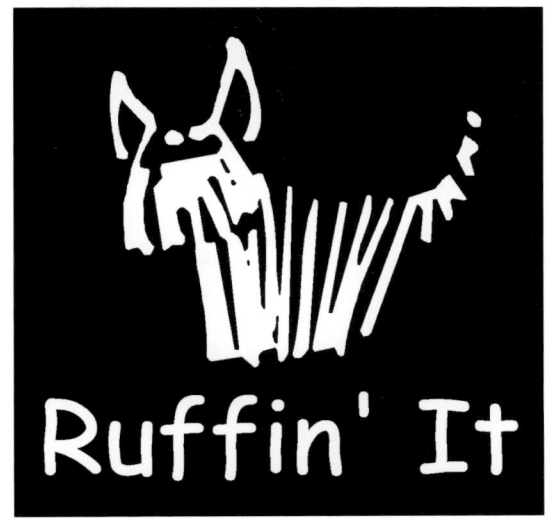

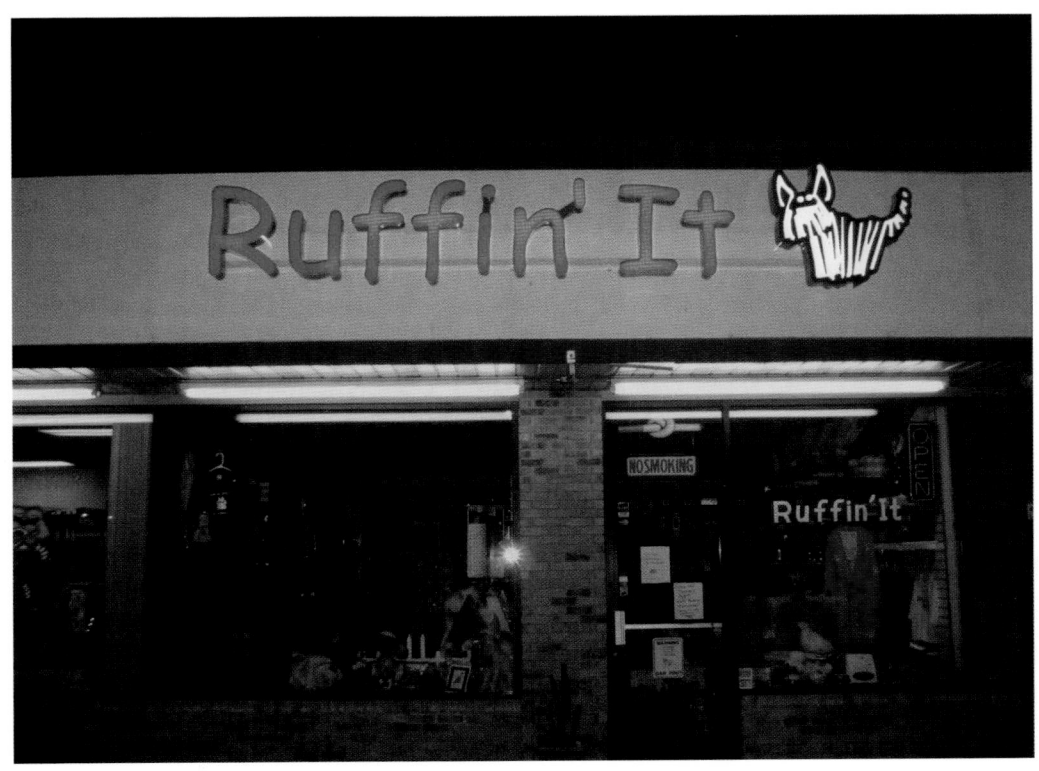

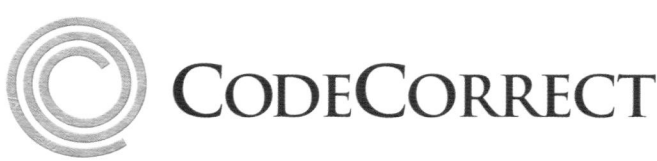

1.

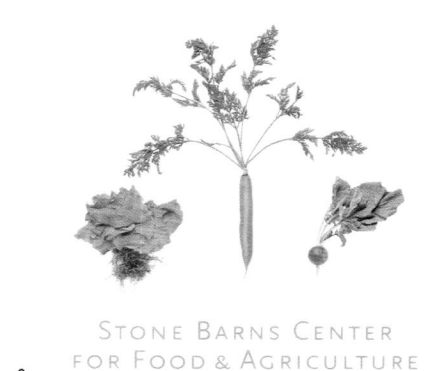

2.

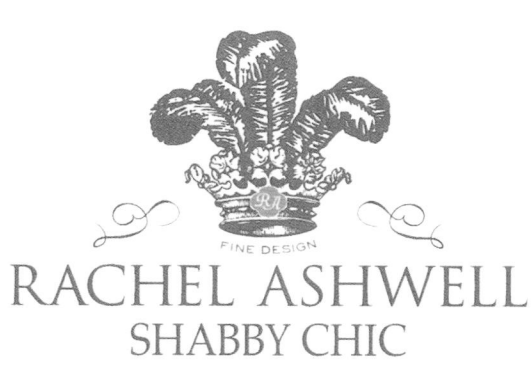

3.

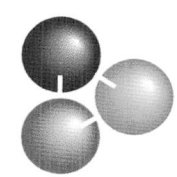

4.

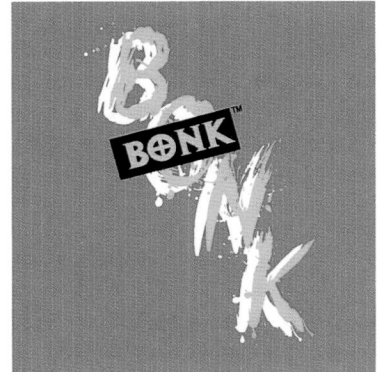

5.

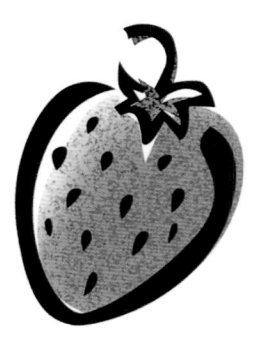

6.

7.

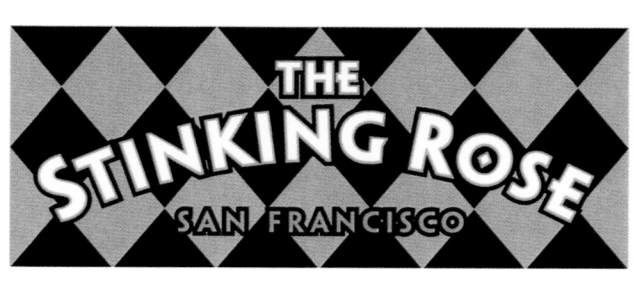

8.

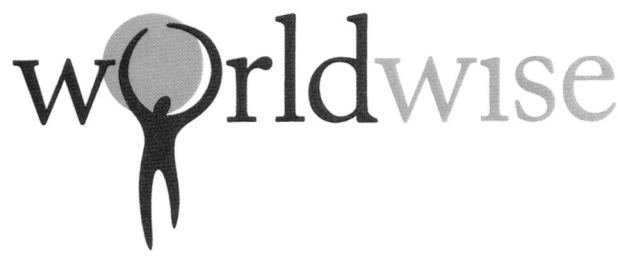

9.

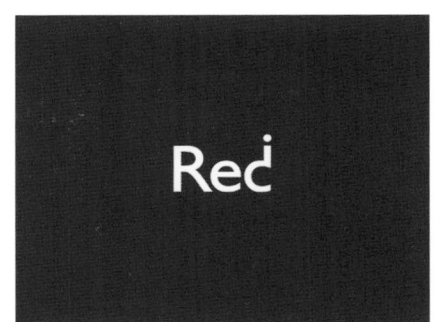

10.

ORANGE

11.

GREEN

12.

blue

13.

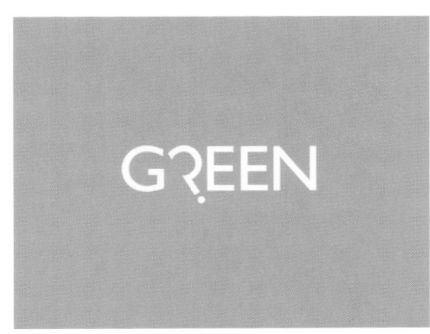

14.

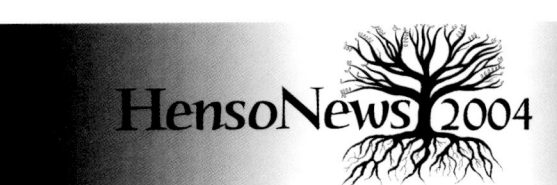

15.

1
Design Firm **Walsh Design**
2
Design Firm **Alexander Isley Inc.**
3
Design Firm **EPOS, Inc.**
4, 5
Design Firm **Shimokochi-Reeves**
6
Design Firm **Sabingrafik, Inc.**
7 - 9
Design Firm **Be Design**
10 - 13
Design Firm **Robert Meyers Design**
14
Design Firm **FIXGO ADVERTISING (M) SDN BHD**
15
Design Firm **Designs on You!**

1.
Client   *CodeCorrect*
Designer   Miriam Lisco
2.
Client   *Stone Barns Center for Food & Agriculture*
Designers   Alex Isley, Tara Benyei
3.
Client   *Rachel Ashwell Shabby Chic*
Designers   Gabrielle Raumberger,
            Samantha Ahdoot,
            Cliff Singontiko

4, 5.
Client   *The Wella Corporation*
Designers   Mamoru Shimokochi,
            Anne Reeves
6.
Client   *Tamansari Beverage*
Designers   Tracy Sabin, Karim Amirgani
7.
Client   *The Stinking Rose*
Designers   Lisa Brussel, Coralie Russo,
            Eric Read, Will Burke
8.
Client   *Mighty Leaf Tea Company*
Designers   Coralie Russo, James Eli
            Eric Read, Will Burke
9.
Client   *Worldwise, Inc.*
Designers   Eric Read, Yusuke Asaka,
            Coralie Russo, Eric Read,
            Will Burke
10 - 13.
Client   *Is It Art?*
Designers   Robert Meyers
14.
Client   Malacca Agriculture
            Developments dn Bhd
Designers   FGA Creative Team
15.
Client   *Henson Family Newsletter*
Designers   Suzanna Stephens,
            Anthony B. Stephens

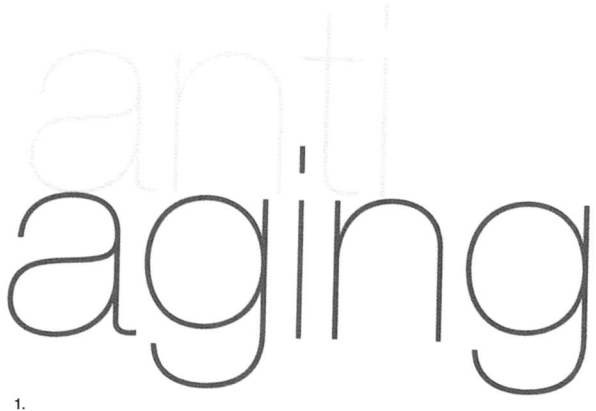

1.

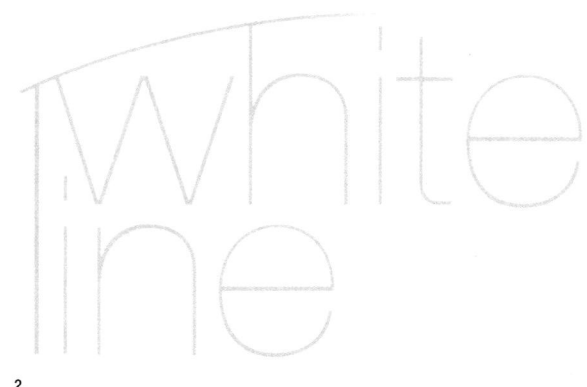

2.

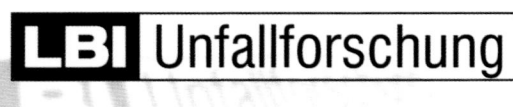

3.

view**point**system

4.

RESOLUTION
L I N E

5.

v o g e l *&* N O L L
v e r l a g

6.

Brüd3r

7.

1 - 7
Design Firm **designbuero**
1, 2.
   Client   *Dr. Temt Laboratories*
   Designer Thomas Stockhammer
3.
   Client   *LBI Unfallforschung*
   Designer Thomas Stockhammer
4.
   Client   *view point system*
   Designer Thomas Stockhammer
5.
   Client   *Dr. Temt Laboratories*
   Designer Thomas Stockhammer
6, 7.
   Client   *DOR Film*
   Designer Thomas Stockhammer

(opposite)
   Client   *Cedar Bluff Middle School*
                    Talented and Gifted Group
Design Firm **Designs On You!**
Designers Suzanna Stephens,
                  Anthony B. Stephens

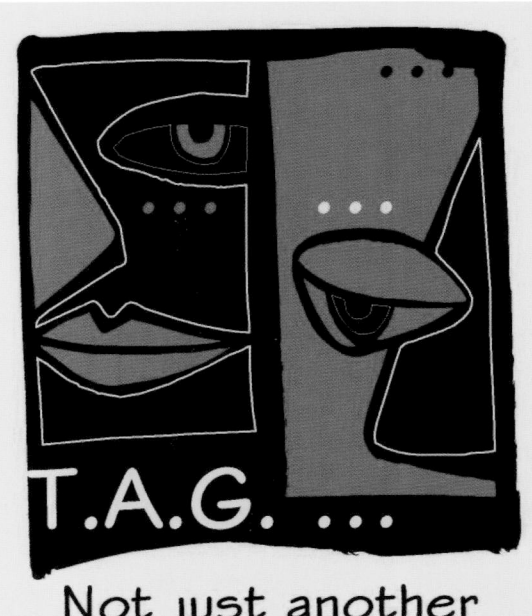

Not just another pretty face!

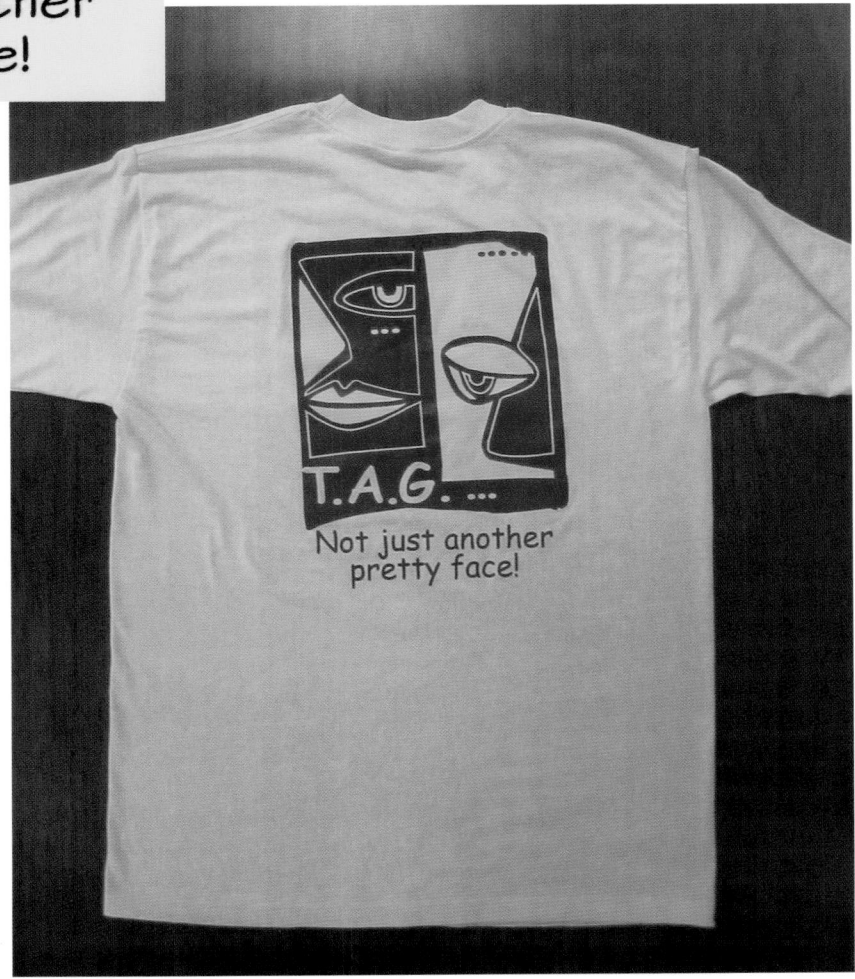

389

**Verizon:
Start-Up Standards**

Verizon Logo Key Applications

▶ Detailed specifications for specific key applications of the logo are being developed and are available through the Corporate Identity Manager.

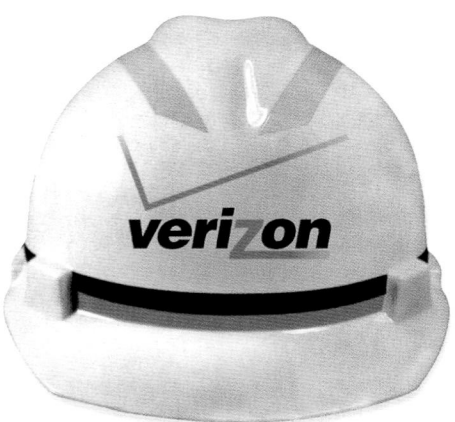

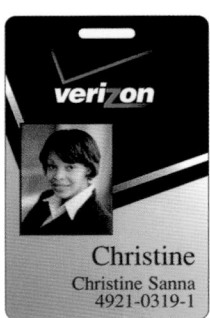

Christine
Christine Sanna
4921-0319-1

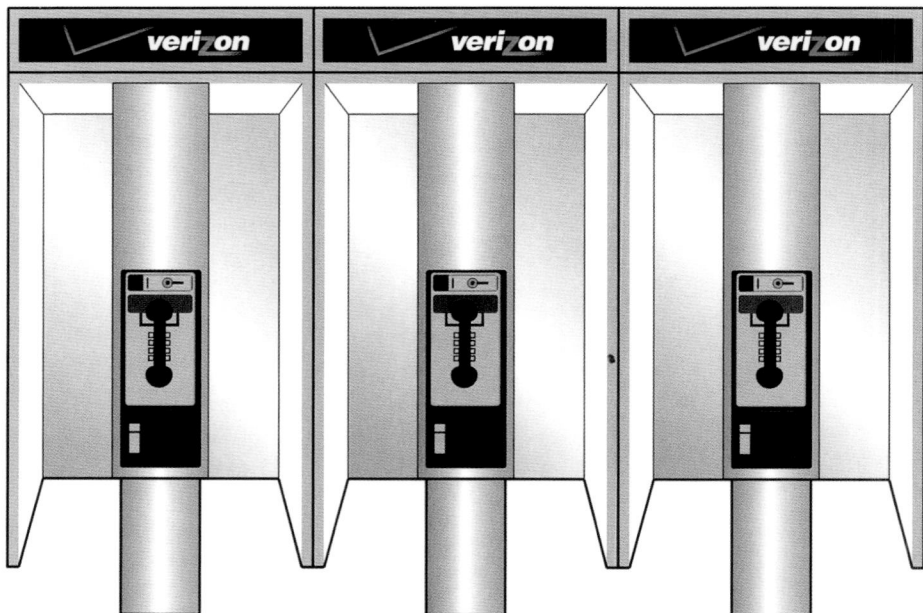

V.3.0 (06/23/00)

390

Verizon Logo Key Applications:
Fleet Examples

▶ Detailed specifications for fleet graphics are being developed and are available through the Corporate Identity Manager.

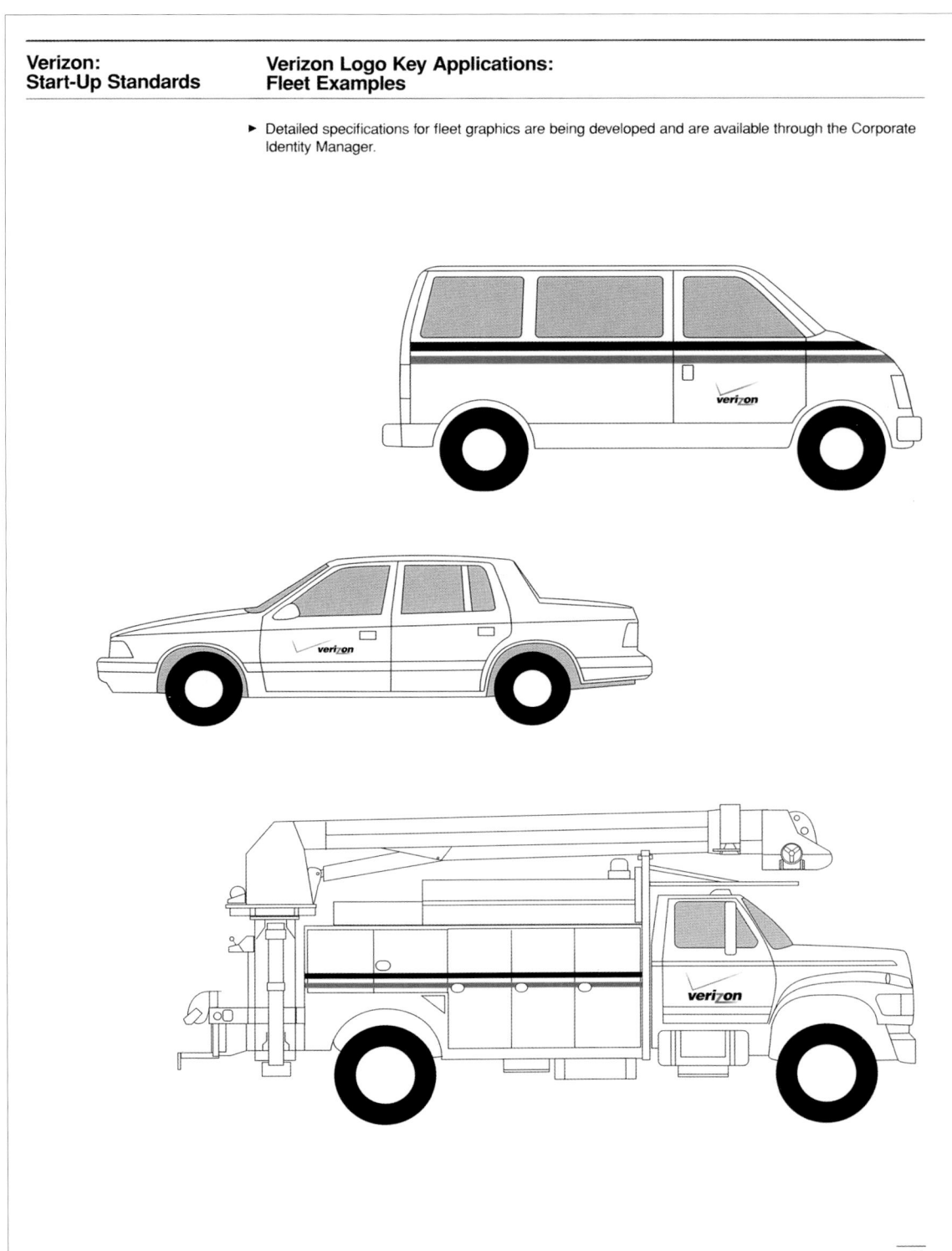

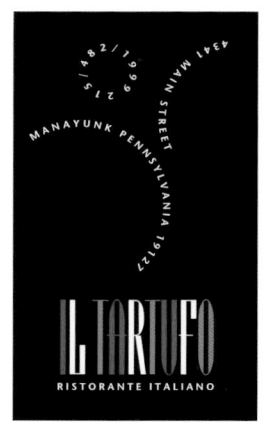

1.

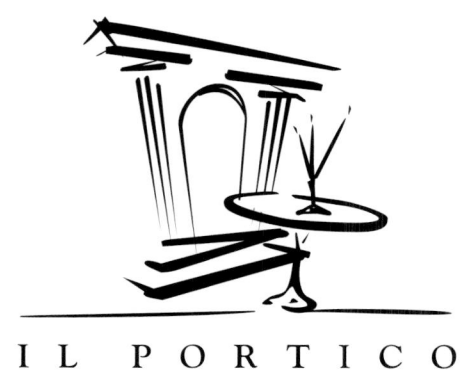

IL PORTICO

2. RISTORANTE ITALIANO

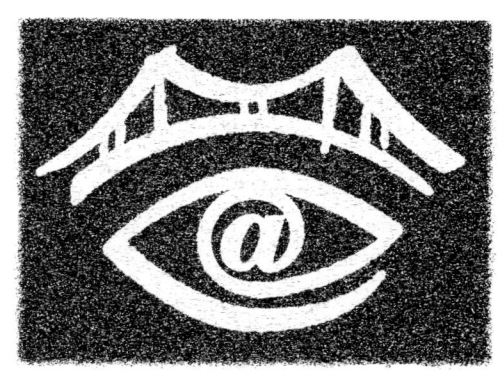

3.

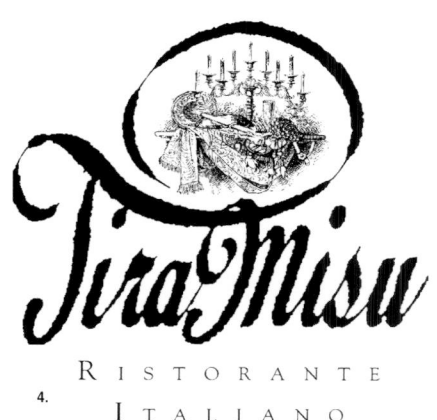

RISTORANTE

4. ITALIANO

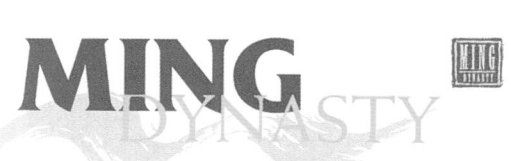

5.

6.

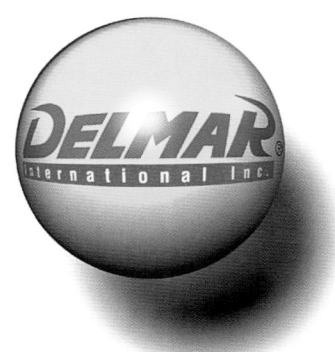

7.

1 - 4
Design Firm **Zygo Communications**
5 - 7
Design Firm **66 communication inc.**
1.
Client   *IL Tartufo*
Designer   Scott Laserow
2.
Client   *IL Portico*
Designer   Scott Laserow
3.
Client   *MindBridge*
Designer   Scott Laserow
4.
Client   *TiraMisu*
Designer   Scott Laserow
5.
Client   *Infinity Industries Inc.*
Designer   Chin C. Yang

6.
Client   *Deco Enterprise Co., Ltd.*
Designer   Chin C. Yang
7.
Client   *Delmar International Inc.*
Designer   Chin C. Yang
(opposite)
Client   *CompanyB, Inc.*
Design Firm **Finished Art, Inc.**
Designers   Donna Johnston, Kannex Fung,
         Barbara Dorn, Luis Fernandez,
         Li-Kim Goh, Mary Jane Hasek,
         Cory Langner, Ake Nimsuwan,
         Larry Peebles, Anne Vongnimitra

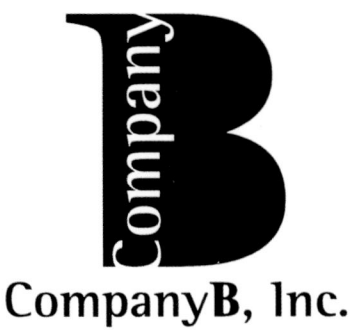

Company**B**, Inc.

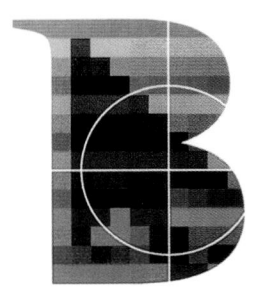

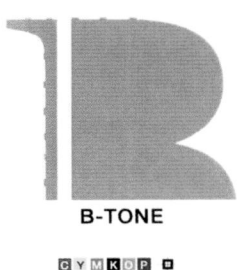

B-TONE

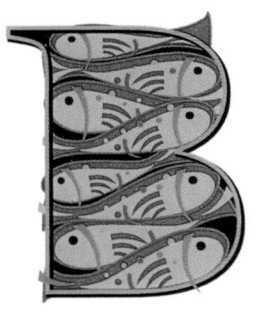

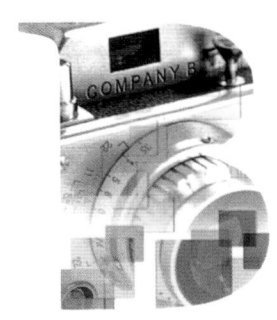

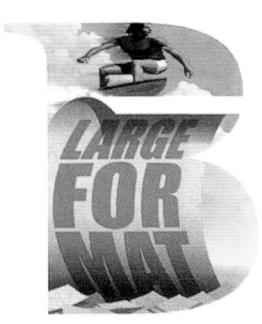

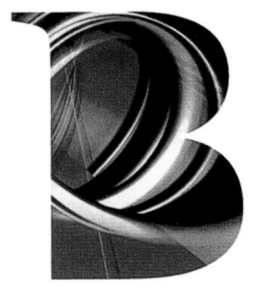

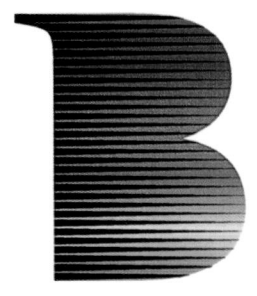

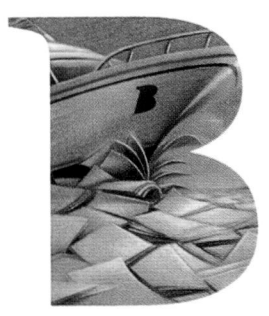

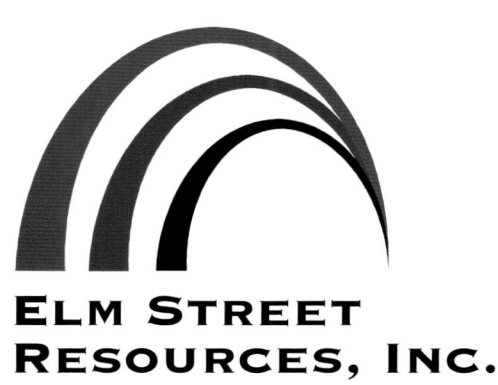

ELM STREET RESOURCES, INC.

1.

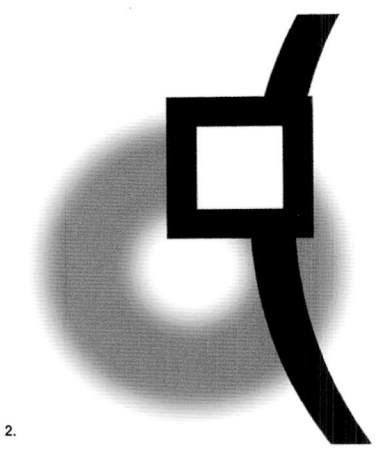

2.

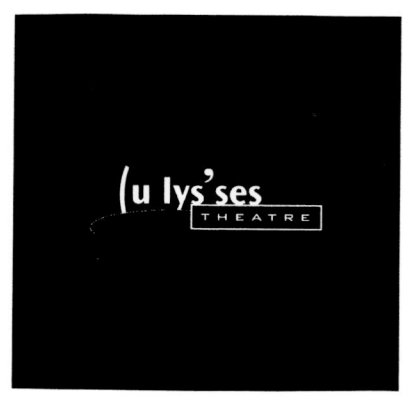

3.

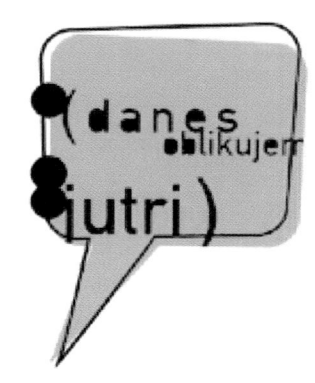

4.

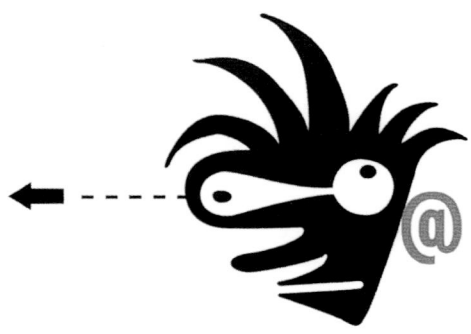

5.

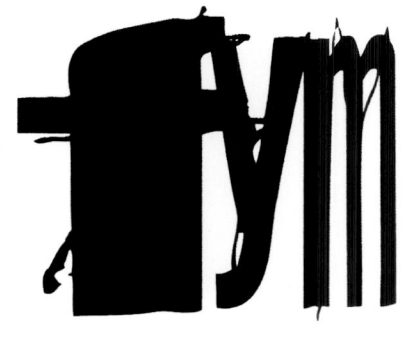

6.

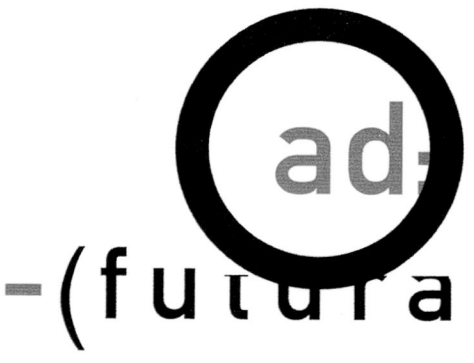

7.

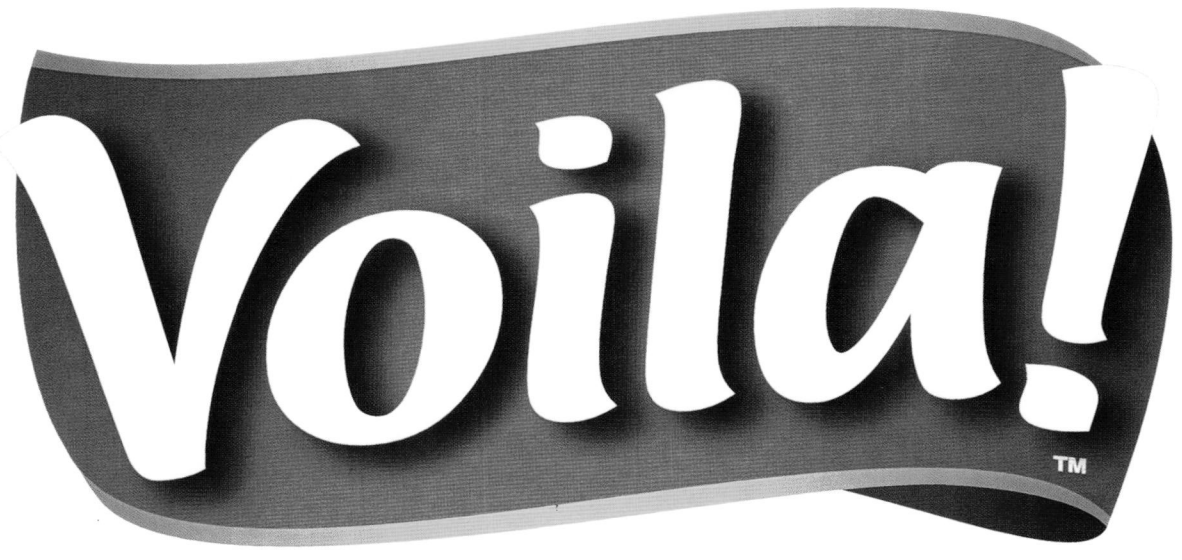

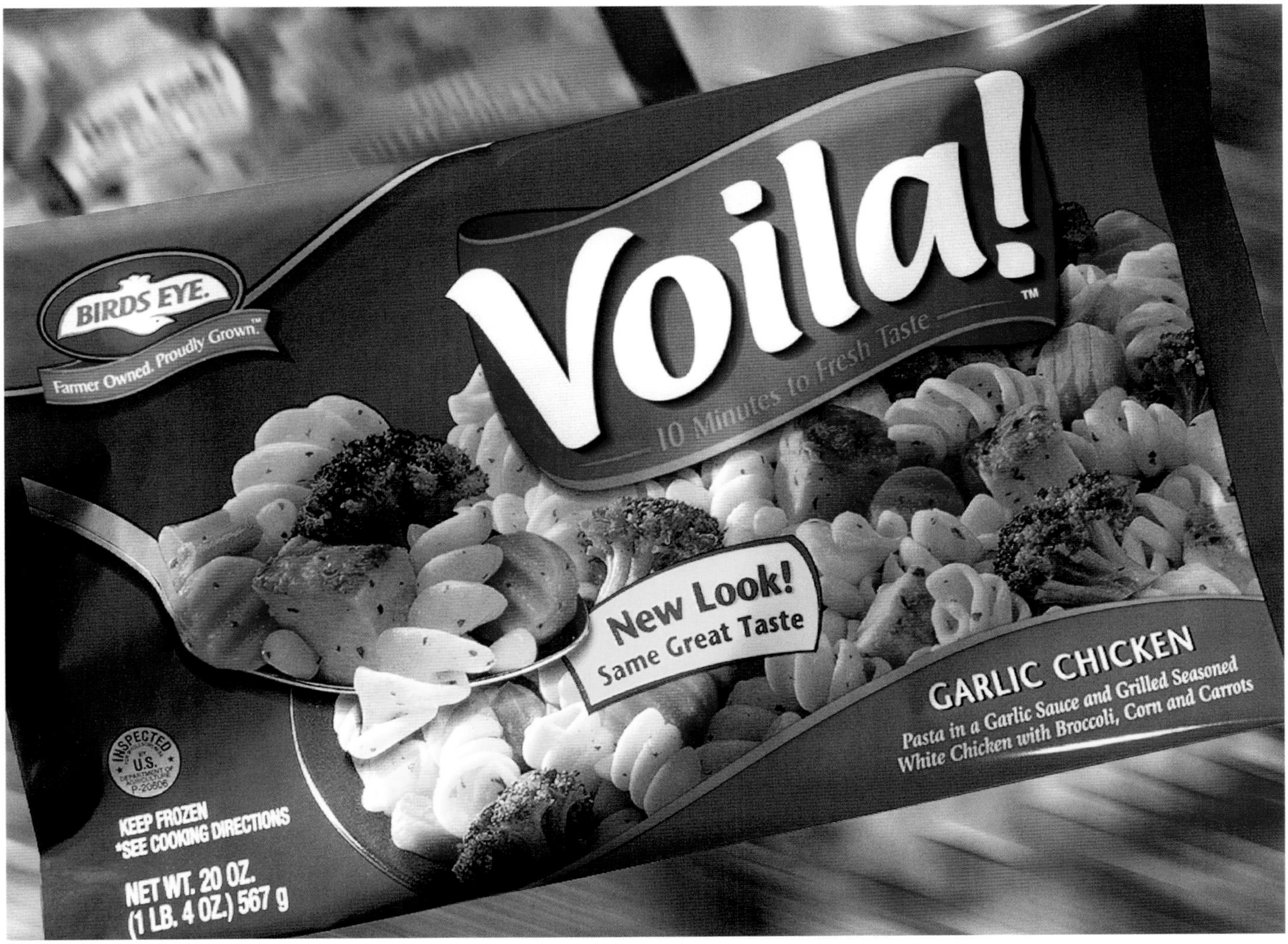

Index